REVELATION

BHGNT

Baylor Handbook on the Greek New Testament
Martin M. Culy
General Editor

OTHER BOOKS IN THIS SERIES

Mark 1–8	Rodney J. Decker
Mark 9–16	Rodney J. Decker
Luke	Martin M. Culy, Mikeal C. Parsons, and Joshua J. Stigall
Acts	Martin M. Culy and Mikeal C. Parsons
2 Corinthians	Fredrick J. Long
Galatians	David A. deSilva
Ephesians	William J. Larkin
Colossians and Philemon	Constantine R. Campbell
James	A. K. M. Adam
1 Peter	Mark Dubis
2 Peter and Jude	Peter H. Davids
1, 2, 3 John	Martin M. Culy

Revelation

A Handbook on the Greek Text

David L. Mathewson

BAYLOR UNIVERSITY PRESS

© 2016 by Baylor University Press
Waco, Texas 76798

All Rights Reserved. No part of this publication may be reproduced, stored in a retrieval system, or transmitted, in any form or by any means, electronic, mechanical, photocopying, recording or otherwise, without the prior permission in writing of Baylor University Press.

Cover Design by Pamela Poll

Library of Congress Cataloging-in-Publication Data

Mathewson, David L., 1963–, author.
  Revelation : a handbook on the Greek text / David L. Mathewson.
    pages cm. — (Baylor handbook on the Greek New Testament)
  Includes bibliographical references and index.
  ISBN 978-1-60258-676-5 (pbk. : alk. paper)
  1. Bible. Revelation—Criticism, Textual. 2. Bible. Revelation. Greek—Versions. I. Title.
  BS2825.52.M383 2016
  228'.077--dc23
                                2015027717

Printed in the United States of America on acid-free paper with a minimum of 30% post-consumer waste recycled content.

To Joyce!

CONTENTS

Series Introduction	xi
Preface	xvii
Abbreviations	xix
Introduction	xxi
Revelation 1:1-3	1
Revelation 1:4-8	4
Revelation 1:9-20	8
Revelation 2:1-7	17
Revelation 2:8-11	23
Revelation 2:12-17	26
Revelation 2:18-29	31
Revelation 3:1-6	39
Revelation 3:7-13	44
Revelation 3:14-22	52
Revelation 4:1-11	58
Revelation 5:1-7	68
Revelation 5:8-14	76
Revelation 6:1-8	81

Revelation 6:9-17	88
Revelation 7:1-8	94
Revelation 7:9-17	98
Revelation 8:1-5	105
Revelation 8:6-13	109
Revelation 9:1-12	115
Revelation 9:13-21	123
Revelation 10:1-11	129
Revelation 11:1-2	139
Revelation 11:3-14	141
Revelation 11:15-19	151
Revelation 12:1-6	155
Revelation 12:7-18	160
Revelation 13:1-8	168
Revelation 13:9-10	175
Revelation 13:11-18	177
Revelation 14:1-5	184
Revelation 14:6-13	189
Revelation 14:14-20	197
Revelation 15:1-8	202
Revelation 16:1-11	209
Revelation 16:12-16	216
Revelation 16:17-21	219
Revelation 17:1-6	222
Revelation 17:7-18	227
Revelation 18:1-8	236
Revelation 18:9-20	244
Revelation 18:21-24	253

Revelation 19:1-10	255
Revelation 19:11-16	263
Revelation 19:17-21	268
Revelation 20:1-10	272
Revelation 20:11-15	279
Revelation 21:1-8	282
Revelation 21:9-21	289
Revelation 21:22-27	296
Revelation 22:1-5	299
Revelation 22:6-9	303
Revelation 22:10-21	306
Glossary	315
Works Cited	321
Grammar Index	325
Author Index	335

SERIES INTRODUCTION

The Baylor Handbook on the Greek New Testament (BHGNT) is designed to guide new readers and seasoned scholars alike through the intricacies of the Greek text. Each handbook provides a verse-by-verse treatment of the biblical text. Unlike traditional commentaries, however, the BHGNT makes no attempt to expound on the theological meaning or significance of the document under consideration. Instead, the handbooks serve as "prequels" to commentary proper. They provide readers of the New Testament with a foundational analysis of the Greek text upon which interpretation may then be established. Readers of traditional commentaries are sometimes dismayed by the fact that even those that are labeled "exegetical" or "critical" frequently have little to say about the mechanics of the Greek text, and all too often completely ignore the more perplexing grammatical issues. In contrast, the BHGNT offers an accessible and comprehensive, though not exhaustive, treatment of the Greek New Testament, with particular attention given to the grammar of the text. In order to make the handbooks more user-friendly, authors have only selectively interacted with secondary literature. Where there is significant debate on an issue, the handbooks provide a representative sample of scholars espousing each position; when authors adopt a less known stance on the text, they generally list any other scholars who have embraced that position.

The BHGNT, however, is more than a reliable guide to the Greek text of the New Testament. Each author brings unique strengths to the task of preparing the handbook. As a result, students and scholars alike will at times be introduced to ways of looking at the Greek language that they have not encountered before. This feature makes the handbooks valuable not only for intermediate and advanced Greek courses, but also for students and scholars who no longer have the luxury of increasing their Greek proficiency within a classroom context. While handbook authors do not consider modern linguistic theory to be a panacea for all questions exegetical, the BHGNT does aim both to help move linguistic insights into the mainstream of New Testament reference works and, at the same time, to help weed out some of the myths about the Greek language that continue to appear in both scholarly and popular treatments of the New Testament.

Using the Baylor Handbook on the Greek New Testament

Each handbook consists of the following features. The introduction draws readers' attention to some of the distinctive features of the biblical text and treats some of the broader issues relating to the text as a whole in a more thorough fashion. In the handbook proper, the biblical text is divided into sections, each of which is introduced with a translation that illustrates how the insights gleaned from the analysis that follows may be expressed in modern English. Following the translation is the heart of the handbook, an extensive analysis of the Greek text. Here, the Greek text of each verse is followed by comments on grammatical, lexical, and text-critical issues. Handbook authors may also make use of other features, such as passage overviews between the translation and notes.

Each page of the handbook includes a header to help readers quickly locate comments on a particular passage. Terminology used in the comments that is potentially unfamiliar is included in a glossary in the back of the handbook and/or cross-referenced with the first occurrence of the expression, where an explanation may be found. Each volume also includes an index that provides a list of grammatical phenomena occurring in the biblical text. This feature provides a valuable resource for students of Greek wanting to study a particular construction more carefully or Greek instructors needing to develop illustrations, exercises, or exams. The handbooks conclude with a bibliography of works cited, providing helpful guidance in identifying resources for further research on the Greek text.

The handbooks assume that users will possess a minimal level of competence with Greek morphology and syntax. Series authors generally utilize traditional labels such as those found in Daniel Wallace's *Greek Grammar Beyond the Basics*. Labels that are drawn from the broader field of modern linguistics are explained at their first occurrence and included in the glossary. Common labels that users may be unfamiliar with are also included in the glossary.

The primary exception to the broad adoption of traditional syntactic labels relates to verb tenses. Most New Testament Greek grammars describe the tense system as being formally fairly simple (only 6 tenses), but functionally complex. The aorist tense, it is frequently said, can function in a wide variety of ways that are associated with labels such as, "ingressive," "gnomic," "constative," "epistolary," "proleptic," and so forth. Similar functional complexity is posited for the other tenses. Positing such "functions," however, typically stems not from a careful analysis of Greek syntax, but rather from grappling with the challenges of translating Greek verbs into English. When we carefully examine the Greek verb tenses themselves, we find that the tense forms do not themselves denote semantic features such as ingressive, iterative, or conative; they certainly do not emphasize such notions; at best they may allow for ingressive, iterative, or conative translations. Although many of the other traditional labels are susceptible to similar critique, the tense labels have frequently led to exegetical claims that go beyond the syntax, e.g., that a particular aorist verb *emphasizes* the beginning of an action. For this reason, we have chosen not to utilize these labels. Instead, where the context points to an ingressive nuance for the action of the verb, this will be incorporated into the translation.

Deponency

Although series authors will vary in the theoretical approaches they bring to the text, the BHGNT has adopted the same general approach on one important issue: deponency. Traditionally, the label "deponent" has been applied to verbs with middle, passive, or middle/passive morphology that are thought to be "active" in meaning. Introductory grammars tend to put a significant number of middle verbs in the New Testament in this category, despite the fact that some of the standard reference grammars have questioned the validity of the label. Robertson (332), for example, argues that the label "should not be used at all."

In recent years, a number of scholars have taken up Robertson's quiet call to abandon this label. Carl Conrad's posts on the B-Greek Internet discussion list (beginning in 1997) and his subsequent formalization of those concerns in unpublished papers available on his website have helped flesh out the concerns raised by earlier scholars. In a recent article, Jonathan Pennington (61–64) helpfully summarizes the rationale for dispensing with the label, maintaining that widespread use of the term "deponent" stems from two key factors: (1) the tendency to attempt to analyze Greek syntax through reference to English translation — if a workable translation of a middle form appears "active" in English, we conclude that the verb must be active in meaning even though it is middle in form; and (2) the imposition of Latin categories on Greek grammar. Pennington concludes that "most if not all verbs that are considered 'deponent' are in fact truly middle in meaning" (61). The questions that have been raised regarding deponency as a syntactic category, then, are not simply issues that interest a few Greek scholars and linguists but have no bearing on how one understands the text. Rather, if these scholars are correct, the notion of deponency has, at least in some cases, effectively obscured the semantic significance of the middle voice, leading to imprecise readings of the text (see also Bakker and Taylor).

It is not only middle voice verbs, however, that are the focus of attention in this debate. Conrad, Pennington, and others also maintain that deponency is an invalid category for passive verbs that have traditionally been placed in this category. To account for putative passive deponent verbs, these scholars have turned to the evolution of voice morphology in the Greek language. They draw attention to the fact that middle morphology was being replaced by passive morphology (the -θη- morpheme) during the Koine period (see esp. Conrad, 3, 5–6; cf. Pennington, 68; Taylor, 175; Caragounis, 153). Consequently, in the Common Era we find "an increasing number of passive forms without a distinctive passive idea ... replacing older middle forms" (Pennington, 68). This diachronic argument leads Conrad (5) to conclude that the -θη- morpheme should be treated as a middle/passive rather than a passive morpheme. Such arguments have a sound linguistic foundation and raise serious questions about the legitimacy of the notion "passive deponent."

Should, then, the label "deponent" be abandoned altogether? While more research needs to be done to account for middle/passive morphology in Koine Greek fully, the arguments, which are very briefly summarized above, are both compelling and exegetically significant. "The middle voice needs to be understood in its own status and function as indicating that the subject of a verb is the focus of the verb's action or state" (Conrad, 3; cf. Taylor, 174). Consequently, users of the BHGNT will discover that verbs that are typically labeled "deponent," including some with -θη- morphology, tend to be listed as "middle."

In recognizing that so-called deponent verbs should be viewed as true middles, users of the BHGNT should not fall into the trap of concluding that the middle form emphasizes the subject's involvement in the action of the verb. At times, the middle voice appears simply to be a morphological flag indicating that the verb is intransitive. More frequently, the middle morphology tends to be driven by the "middle" semantics of the verb itself. In other words, the middle voice is sometimes used with the verb not in order to place a focus on the subject's involvement in the action, but precisely because the sense of the lexical form itself involves subject focus.

It is the hope of Baylor University Press, the series editor, and each of the authors that these handbooks will help advance our understanding of the Greek New Testament, be used to further equip the saints for the work of ministry, and fan into flame a love for the Greek New Testament among a new generation of students and scholars.

Martin M. Culy
Series Editor

PREFACE

I have learned much about both Greek grammar and the book of Revelation from writing this book. Working through every grammatical detail in this fascinating Greek text has been a graduate course in advanced Greek grammar! But as the following notes will testify, I have had many reliable guides along the way. As I suspect is true with many volumes in this series, this one was written in the midst of a busy seminary teaching schedule. At times I have had to "chip away" at chapters and sections here and there; at rare moments I have had longer stretches of uninterrupted time to focus on this project. The result, I hope, is still an evenness in the treatment of the grammar. I would like to thank Marty Culy for the initial invitation to contribute the volume on Revelation to the Baylor Handbook on the Greek Text series. Furthermore, I must say that it has been an absolute blessing to work with Marty as the editor of my manuscript. Even in the midst of a number of personal issues and life changes, he was able to make my manuscript his last one before turning over the editorship of this series. I have learned much from Marty's comments, which were always incisive, challenging, and thought-provoking. His linguistic expertise saved me from countless errors, and this volume is all the better because of his careful attention and guidance. In addition, I would like to thank Baylor Press for publishing this work, and allowing me to participate in this project. Furthermore, I want to thank the faculty and my students at Denver Seminary for their interest in and support of my completion of this project. But I would be remiss if I did not express my extreme love and gratitude to my wife, Joyce, who has always been encouraging and supportive in my research and writing. I don't know how many times she walked through the door of our home this past couple of years as I worked on this volume to find me sitting on the couch with computer in hand, surrounded by stacks of commentaries, grammars, and lexicons! I cannot express how much I appreciate her and all the help she is to me. It is to her that I dedicate this book!

ABBREVIATIONS

1st	first person
2nd	second person
3rd	third person
acc	accusative
act	active
al	other manuscripts
aor	aorist
BDAG	F. Danker, *A Greek-English Lexicon of the NT*, 2000
BDF	F. W. Blass, A. Debrunner, and R. W. Funk. *A Greek Grammar of the NT*
CEB	Common English Bible
CEV	Contemporary English Version
ch(s).	chapter(s)
dat	dative
ESV	English Standard Version
fem	feminine
fut	future
gen	genitive
impf	imperfect
impv	imperative
ind	indicative
inf	infinitive
KJV	King James Version
LN	Louw and Nida, *Greek-English Lexicon*
LSJ	Liddell, Scott, Jones, *A Greek-English Lexicon*
LXX	Septuagint
masc	masculine
mid	middle
NASB	New American Standard Bible

NET	New English Translation
neut	neuter
NIV	New International Version
NLT	New Living Translation
nom	nominative
NP	noun phrase
NRSV	New Revised Standard Version
NT	New Testament
opt	optative
OT	Old Testament
pass	passive
pc	a few other manuscripts
pl	plural
plprf	pluperfect
pm	a great many other manuscripts
PP	prepositional phrase
pres	present
prf	perfect
ptc	participle
RSV	Revised Standard Version
sg	singular
subj	subjunctive
s.v.	under the word (sub verbo)
TEV	Today's English Version
voc	vocative

INTRODUCTION

Although the book of Revelation claims to be an "unsealed" book (22:10), it still remains sealed for many students, taxing even the most seasoned scholar. In addition to its strange and complex symbolism found throughout the book, Revelation's grammar has been a particular source of contention for interpreters. Though at times John's grammar is relatively straightforward and familiar to the student of NT Greek, at other times it is some of the most challenging in the NT. The following pages attempt to wrestle with the language of John's Apocalypse to make sense of its grammatical contours and other details of the Greek text. I do not attempt to be exhaustive and treat every grammatical, lexical, or textual issue in the Apocalypse in detail. Rather, I have tried to focus on some of the more important and problematic issues. The level of confidence that I have arrived at the correct conclusion on all issues varies from issue to issue and verse to verse. At times I will be content to suggest the most likely possibilities; but the overall goal is to provide a guide through the details of the Greek text of Revelation that will serve the student of Revelation in coming to grips with the language of this unique book. In so doing, I have tried as much as possible to avoid commentary on this or that verse or issue, not repeating what can be found in any standard commentary on the Apocalypse, though at times some commentary inevitably intrudes. Rather, this handbook focuses on the linguistic dimensions of the text of the Apocalypse. Like other works in this series, I have also tried to implement, when possible and appropriate, insights from modern linguistics (see "Verbal Aspect" below) in probing the language of the book.

In the following sections of the Introduction I have chosen to summarize very briefly a number of important issues that are integrally related to the treatment of the Greek text of the Apocalypse. These issues are: the literary style and genre of Revelation, the issue of the Greek of

Revelation and Semitic influence, verbal aspect and its significance for interpreting verb tenses in Revelation, and the interpretation of participles. Again, the intention is not to be exhaustive, but to sketch out the broad issues and implications for the treatment of the Greek text of Revelation in the rest of this handbook.

Literary Genre and Style of Revelation

There is now fairly widespread agreement among scholars that the book or Revelation consists of a unique blend of three literary types (though it is not so clear that the ancient, first readers would have so sharply distinguished them): prophecy, apocalypse, and epistle (Aune, 1.lxx-xc; Osborne, 12–15). As a prophecy, the book of Revelation should be seen as having a strong hortatory appeal (i.e., the common description of prophecy as more "forthtelling" than "foretelling"). Revelation functions to motivate its readers to unqualified allegiance to God and the Lamb in the face of competing claims for their allegiance and worship. Furthermore, much of John's language and imagery comes from his prophetic predecessors (e.g., Isaiah, Ezekiel, Daniel), which at times may explain the lexical meaning of different words or grammatical constructions. As an epistle, Revelation is meant to address the specific situation of the audience (Revelation is just as occasional as any of Paul's letters) and to exhort them to respond in obedience to its hortatory message. However, while the entire book functions as a letter, apart from the epistolary introduction (1:4-8) and closing (22:22), which bracket the work, the rest of the Apocalypse does not develop like a letter form (Thanksgiving, Body, etc.). On the other hand, direct address of the audience through hortatory appeal brackets the book (1:1-8; chaps. 2–3; 22:6-21), and interspersed throughout the narrative are calls to calculate (e.g., 13:18) or to endure (e.g., 13:9-10). The generic category that has received most of the attention when it comes to analyzing Revelation is 'apocalypse'. As an apocalypse, Revelation records the visionary experience of a seer (John, in 1:9) conveyed in ubiquitous and sometimes graphic symbolism within a narrative framework. According to Aune, as an apocalypse Revelation is "a first person prose narrative, with an episodic structure consisting of revelatory visions" (1.lxxxii). In other words, Revelation is an account of the seer's visionary experience that develops as a story, or narrative, with a sequential series of visionary segments in an episodic structure. Therefore, for purposes of analyzing verbal aspect and discourse prominence (see below), the way that verbal aspect functions in narrative can be applied to the book of Revelation. This also suggests that the overarching temporal orientation of Revelation is past-time (it narrates what John saw), though it also contains visionary material that is perhaps timeless and/or future referring (Mathewson 2010, 46).

The main visionary segments in Revelation are frequently introduced by καί εἶδον, which marks off the main segments of John's vision (see on 5:1). Furthermore, while these segments are prefaced by the first person εἶδον (and/or ἤκουσα), the visions themselves are generally cast in the third person depicting what John saw (Mathewson 2010, 46), though at times John plays a role within his vision (5:4; 11:1). Another stylistic feature of Revelation is the use of the ubiquitous conjunction καί to string together clauses and paragraphs. According to Aune, 245 of 337 sentences in the Apocalypse begin with καί (1.cxci). Other conjunctions are relatively sparse in comparison. The conjunction δέ occurs only seven times in Revelation (1:14; 2:5, 16, 24; 10:2; 19:12; 21:8). It generally functions to indicate a step or new development, often used to focus attention on a facet of the vision or to indicate contrast. The particle οὖν, a marker of development (Runge, 43), occurs a mere six times (1:19; 2:5, 16; 3:3 [2×], 19). All but one occur in the seven messages to the churches, where it functions to signal logical development. The conjunction γάρ, which introduces material that strengthens or supports previous material, occurs only sixteen times (1:3; 3:2; 9:19 [2x]; 13:18; 14:4, 13; 16:14; 17:17; 19:8, 10; 21:1, 22, 23, 25; 22:10).

This profile suggests that Revelation as a narrative develops episodically, primarily stringing together sentences and episodes without grammatically signaling logical development and argumentation. One important way that the author establishes cohesion in his discourse is through the use of the anaphoric article. Frequently when an entity is mentioned for the first time it will be anarthrous (lacking the article). Subsequent mentions of the entity will have the article, which functions to point back (anaphoric) to the first mention of the entity. Thus, ἀρνίου is anarthrous the first time it is mentioned in 5:6. All subsequent references to the Lamb in Revelation include the anaphoric article (5:8, 12, 13; 6:1, 16; 7:9, 10, 14, 17; 12:11; 13:8; 14:1, 4 [2x], 10; 15:3; 17:14 [2x]; 19:7, 9; 21:14, 22, 23, 27; 22:1, 3). The θρόνος of God and the Lamb is introduced without an article in 4:2, but in every subsequent occurrence in Revelation the reference to this throne is articular, anaphorically pointing back to the first mention in 4:2 (4:2, 3, 4, 5 [2x], 6 [3x], 9, 10; 5:1, 6, 7, 11, 13; 6:16; 7:9, 10, 11 [2x], 15 [2x], 17; 8:3; 11:16; 12:5; 14:3; 16:10, 17; 19:4, 15; 21:3, 5; 22:1, 3; the only exceptions are thrones that belong to other beings: twenty-four elders; Satan). Other important expressions that follow the same pattern are, e.g., βιβλίον (5:1), θηρίον (13:1; see chap. 17), εἴκοσι τέσσαρας πρεσβυτέρους (4:4), and σφραγῖσιν ἑπτά (5:1).

One other important sylistic feature is the numerous verbless clauses throughout the visions. For example, Rev 4:2b-8 has fourteen verbless clauses, which usually consist of a nominative subject and a predicate, sometimes containing participial forms. As Porter notes, "The simple nominative itself may form its own clause in Greek. ... [T]he 'unmarked' case could be used on its own to form a clause, that is, simply to specify the nominal idea" (1992, 85). Similarly, Thompson states that "a noun clause contains no finite verb. ... It stresses the subject's state of being, its existence ..." (83). This has the effect of making Rev 4, for example, highly descriptive and more static since few indicative verb forms are present to carry the narrative along.

The Language of Revelation and Semitic Influence

As noted above, one of the most significant challenges in interpreting the book of Revelation is coming to grips with its language. Revelation is well-known for its grammatical solecisms. One of the more common types of grammatical incongruity is the lack of concord in case and gender with nouns and participles. The most well-known example of John's grammatical "blunders" is found in 1:4 where the phrase ὁ ὢν καὶ ὁ ἦν καὶ ὁ ἐρχόμενος following the preposition ἀπό should be in the genitive case rather than the nominative. In 17:3 the participle ἔχων (nominative masculine) does not match up in gender and case with the noun that it apparently modifies, θηρίον (accusative neuter). For discussion, see 1:4 and 17:3 below.

One common explanation for John's grammatical anomalies is to posit some level of Semitic influence. In this view, underlying the "unique" grammar of Revelation is the Semitic (Hebrew or Aramaic) grammatical system (Charles, Thompson, Mussies; cf. Schmidt). Charles' dictum is well known: "while he writes in Greek, he thinks in Hebrew" (I.cxliii). Similarly, Thompson suggests that in Revelation "the Greek language is little more than a membrane, stretched tightly over a Semitic framework" (108). Or, as Aune argues, "The Greek of Revelation is the most peculiar Greek in the NT, in part because it exhibits interference from Semitic languages, perhaps both Hebrew and Aramaic" (1.clxii). Thompson goes even further by characterizing the Greek of Revelation as "Jewish Greek" (108; cf. Turner, 9).

If this consensus perspective is correct, then John's 'strange' grammar should be evaluated according to Semitic rather than Greek standards. However, the following observations are important to keep in mind. As Porter has reminded us (1989b, 587), it is important to distinguish three levels of influence: (1) *translation* of an underlying Semitic source; (2) *enhancement* of a rare though acceptable construction through

Semitic influence; and (3) *intervention*, where a construction that is unparalleled in Greek is due to Semitic influence. Simply to label a construction a "Semitism" does not tell us what level of influence is present. Very frequently, what is deemed a Semitism turns out to be an acceptable (even if uncommon) Greek construction, the frequency of which has been enhanced by Semitic influence (Porter 1989b). Therefore, I will generally not appeal to Semitic influence (especially in the third sense above) to explain the language of Revelation unless a construction cannot be accounted for by any other means. This also means that it is unnecessary, and probably illegitimate, to talk about a Semitized or Jewish Greek to describe the kind of Greek present in the Apocalypse. If the meaning of John's grammar and lexical items is to be found solely in Hebrew and not in Greek ("John writes in Greek, but thinks in Hebrew"), then one must ask why John bothered to write in Greek at all if he did not intend to communicate Greek meanings (Mathewson 2010, 178). However, as "the messages to the seven churches clearly indicate (Revelation 2-3) ... John was writing to churches in Asia Minor, thoroughly ensconced in Greek culture and at the center of Imperial Roman rule" (Mathewson 2010, 178-79). In such a context, where John's readers used Greek every day as the common language of commerce, it is difficult to think that anyone would have thought that John was writing, at least for the most part, in anything other than the Hellenistic Greek of the day. Therefore, I will approach the grammar of Revelation from the perspective that it can best be made sense of according to the standards of Koine Greek of the first century, though this does not rule out some level of Semitic influence.

Verbal Aspect

Like other works in the series, this contribution attempts to take into account recent advances in linguistics as applied to the Greek of the NT. Recently, there has been much interest in and discussion of verbal aspect as a semantic category that accounts for the Greek verb tense forms (Porter 1989a, Fanning, McKay 1994, Decker, Campbell 2007). While in the past it was common to see Greek verb tenses as indicating both the time of the action (at least in the indicative mood) and kind of action (how the action actually took place), there is now widespread agreement that the primary semantic feature grammaticalized in the verb tense endings is verbal aspect, or how the author chose to portray the action. One significant implication of this research is that traditional conceptions of the tenses are inadequate and too limited. For example, it is frequently thought that the aorist tense indicates punctiliar or specific action, whereas the present tense indicates action that is ongoing, durative, continuous, or habitual. The perfect tense form is often seen as a combination of both of these: a past definite action with ongoing results into the present. These conceptions primarily describe the nature of the action itself. However, verbal aspect studies have shifted the focus from the objective reality of the action, which can only be determined by the broader context, to the subjective viewpoint of the author on the action, which is indicated by the verb tense form chosen by the author. The aorist tense form simply looks at the action externally, as a complete whole, irrespective of the length of the action. The present tense looks at the action as in progress, as unfolding and developing. It is an internal view of the action in that it looks at the action's internal makeup. The meaning of the perfect tense form is debated. Porter 1989 and McKay 1994 have argued for a stative meaning for this tense: the action is viewed as a complex state of affairs. Campbell, however, has recently suggested that the perfect tense form is imperfective aspect (like the present tense) with a more heightened level of proximity to the action than the present tense (Campbell 2007, 161–211). For the purposes of this handbook I will follow Porter 1989 and McKay 1994.

Verbal aspect is a particularly helpful model for interpreting the tenses in Revelation, since the author shifts back and forth between all the major tense forms in his visionary segments while often referring to the same temporal frame—an account of a past visionary experience (for one example of a comprehensive treatment of the tenses in Revelation in light of verbal aspect, see Mathewson 2010). This suggests that the author is not using the verb tenses primarily to communicate temporal information. Rather, the author's use of the various tense forms in the context of his narrative account of his visionary experience may be explained in light of verbal aspect, or how the author wants to portray the various verbal processes that make up his visionary narrative.

There has been much discussion recently on the relationship of verbal aspect to discourse prominence. Some maintain that in addition to indicating the author's perspective on the action, aspect also signals different levels of prominence in the discourse. Although there is still disagreement on this issue, for the following analysis of the text of Revelation, I will adopt the following perspective. To begin, it must be said that prominence is not part of the inherent meanings of the various verbal aspects, but rather is one possible way that aspect can function pragmatically within discourse. In narrative, the aorist tense is the basic form used to narrate the main events and carry the main storyline along. The imperfect tense form is often used to indicate action that is remote from the main storyline, i.e., it narrates supplemental and background information. By contrast, the present tense is used to indicate foreground information in the narrative (the so-called "historical present"; see below on 4:5 on ἐκπορεύονται). It is used to introduce a new scene, to introduce significant speech or characters, or signal an important transition in the narrative. The perfect tense form seems to function in Revelation as another way (along with the present) of signaling prominence. Though some are convinced that by the time of Revelation the perfect is losing its semantic force, the author frequently uses aorist and present forms of the same verbs found in the perfect (e.g., λαμβάνω), sometimes in the same context, suggesting that the perfect was a deliberate choice on the part of the author. This suggests that the perfect still retains its semantic force. Campbell (2007, 187) notes that the perfect tense is very rare in narrative (though it occurs in speech, in Luke for example). Revelation, however, has a number of passages where the perfect tense occurs in the author's narrative (e.g. 5:7; 7:14; 8:5; 12:4; 13:8; 17:8; 19:13).

Since Revelation is a narrative of the author's visionary experience (see "Literary Genre and Style of Revelation" above), the above scheme can be applied to Revelation. Although we should not conclude that verbal aspect always functions in the same manner in Revelation, in the following analysis I have tried to demonstrate where I see verbal aspect serving to indicate levels of prominence. The most fruitful instances are where the same verb is used with different aspects in a section of the vision, sometimes used in contrast with each other, or where there are shifts from a pattern of tense forms (e.g., the present or perfect tense intruding into a context dominated by aorists), or where they occur with other indicators of prominence. While verbal aspect is not the only means of doing so, it can be one important way to indicate prominence in discourse.

A further implication of verbal aspect can be seen in the fact that in the analysis of verb forms in this handbook I have avoided the common, traditional labels used of Greek tenses in most grammars: "progressive present," "conative present," "inceptive imperfect," "constative aorist," "ingressive aorist," "culminative aorist," "intensive perfect," and so on. These popular labels are more appropriate to the broader context rather than the verb tenses (aspects) themselves. Such information only comes from contextual indicators, if these meanings are present at all, not the verb tense forms themselves. Verbal aspect only indicates how the author chooses to portray the action, and it is illegitimate to import all of the information from the context onto the meaning of the aspects themselves (in the same way that it is a lexical fallacy to import all the information from the context onto a given word). Therefore, such labels are probably better abandoned in descriptions of the function of the various aspects in the Greek NT.

Participles

Participles dot the grammatical landscape of Revelation, and Revelation reveals the full range of participle functions. In the analysis of participles that function as adverbial modifiers (Porter 1992, 187), this handbook has tentatively used labels such as "causal," "temporal," "manner," "means," "concessive," "conditional," "purpose," "result," commonly found in most grammars (see Wallace, 622–40). However, it needs to be noted that it is probably inaccurate to give these labels to the participles themselves. As Robertson says, "it must be distinctly noted, the participle does not express time, manner, cause, purpose, condition or concession. These ideas (cause, manner, time, etc.) are not in the participle, but are merely suggested by the context, if at all" (1124). Therefore, these labels are not different kinds of participles, nor are these meanings communicated by the participle. Rather, they are rhetorical labels that may describe the meaning of the *entire participial clause in relationship to its surrounding context*. The participle itself is not marked for these meanings. If the author wanted to indicate time, cause, means, manner, or these other adverbial functions, he had clear means of doing so (e.g., clauses introduced by ὅτι, ἐάν, ἵνα, ὅτε, ὡς, etc.). Participles themselves are indeterminate when it comes to this information. In the absence of clear contextual indicators, it might be better not to insist on these labels, and sometimes more than one could fit. All that the adverbial participle does is to indicate the circumstances under which the action of the controlling verb (the verb it modifies) takes place. Therefore, I have used these labels tentatively in my analysis of the Greek text, but with the above caveats in mind.

If the participles do not indicate these kinds of meanings, how do they function, and how are they important for exegesis? An important factor in analyzing adverbial participles is to observe their position in relationship to the main (nuclear) verb that they modify. The participle is used to prioritize information in relationship to the main verb. As Runge notes, "The most important thing to understand about the participle is the idea of prioritization of action" (Runge, 247). In other words, certain actions (participles) play a subordinate, modifying role, over against the main focus, which is the action of the main verb. They either provide background, prerequisite information, or they further explain and describe in more detail the action of the main verb. If the participle *precedes* the main verb it usually communicates background or action that is prerequisite to the main verb, especially when it is in the perfective aspect. The participle signals information that is of secondary importance to the action of the main verb (Runge, 249). For example, in Rev 1:12 the aorist participle ἐπιστρέψας precedes the main verb εἶδον and thus indicates background information or prerequisite action to the action of the main verb. In contrast, when the participle *follows* the main verb, it typically elaborates "the action of the main verb, often providing more specific explanation of what is meant by the main action" (Runge, 262). For example, in Rev 18:19 the main verb ἔκραζον is followed by two present participles, κλαίοντες καὶ πενθοῦντες. One could ask whether one of the traditional labels fits (perhaps "means" or "manner"). It is far more important, however, to recognize that the participles follow the main verb and therefore serve to further explain the main verb and what it entails.

One important pattern found in the Apocalypse is the clustering of perfect participles around key participants. When an important participant is introduced for the first time, it is often signaled by a cluster of perfect participle forms which function to draw attention to it: The Son of Man in 1:13, 15 (ἐνδεδυμένον, περιεζωσμένον, πεπυρωμένης); the scroll in 5:1 (γεγραμμένον, κατεσφραγισμένον); the Lamb in 5:6 (ἑστηκὸς, ἐσφαγμένον, ἀπεσταλμένοι); the 144,000 in 7:4-8 (ἐσφραγισμένων, ἐσφραγισμένοι three times); the great multitude in 7:9 (ἑστῶτες, περιβεβλημένους); the two witnesses in 11:3-4 (περιβεβλημένοι, ἑστῶτες); the victorious saints in 14:1-3 (ἑστός, γεγραμμένον, ἠγορασμένοι); the overcomers by the sea in 15:2 (μεμιγμένην, ἑστῶτας); the angels who pour out the last plagues in 15:6 (ἐνδεδυμένοι, περιεζωσμένοι); the harlot/Babylon in 17:4 (περιβεβλημένη, κεχρυσωμένη; cf. 18:16); the warrior Messiah in 19:12-16 (γεγραμμένον, περιβεβλημένος, γεγραμμένον, βεβαμμένον); the bride/New Jerusalem in 21:2 (ἡτοιμασμένην, κεκοσμημένην). Several of these participles also probably serve to draw attention to the OT background (Mathewson 2010, 107).

A HANDBOOK ON THE GREEK TEXT OF REVELATION

Revelation 1:1-3

¹The revelation of Jesus Christ which God gave to him to show to his servants the things that must come to pass soon, and he showed it, by sending him, through his angel to his servant, John, ²who bears witness to the word of God and the testimony of Jesus Christ, as much as he saw. ³Blessed is the one who reads and those who hear the words of the prophecy and who keep the things written in it, for the time is near.

1:1 Ἀποκάλυψις Ἰησοῦ Χριστοῦ ἣν ἔδωκεν αὐτῷ ὁ θεὸς δεῖξαι τοῖς δούλοις αὐτοῦ ἃ δεῖ γενέσθαι ἐν τάχει, καὶ ἐσήμανεν ἀποστείλας διὰ τοῦ ἀγγέλου αὐτοῦ τῷ δούλῳ αὐτοῦ Ἰωάννῃ,

Ἀποκάλυψις. Nominative absolute. This construction using the nominative case often occurs in the titles to books (Wallace, 49–50). The nominative could also be viewed as the use of the nominative to form its own clause, consistent with its function of specifying a nominal idea (Porter 1992, 85).

Ἰησοῦ Χριστοῦ. Genitive of source or subjective genitive. There has been some question over the function of the genitive (Beale, 183). It is possible that Ἰησοῦ Χριστοῦ could be understood as an objective genitive; Jesus is the main content of the revelation. However, given the emphasis on the chain of communication in verses 1-3, Jesus Christ should be understood as the source or subject of the act of the unveiling. It is illegitimate to appeal to a category of "plenary genitive" to suggest that both subjective and objective are in mind, as Wallace does (120–21). This is a matter of semantic ambiguity, not a grammatical function.

ἥν. Accusative direct object of ἔδωκεν.

ἔδωκεν. Aor act ind 3rd sg δίδωμι.

αὐτῷ. Dative indirect object of ἔδωκεν.
ὁ θεὸς. Nominative subject of ἔδωκεν.
δεῖξαι. Aor act inf δείκνυμι (purpose).
τοῖς δούλοις. Dative indirect object of δεῖξαι.
αὐτοῦ. Possessive genitive.
ἅ. Accusative subject of the infinitive γενέσθαι. The relative pronoun introduces a headless relative clause. The entire clause functions as the direct object of δεῖξαι.
δεῖ. Pres act ind 3rd sg δεῖ (impersonal).
γενέσθαι. Aor mid inf γίνομαι (complementary). It is also possible to view γενέσθαι as the subject of δεῖ: "to come about is necessary" (Wallace, 600–601).
ἐν τάχει. Temporal. The force of this expression has been the subject of some debate. One possibility is that it refers to the nearness of the time at which the events in Revelation will be fulfilled ("soon"), an expression of imminence. The other main option is that it refers to the speed with which the events in Revelation will be fulfilled when they begin to take place ("quickly" or "suddenly"). Based on the expression in 1:3 (καιρὸς ἐγγύς) the former explanation is to be preferred (Osborne, 54). Thus, this expression is referring to the temporal nearness of the fulfillment of these events.
ἐσήμανεν. Aor act ind 3rd sg σημαίνω. The term suggests "to cause something to be both specific and clear" (LN 33.153). However, in apocalyptic literature and here in Revelation it seems to carry the notion of signifying by means of symbols (Osborne, 55; Aune, 1.15; Beale, 182).
ἀποστείλας. Aor act ptc masc nom sg ἀποστέλλω (means, but see the Introduction on "Participles").
διὰ τοῦ ἀγγέλου. Intermediate agent. The primary agents of the revelation are God and Jesus Christ.
τῷ δούλῳ. Dative indirect object of ἐσήμανεν.
αὐτοῦ. Possessive genitive.
Ἰωάννῃ. Dative in apposition to τῷ δούλῳ.

1:2 ὃς ἐμαρτύρησεν τὸν λόγον τοῦ θεοῦ καὶ τὴν μαρτυρίαν Ἰησοῦ Χριστοῦ ὅσα εἶδεν.

ὅς. Nominative subject of ἐμαρτύρησεν.
ἐμαρτύρησεν. Aor act ind 3rd sg μαρτυρέω. Aune says that the aorist is analogous to the so-called "epistolary aorist," where what is present from John's standpoint will be past from the perspective of the readers (1.6; see also Smalley, 30). From the standpoint of verbal aspect, the aorist refers to the writing of the entire content of the book from John's perspective. In this case the aorist could be translated "who bears witness."

τὸν λόγον ... καὶ τὴν μαρτυρίαν. Accusative direct object of ἐμαρτύρησεν.

τοῦ θεοῦ. Genitive of source or subjective genitive (God is the subject of the act of speaking).

Ἰησοῦ Χριστοῦ. Subjective genitive. Though this could be an objective genitive ("the testimony about Jesus Christ"), the fact that Jesus Christ is the revealer of the revelation in 1:1-2 suggests that he is the subject of the act of testifying ("the testimony which Jesus gave").

ὅσα. Accusative direct object of εἶδεν.

εἶδεν. Aor act ind 3rd sg ὁράω.

1:3 Μακάριος ὁ ἀναγινώσκων καὶ οἱ ἀκούοντες τοὺς λόγους τῆς προφητείας καὶ τηροῦντες τὰ ἐν αὐτῇ γεγραμμένα, ὁ γὰρ καιρὸς ἐγγύς.

Μακάριος. Predicate adjective of a verbless clause. The term μακάριος suggests "pertaining to being happy, with the implication of favorable circumstances" (LN 25.119). The favorable circumstances are probably to be understood as the eschatological reward described in the rest of the book in light of ὁ γὰρ καιρὸς ἐγγύς, which follows.

ὁ ἀναγινώσκων καὶ οἱ ἀκούοντες ... καὶ τηροῦντες. Nominative subject of a verbless clause.

ὁ ἀναγινώσκων. Pres act ptc masc nom sg ἀναγινώσκω (substantival).

οἱ ἀκούοντες. Pres act ptc masc nom pl ἀκούω (substantival).

λόγους. Accusative direct object of ἀναγινώσκων and ἀκούοντες.

τῆς προφητείας. This could be taken as an attributive genitive (the prophetic words), or more likely as an epexegetical genitive (the words that constitute this prophecy; Aune, 1.7).

τηροῦντες. Pres act ptc masc nom pl τηρέω (substantival). The article οἱ with ἀναγινώσκων governs τηροῦντες as well.

τὰ ... γεγραμμένα. Prf pass ptc neut acc pl γράφω (substantival). Accusative direct object of τηροῦντες.

ἐν αὐτῇ. Locative.

γὰρ. Causal. "[A] motive for hearing and keeping" (Swete, 3), but probably also the reason for the pronouncement of blessing. More specifically, "γάρ constrains the reader to interpret the material it introduces as *strengthening* an assertion or assumption that has been presented in or implied by the immediate context" (Levinsohn 2000, 69). Whether that strengthening entails cause or explanation, etc. is determined by the context in which it occurs.

καιρὸς. Nominative subject of a verbless clause.

ἐγγύς. Predicate of a verbless clause.

Revelation 1:4-8

⁴John, to the seven churches which are in Asia; grace and peace to you from the One Who is, Who Was, and Who is Coming, and from the seven spirits which are before his throne, ⁵and from Jesus Christ, the faithful witness, the firstborn from the dead and the ruler over the kings of the earth. To him who loved us and freed us from our sins by his blood ⁶and made us a kingdom, priests to his God and Father, to him (be) glory and power forever and ever. Amen. ⁷Look, he is coming with the clouds, and every eye will see him, even those who pierced him, and all the tribes of the earth will mourn over him. Yes, amen. ⁸"I am the Alpha and the Omega," says the Lord God, "the One Who Is, Who Was, and Who Is Coming, the Almighty One."

1:4 Ἰωάννης ταῖς ἑπτὰ ἐκκλησίαις ταῖς ἐν τῇ Ἀσίᾳ· χάρις ὑμῖν καὶ εἰρήνη ἀπὸ ὁ ὢν καὶ ὁ ἦν καὶ ὁ ἐρχόμενος καὶ ἀπὸ τῶν ἑπτὰ πνευμάτων ἃ ἐνώπιον τοῦ θρόνου αὐτοῦ

Ἰωάννης. Nominative absolute in an epistolary address (see Wallace, 49–51).

ταῖς ἑπτὰ ἐκκλησίαις. Dative of recipient in a verbless clause. This construction is common in epistolary openings: "X *to* Y, Greetings."

ταῖς ἐν τῇ Ἀσίᾳ. The article functions as an adjectivizer, turning the locative PP into an attributive modifier of ταῖς ἑπτὰ ἐκκλησίαις. Lit. "the in-Asia churches." This construction is often translated with a relative pronoun in English ("*which* are in Asia"), though this does not mean that the article is functioning as a relative pronoun.

χάρις . . . καὶ εἰρήνη. Nominative absolute in an epistolary salutation.

ὑμῖν. Dative of advantage.

ἀπὸ ὁ ὢν καὶ ὁ ἦν καὶ ὁ ἐρχόμενος. Source. This PP is one of the first clear examples of John's numerous solecisms. Here the preposition ἀπό is followed by the nominative case (ὁ) rather than the expected genitive (τοῦ). There is broad agreement that the grammatical incongruity is intentional (in the very next clause the author uses the construction "correctly" with the genitive: ἀπὸ τῶν ἑπτὰ πνευμάτων; Robertson, 459). The most likely explanation is that by the grammatical incongruity the author wishes to draw attention to the titular nature of this expression and the OT text from which it comes: Exod 3:14: ἐγώ εἰμι ὁ ὤν. See Wallace, 63–64; Beale, 188–89. Some scribes (𝔐) attempted to alleviate the grammatical incongruity be inserting the genitive θεοῦ between ἀπό and ὁ ὤν.

ὁ ὤν. Pres act ptc masc nom sg εἰμί (substantival). See also ἀπὸ ὁ ὢν καὶ ὁ ἦν καὶ ὁ ἐρχόμενος above on the grammar.

ὁ ἦν. Impf act ind 3rd sg εἰμί. The shift from the present participle of εἰμί (ὤν) to the imperfect indicative ἦν, though grammatically awkward, can be explained by the lack of an imperfect participle form in analogy to ὁ ὤν. The author wants to communicate a temporal piece of information here with the remote imperfect form, and therefore switches to the indicative ἦν since there is no imperfect participle form (Swete, 5). The article is used in analogy with ὁ ὤν and ὁ ἐρχόμενος. See also ἀπὸ ὁ ὤν καὶ ὁ ἦν καὶ ὁ ἐρχόμενος above on the grammar.

ὁ ἐρχόμενος. Pres mid ptc masc nom sg ἔρχομαι (substantival). See also ἀπὸ ὁ ὤν καὶ ὁ ἦν καὶ ὁ ἐρχόμενος above on the grammar.

ἀπὸ τῶν ἑπτὰ πνευμάτων. Source. Here the author reverts back to the more grammatically "appropriate" genitive case following ἀπό.

ἅ. Nominative subject of a verbless clause.

ἐνώπιον τοῦ θρόνου. Locative.

αὐτοῦ. Possessive genitive.

1:5 καὶ ἀπὸ Ἰησοῦ Χριστοῦ, ὁ μάρτυς, ὁ πιστός, ὁ πρωτότοκος τῶν νεκρῶν καὶ ὁ ἄρχων τῶν βασιλέων τῆς γῆς. Τῷ ἀγαπῶντι ἡμᾶς καὶ λύσαντι ἡμᾶς ἐκ τῶν ἁμαρτιῶν ἡμῶν ἐν τῷ αἵματι αὐτοῦ,

ἀπὸ Ἰησοῦ Χριστοῦ. Source.

ὁ μάρτυς, ὁ πιστός. Nominative in apposition to Ἰησοῦ Χριστοῦ. Grammatical incongruity is created by having a nominative noun in apposition to a genitive noun (see also πρωτότοκος and ἄρχων below). While this is sometimes seen as another example of John's unconventional Greek, the nominative form probably preserves its function as designating a title (Robertson, 458) and draws attention to its OT background (Ps 89:37; see Beale, 192). The effect of the incongruity, then, is to draw attention to these titles. Both NA[28] and UBS[5] place a comma between ὁ μάρτυς and ὁ πιστός, suggesting that ὁ πιστός functions substantively as a separate designation of Christ (making four designations in total in this verse). However, it is more likely that ὁ πιστός stands in attributive relationship to ὁ μάρτυς ("faithful witness") and that there are only three designations for Christ here (the other two being ὁ πρωτότοκος and ὁ ἄρχων), perhaps in analogy to the threefold formula for God (ὁ ὤν καὶ ὁ ἦν καὶ ὁ ἐρχόμενος) in verse 4.

ὁ πρωτότοκος. Nominative in apposition to Ἰησοῦ Χριστοῦ.

τῶν νεκρῶν. Genitive of separation or partitive genitive.

ὁ ἄρχων. Nominative in apposition to Ἰησοῦ Χριστοῦ.

τῶν βασιλέων. Genitive of subordination (see Wallace, 103).

τῆς γῆς. Genitive of subordination (kings over the earth).

Τῷ ἀγαπῶντι. Pres act ptc masc dat sg ἀγαπάω (substantival). Dative of possession in a doxology. This constitutes an example of a topic construction in the form of a left dislocation (Runge, 287–93) where an entity is detached from the main clause and placed outside it at the beginning. According to Runge, "The new entity is dislocated at the beginning of the clause and then resumed in the main clause through the use of a pronominal trace" (289). Here the construction Τῷ ἀγαπῶντι is picked up again in the main clause by the dative αὐτῷ in verse 6. The function of this construction is to shift the topic and attract more attention to it.

ἡμᾶς. Accusative direct object of ἀγαπῶντι.

λύσαντι. Pres act ptc masc dat sg λύω (substantival). Dative of possession in a doxology. Topic construction (see Τῷ ἀγαπῶντι above).

ἡμᾶς. Accusative direct object of λύσαντι.

ἐκ τῶν ἁμαρτιῶν. Separation.

ἐν τῷ αἵματι. Instrumental. "Blood" is a metonymy for "death," substituting the means (shedding of blood) for the effect (death). A metonymy is a figure of speech where a term is used in place of another with which it is associated.

αὐτοῦ. Possessive genitive.

1:6 καὶ ἐποίησεν ἡμᾶς βασιλείαν, ἱερεῖς τῷ θεῷ καὶ πατρὶ αὐτοῦ, αὐτῷ ἡ δόξα καὶ τὸ κράτος εἰς τοὺς αἰῶνας [τῶν αἰώνων]· ἀμήν.

ἐποίησεν. Aor act ind 3rd sg ποιέω. The grammar appears awkward at this point. One would expect a participle ποιήσαντι to correspond to the ἀγαπῶντι and λύσαντι in the preceding verse, rather than the finite verb form ἐποίησεν. The shift to a participle from a finite verb occurs several times in Revelation and has sometimes been explained as a Hebraism (Charles, 1.15; Mussies, 326; Thompson, 66–67), though this grammatical phenomenon was not unknown in extra-biblical Greek (Porter 1989a, 140; BDF §468). It is also possible that the finite verb introduced by καὶ indicates a parenthetical construction: "To the one who freed us from our sins by his blood—indeed, he made us a kingdom, priests to his God and Father—to him be the glory." Several witnesses (no doubt secondary) change ἐποίησεν to ποιήσαντι to conform to the preceding participles (046 1854 *pc*).

ἡμᾶς. Accusative direct object of ἐποίησεν.

βασιλείαν. Complement in an object-complement double accusative construction.

ἱερεῖς. Accusative in apposition to βασιλείαν.

τῷ θεῷ καὶ πατρὶ. Dative of advantage.

αὐτοῦ. Genitive of relationship.

αὐτῷ. Dative of possession in a doxology. The pronoun picks up the topic introduced by Τῷ ἀγαπῶντι ... καὶ λύσαντι in verse 5 (see v. 5 on Τῷ ἀγαπῶντι).

ἡ δόξα καὶ τὸ κράτος. Nominative subject of verbless clause.

εἰς τοὺς αἰῶνας [τῶν αἰώνων]. Temporal. Lit. "into the ages [of ages]," a formula common in doxologies (BDAG, 32.1.b). The bracketed [τῶν αἰώνων] is found in ℵ² C 046 1006 1611 1841 1854 2053 2062 2329 2351 𝔐, but omitted in 𝔓¹⁸ A P 2050. Most likely the bracketed words were added due to conformity to the use of this formula elsewhere in Revelation (1:18; 4:9, 10; 5:13; 7:12; 10:6; 11:15; 14:11; 15:7; 19:13; 20:10; 22:5) where the genitive τῶν αἰώνων is included.

1:7 Ἰδοὺ ἔρχεται μετὰ τῶν νεφελῶν, καὶ ὄψεται αὐτὸν πᾶς ὀφθαλμὸς καὶ οἵτινες αὐτὸν ἐξεκέντησαν, καὶ κόψονται ἐπ' αὐτὸν πᾶσαι αἱ φυλαὶ τῆς γῆς. ναί, ἀμήν.

Ἰδού. A marker of attention that deictically functions to make the following statement emphatic. Formally, ἰδού is the aor mid impv of εἶδον (BDAG, 468). Throughout the rest of Revelation, a common pattern is for the nominative to follow ἰδού (1:7, 18; 2:10; 4:1-2; 5:5; 6:2, 5, 8; 7:9; 9:12; 11:14; 12:3; 14:1, 14; 19:11; 21:3) and the accusative to follow εἶδον (1:12, 17; 5:1, 2, 6; 6:9; 7:1, 2; 8:2; 9:1, 17; 10:1, 5; 14:6; 15:1, 2; 16:13; 17:3, 6; 18:1; 19:11, 17, 19; 20:1, 4, 11, 12; 21:1, 2, 22).

ἔρχεται. Pres mid ind 3rd sg ἔρχομαι. The present tense has future reference here. This is common with verbs of "coming" and "going" (McKay 1994, 41).

μετὰ τῶν νεφελῶν. Manner or association.

ὄψεται. Fut mid ind 3rd sg ὁράω.

αὐτόν. Accusative direct object of ὄψεται.

πᾶς ὀφθαλμός. Nominative subject of ὄψεται.

καί. Ascensive: "even."

οἵτινες. Nominative subject of ἐξεκέντησαν. The relative pronoun introduces a headless relative clause. The entire clause functions as the subject of an implied ὄψεται.

αὐτόν. Accusative direct object of ἐξεκέντησαν.

ἐξεκέντησαν. Aor act ind 3rd pl ἐκκεντέω.

κόψονται. Fut mid ind 3rd pl κόπτω. In the active voice κόπτω means "to cut (off)," but with the middle voice it means to "beat one's breast as an act of mourning" (BDAG, 559.2).

ἐπ' αὐτόν. The preposition ἐπί can indicate the object towards which feelings or actions are directed (BDAG, 365.6.c). Here it indicates the object of the mourning.

πᾶσαι αἱ φυλαί. Nominative subject of κόψονται.

τῆς γῆς. Genitive of location.

ναί, ἀμήν. An emphatic way of affirming the preceding statement.

1:8 Ἐγώ εἰμι τὸ ἄλφα καὶ τὸ ὦ, λέγει κύριος ὁ θεός, ὁ ὢν καὶ ὁ ἦν καὶ ὁ ἐρχόμενος, ὁ παντοκράτωρ.

The expansion in this verse through the piling up of modifiers draws attention to the identity of the one now speaking.

Ἐγώ. Nominative subject of εἰμι.

εἰμι. Pres act ind 1st sg εἰμί. In most of its present indicative forms εἰμί is an enclitic, which means that it is grammatically free, but phonologically bound to the preceding word. Hence, it tends to give its accent to the preceding word, as is the case here.

τὸ ἄλφα καὶ τὸ ὦ. Predicate nominative of εἰμι. The expression constitutes a merism (stating the two extremes on a spectrum in order to also emphasize everything in between; Beale, 199). Several manuscripts (א' 1854 2050 2329 2351) insert ἀρχὴ καὶ τέλος here, probably in conformity to the fuller formula in 21:6; 22:13. There is an apparent imbalance between the way the first and last letters of the Greek alphabet are written here, with one written out and the other simply listed in letter form. Though the first letter of the Greek alphabet was written ἄλφα early on, the letter Ω was not written out as ὦ μέγα until around the 7th century A.D., perhaps to distinguish it from ὃ μικρόν (see LJS, 2029; Aune, 1.51).

λέγει. Pres act ind 3rd sg λέγω.

κύριος. Nominative subject of λέγει.

ὁ θεός. Nominative in apposition to κύριος.

ὁ ὢν καὶ ὁ ἦν καὶ ὁ ἐρχόμενος. Nominative in apposition to κύριος ὁ θεός. On this threefold designation, see 1:4.

ὁ παντοκράτωρ. Nominative in apposition to κύριος.

Revelation 1:9-20

⁹I, John, your brother and companion in the tribulation and kingdom and endurance in Jesus, was on the island called Patmos because of the word of God and the testimony about Jesus. ¹⁰I was in the Spirit on the Lord's Day and I heard behind me a mighty voice like a trumpet ¹¹saying, "Write what you see in a scroll and send it to the seven churches, to Ephesus, and to Smyrna, and to Pergamum, and to Thyatira, and to Sardis, and to Philadelphia, and to Laodicea." ¹²And I turned to see the voice which was speaking with me, and when I turned I saw seven golden lampstands ¹³and in the midst of the lampstands (I saw) one like a son of man clothed with a long robe and a golden belt encircling his chest. ¹⁴And his head and white hair were like white wool, like snow, and his eyes were like a flame of fire, ¹⁵and his feet were like bronze refined in a furnace and his voice was like the sound of many waters, ¹⁶and he

had in his right hand seven stars and a sharp double-edged sword came out of his mouth and his appearance was like the sun shining in all its strength. [17]And when I saw him, I fell at his feet as if dead, and he placed his right hand on me, saying, "Do not fear! I am the first and the last [18]and the living one, and I was dead and, look, I am living forever and ever and I have the keys of death and Hades. [19]Therefore, write what you see, the things that are and the things that are about to take place after these. [20](This is) the mystery of the seven stars which you saw in my right hand and the seven golden lampstands: The seven stars are the angels of the seven churches and the lampstands are the seven churches."

1:9 Ἐγὼ Ἰωάννης, ὁ ἀδελφὸς ὑμῶν καὶ συγκοινωνὸς ἐν τῇ θλίψει καὶ βασιλείᾳ καὶ ὑπομονῇ ἐν Ἰησοῦ, ἐγενόμην ἐν τῇ νήσῳ τῇ καλουμένῃ Πάτμῳ διὰ τὸν λόγον τοῦ θεοῦ καὶ τὴν μαρτυρίαν Ἰησοῦ.

Ἐγώ. Nominative subject of ἐγενόμην.

Ἰωάννης. Nominative in apposition to Ἐγώ.

ὁ ἀδελφὸς ... καὶ συγκοινωνός. Nominative in apposition to Ἰωάννης.

ὑμῶν. Genitive of relationship.

ἐν τῇ θλίψει καὶ βασιλείᾳ καὶ ὑπομονῇ. Indicates the thing in which one shares, though elsewhere in the NT συγκοινωνός occurs with the genitive of the thing shared (BDAG, 952).

ἐν Ἰησοῦ. Locative, in a metaphorical sense. This is probably to be understood in a similar way to ἐν Χριστῷ. At least one witness (A) reads ἐν Χριστῷ here. Aune thinks that it is problematic to read ἐν Ἰησοῦ with τῇ θλίψει, and so ἐν Ἰησοῦ should only be taken as modifying βασιλείᾳ καὶ ὑπομονῇ (Aune, 1.75–76). However, it is best to take ἐν Ἰησοῦ as modifying all three substantives, which are governed by the single article τῇ.

ἐγενόμην. Aor mid ind 1st sg γίνομαι.

ἐν τῇ νήσῳ. Locative.

τῇ καλουμένῃ. Pres act ptc fem dat sg καλέω (attributive).

Πάτμῳ. Along with νήσῳ this is part of a double dative construction with a passive verb from a double accusative construction with an active verb (Culy 2009, 87–92): "(I) call the island Patmos." By turning the verb into a passive, the direct object becomes the subject and the other noun is the complement: "The island called Patmos."

διὰ τὸν λόγον ... καὶ τὴν μαρτυρίαν. Cause.

τοῦ θεοῦ. Genitive of source or subjective genitive.

Ἰησοῦ. Objective genitive. Here Jesus is the object of John's activity of witnessing. It is unlikely that Beale is correct in concluding that the genitive is both subjective and objective (202), since this is a matter of semantic ambiguity rather than a grammatical category.

1:10 ἐγενόμην ἐν πνεύματι ἐν τῇ κυριακῇ ἡμέρᾳ καὶ ἤκουσα ὀπίσω μου φωνὴν μεγάλην ὡς σάλπιγγος

ἐγενόμην. Aor mid ind 1st sg γίνομαι.
ἐν πνεύματι. Locative, in a metaphorical sense. The primary debate is whether πνεύματι refers to the human spirit or the Holy Spirit. Given John's dependence on Ezekiel (cf. 43:5) the latter is to be preferred.
ἐν τῇ κυριακῇ ἡμέρᾳ. Temporal. The reference most likely is to Sunday, the day of the Christians' worship (Aune, 1.84).
ἤκουσα. Aor act ind 1st sg ἀκούω.
ὀπίσω μου. Locative.
φωνὴν μεγάλην. Accusative direct object of ἤκουσα.
ὡς σάλπιγγος. Comparative.
σάλπιγγος. Genitive of source ("as from a trumpet") or subjective genitive ("sound as made by a trumpet").

1:11 λεγούσης· ὃ βλέπεις γράψον εἰς βιβλίον καὶ πέμψον ταῖς ἑπτὰ ἐκκλησίαις, εἰς Ἔφεσον καὶ εἰς Σμύρναν καὶ εἰς Πέργαμον καὶ εἰς Θυάτειρα καὶ εἰς Σάρδεις καὶ εἰς Φιλαδέλφειαν καὶ εἰς Λαοδίκειαν.

λεγούσης. Pres act ptc fem gen sg λέγω. On the use of the participle λεγούσης to introduce speech, see 1:17 below on λέγων. The participle functions as the complement in an object-complement double case construction with φωνὴν μεγάλην in verse 10 serving as the object. Although one would expect an accusative participle, the case here has probably been attracted to the genitive of σάλπιγγος. One witness (א[2]) corrects the participle to λεγούσαν.
ὅ. Accusative direct object of βλέπεις. The relative pronoun introduces a headless relative clause. The entire clause functions as the direct object of γράψον. The relative clause comes at the beginning for emphasis.
βλέπεις. Pres act ind 2nd sg βλέπω. The present tense refers to the contents of the entire book, which John has not yet seen.
γράψον. Aor act impv 2nd sg γράφω. The aorist here refers to the writing of the entire book. The command to write occurs eleven more times in Revelation (1:19; 2:1, 8, 12, 18; 3:1, 7, 14; 14:13; 19:9; 21:5), all in the aorist tense.
εἰς βιβλίον. Locative.
πέμψον. Aor act impv 2nd sg πέμπω.
ταῖς ἑπτὰ ἐκκλησίαις. Dative indirect object of πέμψον.

εἰς Ἔφεσον ... καὶ εἰς Λαοδίκειαν. Although the preposition εἰς may be synonymous with the dative ἐκκλησίαις (Osborne, 101), it could carry the idea of direction or motion toward (Moule, 68). The construction εἰς + "name of city" functions to enumerate in detail the ἑπτὰ ἐκκλησίαις.

1:12 Καὶ ἐπέστρεψα βλέπειν τὴν φωνὴν ἥτις ἐλάλει μετ' ἐμοῦ, καὶ ἐπιστρέψας εἶδον ἑπτὰ λυχνίας χρυσᾶς

ἐπέστρεψα. Aor act ind 1st sg ἐπιστρέφω.
βλέπειν. Pres act inf βλέπω (purpose).
τὴν φωνὴν. Accusative direct object of βλέπειν.
ἥτις. Nominative subject of ἐλάλει.
ἐλάλει. Impf act ind 3rd sg λαλέω. The implication of the imperfect here may be that John turned (ἐπέστρεψα) while the voice was in the process of speaking (ἐλάλει) with him.
μετ' ἐμοῦ. Association.
ἐπιστρέψας. Aor act ptc masc nom sg ἐπιστρέφω (temporal).
εἶδον. Aor act ind 1st sg ὁράω.
ἑπτὰ λυχνίας χρυσᾶς. Accusative direct object of εἶδον.

1:13 καὶ ἐν μέσῳ τῶν λυχνιῶν ὅμοιον υἱὸν ἀνθρώπου ἐνδεδυμένον ποδήρη καὶ περιεζωσμένον πρὸς τοῖς μαστοῖς ζώνην χρυσᾶν.

ἐν μέσῳ τῶν λυχνιῶν. Locative.
ὅμοιον υἱὸν. Accusative direct object of εἶδον (v. 12). Normally ὅμοιον occurs with the dative of the thing to which something is compared (BDAG, 706.a). In this case we would expect υἱῷ after ὅμοιον (cf. 1:15; 2:18; 4:3, 6, 7, etc.). The dative υἱῷ is, in fact, found in A C 1006 1611 1854 2053 2062 2351 2681. It is possible that υἱόν has been attracted to the case of ὅμοιον to produce this solecism (Aune, 1.65). However, it is more likely that this apparent grammatical irregularity is due to the author's desire to draw attention to the OT allusion (Dan 7:13), since the only other place that this exact same phrase occurs is in 14:14 (ὅμοιον υἱὸν ἀνθρώπου), a clear allusion to Dan 7:13. It is improbable that the author used ὅμοιον like ὡς here, since in the 19 other times John used ὅμοιον (outside of 1:13 and 14:14), it is followed by the dative (contra Aune, 1.65). The accusative here seems to be deliberate. The accusative of ὅμοιον is due to the fact that either (1) it is the direct object of "I saw" in verse 12, or (2) it modifies the participles ἐνδεδυμένον and περιεζωσμένον. See below.
ἀνθρώπου. Genitive of relationship.

ἐνδεδυμένον. Prf mid ptc masc acc sg ἐνδύω. The participle could be attributive, in which case it modifies "one like a son of man." It could also be substantival, in which case it functions as the direct object of "I saw" in verse 12: "I saw one clothed … and girded about … like a son of man."

ποδήρη. Accusative direct object of ἐνδεδυμένον. ποδήρης is a hapax legemenon and occurs only here in the NT. This term literally means "reaching to the feet" (BDAG, 838; Moulton-Milligan, 522), but here refers to "a long robe reaching to the feet" (LN 6.175).

περιεζωσμένον. Prf mid ptc masc acc sg περιζώννυμι. On the function of this participle, see ἐνδεδυμένον above. The clustering of perfect participle forms around υἱὸν ἀνθρώπου functions to draw attention to this figure.

πρὸς τοῖς μαστοῖς. Locative. The preposition πρός occurs only 6 times in the entire NT with the dative case. For πρός indicating position with the dative ("around"), see Porter 1992, 174; BDAG, 874.2.a.

ζώνην χρυσᾶν. Accusative direct object of περιεζωσμένον.

1:14 ἡ δὲ κεφαλὴ αὐτοῦ καὶ αἱ τρίχες λευκαὶ ὡς ἔριον λευκόν ὡς χιὼν καὶ οἱ ὀφθαλμοὶ αὐτοῦ ὡς φλὸξ πυρός

δέ. The sequence of clauses introduced by καί is broken by a clause introduced by δέ. δέ is used to indicate that the author signals a new or distinct development in the story (cf. Runge, 31). It is used six other times in Revelation: 2:5, 16, 24; 10:2; 19:12; 21:8. Perhaps here, after introducing and describing the Son of Man's overall dress in v. 13, the author now signals a development with δέ where he begins to enumerate in detail specific features of the Son of Man. The δέ thus functions to shift the focus to the Son of Man's head and face.

ἡ … κεφαλὴ … καὶ αἱ τρίχες. Nominative subject of a verbless clause.

αὐτοῦ. Possessive genitive.

λευκαί. Predicate adjective of a verbless clause.

ὡς ἔριον λευκόν. Comparison.

ὡς χιών. Comparison. This comparative clause stands in apposition to the preceding one.

οἱ ὀφθαλμοί. Nominative subject of a verbless clause.

αὐτοῦ. Possessive genitive.

ὡς φλόξ. Comparison.

πυρός. Attributive genitive.

1:15 καὶ οἱ πόδες αὐτοῦ ὅμοιοι χαλκολιβάνῳ ὡς ἐν καμίνῳ πεπυρωμένης καὶ ἡ φωνὴ αὐτοῦ ὡς φωνὴ ὑδάτων πολλῶν,

οἱ πόδες. Nominative subject of a verbless clause.

αὐτοῦ. Possessive genitive.

ὅμοιοι. Predicate adjective of a verbless clause.

χαλκολιβάνῳ. Dative complement of ὅμοιοι. The precise meaning of this compound word (χαλκός and λίβανος) is problematic since it occurs only here and in 2:18 in the NT, though there is widespread agreement that some kind of metal is in mind (copper, brass, or bronze). BDAG defines it as "an exceptionally fine type of metal or alloy" (1076). See the discussion in Hemer, 111–17. Most English translations opt for polished brass or bronze.

ὡς . . . πεπυρωμένης. Manner. For this use of ὡς, see BDAG, 1103.1.a.

ἐν καμίνῳ. Manner or means.

πεπυρωμένης. Prf pass ptc fem gen sg πυρόω (genitive absolute). The case and gender of this participle is problematic (another example of Revelation's grammatical solecism), since there seems to be no antecedent to which it is grammatically connected. The readings found in ℵ 2050 2045 2053 2062 (πεπυρωμένῳ) and 025 046 2351 𝔐 syr^h (πεπυρωμένοι) are obvious attempts to correct the grammar. It could take its gender from the feminine καμίνῳ (Aune, 1.65–66; Osborne, 102), or possibly χαλκολιβάνῳ if that is understood as a feminine noun (Aune, 1.66). Beale (210) thinks it is possible that it is designed to draw attention to an allusion to Daniel (Theodotian) 3:21, 23, 26, though the correspondence is not that close. Aune is probably correct when he understands this as a genitive absolute construction, where αὐτῆς is omitted (1.66). The assumed subject of the participle would be καμίνῳ or χαλκολιβάνῳ ("his feet were like bronze as it is burning in a furnace").

ἡ φωνή. Nominative subject of a verbless clause.

ὡς φωνή. Comparison.

ὑδάτων πολλῶν. Genitive of source or subjective genitive.

1:16 καὶ ἔχων ἐν τῇ δεξιᾷ χειρὶ αὐτοῦ ἀστέρας ἑπτὰ καὶ ἐκ τοῦ στόματος αὐτοῦ ῥομφαία δίστομος ὀξεῖα ἐκπορευομένη καὶ ἡ ὄψις αὐτοῦ ὡς ὁ ἥλιος φαίνει ἐν τῇ δυνάμει αὐτοῦ.

ἔχων. Pres act ptc masc nom sg ἔχω. The function of the participial form of ἔχω in Revelation is often difficult to determine. It frequently occurs as a nominative masculine, even when the verb or noun it modifies requires a different case and/or number (1:16; 4:8; 9:14; 10:2; 14:14; 17:3; 19:12). In addition, it is often unclear how it functions. At times it appears to be an example of the participle used as a finite verb (see below). At other times the participle appears to be a more loosely appended as a further descriptive feature (Robertson, 414), parenthetically, or the predicate of a verbless cluase. The grammatical incongruity here may function to draw attention to the description that follows. The participle here in 1:16 is used like a finite verb (i.e., ἔχει or εἴχεν) as part of a periphrastic construction with an implied ἦν. There are several examples of this use of the participle in Revelation.

ἐν τῇ δεξιᾷ χειρί. Locative. In the OT, the "right hand" of God is a metaphor for God's power and authority (Exod 15:6; Pss 18:35; 20:6; 63:8; Isa 41:10; 48:13).

ἀστέρας ἑπτά. Accusative direct object of ἔχων.

αὐτοῦ. Possessive genitive.

ἐκ τοῦ στόματος. Source.

αὐτοῦ. Possessive genitive.

ῥομφαία δίστομος ὀξεῖα. Nominative subject of (ἦν) ἐκπορευομένη.

ἐκπορευομένη. Pres mid ptc fem nom sg ἐκπορεύομαι. It is possible that this is a further example of the use of a participle as part of a periphrastic construction with an implied ἦν. See ἔχων above. This is consistent with the pattern of a series of equative clauses with an assumed ἦν.

ἡ ὄψις. Nominative subject of a verbless clause.

ὡς ὁ ἥλιος. Comparison.

ὁ ἥλιος. Nominative subject of φαίνει.

φαίνει. Pres act ind 3rd sg φαίνω. The present tense is used omnitemporally (gnomically) to refer to a recurring process in nature (Porter 1992, 32).

ἐν τῇ δυνάμει. Manner.

αὐτοῦ. Subjective genitive.

1:17 Καὶ ὅτε εἶδον αὐτόν, ἔπεσα πρὸς τοὺς πόδας αὐτοῦ ὡς νεκρός, καὶ ἔθηκεν τὴν δεξιὰν αὐτοῦ ἐπ' ἐμὲ λέγων· μὴ φοβοῦ· ἐγώ εἰμι ὁ πρῶτος καὶ ὁ ἔσχατος

ὅτε. Introduces a temporal clause.

εἶδον. Aor act ind 1st sg ὁράω.

αὐτόν. Accusative direct object of εἶδον.

ἔπεσα. Aor act ind 1st sg πίπτω.

πρὸς τοὺς πόδας. Locative.

αὐτοῦ. Possessive genitive.

ὡς νεκρός. Manner.

ἔθηκεν. Aor act ind 3rd sg τίθημι.

τὴν δεξιὰν. Accusative direct object of ἔθηκεν. On the meaning of δεξιάν, see verse 16.

αὐτοῦ. Possessive genitive.

ἐπ' ἐμὲ. Locative.

λέγων. Pres act ptc masc nom sg λέγω (manner). Introduces a quotation. The present participial form of λέγω is used numerous times throughout Revelation to introduce the speech of various individuals and groups. While some have labeled this a Semitism due to its extensive occurrence in the LXX to translate the Hebrew infinitive absolute לֵאמֹר (Thompson, 69–70), parallels in extra-biblical Greek literature suggest that it is acceptable Greek. At best, its usage in Revelation may have been enhanced by the LXX (Porter 1989a, 138–39; 1989b, 590).

φοβοῦ. Pres mid impv 2nd sg φοβέομαι (prohibition). At one time it was customary to interpret present prohibitions (present imperatives with μή) as commands to cease an activity already going on ("stop..."; see Charles, 1.cxxvi). However, the present imperative with μή does not necessarily indicate the cessation of an activity already in process (see Wallace, 714–17; McKay 1992; Mathewson 1996). It only forbids an action viewed as a process. Whether the action is actually taking place or not can only be determined by the context (see Boyer 1987). However, here it would be legitimate to *translate* it "stop fearing," but only because the *immediately preceding clause* makes it clear that the seer is already gripped with fear at the time the prohibition is given.

ἐγώ. Nominative subject of εἰμί.

εἰμι. Pres act ind 1st sg εἰμί. For the loss of accent, see 1:8.

ὁ πρῶτος καὶ ὁ ἔσχατος καὶ ὁ ζῶν. Predicate nominative.

1:18 καὶ ὁ ζῶν, καὶ ἐγενόμην νεκρὸς καὶ ἰδοὺ ζῶν εἰμι εἰς τοὺς αἰῶνας τῶν αἰώνων καὶ ἔχω τὰς κλεῖς τοῦ θανάτου καὶ τοῦ ᾅδου.

ὁ ζῶν. Pres act ptc masc nom sg ζάω (substantival). Predicate nominative.

ἐγενόμην. Aor mid ind 1st sg γίνομαι.

νεκρός. Predicate adjective.

ἰδού. A marker of attention that deictically functions to make the following statement emphatic. On the form, see 1:7. Here it draws attention to the state of Christ being alive in contrast to being dead.

ζῶν. Pres act ptc masc nom sg ζάω (present periphrastic). In contrast to the aorist ἐγενόμην with reference to Jesus' death, the use of the present periphrastic construction with ἰδού and the fronting of the participle before εἰμι draw attention to Jesus' state of being alive. As Porter says, "Grammarians who wish to stress that the periphrastic is more emphatic or significant, or that it draws attention to the participle and its modifiers, are probably correct" (1992, 46).

εἰμι. Pres act ind 1st sg εἰμί. On the loss of accent, see 1:8.

εἰς τοὺς αἰῶνας τῶν αἰώνων. Temporal. Lit. "unto the ages of the ages." In this expression for eternity (BDAG, 32.1.b) the double use of αἰών may be emphatic (LN 67.95).

ἔχω. Pres act ind 1st sg ἔχω.

τὰς κλεῖς. Accusative direct object of ἔχω.

τοῦ θανάτου καὶ τοῦ ᾅδου. Possessive genitive. Or the idea might be "the keys to death and Hades."

1:19 γράψον οὖν ἃ εἶδες καὶ ἃ εἰσὶν καὶ ἃ μέλλει γενέσθαι μετὰ ταῦτα.

γράψον. Aor act impv 2nd sg γράφω.

οὖν. Inferential. John is commanded to write based on the fact that the exalted Son of Man has overcome death and is alive.

ἃ. Accusative direct object of εἶδες. The relative pronoun introduces a headless relative clause. The entire clause, together with the other conjoined relative clauses (ἃ εἶδες καὶ ἃ εἰσὶν καὶ ἃ μέλλει γενέσθαι μετὰ ταῦτα), functions as the direct object of γράψον.

εἶδες. Aor act ind 2nd sg ὁράω. The aorist tense probably refers to the contents of the entire book of Revelation, not only to what he just saw, and can be translated "what you see."

καὶ. The first καί here may function in an epexegetical manner: "Write what you see, *that is,* the things that are and the things that are about to take place after these things."

ἃ. Nominative subject of εἰσίν. The relative pronoun introduces a headless relative clause. See also the first ἃ above.

εἰσὶν. Pres act ind 3rd sg εἰμί.

ἃ. Nominative subject of μέλλει. The relative pronoun introduces a headless relative clause. See also the first ἃ above.

μέλλει. Pres act ind 3rd sg μέλλω.

γενέσθαι. Aor mid inf γίνομαι (complementary). Some manuscripts read the present infinitive γίνεσθαι (ℵ² A 1006 1611 1841 1854 2053 2062 2329 2351 2681). The frequency of μέλλω with a present infinitive in the NT may account for the present tense variant here (see Aune, 1.67), making the aorist the more difficult reading.

μετὰ ταῦτα. Temporal. The antecedent of ταῦτα is difficult to determine. Although some have limited it to a specific section of Revelation, such as chs. 4–22, ταῦτα more likely refers anaphorically back to ἃ εἰσίν in the previous clause, with ἃ εἰσίν being a reference to the present time of the readers. Beale (155) argues that μέλλει γενέσθαι μετὰ ταῦτα draws on Dan 2:28, 29 (δεῖ γενέσθαι ἐπ' ἐσχάτων τῶν ἡμερῶν; Dan 2:28, 45 Theod: δεῖ γενέσθαι μετὰ ταῦτα). In this case, the intent would be to draw attention to the fulfillment of Daniel's latter days. In any case, the entire clause ἃ μέλλει γενέσθαι μετὰ ταῦτα refers to events that will transpire in the future from the standpoint of the readers. It is doubtful, however, that either of these two phrases can be used to form a clear outline of the Apocalypse (contra Charles, 1.33).

1:20 τὸ μυστήριον τῶν ἑπτὰ ἀστέρων οὓς εἶδες ἐπὶ τῆς δεξιᾶς μου καὶ τὰς ἑπτὰ λυχνίας τὰς χρυσᾶς· οἱ ἑπτὰ ἀστέρες ἄγγελοι τῶν ἑπτὰ ἐκκλησιῶν εἰσιν καὶ αἱ λυχνίαι αἱ ἑπτὰ ἑπτὰ ἐκκλησίαι εἰσίν.

τὸ μυστήριον. The grammar here is difficult. Apparently this word and τὰς ἑπτὰ λυχνίας τὰς χρυσᾶς are both in the accusative case (the neuter τὸ μυστήριον could be either nominative or accusative), but do not appear to be the object of any verb (e.g., γράψον in v. 19). They could be the direct object of an assumed εἶδον (Mussies, 100), but the "mystery" seems to refer to the interpretation of what John saw (Aune, 1.67) as is indicated by the relative clause οὓς εἶδες, which follows "seven stars." Smalley argues that it is a rare instance of an accusative absolute (57; see Charles, 1.33–34). Aune thinks that τὸ μυστήριον is a nominative absolute, and τὰς ἑπτὰ λυχνίας τὰς χρυσᾶς has been attracted to the accusative case of the relative pronoun οὓς (1.68). It is also possible to treat this construction as an accusative of respect ("as for the mystery"; Wallace, 203–4), though Wallace says this is rare and should only be appealed to as a last resort. It is probably best to take the accusative case of both τὸ μυστήριον τῶν ἑπτὰ ἀστέρων and τὰς ἑπτὰ λυχνίας τὰς χρυσᾶς as direct objects of an implied verb, such as "I will explain" or "I will interpret."

τῶν ἑπτὰ ἀστέρων. Epexegetical genitive.

οὓς. Accusative direct object of εἶδες. The (masculine) antecedent is ἀστέρων.

εἶδες. Aor act ind 2nd sg ὁράω.

ἐπὶ τῆς δεξιᾶς. Locative.

τὰς ἑπτὰ λυχνίας τὰς χρυσᾶς. See τὸ μυστήριον above.

οἱ ἑπτὰ ἀστέρες. Nominative subject of the following εἰσιν. The article distinguishes the subject from the predicate nominative.

ἄγγελοι. Predicate nominative.

τῶν ἑπτὰ ἐκκλησιῶν. Genitive of subordination ("angels over the seven churches").

εἰσιν. Pres act ind 3rd pl εἰμί. On the loss of accent, see 1:8.

αἱ λυχνίαι αἱ ἑπτά. Nominative subject of the following εἰσίν. The article with λυχνίαι distinguishes the subject from the predicate nominative.

ἑπτὰ ἐκκλησίαι. Predicate nominative of εἰσίν.

εἰσίν. Pres act ind 3rd pl εἰμί.

Revelation 2:1-7

¹To the angel of the church in Ephesus write: The one who holds the seven stars in his right hand, who walks in the midst of the seven

golden lampstands says these things: ²I know your works and your labor and endurance and that you are not able to tolerate evil ones, and you test those who call themselves apostles and are not, and you have found them (to be) liars, ³and you have endurance and you have borne up because of my name, and you have not grown weary. ⁴But I have against you that you have left your first love. ⁵Therefore, remember from where you have fallen and repent and do the first works. But if (you do) not, I am coming against you and I will remove your lampstand from its place, if you do not repent. ⁶But you have this, you hate the works of the Nicolaitans, which I also hate. ⁷The one who has ears should listen to what the Spirit is saying to the churches. To the one who overcomes I will give to eat from the tree of life, which is in the paradise of God.

2:1 Τῷ ἀγγέλῳ τῆς ἐν Ἐφέσῳ ἐκκλησίας γράψον· Τάδε λέγει ὁ κρατῶν τοὺς ἑπτὰ ἀστέρας ἐν τῇ δεξιᾷ αὐτοῦ, ὁ περιπατῶν ἐν μέσῳ τῶν ἑπτὰ λυχνιῶν τῶν χρυσῶν·

Τῷ ἀγγέλῳ. Dative indirect object of γράψον.

τῆς . . . ἐκκλησίας. Possessive genitive or genitive of subordination.

ἐν Ἐφέσῳ. Locative.

γράψον. Aor act impv 2nd sg γράψω. In each of the messages to the churches, everything following the command γράψον functions as its direct object.

Τάδε. Accusative (neut pl from ὅδε) direct object of λέγει. In each of its seven uses in chs. 2–3, Τάδε is used cataphorically to refer to the message that follows. The expression Τάδε λέγει was used in the OT (LXX) around 250 times to introduce prophetic oracles spoken by God to the prophets. The expression was obsolete by the NT time and would have had an "antique ring" to it, not unlike the expression "thus saith" (Aune, 1.141). This formula occurs here and in 2:9, 12, 18; 3:1, 7, 14, as well as once in Acts 21:11. The use of this expression to refer to the words of Jesus here suggests that Christ's words are treated on the same level as YHWH's in the past (Beale, 229).

λέγει. Pres act ind 3rd sg λέγω.

ὁ κρατῶν. Pres act ptc masc nom sg κρατέω (substantival). Nominative subject of λέγει.

τοὺς ἑπτὰ ἀστέρας. Accusative direct object of κρατῶν.

ἐν τῇ δεξιᾷ. Locative.

αὐτοῦ. Possessive genitive.

ὁ περιπατῶν. Pres act ptc masc nom sg περιπατέω (substantival). Nominative in apposition to ὁ κρατῶν.

ἐν μέσῳ. Locative.

τῶν ἑπτὰ λυχνιῶν τῶν χρυσῶν. Partitive genitive.

2:2 οἶδα τὰ ἔργα σου καὶ τὸν κόπον καὶ τὴν ὑπομονήν σου καὶ ὅτι οὐ δύνῃ βαστάσαι κακούς, καὶ ἐπείρασας τοὺς λέγοντας ἑαυτοὺς ἀποστόλους καὶ οὐκ εἰσὶν καὶ εὗρες αὐτοὺς ψευδεῖς,

οἶδα. Prf act ind 1st sg οἶδα. Though often treated as a perfect tense with present tense meaning, along with the stative semantics of οἶδα, the perfect tense should be given its full stative force, irrespective of how we translate it into English. Lit. "I am in the state of knowing" (see McKay 1981). The rest of verses 2-3 functions as the content of οἶδα.

τὰ ἔργα ... καὶ τὸν κόπον καὶ τὴν ὑπομονήν. Accusative direct object of οἶδα. Charles (1.49) places a comma after ἔργα σου, making the following καί epexegetical: the works consist of τὸν κόπον καὶ τὴν ὑπομονήν.

σου ... σου. Subjective genitive.

ὅτι. Introduces a content clause that is the clausal complement of οἶδα.

δύνῃ. Pres mid ind 2nd sg δύναμαι. The verbs throughout chs. 2-3 addressing the churches are generally singular since the angel of each of the churches is being addressed.

βαστάσαι. Aor act inf βαστάζω (complementary).

κακούς. Accusative direct object of βαστάσαι.

ἐπείρασας. Aor act ind 2nd sg πειράζω.

τοὺς λέγοντας. Pres act ptc masc acc pl λέγω (substantival). Accusative direct object of ἐπείρασας.

ἑαυτούς. Accusative direct object of λέγοντας.

ἀποστόλους. Complement in an object-complement double accusative construction.

καί. Aune (1.134) confuses grammar and translation by treating this καί as adversative. Any adversative notion comes from the semantic relationship between the two clauses, not from the καί itself, which simply signals continuity between the two clauses.

εἰσὶν. Pres act ind 3rd pl εἰμί. On the shift from the participle to a finite verb, see 1:6 on ἐποίησεν.

εὗρες. Aor act ind 2nd sg εὑρίσκω.

αὐτούς. Accusative direct object of εὗρες.

ψευδεῖς. Complement in an object-complement double accusative construction.

2:3 καὶ ὑπομονὴν ἔχεις καὶ ἐβάστασας διὰ τὸ ὄνομά μου καὶ οὐ κεκοπίακες.

ὑπομονήν. Accusative direct object of ἔχεις.

ἔχεις. Pres act ind 2nd sg ἔχω.

ἐβάστασας. Aor act ind 2nd sg βαστάζω.

διὰ τὸ ὄνομά. Cause. The accenting is due to the enclitic μου that follows.

μου. Possessive genitive.

κεκοπίακες. Prf act ind 2nd sg κοπιάω. Instead of κεκοπίακες (A C *pc*) some manuscripts have ἐκοπίασας (א 𝔐). This textual issue is difficult. The aorist reading may be an attempt to conform to the aorist ἐβάστασας. However, the aorist reading is widely attested and has the support of א.

2:4 ἀλλὰ ἔχω κατὰ σοῦ ὅτι τὴν ἀγάπην σου τὴν πρώτην ἀφῆκες.

ἀλλά. Adversative. Here the conjunction introduces a contrast and provides a corrective (see Runge, 56) to the previous positive evaluation by introducing the primary accusation.

ἔχω. Pres act ind 1st sg ἔχω.

κατὰ σοῦ. Opposition.

ὅτι. Introduces a content clause that is the clausal complement of ἔχω.

τὴν ἀγάπην . . . τὴν πρώτην. Accusative direct object of ἀφῆκες. There is debate as to whether the "love" here is directed toward other members of the church (Smalley, 61) or to Jesus (Beale, 230) or both (Osborne, 115–16). Beale thinks that, given the emphasis on witness, the idea is that "they no longer expressed their former zealous love for Jesus *by witnessing to him in the world*" (230, emphasis in original).

σου. Subjective genitive.

ἀφῆκες. Aor act ind 2nd sg ἀφίημι.

2:5 μνημόνευε οὖν πόθεν πέπτωκας καὶ μετανόησον καὶ τὰ πρῶτα ἔργα ποίησον· εἰ δὲ μή, ἔρχομαί σοι καὶ κινήσω τὴν λυχνίαν σου ἐκ τοῦ τόπου αὐτῆς, ἐὰν μὴ μετανοήσῃς.

μνημόνευε. Pres act impv 2nd sg μνημονεύω. The present imperative μνημόνευε introduces the main hortatory line of thought: their need to recall their state, which is indicated by the stative aspect πέπτωκας (perhaps to emphasize its gravity). The present imperative functions as an impetus for the imperatives to repent and do the first works summarized in the aorists μετανόησον and ποίησον. It is a misunderstanding of the present tense to interpret it as indicating the constant need for spiritual recollection (contra Smalley, 62) or ongoing action (contra Osborne, 117 n. 18). See the Introduction on "Verbal Aspect."

οὖν. Inferential.

πόθεν. An "interrogative expression of extension from a local source, *from what place? from where?*" (BDAG, 838.1).
πέπτωκας. Prf act ind 2nd sg πίπτω. On the aspect, see 2:3 on κεκοπίακες.
μετανόησον. Aor act impv 2nd sg μετανοέω.
τὰ πρῶτα ἔργα. Accusative direct object of ποίησον.
ποίησον. Aor act impv 2nd sg ποιέω.
εἰ δὲ μή. This combination of particles after an affirmative clause can be translated "if not" or "otherwise" (BDAG, 278.6.d; BDF §480).
ἔρχομαί. Pres mid ind 1st sg ἔρχομαι. The present tense is future referring (see 1:7). The accenting is due to the enclitic σοι that follows. Some witnesses (𝔐 *pc*) insert ταχύ after ἔρχομαί σοι probably in analogy to 2:16; 3:11; 11:14; 22:7, 12, 20.
σοι. Dative of location.
κινήσω. Fut act ind 1st sg κινέω.
τὴν λυχνίαν. Accusative direct object of κινήσω: "to cause someth. to be moved from its customary or established place" (BDAG, 545.1).
σου. Possessive genitive.
ἐκ τοῦ τόπου. Separation.
αὐτῆς. Possessive genitive.
ἐάν. Introduces the protasis of a third-class condition, which Porter notes "is more tentative and simply projects some action or event for hypothetical consideration" (1992, 262) and contains no indication of the probability of the condition's fulfillment (e.g., the dubious "future more probable"). The protasis of conditional sentences usually precedes the primary clause (apodosis). By placing the protasis last and repeating the verb μετανοέω from the beginning of the sentence, the author foregrounds the need for repentance in order to avoid Jesus' coming to them in judgment. It is probable that the third-class condition here functions in a hortatory manner, or to support the hortatory intentions of the imperatives in the surrounding discourse (see Culy 2004, 14). This observation has more force when it is observed that ἐάν + subjunctive occur only in hortatory sections of the Apocalypse (2:5, 22; 3:3, 20; 22:18, 19).
μετανοήσῃς. Aor act subj 2nd sg μετανοέω. Subjunctive with ἐάν.

2:6 ἀλλὰ τοῦτο ἔχεις, ὅτι μισεῖς τὰ ἔργα τῶν Νικολαϊτῶν ἃ κἀγὼ μισῶ.

ἀλλά. Adversative. Here it functions to contrast with the previous negative evaluation of the Ephesians.
τοῦτο. Accusative direct object of ἔχεις. τοῦτο cataphorically refers to the ὅτι clause that follows.
ἔχεις. Pres act ind 2nd sg ἔχω.

ὅτι. Introduces a content clause that is epexegetical to the demonstrative τοῦτο.
μισεῖς. Pres act ind 2nd sg μισέω.
τὰ ἔργα. Accusative direct object of μισεῖς.
τῶν Νικολαϊτῶν. Subjective genitive.
ἅ. Accusative direct object of μισῶ.
κἀγώ. A shortened form (crasis) of καὶ ἐγώ. ἐγώ is the nominative subject of μισῶ.
μισῶ. Pres act ind 1st sg μισέω.

2:7 Ὁ ἔχων οὖς ἀκουσάτω τί τὸ πνεῦμα λέγει ταῖς ἐκκλησίαις. Τῷ νικῶντι δώσω αὐτῷ φαγεῖν ἐκ τοῦ ξύλου τῆς ζωῆς, ὅ ἐστιν ἐν τῷ παραδείσῳ τοῦ θεοῦ.

Ὁ ἔχων. Pres act ptc masc nom sg ἔχω (substantival). Nominative subject of ἀκουσάτω. It is unnecessary to treat this as a substantival participle functioning as a protasis of a conditional clause under Semitic influence as Thompson does (95).
οὖς. Accusative direct object of ἔχων.
ἀκουσάτω. Aor act impv 3rd sg ἀκούω. As Wallace correctly notes, the third person imperative is just as strongly directive as the second person forms (486). The traditional way of translating it as "Let him/her . . ." could easily lead to confusion, since it could imply permission (Wallace, 486 n. 97). But its force is still imperatival, not permissive. Perhaps a better way to translate third person imperatives would be "He/she should/must. . . ." The function of the third person imperative in this context may be to focus on the subject who is commanded to perform the action: Ὁ ἔχων οὖς.
τί. Accusative direct object of λέγει. The interrogative pronoun introduces a clause that functions as the syntactic complement of ἀκουσάτω.
λέγει. Pres act ind 3rd sg λέγω.
ταῖς ἐκκλησίαις. Dative indirect object of λέγει.
Τῷ νικῶντι. Pres act ptc masc dat sg νικάω (substantival). The dative τῷ νικῶντι functions as the indirect object of δώσω, which anticipates and is resumed by the pronoun αὐτῷ. This is a topic construction that functions to draw attention to the topic of overcoming (see 1:5 on Τῷ ἀγαπῶντι . . . καὶ λύσαντι).
δώσω. Fut act ind 1st sg δίδωμι.
αὐτῷ. Dative indirect object of δώσω. The pronoun picks up the topic introduced by Τῷ νικῶντι at the beginning of the clause.
φαγεῖν. Aor act inf ἐσθίω (substantival, direct object of δώσω).
ἐκ τοῦ ξύλου. Partitive or source. The PP functions as the direct object of φαγεῖν. As Turner observes, "the partitive ἀπό and ἐκ [introduce] a

phrase which can stand independently of a noun as subject or object of a verb" (208). This may be part of an elliptical expression: "Eat the fruit of the tree" (Aune, 1.135). For ἐκ + genitive + δίδωμι, see also 1 John 4:13. The idea accompanying this construction may be that no one person at any one time exhausts the tree of life (see Rev 22:2).

τῆς ζωῆς. The idea communicated by the genitive seems to be "the tree that gives life." Wallace (106–7) labels this a genitive of product.

ὅ. Nominative subject of ἐστιν.

ἐστιν. Pres act ind 3rd sg εἰμί. For the loss of accent, see 1:8.

ἐν τῷ παραδείσῳ. Locative.

τοῦ θεοῦ. Possessive genitive. A number of manuscripts include the pronoun μου after θεοῦ (𝔐ᴷ *pc*), most likely due to its usage with θεοῦ in 3:2 and 3:12 (4×) (Metzger, 664).

Revelation 2:8-11

⁸And to the angel of the church in Smyrna write: The First and the Last, who was dead and is alive, says these things: ⁹I know your tribulation and poverty, but you are rich, and (I know) the blasphemy from those who say they are Jews and are not, but are the synagogue of Satan. ¹⁰Do not fear what you are about to suffer. Look, the devil is about to throw some of you into prison in order that you might be tested and you will have tribulation for ten days. Be faithful until death, and I will give you the crown of life. ¹¹The one who has ears should listen to what the Spirit is saying to the churches. The one who overcomes will not be harmed at all by the second death.

2:8 Καὶ τῷ ἀγγέλῳ τῆς ἐν Σμύρνῃ ἐκκλησίας γράψον· Τάδε λέγει ὁ πρῶτος καὶ ὁ ἔσχατος, ὃς ἐγένετο νεκρὸς καὶ ἔζησεν·

τῷ ἀγγέλῳ. Dative indirect object of γράψον.

τῆς ... ἐκκλησίας. Possessive genitive or genitive of subordination.

ἐν Σμύρνῃ. Locative.

γράψον. Aor act impv 2nd sg γράφω.

Τάδε. Accusative direct object of λέγει. On the form, see 2:1.

λέγει. Pres act ind 3rd sg λέγω.

ὁ πρῶτος καὶ ὁ ἔσχατος. Nominative subject of λέγει.

ὅς. Nominative subject of ἐγένετο ... καὶ ἔζησεν.

ἐγένετο. Aor mid ind 3rd sg γίνομαι.

νεκρός. Predicate nominative of ἐγένετο.

ἔζησεν. Aor act ind 3rd sg ζάω. While some commentators and grammars give the aorist an "ingressive (inceptive)" meaning ("came to life") (Wallace, 559; Aune, 1.157), this depends more on the contrast with ἐγένετο νεκρὸς and on English translation than on the semantics of the aorist tense form. Here the aorist simply summarizes the state of Jesus being alive in contrast to his prior state of being dead. Therefore, it may be best to refrain from making too much of an ingressive notion here. See Introduction on "Verbal Aspect."

2:9 οἶδά σου τὴν θλῖψιν καὶ τὴν πτωχείαν, ἀλλὰ πλούσιος εἶ, καὶ τὴν βλασφημίαν ἐκ τῶν λεγόντων Ἰουδαίους εἶναι ἑαυτοὺς καὶ οὐκ εἰσὶν ἀλλὰ συναγωγὴ τοῦ σατανᾶ.

οἶδά. Prf act ind 1st sg οἶδά. On the tense, see 2:2. The accenting is due to the enclitic σου that follows.

σου. Subjective genitive (the tribulation and poverty that you experience). Placed before the head term it modifies for prominence. σου probably modifies both θλῖψιν and πτωχείαν.

τὴν θλῖψιν καὶ τὴν πτωχείαν. Accusative direct object of οἶδά. ℵ and 𝔐 insert τὰ ἔργα καί before τὴν θλῖψιν καὶ τὴν πτωχείαν probably on the basis of its inclusion in 2:2.

ἀλλὰ. Introduces a contrast to their poverty (πτωχείαν). As Runge notes on ἀλλά, "The constraint that it brings to bear is a 'correction' of some aspect of the preceding context" (56).

πλούσιος. Predicate nominative.

εἶ. Pres act ind 2nd sg εἰμί.

τὴν βλασφημίαν. Accusative direct object of οἶδά.

ἐκ τῶν λεγόντων. Source (Charles, 1.56: "proceeding from").

τῶν λεγόντων. Pres act ptc masc gen pl λέγω (substantival).

Ἰουδαίους. Predicate accusative of εἶναι.

εἶναι. Pres act inf εἰμί (indirect discourse). Direct speech would require the first person ("We are Jews").

ἑαυτοὺς. Accusative subject of εἶναι.

εἰσὶν. Pres act ind 3rd pl εἰμί. On the shift from the participle to a finite verb, see 1:6 on ἐποίησεν (see 2:2).

ἀλλὰ. The conjunction draws a contrast and introduces a correction to their claim to be Jews.

συναγωγὴ. Predicate nominative of a verbless clause.

τοῦ σατανᾶ. Possessive genitive.

2:10 μηδὲν φοβοῦ ἃ μέλλεις πάσχειν. ἰδοὺ μέλλει βάλλειν ὁ διάβολος ἐξ ὑμῶν εἰς φυλακὴν ἵνα πειρασθῆτε καὶ ἕξετε θλῖψιν ἡμερῶν δέκα. γίνου πιστὸς ἄχρι θανάτου, καὶ δώσω σοι τὸν στέφανον τῆς ζωῆς.

μηδὲν. This could be an accusative direct object of φοβοῦ. According to Caragounis the territory of μή "is now being increasingly invaded by

[its] neuter compound … μηδέν" (231). If this is the case, μηδέν φοβοῦ may simply function as a present prohibition ("do not fear"). A number of manuscripts (A C 046 2050 *pc*) have μή instead of μηδέν. However, it is more likely that we should take this as an adverbial accusative, "not at all" or "in no way" (BDAG, 647.2.b.β): "Do not fear at all what you are about to suffer."

φοβοῦ. Pres mid impv 2nd sg φοβέομαι.

ἅ. Accusative direct object of πάσχειν. The relative pronoun ἅ introduces a headless relative clause. The entire clause could function in apposition to μηδέν, if μηδέν is the direct object of φοβοῦ. If this is the case, ἅ (pl) lacks agreement in number with μηδέν (sg). On the other hand, if μηδέν functions as an adverbial accusative with φοβοῦ, then the entire headless relative clause introduced by ἅ functions as the direct object of φοβοῦ ("do not fear what things you are about to suffer").

μέλλεις. Pres act ind 2nd sg μέλλω.

πάσχειν. Pres act inf πάσχω (complementary).

ἰδού. A marker of attention that deictically functions to make the following statement emphatic. On the form, see 1:7.

μέλλει. Pres act ind 3rd sg μέλλω.

βάλλειν. Pres act inf βάλλω (complementary).

ὁ διάβολος. Nominative subject of μέλλει.

ἐξ ὑμῶν. Partitive. The PP functions as the direct object of βάλλειν. This may be an elliptical expression: *τίνας ἐξ ὑμῶν*.

εἰς φυλακὴν. Locative.

ἵνα. Introduces a purpose clause.

πειρασθῆτε. Aor pass subj 2nd pl πειράζω. Subjunctive with ἵνα.

ἕξετε. Fut act ind 2nd pl ἔχω. It is possible that this is one of several examples in Revelation of a future tense being used in place of an aorist subjunctive (following ἵνα). On the possible significance of this construction, see 3:9 on ἥξουσιν. However, it is more likely that the καί does not connect ἕξετε with the subjunctive πειρασθῆτε as part of the ἵνα clause, but with μέλλει preceding it: "The devil is about to … and you will have."

ἡμερῶν δέκα. Genitive of time.

γίνου. Pres mid impv 2nd sg γίνομαι.

πιστὸς. Predicate adjective.

ἄχρι θανάτου. Temporal.

δώσω. Fut act ind 1st sg δίδωμι.

σοι. Dative indirect object of δώσω.

τὸν στέφανον. Accusative direct object of δώσω. The term στέφανος literally refers to "a wreath consisting either of foliage or precious metals formed to resemble foliage and worn as a symbol of honor, victory, or a badge of high office" (LN 6.192). Metaphorically, it could signify "a prize or reward given as the result of oustanding performance" (LN 57.121).

τῆς ζωῆς. Epexegetical genitive ("the crown which is life").

2:11 Ὁ ἔχων οὖς ἀκουσάτω τί τὸ πνεῦμα λέγει ταῖς ἐκκλησίαις. Ὁ νικῶν οὐ μὴ ἀδικηθῇ ἐκ τοῦ θανάτου τοῦ δευτέρου.

Ὁ ἔχων. Pres act ptc masc nom sg ἔχω (substantival). Nominative subject of ἀκουσάτω.

οὖς. Accusative direct object of ἔχων.

ἀκουσάτω. Pres act impv 3rd sg ἀκούω. On the force of the third person imperative, see 2:7 on ἀκουσάτω.

τί. Accusative direct object of λέγει. The interrogative pronoun introduces a clause that functions as the syntactic complement of ἀκουσάτω.

τὸ πνεῦμα. Nominative subject of λέγει.

λέγει. Pres act ind 3rd sg λέγω.

ταῖς ἐκκλησίαις. Dative indirect object of λέγει.

Ὁ νικῶν. Pres act ptc masc nom sg νικάω (substantival). Nominative subject of ἀδικηθῇ.

ἀδικηθῇ. Aor pass subj 3rd sg ἀδικέω. The subjunctive is used with οὐ μὴ, which expresses emphatic negation.

ἐκ τοῦ θανάτου τοῦ δευτέρου. Instrumental. For this usage of ἐκ, see Porter 1992, 155.

Revelation 2:12-17

[12]And to the angel of the church in Pergamum write: The one who has the sharp, two-edged sword says these things: [13]I know where you live, where the throne of Satan is, and you hold on to my name and you have not denied your faith in me, even in the days of Antipas, my witness, my faithful one, who was put to death among you, where Satan lives. [14]But I have a few things against you, that you have there some who hold to the teaching of Balaam, who taught Balak to throw a stumbling block before the sons of Israel to eat food sacrificed to idols and to commit sexual immorality. [15]In the same way, you also have some who cling to the teaching of the Nicolatians likewise. [16]Repent, therefore. And if not, I will come against you soon and make war with them with the sword from my mouth. [17]The one who has ears should listen to what the Spirit is saying to the churches. I will give to the one who overcomes the hidden manna, and I will give a white stone to him, and upon the stone a new name written which no one knows except the one who receives it.

2:12 Καὶ τῷ ἀγγέλῳ τῆς ἐν Περγάμῳ ἐκκλησίας γράψον· Τάδε λέγει ὁ ἔχων τὴν ῥομφαίαν τὴν δίστομον τὴν ὀξεῖαν·

τῷ ἀγγέλῳ. Dative indirect object of γράψον.
τῆς... ἐκκλησίας. Possessive genitive or genitive of subordination.
ἐν Περγάμῳ. Locative.
γράψον. Aor act impv 2nd sg γράψω.
Τάδε. Accusative direct object of λέγει. On the form, see 2:1.
λέγει. Pres act ind 3rd sg λέγω.
ὁ ἔχων. Pres act ptc masc nom sg ἔχω (substantival). Nominative subject of λέγει.
τὴν ῥομφαίαν τὴν δίστομον τὴν ὀξεῖαν. Accusative direct object of ἔχων. The article τήν is probably anaphoric, referring back to the mention of the sword in 1:16.

2:13 οἶδα ποῦ κατοικεῖς, ὅπου ὁ θρόνος τοῦ σατανᾶ, καὶ κρατεῖς τὸ ὄνομά μου καὶ οὐκ ἠρνήσω τὴν πίστιν μου καὶ ἐν ταῖς ἡμέραις Ἀντιπᾶς ὁ μάρτυς μου ὁ πιστός μου, ὃς ἀπεκτάνθη παρ' ὑμῖν, ὅπου ὁ σατανᾶς κατοικεῖ.

οἶδα. Prf act ind 1st sg οἶδα. On the tense, see 2:2. Some manuscripts (𝔐) insert τὰ ἔργά σου καί after οἶδα, perhaps due to the fact that the phrases τὰ ἔργά σου or σου τὰ ἔργα commonly occur after οἶδα elsewhere in Rev 2–3 (2:2, 19; 3:1, 8, 15).
ποῦ. Locative. Here it introduces a clause that functions as the syntactic complement of οἶδα.
κατοικεῖς. Pres act ind 2nd sg κατοικέω.
ὅπου. Locative. The local adverb ὅπου substitutes for a relative pronoun (Caragounis, 193), here functioning as the predicate of a verbless clause. The entire clause ὅπου ὁ θρόνος τοῦ σατανᾶ stands in apposition to ποῦ κατοικεῖς.
ὁ θρόνος. Nominative subject of a verbless clause.
τοῦ σατανᾶ. Possessive genitive. If θρόνος signifies the idea of ruling and sovereignty, it is also possible to take this as a subjective genitive. "Satan is enthroned and holds his court" (Smalley, 68).
κρατεῖς. Pres act ind 2nd sg κρατέω.
τὸ ὄνομά. Accusative direct object of κρατεῖς. The accenting is due to the enclitic μου that follows.
μου. Possessive genitive.
ἠρνήσω. Aor mid ind 2nd sg ἀρνέομαι. Smalley is incorrect to conclude, based on the aorist, that this refers to "one particular moment in the past" (69). The aorist simply summarizes the entirety of their response.

τὴν πίστιν. Accusative direct object of ἠρνήσω.
μου. Objective genitive ("faith in me").
καί. Ascensive: "even."
ἐν ταῖς ἡμέραις. Temporal.
Ἀντιπᾶς. Though an indeclinable name, Ἀντιπᾶς functions as a genitive here. The idea appears to be "the days when Antipas lived."
ὁ μάρτυς ... ὁ πιστός. Nominative in apposition to Ἀντιπᾶς, which syntactically should be genitive. The nominative form can be explained along similar lines as 1:5, where ὁ μάρτυς and ὁ πιστός are also epexegetical to a genitive (Ἰησοῦ Χριστοῦ) as a title of Jesus Christ. The use of the nominative here draws attention to the connection between Christ and Antipas, who is Christ's faithful witness. Apparently, unlike the expression in 1:5, here grammatically two descriptions are intended (as opposed to an attributive construction: "my faithful witness"; see 1:5). This would be enhanced by the repetition of μου after both μάρτυς and πιστός: "my witness, my faithful one." However, a number of manuscripts omit the second μου after ὁ πιστός (ℵ P 046 1006 1611 1841 1854 2329 𝔐). The second μου found in A C 2050 2053 2351 could be a scribal addition to conform to the first part of the construction ὁ μάρτυς μου. The second item, ὁ πιστός, stands in apposition to the first one, ὁ μάρτυς.
μου ... μου. Objective genitive.
ὅς. Nominative subject of ἀπεκτάνθη.
ἀπεκτάνθη. Aor pass ind 3rd sg ἀποκτείνω.
παρ' ὑμῖν. Locative.
ὅπου. Locative. See on ὅπου above. Introduces a clause that modifies παρ' ὑμῖν.
ὁ σατανᾶς. Nominative subject of κατοικεῖ.
κατοικεῖ. Pres act ind 3rd sg κατοικέω.

2:14 ἀλλ' ἔχω κατὰ σοῦ ὀλίγα ὅτι ἔχεις ἐκεῖ κρατοῦντας τὴν διδαχὴν Βαλαάμ, ὃς ἐδίδασκεν τῷ Βαλὰκ βαλεῖν σκάνδαλον ἐνώπιον τῶν υἱῶν Ἰσραὴλ φαγεῖν εἰδωλόθυτα καὶ πορνεῦσαι.

ἀλλ'. The conjunction draws a contrast with and corrective to the preceding positive evaluation of the church in Pergamum.
ἔχω. Pres act ind 1st sg ἔχω.
κατὰ σοῦ. Opposition.
ὀλίγα. Accusative direct object of ἔχω.
ὅτι. Introduces a content clause that is epexegetical to ὀλίγα.
ἔχεις. Pres act ind 2nd sg ἔχω.
ἐκεῖ. Locative.

κρατοῦντας. Pres act ptc masc acc pl κρατέω (substantival). Accusative direct object of ἔχεις.

τὴν διδαχὴν. Accusative direct object of κρατοῦντας.

Βαλαάμ. This could be an objective genitive ("the teaching *about* Balaam"), but more likely given the OT background it is a subjective genitive ("the teaching that Balaam taught," see Osborne, 143).

ὅς. Nominative subject of ἐδίδασκεν.

ἐδίδασκεν. Impf act ind 3rd sg διδάσκω. It is reading too much into the tense to conclude with Osborne (144 n. 9) that the imperfect pictures the ongoing teaching of Balaam (see the Introduction on "Verbal Aspect").

τῷ Βαλάκ. Dative indirect object of ἐδίδασκεν. The article τῷ clarifies the case of the indeclinable Βαλάκ.

βαλεῖν. Aor act inf βάλλω (direct object of ἐδίδασκεν).

σκάνδαλον. Accusative direct object of βαλεῖν.

ἐνώπιον τῶν υἱῶν. Locative.

Ἰσραὴλ. Genitive of relationship.

φαγεῖν. Aor act inf ἐσθίω (purpose, or perhaps epexegetical to σκάνδαλον).

εἰδωλόθυτα. Accusative direct object of φαγεῖν. This term refers to meat (or possibly food) that is sacrificed to idols. According to Aune, "Part of the flesh of victims sacrificed in Greek temples was consumed by priests and worshipers on the premises, while the rest was sold to the public in the marketplace" (1.186). It is difficult to determine the precise situation John envisions. There are a number of possibilities: (1) participation in a temple meal; (2) accepting meat distributed during a religious festival; (3) eating meat purchased at a marketplace that had earlier been part of a pagan sacrifice; (4) participation in a sacral meal as part of an association (see Aune, 1.186). Most likely what is envisioned here is eating food in the context of idolatrous worship, perhaps in connection with meals celebrated within trade guilds.

πορνεῦσαι. Aor act inf πορνεύω (purpose, or perhaps epexegetical to σκάνδαλον). Πορνεύω is probably used here metaphorically of worshiping idols (Beale, 250).

2:15 οὕτως ἔχεις καὶ σὺ κρατοῦντας τὴν διδαχὴν [τῶν] Νικολαϊτῶν ὁμοίως.

οὕτως. Manner.
ἔχεις. Pres act ind 2nd sg ἔχω.
καὶ. Ascensive: "also."
σύ. Nominative subject of ἔχεις.
κρατοῦντας. Pres act ptc masc acc pl κρατέω (direct object of ἔχεις).

τὴν διδαχὴν. Accusative direct object of κρατοῦντας.
[τῶν] Νικολαϊτῶν. Subjective genitive (see also 2:14 on Βαλαάμ).
ὁμοίως. Expresses a similarity with the preceding "those who grasp the teaching" of Balaam (v. 14). Charles thinks ὁμοίως refers back to the Ephesian church in 2:6 (1.64). However, the proposed reference is probably too far removed. Rather, οὕτως ... ὁμοίως is an emphatic way of equating those who hold (κρατοῦντας) to the teaching of the Nicolatians with those who hold to the teaching of Balaam in verse 14.

2:16 μετανόησον οὖν· εἰ δὲ μή, ἔρχομαί σοι ταχὺ καὶ πολεμήσω μετ' αὐτῶν ἐν τῇ ῥομφαίᾳ τοῦ στόματός μου.

μετανόησον. Aor act impv 2nd sg μετανοέω.
οὖν. Inferential.
εἰ δὲ μή. See 2:5 above.
ἔρχομαί. Pres mid ind 1st sg ἔρχομαι. The present tense is future referring (cf. the future πολεμήσω below). The accenting is due to the enclitic σοι that follows.
σοι. Dative of location.
ταχὺ. Temporal. ταχύ can indicate the speed in which an activity or event takes place ("quickly"), or "a relatively brief period of time subsequent to another point of time" ("soon") (BDAG, 993.2). In the context of judgment it makes sense to see the emphasis on the nearness of the coming in judgment, rather than the speed with which it will take place.
πολεμήσω. Fut act ind 1st sg πολεμέω.
μετ' αὐτῶν. Association. Harris says that μετά can carry the meaning "against" (164). While this is a valid *translation* based on the context, it is uncertain that this is the *meaning* of the preposition. Μετά still probably carries the idea of "accompaniment" (to engage in battle with). The antecedent of αὐτῶν is those who hold to the teachings of Balaam and the Nicolatians in verses 14-15.
ἐν τῇ ῥομφαίᾳ. Instrumental.
τοῦ στόματός. Genitive of source. The accenting is due to the enclitic μου that follows.
μου. Possessive genitive.

2:17 Ὁ ἔχων οὖς ἀκουσάτω τί τὸ πνεῦμα λέγει ταῖς ἐκκλησίαις. Τῷ νικῶντι δώσω αὐτῷ τοῦ μάννα τοῦ κεκρυμμένου καὶ δώσω αὐτῷ ψῆφον λευκήν, καὶ ἐπὶ τὴν ψῆφον ὄνομα καινὸν γεγραμμένον ὃ οὐδεὶς οἶδεν εἰ μὴ ὁ λαμβάνων.

Ὁ ἔχων. Pres act ptc masc nom sg ἔχω (substantival). Nominative subject of ἀκουσάτω.

ἀκουσάτω. Pres act impv 3rd sg ἀκούω. On the force of the third person imperative, see 2:7 on ἀκουσάτω.
τί. Accusative direct object of λέγει. The interrogative pronoun introduces a clause that functions as the syntactic complement of ἀκουσάτω.
τὸ πνεῦμα. Nominative subject of λέγει.
λέγει. Pres act ind 3rd sg λέγω.
ταῖς ἐκκλησίαις. Dative indirect object of λέγει.
Τῷ νικῶντι. Pres act ptc masc dat sg νικάω (substantival). Topic construction (see 1:5).
δώσω. Fut act ind 1st sg δίδωμι.
αὐτῷ. Dative indirect object of δώσω. The pronoun picks up the topic introduced by τῷ νικῶντι.
τοῦ μάννα. Partitive genitive, functioning as the direct object of δώσω. This may be an elliptical construction: τινας τοῦ μάννα. On the function of partitive constructions as subject or object of a verb, see 2:7 ἐκ τοῦ ξύλου. The idea may be that no one person at any one time exhausts the manna.
τοῦ κεκρυμμένου. Prf pass ptc neut gen sg κρύπτω (attributive).
δώσω. Fut act ind 1st sg δίδωμι.
αὐτῷ. Dative indirect object of δώσω.
ψῆφον λευκὴν. Accusative direct object of δώσω. On the various possible backgrounds and associations for a white stone, see Beale, 252–53.
ἐπὶ τὴν ψῆφον. Locative.
ὄνομα καινὸν. Nominative subject of a verbless clause: "There will be a new name written."
γεγραμμένον. Prf pass ptc neut acc sg γράφω (attributive).
ὃ. Accusative direct object of οἶδεν.
οὐδεὶς. Nominative subject of οἶδεν.
οἶδεν. Prf act ind 3rd sg οἶδα.
εἰ μὴ. Louw and Nida describe this as "a marker of contrast by designating an exception" (89.131). Runge explains this construction (negation + exception) where an entire set is negated ("no one knows"), but then an item is added through the exception ("except the one receiving"). "The effect of creating a set, and then adding one member back is to attract additional attention to the excepted item . . ." (86).
ὁ λαμβάνων. Pres act ptc masc nom sg λαμβάνω (substantival). Nominative subject of an implied οἶδεν.

Revelation 2:18-29

[18]And to the angel of the church in Thyatira write: The Son of God, the one who has his eyes as flames of fire and his feet like burnished

bronze says these things: ¹⁹I know your works, that is, your love and faith and service and endurance, and (that) your last works are greater than your first. ²⁰But I have against you that you tolerate the woman Jezebel, who calls herself a prophetess and teaches and leads astray my servants to commit sexual immorality and to eat food offered to idols. ²¹And I gave her time in order that she might repent, but she is not willing to repent from her sexual immorality. ²²Look, I am throwing her on a bed and those who have committed adultery with her into great tribulation, if they do not repent from her works. ²³And I will kill her children with death, and all the churches will know that I am the one who searches minds and hearts, and I will give to each of you according to your works. ²⁴But to the rest of you in Thyatira I say, (to) as many as do not hold to this teaching, who do not know the deep things of Satan as they are called: I do not place any other burden upon you; ²⁵however, cling to what you have until I come. ²⁶The one who overcomes and keeps my works until the end, I will give to that person authority over the nations, ²⁷and I will shepherd them with an iron rod, as when jars made of clay are shattered, ²⁸just as I have received from my father. I will also give to that person the morning star. ²⁹The one who has ears should listen to what the Spirit is saying to the churches.

2:18 Καὶ τῷ ἀγγέλῳ τῆς ἐν Θυατίροις ἐκκλησίας γράψον· Τάδε λέγει ὁ υἱὸς τοῦ θεοῦ, ὁ ἔχων τοὺς ὀφθαλμοὺς αὐτοῦ ὡς φλόγα πυρὸς καὶ οἱ πόδες αὐτοῦ ὅμοιοι χαλκολιβάνῳ·

    τῷ ἀγγέλῳ. Dative indirect object of γράψον.
    τῆς ... ἐκκλησίας. Possessive genitive or genitive of subordination.
    ἐν Θυατίροις. Locative.
    γράψον. Aor act impv 2nd sg γράφω.
    Τάδε. Accusative direct object of λέγει. On the form, see 2:1.
    λέγει. Pres act ind 3rd sg λέγω.
    ὁ υἱὸς. Nominative subject of λέγει.
    τοῦ θεοῦ. Genitive of relationship.
    ὁ ἔχων. Pres act ptc masc nom sg ἔχω (substantival). Nominative in apposition to ὁ υἱὸς.
    τοὺς ὀφθαλμοὺς. Accusative direct object of ἔχων.
    αὐτοῦ. Possessive genitive.
    ὡς φλόγα. Comparision.
    πυρὸς. Attributive genitive or genitive of content ("consisting of fire").
    οἱ πόδες. Nominative subject of a verbless clause.
    αὐτοῦ. Possessive genitive.
    ὅμοιοι. Predicate adjective of a verbless clause.
    χαλκολιβάνῳ. Dative complement of ὅμοιος.

2:19 οἶδά σου τὰ ἔργα καὶ τὴν ἀγάπην καὶ τὴν πίστιν καὶ τὴν διακονίαν καὶ τὴν ὑπομονήν σου, καὶ τὰ ἔργα σου τὰ ἔσχατα πλείονα τῶν πρώτων.

οἶδά. Prf act ind 1st sg οἶδά. On the tense, see 2:2. The accenting is due to the enclitic σου that follows.
σου. Subjective genitive. Placed before the head term it modifies for prominence.
τὰ ἔργα καὶ τὴν ἀγάπην ... καὶ τὴν ὑπομονήν. Accusative direct object of οἶδά.
καὶ. The first καὶ following ἔργα should be understood as epexegetical.
σου. Subjective genitive. Modifies the entire string of nouns τὴν ἀγάπην καὶ τὴν πίστιν καὶ τὴν διακονίαν καὶ τὴν ὑπομονήν.
τὰ ἔργα ... τὰ ἔσχατα. Nominative subject of a verbless clause. The καὶ begins a new clause.
σου. Subjective genitive.
πλείονα. Predicate adjective of a verbless clause. This is the only example of a comparative adjective form in the Apocalypse (Mussies, 138).
τῶν πρώτων. Genitive of comparison.

2:20 ἀλλὰ ἔχω κατὰ σοῦ ὅτι ἀφεῖς τὴν γυναῖκα Ἰεζάβελ, ἡ λέγουσα ἑαυτὴν προφῆτιν καὶ διδάσκει καὶ πλανᾷ τοὺς ἐμοὺς δούλους πορνεῦσαι καὶ φαγεῖν εἰδωλόθυτα.

ἀλλὰ. Introduces a contrast to the previous positive evaluation in verse 19.
ἔχω. Pres act ind 1st sg ἔχω.
κατὰ σοῦ. Opposition.
ὅτι. Introduces a content clause that is the clausal complement of ἔχω.
ἀφεῖς. Pres act ind 2nd sg ἀφίημι.
τὴν γυναῖκα. Accusative direct object of ἀφεῖς.
Ἰεζάβελ. Accusative in apposition to τὴν γυναῖκα.
λέγουσα. Pres act ptc fem nom sg λέγω (substantival). The case of λέγουσα (nominative) is grammatically incongruous with the noun it modifies, τὴν γυναῖκα Ἰεζάβελ (accusative). In an attempt to correct the syntax ℵ¹ 1854 2050 𝔐^A change the participle to accusative (λέγουσαν). Beale argues that rather than careless grammar the nominative is used to draw attention to the OT allusion: LXX 1 Kgdms 20:5, 7 (263). Robertson says the participle is loosely connected (414). It is also possible to take the participle as parenthetical: "The woman, Jezebel—the one who calls herself a prophet and teaches. . . ."

ἑαυτὴν. Accusative direct object of λέγουσα.

προφῆτιν. Complement in an object-complement double accusative construction.

διδάσκει. Pres act ind 3rd sg διδάσκω. On the shift from the participle to a finite verb, see 1:6 on ἐποίησεν.

πλανᾷ. Pres act ind 3rd sg πλανάω.

τοὺς ἐμοὺς δούλους. Accusative direct object of διδάσκει and πλανᾷ. This is the only place in Revelation where a possessive adjective (ἐμούς) is used. Possession is usually shown with a personal pronoun in the genitive case (e.g., αὐτοῦ).

πορνεῦσαι. Aor act inf πορνεύω (result). On the meaning of πορνεύω, see 2:14.

φαγεῖν. Aor act inf ἐσθίω. On the function, see πορνεῦσαι above.

εἰδωλόθυτα. Accusative direct object of φαγεῖν. On the meaning of εἰδωλόθυτα, see 2:14.

2:21 καὶ ἔδωκα αὐτῇ χρόνον ἵνα μετανοήσῃ, καὶ οὐ θέλει μετανοῆσαι ἐκ τῆς πορνείας αὐτῆς.

ἔδωκα. Aor act ind 1st sg δίδωμι.

αὐτῇ. Dative indirect object of ἔδωκα.

χρόνον. Accusative direct object of ἔδωκα.

ἵνα. It is possible that ἵνα introduces a clause that is epexegetical to χρόνον. However, it may be better to take it as introducing a clause that expresses the purpose of ἔδωκα.

μετανοήσῃ. Aor act subj 3rd sg μετανοέω. Subjunctive with ἵνα.

καί. Although Aune (1.197) takes the conjunction as adversative, this reflects the semantic relationship between the clauses and the necessities of English translation. The καί itself simply indicates continuity.

θέλει. Pres act ind 3rd sg θέλω. The more marked present tense may contrast with the aorist ἔδωκα to carry forward the discourse by emphasizing Jezebel's refusal to repent despite the opportunity given to her.

μετανοῆσαι. Aor act inf μετανοέω (complementary).

ἐκ τῆς πορνείας. Separation. The verb μετανοέω occurs elsewhere with ἐκ + genitive indicating that from which one turns away (cf. 2:22; 9:20, 21; 16:11).

αὐτῆς. Subjective genitive.

2:22 ἰδοὺ βάλλω αὐτὴν εἰς κλίνην καὶ τοὺς μοιχεύοντας μετ' αὐτῆς εἰς θλῖψιν μεγάλην, ἐὰν μὴ μετανοήσωσιν ἐκ τῶν ἔργων αὐτῆς,

ἰδού. A marker of attention that deictically functions to make the following statement emphatic. On the form, see 1:7.

βάλλω. Pres act ind 1st sg βάλλω. The present tense is future referring ("I am going to/about to throw"). Some manuscripts (ℵ² P *pc*) have the future βαλῶ. There is no reason to attribute the future usage of the present tense to Semitic influence (the Hebrew participle) as Thompson does (32; see also Charles, 1.71), since the Greek present tense can have future time implicature (Porter 1992, 32; McKay 1994, 41).

αὐτήν. Accusative direct object of βάλλω.

εἰς κλίνην. Locative.

τοὺς μοιχεύοντας. Pres act ptc masc acc pl μοιχεύω (direct object of an implied βάλλω).

μετ᾽ αὐτῆς. Association.

εἰς θλῖψιν μεγάλην. Locative.

ἐάν. Introduces the protasis of a third-class conditional sentence. On the function of the third-class condition, see 2:5 on ἐάν.

μετανοήσωσιν. Aor act subj 3rd pl μετανοέω. Subjunctive with ἐάν.

ἐκ τῶν ἔργων. Separation. On ἐκ + genitive following μετανοέω, see 2:21 above.

αὐτῆς. Subjective genitive.

2:23 καὶ τὰ τέκνα αὐτῆς ἀποκτενῶ ἐν θανάτῳ. καὶ γνώσονται πᾶσαι αἱ ἐκκλησίαι ὅτι ἐγώ εἰμι ὁ ἐραυνῶν νεφροὺς καὶ καρδίας, καὶ δώσω ὑμῖν ἑκάστῳ κατὰ τὰ ἔργα ὑμῶν.

τὰ τέκνα. Accusative direct object of ἀποκτενῶ.

αὐτῆς. Genitive of relationship.

ἀποκτενῶ. Fut act ind 1st sg ἀποκτείνω.

ἐν θανάτῳ. Manner or instrumental. Porter (1992, 98–99) correctly observes that the instrumental, manner, and causal usages of the dative are difficult, and sometimes unnecessary, to distinguish. The PP functions to intensify the act of killing. The construction ἀποκτενῶ ἐν θανάτῳ may be due to Semitic influence (Aune, 1.198).

γνώσονται. Fut mid ind 3rd pl γινώσκω.

πᾶσαι αἱ ἐκκλησίαι. Nominative subject of γνώσονται.

ὅτι. Introduces a content clause that is the clausal complement (direct discourse) of γνώσονται.

ἐγώ. Nominative subject of εἰμι.

εἰμι. Pres act ind 1st sg εἰμί. On the loss of accent, see 1:8.

ὁ ἐραυνῶν. Pres act ptc masc nom sg ἐραυνάω (substantival). Predicate nominative.

νεφροὺς καὶ καρδίας. Accusative direct object of ἐραυνῶν. Lit. "kidneys and hearts." Both nouns are used metaphorically to refer to the totality of one's inner being (Osborne, 161).

δώσω. Fut act ind 1st sg δίδωμι. Grammatically there is no direct object of δώσω.

ὑμῖν ἑκάστῳ. Dative indirect object.

κατὰ τὰ ἔργα. Standard.

ὑμῶν. Subjective genitive.

2:24 ὑμῖν δὲ λέγω τοῖς λοιποῖς τοῖς ἐν Θυατίροις, ὅσοι οὐκ ἔχουσιν τὴν διδαχὴν ταύτην, οἵτινες οὐκ ἔγνωσαν τὰ βαθέα τοῦ σατανᾶ ὡς λέγουσιν· οὐ βάλλω ἐφ' ὑμᾶς ἄλλο βάρος,

ὑμῖν. Dative indirect object of λέγω. The indirect object is fronted here to draw attention to the contrast between the children of Jezebel (v. 23) and the rest who do not hold to her teaching (v. 24).

δέ. The δέ indicates a new development in the argument: The rest of those in Thyatira.

λέγω. Pres act ind 1st sg λέγω.

τοῖς λοιποῖς. Dative in apposition to ὑμῖν.

τοῖς ἐν Θυατίροις. The article functions as an adjectivizer, turning the locative PP into an attributive modifier of λοιποῖς (lit. "to the in-Thyatira rest").

ὅσοι. Nominative subject of ἔχουσιν.

ἔχουσιν. Pres act ind 3rd pl ἔχω.

τὴν διδαχὴν ταύτην. Accusative direct object of ἔχουσιν.

οἵτινες. Nominative subject of ἔγνωσαν. The entire clause stands in apposition to the ὅσοι clause.

ἔγνωσαν. Aor act ind 3rd pl γινώσκω. The aorist is present referring temporally.

τὰ βαθέα. Accusative direct object of ἔγνωσαν.

τοῦ σατανᾶ. Genitive of source.

ὡς λέγουσιν. Manner. This construction constitutes an impersonal use of a plural verb, which can be translated as a passive ("as it is said" or "as they say"). As McKay notes, "such plurals may be influenced by a Semitic idiom in which a plural verb with a completely vague subject is used in the active in circumstances where English, and normally also Greek, would need a passive" (1994, 19). See also 10:11 on λέγουσίν.

λέγουσιν. Pres act ind 3rd pl λέγω.

βάλλω. Pres act ind 1st sg βάλλω.

ἐφ' ὑμᾶς. Locative.

ἄλλο βάρος. Accusative direct object of βάλλω.

2:25 πλὴν ὃ ἔχετε κρατήσατε ἄχρις οὗ ἂν ἥξω.

πλὴν. "This particle is an adverb which seems to have taken on an adversative conjunctive sense" (Porter 1992, 215).

ὅ. Accusative direct object of ἔχετε. The relative pronoun introduces a headless relative clause. The entire clause (ὃ ἔχετε) functions as the direct object of κρατήσατε.

ἔχετε. Pres act ind 2nd sg ἔχω.

κρατήσατε. Aor act impv 2nd pl κρατέω. The aorist imperative cannot here refer to a single act, since it temporally extends to the coming of the Lord (Porter 1989a, 354).

ἄχρις οὗ ἄν. Temporal. Here ἄχρις and the relative οὗ function as a conjunction "*until the time when*" (BDAG, 160–61.1.b.α). The particle ἄν makes the construction indefinite, adding an element of contingency or condition: "Until the time whenever."

ἥξω. Aor act subj 1st sg ἥκω. Subjunctive with ἄν.

2:26 Καὶ ὁ νικῶν καὶ ὁ τηρῶν ἄχρι τέλους τὰ ἔργα μου, δώσω αὐτῷ ἐξουσίαν ἐπὶ τῶν ἐθνῶν

ὁ νικῶν. Pres act ptc masc nom sg νικάω (substantival). Topic construction (see 1:5). This construction, often described as a "hanging nominative," introduces a clause that lacks *grammatical* agreement with the main clause, though in *sense* it is linked with an element (usually a pronoun) in the main clause (Porter 1992, 86). Here ὁ νικῶν καὶ ὁ τηρῶν are picked up by the dative αὐτῷ of the main clause.

ὁ τηρῶν. Pres act ptc masc nom sg τηρέω (substantival). On the function, see νικῶν above.

ἄχρι τέλους. Temporal.

τὰ ἔργα. Accusative direct object of ὁ τηρῶν.

μου. Subjective genitive.

δώσω. Fut act ind 1st sg δίδωμι.

αὐτῷ. Dative indirect object of δώσω. The pronoun picks up the topic introduced by ὁ νικῶν καὶ ὁ τηρῶν.

ἐξουσίαν. Accusative direct object of δώσω.

ἐπὶ τῶν ἐθνῶν. ἐπί with the genitive is a "marker of power, authority, control of or over someone or someth." (BDAG, 365.9.a).

2:27 καὶ ποιμανεῖ αὐτοὺς ἐν ῥάβδῳ σιδηρᾷ ὡς τὰ σκεύη τὰ κεραμικὰ συντρίβεται,

ποιμανεῖ. Fut act ind 3rd sg ποιμαίνω. The language in this verse closely parallels LXX Ps 2:9. While ποιμαίνω can generally mean "to shepherd" in terms of protecting, leading, guiding, or ruling (BDAG, 842.2.a), it can also be used of an activity that has destructive results.

That the latter is intended here is suggested by the the metaphor of shattering vessels at the end of the verse (see below).

αὐτούς. Accusative direct object of ποιμανεῖ.
ἐν ῥάβδῳ σιδηρᾷ. Instrumental or manner.
ὡς τὰ σκεύη τὰ κεραμικὰ. Comparison.
τὰ σκεύη τὰ κεραμικὰ. Nominative subject of συντρίβεται.
συντρίβεται. Pres pass ind 3rd sg συντρίβω. Here the present tense is timeless (gnomic), used in a proverbial type of statement.

2:28 ὡς κἀγὼ εἴληφα παρὰ τοῦ πατρός μου, καὶ δώσω αὐτῷ τὸν ἀστέρα τὸν πρωϊνόν.

ὡς κἀγώ. Comparison.
κἀγώ. On the form, see on 2:6. The καί functions ascensively: "Even." The ἐγώ is the nominative subject of εἴληφα.
εἴληφα. Prf act ind 1st sg λαμβάνω. The perfect indicative εἴληφα occurs five times in Revelation (2:28; 3:3; 5:7; 8:5; 11:17). The perfect form may function here emphasizing Jesus' reception of the morning star perhaps to highlight his authority to give it to his followers in the next clause (δώσω αὐτῷ τὸν ἀστέρα τὸν πρωϊνόν). For more details on the tense form of εἴληφα, see 5:7.
παρὰ τοῦ πατρός. Source.
μου. Genitive of relationship.
δώσω. Fut act ind 1st sg δίδωμι.
αὐτῷ. Dative indirect object of δώσω. The antecedent of αὐτῷ is the αὐτῷ (which refers to the ὁ νικῶν καὶ ὁ τηρῶν) in verse 26.
τὸν ἀστέρα τὸν πρωϊνόν. Accusative direct object of δώσω.

2:29 Ὁ ἔχων οὖς ἀκουσάτω τί τὸ πνεῦμα λέγει ταῖς ἐκκλησίαις.

Ὁ ἔχων. Pres act ptc masc nom sg ἔχω (substantival). Nominative subject of ἀκουσάτω.
οὖς. Accusative direct object of ὁ ἔχων.
ἀκουσάτω. Pres act impv 3rd sg ἀκούω. On the force of the third person imperative, see 2:7 on ἀκουσάτω.
τί. Accusative direct object of λέγει. The interrogative pronoun introduces a clause that functions as the syntactic complement of ἀκουσάτω.
τὸ πνεῦμα. Nominative subject of λέγει.
λέγει. Pres act ind 3rd sg λέγω.
ταῖς ἐκκλησίαις. Dative indirect object of λέγει.

Revelation 3:1-6

¹And to the angel of the church in Sardis, write: The one who holds the seven spirits of God and the seven stars says these things: I know your works, that you have a reputation that you live, but you are dead. ²Become watchful and strengthen what remains, which is about to die, for I have not found your works complete before my God. ³Therefore, remember how you received and heard, and then keep it and repent. So then, if you are not watchful, I will come as a thief, and you will certainly not know at what hour I will come against you. ⁴But you have a few names in Sardis who have not soiled their clothes, and they will walk with me in white, for they are worthy. ⁵The one who overcomes will be so dressed in white clothes and I will by no means wipe out his name from the book of life, and I will confess his name before my father and before his angels. ⁶The one who has ears should listen to what the Spirit is saying to the churches.

3:1 Καὶ τῷ ἀγγέλῳ τῆς ἐν Σάρδεσιν ἐκκλησίας γράψον· Τάδε λέγει ὁ ἔχων τὰ ἑπτὰ πνεύματα τοῦ θεοῦ καὶ τοὺς ἑπτὰ ἀστέρας· οἶδά σου τὰ ἔργα ὅτι ὄνομα ἔχεις ὅτι ζῇς, καὶ νεκρὸς εἶ.

τῷ ἀγγέλῳ. Dative indirect object of γράψον.
τῆς . . . ἐκκλησίας. Possessive genitive or genitive of subordination.
ἐν Σάρδεσιν. Locative.
γράψον. Aor act impv 2nd sg γράψω.
Τάδε. Accusative direct object of λέγει. On the form, see 2:1.
λέγει. Pres act ind 3rd sg λέγω.
ὁ ἔχων. Pres act ptc masc nom sg ἔχω (substantival). Nominative subject of λέγει.
τὰ ἑπτὰ πνεύματα . . . καὶ τοὺς ἑπτὰ ἀστέρας. Accusative direct object of ἔχων.
τοῦ θεοῦ. Possessive genitive or genitive of source.
οἶδά. Prf act ind 1st sg οἶδα. On the tense, see 2:2.
σου. Subjective genitive. Placed before the head term it modifies for prominence.
τὰ ἔργα. Accusative direct object of οἶδά.
ὅτι. Introduces a content clause that is epexegetical to τὰ ἔργα.
ὄνομα. Accusative direct object of ἔχεις. The term ὄνομα here means "reputation" (LN 3.265).
ἔχεις. Pres act ind 2nd sg ἔχω.
ὅτι. Introduces a clause that is epexegetical to ὄνομα.
ζῇς. Pres act ind 2nd sg ζάω.

καί. Though Aune classifies καί here as adversative (1.215, καί *adversativum*), this is due not to the meaning of καί but to the semantic contrast between the two lexical items ζῇς and νεκρός. The καί simply expresses continuity.

νεκρὸς. Predicate adjective.

εἶ. Pres act ind 2nd sg εἰμί.

3:2 γίνου γρηγορῶν καὶ στήρισον τὰ λοιπὰ ἃ ἔμελλον ἀποθανεῖν, οὐ γὰρ εὕρηκά σου τὰ ἔργα πεπληρωμένα ἐνώπιον τοῦ θεοῦ μου.

γίνου. Pres mid impv 2nd sg γίνομαι.

γρηγορῶν. Pres act ptc masc nom sg γρηγορέω (present periphrastic; the imperative of γίνομαι used with a present participle is equivalent to a present imperative). This construction draws attention to the aspect of the participle.

στήρισον. Aor act impv 2nd sg στηρίζω.

τὰ λοιπά. Accusative direct object of στήρισον. Aune says that the neuter τὰ λοιπά refers to people (1.216). However, it more likely refers to the works that Jesus finds deficient in the rest of the verse (τὰ ἔργα).

ἅ. Nominative subject of ἔμελλον.

ἔμελλον. Impf act ind 3rd pl μέλλω. Constructions with imperfect verbs complemented by an infinitive frequently do not refer to past time (Porter 1992, 34–35). The imperfect does not imply that the process of dying has been going on for some time (contra Osborne, 175). See also "Verbal Aspect" in the Introduction.

ἀποθανεῖν. Aor act inf ἀποθνῄσκω (complementary).

γάρ. Introduces explanatory material that strengthens or supports what precedes (Runge, 52).

εὕρηκά. Prf act ind 1st sg εὑρίσκω. The use of the perfect tense draws attention to the reason for the preceding imperatives: They have been investigated and "have been tried and found wanting" (Osborne, 175). The accenting is due to the enclitic σου that follows.

σου. Subjective genitive. Placed before the head term it modifies for prominence.

τὰ ἔργα. Accusative direct object of εὕρηκά.

πεπληρωμένα. Prf pass ptc masc acc pl πληρόω. Complement in an object-complement double accusative construction.

ἐνώπιον τοῦ θεοῦ. Though this could be locative, it is more likely that ἐνώπιον marks "a participant whose viewpoint is relevant to an event—'in the sight of, in the opinion of, in the judgment of'" (LN 90.20).

μου. Genitive of subordination.

3:3 μνημόνευε οὖν πῶς εἴληφας καὶ ἤκουσας καὶ τήρει καὶ μετανόησον. ἐὰν οὖν μὴ γρηγορήσῃς, ἥξω ὡς κλέπτης, καὶ οὐ μὴ γνῷς ποίαν ὥραν ἥξω ἐπὶ σέ.

μνημόνευε. Pres act impv 2nd sg μνημονεύω. The present tense here is used of a specific command. Osborne reads too much into the tense when he concludes that it indicates "a continual recall" (176). See "Verbal Aspect" in the Introduction.

οὖν. Inferential.

πῶς εἴληφας καὶ ἤκουσας. The interrogative clause functions as a clausal complement of μνημόνευε. The interrogative πῶς indicates the manner in which they welcomed and heard what they were taught.

εἴληφας. Prf act ind 2nd sg λαμβάνω. The aorist ἤκουσας summarizes the way the word of God came to them, with their reception in the perfect tense (εἴληφας) being the highlighted element of the pair (Mathewson 2010, 97–98). The hearing forms the basis for their receiving the message. The order "received" and "heard" seems strange. Logically, the hearing would precede the act of receiving. This inversion is an example of the rhetorical device hysteron-proteron (last-first). This is most likely the author's way of foregrounding the more important element of the pair: The receiving (Resseguie, 51). This is further supported by the use of the perfect tense form εἴληφας. Though some think that the perfect εἴληφας has the force of an aorist (Mussies, 338), the fact that it occurs in tandem with an aorist tense form or that they are translated as aorists in English does not mean that the two forms are semantically synonymous (see also 5:7 on εἴληφεν). Neither is Smalley correct that the "faith of the Sardians came by 'hearing' the gospel at a particular moment in time (aorist); but on that occasion they received the faith as an ongoing trust (perfect)" (82; also Swete, 50). Both verbs refer to aspects of the reception of the gospel. The difference is in verbal aspect, or the author's conception of the processes (see "Verbal Aspect" in the Introduction).

ἤκουσας. Aor act ind 2nd sg ἀκούω.

καὶ. The καί preceding τήρει links τήρει with the imperative μνημόνευε, not with ἤκουσας.

τήρει. Pres act impv 2nd sg τηρέω. The aorist imperative μετανόησον forms the basis for the command to keep what they received, which is expressed in the present imperative τήρει viewing the action as a process.

μετανόησον. Aor act impv 2nd sg μετανοέω. For the shift from the present to the aorist imperative, see τήρει above. Logically, the repenting would precede the act of keeping. This inversion is another example of hysteron-proteron. See comment on εἴληφας above.

ἐάν. Introduces the protasis of a third-class conditional sentence (see 2:5 on ἐάν).

οὖν. Resumptive.
γρηγορήσῃς. Aor act subj 2nd sg γρηγορέω. Subjunctive with ἐάν.
ἥξω. Fut act ind 1st sg ἥκω.
ὡς κλέπτης. Manner.
κλέπτης. Nominative subject of an implied ἥκει.
γνῷς. Aor act subj 2nd sg γινώσκω. The subjunctive is used with οὐ μὴ, which expresses emphatic negation.
ποίαν ὥραν ἥξω ἐπὶ σέ. The entire clause functions as the complement of γνῷς.
ποίαν ὥραν. Adverbial accusative expressing time. According to Robertson (740), ποίαν here has lost its qualitative sense.
ἥξω. Fut act ind 1st sg ἥκω.
ἐπὶ σέ. The preposition ἐπί here with the accusative is a marker of opposition: "Against" (BDAG, 366.12.b).

3:4 ἀλλὰ ἔχεις ὀλίγα ὀνόματα ἐν Σάρδεσιν ἃ οὐκ ἐμόλυναν τὰ ἱμάτια αὐτῶν, καὶ περιπατήσουσιν μετ' ἐμοῦ ἐν λευκοῖς, ὅτι ἄξιοί εἰσιν.

ἀλλὰ. Draws a contrast with the previous negative evaluation in verse 3.
ἔχεις. Pres act ind 2nd sg ἔχω.
ὀλίγα ὀνόματα. Accusative direct object of ἔχεις. The word ὀνόματα ("names") refers to "people" (LN 9.19) by the figure of speech of synecdoche, substituting a part (a person's name) for the whole (the entire person). Perhaps it is meant to contrast with those who have an ὄνομα (reputation) in verse 1.
ἐν Σάρδεσιν. Locative.
ἃ. Nominative subject of ἐμόλυναν.
ἐμόλυναν. Aor act ind 3rd pl μολύνω. Neuter plurals commonly take singular verbs, unless they refer to personal beings in the Apocalypse. Here since the relative pronoun refers back to names, which refer to "people," the plural ἐμόλυναν is used.
τὰ ἱμάτια. Accusative direct object of ἐμόλυναν.
αὐτῶν. Possessive genitive.
περιπατήσουσιν. Fut act ind 3rd pl περιπατέω.
μετ' ἐμοῦ. Association.
ἐν λευκοῖς. Manner.
ὅτι. Introduces a causal clause that provides the reason why they will walk with Christ dressed in white.
ἄξιοί. Predicate nominative. The accenting is due to the enclitic εἰσιν that follows.
εἰσιν. Pres act ind 3rd pl εἰμί. On the loss of accent, see 1:8.

3:5 Ὁ νικῶν οὕτως περιβαλεῖται ἐν ἱματίοις λευκοῖς καὶ οὐ μὴ ἐξαλείψω τὸ ὄνομα αὐτοῦ ἐκ τῆς βίβλου τῆς ζωῆς καὶ ὁμολογήσω τὸ ὄνομα αὐτοῦ ἐνώπιον τοῦ πατρός μου καὶ ἐνώπιον τῶν ἀγγέλων αὐτοῦ.

Ὁ νικῶν. Pres act ptc masc nom sg νικάω (substantival). Nominative subject of περιβαλεῖται.

οὕτως. Manner. Here it cataphorically points forward to the PP ἐν ἱματίοις λευκοῖς, which indicates the manner of the clothing.

περιβαλεῖται. Fut mid ind 3rd sg περιβάλλω.

ἐν ἱματίοις λευκοῖς. Manner or instrumental.

ἐξαλείψω. Fut act ind 1st sg ἐξαλείφω. The double negative (οὐ μή) occurring with the future tense is an emphatic way of negating something. The entire expression, "I will not wipe out his name from the book of life," reflects a rhetorical figure of speech known as a litotes, the use of understatement to emphasize a point, usually by negating its opposite (e.g., "How are you?" "Not bad!" = "I am doing fine"; see Black, 135). Thus "I will not wipe out his name from the book of life" is a rhetorically emphatic way of saying "I will keep you."

τὸ ὄνομα. Accusative direct object of ἐξαλείψω.

αὐτοῦ. Possessive genitive.

ἐκ τῆς βίβλου. Separation.

τῆς ζωῆς. Attributive genitive.

ὁμολογήσω. Fut act ind 1st sg ὁμολογέω.

τὸ ὄνομα. Accusative direct object of ὁμολογήσω.

αὐτοῦ. Possessive genitive.

ἐνώπιον τοῦ πατρός. Locative.

μου. Genitive of relationship.

ἐνώπιον τῶν ἀγγέλων. Locative.

αὐτοῦ. Possessive genitive.

3:6 Ὁ ἔχων οὖς ἀκουσάτω τί τὸ πνεῦμα λέγει ταῖς ἐκκλησίαις.

Ὁ ἔχων. Pres act ptc masc nom sg ἔχω (substantival). Nominative subject of ἀκουσάτω.

οὖς. Accusative direct object of ἔχων.

ἀκουσάτω. Aor act impv 3rd sg ἀκούω. On the force of the third person imperative, see 2:7 on ἀκουσάτω.

τί. Accusative direct object of λέγει. The interrogative pronoun introduces a clause that functions as the syntactic complement of ἀκουσάτω.

τὸ πνεῦμα. Nominative subject of λέγει.

λέγει. Pres act ind 3rd sg λέγω.

ταῖς ἐκκλησίαις. Dative indirect object of λέγει.

Revelation 3:7-13

⁷And to the angel of the church in Philadelphia write: The holy one, the true one, the one who has the key of David, who opens and no one shall shut, and who shuts and no one opens, says these things: ⁸I know your works; behold I have caused a door to stand open before you, which no one is able to shut. Because you have little power and you have kept my word, and you have not denied my name, ⁹look, I am going to make those from the synagogue of Satan who say that they are Jews and they are not but they are lying—look, I am going to make them come and bow down before your feet and acknowledge that I love you. ¹⁰Because you have kept the word of my endurance, I will also keep you from the hour of testing which is about to come upon the whole inhabited world in order to test those who dwell upon the earth. ¹¹I am coming soon; hold on to what you have, in order that no one might take your crown. ¹²I will make the one who overcomes a pillar in the temple of my God and they will never again go outside of it and I will write upon them the name of my God and the name of the city of my God, the New Jerusalem which comes down out of heaven from my God, and (I will write upon them) my new name. ¹³The one who has ears should listen to what the Spirit is saying to the churches.

3:7 Καὶ τῷ ἀγγέλῳ τῆς ἐν Φιλαδελφείᾳ ἐκκλησίας γράψον· Τάδε λέγει ὁ ἅγιος, ὁ ἀληθινός, ὁ ἔχων τὴν κλεῖν Δαυίδ, ὁ ἀνοίγων καὶ οὐδεὶς κλείσει καὶ κλείων καὶ οὐδεὶς ἀνοίγει·

    τῷ ἀγγέλῳ. Dative indirect object of γράψον.
    τῆς . . . ἐκκλησίας. Possessive genitive or genitive of subordination.
    ἐν Φιλαδελφείᾳ. Locative.
    γράψον. Aor act impv 2nd sg γράψω.
    Τάδε. Accusative direct object of λέγει. On the form, see 2:1.
    λέγει. Pres act ind 3rd sg λέγω.
    ὁ ἅγιος. Nominative subject of λέγει.
    ὁ ἀληθινός. Nominative in apposition to ὁ ἅγιος. It could also function as an attributive modifier of ὁ ἅγιος.
    ὁ ἔχων. Pres act ptc masc nom sg ἔχω (substantival). Nominative in apposition to ὁ ἅγιος.
    τὴν κλεῖν. Accusative direct object of ὁ ἔχων.
    Δαυίδ. Possessive genitive. As a name, Δαυίδ is an indeclinable noun and its case must be inferred from its function in the context.
    ὁ ἀνοίγων. Pres act ptc masc nom sg ἀνοίγω (substantival). Nominative in apposition to ὁ ἅγιος. The four verbal forms in the last clause of

this verse form a chiasm (ABBA pattern): open . . . shut/ shut . . . open (Smalley, 88).

οὐδεὶς. Nominative subject of κλείσει.

κλείσει. Fut act ind 3rd sg κλείω.

κλείων. Pres act ptc masc nom sg κλείω (substantival). Nominative in apposition to ὁ ἅγιος.

οὐδεὶς. Nominative subject of ἀνοίγει.

ἀνοίγει. Pres act ind 3rd sg ἀνοίγω. Probably to conform to the future κλείσει above, some manuscripts read the future ἀνοίξει (ℵ 1006 1841 2050 2329 2344 𝔐) rather than the present ἀνοίγει.

3:8 οἶδά σου τὰ ἔργα, ἰδοὺ δέδωκα ἐνώπιόν σου θύραν ἠνεῳγμένην, ἣν οὐδεὶς δύναται κλεῖσαι αὐτήν, ὅτι μικρὰν ἔχεις δύναμιν καὶ ἐτήρησάς μου τὸν λόγον καὶ οὐκ ἠρνήσω τὸ ὄνομά μου.

οἶδά. Prf act ind 1st sg οἶδα. On the tense, see 2:2. The accenting is due to the enclitic σου that follows.

σου. Subjective genitive. Placed before the head term it modifies for prominence.

τὰ ἔργα. Accusative direct object of οἶδά. The syntax of this verse and verses 9-10 is unclear. Because the expression of the knowledge of works is followed elsewhere by an indication of the content of those works, sometimes in the form of a clause introduced by ὅτι (see 3:1, 15), some scholars such as Charles, Mounce, Smalley, Beale, and Osborne argue that the clause introduced by ἰδού that follows (ἰδοὺ δέδωκα . . . κλεῖσαι αὐτήν) forms a parenthesis, and the ὅτι clause that follows (see below) indicates the content of the "works" as in 3:1, 15 (Charles, 1.86–87; Swete, 54; Mounce, 117; Smalley, 89; Beale, 286; Osborne, 188–89). This way of construing the clauses is also followed in UBS[3] by placing a dash before and after ἰδοὺ δέδωκα . . . κλεῖσαι αὐτήν, but is not observed in UBS[5]. However, it is probably better to take ἰδοὺ δέδωκα . . . κλεῖσαι αὐτήν as a new sentence rather than a parenthesis, with οἶδά σου τὰ ἔργα here in verse 8 constituting a separate clause containing no explicit expression of the content of ἔργα (e.g., Aune, 1.228; NASB, NRSV, NIV, which place a full stop after "works"). The clause introduced by ὅτι below would then function to introduce a causal clause, explaining the reason that the church is given an open door, rather than the content of ἔργα.

ἰδοὺ. A marker of attention that deictically functions to make the following statement emphatic. On the form, see on 1:7.

δέδωκα. Prf act ind 1st sg δίδωμι. Perhaps the perfect tense form functions to provide a contrast between what Christ gives (present tense διδῶ) and those of the synagogue of Satan (v. 9) have given.

ἐνώπιόν σου. Locative. The accenting can be explained by the enclitic σου that follows.

θύραν. Accusative direct object of δέδωκα.

ἠνεῳγμένην. Prf pass ptc fem acc sg ἀνοίγω (attributive). On the possible significance of the perfect tense, see above on δέδωκα.

ἥν. Accusative direct object of κλεῖσαι.

οὐδεὶς. Nominative subject of δύναται.

δύναται. Pres mid ind 3rd sg δύναμαι.

κλεῖσαι. Aor act inf κλείω (complementary).

αὐτήν. Accusative direct object of κλεῖσαι. The personal pronoun is redundant following the accusative relative pronoun ἥν (lit. "which no one is able to shut *it*"). This construction occurs elsewhere in Revelation: 7:2, 9; 12:6, 14; 13:8, 12; 17:9; 19:9; 20:8. This may be an example of Semitic influence (Turner, 325; Zerwick, §§201–3; Caragounis, 148), though examples of this construction can also be found in Hellenistic Greek (Aune, 1.229; Robertson, 722). However, it is rare outside of Revelation and is more common in the LXX (Robertson, 722). This construction probably functions to place greater emphasis on the antecedent: here, the open door.

ὅτι. Introduces a causal clause. It is possible that this ὅτι clause goes with what follows (see translation).

μικρὰν ... δύναμιν. Accusative direct object of ἔχεις.

ἔχεις. Pres act ind 2nd sg ἔχω.

ἐτήρησάς. Aor act ind 2nd sg τηρέω. The accenting is due to the enclitic μου that follows. Smalley (89) incorrectly concludes that because the verbs ἐτήρησάς and ἠρνήσω are in the aorist tense the author has a specific occasion in mind. The aorist simply views the action as a complete whole. See "Verbal Aspect" in the Introduction.

μου. Genitive of source or subjective genitive. Placed before the head term it modifies for prominence. It may also function to create a balance (with the two elements in reverse order) with the end of the verse: μου τὸν λόγον ... τὸ ὄνομά μου.

τὸν λόγον. Accusative direct object of ἐτήρησας.

καὶ. Aune argues that καί here functions to introduce "the consequences of the action in the previous clause" (1.230). This does not mean that "consequence" is the meaning of καί, but only that it introduces a clause that semantically may indicate the consequences of the preceding clause. The καί simply indicates continuity.

ἠρνήσω. Aor mid ind 2nd sg ἀρνέομαι.

τὸ ὄνομά. Accusative direct object of ἠρνήσω. The accenting is due to the enclitic μου that follows.

μου. Possessive genitive.

3:9 ἰδοὺ διδῶ ἐκ τῆς συναγωγῆς τοῦ σατανᾶ τῶν λεγόντων ἑαυτοὺς Ἰουδαίους εἶναι, καὶ οὐκ εἰσὶν ἀλλὰ ψεύδονται. ἰδοὺ ποιήσω αὐτοὺς ἵνα ἥξουσιν καὶ προσκυνήσουσιν ἐνώπιον τῶν ποδῶν σου καὶ γνῶσιν ὅτι ἐγὼ ἠγάπησά σε.

ἰδού. A marker of attention that deictically functions to make the following statement emphatic. On the form, see 1:7.

διδῶ. Pres act ind 1st sg δίδωμι. Here δίδωμι may be used in the sense of "cause" (BDAG, 242.4; LN 90.51). The form διδῶ only here in 3:9 reflects a transition to the replacement of -μι with -ω, hence διδόω (see BDF §94.1; Charles, 1.88; Aune, 1.229-30; 𝔐 reads δίδωμι). The present tense is future referring. The present tense may also contrast with the perfect δέδωκα in verse 8, so that the author may be highlighting the contrast between what Christ has given the church (v. 8) and what he now gives unbelieving Jews (v. 9; see Mathewson 2010, 105). ἰδοὺ διδῶ is resumed with ἰδοὺ ποιήσω that follows.

ἐκ τῆς συναγωγῆς. Partitive. Functions as the direct object of διδῶ. This may be an elliptical expression: τίνας ἐκ τῆς συναγωγῆς. On the function of partitive constructions as subject or object of a verb, see 2:7 on ἐκ τοῦ ξύλου.

τοῦ σατανᾶ. Possessive genitive.

τῶν λεγόντων. Pres act ptc masc gen pl λέγω (substantival). The participle stands in apposition to ἐκ τῆς συναγωγῆς. The plural is according to sense, reflecting the sense of ἐκ τῆς συναγωγῆς (the members of the synagogue).

ἑαυτούς. Accusative subject of εἶναι.

Ἰουδαίους. Predicate accusative of εἶναι.

εἶναι. Pres act inf εἰμί (indirect discourse).

εἰσὶν. Pres act ind 3rd pl εἰμί. On the shift from a participle to a finite verb, see 1:6 on ἐποίησεν.

ἀλλά. Draws a contrast with the claim to be Jews, which the author denies.

ψεύδονται. Pres mid ind 3rd pl ψεύδομαι.

ἰδού. A marker of attention that deictically functions to make the following statement emphatic. On the form, see 1:7. ἰδοὺ ποιήσω resumes ἰδοὺ διδῶ at the beginning of the verse.

ποιήσω. Fut act ind 1st sg ποιέω. Here ποιήσω connotes causality and is complemented by a ἵνα clause (BDAG, 840.2.h). See also below on ἵνα. The shift from the causal use of δίδωμι (see above) to the causal use of ποιέω here may only be stylistic.

αὐτούς. Accusative direct object of ποιήσω.

ἵνα. Though it is possible to take the ἵνα here as introducing a final or result clause (Aune, 1.230; Charles, 1.88), it is more likely that it functions as a content clause in the place of an infinitive as a complement of the verb ποιήσω in a causative construction (BDF §392.1e; Robertson, 922): "I will cause them to come and bow down." More specifically, McKay thinks this is an example of a ἵνα clause functioning in place of an infinitive to indicate an indirect command (1994, 116).

ἥξουσιν. Fut act ind 3rd pl ἥκω. This is one of many examples of John's use of the future where one would expect a subjunctive (here after ἵνα). Robertson (984) notes that ἵνα was not used with the future indicative in classical Greek. The similarity in form and sense between the future and subjunctive probably accounts for this usage (984). The future is used after ἵνα ten times in Revelation (3:9; 6:4, 11; 8:3; 9:4, 5, 20; 13:12; 14:13; 22:14). Usually there are variant readings in manuscripts with the subjunctive in these instances. Grammarians and commentators have long noted the usage of the future where the subjunctive is expected in Revelation (Robertson, 960–61; BDF, §§369, 78; Mussies, 242; Aune, 1.clxxxvi). Caragounis (117 n. 100) suggests that although the most common form was still ἵνα with the subjunctive, the indicative was beginning to be used during this time with no apparent difference in meaning. However, if the choice of the future is intentional, Porter suggests, "Where a choice is offered between the Subjunctive and the Future, the Future is the more heavily marked semantically" indicating what can be expected to take place (1989a, 414). Porter notes parallels to this in classical literature (415). A number of scribes replaced the future with what was felt to be the more "appropriate" subjunctive (046 1611 1841 1854 2344 2351 *pm* read ἥξωσιν).

προσκυνήσουσιν. Fut act ind 3rd pl προσκυνέω. On the future in place of the subjunctive, see ἥξουσιν above. 046 1611 1841 1854 2053 2344 2351 *pm* have the subjunctive προσκυνήσωσιν.

ἐνώπιον τῶν ποδῶν. Locative.

σου. Possessive genitive.

γνῶσιν. Aor act subj 3rd pl γινώσκω. Subjunctive with ἵνα. The author switches back to the subjunctive with ἵνα.

ὅτι. Introduces a content clause that is the clausal complement of γνῶσιν.

ἐγὼ. Nominative subject of ἠγάπησά.

ἠγάπησά. Aor act ind 1st sg ἀγαπάω. The aorist tense of ἠγάπησα here is often translated "I have loved" and treated as an aorist with perfective force (see Aune, 1.231). However, this depends more on English translation concerns than the semantics of the aorist form (see "Verbal Aspect" in the Introduction). More likely, this is an example of a present referring, or possibly a timeless, use of the aorist reflected in the translation "I love you." There is no need to attribute this use of the aorist to Semitic influence, as Thompson proposes (40), since the aorist can occur in a variety of temporal contexts (Porter 1992, 35–39). The accenting is due to the enclitic σε that follows.

σε. Accusative direct object of ἠγάπησά.

3:10 ὅτι ἐτήρησας τὸν λόγον τῆς ὑπομονῆς μου, κἀγώ σε τηρήσω ἐκ τῆς ὥρας τοῦ πειρασμοῦ τῆς μελλούσης ἔρχεσθαι ἐπὶ τῆς οἰκουμένης ὅλης πειράσαι τοὺς κατοικοῦντας ἐπὶ τῆς γῆς.

ὅτι. Introduces a causal clause. Though causal clauses tend to be sentence final, here the causal clause is sentence initial (Runge, 208). By placing the causal clause at the beginning of the sentence, the author provides a causal "frame of reference" (208–9). The readers have kept Christ's word, which forms the basis for what Christ will do for them in the clause that follows.

ἐτήρησας. Aor act ind 2nd sg τηρέω.

τὸν λόγον. Accusative direct object of ἐτήρησας.

τῆς ὑπομονῆς. Objective genitive ("the word concerning/about endurance").

μου. Subjective genitive. There is some question regarding what μου modifies. It would seem naturally to go with the term immediately preceding it, τῆς ὑπομονῆς, so that the entire phrase should be rendered "the word concerning my (Christ's) endurance" (see Charles, 1.89; Swete, 56). Most likely, however, the genitive μου modifies the entire phrase τὸν λόγον τῆς ὑπομονῆς (Aune, 1.231), and should be rendered "my word of patient endurance" (NRSV; see also NIV: "my command to endure patiently"). Therefore, it is semantically equivalent to ἐτήρησάς μου τὸν λόγον in verse 8.

κἀγώ. On the form, see 2:6. ἐγώ is the nominative subject of τηρήσω.

σε. Accusative direct object of τηρήσω. The fronting of the direct object before the verb is emphatic, perhaps to draw attention to what Christ will do for them since they have kept his word.

τηρήσω. Fut act ind 1st sg τηρέω.

ἐκ τῆς ὥρας. Separation. There has been some debate whether this construction (τηρήσω ἐκ) implies preservation outside of the hour of testing ("remove from"), or preservation within/in the midst of the hour of testing ("protect from"). Given the parallels with John 17:15 (τηρήσῃς ἐκ τοῦ πονηροῦ), and the fact that in Revelation God's people experience trials, tribulations, and persecution, most commentators opt for the latter explanation (see Aune, 1.239–40; Osborne, 192–94; Beale, 287–92).

τοῦ πειρασμοῦ. The idea communicated by the genitive seems to be "the hour when testing takes place."

τῆς μελλούσης. Pres act ptc fem gen sg μέλλω (attributive).

ἔρχεσθαι. Pres mid inf ἔρχομαι (complementary).
ἐπὶ τῆς οἰκουμένης ὅλης. Locative.
πειράσαι. Aor act inf πειράζω (purpose).
τοὺς κατοικοῦντας. Pres act ptc masc acc pl κατοικέω (substantival). Accusative direct object of πειράσαι. This is a favorite designation of the author to refer to those who are in collusion with the Beast and who oppress God's people.
ἐπὶ τῆς γῆς. Locative.

3:11 ἔρχομαι ταχύ· κράτει ὃ ἔχεις, ἵνα μηδεὶς λάβῃ τὸν στέφανόν σου.

ἔρχομαι. Pre mid ind 1st sg ἔρχομαι.
ταχύ. Temporal. On the force of ταχύ, see 1:1 on ἐν τάχει. "The emphasis ... is on imminence, not swiftness" (Osborne, 194 n. 24).
κράτει. Pres act impv 2nd sg κρατέω.
ὅ. Accusative direct object of ἔχεις. The relative pronoun introduces a headless relative clause. The entire clause functions as the direct object of κράτει.
ἔχεις. Pres act ind 2nd sg ἔχω.
ἵνα. Introduces a purpose clause.
μηδεὶς. Nominative subject of λάβῃ.
λάβῃ. Aor act subj 3rd sg λαμβάνω. Subjunctive with ἵνα.
τὸν στέφανόν. Accusative direct object of λάβῃ. The accenting is due to the enclitic σου which follows.
σου. Possessive genitive.

3:12 Ὁ νικῶν ποιήσω αὐτὸν στῦλον ἐν τῷ ναῷ τοῦ θεοῦ μου καὶ ἔξω οὐ μὴ ἐξέλθῃ ἔτι καὶ γράψω ἐπ' αὐτὸν τὸ ὄνομα τοῦ θεοῦ μου καὶ τὸ ὄνομα τῆς πόλεως τοῦ θεοῦ μου, τῆς καινῆς Ἰερουσαλὴμ ἡ καταβαίνουσα ἐκ τοῦ οὐρανοῦ ἀπὸ τοῦ θεοῦ μου, καὶ τὸ ὄνομά μου τὸ καινόν.

Ὁ νικῶν. Pres act ptc masc nom sg νικάω (substantival). Topical construction (see 1:5). Ὁ νικῶν is resumed by the pronoun αὐτόν.
ποιήσω. Fut act ind 1st sg ποιέω.
αὐτὸν. Accusative direct object of ποιήσω. The pronoun picks up the topic introduced by ὁ νικῶν.
στῦλον. Complement in an object-complement double accusative construction.
ἐν τῷ ναῷ. Locative.
τοῦ θεοῦ. Possessive genitive.
μου. Genitive of subordination.
ἔξω. Locative.

ἐξέλθῃ. Aor act subj 3rd sg ἐξέρχομαι. The subjunctive is used with οὐ μὴ, which expresses emphatic negation.
ἔτι. BDAG (400.1.b) suggests that οὐ μή with ἔτι implies "*never again.*"
γράψω. Fut act ind 1st sg γράφω.
ἐπ' αὐτὸν. Locative.
τὸ ὄνομα. Accusative direct object of γράψω.
τοῦ θεοῦ. Possessive genitive.
μου. Genitive of subordination.
τὸ ὄνομα. Accusative direct object of γράψω.
τῆς πόλεως. Possessive genitive.
τοῦ θεοῦ. Possessive genitive.
μου. Genitive of subordination.
τῆς καινῆς Ἰερουσαλὴμ. Genitive in apposition to τῆς πόλεως. What is written on the overcomer is the name "New Jerusalem." On the issue of the different Greek spellings for Jerusalem, see Aune, 1.232.
ἡ καταβαίνουσα. Pres act ptc fem nom sg καταβαίνω (substantival). This construction appears to be a grammatical incongruity, in that the participle καταβαίνουσα is nominative whereas the thing that it refers to, τῆς καινῆς Ἰερουσαλήμ, is genitive. This should probably be understood as a parenthetical use of the participle: "The New Jerusalem—the one that comes down out of heaven from God—and my new name." ℵ[2] "corrects" it to the genitive τῆς καταβαινούσης.
ἐκ τοῦ οὐρανοῦ. Source.
ἀπὸ τοῦ θεοῦ. Source. While both ἐκ and ἀπό express the source or origin of the city (Aune says "from God" is redundant, 1.243), ἀπό can be used of the direct originator of an action (BDAG, 106.5.d).
μου. Genitive of subordination.
τὸ ὄνομά ... τὸ καινόν. Accusative direct object of γράψω. The accenting of ὄνομά is due to the enclitic μου that follows.
μου. Possessive genitive.

3:13 Ὁ ἔχων οὖς ἀκουσάτω τί τὸ πνεῦμα λέγει ταῖς ἐκκλησίαις.

Ὁ ἔχων. Pres act ptc masc nom sg ἔχω (substantival). Nominative subject of ἀκουσάτω.
οὖς. Accusative direct object of ἔχων.
ἀκουσάτω. Aor act impv 3rd sg ἀκούω. On the force of the third person imperative, see 2:7 on ἀκουσάτω.
τί. Accusative direct object of λέγει. The interrogative pronoun introduces a clause that functions as the syntactic complement of ἀκουσάτω.
τὸ πνεῦμα. Nominative subject of λέγει.
λέγει. Pres act ind 3rd sg λέγω.
ταῖς ἐκκλησίαις. Dative indirect object of λέγει.

Revelation 3:14-22

¹⁴And to the angel of the church in Laodicea write: The "Amen," the faithful and true witness, the beginning of the creation of God says these things: ¹⁵I know your works, that you are neither cold nor hot. I wish that you were either cold or hot. ¹⁶So because you are lukewarm and neither hot nor cold, I am about to vomit you out of my mouth! ¹⁷Because you say, "I am rich and I am wealthy, and in no way do I have need," and you do not know that you are really miserable and pitiful and poor and blind and naked, ¹⁸I counsel you to buy from me gold that is purified with fire in order than you might be rich, and white garments in order that you might be clothed and that the shame of your nakedness might not be revealed, and medication to apply to your eyes in order that you might see. ¹⁹As many as I love, I reprove and discipline. Therefore, be zealous and repent. ²⁰Look, I stand at the door and knock. If anyone hears my voice and opens the door, I will come in to them and will dine with them, and they with me. ²¹I will give to the one who overcomes the right to sit with me on my throne, just as I overcame and sat with my father on his throne. ²²The one who has ears should listen to what the Spirit is saying to the churches.

3:14 Καὶ τῷ ἀγγέλῳ τῆς ἐν Λαοδικείᾳ ἐκκλησίας γράψον· Τάδε λέγει ὁ ἀμήν, ὁ μάρτυς ὁ πιστὸς καὶ ἀληθινός, ἡ ἀρχὴ τῆς κτίσεως τοῦ θεοῦ·

τῷ ἀγγέλῳ. Dative indirect object of γράψον.

τῆς ... ἐκκλησίας. Possessive genitive or genitive of subordination.

ἐν Λαοδικείᾳ. Locative.

γράψον. Aor act impv 2nd sg γράφω.

Τάδε. Accusative direct object of λέγει. On the form, see 2:1.

λέγει. Pres act ind 3rd sg λέγω.

ὁ Ἀμήν. Nominative subject of λέγει. Ἀμήν is a transliteration of the Hebrew אמן. The meaning of the title is further explicated by ὁ πιστὸς καὶ ἀληθινός which follows, and probably echoes LXX Isa 65:16 where אמן is translated ἀληθινόν (see Beale, 299).

ὁ μάρτυς ὁ πιστὸς καὶ ἀληθινός. Nominative in apposition to ὁ Ἀμήν.

ἡ ἀρχὴ. Nominative in apposition to ὁ Ἀμήν. ἀρχή could have the sense "first cause, origin" (LN 89.16) or "ruler."

τῆς κτίσεως. Objective genitive, if ἀρχή means "origin." If ἀρχή means "ruler," τῆς κτίσεως could be a genitive of subordination ("ruler over the creation of God"). In either case, Christ's sovereignty in relation to creation is being emphasized.

τοῦ θεοῦ. Subjective genitive.

Revelation 3:14-16

3:15 οἶδά σου τὰ ἔργα ὅτι οὔτε ψυχρὸς εἶ οὔτε ζεστός. ὄφελον ψυχρὸς ἦς ἢ ζεστός.

οἶδά. Prf act ind 1st sg οἶδα. On the tense, see 2:2. The accenting is due to the enclitic σου that follows.
σου. Subjective genitive. Placed before the head term it modifies for prominence.
τὰ ἔργα. Accusative direct object of οἶδά.
ὅτι. Introduces a content clause that is epexegetical to τὰ ἔργα.
ψυχρὸς. Predicate adjective.
εἶ. Pres act ind 2nd sg εἰμί.
ζεστός. Predicate adjective.
ὄφελον. McKay notes that ὄφελον is a particle that expresses an excluded wish: "An excluded wish is usually expressed by means of ὄφελον with a secondary tense of the indicative, usually imperfect or aorist [here in Rev 3:15 the imperfect ἦς]. . . . [T]he possibility of fulfillment . . . has already been excluded by the existing state of affairs or by irreversable events in the past" (1994, 86-87).
ψυχρὸς. Predicate adjective.
ἦς. Impf act ind 2nd sg εἰμί. The imperfect tense with ὄφελον expresses present time (Porter 1989a, 209).
ζεστός. Predicate adjective.

3:16 οὕτως ὅτι χλιαρὸς εἶ καὶ οὔτε ζεστὸς οὔτε ψυχρός, μέλλω σε ἐμέσαι ἐκ τοῦ στόματός μου.

οὕτως. The particle is used here to draw an inference (cf. Porter 1992, 215).
ὅτι. Introduces a causal clause. On the position of the ὅτι clause, see 3:10. The emphasis is on the cause of Jesus' response in the remainder of the clause.
χλιαρὸς. Predicate adjective.
εἶ. Pres act ind 2nd sg εἰμί.
ζεστὸς. Predicate adjective.
ψυχρός. Predicate adjective.
μέλλω. Pres act ind 1st sg μέλλω.
σε. Accusative direct object of ἐμέσαι.
ἐμέσαι. Aor act inf ἐμέω (complementary).
ἐκ τοῦ στόματός. Separation. The accenting is due to the enclitic μου that follows.
μου. Possessive genitive.

3:17 ὅτι λέγεις ὅτι πλούσιός εἰμι καὶ πεπλούτηκα καὶ οὐδὲν χρείαν ἔχω, καὶ οὐκ οἶδας ὅτι σὺ εἶ ὁ ταλαίπωρος καὶ ἐλεεινὸς καὶ πτωχὸς καὶ τυφλὸς καὶ γυμνός,

ὅτι. Introduces a causal clause that provides a reason for verse 18. On the position of the ὅτι clause, see 3:10.
λέγεις. Pres act ind 2nd sg λέγω.
ὅτι. Introduces a content clause that is the clausal complement (direct discourse) of λέγεις.
πλούσιός. Predicate adjective. The accenting is due to the enclitic εἰμι that follows.
εἰμι. Pres act ind 1st sg εἰμί. On the loss of accent, see 1:8.
πεπλούτηκα. Prf act ind 1st sg πλουτέω. The perfect tense here functions to draw attention to the state of being rich as part of the self-evaluation of the Laodiceans based on their wealth and status, in contrast to Christ's (true) evaluation of them in the second half of the verse.
οὐδὲν. The accusative functions adverbially: "In no way," "in no respect" (BDAG, 735.2.b.γ).
χρείαν. Accusative direct object of ἔχω.
ἔχω. Pres act ind 1st sg ἔχω.
οἶδας. Prf act ind 2nd sg οἶδα. On the perfect of οἶδα, see 2:2.
ὅτι. Introduces a clausal complement of οἶδας.
εἶ. Pres act ind 2nd sg εἰμί.
ὁ ταλαίπωρος . . . καὶ γυμνός. Predicate adjective.

3:18 συμβουλεύω σοι ἀγοράσαι παρ' ἐμοῦ χρυσίον πεπυρωμένον ἐκ πυρὸς ἵνα πλουτήσῃς, καὶ ἱμάτια λευκὰ ἵνα περιβάλῃ καὶ μὴ φανερωθῇ ἡ αἰσχύνη τῆς γυμνότητός σου, καὶ κολλ[ο]ύριον ἐγχρῖσαι τοὺς ὀφθαλμούς σου ἵνα βλέπῃς.

συμβουλεύω. Pres act ind 1st sg συμβουλεύω.
σοι. Dative direct object of συμβουλεύω.
ἀγοράσαι. Aor act inf ἀγοράζω (indirect discourse).
παρ' ἐμοῦ. Source.
χρυσίον. Accusative direct object of ἀγοράσαι.
πεπυρωμένον. Prf pass ptc neut acc sg πυρόω (attributive).
ἐκ πυρὸς. Means.
ἵνα. Introduces a purpose clause.
πλουτήσῃς. Aor act subj 2nd sg πλουτέω. Subjunctive with ἵνα.
ἱμάτια λευκὰ. Accusative direct object of an implied ἀγοράσαι.
ἵνα. Introduces a purpose clause.
περιβάλῃ. Aor mid subj 2nd sg περιβάλλω. Subjunctive with ἵνα.
φανερωθῇ. Aor mid or pass subj 3rd sg φανερόω. Subjunctive with ἵνα.

ἡ αἰσχύνη. Nominative subject of φανερωθῇ.
τῆς γυμνότητός. Attributive genitive ("shameful nakedness") or genitive of source ("shame brought about by your nakedness"). The accenting is due to the enclitic σου that follows.
σου. Possessive genitive.
κολλ[ο]ύριον. Accusative direct object of an implied ἀγοράσαι. "[A] medical compound applied to the eyes, *eye-salve*" (BDAG 556).
ἐγχρῖσαι. Aor act inf ἐγχρίω (purpose). Probably reflecting conformity with the other clauses beginning with ἵνα in this verse, 1006 1611 1841 2351 𝔐^K have ἵνα ἐγχρίσῃ rather than the infinitive ἐγχρῖσαι.
τοὺς ὀφθαλμούς. Accusative direct object of ἐγχρῖσαι.
σου. Possessive genitive.
ἵνα. Introduces a purpose clause.
βλέπῃς. Pres act subj 2nd sg βλέπω. Subjunctive with ἵνα.

3:19 ἐγὼ ὅσους ἐὰν φιλῶ ἐλέγχω καὶ παιδεύω· ζήλευε οὖν καὶ μετανόησον.

ἐγώ. Nominative subject of ἐλέγχω. The pronoun is emphatic. The placing of ἐγώ first before the correlative pronoun draws attention to what Christ does as the basis for the readers to be zealous and repent.
ὅσους ἐὰν φιλῶ. The combination of ὅσος (quantitative correlative pronoun; Porter, 1992, 134) with ἐάν functions to make the expression more general or indefinite (BDAG, 729.2, "whoever," lit. "as many as ever"). The entire headless correlative clause construction functions as the direct object of ἐλέγχω καὶ παιδεύω.
ὅσους. Accusative direct object of φιλῶ.
φιλῶ. Pres act ind 1st sg φιλέω.
ἐλέγχω. Pres act ind 1st sg ἐλέγχω.
παιδεύω. Pres act ind 1st sg παιδεύω.
ζήλευε. Pres act impv 2nd sg ζηλεύω. The present tense could emphasize and describe the condition for their repentance, summarized with the aorist μετανόησον.
οὖν. Inferential.
μετανόησον. Aor act impv 2nd sg μετανοέω.

3:20 Ἰδοὺ ἕστηκα ἐπὶ τὴν θύραν καὶ κρούω· ἐάν τις ἀκούσῃ τῆς φωνῆς μου καὶ ἀνοίξῃ τὴν θύραν, [καὶ] εἰσελεύσομαι πρὸς αὐτὸν καὶ δειπνήσω μετ' αὐτοῦ καὶ αὐτὸς μετ' ἐμοῦ.

Ἰδού. A marker of attention that deictically functions to make the following statement emphatic. On the form, see 1:7. Here it emphasizes the invitation by Christ that follows.

ἕστηκα. Prf act ind 1st sg ἵστημι. In the indicative mood ἵστημι occurs three times in the perfect tense, four times as an aorist, once in the future, and once as a pluperfect. In addition it occurs 11 times as a perfect participle. Thompson (44–45) thinks that it is odd that the perfect tense is used in conjunction with the present (κρούω) and postulates that it is due to Semitic influence. However, the presence of aorist forms and a future form of ἵστημι in Revelation suggests that the author's choice is probably intentional here. Temporally, the perfect tense here refers to present time. The perfect tense emphasizes the state of Christ standing, and functions "to highlight Christ's climactic, present invitation to the readers as a powerful motivation to repent (v. 19)" (Mathewson 2010, 103).

ἐπὶ τὴν θύραν. Locative. ἐπί can be used with the sense of "*at, by, near someone or someth.*" (BDAG, 363.1.b.γ).

κρούω. Pres act ind 1st sg κρούω. Smalley reads too much into the present tense when he incorrectly concludes that the present "implies a repeated and gentle request for entry" (101). See "Verbal Aspect" in the Introduction.

ἐάν. Introduces the protasis of a third-class conditional sentence (see 2:5 on ἐάν).

τις. Nominative subject of ἀκούσῃ.

ἀκούσῃ. Aor act subj 3rd sg ἀκούω. Subjunctive with ἐάν.

τῆς φωνῆς. Genitive direct object of ἀκούσῃ. In the NT ἀκούω takes its object in either the accusative or genitive case. One suggestion for the distinction is that the accusative case is used when something is heard and understood, whereas the genitive indicates only the hearing (i.e., understanding vs. hearing; see Robertson, 506). However, this distinction is hard to maintain in Revelation and elswhere in the NT (Wallace, 133). In Revelation the verb ἀκούω is followed by a word as its object (not including entire clauses or ὡς constructions) in the accusative sixteen times (1:3, 10; 4:1; 5:11, 13; 6:7; 7:4; 9:13, 16; 10:4, 8; 12:10; 14:2 [2×]; 18:4; 22:5) and in the genitive eleven times (3:20; 6:1, 3, 5; 8:13; 11:12; 14:13; 16:1, 5, 7; 21:3). The distinction between hearing with the genitive and understanding with the accusative does not hold when these texts are examined, since both the genitive and accusative cases are used with voices that are apparently heard and understood. Taking the genitive with ἀκούω here as indicating merely hearing the voice of Christ, but not understanding it, clearly does not fit the context.

μου. Possessive genitive or genitive of source.

ἀνοίξῃ. Aor act subj 3rd sg ἀνοίγω. Subjunctive with ἐάν.

τὴν θύραν. Accusative direct object of ἀνοίξῃ.

εἰσελεύσομαι. Fut mid ind 1st sg εἰσέρχομαι.

πρὸς αὐτὸν. πρός indicates "extension toward a goal, with the probability of some type of implied interaction or reciprocity" (LN 84.18).
δειπνήσω. Fut act ind 1st sg δειπνέω.
μετ' αὐτοῦ. Accompaniment.
αὐτὸς. Nominative subject of an implied δειπνήσει.
μετ' ἐμοῦ. Accompaniment.

3:21 Ὁ νικῶν δώσω αὐτῷ καθίσαι μετ' ἐμοῦ ἐν τῷ θρόνῳ μου, ὡς κἀγὼ ἐνίκησα καὶ ἐκάθισα μετὰ τοῦ πατρός μου ἐν τῷ θρόνῳ αὐτοῦ.

Ὁ νικῶν. Pres act ptc masc nom sg νικάω (substantival). Topic construction (see 1:5). The topic is resumed with the pronoun αὐτῷ below.
δώσω. Fut act ind 1st sg δίδωμι. Here δίδωμι may be used in the sense of "to grant, allow" (BDAG, 243.13).
αὐτῷ. Dative indirect object of δώσω. The pronoun picks up the topic ὁ νικῶν.
καθίσαι. Aor act inf καθίζω (substantival). The infinitive functions as the direct object of δώσω.
μετ' ἐμοῦ. Accompaniment.
ἐν τῷ θρόνῳ. Locative.
μου. Possessive genitive.
ὡς. Comparison.
κἀγὼ. On the form, see 2:6. ἐγώ is the nominative subject of ἐνίκησα καὶ ἐκάθισα. The καί functions ascensively: "also."
ἐνίκησα. Aor act ind 1st sg νικάω.
ἐκάθισα. Aor act ind 1st sg καθίζω.
μετὰ τοῦ πατρός. Accompaniment.
μου. Genitive of relationship.
ἐν τῷ θρόνῳ. Locative.
αὐτοῦ. Possessive genitive.

3:22 Ὁ ἔχων οὖς ἀκουσάτω τί τὸ πνεῦμα λέγει ταῖς ἐκκλησίαις.

Ὁ ἔχων. Pres act ptc masc nom sg ἔχω (substantival). Nominative subject of ἀκουσάτω.
οὖς. Accusative direct object of ἔχων.
ἀκουσάτω. Aor act impv 3rd sg ἀκούω. On the force of the third person imperative, see 2:7.
τί. Accusative direct object of λέγει. The interrogative pronoun introduces a clause that functions as the syntactic complement of ἀκουσάτω.
τὸ πνεῦμα. Nominative subject of λέγει.
λέγει. Pres act ind 3rd sg λέγω.
ταῖς ἐκκλησίαις. Dative indirect object of λέγει.

Revelation 4:1-11

¹After these things I looked, and look there was a door to heaven standing open and the first voice which I heard as a trumpet speaking with me saying, "Come up here, and I will show you that which is necessary to take place after these things." ²Immediately I was in the spirit, and look, a throne was set in heaven, and on the throne there was one sitting on it, ³and the one who was sitting on it was like a stone of jasper and ruby in appearance, and a rainbow encircled the throne that was like emerald in appearance. ⁴And surrounding the throne were twenty-four thrones, and upon the thrones were seated twenty-four elders, clothed in white garments, and upon their heads were golden crowns. ⁵And from the throne came lightening and sounds and thunder, and seven lamps of fire were burning before the throne, which are the seven spirits of God. ⁶And before the throne was something like a glassy sea like crystal. And in the midst of the throne and around the throne were four living creatures full of eyes in front and in back. ⁷And the first living creature was like a lion, and the second living creature like an ox, and the third living creature had a face as a human being, and the forth living creature was like an eagle flying. ⁸And each of the four living creatures, which had six wings apiece, were full of eyes outside and within. And they did not have rest day and night, saying, "Holy, holy, holy is the Lord, God, the Almighty, who was and who is and who is coming." ⁹And whenever the living creatures give glory and honor and thanksgiving to the one sitting on the throne, who lives for ever and ever, ¹⁰the twenty-four elders will fall before the one seated on the throne and they will worship the one who lives forever and ever, and they will throw their crowns before the throne saying, ¹¹"You are worthy, our Lord and God, to receive glory and honor and dominion for you created all things, and by your will they existed and were created."

4:1 Μετὰ ταῦτα εἶδον, καὶ ἰδοὺ θύρα ἠνεῳγμένη ἐν τῷ οὐρανῷ, καὶ ἡ φωνὴ ἡ πρώτη ἣν ἤκουσα ὡς σάλπιγγος λαλούσης μετ' ἐμοῦ λέγων· ἀνάβα ὧδε, καὶ δείξω σοι ἃ δεῖ γενέσθαι μετὰ ταῦτα.

Overall, Rev 4 is of a different character than Rev 5 because indicative verbs, which carry the story forward, are less frequent in Rev 4; instead verbless clauses or participles predominate. Revelation 4 contains numerous nominal clauses containing a subject and sometimes a predicate nominative or adjective, or participle with no indicative verb, rather than sentences with an indicative verb filling the predicate slot in the sentence. As Porter says, "The simple nominative itself may form its own clause in Greek. . . . [T]he 'unmarked' case could be used on its own to form a clause, that is, simply to specify the nominal idea" (1992, 85). In Rev 5 indicative verbs are more predominant and function to communicate activity and move the story along. In other words, linguistically Rev 4 provides the setting for Rev 5, in that Rev 4 is highly descriptive and more static, whereas Rev 5 relates activities and processes. As Thompson states, "A noun clause contains no finite verb . . . It stresses the subject's state of being, its existence" (83). Thus, the main focus in this section is Rev 5 since it is where all the action takes place.

Μετὰ ταῦτα. Temporal. The antecedent of ταῦτα is anaphorically the seven messages of Rev 2-3, perhaps also including Rev 1. The main function of Μετὰ ταῦτα is to indicate visionary sequence, not that the events of Rev 4-5 took place chronologically after Rev 1-3.

εἶδον. Aor act ind 1st sg ὁράω.

ἰδού. A marker of attention that deictically functions to make the following statement emphatic. On the form, see 1:7. Here it draws attention to the open door that sets the stage for John's visionary experience.

θύρα. Nominative subject of a verbless clause. On verbless clauses, see above. John usually uses the accusative case after εἶδον. However, the nominative occurs following ἰδού (4:1, 2; 6:2, 5, 8; 7:9; 14:4; 19:11).

ἠνεῳγμένη. Prf pass ptc fem nom sg ἀνοίγω (attributive).

ἐν τῷ οὐρανῷ. Locative.

ἡ φωνὴ ἡ πρώτη. Nominative subject of a verbless clause. This phrase specifies the voice as the same one that spoke to John in 1:10. Both voices are identified with ὡς σάλπιγγος.

ἥν. Accusative direct object of ἤκουσα.

ἤκουσα. Aor act ind 1st sg ἀκούω.

ὡς σάλπιγγος. Comparison. σάλπιγγος could be a genitive of source ("as from a trumpet") or subjective genitive ("sound made by a trumpet"). However, it may be preferrable to see it as a genitive direct object of an implied verb of hearing (ἀκούω): "as *hearing* a trumpet."

λαλούσης. Pres act ptc fem gen sg λαλέω (attributive). The genitive case of the participle seems awkward here, and may have been attracted to the genitive case of σάλπιγγος. The same attraction of λαλούσης to σάλπιγγος occurs also in 1:10-11. In support of this, several manuscripts have attempted to correct this with λαλοῦσα (2329 *pc*) or λεγοῦσα (1854). Another option is that the participle should be accusative, and functions as the complement in an object-complement double accusative construction with ἥν. ℵ corrects the participle to the accusative λαλοῦσαν. Beale (318) thinks that the genitive case is a deliberate attempt by the author to draw attention to an OT allusion to Exod 19:16-19. But it is probably best to take the participle as attributive modifying the genitive σάλπιγγος.

μετ' ἐμοῦ. Association or accompaniment.

λέγων. Pres act ptc masc nom sg λέγω (manner). On the usage of λέγων to introduce speech, see 1:17 on λέγων. The masculine gender of the participle is problematic grammatically, since it is the voice (feminine ἡ φωνή) that is speaking. Perhaps the gender has been determined according to sense. Though the voice is strictly anonymous here, based on the parallels with 1:10-11 Osborne (224n3) thinks that it is Christ who is speaking here, which would account for the masculine participle (according to sense). This has support in view of the identification of the voice here as the voice that John first heard speaking to him, which is identified as Christ's voice in 1:15-16. Some manuscripts have corrected the participle to read λέγουσα (ℵ¹ 𝔐ᴬ). It is also possible that the nominative masculine indicates that the participle functions as a finite verb. On this use of the participle, see 1:16 on ἔχων.

ἀνάβα. Aor act impv 2nd sg ἀναβαίνω.

ὧδε. Locative/Spatial. Refers to a location relative to the speaker.

δείξω. Fut act ind 1st sg δείκνυμι.

σοι. Dative indirect object of δείξω.

ἅ. Accusative subject of γενέσθαι. The relative pronoun introduces a headless relative clause. The entire clause functions as the direct object of δείξω.

δεῖ. Pres act ind 3rd sg δεῖ (impersonal).

γενέσθαι. Aor mid inf γίνομαι (complementary). It is also possible that γενέσθαι is the subject of δεῖ: "To come about is necessary" (Wallace, 600–1), though seeing γενέσθαι as complementary to δεῖ is probably preferred.

μετὰ ταῦτα. Temporal. The precise antecedent of ταῦτα is difficult to determine. It is possible that it is simply an expression indicating the future referring nature of much of the book. See on 1:19.

4:2 Εὐθέως ἐγενόμην ἐν πνεύματι, καὶ ἰδοὺ θρόνος ἔκειτο ἐν τῷ οὐρανῷ, καὶ ἐπὶ τὸν θρόνον καθήμενος,

Εὐθέως. Temporal. Indicates "a point in time immediately subsequent to a previous point of time" (LN 67.53). Only occurs here in Revelation.

ἐγενόμην. Aor mid ind 1st sg γίνομαι.

ἐν πνεύματι. Locative, in a metaphorical sense. See 1:10.

ἰδού. A marker of attention that deictically functions to make the following statement emphatic. On the form, see 1:7. Here it draws attention to a central element of the vision, the throne and more importantly, the one seated on it.

θρόνος. Nominative subject of ἔκειτο. Throughout Revelation the nominative follows ἰδού (see 1:7 on ἰδού). θρόνος is anarthrous here because it is introduced for the first time in the narrative. It occurs subsequently in Rev 4–5 with the article, which functions anaphorically to point back to this first mention of the θρόνος. "Anaphoric usage of the article is its backward-looking use. The Greek article may occur with subsequent instances of a substantive to refer back to or 'resume' the substantive's initial use" (Porter, 1992, 106; see Levinsohn 2000, 150). Here it introduces a new theme. The term θρόνος occurs fourteen times in this chapter suggesting an important semantic chain.

ἔκειτο. Impf mid or pass ind 3rd sg κεῖμαι.

ἐν τῷ οὐρανῷ. Locative.

ἐπὶ τὸν θρόνον. Locative. In the construction "the one seated upon the throne" the preposition ἐπί is followed by "throne" in all three cases in Rev 4: accusative (v. 2; see also θρόνους in v. 4); dative (v. 9, following ℵ A 1854 2050); and genitive (v. 10). For ἐπί and the genitive elsewhere in Revelation, see 5:1, 7; 6:16; 7:15; for ἐπί and the dative, see 5:13; 7:10; 19:4; 21:5. It is difficult to discern a distinction of meaning in Revelation between these three cases used with ἐπί (Harris, 137).

καθήμενος. Pres mid ptc masc nom sg κάθημαι (substantival). Nominative subject of a verbless clause. Like θρόνος above, καθήμενος is anarthrous here the first time it is introduced. Subsequent references to καθήμενος will include the anaphoric article since they point back to this first mention.

4:3 καὶ ὁ καθήμενος ὅμοιος ὁράσει λίθῳ ἰάσπιδι καὶ σαρδίῳ, καὶ ἶρις κυκλόθεν τοῦ θρόνου ὅμοιος ὁράσει σμαραγδίνῳ.

ὁ καθήμενος. Pres mid ptc masc nom sg κάθημαι (substantival). Nominative subject of a verbless clause. The article is anaphoric pointing back to the first mention in verse 2.

ὅμοιος. Predicate adjective of a verbless clause.

ὁράσει. Dative of respect/reference.

λίθῳ ἰάσπιδι καὶ σαρδίῳ. Dative complement of ὅμοιος.

ἶρις. Nominative subject of a verbless clause. The reading ἱερεῖς found in ℵ* A 2329 is probably due to confusion in hearing since ἶρις and ἱερεῖς were pronounced the same way (Caragounis, 495–96).

κυκλόθεν τοῦ θρόνου. Locative. κυκλόθεν is an "improper" preposition (Moule, 85) that takes the genitive. The article before θρόνου and all subsequent mentions of θρόνος in Rev 4 are anaphoric, pointing back to its first mention in verse 2.

ὅμοιος. Predicate adjective of a verbless clause.

ὁράσει. Dative of respect/reference.

σμαραγδίνῳ. Dative complement of ὅμοιος.

4:4 Καὶ κυκλόθεν τοῦ θρόνου θρόνους εἴκοσι τέσσαρες, καὶ ἐπὶ τοὺς θρόνους εἴκοσι τέσσαρας πρεσβυτέρους καθημένους περιβεβλημένους ἐν ἱματίοις λευκοῖς καὶ ἐπὶ τὰς κεφαλὰς αὐτῶν στεφάνους χρυσοῦς.

κυκλόθεν τοῦ θρόνου. Locative. See also verse 3. The article before θρόνου is anaphoric.

θρόνους εἴκοσι τέσσαρες. The accusative seems to be functioning as the direct object of an implied εἶδον (see 4:1), though the author has used a string of nominative forms up until now to specify the features of John's vision in this chapter following ἰδού. θρόνους εἴκοσι τέσσαρες begins a series of accusatives (εἴκοσι τέσσαρας πρεσβυτέρους, καθημένους, περιβεβλημένους, στεφάνους χρυσοῦς) in verse 4 that all probably function as the direct object of an implied εἶδον. The shift in case marks a shift away from the throne to a new topic: the thrones of the twenty-four elders. θρόνους is anarthrous because it is introducing for the first time the twenty-four separate thrones (different from the θρόνος already mentioned in vv. 2-3) upon which the elders sit.

ἐπὶ τοὺς θρόνους. Locative.

εἴκοσι τέσσαρας πρεσβυτέρους. Accusative direct object of an implied εἶδον (see 4:1).

καθημένους. Pres mid ptc masc acc pl κάθημαι. The participle may function attributively. However, if εἶδον is implied, καθημένους may function as the complement in an object-complement double accusative construction with εἴκοσι τέσσαρας πρεσβυτέρους.

περιβεβλημένους. Prf mid ptc masc acc pl περιβάλλω (attributive).

ἐν ἱματίοις λευκοῖς. Manner.

ἐπὶ τὰς κεφαλὰς. Locative.

αὐτῶν. Possessive genitive.

στεφάνους χρυσοῦς. Accusative direct object of an implied εἶδον (see 4:1).

4:5 Καὶ ἐκ τοῦ θρόνου ἐκπορεύονται ἀστραπαὶ καὶ φωναὶ καὶ βρονταί, καὶ ἑπτὰ λαμπάδες πυρὸς καιόμεναι ἐνώπιον τοῦ θρόνου, ἅ εἰσιν τὰ ἑπτὰ πνεύματα τοῦ θεοῦ,

ἐκ τοῦ θρόνου. Source.

ἐκπορεύονται. Pres mid ind 3rd pl ἐκπορεύομαι. This is the first clear example in Revelation of the so-called "historical" or narrative present. Scholars have long recognized the usage of the Greek present tense in past-time contexts in narrative. This creates a difficulty for a strictly time-based (present time) approach to the Greek tenses. Therefore, several different explanations have been provided for this use of the present tense (for a survey of the various theories, see Porter 1992, 30–31; Campbell 2007, 57–65). The most likely explanation is that the author uses the present tense in order to view an action as unfolding, or in progress (see "Verbal Aspect" in the Introduction; Campbell 2007, 35–76). The present tense in narrative marks as prominent or foregrounds something in the discourse, often an event or events that follow the "historical" present. The two most likely reasons for its discourse-prominence function are (1) the present is the more heavily marked tense form over against the aorist (Porter 1992, 31); and (2) the present tense is used unexpectedly from its normal occurrence in present time contexts; there is a mismatch between the tense and the context (Runge, 125–43). The present tense, which looks at an action as unfolding or in progress, could be seen as slowing down the narrative (Campbell 2007, 54) in order to focus attention on an upcoming element. Here ἐκπορεύονται functions to foreground or refocus attention on the throne after describing the twenty-four thrones belonging to the elders, by describing the phenomena that come from the throne. "The eye of the Seer returns to the central Throne" (Swete, 69).

 ἀστραπαὶ καὶ φωναὶ καὶ βρονταί. Nominative subject of ἐκπορεύονται.

 ἑπτὰ λαμπάδες. Nominative subject of a verbless clause.

 πυρὸς. Attributive genitive.

 καιόμεναι. Pres mid ptc fem nom pl καίω (attributive).

 ἐνώπιον τοῦ θρόνου. Locative.

 ἅ. Nominative subject of εἰσιν. The antecedent of ἅ is ἑπτὰ λαμπάδες. We would expect the relative pronoun to be feminine (αἵ), as we find in some manuscripts (1006 1841 𝔐ᴷ), rather than neuter, since it modifies λαμπάδες. It appears that the gender of the relative pronoun has been attracted to τὰ ἑπτὰ πνεύματα to which it is linked by the copulative εἰσιν.

 εἰσιν. Pres act ind 3rd pl εἰμί. On the loss of accent, see 1:8. Sometimes the neuter plural subject, which usually takes a singular verb, takes a plural verb as it does here. This is sometimes true of πνεύματα when used of personal beings (Turner, 313).

 τὰ ἑπτὰ πνεύματα. Predicate nominative.

 τοῦ θεοῦ. Possessive genitive or genitive of source.

4:6 καὶ ἐνώπιον τοῦ θρόνου ὡς θάλασσα ὑαλίνη ὁμοία κρυστάλλῳ. Καὶ ἐν μέσῳ τοῦ θρόνου καὶ κύκλῳ τοῦ θρόνου τέσσαρα ζῷα γέμοντα ὀφθαλμῶν ἔμπροσθεν καὶ ὄπισθεν·

 ἐνώπιον τοῦ θρόνου. Locative.

 ὡς θάλασσα ὑαλίνη. Comparison. This clause functions as the subject of a verbless clause.

ὁμοία. Comparison.
κρυστάλλῳ. Dative complement of ὅμοιος.
ἐν μέσῳ τοῦ θρόνου. Locative.
κύκλῳ τοῦ θρόνου. Locative. Dative of κύκλος fixed as an adverb "pert. to encirclement, *around*" (BDAG, 574.1) and used here as a preposition (Moule, 85). The occurrence of this expression following ἐν μέσῳ τοῦ θρόνου ("in the midst of the throne") creates a conceptual difficulty, since it is hard to see how the four living creatures can be both around the throne and in the midst of the throne (Aune, 1.271–72). BDAG understands ἐν μέσῳ as around the throne, "but *between* the throne and a more remote point" (635.1.b). It may be better to take ἐν μέσῳ with the notion of being in the immediate vicinity (Mounce, 137), or right next to the throne, surrounding it. The two expressions together would portray the four living creatures as in close proximity to the throne and all around it. Harris takes ἐν μέσῳ with κύκλῳ as indicating "'in close proximity to the throne' or 'around (*on every side of*) the throne'" (46).
τέσσαρα ζῷα. Nominative subject of a verbless clause.
γέμοντα. Pres act ptc neut nom pl γέμω (attributive).
ὀφθαλμῶν. Genitive complement of γέμω ("to be full of something," BDAG, 191.a).
ἔμπροσθεν καὶ ὄπισθεν. Locative. Lit. "in front and behind."

4:7 καὶ τὸ ζῷον τὸ πρῶτον ὅμοιον λέοντι καὶ τὸ δεύτερον ζῷον ὅμοιον μόσχῳ καὶ τὸ τρίτον ζῷον ἔχων τὸ πρόσωπον ὡς ἀνθρώπου καὶ τὸ τέταρτον ζῷον ὅμοιον ἀετῷ πετομένῳ.

τὸ ζῷον τὸ πρῶτον. Nominative subject of a verbless clause.
ὅμοιον. Predicate adjective of a verbless clause.
λέοντι. Dative complement of ὅμοιος.
τὸ δεύτερον ζῷον. Nominative subject of a verbless clause.
ὅμοιον. Predicate adjective of a verbless clause.
μόσχῳ. Dative complement of ὅμοιον.
τὸ τρίτον ζῷον. Nominative subject of a verbless clause.
ἔχων. Pres act ptc masc nom sg ἔχω. This may be another example of the participle functioning as a finite verb (see 1:16 on ἔχων). The masculine gender does not match the neuter gender of ζῷον. This could be the result of confusion in sound between ο and ω (Robertson, 412; Aune, 1.272), with ℵ 𝔐 reading the neuter ἔχον. However, it may be more likely that this is a scribal attempt to conform the participles to the neuter ζῷον. The masculine ἔχων is probably a construction according to sense, where the neuter ζῷον represents a living being (Osborne, 235 n.27).
τὸ πρόσωπον. Accusative direct object of ἔχων.

ὡς ἀνθρώπου. Comparison.
ἀνθρώπου. Possessive genitive ("as belonging to a man").
τὸ τέταρτον ζῷον. Nominative subject of a verbless clause.
ὅμοιον. Predicate adjective of a verbless clause.
ἀετῷ. Dative complement of ὅμοιος.
πετομένῳ. Pres mid ptc masc dat sg πέτομαι (attributive).

4:8 καὶ τὰ τέσσαρα ζῷα, ἓν καθ' ἓν αὐτῶν ἔχων ἀνὰ πτέρυγας ἕξ, κυκλόθεν καὶ ἔσωθεν γέμουσιν ὀφθαλμῶν, καὶ ἀνάπαυσιν οὐκ ἔχουσιν ἡμέρας καὶ νυκτὸς λέγοντες· ἅγιος ἅγιος ἅγιος κύριος ὁ θεὸς ὁ παντοκράτωρ, ὁ ἦν καὶ ὁ ὢν καὶ ὁ ἐρχόμενος.

τὰ τέσσαρα ζῷα. Nominative subject of γέμουσιν.
ἓν καθ' ἕν. This construction conveys a distributive sense: "each one" (BDAG, 293.5.e).
αὐτῶν. Partitive genitive.
ἔχων. Pres act ptc masc nom sg ἔχω. The participle could be understood attributively (modifying ἕν), or function as a finite verb in a sort of parenthetical statement (see 1:16 on ἔχων). The masculine gender of ἔχων does not match the neuter gender of ζῷα and ἕν. This is probably due to the fact that τὰ τέσσαρα ζῷα refers to living beings, or possibly to signal that the participle functions as a finite verb (see 4:7 on ἔχων).
ἀνὰ ... ἕξ. With numbers ἀνά has a distributive sense, "each" or "apiece" (BDAG, 58.3): "Six wings apiece."
πτέρυγας. Accusative direct object of ἔχων.
κυκλόθεν καὶ ἔσωθεν. Locative: "All around and within" (BDAG, 398.2).
γέμουσιν. Pres act ind 3rd pl γέμω.
ὀφθαλμῶν. See verse 4 on ὀφθαλμῶν.
ἀνάπαυσιν. Accusative direct object of ἔχουσιν. Nida explains that "'to cease' is not an event in and of itself but merely an aspect of some other event" (100). That is, ἀνάπαυσιν combines with ἔχουσιν "to form an aspect of the participle λέγοντες" (100). The entire clause ἀνάπαυσιν οὐκ ἔχουσιν ἡμέρας καὶ νυκτὸς λέγοντες could be translated "and they did not cease speaking day and night."
ἔχουσιν. Pres act ind 3rd pl ἔχω.
ἡμέρας καὶ νυκτὸς. Genitive of time. This construction in the genitive case occurs four other times in Revelation: 7:15; 12:10; 14:11; 20:10. Though the genitive of time is often considered to indicate "kind of time," this construction with these words ("day" and "night") may be idiomatic, and so the notion of "kind of time" should not be pressed.
λέγοντες. Pres act ptc masc nom pl λέγω (manner). On the usage of λέγοντες to introduce speech, see 1:17 on λέγων.

ἅγιος ἅγιος ἅγιος. Predicate adjective of a verbless clause.
κύριος. Nominative subject of a verbless clause.
ὁ θεὸς. Nominative in apposition to κύριος.
ὁ παντοκράτωρ. Nominative in apposition to κύριος.
ὁ ἦν καὶ ὁ ὢν καὶ ὁ ἐρχόμενος. The entire phrase is in apposition to κύριος. On this phrase and the form and function of its constituents, see 1:4.

4:9 Καὶ ὅταν δώσουσιν τὰ ζῷα δόξαν καὶ τιμὴν καὶ εὐχαριστίαν τῷ καθημένῳ ἐπὶ τῷ θρόνῳ τῷ ζῶντι εἰς τοὺς αἰῶνας τῶν αἰώνων,

ὅταν. Introduces an indefinite temporal clause. There is some debate as to whether ὅταν with the future indicates a particular future event (Aune, 1.273, 307) or is a more general reference to a repeated event. The clause introduced by ὅταν modifies the falling down (πεσοῦνται) and worshiping (προσκυνήσουσιν) of the twenty-four elders in verse 10. The entire construction in verses 9-10 functions similarly to a conditional construction: the falling down of the elders (v. 10) is conditioned upon the worship of the four living creatures expressed in the ὅταν clause (v. 9). When in Revelation do these two events take place? Smalley (123) sees verses 9-10 fulfilled in the eschaton, but incorrectly draws this conclusion based simply on the future tense forms. Thompson (45–47) takes verses 9-10 to be past referring, perhaps to verse 8. He bases this on his assumption that the future has been influenced by the imperfect of the Hebrew verbal system, and the assumption that verses 9-10 must refer to something within Rev 4 (Mathewson 2010, 113). Aune (1.307), Mussies (345), and Beale (334, who also thinks 5:8-12 should be included) find the fulfillment of the ὅταν clause in 5:13-14, since when all creation gives glory to God in 5:13-14 the elders bow down. It is also possible that ὅταν + future in 4:9 and the futures in 4:10 should not be restricted to 5:13-14, but should include other instances in Revelation where the elders fall down along with the four living creatures and worship in response to God's manifestation of his salvation and judgment (7:11; 19:4; cf. 11:16, though there is no mention of the four living creatures; Charles, 1.127). Most likely, we should understand ὅταν as referring to a specific event, since in almost all of its other occurrences in Revelation it refers to something specific in the context (8:1, 10:7, 11:7, 12:4, 17:10, 18:9, 20:7). Aune, Mussies, and Beale are probably correct in identifying the referent as 5:13-14 in the following chapter.

δώσουσιν. Fut act ind 3rd pl δίδωμι. Future with ὅταν. On the future in place of the subjunctive, see 3:9 on ἥξουσιν.

τὰ ζῷα. Nominative subject of δώσουσιν.
δόξαν καὶ τιμὴν καὶ εὐχαριστίαν. Accusative direct object of δώσουσιν.
τῷ καθημένῳ. Pres mid ptc masc dat sg κάθημαι (substantival). Dative indirect object of δώσουσιν.
ἐπὶ τῷ θρόνῳ. Locative.
τῷ ζῶντι. Pres act ptc masc dat sg ζάω (attributive).
εἰς τοὺς αἰῶνας τῶν αἰώνων. Temporal (see 1:18).

4:10 πεσοῦνται οἱ εἴκοσι τέσσαρες πρεσβύτεροι ἐνώπιον τοῦ καθημένου ἐπὶ τοῦ θρόνου καὶ προσκυνήσουσιν τῷ ζῶντι εἰς τοὺς αἰῶνας τῶν αἰώνων καὶ βαλοῦσιν τοὺς στεφάνους αὐτῶν ἐνώπιον τοῦ θρόνου λέγοντες·

πεσοῦνται. Fut mid ind 3rd pl πίπτω. See verse 9 on ὅταν.
οἱ εἴκοσι τέσσαρες πρεσβύτεροι. Nominative subject of πεσοῦνται.
ἐνώπιον τοῦ καθημένου. Locative.
τοῦ καθημένου. Pres mid ptc masc gen sg κάθημαι (substantival).
ἐπὶ τοῦ θρόνου. Locative.
προσκυνήσουσιν. Fut act ind 3rd pl προσκυνέω. See verse 9 on ὅταν.
τῷ ζῶντι. Pres act ptc masc dat sg ζάω (substantival). Dative direct object of προσκυνήσουσιν. The verb προσκυνέω, when it takes an object, occurs throughout Revelation with its object in either the dative (4:10; 7:11; 11:16; 13:14 [2×], 15; 14:17; 16:2; 19:4, 10, 20; 22:9) or the accusative case (9:20; 13:8, 12; 14:9, 11; 20:4). Wallace (172–73) suggests a possible explanation: the dative is used for worship of the true Deity, and the accusative used for worship of false deities. This pattern, however, does not fit all instances. A better explanation may be that neuter objects (e.g., θηρίον) occur in the accusative case, whereas masculine (θεός or references to God, δράκων) or feminine (εἰκών) objects occur in the dative case—though the neuter noun θηρίον is found in the dative in 13:4 according to NA[28]/UBS[5] (but see 13:4 for a discussion of the textual problem).
εἰς τοὺς αἰῶνας τῶν αἰώνων. Temporal (see 1:18).
βαλοῦσιν. Fut act ind 3rd pl βάλλω.
τοὺς στεφάνους. Accusative direct object of βαλοῦσιν.
αὐτῶν. Possessive genitive.
ἐνώπιον τοῦ θρόνου. Locative.
λέγοντες. Pres act ptc masc nom pl λέγω (manner). On the usage of λέγοντες to introduce speech, see 1:17 on λέγων.

4:11 ἄξιος εἶ, ὁ κύριος καὶ ὁ θεὸς ἡμῶν, λαβεῖν τὴν δόξαν καὶ τὴν τιμὴν καὶ τὴν δύναμιν, ὅτι σὺ ἔκτισας τὰ πάντα καὶ διὰ τὸ θέλημά σου ἦσαν καὶ ἐκτίσθησαν.

ἄξιος. Predicate adjective.
εἶ. Pres act ind 2nd sg εἰμί.
ὁ κύριος καὶ ὁ θεὸς. Nominative used as a vocative of address.
ἡμῶν. Genitive of subordination.
λαβεῖν. Aor act inf λαμβάνω (epexegetical to ἄξιος; see Wallace, 607).
τὴν δόξαν καὶ τὴν τιμὴν καὶ τὴν δύναμιν. Accusative direct object of λαβεῖν.
ὅτι. Introduces a causal clause.
σὺ. Nominative subject of ἔκτισας. The inclusion of σύ is emphatic.
ἔκτισας. Aor act ind 2nd sg κτίζω. Aune thinks that the aorist is used here with the semantic value of a perfect tense form (1.clxxxvii). However, this probably confuses translation with the semantics of the tense form (see 3:9 on ἠγάπησά).
τὰ πάντα. Accusative direct object of ἔκτισας.
διὰ τὸ θέλημά. Cause. The accenting of θέλημά is due to the enclitic σου that follows.
σου. Subjective genitive.
ἦσαν. Impf act ind 3rd pl εἰμί. The idea is that all things "existed" (Aune, 1.312).
ἐκτίσθησαν. Aor pass ind 3rd pl κτίζω. It is strange that the existence of all things (ἦσαν) precedes their coming into existence (ἐκτίσθησαν). This is probably another example of hysteron-proteron (see 3:3 on εἴληφας).

Revelation 5:1-7

¹And I saw a scroll in the right hand of the one sitting on the throne; it was written on the inside and on the back, sealed with seven seals. ²And I saw a mighty angel proclaiming with a loud voice, "Who is worthy to open the scroll and to break its seals?" ³But no one in heaven or upon the earth or under the earth was able to open the scroll or to look at its contents. ⁴And I wept greatly, because no one was found worthy to open the scroll or to look at its contents. ⁵And one of the elders said to me, "Stop weeping. Look, the lion from the tribe of Judah, the root of David, has conquered so that he can open the scroll and its seven seals." ⁶And I saw among the throne and the four living creatures, and among the elders, a lamb standing as slain and having seven horns and seven eyes, which are the seven spirits of God sent out into all the earth. ⁷And he went and took (the scroll) from the right hand of the one sitting on the throne.

5:1 Καί εἶδον ἐπὶ τὴν δεξιὰν τοῦ καθημένου ἐπὶ τοῦ θρόνου βιβλίον γεγραμμένον ἔσωθεν καὶ ὄπισθεν κατεσφραγισμένον σφραγῖσιν ἑπτά.

The piling up of modifiers in this verse (prepositional phrases, participle clauses) around the head term βιβλίον functions to make it prominent and a significant feature of the visionary narrative.

Καί εἶδον. This phrase reflects John's style of introducing and punctuating his visions as he moves from visionary segment to segment. According to Aune (1.338), καί εἶδον can (1) introduce a new visionary narrative, (2) introduce a major scene within a continuing vision narrative, or (3) function to focus on a new or important figure or activity within a vision. Καί εἶδον functions to focus on new actors or actions within the vision in 5:2 (the angel who announces the dilemma, and John's response), 5:6 (the appearance of the slain Lamb), and 5:11 (the universal worship of the Lamb).

εἶδον. Aor act ind 1st sg ὁράω.

ἐπὶ τὴν δεξιὰν. Locative. Modifies βιβλίον.

τοῦ καθημένου. Pres mid ptc masc gen sg κάθημαι (substantival). Possessive genitive.

ἐπὶ τοῦ θρόνου. Locative.

βιβλίον. Accusative direct object of εἶδον. βιβλίον lacks the article since it is the first time it is introduced. Subsequent mentions of βιβλίον in this scene have an article, anaphorically pointing back to this first mention of the scroll (see vv. 2, 3, 4, 5, 8, 9).

γεγραμμένον. Prf pass ptc neut acc sg γράφω. Complement in an object-complement double accusative construction.

ἔσωθεν καὶ ὄπισθεν. Locative: "Inside and on the back" (BDAG, 715.2). This designation has led most scholars to see the scroll as an opistograph, a document written on both sides reflecting Ezek 2:9-10 (Aune, 1.322; Smalley, 128; Beale, 337).

κατεσφραγισμένον. Prf pass ptc neut acc sg κατασφραγίζω (attributive).

σφραγῖσιν ἑπτά. Dative of instrument (Wallace, 168, labels this a "Cognate Dative"; grammatically, it still functions to indicate instrument). The first mention of σφραγῖσιν is anarthrous, while subsequent references to the seals contain the anaphoric article, which points the reader back to this first mention of the seals (see vv. 2, 5, 9; see also on βιβλίον above).

5:2 καὶ εἶδον ἄγγελον ἰσχυρὸν κηρύσσοντα ἐν φωνῇ μεγάλῃ· τίς ἄξιος ἀνοῖξαι τὸ βιβλίον καὶ λῦσαι τὰς σφραγῖδας αὐτοῦ;

καὶ εἶδον. Functions to introduce a new scene with new actors and actions within the vision (vv. 2-5): the angel who announces the dilemma, the response of John to the dilemma, and the counter-response of the elder.

εἶδον. Aor act ind 1st sg ὁράω.

ἄγγελον ἰσχυρὸν. Accusative direct object of εἶδον.

κηρύσσοντα. Pres act ptc masc acc pl κηρύσσω. Complement in an object-complement double accusative construction.

ἐν φωνῇ μεγάλῃ. Instrumental.

τίς. Nominative subject of a verbless clause. Introduces a direct question that will be answered in the rest of the chapter.

ἄξιος. Predicate adjective of a verbless clause.

ἀνοῖξαι. Aor act inf ἀνοίγω (epexegetical to ἄξιος).

τὸ βιβλίον. Accusative direct object of ἀνοῖξαι.

λῦσαι. Aor act inf λύω (epexegetical to ἄξιος). Logically, the loosing of the seals would precede the opening of the scroll. This inversion is an example of hysteron-proteron (see 3:3 on εἴληφας). This is most likely the author's way of foregrounding the more important element of the pair: opening the scroll (Resseguie, 51; Swete, 76).

τὰς σφραγῖδας. Accusative direct object of λῦσαι.

αὐτοῦ. Possessive genitive or objective genitive.

5:3 καὶ οὐδεὶς ἐδύνατο ἐν τῷ οὐρανῷ οὐδὲ ἐπὶ τῆς γῆς οὐδὲ ὑποκάτω τῆς γῆς ἀνοῖξαι τὸ βιβλίον οὔτε βλέπειν αὐτό.

οὐδεὶς. Nominative subject of ἐδύνατο. The subject shifts the topic from the angel in verse 2 to no one being found who is worthy to open the book.

ἐδύνατο. Impf mid ind 3rd sg δύναμαι. In narrative, the main action of the storyline is carried along by aorist indicative verbs in the primary (independent) clauses, while offline information is often communicated by the imperfect tense form. Here offline information is indicated by the more remote imperfect ἐδύνατο: the inability of any one (οὐδείς) to open the scroll.

ἐν τῷ οὐρανῷ οὐδὲ ἐπὶ τῆς γῆς οὐδὲ ὑποκάτω τῆς γῆς. Locative. Together these three PPs are all-encompassing and are a way of saying "nowhere in the entire universe" (Aune, 1.348).

ἀνοῖξαι. Aor act inf ἀνοίγω (complementary to ἐδύνατο).

τὸ βιβλίον. Accusative direct object of ἀνοῖξαι.

βλέπειν. Pres act inf βλέπω (complementary to ἐδύνατο). Osborne (252 n. 5) explains the contrast between the aorist ἀνοῖξαι and the present βλέπειν as that between a single opening and a careful perusal. However, this relies too much on a common misunderstanding of the aorist (punctiliar action) and the present (continuous, durative action) that confuses aspect and *Aktionsart* (kind of action), or the meaning of the tense forms themselves and how the action occurred as determined by context (see "Verbal Aspect" in the Introduction). Here, the opposition between the aorist and present is best understood in terms of the author's depiction of the processes (aspect). The aorist ἀνοῖξαι functions as the backdrop to the act of looking into the scroll described with the present infinitive (βλέπειν).

αὐτό. Accusative direct object of βλέπειν. I have translated βλέπειν αὐτό "to look at its contents," since the idea is not just looking at the physical scroll, but rather at what it contains.

5:4 καὶ ἔκλαιον πολύ, ὅτι οὐδεὶς ἄξιος εὑρέθη ἀνοῖξαι τὸ βιβλίον οὔτε βλέπειν αὐτό.

ἔκλαιον. Impf act ind 1st sg κλαίω. The imperfect tense here has been interpreted in various ways. Some have interpreted it inceptively ("I began weeping"). Relying on conceptions of the imperfect as indicating durative or continuous action, Smalley (130) thinks that the imperfect implies that John has already been weeping for some time. Both conceptions are inappropriate. Apart from clear contextual features, it is illegitimate to think that the imperfect emphasizes an inceptive notion. And the imperfect itself says nothing about the duration of the action (contra Smalley, 130; Swete, 77). It simply looks at the action as developing or unfolding (see "Verbal Aspect" in the Introduction). Here the more remote imperfect form is used of the author's weeping. The more significant (foregrounded) act of speaking will come in the next clause, where one of the elders introduces the solution to John's dilemma with a more heavily marked present form (λέγει).

πολύ. Manner.

ὅτι. Introduces a causal clause.

οὐδεὶς. Nominative subject of εὑρέθη.

ἄξιος. Along with οὐδείς this is part of a double nominative construction with a passive verb from a double accusative construction: "(I) find no one worthy" (see Culy 2009, 83–87; see also 1:9 on Πάτμῳ).

εὑρέθη. Aor pass ind 3rd sg εὑρίσκω. The use of the passive allows the emphasis to be placed on the subject οὐδείς in this clause. There is no agent expressed, so it is left unclear who did the "searching." It could

be John, God, the angel, or it could be intentionally unspecified so that the idea is simply, "There was no one found worthy."
    ἀνοῖξαι. Aor act inf ἀνοίγω (epexegetical to ἄξιος).
    τὸ βιβλίον. Accusative direct object of ἀνοῖξαι.
    βλέπειν. Pres act inf βλέπω (epexegetical to ἄξιος).
    αὐτό. Accusative direct object of βλέπειν.

5:5 καὶ εἷς ἐκ τῶν πρεσβυτέρων λέγει μοι· μὴ κλαῖε, ἰδοὺ ἐνίκησεν ὁ λέων ὁ ἐκ τῆς φυλῆς Ἰούδα, ἡ ῥίζα Δαυίδ, ἀνοῖξαι τὸ βιβλίον καὶ τὰς ἑπτὰ σφραγῖδας αὐτοῦ.

    εἷς. Nominative subject of λέγει. Though it is possible that εἷς is being used with the sense of an indefinite pronoun τις (Smalley, 195), it is more likely that here it still retains its function as an ordinal, "one," since it is followed by the partitive construction (ἐκ τῶν πρεσβυτέρων) referring to a group that has already been numbered (4:4).
    ἐκ τῶν πρεσβυτέρων. Partitive.
    λέγει. Pres act ind 3rd sg λέγω. Historical or narrative present (see 4:5 on ἐκπορεύονται). The present tense introducing the speech of the elder draws attention to what the elder said, the solution to the dilemma from verses 3-4, and contrasts with the remote imperfect tense form, which records the seers weeping in verse 4 (ἔκλαιον).
    μοι. Dative indirect object of λέγει.
    μὴ κλαῖε. Pres act impv 2nd sg κλαίω (prohibition). On the present prohibition, see 1:17. While the present prohibition does not by itself indicate the cessation of an action already in progress ("stop weeping"), since the *context* here (v. 4) indicates that John is already weeping (using the same verb: ἔκλαιον), it is appropriate to *translate* it "stop weeping."
    ἰδοὺ. A marker of attention that deictically functions to make the following statement emphatic. Here it draws attention to the announcement of the solution to the dilemma of verses 3-4. On the form, see 1:7.
    ἐνίκησεν. Aor act ind 3rd sg νικάω. Osborne (253) may be correct that this refers to Jesus' sacrificial death, but errs in basing this on a misunderstanding of the aorist as punctiliar.
    ὁ λέων. Nominative subject of ἐνίκησεν.
    ὁ ἐκ τῆς φυλῆς Ἰούδα. The article functions as an adjectivizer, turning the PP (source) into an attributive modifier of λέων: Lit. "the out-of-the-tribe-of-Judah lion." Although such constructions are usually translated using a relative clause in English ("the lion *which is* from the tribe of Judah") this does not mean that the article functions as a relative pronoun.
    Ἰούδα. Epexegetical genitive.
    ἡ ῥίζα. Nominative in apposition to λέων.

Δαυίδ. Genitive of source: "The root from David," in line with its OT background (Isa 11:1, 10). Smalley interprets it as "a branch from David's root" (130). The piling up of phrases with reference to Christ is an example of "overspecification," that is, providing more information than necessary. Here it shifts the focus to Christ and also draws attention to the OT background of the titles.

ἀνοῖξαι. Aor act inf ἀνοίγω (result). Alternatively, there could be an ellipsis here. It could be that an infinitive of δύναμαι is implied and ἀνοῖξαι is complementary: "He conquered so that he is able to open the scroll." This finds support in verse 3 above. Or it is possible that ἀνοῖξαι here should be seen as epexegetical to an implied ἄξιος as it is in verse 4 above: "He conquered so that he is worthy to open the scroll."

τὸ βιβλίον καὶ τὰς ἑπτὰ σφραγῖδας. Accusative direct object of ἀνοῖξαι.

αὐτοῦ. Possessive genitive or objective genitive.

5:6 Καὶ εἶδον ἐν μέσῳ τοῦ θρόνου καὶ τῶν τεσσάρων ζῴων καὶ ἐν μέσῳ τῶν πρεσβυτέρων ἀρνίον ἑστηκὸς ὡς ἐσφαγμένον ἔχων κέρατα ἑπτὰ καὶ ὀφθαλμοὺς ἑπτὰ οἵ εἰσιν τὰ [ἑπτὰ] πνεύματα τοῦ θεοῦ ἀπεσταλμένοι εἰς πᾶσαν τὴν γῆν.

The significant expansion of the ἀρνίον in this verse by means of participial clauses and prepositional phrases functions to draw attention to this feature in the vision, making the Lamb highly prominent.

Καί εἶδον. Introduces a new scene in the visionary narrative.

εἶδον. Aor act ind 1st sg ὁράω.

ἐν μέσῳ τοῦ θρόνου καὶ τῶν τεσσάρων ζῴων καὶ ἐν μέσῳ τῶν πρεσβυτέρων. Locative/Spatial. The resultant spatial picture is somewhat difficult to visualize (if we are even meant to picture it!). It could suggest that the Lamb is on the throne, which sits in the middle of the living creatures and the elders. But this seems unlikely since the Lamb does not approach the throne until verse 7. The construction could suggest that the Lamb stands between the throne and the creatures, and the elders. However, μέσος can also mean "a position within an area determined by other objects and distributed among such objects" (LN 83.9). In this case it should be translated "among" (BDAG, 635.2.b). The Lamb is standing among the objects mentioned: the throne, living creatures, and elders (Aune, 1.352; Beale, 350; Osborne, 255).

ἀρνίον. Accusative direct object of εἶδον. ἀρνίον is a diminutive form of ἀρήν (lit. "a small lamb"). However, it has lost its diminutive value and the diminutive force should not be pressed here (Mussies, 108; BDAG, 133). Although the reference to having "horns" may suggest that the term should be translated "ram" (Aune, 1.323), the OT sacrificial background suggests the translation "lamb" (Smalley, 131–32). John uses ἀρνίον twenty-eight times in the book with reference to Christ. ἀρνίον is anarthrous since it is introduced here for the first time. Subsequent references have the anaphoric article (see vv. 12, 13; see also 4:1 on βιβλίον).

ἑστηκὸς. Prf act ptc neut acc sg ἵστημι. Complement in an object-complement double accusative construction. Along with the significant expansion in this verse, the cluster of three perfect participles (ἑστηκός, ἐσφαγμένον, ἀπεσταλμένοι) to introduce the Lamb functions to draw attention to the Lamb as the significant and focal point of the vision.

ὡς ἐσφαγμένον. Comparative indicating manner. Here ὡς indicates not that the Lamb only appeared to be slain but really was not, but that the lamb appeared to be slain, though he is in reality alive (Aune, 1.353; Smalley, 132).

ἐσφαγμένον. Prf pass ptc neut acc sg σφάζω (substantival). In comparative constructions such as this the participle is best taken as substantival: "As one who is slain."

ἔχων. Pres act ptc masc nom sg ἔχω. This participle constitutes one of John's grammatical anomalies. It is both masculine and nominative, though the noun it appears to modify, ἀρνίον, is neuter and accusative. It is possible that this is to be explained as a construction according to sense since the Lamb is Christ, though ἑστηκός and ἐσφαγμένον are both neuter, making this explanation less likely. The participle of ἔχω commonly occurs in the nominative masculine even when it does not agree in case and/or gender with the noun or verb it modifies (Robertson, 414). Here the masculine gender, following the two neuter participles, is probably intentional and is meant to draw attention to this startling feature of the slain Lamb: it has horns and eyes! See also 1:16 on ἔχων. Some manuscripts read ἔχον (𝔐). It is possible that this was an attempt by scribes to conform to the neuter ἀρνίον.

κέρατα ἑπτὰ καὶ ὀφθαλμοὺς ἑπτά. Accusative direct object of ἔχων.

οἵ. Nominative subject of εἰσιν. On the masculine with a neuter antecedent, see on ἀπεσταλμένοι below.

εἰσιν. Pres act ind 3rd pl εἰμί. On the loss of accent, see 1:8.

τὰ [ἑπτὰ] πνεύματα. Predicate nominative.

τοῦ θεοῦ. Possessive genitive or genitive of source (since the spirits are sent out, ἀπεσταλμένοι).

ἀπεσταλμένοι. Prf pass ptc masc nom pl ἀποστέλλω (attributive). The masculine participle modifies a neuter noun (πνεύματα). The masculine ἀπεσταλμένοι is probably a construction according to sense, where the neuter πνεύματα represents a living being (see 4:7 on ἔχων). On the significance of the perfect tense, see ἑστηκὸς above.

εἰς πᾶσαν τὴν γῆν. Spatial. Indicates movement toward (Porter 1992, 152).

5:7 καὶ ἦλθεν καὶ εἴληφεν ἐκ τῆς δεξιᾶς τοῦ καθημένου ἐπὶ τοῦ θρόνου.

ἦλθεν. Aor act ind 3rd sg ἔρχομαι. The storyline of the vision is resumed in 5:7 with the aorist ἦλθεν. Also, in contrast to the verbs in verses 4-5, where the processes were verbs of weeping and speaking, here the verbs are verbs of action, so that the Lamb is associated with processes depicting activities.

εἴληφεν. Prf act ind 3rd sg λαμβάνω. There has been much discussion regarding the use of the perfect tense εἴληφεν here in the midst of aorists. Scholars have long noted the mixing of aorist with perfect tense forms in places in Revelation (Mathewson 2010, 91). One suggestion is that this should be labeled a "dramatic perfect," which is used to make a past event vivid (Young, 128). However, this seems to depend on an understanding of the perfect tense as including present results, so that looking at a past event from the standpoint of present results makes it more vivid. More commonly, several commentators and grammarians have concluded that this is an aoristic use of the perfect, where in the context of other aorists the notion of state or existing results has been diminished or lost so that it functions as an aorist (Beale, 357; Fanning, 303; Mussies, 338; BDF §343; Caragounis, 110; Wallace, 579). This is often coupled with the observation that the perfect tense is losing its force by this time and is being confused with the aorist. This assessment of εἴληφεν is also based on an understanding of the perfect as including "present results" in its definition, which does not seem to be present in this context (Fanning, 301-3). Further, Zerwick (§289) posits that the lack of discernible reduplication would have led to εἴληφεν being regarded as an aorist. All of this, however, overlooks the fact that the author uses the aorist tense of λαμβάνω elsewhere in Revelation, including the very next indicative verb in verse 8 (ἔλαβεν; see the non-indicative aorist forms in vv. 9, 12), suggesting that the author's selection of εἴληφεν was intentional and that the perfect here should be given its full stative force, irrespective of how we translate it (Mathewson 2010, 128). "Failure to make a translational distinction does not minimize semantic value or contrast" (Porter 1989a, 265). Both of the above conceptions are further hampered by the need to reconcile a past event with an understanding of the perfect that includes present results. However, if the perfect tense semantically indicates a state of affairs (see "Verbal Aspect" in the Introduction), rather than "present results," there should be little difficulty in seeing perfect tense forms used in past time contexts, along with aorists. The force of the perfect in past time contexts is often difficult to render in English translation (see the awkward attempt of Swete, 79: "And I saw him go (aor.) and now he has taken"). Yet this does not mean that the perfect is semantically equivalent to an aorist. In breaking the pattern of aorists, the perfect tense functions to draw attention to this action as the highpoint of the vision, for it is here that the transition of the scroll from the hand of the one seated on the throne to the Lamb, the only one worthy to open the scroll, now takes place. The author marks this scene with the perfect tense form. For more on the force of the perfect in the NT, see McKay 1981.

ἐκ τῆς δεξιᾶς. Separation. βιβλίον appears to be the implied object of εἴληφεν and is made explicit in several witnesses (1006 1841 2050 *pc*).

τοῦ καθημένου. Pres mid ptc masc gen sg κάθημαι (substantival). Possessive genitive.

ἐπὶ τοῦ θρόνου. Locative.

Revelation 5:8-14

⁸And when he took the scroll, the four living creatures and the twenty four elders fell before the Lamb, each one having a harp and golden bowls full of incense, which are the prayers of the saints. ⁹And they sang a new song, saying, "You are worthy to take the scroll and to open its seals, for you were slain and by your blood you redeemed for God (those) from every tribe, tongue, people, and nation, ¹⁰and you have made them a kingdom and priests to our God, and they will reign upon the earth." ¹¹And I looked, and I heard the sound of many angels around the throne, and of the living creatures and of the elders, and their number was myriads of myriads, and thousands of thousands, ¹²saying with a loud voice, "Worthy is the Lamb who was slain to receive power and wealth and wisdom and strength and honor and glory and praise." ¹³And every created thing that is in heaven and upon the earth and under the earth and in the sea, and everything in them I heard saying, "To the one who is sitting upon the throne and to the Lamb is praise and honor and glory and strength for ever and ever." ¹⁴And the four living creatures said, "Amen." And the elders fell down and worshiped.

5:8 Καὶ ὅτε ἔλαβεν τὸ βιβλίον, τὰ τέσσαρα ζῷα καὶ οἱ εἴκοσι τέσσαρες πρεσβύτεροι ἔπεσαν ἐνώπιον τοῦ ἀρνίου ἔχοντες ἕκαστος κιθάραν καὶ φιάλας χρυσᾶς γεμούσας θυμιαμάτων, αἵ εἰσιν αἱ προσευχαὶ τῶν ἁγίων,

ὅτε. Introduces a temporal clause.

ἔλαβεν. Aor act ind 3rd sg λαμβάνω. The reverting from the perfect εἴληφεν back to the aorist in a subordinate clause has the effect here of drawing attention to the witnesses who "fall down" (ἔπεσαν) in the following primary clause (McKay 1994, 50).

τὸ βιβλίον. Accusative direct object of ἔλαβεν.

τὰ τέσσαρα ζῷα καὶ οἱ εἴκοσι τέσσαρες πρεσβύτεροι. Nominative subject of ἔπεσαν.

ἔπεσαν. Aor act ind 3rd sg πίπτω.

ἐνώπιον τοῦ ἀρνίου. Locative.

ἔχοντες. Pres act ptc masc nom pl ἔχω. It is possible that the participle functions adverbially indicating manner. However, it could also function attributively modifying ἕκαστος.

ἕκαστος. Nominative subject of ἔχοντες. The singular ἕκαστος is used with a plural participle ἔχοντες. This can be explained by the fact that ἕκαστος carries a distributive sense (BDAG, 298). See also Rev 20:13.

κιθάραν καὶ φιάλας χρυσᾶς. Accusative direct object of ἔχοντες.

γεμούσας. Pres act ptc fem acc pl γέμω (attributive).

θυμιαμάτων. Genitive complement of γεμούσας.

αἵ. Nominative subject of εἰσιν. αἵ does not match its antecedent (θυμιαμάτων) in gender (αἵ is feminine; θυμιαμάτων is neuter). The pronoun αἵ, as the subject of the relative clause, appears to get its gender from attraction to the predicate nominative προσευχαί, to which it is linked by εἰσιν.

εἰσιν. Pres act ind 3rd pl εἰμί. On the loss of accent, see 1:8.

αἱ προσευχαὶ. Predicate nominative.

τῶν ἁγίων. Subjective genitive.

5:9 καὶ ᾄδουσιν ᾠδὴν καινὴν λέγοντες· ἄξιος εἶ λαβεῖν τὸ βιβλίον καὶ ἀνοῖξαι τὰς σφραγῖδας αὐτοῦ, ὅτι ἐσφάγης καὶ ἠγόρασας τῷ θεῷ ἐν τῷ αἵματί σου ἐκ πάσης φυλῆς καὶ γλώσσης καὶ λαοῦ καὶ ἔθνους

ᾄδουσιν. Pres act ind 3rd pl ᾄδω. Historical or narrative present (see 4:5 on ἐκπορεύονται). Following the narrative aorist (ἔπεσαν, v. 8) the present tense draws attention to the following song that is sung.

ᾠδὴν καινὴν. Accusative direct object of ᾄδουσιν. This type of accusative is often labeled a "cognate accusative" due to the fact that the noun and verb come from the same root. However, grammatically it simply functions as a direct object.

λέγοντες. Pres act ptc masc nom pl λέγω (manner). On the use of λέγοντες to introduce speech, see 1:17 on λέγων. This participle of "saying" has suggested to some that ᾄδουσιν should be translated "chanted," rather than "sung" (Aune, 1.325; Smalley, 136). However, the present participle of λέγω is typically used simply to introduce speech.

ἄξιος. Predicate nominative.
εἶ. Pres act ind 2nd sg εἰμί.
λαβεῖν. Aor act inf λαμβάνω (epexegetical to ἄξιος).
τὸ βιβλίον. Accusative direct object of λαβεῖν.
ἀνοῖξαι. Aor act inf ἀνοίγω (epexegetical to ἄξιος).
τὰς σφραγῖδας. Accusative direct object of ἀνοῖξαι.
αὐτοῦ. Possessive genitive or objective genitive.
ὅτι. Introduces a causal clause.
ἐσφάγης. Aor pass ind 2nd sg σφάζω.
ἠγόρασας. Aor act ind 2nd sg ἀγοράζω. It is possible that the aorists ἠγόρασας and ἐποίησας are timeless (Charles, 1.cxxv).
τῷ θεῷ. Dative of advantage. Several manuscripts add ἡμᾶς either before (2050 2344 *al*) or after (ℵ P 046 1006 1611 1841 2053 2329 2351 𝔐) or to replace (1 *pc*) τῷ θεῷ. According to Metzger (666), τῷ θεῷ (A) best accounts for the rise of these other readings, since scribes would have wanted to provide a more specific object after ἠγόρασας than ἐκ πάσης φυλῆς καὶ γλώσσης καὶ λαοῦ καὶ ἔθνους.
ἐν τῷ αἵματί. Instrumental. Moule (77) classifies this as a dative of price, which he says is an extension of the instrumental usage (see also Robertson, 589). This probably depends more on lexical factors ("purchased," "blood") than grammar. The accenting is due to the enclitic σου that follows. "Blood" is a metonymy for "death," substituting the means (shedding of blood) for the effect (death).
σου. Possessive genitive.
ἐκ πάσης φυλῆς καὶ γλώσσης καὶ λαοῦ καὶ ἔθνους. Partitive. The PP functions as the object of ἠγόρασας. This may be an elliptical expression: τίνας ἐκ πάσης φυλῆς καὶ γλώσσης καὶ λαοῦ καὶ ἔθνους. γλώσσης stands for "language" by metonymy. A form of this fourfold designation occurs seven times in Revelation (5:9; 7:9; 10:11; 11:9; 13:7; 14:6; 17:15).

5:10 καὶ ἐποίησας αὐτοὺς τῷ θεῷ ἡμῶν βασιλείαν καὶ ἱερεῖς, καὶ βασιλεύσουσιν ἐπὶ τῆς γῆς.

ἐποίησας. Aor act ind 2nd sg ποιέω.
αὐτοὺς. Accusative direct object of ἐποίησας.
τῷ θεῷ. Dative of advantage.
ἡμῶν. Genitive of subordination.
βασιλείαν καὶ ἱερεῖς. Complement in an object-complement double accusative construction.
βασιλεύσουσιν. Fut act ind 3rd pl βασιλεύω. The future tense reading is found in ℵ P 205 209 1854 2050 2053 2344 2351, while the present tense βασιλεύουσιν is found in A 1006 1611 1841 2329 𝔐. Beale (362–63) argues on the basis of the more "difficult reading" that the present

tense should be preferred. Primarily for contextual reasons, most commentators favor the future as the correct reading (Smalley, 109). This text likely anticipates the future rule of the saints in 20:6. Metzger (666–67) further argues that Codex A also reads the present tense instead of the future for the same verb in 20:6. However, even if the present tense form is accepted as the original reading, the present is often understood as futuristic (Osborne, 268), so that there is little difference in overall meaning.

ἐπὶ τῆς γῆς. Though this could be locative, more likely the preposition ἐπί with the genitive indicates that over which someone exercises authority following βασιλεύσουσιν (BDAG, 365.9.a). Cf. Luke 1:33 (with the accusative).

5:11 Καὶ εἶδον, καὶ ἤκουσα φωνὴν ἀγγέλων πολλῶν κύκλῳ τοῦ θρόνου καὶ τῶν ζῴων καὶ τῶν πρεσβυτέρων, καὶ ἦν ὁ ἀριθμὸς αὐτῶν μυριάδες μυριάδων καὶ χιλιάδες χιλιάδων

Καὶ εἶδον. Introduces a new segment within the larger vision (Charles, 1.148).
εἶδον. Aor act ind 1st sg ὁράω.
ἤκουσα. Aor act ind 1st sg ἀκούω.
φωνὴν. Accusative direct object of ἤκουσα.
ἀγγέλων πολλῶν ... καὶ τῶν ζῴων καὶ τῶν πρεσβυτέρων. Genitive of source or subjective genitive. The καί connects τῶν ζῴων and τῶν πρεσβυτέρων with ἀγγέλων, and not with κύκλῳ τοῦ θρόνου.
κύκλῳ τοῦ θρόνου. Locative.
ἦν. Impf act ind 3rd sg εἰμί.
ὁ ἀριθμὸς. Nominative subject of ἦν.
αὐτῶν. Objective genitive. The antecedent is ἀγγέλων πολλῶν rather than the living creatures and elders, the latter two groups already being numbered (4:4, 6, 10; 5:6, 8).
μυριάδες ... καὶ χιλιάδες. Predicate nominative.
μυριάδων ... χιλιάδων. The genitive function is difficult (and perhaps unnecessary) to specify. Robertson (502) does not appear to be correct in labeling it a partitive genitive, since the idea does not seem to be that only a part of the larger whole worships the Lamb. The entire phrase μυριάδες μυριάδων καὶ χιλιάδες χιλιάδων indicates a vast number that cannot (paradoxically) be numbered (a myriad was literally about ten thousand; BDAG, 661.2) and reflects an allusion to Dan 7:10. Perhaps the English translation "myriads times myriads, and thousands times thousands" captures the correct sense.

5:12 λέγοντες φωνῇ μεγάλῃ· ἄξιον ἐστιν τὸ ἀρνίον τὸ ἐσφαγμένον λαβεῖν τὴν δύναμιν καὶ πλοῦτον καὶ σοφίαν καὶ ἰσχὺν καὶ τιμὴν καὶ δόξαν καὶ εὐλογίαν.

λέγοντες. Pres act ptc masc nom pl λέγω (manner). On the use of λέγοντες to introduce speech, see 1:17 on λέγων. The gender and number of the participle (masculine and plural) seems to be determined by the reference to the μυριάδες . . . καὶ χιλιάδες.

φωνῇ μεγάλῃ. Dative of instrument. Wallace prefers the label "cognate dative" (168–69), though "voice" is not lexically cognate to "saying." It functions to indicate instrument.

ἄξιον. Predicate nominative.

ἐστιν. Pres act ind 3rd sg εἰμί. On the loss of accent, see 1:8.

τὸ ἀρνίον. Nominative subject of ἐστιν.

τὸ ἐσφαγμένον. Prf pass ptc neut nom sg σφάζω (attributive). The perfect tense picks up the reference to the slain Lamb from verse 6 (ἐσφαγμένον).

λαβεῖν. Aor act inf λαμβάνω (epexegetical to ἄξιον).

τὴν δύναμιν καὶ πλοῦτον καὶ σοφίαν καὶ ἰσχὺν καὶ τιμὴν καὶ δόξαν καὶ εὐλογίαν. Accusative direct object of λαβεῖν. The fact that this is a series of seven is probably intentional given the role the number seven plays throughout the Apocalypse.

5:13 καὶ πᾶν κτίσμα ὃ ἐν τῷ οὐρανῷ καὶ ἐπὶ τῆς γῆς καὶ ὑποκάτω τῆς γῆς καὶ ἐπὶ τῆς θαλάσσης καὶ τὰ ἐν αὐτοῖς πάντα ἤκουσα λέγοντας· τῷ καθημένῳ ἐπὶ τῷ θρόνῳ καὶ τῷ ἀρνίῳ ἡ εὐλογία καὶ ἡ τιμὴ καὶ ἡ δόξα καὶ τὸ κράτος εἰς τοὺς αἰῶνας τῶν αἰώνων.

πᾶν κτίσμα. Accusative direct object of ἤκουσα. The direct object is fronted to make prominent this final group, which encompasses the entirety of creation. The phrase τὰ . . . πάντα resumes πᾶν κτίσμα before the main verb forming a sort of inclusio around the entire section (πᾶν/πάντα).

ὅ. Nominative subject of a verbless relative clause.

ἐν τῷ οὐρανῷ καὶ ἐπὶ τῆς γῆς καὶ ὑποκάτω τῆς γῆς καὶ ἐπὶ τῆς θαλάσσης. Locative. This is an all-encompassing expression that indicates "everything in the entire universe" (see 5:3).

τὰ . . . πάντα. Accusative direct object of ἤκουσα. Resumes the πᾶν at the beginning of the clause.

ἐν αὐτοῖς. Locative.

ἤκουσα. Aor act ind 1st sg ἀκούω.

λέγοντας. Pres act ptc masc acc pl λέγω. Complement in an object-complement double accusative construction with κτίσμα . . . πάντα.

On the use of the participle λέγοντας to introduce speech, see 1:17 on λέγων. The participle is masculine, rather than neuter, perhaps to agree conceptually with "the sense of personified voices" (Beale, 366).

τῷ καθημένῳ. Pres mid ptc masc dat sg κάθημαι (substantival). Dative of possession in a verbless clause in a doxology (cf. 1 Pet 4:11).

ἐπὶ τῷ θρόνῳ. Locative.

τῷ ἀρνίῳ. Dative of possession (see τῷ καθημένῳ above).

ἡ εὐλογία . . . τὸ κράτος. Nominative subject of a verbless clause.

εἰς τοὺς αἰῶνας τῶν αἰώνων. Temporal (see 1:18). This expression is often used in doxologies (BDAG, 32.1.b).

5:14 καὶ τὰ τέσσαρα ζῷα ἔλεγον· ἀμήν. καὶ οἱ πρεσβύτεροι ἔπεσαν καὶ προσεκύνησαν.

τὰ τέσσαρα ζῷα. Nominative subject of ἔλεγον.

ἔλεγον. Impf act ind 3rd pl λέγω. The imperfect indicates offline information, perhaps to focus attention on the falling and worship of the elders in fulfillment of 4:9-10. Here a plural verb occurs with a neuter plural subject rather than the usual singular verb (Wallace, 400). This is common in Revelation when the subject refers to living beings.

ἀμήν. Functions as the complement of ἔλεγον. A "strong affirmation of what is declared" (LN 72.6).

οἱ πρεσβύτεροι. Nominative subject of ἔπεσαν καὶ προσεκύνησαν.

ἔπεσαν. Aor act ind 3rd pl πίπτω. Following the offline imperfect form (ἔλεγον) the two aorist forms ἔπεσαν and προσεκύνησαν resume the storyline and move this scene to its conclusion.

προσεκύνησαν. Aor act ind 3rd pl προσκυνέω.

Revelation 6:1-8

[1]And I saw when the Lamb opened one (the first) of the seven seals, and I heard one of the four living creatures saying in a thunderous voice, "Come!" [2]And I saw, and look, (there was) a white horse, and the one sitting on it was holding a bow, and a crown was given to him and he came conquering and in order that he might conquer. [3]And when he opened the second seal, I heard the second living creature saying, "Come!" [4]And another horse, a red one, came, and to the one sitting on it was given the ability to take peace from the earth, in order that (people) would slaughter one another, and a great sword was given to him. [5]And when he opened the third seal, I heard the third living creature saying, "Come!" And I saw, and look, there was a black horse, and the one sitting on it was holding a scale in his hand. [6]And I heard (something) like a voice in the midst of the four living creatures saying, "A quart of wheat for a

denarius, and three quarts of barley for a denarius, and do not harm the oil and the wine." ⁷And when he opened the fourth seal, I heard the voice of the fourth living creature saying, "Come!" ⁸And I saw, and look, there was a pale horse and the one sitting on it was named Death, and Hades followed behind him and they were given authority over a fourth of the earth to kill with the sword and famine and death and by the wild animals on the earth.

6:1 Καὶ εἶδον ὅτε ἤνοιξεν τὸ ἀρνίον μίαν ἐκ τῶν ἑπτὰ σφραγίδων, καὶ ἤκουσα ἑνὸς ἐκ τῶν τεσσάρων ζῴων λέγοντος ὡς φωνὴ βροντῆς· ἔρχου.

Καὶ εἶδον. Introduces a new and major scene within the visionary narrative.

εἶδον. Aor act ind 1st sg ὁράω.

ὅτε. Introduces a temporal clause that seems to function as the syntactic complement of εἶδον.

ἤνοιξεν. Aor act ind 3rd sg ἀνοίγω.

τὸ ἀρνίον. Nominative subject of ἤνοιξεν. The article is anaphoric, referring back to the first mention of ἀρνίον in 5:6. The Lamb is the implied subject of the remaining occurrences of ἤνοιξεν with each seal (vv. 3, 5, 7, 9, 12).

μίαν. Accusative direct object of ἤνοιξεν. Aune (2.379) and BDF (§247.1) think that μίαν should be understood as equivalent to πρώτην ("*first* of the seven seals"). However, with the partitive construction ἐκ τῶν ἑπτὰ σφραγίδων following μίαν (see also ἑνὸς ἐκ τῶν τεσσάρων), it is probably better to understand it in its usual sense as "*one* of the seven seals," though in the context the implication is that it is the *first* one in a series of seven.

ἐκ τῶν ἑπτὰ σφραγίδων. Partitive.

ἤκουσα. Aor act ind 1st sg ἀκούω.

ἑνὸς. Genitive direct object of ἤκουσα.

ἐκ τῶν τεσσάρων ζῴων. Partitive.

λέγοντος. Pres act ptc masc or neut gen sg λέγω. Complement in an object-complement double genitive construction with ἑνός. On the use of the participle λέγοντος to introduce speech, see 1:17 on λέγων.

ὡς φωνὴ. Manner.

βροντῆς. Attributive genitive.

ἔρχου. Pres mid impv 2nd sg ἔρχομαι. The traditional understanding of present imperatives is that they command an action as continuous or ongoing (Moule, 20). However, in this context this understanding of the present imperative does not work. The horses are not commanded to continually come. Here the present tense is used of a specific command.

Along with verse 2a, several manuscripts read ἔρχου καὶ ἴδε. καὶ εἶδον καὶ ἰδού (ℵ 2329 2344). The variant ἔρχου καὶ ἴδε. καὶ ἰδού is found in 𝔐ᴷ. The effect of these variants is that John, rather than the four horses, would be the one addressed by the living creature. Beale (374) thinks that the alteration is intentional and a result of the theological difficulty created by God commanding such horses to inflict suffering on earth. The same variant found in verses 3, 5, 7 suggests that it is intentional. The reading ἔρχου καὶ ἴδε. καὶ εἶδον καὶ ἰδού found in ℵ et al. is probably a conflation of the original reading ἔρχου. καὶ εἶδον, καὶ ἰδού and the reading ἔρχου καὶ ἴδε. καὶ ἰδού in 𝔐ᴷ. According to Metzger (667), the reading ἔρχου. καὶ εἶδον, καὶ ἰδού adopted in UBS[5] (see NA[28]) is well supported in A C P 1 1006 1611 1854 2053 *al*.

6:2 καὶ εἶδον, καὶ ἰδοὺ ἵππος λευκός, καὶ ὁ καθήμενος ἐπ' αὐτὸν ἔχων τόξον καὶ ἐδόθη αὐτῷ στέφανος καὶ ἐξῆλθεν νικῶν καὶ ἵνα νικήσῃ.

εἶδον. Aor act ind 1st sg ὁράω. εἶδον has been altered to ἴδε in 𝔐ᴷ (see 6:1 on ἔρχου).

ἰδού. A marker of attention that deictically functions to make the following statement emphatic. On the form, see 1:7.

ἵππος λευκός. Nominative subject of a verbless clause.

ὁ καθήμενος. Pres mid ptc masc nom sg κάθημαι (substantival). Nominative subject of a verbless clause. Aune translates it as "cavalier" (2.380).

ἐπ' αὐτὸν. Locative.

ἔχων. Pres act ptc masc nom sg ἔχω. This could be an attributive use of the participle or an example of the participle functioning as an indicative verb in the clause (see 1:16 on ἔχων).

τόξον. Accusative direct object of ἔχων.

ἐδόθη. Aor pass ind 3rd sg δίδωμι. The passive form of δίδωμι throughout this section suggests that the riders only act by permission.

στέφανος. Nominative subject of ἐδόθη.

αὐτῷ. Dative indirect object of ἐδόθη. Antecedent is ὁ καθήμενος.

ἐξῆλθεν. Aor act ind 3rd sg ἐξέρχομαι.

νικῶν. Pres act ptc masc nom sg νικάω (manner).

ἵνα. Introduces a purpose clause.

νικήσῃ. Aor act subj 3rd sg νικάω. Subjunctive with ἵνα. The repetition of νικάω in the ἵνα clause adds force to the statement.

6:3 Καὶ ὅτε ἤνοιξεν τὴν σφραγῖδα τὴν δευτέραν, ἤκουσα τοῦ δευτέρου ζῴου λέγοντος· ἔρχου.

ὅτε. Introduces a temporal clause.

ἤνοιξεν. Aor act ind 3rd sg ἀνοίγω.

τὴν σφραγῖδα τὴν δευτέραν. Accusative direct object of ἤνοιξεν.
ἤκουσα. Aor act ind 1st sg ἀκούω.
τοῦ δευτέρου ζῴου. Genitive direct object of ἤκουσα.
λέγοντος. Pres act ptc masc gen sg λέγω. Complement in an object-complement double genitive construction. The double genitive is due to ἤκουσα here taking its object in the genitive case. On the use of the participle λέγοντος to introduce speech, see 1:17 on λέγων.
ἔρχου. Pres mid impv 2nd sg ἔρχομαι. On the text-critical issues, see on 6:1.

6:4 καὶ ἐξῆλθεν ἄλλος ἵππος πυρρός, καὶ τῷ καθημένῳ ἐπ' αὐτὸν ἐδόθη αὐτῷ λαβεῖν τὴν εἰρήνην ἐκ τῆς γῆς καὶ ἵνα ἀλλήλους σφάξουσιν καὶ ἐδόθη αὐτῷ μάχαιρα μεγάλη.

ἐξῆλθεν. Aor act ind 3rd sg ἐξέρχομαι.
ἄλλος ἵππος πυρρός. Nominative subject of ἐξῆλθεν. ἄλλος functions to distinguish this horse from the "previously mentioned subj." (BDAG, 46.1.b), which was the white horse in verse 2. The translation, "another horse, a red one," is meant to clarify that what John sees is another horse, which he describes as red, not another red horse.
τῷ καθημένῳ. Pres mid ptc masc dat sg κάθημαι (substantival). Topic construction (see Τῷ ἀγαπῶντι in 1:5). Dative indirect object of ἐδόθη, which is picked up with the αὐτῷ.
ἐπ' αὐτὸν. Locative.
ἐδόθη. Aor pass ind 3rd sg δίδωμι.
αὐτῷ. Dative indirect object of ἐδόθη. αὐτῷ resumes τῷ καθημένῳ. This construction probably draws attention to the one seated on the horse.
λαβεῖν. Aor act inf λαμβάνω (substantival). Functions as the subject of the passive ἐδόθη ("to take peace was given to him").
τὴν εἰρήνην. Accusative direct object of λαβεῖν.
ἐκ τῆς γῆς. Separation.
ἵνα. According to Smalley (151–52) the ἵνα should be seen as parallel to the infinitive λαβεῖν. It is possible, then, that it should be taken as equivalent to an infinitive construction and introducing a further subject of the passive ἐδόθη.
ἀλλήλους. Accusative direct object of σφάξουσιν. Though the grammatical direct object of the verb, the reciprocal pronoun ἀλλήλους implies that the members of this group perform the action toward each other (see BDAG, 46).
σφάξουσιν. Fut act ind 3rd pl σφάζω. On the use of the future in place of the subjunctive after ἵνα, see 3:9 on ἥξουσιν. ℵ 𝔐 predictably "correct" the future to the subjunctive σφάξωσιν.

ἐδόθη. Aor pass ind 3rd sg δίδωμι.
αὐτῷ. Dative indirect object of ἐδόθη.
μάχαιρα μεγάλη. Nominative subject of ἐδόθη.

6:5 Καὶ ὅτε ἤνοιξεν τὴν σφραγῖδα τὴν τρίτην, ἤκουσα τοῦ τρίτου ζῴου λέγοντος· ἔρχου. καὶ εἶδον, καὶ ἰδοὺ ἵππος μέλας, καὶ ὁ καθήμενος ἐπ' αὐτὸν ἔχων ζυγὸν ἐν τῇ χειρὶ αὐτοῦ.

ὅτε. Introduces a temporal clause.
ἤνοιξεν. Aor act ind 3rd sg ἀνοίγω.
τὴν σφραγῖδα τὴν τρίτην. Accusative direct object of ἤνοιξεν.
ἤκουσα. Aor act ind 1st sg ἀκούω.
τοῦ τρίτου ζῴου. Genitive direct object of ἤκουσα.
λέγοντος. Pres act ptc masc gen sg λέγω. Complement in an object-complement double genitive construction with τοῦ τρίτου ζῴου. On the use of the participle λέγοντος to introduce speech, see 1:17 on λέγων.
ἔρχου. Pres mid impv 2nd sg ἔρχομαι. On the text-critical issues, see on 6:1.
εἶδον. Aor act ind 1st sg ὁράω.
ἰδοὺ. A marker of attention that deictically functions to make the following statement emphatic. On the form, see 1:7.
ἵππος μέλας. Nominative subject of a verbless clause.
ὁ καθήμενος. Pres mid ptc masc nom sg κάθημαι (substantival). Nominative subject of a verbless clause.
ἐπ' αὐτὸν. Locative.
ἔχων. Pres act ptc masc nom sg ἔχω. This could be an attributive use of the participle. It could also be an example of the participle functioning as an indicative verb in the clause (see 1:16 on ἔχων).
ζυγὸν. Accusative direct object of ἔχων. A ζυγός was "a balance scale" (LN 6.214). As Louw and Nida go on to explain, "Ancient balance scales often consisted of a rod held by a cord in the middle and with pans attached to both ends. Weights could be placed in one pan, while the item to be weighed would be placed in the other" (6.214).
ἐν τῇ χειρὶ. Locative.
αὐτοῦ. Possessive genitive.

6:6 καὶ ἤκουσα ὡς φωνὴν ἐν μέσῳ τῶν τεσσάρων ζῴων λέγουσαν· χοῖνιξ σίτου δηναρίου καὶ τρεῖς χοίνικες κριθῶν δηναρίου, καὶ τὸ ἔλαιον καὶ τὸν οἶνον μὴ ἀδικήσῃς.

ἤκουσα. Aor act ind 1st sg ἀκούω.
ὡς φωνὴν. Comparison. Functions as the direct object of ἤκουσα. Most English translations insert an implied "sound" or "something" to read more smoothly and to reflect an elliptical construction.

ἐν μέσῳ τῶν τεσσάρων ζῴων. Locative.

λέγουσαν. Pres act ptc fem acc sg λέγω. Complement in an object-complement double accusative construction with φωνήν. On the use of the participle λέγουσαν to introduce speech, see 1:17 on λέγων.

χοῖνιξ. Nominative subject of a verbless clause. A χοῖνιξ was a dry measure often used for grain, which was roughly equivalent to one quart or liter (BDAG, 1086).

σίτου. Genitive of content.

δηναρίου. Genitive of price. The δηνάριον was a unit of currency in the Roman world that was a typical day's wage (Smalley, 153).

τρεῖς χοίνικες. Nominative subject of a verbless clause.

κριθῶν. Genitive of content.

δηναρίου. Genitive of price.

τὸ ἔλαιον καὶ τὸν οἶνον. Accusative direct object of ἀδικήσῃς.

ἀδικήσῃς. Aor act subj 2nd sg ἀδικέω (prohibition). Traditionally, it has been thought that the aorist prohibition (aorist subjunctive with μή) was to be interpreted ingressively: a command not to begin an action ("no devestation has yet taken place"; Smalley, 154; cf. Aune, 2.381). However, while this may be true in several contexts, based on verbal aspect (see "Verbal Aspect" in the Introduction) the aorist prohibition only prohibits an action as a complete whole, and whether the action is already taking place ("stop") or not ("do not start") can only be determined by the broader context. Here, the context may suggest that the action has not yet taken place, since the rider has just been summoned to ride out upon the earth. If this is the case, the prohibition is preventative ("Do not harm"). The aorist prohibition here forbids the action as a whole.

6:7 Καὶ ὅτε ἤνοιξεν τὴν σφραγῖδα τὴν τετάρτην, ἤκουσα φωνὴν τοῦ τετάρτου ζῴου λέγοντος· ἔρχου.

ὅτε. Introduces a temporal clause.

ἤνοιξεν. Aor act ind 3rd sg ἀνοίγω.

τὴν σφραγῖδα τὴν τετάρτην. Accusative direct object of ἤνοιξεν.

ἤκουσα. Aor act ind 1st sg ἀκούω.

φωνὴν. Accusative direct object of ἤκουσα.

τοῦ τετάρτου ζῴου. Genitive of source or subjective genitive.

λέγοντος. Pres act ptc neut gen sg λέγω. Complement in an object-complement double case construction with φωνήν. The participle is grammatically incongruous. Although we might expect a feminine accusative participle rather than the neuter genitive λέγοντος, the neuter genitive has been influenced by τοῦ τετάρτου ζῴου immediately preceding it (the one actually doing the speaking). On the use of the participle λέγοντος to introduce speech, see 1:17 on λέγων.

ἔρχου. Pres mid impv 2nd sg ἔρχομαι. On the text-critical issues, see 6:1.

6:8 καὶ εἶδον, καὶ ἰδοὺ ἵππος χλωρός, καὶ ὁ καθήμενος ἐπάνω αὐτοῦ ὄνομα αὐτῷ [ὁ] θάνατος, καὶ ὁ ᾅδης ἠκολούθει μετ' αὐτοῦ καὶ ἐδόθη αὐτοῖς ἐξουσία ἐπὶ τὸ τέταρτον τῆς γῆς ἀποκτεῖναι ἐν ῥομφαίᾳ καὶ ἐν λιμῷ καὶ ἐν θανάτῳ καὶ ὑπὸ τῶν θηρίων τῆς γῆς.

εἶδον. Aor act ind 1st sg ὁράω.

ἰδοὺ. A marker of attention that deictically functions to make the following statement emphatic. On the form, see 1:7.

ἵππος χλωρός. Nominative subject of a verbless clause. Here χλωρός should be understood as "pale greenish gray" and was "evidently regarded as typical of a corpse, since the color is used as a symbol of death" (LN 79.35).

ὁ καθήμενος. Pres mid ptc masc nom sg κάθημαι (substantival). Topic construction (see Τῷ ἀγαπῶντι in 1:5), which draws attention to the the one seated on the horse (see Runge, 290–91). This so-called "hanging nominative" (see 2:26 on ὁ νικῶν) gets picked up by the following αὐτῷ.

ἐπάνω αὐτοῦ. Locative. For ἐπάνω as a preposition, see BDAG (359.1.b). The reason for the switch from ἐπί with the first three horsemen to ἐπάνω here for the fourth horseman is unclear. Perhaps it is to draw attention to the last rider and the plague associated with him.

ὄνομα. This is often labeled a parenthetical nominative (BDF §144; Aune, 1.clxix). However, it is better to analyze it as a nominative subject of a verbless clause (see Porter 1992, 85), following the topic construction ὁ καθήμενος ἐπάνω αὐτοῦ which gets picked up with the dative in the verbless clause: "The one seated on it, his name is death."

αὐτῷ. Dative of possession or reference. The antecedent is ὁ καθήμενος.

[ὁ] θάνατος. Predicate nominative of a verbless clause.

ὁ ᾅδης. Nominative subject of ἠκολούθει.

ἠκολούθει. Impf act ind 3rd sg ἀκολουθέω.

μετ' αὐτοῦ. Accompaniment.

ἐδόθη. Aor pass ind 3rd sg δίδωμι.

αὐτοῖς. Dative indirect object of ἐδόθη. Beale (383) argues that the pronoun refers to all four horsemen. However, it is more likely that the antecedents are [ὁ] θάνατος and ὁ ᾅδης since they are the closest antecedents.

ἐξουσία. Nominative subject of ἐδόθη.

ἐπὶ τὸ τέταρτον. Here ἐπί is a "marker of power, authority, control of or over someone or someth." (BDAG, 365).
τῆς γῆς. Partitive genitive.
ἀποκτεῖναι. Aor act inf ἀποκτείνω (epexegetical to ἐξουσία).
ἐν ῥομφαίᾳ καὶ ἐν λιμῷ καὶ ἐν θανάτῳ. Instrumental.
ὑπὸ τῶν θηρίων. Agency, used of animate beings in contrast to the instrumental ἐν used of inanimate objects or processes (Porter 1992, 179). It is doubtful that Wallace is correct that this is an example of intermediate agency (432 n. 74).
τῆς γῆς. Attributive genitive or genitive expressing location.

Revelation 6:9-17

⁹And when he opened the fifth seal, I saw under the altar the souls of those who were slain because of the word of God and because of the testimony that they had. ¹⁰And they cried out in a loud voice saying, "How long, O Lord, holy and true, will you not judge and avenge our blood shed by those who dwell upon the earth?" ¹¹And they were each given a white robe and were told to rest for a little while longer until the number of their fellow servants and their brothers, who are about to be put to death as they also were, was completed. ¹²And I saw when he opened the sixth seal, and there was a strong earthquake and the sun became black as sackcloth made of hair and the whole moon became (red) like blood ¹³And the stars of heaven fell to the earth, as a fig tree throws off its figs when shaken by a strong wind, ¹⁴and the sky disappeared as a scroll that is rolled up, and every mountain and island was removed from their place. ¹⁵And the kings of the earth and the magnates and the military commanders, and the rich and the strong, and every slave and free person hid themselves in the caves and in the rocks of the mountains. ¹⁶And they said to the mountains and rocks, "Fall on us and hide us from the face of the one sitting on the throne and from the wrath of the lamb, ¹⁷for the great day of their wrath has come, and who is able to stand?"

6:9 Καὶ ὅτε ἤνοιξεν τὴν πέμπτην σφραγῖδα, εἶδον ὑποκάτω τοῦ θυσιαστηρίου τὰς ψυχὰς τῶν ἐσφαγμένων διὰ τὸν λόγον τοῦ θεοῦ καὶ διὰ τὴν μαρτυρίαν ἣν εἶχον.

ὅτε. Introduces a temporal clause.
ἤνοιξεν. Aor act ind 3rd sg ἀνοίγω.
τὴν πέμπτην σφραγῖδα. Accusative direct object of ἤνοιξεν.
εἶδον. Aor act ind 1st sg ὁράω.
ὑποκάτω τοῦ θυσιαστηρίου. Locative. The θυσιαστηρίου probably refers to the heavenly counterpart of the OT altar of burnt offering (Osborne, 284; Aune, 2.405).

τὰς ψυχὰς. Accusative direct object of εἶδον. The ψυχή is the "seat and center of life that transcends the earthly" (BDAG, 1099.2.d).
τῶν ἐσφαγμένων. Prf pass ptc masc gen pl σφάζω (substantival). Possessive genitive.
διὰ τὸν λόγον. Cause.
τοῦ θεοῦ. Genitive of source or subjective genitive.
διὰ τὴν μαρτυρίαν. Cause.
ἥν. Accusative direct object of εἶχον.
εἶχον. Impf act ind 3rd pl ἔχω.

6:10 καὶ ἔκραξαν φωνῇ μεγάλῃ λέγοντες· ἕως πότε, ὁ δεσπότης ὁ ἅγιος καὶ ἀληθινός, οὐ κρίνεις καὶ ἐκδικεῖς τὸ αἷμα ἡμῶν ἐκ τῶν κατοικούντων ἐπὶ τῆς γῆς;

ἔκραξαν. Aor act ind 3rd pl κράζω.
φωνῇ μεγάλῃ. Dative of instrument or dative of manner.
λέγοντες. Pres act ptc masc nom pl λέγω (manner). On the use of λέγοντες to introduce speech, see 1:17 on λέγων.
ἕως πότε. ἕως is used as a preposition with an adverb of time (BDAG, 422–423.1). Here with πότε it introduces a question and can be translated, "How long?"
ὁ δεσπότης. Nominative used for vocative (direct address). A term which suggests "one who holds complete power or authority over another" (LN 37.63).
ὁ ἅγιος καὶ ἀληθινός. Nominative in apposition to ὁ δεσπότης. The article indicates that both adjectives function as substantives.
κρίνεις. Pres act ind 2nd sg κρίνω.
ἐκδικεῖς. Pres act ind 2nd sg ἐκδικέω. Though grammatically the καί simply links the two verbs, κρίνεις ("judge") and ἐκδικεῖς ("avenge"), semantically ἐκδικεῖς provides a more specific explanation of the judgment in κρίνεις.
τὸ αἷμα. Accusative direct object of ἐκδικεῖς. "Blood" is a metonymy for "death," substituting the means (blood) for the effect (death).
ἡμῶν. Possessive genitive.
ἐκ τῶν κατοικούντων. It is possible that the PP designates the persons "*on* whom vengeance is taken, or who is punished" (BDAG, 301.2; see Charles, 2.405; Mounce, 157). However, it is preferable to take it as the cause or source of the shedding of blood: "the bloodshed by those dwelling on the earth." This understanding is supported by the similar construction in 19:2, which has ἐκ χειρὸς αὐτῆς ("by her hand"; see Aune, 2.384).
τῶν κατοικούντων. Pres act ptc masc gen pl κατοικέω (substantival).
ἐπὶ τῆς γῆς. Locative.

6:11 καὶ ἐδόθη αὐτοῖς ἑκάστῳ στολὴ λευκὴ καὶ ἐρρέθη αὐτοῖς ἵνα ἀναπαύσονται ἔτι χρόνον μικρόν, ἕως πληρωθῶσιν καὶ οἱ σύνδουλοι αὐτῶν καὶ οἱ ἀδελφοὶ αὐτῶν οἱ μέλλοντες ἀποκτέννεσθαι ὡς καὶ αὐτοί.

ἐδόθη. Aor pass ind 3rd sg δίδωμι.
αὐτοῖς ἑκάστῳ. Dative indirect object of ἐδόθη. ἕκαστος adds a distributive notion.
στολὴ λευκὴ. Nominative subject of ἐδόθη.
ἐρρέθη. Aor pass ind 3rd sg λέγω.
αὐτοῖς. Dative indirect object of ἐρρέθη.
ἵνα. Here the ἵνα is used in place of an infinitive to express an indirect command (McKay 1994, 116). With the passive ἐρρέθη the entire clause introduced by ἵνα functions as the subject of ἐρρέθη.
ἀναπαύσονται. Fut mid ind 3rd pl ἀναπαύω. On the use of the future in place of the subjunctive, see 3:9 on ἥξουσιν.
ἔτι χρόνον μικρόν. Temporal.
ἕως πληρωθῶσιν καὶ οἱ σύνδουλοι αὐτῶν καὶ οἱ ἀδελφοὶ αὐτῶν οἱ μέλλοντες ἀποκτέννεσθαι. Lit. "until both their fellow servants and their brothers who are about to be killed might be fulfilled."
ἕως. Introduces a temporal clause, further specifying the limit of ἔτι χρόνον μικρόν.
πληρωθῶσιν. Aor pass subj 3rd pl πληρόω. Subjunctive with ἕως.
οἱ σύνδουλοι . . . καὶ οἱ ἀδελφοὶ. Nominative subject of πληρωθῶσιν.
αὐτῶν . . . αὐτῶν. Genitive of relationship.
οἱ μέλλοντες. Pres act ptc masc nom pl μέλλω (attributive).
ἀποκτέννεσθαι. Pres pass inf ἀποκτέννω (complementary).
ὡς . . . αὐτοί. Manner.
καὶ. Ascensive: "also."
αὐτοί. Nominative subject of an implied form of ἀποκτέννω: "as also they *had been killed*."

6:12 Καὶ εἶδον ὅτε ἤνοιξεν τὴν σφραγῖδα τὴν ἕκτην, καὶ σεισμὸς μέγας ἐγένετο καὶ ὁ ἥλιος ἐγένετο μέλας ὡς σάκκος τρίχινος καὶ ἡ σελήνη ὅλη ἐγένετο ὡς αἷμα

εἶδον. Aor act ind 1st sg ὁράω.
ὅτε. Introduces a temporal clause.
ἤνοιξεν. Aor act ind 3rd sg ἀνοίγω.
τὴν σφραγῖδα τὴν ἕκτην. Accusative direct object of ἤνοιξεν.
σεισμὸς μέγας. Nominative subject of ἐγένετο.
ἐγένετο. Aor mid ind 3rd sg γίνομαι.
ὁ ἥλιος. Nominative subject of the following ἐγένετο.

ἐγένετο. Aor mid ind 3rd sg γίνομαι.
μέλας. Predicate adjective.
ὡς σάκκος. Comparison.
σάκκος. Nominative subject of an elliptical comparative clause: "like sackcloth of hair (is black)."
τρίχινος. Attributive genitive: "sackcloth *consisting of hair*" or "*hairy* sackcloth" (LN 8.13).
ἡ σελήνη ὅλη. Nominative subject of ἐγένετο.
ἐγένετο. Aor mid ind 3rd sg γίνομαι.
ὡς αἷμα. Comparison. The comparative clause serves as the predicate of ἐγένετο.

6:13 καὶ οἱ ἀστέρες τοῦ οὐρανοῦ ἔπεσαν εἰς τὴν γῆν, ὡς συκῆ βάλλει τοὺς ὀλύνθους αὐτῆς ὑπὸ ἀνέμου μεγάλου σειομένη,

οἱ ἀστέρες. Nominative subject of ἔπεσαν.
τοῦ οὐρανοῦ. Genitive of location.
ἔπεσαν. Aor act ind 3rd pl πίπτω.
εἰς τὴν γῆν. Locative. The preposition εἰς can be used of "movement directed at the surface of an area" (BDAG, 289.1.a.γ).
ὡς. Comparison.
συκῆ. Nominative subject of βάλλει.
βάλλει. Pres act ind 3rd sg βάλλω. Here the present tense is used in an omnitemporal context in a gnomic type statement. This use of the present tense speaks "of regularly occuring actions" and is common especially with actions that "recur in nature" (Porter 1992, 32). While all the tense forms can be used of omnitemporal actions, the present tense is used to view the action as in progress, depicting it according to its internal structure (Porter 1989a, 225). See "Verbal Aspect" in the Introduction.
τοὺς ὀλύνθους. Accusative direct object of βάλλει.
αὐτῆς. Possessive genitive.
ὑπὸ ἀνέμου μεγάλου. Means. Although unusual, here ὑπό rather than ἐν (with the dative) refers to an impersonal agent.
σειομένη. Pres pass ptc fem nom sg σείω (temporal if modifying βάλλει, or possibly attributive modifying συκῆ).

6:14 καὶ ὁ οὐρανὸς ἀπεχωρίσθη ὡς βιβλίον ἑλισσόμενον καὶ πᾶν ὄρος καὶ νῆσος ἐκ τῶν τόπων αὐτῶν ἐκινήθησαν.

ὁ οὐρανὸς. Nominative subject of ἀπεχωρίσθη.
ἀπεχωρίσθη. Aor pass ind 3rd sg ἀποχωρίζω. On the meaning, see ἑλισσόμενον below.

ὡς βιβλίον. Comparison.

βιβλίον. Nominative subject of an implied verb (ἀπεχωρίσθη).

ἑλισσόμενον. Pres pass ptc neut nom sg ἑλίσσω (attributive). The point of comparison between heaven being split and a scroll being rolled up is not quite clear. While ἀποχωρίζω can mean "to separate, to split up," Louw and Nida also suggest that it can mean "to move away from a normal location, with the implication of disappearing" (15.14). This is probably how the word should be taken here and is the only sense that makes sense of the comparison. The heavens will be removed or will disappear, in the same way that an open scroll is rolled up and recedes (see also Osborne, 293).

πᾶν ὄρος καὶ νῆσος. Nominative subject of ἐκινήθησαν.

ἐκ τῶν τόπων. Separation.

αὐτῶν. Possessive genitive.

ἐκινήθησαν. Aor pass ind 3rd pl κινέω.

6:15 Καὶ οἱ βασιλεῖς τῆς γῆς καὶ οἱ μεγιστᾶνες καὶ οἱ χιλίαρχοι καὶ οἱ πλούσιοι καὶ οἱ ἰσχυροὶ καὶ πᾶς δοῦλος καὶ ἐλεύθερος ἔκρυψαν ἑαυτοὺς εἰς τὰ σπήλαια καὶ εἰς τὰς πέτρας τῶν ὀρέων

οἱ βασιλεῖς ... καὶ πᾶς δοῦλος καὶ ἐλεύθερος. Nominative subject of ἔκρυψαν. This list covers the broad socio-economic spectrum of first-century Rome. οἱ μεγιστᾶνες refers to "a person of high rank" (BDAG, 625). A χιλίαρχος is a high-ranking military general, a *tribunus militum*, which was a commander of a cohort of about a thousand men (Aune, 2.386).

τῆς γῆς. Genitive of location or genitive of description.

ἔκρυψαν. Aor act ind 3rd pl κρύπτω.

ἑαυτοὺς. Accusative direct object of ἔκρυψαν.

εἰς τὰ σπήλαια. Locative. Although there may be some overlap with the preposition ἐν, the preposition εἰς probably still carries its local meaning of "entry into" (see Porter 1992, 151–53).

εἰς τὰς πέτρας. Locative. On εἰς, see εἰς τὰ σπήλαια above.

τῶν ὀρέων. Possessive genitive or genitive of location.

6:16 καὶ λέγουσιν τοῖς ὄρεσιν καὶ ταῖς πέτραις· πέσετε ἐφ' ἡμᾶς καὶ κρύψατε ἡμᾶς ἀπὸ προσώπου τοῦ καθημένου ἐπὶ τοῦ θρόνου καὶ ἀπὸ τῆς ὀργῆς τοῦ ἀρνίου,

λέγουσιν. Pres act ind 3rd pl λέγω. Historical or narrative present (see 4:5 on ἐκπορεύονται). The present tense may function to draw attention to the desperate plea of those who face God's and the Lamb's wrath.

τοῖς ὄρεσιν καὶ ταῖς πέτραις. Dative indirect object of λέγουσιν. This is an example of personification (the mountains and rocks are addressed as animate objects).

πέσετε. Aor act impv 2nd pl πίπτω.

ἐφ' ἡμᾶς. Locative.

κρύψατε. Aor act impv 2nd pl κρύπτω.

ἡμᾶς. Accusative direct object of κρύψατε.

ἀπὸ προσώπου. Separation. προσώπου refers to the personal presence of the one sitting on the throne (BDAG, 887–888.1.b).

τοῦ καθημένου. Pres mid ptc masc gen sg κάθημαι (substantival). Possessive genitive.

ἐπὶ τοῦ θρόνου. Locative.

ἀπὸ τῆς ὀργῆς. Separation.

τοῦ ἀρνίου. Subjective genitive.

6:17 ὅτι ἦλθεν ἡ ἡμέρα ἡ μεγάλη τῆς ὀργῆς αὐτῶν, καὶ τίς δύναται σταθῆναι;

ὅτι. Introduces a causal clause.

ἦλθεν. Aor act ind 3rd sg ἔρχομαι. This is an example of an aorist that refers to an event that has just happened and that extends into the present time of the speaker ("has come and is now present"; see Mathewson 2010, 55–56).

ἡ ἡμέρα ἡ μεγάλη. Nominative subject of ἦλθεν.

τῆς ὀργῆς. The genitive seems to carry the notion of "the day when their wrath occurs."

αὐτῶν. Subjective genitive. Antecedent is God and the Lamb (v. 16). The singular αὐτοῦ is attested in A 𝔐, while the plural αὐτῶν included in NA[28]/UBS[5] is supported by ℵ C 1611 1854 2053 2329 2344 *pc*. While the plural has good manuscript support, arriving at a decision is not easy. Metzger (669) thinks that the singular is the easier reading, which was an attempt to remove the ambiguity of αὐτῶν, and so the plural is to be preferred. This may find support in the fact that the day of wrath is associated with the Lamb in verse 16. However, it is not clear why Metzger thinks the plural is ambiguous, since the one seated on the throne and the Lamb have just been mentioned in verse 16. It is just as possible that the singular αὐτοῦ was ambiguous, since both the Lamb and the one seated on the throne are mentioned in verse 16, and the plural may have been introduced to conform to both the Lamb and the one seated on the throne (Beale, 402), making αὐτοῦ the more difficult reading. If the singular is the correct reading, the antecedent could be ambiguous and it could be understood as an example of John's heightened Christology and trinitarian thought (see 11:15; 22:3, 4).

τίς. Nominative subject of δύναται. Introduces a question.
δύναται. Pres mid ind 3rd sg δύναμαι.
σταθῆναι. Aor mid inf ἵστημι (complementary).

Revelation 7:1-8

¹After this I saw four angels standing at the four corners of the earth, grasping the four winds of the earth in order that the wind might not blow upon the earth nor upon the sea, nor against every tree. ²And I saw another angel coming up from the east having the seal of the living God, and he cried out with a loud voice to the four angels who were given (authority) to harm the earth and the sea ³saying, "Do not harm the earth or the sea or the trees, until we seal the servants of our God upon their foreheads." ⁴And I heard the number of those who were sealed, one hundred and forty-four thousand, sealed from every tribe of the sons of Israel. ⁵From the tribe of Judah twelve thousand were sealed, from the tribe of Reuben twelve thousand, from the tribe of Gad twelve thousand, ⁶from the tribe of Asher twelve thousand, from the tribe of Naphtali twelve thousand, from the tribe of Manasseh twelve thousand, ⁷from the tribe of Simeon twelve thousand, from the tribe of Levi twelve thousand, from the tribe of Issachar twelve thousand, ⁸from the tribe of Zebulon twelve thousand, from the tribe of Joseph twelve thousand, from the tribe of Benjamin twelve thousand were sealed.

7:1 Μετὰ τοῦτο εἶδον τέσσαρας ἀγγέλους ἑστῶτας ἐπὶ τὰς τέσσαρας γωνίας τῆς γῆς, κρατοῦντας τοὺς τέσσαρας ἀνέμους τῆς γῆς ἵνα μὴ πνέῃ ἄνεμος ἐπὶ τῆς γῆς μήτε ἐπὶ τῆς θαλάσσης μήτε ἐπὶ πᾶν δένδρον.

This section of the vision consists of two visionary segments marked off by μετὰ τοῦτο εἶδον in 7:1 (144,000) and μετὰ ταῦτα εἶδον in 7:9 (the innumerable multitude).

Μετὰ τοῦτο. Temporal. The antecedent of τοῦτο anaphorically is the seal sequence in ch. 6. This does not suggest that the events narrated in 7:1-17 occur chronologically after the events of ch. 6, but only that this was the sequence in which John himself saw them (Beale, 406). Blount (149) makes a similar comment on Μετὰ ταῦτα in verse 9.

εἶδον. Aor act ind 1st sg ὁράω.

τέσσαρας ἀγγέλους. Accusative direct object of εἶδον.

ἑστῶτας. Prf act ptc masc acc pl ἵστημι. Complement in an object-complement double accusative construction. The perfect tense (stative aspect) highlights the posture of the angels in relation to their function of holding back (present participle κρατοῦντας) the winds.

ἐπὶ τὰς τέσσαρας γωνίας. Locative.

τῆς γῆς. Partitive genitive.

κρατοῦντας. Pres act ptc masc acc pl κρατέω. This participle could either be attributive, or function adverbially to indicate manner, modifying ἑστῶτας.

    τοὺς τέσσαρας ἀνέμους. Accusative direct object of κρατοῦντας.

    τῆς γῆς. Possessive genitive or genitive expressing location.

    ἵνα. Introduces a purpose clause.

    πνέῃ. Pres act subj 3rd sg πνέω. Subjunctive with ἵνα.

    ἄνεμος. Nominative subject of πνέῃ.

    μὴ ... μήτε ... μήτε. "Not ... nor ... nor" (BDF §445.1).

    ἐπὶ τῆς γῆς μήτε ἐπὶ τῆς θαλάσσης μήτε ἐπὶ πᾶν δένδρον. Locative. ἐπί and the accusative indicate movement against, i.e., the wind blows against the trees (Smalley, 180).

    μήτε ἐπὶ πᾶν δένδρον. This phrase could be translated "nor on any tree" (Aune, 2.427).

7:2 Καὶ εἶδον ἄλλον ἄγγελον ἀναβαίνοντα ἀπὸ ἀνατολῆς ἡλίου ἔχοντα σφραγῖδα θεοῦ ζῶντος, καὶ ἔκραξεν φωνῇ μεγάλῃ τοῖς τέσσαρσιν ἀγγέλοις οἷς ἐδόθη αὐτοῖς ἀδικῆσαι τὴν γῆν καὶ τὴν θάλασσαν

    εἶδον. Aor act ind 1st sg ὁράω. Here εἶδον introduces a new element in the vision begun at 7:1.

    ἄλλον ἄγγελον. Accusative direct object of εἶδον. ἄγγελον is anarthrous since this participant is mentioned here for the first time.

    ἀναβαίνοντα. Pres act ptc masc acc sg ἀναβαίνω. Complement in an object-complement double accusative construction.

    ἀπὸ ἀνατολῆς ἡλίου. Source.

    ἀνατολῆς ἡλίου. Lit. the "rising of the sun," referring to the position of the sun in the *east* (BDAG, 74.2.a).

    ἡλίου. Subjective genitive (Aune, 2.427).

    ἔχοντα. Pres act ptc masc acc sg ἔχω (manner).

    σφραγῖδα. Accusative direct object of ἔχοντα. According to BDAG, this noun refers to "the instrument used for sealing or stamping, *signet*" (980.1; see also v. 3 on σφραγίσωμεν).

    θεοῦ. Possessive genitive. This seems more likely than a subjective genitive (Osborne, 308), since it is the angel who performs the act of sealing.

    ζῶντος. Pres act ptc masc gen sg ζάω (attributive).

    ἔκραξεν. Aor act ind 3rd sg κράζω.

    φωνῇ μεγάλῃ. Dative of instrument or dative of manner.

    τοῖς τέσσαρσιν ἀγγέλοις. Dative indirect object of ἔκραξεν. The article is anaphoric, referring back to the first mention of this group in verse 1.

    οἷς. Dative indirect object of ἐδόθη.

ἐδόθη. Aor pass ind 3rd sg δίδωμι.

αὐτοῖς. Dative indirect object of ἐδόθη. An example of the redundant use of the pronoun, which picks up the relative pronoun οἷς (McKay 1994, 150, thinks this is an Aramaic idiom not unknown in Greek; Aune, 2.427). On this construction, see 3:8 on αὐτήν. This construction probably functions to draw attention to the antecedent: τέσσαρσιν ἀγγέλοις.

ἀδικῆσαι. Aor act inf ἀδικέω (subject of the passive ἐδόθη). In light of the similar construction in 6:8 (ἐδόθη αὐτοῖς ἐξουσία) this could be an elliptical construction where ἐξουσία is implied (ἐδόθη αὐτοῖς ἐξουσία ἀδικῆσαι), in which case the infinitive would be epexegetical to the implied ἐξουσία. If so, the entire elliptical construction would be the subject of ἐδόθη. Here ἀδικῆσαι carries the meaning "to cause damage to or mistreat" (BDAG, 20.2).

τὴν γῆν καὶ τὴν θάλασσαν. Accusative direct object of ἀδικῆσαι.

7:3 λέγων· μὴ ἀδικήσητε τὴν γῆν μήτε τὴν θάλασσαν μήτε τὰ δένδρα, ἄχρι σφραγίσωμεν τοὺς δούλους τοῦ θεοῦ ἡμῶν ἐπὶ τῶν μετώπων αὐτῶν.

λέγων. Pres act ptc masc nom sg λέγω (manner). On the use of the participle λέγων to introduce speech, see 1:17 on λέγων.

ἀδικήσητε. Aor act subj 2nd pl ἀδικέω (prohibition). In this context μὴ ἀδικήσητε could function to forbid an action from beginning, but more likely it refers to the entire period of time leading up to the sealing deictically indicated by ἄχρι (see below). The aorist prohibition simply forbids the entire action (see also 6:6 on ἀδικήσῃς).

μὴ ... μήτε ... μήτε. "Not ... nor ... nor."

τὴν γῆν μήτε τὴν θάλασσαν μήτε τὰ δένδρα. Accusative direct object of ἀδικήσητε.

ἄχρι. Introduces a temporal clause indicating time up to which (Porter 1992, 242).

σφραγίσωμεν. Aor act subj 1st pl σφραγίζω. Subjunctive with ἄχρι. According to BDAG, σφραγίσωμεν here means "to mark with a seal as a means of identification" (980.3). However, in the context of the four winds being held back so that they are not able to harm the earth, the notion of "protection" or "security" is certainly present.

τοὺς δούλους. Accusative direct object of σφραγίσωμεν.

τοῦ θεοῦ. Possessive genitive.

ἡμῶν. Genitive of subordination.

ἐπὶ τῶν μετώπων. Locative.

αὐτῶν. Possessive genitive.

7:4 Καὶ ἤκουσα τὸν ἀριθμὸν τῶν ἐσφραγισμένων, ἑκατὸν τεσσεράκοντα τέσσαρες χιλιάδες, ἐσφραγισμένοι ἐκ πάσης φυλῆς υἱῶν Ἰσραήλ·

ἤκουσα. Aor act ind 1st sg ἀκούω.
τὸν ἀριθμὸν. Accusative direct object of ἤκουσα.
τῶν ἐσφραγισμένων. Prf pass ptc masc gen pl σφραγίζω (substantival). Objective genitive. The perfect tense (stative aspect) may draw attention to the sealing to emphasize their state of protection from the judgments that are about to be unleashed.
ἑκατὸν τεσσεράκοντα τέσσαρες χιλιάδες. Nominative subject of a verbless clause: "(there were) one hundred and forty-four thousand." The nominative case simply specifies the nominal idea to form its own clause (Porter 1992, 85).
ἐσφραγισμένοι. Prf pass ptc masc nom pl σφραγίζω. The nominative could be in apposition to ἑκατὸν τεσσαράκοντα τέσσαρες χιλιάδες. It is also possible that it is attributive: "one hundred and forty-four thousand *who were* sealed." The repetition of the participial form of σφραγίζω draws attention to the protection of God's people from the subsequent judgments.
ἐκ πάσης φυλῆς. Partitive or possibly source.
υἱῶν. Genitive of source or epexegetical genitive.
Ἰσραήλ. Genitive of relationship.

7:5-8 ἐκ φυλῆς Ἰούδα δώδεκα χιλιάδες ἐσφραγισμένοι, ἐκ φυλῆς Ῥουβὴν δώδεκα χιλιάδες, ἐκ φυλῆς Γὰδ δώδεκα χιλιάδες, ἐκ φυλῆς Ἀσὴρ δώδεκα χιλιάδες, ἐκ φυλῆς Νεφθαλὶμ δώδεκα χιλιάδες, ἐκ φυλῆς Μανασσῆ δώδεκα χιλιάδες, ἐκ φυλῆς Συμεὼν δώδεκα χιλιάδες, ἐκ φυλῆς Λευὶ δώδεκα χιλιάδες, ἐκ φυλῆς Ἰσσαχὰρ δώδεκα χιλιάδες, ἐκ φυλῆς Ζαβουλὼν δώδεκα χιλιάδες, ἐκ φυλῆς Ἰωσὴφ δώδεκα χιλιάδες, ἐκ φυλῆς Βενιαμὶν δώδεκα χιλιάδες ἐσφραγισμένοι.

The itemization of the number of those sealed from each of the twelve tribes stands in apposition to ἑκατὸν τεσσαράκοντα τέσσαρες χιλιάδες and ἐσφραγισμένοι ἐκ πάσης φυλῆς υἱῶν Ἰσραήλ as a further elaboration on the specific division of the 144,000 according to each of the twelve tribes.

ἐκ φυλῆς. See verse 4 above.
δώδεκα χιλιάδες. Nominative subject in a verbless clause: "From the tribe of Judah (there were) twelve thousand."
ἐσφραγισμένοι. Prf pass ptc masc nom pl σφραγίζω (attributive). The participle could also plausibly be read as substantival: "twelve thousand sealed ones." ἐσφραγισμένοι in verse 8 forms an inclusio with ἐσφραγισμένοι in verse 5.

Revelation 7:9-17

⁹After these things I saw, and look, a great multitude, which no one was able to number, from every nation and tribe and people and language, standing before the throne and before the Lamb, dressed in white robes and (there were) palm leaves in their hands. ¹⁰And they cried out with a loud voice, saying, "Salvation belongs to our God who is seated upon the throne, and to the Lamb." ¹¹And all the angels stood around the throne and around the elders and around the four living creatures, and they fell before the throne upon their faces and they worshiped God ¹²saying, "Amen, praise and glory and wisdom and thanksgiving and honor and power and strength belong to our God for ever and ever, amen." ¹³And one of the elders answered saying to me, "Who are these who are clothed in white robes and from where have they come?" ¹⁴And I said to him, "My lord, you know." And he said to me, "These are the ones who have come out of the great tribulation and they have washed their robes and have made them white with the blood of the Lamb. ¹⁵For this reason, they are before the throne of God and they serve him day and night in his temple, and the one sitting upon the throne will dwell with them. ¹⁶They will not hunger any longer nor will they thirst any longer, nor will the sun fall on them nor any burning heat, ¹⁷for the Lamb in the midst of the throne will shepherd them and he shall lead them to springs of living water, and God will wipe away every tear from their eyes."

7:9 Μετὰ ταῦτα εἶδον, καὶ ἰδοὺ ὄχλος πολύς, ὃν ἀριθμῆσαι αὐτὸν οὐδεὶς ἐδύνατο, ἐκ παντὸς ἔθνους καὶ φυλῶν καὶ λαῶν καὶ γλωσσῶν ἑστῶτες ἐνώπιον τοῦ θρόνου καὶ ἐνώπιον τοῦ ἀρνίου περιβεβλημένους στολὰς λευκάς καὶ φοίνικες ἐν ταῖς χερσὶν αὐτῶν,

Aune notices the tense sequence that occurs in this section: aorist tense verbs, followed by present tense verbs, followed by future tense verbs (2.438; see also Mussies, 334–35). But as Aune notes, the sequence is not followed exactly. This makes it unlikely that ch. 7 can be read according to a strict temporal sequence (past, present, and future elements). Rather, consistent with verbal aspect, the verb tense forms indicate the author's perspective on the action (see "Verbal Aspect" in the Introduction; Mathewson 2010, 129–30). While verses 15-17 end with a concentration of future tense verbs, the key is to understand that these verses are still part of the speech of the elder to John (see the translation above), rather than part of the narrated vision. In other words, "The elder now articulates the expected [future] reward of those seen in the vision in vv. 9-10" (Mathewson 2010, 133).

Μετὰ ταῦτα. Temporal. On this phrase, see 7:1. The antecedent is 7:1-8.

εἶδον. Aor act ind 1st sg ὁράω.

ἰδού. A marker of attention that deictically functions to make the following statement emphatic. On the form, see 1:7. Here it draws attention to the great multitude.

ὄχλος πολύς. Nominative subject of a verbless clause.

ὅν. Accusative direct object of ἀριθμῆσαι.

ἀριθμῆσαι. Aor act inf ἀριθμέω (complementary).

αὐτόν. An example of the redundant use of the pronoun, which picks up ὅν (see 3:8 on αὐτήν). This construction probably functions to add greater emphasis to the antecedent: ὄχλος πολύς.

οὐδείς. Nominative subject of ἐδύνατο.

ἐδύνατο. Impf mid ind 3rd sg δύναμαι.

ἐκ παντὸς ἔθνους καὶ φυλῶν καὶ λαῶν καὶ γλωσσῶν. Source or partitive. Modifies ὄχλος. There is a grammatical awkwardness with the singular παντὸς ἔθνους being followed by a group of plural nouns (φυλῶν καὶ λαῶν καὶ γλωσσῶν). Aune argues that the first construction παντὸς ἔθνους should be taken in a distributive sense ("every nation"), and that the distributive sense of παντός is to be extended to the plural nouns that follow (2.428). A more likely solution (not necessarily in conflict with Aune) is that this may be the author's way of drawing attention to the OT Abrahamic promise as the background (Bauckham, 224–25). In particular, ὄχλος *πολύς* ... ἐκ παντὸς *ἔθνους* echoes the patriarchal promise in LXX Gen 17:4: πλήθους ἐθνῶν (Bauckham, 225). Furthermore, other than 14:6, this is the only place where "every nation" occurs first in occurrences of the fourfold formula (5:9; 10:11; 11:9; 13:7; 14:6; 17:15).

ἑστῶτες. Prf act ptc masc nom pl ἵστημι. Complement in a subject-complement double nominative construction with ὄχλος πολύς. The two perfect participles ἑστῶτες and περιβεβλημένους help to highlight and introduce a new and significant feature in the discourse (see ἰδού above). The plural participle modifying the singular ὄχλος πολύς is according to sense, ὄχλος being a collective noun (Charles, 1.cxli). Also, the "great crowd" consists of those "from every nation, tribe, people, and language."

ἐνώπιον τοῦ θρόνου καὶ ἐνώπιον τοῦ ἀρνίου. Locative.

περιβεβλημένους. Prf mid ptc masc acc pl περιβάλλω. Rather than the expected nominative case, the accusative case could be accounted for by the author reverting to the accusative as the substantival direct object of εἶδον (Aune, 2.429; Robertson, 441). Several manuscripts correct the participle to the nominative περιβεβλημένοι (א² P 1854 2053 2329 2344 2351 𝔐ᴬ).

στολὰς λευκάς. Accusative direct object of περιβεβλημένους.

φοίνικες. Nominative subject of a verbless clause. א* 2351 𝔐ᴷ have the accusative φοίνικας, probably in conformity to the preceding accusative περιβεβλημένους or because it was thought to function as the direct object of εἶδον.

ἐν ταῖς χερσὶν. Locative.

αὐτῶν. Possessive genitive.

7:10 καὶ κράζουσιν φωνῇ μεγάλῃ λέγοντες· ἡ σωτηρία τῷ θεῷ ἡμῶν τῷ καθημένῳ ἐπὶ τῷ θρόνῳ καὶ τῷ ἀρνίῳ.

κράζουσιν. Pres act ind 3rd pl κράζω. Historical or narrative present (see 4:5 on ἐκπορεύονται). Here it draws attention to the speech of the great multitude. The plural used with reference to the singular ὄχλος πολύς is an example of a construction according to sense with a collective noun (ὄχλος).

φωνῇ μεγάλῃ. Dative of instrument or dative of manner.

λέγοντες. Pres act ptc masc nom pl λέγω (manner). On the use of λέγοντες to introduce speech, see 1:17 on λέγων.

ἡ σωτηρία. Nominative subject of a verbless clause.

τῷ θεῷ. Dative of possession in a verbless clause in a doxology (see 5:13).

ἡμῶν. Genitive of subordination.

τῷ καθημένῳ. Pres mid ptc masc dat sg κάθημαι (attributive).

ἐπὶ τῷ θρόνῳ. Locative.

τῷ ἀρνίῳ. See τῷ θεῷ above.

7:11 Καὶ πάντες οἱ ἄγγελοι εἱστήκεισαν κύκλῳ τοῦ θρόνου καὶ τῶν πρεσβυτέρων καὶ τῶν τεσσάρων ζῴων καὶ ἔπεσαν ἐνώπιον τοῦ θρόνου ἐπὶ τὰ πρόσωπα αὐτῶν καὶ προσεκύνησαν τῷ θεῷ

πάντες οἱ ἄγγελοι. Nominative subject of εἱστήκεισαν.

εἱστήκεισαν. Plprf act ind 3rd pl ἵστημι. This is the only example of a pluperfect tense in the entire book of Revelation, with the perfect tense of ἵστημι often used of the posture of different persons or groups (see ἑστῶτες in v. 9 above). The pluperfect tense indicates stative aspect, along with the semantic feature of remoteness (like the imperfect tense form; see Porter 1989a, 289), and probably fills in background information. It is difficult to discover a rationale for the use of the pluperfect instead of the perfect tense here. Perhaps the more remote form of the pluperfect was used so as not to distract attention from the great multitude which stands (perfect ἑστῶτες) before the throne and cries out (present κράζουσιν), or perhaps the more remote pluperfect form portrays the angels as standing spatially further from the throne, encircling all the other groups (Mathewson 2010, 131–32). It is doubtful that Wallace is correct in thinking the pluperfect here occurs without aspectual significance (586), due to the fact that ἵστημι occurs in Revelation in aorist, future and perfect tense forms, suggesting a choice on the part of the author. Mussies (347) is also incorrect that the pluperfect here is simply equivalent to the imperfect.

κύκλῳ τοῦ θρόνου καὶ τῶν πρεσβυτέρων καὶ τῶν τεσσάρων ζῴων. Locative. The picture seems to be that the throne is surrounded by the elders and living creatures (see 4:4-6), and the great multitude. All the angels then would encircle the entire group, though it is unlikely that the author is concerned with a precise spatial visualization since they fall before the throne in the next clause.

ἔπεσαν. Aor act ind 3rd pl πίπτω.

ἐνώπιον τοῦ θρόνου. Locative.

ἐπὶ τὰ πρόσωπα. Locative.

αὐτῶν. Possessive genitive.

προσεκύνησαν. Aor act ind 3rd pl προσκυνέω.

τῷ θεῷ. Dative direct object of προσεκύνησαν (see 4:10).

7:12 λέγοντες· ἀμήν, ἡ εὐλογία καὶ ἡ δόξα καὶ ἡ σοφία καὶ ἡ εὐχαριστία καὶ ἡ τιμὴ καὶ ἡ δύναμις καὶ ἡ ἰσχὺς τῷ θεῷ ἡμῶν εἰς τοὺς αἰῶνας τῶν αἰώνων· ἀμήν.

λέγοντες. Pres act ptc masc nom pl λέγω (manner). On the use of λέγοντες to introduce speech, see 1:17 on λέγων.

ἀμήν ... ἀμήν. The rest of the verse functions as the complement of λέγοντες. A "strong affirmation of what is declared" (LN 72.6).

ἡ εὐλογία καὶ ἡ δόξα καὶ ἡ σοφία καὶ ἡ εὐχαριστία καὶ ἡ τιμὴ καὶ ἡ δύναμις καὶ ἡ ἰσχὺς. Nominative subject of a verbless clause. The fact that this is a series of seven is probably intentional given the role the number seven plays throughout the Apocalypse.

τῷ θεῷ. Dative of possession in a verbless clause in a doxology (see v. 10 on τῷ θεῷ).

ἡμῶν. Genitive of subordination.

εἰς τοὺς αἰῶνας τῶν αἰώνων. Temporal. On this construction, see 1:18. Given the use of similar temporal expressions in doxologies elsewhere (1:6; 5:13), the PP likely refers to the eternal duration of praise here, rather than to God as eternal (contra Osborne, 323).

7:13 Καὶ ἀπεκρίθη εἷς ἐκ τῶν πρεσβυτέρων λέγων μοι· οὗτοι οἱ περιβεβλημένοι τὰς στολὰς τὰς λευκὰς τίνες εἰσὶν καὶ πόθεν ἦλθον;

ἀπεκρίθη. Aor mid ind 3rd sg ἀποκρίνομαι. On the voice, see "Deponency" in the Series Introduction.

εἷς. Nominative subject of ἀπεκρίθη. Introduces a switch in subject. On the use of εἷς followed by ἐκ + genitive as an ordinal rather than an indefinite pronoun, see 5:5 on εἷς (contra Aune, 2.430; BDF §247.2).

ἐκ τῶν πρεσβυτέρων. Partitive.

λέγων. Pres act ptc masc nom sg λέγω (manner). On the use of λέγοντες to introduce speech, see 1:17 on λέγων.

μοι. Dative indirect object of λέγων.

οὗτοι. The entire phrase οὗτοι οἱ περιβεβλημένοι τὰς στολὰς τὰς λευκὰς is a topic construction, which gets picked up by the τίνες. On topic constructions, see 1:5.

οἱ περιβεβλημένοι. Pres mid ptc masc nom pl περιβάλλω (attributive). The use of the near demonstrative οὗτοι further makes the ones clothed in white prominent.

τὰς στολὰς τὰς λευκὰς. Accusative direct object of περιβεβλημένοι.

τίνες. Nominative subject of εἰσίν. Introduces a question. The interrogative pronoun picks up the topic indicated by οὗτοι οἱ περιβεβλημένοι τὰς στολὰς τὰς λευκὰς.

εἰσὶν. Pres act ind 3rd pl εἰμί.

πόθεν. Locative. πόθεν is an "interrogative expression of extension from a local source, *from what place? from where?*" (BDAG, 838.1).

ἦλθον. Aor act ind 3rd pl ἔρχομαι.

7:14 καὶ εἴρηκα αὐτῷ· κύριέ μου, σὺ οἶδας. καὶ εἶπέν μοι· οὗτοί εἰσιν οἱ ἐρχόμενοι ἐκ τῆς θλίψεως τῆς μεγάλης καὶ ἔπλυναν τὰς στολὰς αὐτῶν καὶ ἐλεύκαναν αὐτὰς ἐν τῷ αἵματι τοῦ ἀρνίου.

εἴρηκα. Prf act ind 1st sg εἶπον. Smalley (196) thinks that the perfect tense used alongside of the aorist suggests that εἴρηκα functions as an aorist (cf. Osborne, 323 n. 10; Aune, 2.430; Turner, 69–70; Mussies, 264–65; BDF §343.1; Fanning, 303; Robertson also notes that it lacks reduplication, 902). However, the author uses the suppletive aorist form εἶπέν in the next clause, as well as elsewhere in Revelation, suggesting an intentional choice (Porter 1989a, 279). Further, just because the two tense forms occur in similar contexts does not mean that they are identical in meaning (see also 5:7 on εἴληφεν). Rather, the perfect should be given its full stative force here (see "Verbal Aspect" in the Introduction). In the midst of aorists introducing the speech of the others (ἀπεκρίθη, εἶπέν), the use of the perfect perhaps functions to express the seer's surprise at the elder's question, since the elder should already know (οἶδας) the answer (Mathewson 2010, 131). This also makes Thompson's (45) assessment, that the perfect tense can be ignored since it is a translation of an underlying Hebrew tense, highly problematic.

αὐτῷ. Dative indirect object of εἴρηκα.

κύριέ. Vocative of direct address. The accenting is due to the enclitic μου that follows.

μου. Genitive of subordination.

σὺ. Nominative subject of οἶδας.

οἶδας. Prf act ind 2nd sg οἶδα.

εἶπέν. Aor act ind 3rd sg εἶπον. The accenting is due to the enclitic μοι that follows.

μοι. Dative indirect object of εἶπέν.

οὗτοί. Nominative subject of εἰσιν. Antecedent is οὗτοι οἱ περιβεβλημένοι (v. 13). The accenting is due to the enclitic εἰσιν that follows.

εἰσιν. Pres act ind 3rd pl εἰμί. On the loss of accent, see 1:8.

οἱ ἐρχόμενοι. Pres mid ptc masc nom pl ἔρχομαι (substantival). Predicate nominative. While Charles (1.212) translates the participle "who are coming," the participle seems to be past in its temporal sphere of reference (Aune, 2.430), since it occurs in a vision of the redeemed standing before the throne (v. 9) and answers the question recorded in the aorist ἦλθον in verse 13 above (Mounce, 173 n. 22). While participles do not indicate time, their relationship to time (past, present, future) can be determined by the context.

ἐκ τῆς θλίψεως τῆς μεγάλης. Separation.

ἔπλυναν. Aor act ind 3rd pl πλύνω. On the shift from the participle to a finite verb, see 1:6 on ἐποίησεν.

τὰς στολὰς. Accusative direct object of ἔπλυναν.

αὐτῶν. Possessive genitive.

ἐλεύκαναν. Aor act ind 3rd pl λευκαίνω.

αὐτὰς. Accusative direct object of ἐλεύκαναν.

ἐν τῷ αἵματι. Instrumental or locative (cf. Moule, 75). As Porter notes, "The label 'instrumental' is given to a range of metaphorical extensions of the locative sense of ἐν" (1992, 158).

τοῦ ἀρνίου. Possessive genitive.

7:15 διὰ τοῦτό εἰσιν ἐνώπιον τοῦ θρόνου τοῦ θεοῦ καὶ λατρεύουσιν αὐτῷ ἡμέρας καὶ νυκτὸς ἐν τῷ ναῷ αὐτοῦ, καὶ ὁ καθήμενος ἐπὶ τοῦ θρόνου σκηνώσει ἐπ' αὐτούς.

διὰ τοῦτό. Introduces a cause, with τοῦτό functioning anaphorically to point back to verse 14. The accenting is due to the enclitic εἰσιν that follows.

εἰσιν. Pres act ind 3rd pl εἰμί. On the loss of accent, see 1:8.
ἐνώπιον τοῦ θρόνου. Locative.
τοῦ θεοῦ. Possessive genitive.
λατρεύουσιν. Pres act ind 3rd pl λατρεύω. The present tense is future referring. See the futures σκηνώσει, πεινάσουσιν, διψήσουσιν, ποιμανεῖ, ὁδηγήσει, ἐξαλείψει that follow. The difference may be that the present tense λατρεύουσιν describes what the people will do to God, while the futures are used of what God can be expected to do for his people (Mathewson 2010, 133). The term λατρεύουσιν may carry cultic connotations here, indicating "the carrying out of religious duties, esp. of a cultic nature, by human beings" (BDAG, 587) or "to serve or worship cultically, especially by sacrifice" (Strathmann, 60). However, here it is clear that this "religious service" is rendered not in ritual acts, but in spiritual worship (Osborne, 327).
αὐτῷ. Dative direct object of λατρεύουσιν.
ἡμέρας καὶ νυκτὸς. Genitive of time (see also 4:8).
ἐν τῷ ναῷ. Locative.
αὐτοῦ. Possessive genitive.
ὁ καθήμενος. Pres mid ptc masc nom sg κάθημαι (substantival). Nominative subject of σκηνώσει.
ἐπὶ τοῦ θρόνου. Locative.
σκηνώσει. Fut act ind 3rd sg σκηνόω.
ἐπ' αὐτούς. Locative. σκηνώσει ἐπ' αὐτούς can be taken to mean that God will shelter them or protect them (BDAG, 929), or that God will spread his tent "over" them (Osborne, 329). The antecedent is "those who have come out of the great tribulation" (v. 14).

7:16 οὐ πεινάσουσιν ἔτι οὐδὲ διψήσουσιν ἔτι οὐδὲ μὴ πέσῃ ἐπ' αὐτοὺς ὁ ἥλιος οὐδὲ πᾶν καῦμα,

πεινάσουσιν. Fut act ind 3rd pl πεινάω.
ἔτι . . . ἔτι. Temporal. With the negative οὐ . . . οὐδὲ the expression can be translated "no longer."
διψήσουσιν. Fut act ind 3rd pl διψάω.
πέσῃ. Aor act subj 3rd sg πίπτω. The subjunctive is used with οὐ μή (here οὐδὲ μή), which is an emphatic way of expressing negation.
ὁ ἥλιος οὐδὲ πᾶν καῦμα. Nominative subject of πέσῃ.

7:17 ὅτι τὸ ἀρνίον τὸ ἀνὰ μέσον τοῦ θρόνου ποιμανεῖ αὐτοὺς καὶ ὁδηγήσει αὐτοὺς ἐπὶ ζωῆς πηγὰς ὑδάτων, καὶ ἐξαλείψει ὁ θεὸς πᾶν δάκρυον ἐκ τῶν ὀφθαλμῶν αὐτῶν.

ὅτι. Introduces a causal clause.

τὸ ἀρνίον. Nominative subject of ποιμανεῖ.

τὸ ἀνὰ μέσον τοῦ θρόνου. The preposition ἀνά in combination with μέσος expresses a spatial notion (Young, 89). BDAG (635.1.b) understands the expression ἀνὰ μέσον to mean at the "center of the throne" (see also Harris, 46–47). The article before ἀνὰ μέσον functions as an adjectivizer, turning the PP into an attributive modifier of ἀρνίον. Lit. "the in-the-midst-of the throne Lamb."

ποιμανεῖ. Fut act ind 3rd sg ποιμαίνω. In contrast to 2:27 and 12:5, here ποιμαίνω has the positive connotation of leading, protecting, guiding, or nurturing.

αὐτούς. Accusative direct object of ποιμανεῖ. The antecedent is "those who have come out of the great tribulation."

ὁδηγήσει. Fut act ind 3rd sg ὁδηγέω.

αὐτούς. Accusative direct object of ὁδηγήσει.

ἐπὶ ζωῆς πηγὰς ὑδάτων. Locative.

ζωῆς. Attributive genitive. ζωῆς could modify πηγὰς ("living springs of water"). But it could also modify ὑδάτων ("springs of living water"). The latter is suggested by the other references to "water of life" in Revelation where the genitive ζωῆς modifies "water" (21:6, 22:1; 22:17). The fronting of the genitive before its head term emphasizes the quality of life.

ὑδάτων. Genitive of content ("springs which contain water") or epexegetical genitive.

ἐξαλείψει. Fut act ind 3rd sg ἐξαλείφω.

ὁ θεός. Nominative subject of ἐξαλείψει. Introduces a switch in subject from ἀρνίον.

πᾶν δάκρυον. Accusative direct object of ἐξαλείψει.

ἐκ τῶν ὀφθαλμῶν. Separation.

αὐτῶν. Possessive genitive.

Revelation 8:1-5

¹And when he opened the seventh seal, there was silence in heaven for something like one half hour. ²And I saw the seven angels who stand before God, and seven trumpets were given to them. ³And another angel came and stood at the altar having a gold censer, and much incense was given to him in order that he might offer it with the prayers of all the saints upon the golden altar that is before the throne. ⁴And the smoke of the incense with the prayers of the saints went up from the hand of the angel before God. ⁵And the angel took the censer and filled it with the fire from the altar and threw it upon the earth, and there was thunder and sounds and lightening and an earthquake.

8:1 Καὶ ὅταν ἤνοιξεν τὴν σφραγῖδα τὴν ἑβδόμην, ἐγένετο σιγὴ ἐν τῷ οὐρανῷ ὡς ἡμίωρον.

ὅταν. Introduces a temporal clause. While ὅταν usually introduces an indefinite temporal clause and is followed by a verb in the subjunctive mood or future tense ("whenever"), here it refers to a specific event, the opening of the seventh seal ("when he opened the seventh seal"), and is followed by an indicative verb. Robertson says that "the κοινή writers used ὅταν with the aorist indicative for a definite occurrence" (973). Caragounis (117) notes that this is due to the indicative beginning to compete with the subjunctive. Some manuscripts (ℵ 𝔐) read ὅτε. This was probably to conform to the preceding six seals, which were introduced by ὅτε in 6:1, 3, 5, 7, 9, 12, and perhaps also to conform to the indicative mood of ἤνοιξεν. The NA[28]/UBS[5] (though UBS[5] does not note a variant here) reading is supported by A C 1006 1611 1841.

ἤνοιξεν. Aor act ind 3rd sg ἀνοίγω.

τὴν σφραγῖδα τὴν ἑβδόμην. Accusative direct object of ἤνοιξεν. The opening of the seventh seal picks up the sequence from ch. 6, which was "interrupted" by the two visions in ch. 7.

ἐγένετο. Aor mid ind 3rd sg γίνομαι.

σιγὴ. Nominative subject of ἐγένετο.

ἐν τῷ οὐρανῷ. Locative.

ὡς ἡμίωρον. Here ὡς functions as a marker of approximation (LN 78.42). Rhetorically, the half hour of silence slows the action down and draws attention to significant events (judgments) that are about to take place. The silence may also be so the prayers of the saints in verses 3-4 can be heard (Bauckham, 70–83).

8:2 Καὶ εἶδον τοὺς ἑπτὰ ἀγγέλους οἳ ἐνώπιον τοῦ θεοῦ ἑστήκασιν, καὶ ἐδόθησαν αὐτοῖς ἑπτὰ σάλπιγγες.

εἶδον. Aor act ind 1st sg ὁράω.

τοὺς ἑπτὰ ἀγγέλους. Accusative direct object of εἶδον.

οἵ. Nominative subject of ἑστήκασιν.

ἐνώπιον τοῦ θεοῦ. Locative.

ἑστήκασιν. Prf act ind 3rd pl ἵστημι. The perfect tense may function to highlight the angels' posture in preparation for enacting the trumpet plagues. As Aune (2.483) notes, this is the only example in Revelation of a prf 3rd pl that retains the older -ασι(ν) ending (-καν/αν is used elsewhere in Revelation).

ἐδόθησαν. Aor pass ind 3rd pl δίδωμι.

αὐτοῖς. Dative indirect object of ἐδόθησαν.

ἑπτὰ σάλπιγγες. Nominative subject of ἐδόθησαν. It is possible that the trumpets have their background in ancient warfare where the trumpet was used to deploy troops and cavalry in attacking enemy forces (Aune, 2.497). Trumpets were also "an instrument announcing eschatological judgment" in Jewish apocalyptic literature (Osborne, 343; Charles, 1.225).

8:3 Καὶ ἄλλος ἄγγελος ἦλθεν καὶ ἐστάθη ἐπὶ τοῦ θυσιαστηρίου ἔχων λιβανωτὸν χρυσοῦν, καὶ ἐδόθη αὐτῷ θυμιάματα πολλά, ἵνα δώσει ταῖς προσευχαῖς τῶν ἁγίων πάντων ἐπὶ τὸ θυσιαστήριον τὸ χρυσοῦν τὸ ἐνώπιον τοῦ θρόνου.

ἄλλος ἄγγελος. Nominative subject of ἦλθεν and ἐστάθη.

ἦλθεν. Aor act ind 3rd sg ἔρχομαι.

ἐστάθη. Aor mid ind 3rd sg ἵστημι. On the voice, see "Deponency" in the Series Introduction.

ἐπὶ τοῦ θυσιαστηρίου. Locative. Though some have taken the preposition here to mean that the angel stood "over" the altar (Mounce, 181 n. 15), ἐπί can be used as a "marker of presence or occurrence near an object or area" and thus be translated "at" (BDAG, 363.2.a; see Wallace, 376; so NIV, NASB, NRSV).

ἔχων. Pres act ptc masc nom sg ἔχω (manner). Modifies ἦλθεν καὶ ἐστάθη.

λιβανωτὸν χρυσοῦν. Accusative direct object of ἔχων. While λιβανωτόν is used in the LXX (1 Chron 9:29; 3 Macc 5:2) to refer to incense (its cognate λίβανος refers to "frankincense" in Rev 18:13), here it refers to the censer where the incense is burned (BDAG, 594.2; LN 6.138), as is made clear by its modification by χρυσοῦν (Swete, 108; Smalley, 215).

ἐδόθη. Aor pass ind 3rd sg δίδωμι.

αὐτῷ. Dative indirect object of ἐδόθη.

θυμιάματα πολλά. Nominative subject of ἐδόθη.

ἵνα. Introduces a purpose clause.

δώσει. Fut act ind 3rd sg δίδωμι. On the future in place of the subjunctive after ἵνα, see 3:9 on ἥξουσιν. The object θυμιάματα seems to be implied.

ταῖς προσευχαῖς. The dative has been understood in at least three ways: (1) a dative of respect or association: the prayers go up to heaven in relation to or along with the incense (Robertson, 529; Wallace, 160); (2) a dative of advantage: the incense is offered for the benefit of or on behalf of the prayers (Charles, 1.231; Osborne, 345; BDF §188; Mussies, 99; cf. Zerwick §55); (3) a temporal dative: the incense is offered simultaneously with the prayers, though this use of the dative usually occurs with words specifying a temporal notion (Moule, 43–44; followed by Smalley, 216). Though the latter two notions may indeed be present contextually or theologically, at a grammatical level the first option (association or respect) appears to be the most likely, since the context is not clear as to the specific relationship between the incense and the prayers. The incense goes up in assocation with the prayers of the saints.

τῶν ἁγίων πάντων. Subjective genitive.
ἐπὶ τὸ θυσιαστήριον τὸ χρυσοῦν. Locative.
τὸ ἐνώπιον τοῦ θρόνου. The article functions as an adjectivizer, which turns the entire PP into an attributive modifier of θυσιαστήριον: Lit. "the before-the-throne altar."
ἐνώπιον τοῦ θρόνου. Locative.

8:4 καὶ ἀνέβη ὁ καπνὸς τῶν θυμιαμάτων ταῖς προσευχαῖς τῶν ἁγίων ἐκ χειρὸς τοῦ ἀγγέλου ἐνώπιον τοῦ θεοῦ.

ἀνέβη. Aor act ind 3rd sg ἀναβαίνω.
ὁ καπνὸς. Nominative subject of ἀνέβη.
τῶν θυμιαμάτων. Genitive of source.
ταῖς προσευχαῖς. On the function of the dative, see verse 3 on ταῖς προσευχαῖς.
τῶν ἁγίων. Subjective genitive.
ἐκ χειρὸς. Source.
τοῦ ἀγγέλου. Possessive genitive.
ἐνώπιον τοῦ θεοῦ. Locative.

8:5 καὶ εἴληφεν ὁ ἄγγελος τὸν λιβανωτὸν καὶ ἐγέμισεν αὐτὸν ἐκ τοῦ πυρὸς τοῦ θυσιαστηρίου καὶ ἔβαλεν εἰς τὴν γῆν, καὶ ἐγένοντο βρονταὶ καὶ φωναὶ καὶ ἀστραπαὶ καὶ σεισμός.

εἴληφεν. Prf act ind 3rd sg λαμβάνω. On the significance of the perfect here, see 5:7. In light of the fact that λαμβάνω occurs in the present, aorist (see ἔβαλεν below), and perfect tenses in Revelation, Osborne and others are incorrect in assuming that this is simply a perfect used in place of an aorist (Osborne, 346 n. 13; Fanning, 302–3; Smalley, 217; Caragounis, 154; BDF §343; Wallace, 579). The perfect tense emphasizes the state of the angel in preparation for pouring out the bowl judgments.
ὁ ἄγγελος. Nominative subject of εἴληφεν.
τὸν λιβανωτὸν. Accusative direct object of εἴληφεν. On the meaning, see verse 3.
ἐγέμισεν. Aor act ind 3rd sg γεμίζω.
αὐτὸν. Accusative direct object of ἐγέμισεν.
ἐκ τοῦ πυρὸς. Source.

τοῦ θυσιαστηρίου. Genitive of source or possibly genitive expressing location.

ἔβαλεν. Aor act ind 3rd sg βάλλω. The assumed object of ἔβαλεν is αὐτόν.

εἰς τὴν γῆν. Locative.

ἐγένοντο. Aor mid ind 3rd pl γίνομαι.

βρονταὶ καὶ φωναὶ καὶ ἀστραπαὶ καὶ σεισμός. Nominative subject of ἐγένοντο. Swete (109) is correct that this specifies the *results* of the casting of the fire to earth. This is true at a semantic level, while at a grammatical level the καί before ἐγένοντο simply expresses continuity.

Revelation 8:6-13

⁶And the seven angels who have the seven trumpets prepared themselves in order to sound (them). ⁷And the first (angel) sounded (his) trumpet. And there was hail and fire mixed with blood and it was thrown to the earth, and a third of the earth was burned up and a third of the trees were burned up, and all the green grass was burned up. ⁸And the second angel sounded (his) trumpet. And (something) like a great mountain burning with fire was thrown into the sea, and a third of the sea became blood, ⁹and a third of the living creatures which are in the sea, those that have life, died, and a third of the ships were destroyed. ¹⁰And the third angel sounded (his) trumpet. And a great star burning like a lamp fell from heaven, and it fell upon a third of the rivers and upon the springs of water, ¹¹and the name of the star is called "Wormwood," and a third of the waters became bitter and many people died from the water, because it was made bitter. ¹²And the fourth angel sounded (his) trumpet. And a third of the sun and a third of the moon and a third of the stars were struck, so that a third of them were darkened, and the third of the day did not shine, and the night likewise. ¹³And I saw, and I heard an eagle flying in midheaven, saying with a loud voice, "Woe, Woe, Woe to those who dwell upon the earth because of the remaining blasts of the trumpets of the three angels who are about to sound (them)."

8:6 Καὶ οἱ ἑπτὰ ἄγγελοι οἱ ἔχοντες τὰς ἑπτὰ σάλπιγγας ἡτοίμασαν αὐτοὺς ἵνα σαλπίσωσιν.

οἱ ἑπτὰ ἄγγελοι. Nominative subject of ἡτοίμασαν.

οἱ ἔχοντες. Pres act ptc masc nom pl ἔχω (attributive). Osborne reads too much into the present tense by saying that it "pictures the angels' constant readiness to blow the trumpets" (347 n. 17). The present tense simply looks at the action as in progress without any indication of its duration (see "Verbal Aspect" in the Introduction).

τὰς ἑπτὰ σάλπιγγας. Accusative direct object of ἔχοντες.
ἡτοίμασαν. Aor act ind 3rd pl ἑτοιμάζω.
αὐτούς. Accusative direct object of ἡτοίμασαν. The personal pronoun here functions reflexively. "It is common in Hellenistic Greek for personal pronouns to function as reflexives" (Young, 75). Many manuscripts (ℵ² P 046 1006 1611 1841 1854 2053 2329 𝔐) have the explicitly reflexive form ἑαυτούς.
ἵνα. Introduces a purpose clause.
σαλπίσωσιν. Aor act subj 3rd pl σαλπίζω. Subjunctive with ἵνα.

8:7 Καὶ ὁ πρῶτος ἐσάλπισεν· καὶ ἐγένετο χάλαζα καὶ πῦρ μεμιγμένα ἐν αἵματι καὶ ἐβλήθη εἰς τὴν γῆν, καὶ τὸ τρίτον τῆς γῆς κατεκάη καὶ τὸ τρίτον τῶν δένδρων κατεκάη καὶ πᾶς χόρτος χλωρὸς κατεκάη.

ὁ πρῶτος. Nominative subject of ἐσάλπισεν. Some manuscripts (2329 𝔐^A) add ἄγγελος, which is implied from verse 6 (it is less likely that a scribe would omit ἄγγελος), and perhaps to conform to verses 8, 10, 12; 9:1, 13, all of which include ἄγγελος following the ordinal (though ℵ 2053 omit ἄγγελος in v. 8).
ἐσάλπισεν. Aor act ind 3rd sg σαλπίζω.
ἐγένετο. Aor mid ind 3rd sg γίνομαι. Though the subject of ἐγένετο is plural (χάλαζα καὶ πῦρ) the verb has a singular ending. As Porter notes, "A frequent pattern is to find a singular element closest to a singular verb" (1992, 75). In this type of construction, "The verb, if it stands first, usually agrees with the first subject" (Turner, 313; Charles, 1.cxli; see also 8:7; 9:2, 17; 11:19; 12:10; 18:20; 19:20; 20:11). However, it may be the case that χάλαζα (feminine) and πῦρ (neuter) together are treated as neuter plural (see μεμιγμένα, which modifies them) with a common pattern being that neuter plural subjects take a singular verb (see ἐβλήθη below).
χάλαζα καὶ πῦρ. Nominative subject of ἐγένετο. On the lack of concord in number, see ἐγένετο above.
μεμιγμένα. Prf pass ptc neut nom pl μίγνυμι (attributive). The neuter plural of the participle can be accounted for by the fact that it modifies both the feminine χάλαζα and the neuter πῦρ.
ἐν αἵματι. Accompaniment (see Porter 1992, 158).
ἐβλήθη. Aor pass ind 3rd sg βάλλω. The singular verb with a plural subject is probably due to the fact that χάλαζα καὶ πῦρ are treated as neuter plural (see μεμιγμένα) with a common pattern being that neuter plural subjects take a singular verb. Or the author may have considered χάλαζα καὶ πῦρ a single entity.
εἰς τὴν γῆν. Locative.

καὶ. Aune (2.484) says that the conjunction here indicates result (a καί *consecutivum*). While this is true semantically, at a grammatical level the καί simply continues the visionary sequence.

τὸ τρίτον. Nominative subject of κατεκάη. This fraction throughout this section highlights the partial nature of the judgments; they are not final (Swete, 111).

τῆς γῆς. Partitive genitive.

κατεκάη . . . κατεκάη . . . κατεκάη. Aor mid ind 3rd sg κατακαίω.

τὸ τρίτον. Nominative subject of κατεκάη.

τῶν δένδρων. Partitive genitive.

πᾶς χόρτος χλωρὸς. Nominative subject of κατεκάη.

8:8 Καὶ ὁ δεύτερος ἄγγελος ἐσάλπισεν· καὶ ὡς ὄρος μέγα πυρὶ καιόμενον ἐβλήθη εἰς τὴν θάλασσαν, καὶ ἐγένετο τὸ τρίτον τῆς θαλάσσης αἷμα

ὁ δεύτερος ἄγγελος. Nominative subject of ἐσάλπισεν.

ἐσάλπισεν. Aor act ind 3rd sg σαλπίζω.

ὡς ὄρος μέγα. Comparison. The entire clause functions as the subject of ἐβλήθη, with the actual subject of ἐβλήθη being implicit: "(something) like a great mountain."

πυρὶ. Dative of means or manner.

καιόμενον. Pres mid ptc neut nom sg καίω (attributive).

ἐβλήθη. Aor pass ind 3rd sg βάλλω.

εἰς τὴν θάλασσαν. Locative.

ἐγένετο. Aor mid ind 3rd sg γίνομαι.

τὸ τρίτον. Nominative subject of ἐγένετο.

τῆς θαλάσσης. Partitive genitive.

αἷμα. Predicate nominative of ἐγένετο.

8:9 καὶ ἀπέθανεν τὸ τρίτον τῶν κτισμάτων τῶν ἐν τῇ θαλάσσῃ τὰ ἔχοντα ψυχὰς καὶ τὸ τρίτον τῶν πλοίων διεφθάρησαν.

ἀπέθανεν. Aor act ind 3rd sg ἀποθνῄσκω.

τὸ τρίτον. Nominative subject of ἀπέθανεν.

τῶν κτισμάτων. Partitive genitive.

τῶν ἐν τῇ θαλάσσῃ. The article functions as an adjectivizer, turning the entire PP into an attributive modifier of τῶν κτισμάτων. Lit. "the in-the-sea creatures."

ἐν τῇ θαλάσσῃ. Locative.

τὰ ἔχοντα. Pres act ptc neut nom pl ἔχω (substantival). Stands in apposition to τὸ τρίτον.

ψυχὰς. Accusative direct object of ἔχοντα. On the meaning, see 6:9.

τὸ τρίτον. Nominative subject of διεφθάρησαν.
τῶν πλοίων. Partitive genitive.
διεφθάρησαν. Aor pass ind 3rd pl διαφθείρω. The plural number comes from the genitive τῶν πλοίων rather than the singular subject (Aune, 2.484). Conceptually, a third of all the boats would be plural in number.

8:10 Καὶ ὁ τρίτος ἄγγελος ἐσάλπισεν· καὶ ἔπεσεν ἐκ τοῦ οὐρανοῦ ἀστὴρ μέγας καιόμενος ὡς λαμπὰς καὶ ἔπεσεν ἐπὶ τὸ τρίτον τῶν ποταμῶν καὶ ἐπὶ τὰς πηγὰς τῶν ὑδάτων,

ὁ τρίτος ἄγγελος. Nominative subject of ἐσάλπισεν.
ἐσάλπισεν. Aor act ind 3rd sg σαλπίζω.
ἔπεσεν. Aor act ind 3rd sg πίπτω.
ἐκ τοῦ οὐρανοῦ. Source.
ἀστὴρ μέγας. Nominative subject of ἔπεσεν.
καιόμενος. Pres mid ptc masc nom sg καίω (attributive).
ὡς λαμπὰς. Comparative expressing manner.
ἔπεσεν. Aor act ind 3rd sg πίπτω.
ἐπὶ τὸ τρίτον. Locative.
τῶν ποταμῶν. Partitive genitive.
ἐπὶ τὰς πηγὰς. Locative.
τῶν ὑδάτων. Genitive of content. See also 7:17.

8:11 καὶ τὸ ὄνομα τοῦ ἀστέρος λέγεται ὁ Ἄψινθος, καὶ ἐγένετο τὸ τρίτον τῶν ὑδάτων εἰς ἄψινθον καὶ πολλοὶ τῶν ἀνθρώπων ἀπέθανον ἐκ τῶν ὑδάτων ὅτι ἐπικράνθησαν.

τὸ ὄνομα. Nominative subject of λέγεται.
τοῦ ἀστέρος. Possessive genitive.
λέγεται. Pres pass ind 3rd sg λέγω. Here the present tense is used in an omnitemporal context in a gnomic type statement.
ὁ Ἄψινθος. Though this could be seen as an example of a nominative used of a name or an independent nominative (BDF §144), it is better to see the case here as part of a double nominative construction with a passive verb, derived from the active clause "I call the star wormwood" (see Culy 2009, 83–87). In the passive construction, one noun becomes the nominative subject, and the other becomes the nominative complement. "'Wormwood' is a bitter herb, and water contaminated by it can be poisonous if drunk over a long period" (Beale, 479). The term "wormwood" is derived from the use of the herb medicinally to kill intestinal worms (LN 3.21).
ἐγένετο. Aor mid ind 3rd sg γίνομαι.

τὸ τρίτον. Nominative subject of ἐγένετο.
τῶν ὑδάτων. Partitive genitive.
εἰς ἄψινθον. This construction is sometimes used as a substitute for, or to fill the slot of, the predicate modifier of εἰμί or γίνομαι (less frequently with λογίζομαι) (Wallace, 47; Robertson, 458). Although this construction in the NT is often attributed to Semitic influence, there are examples in non-biblical Greek (see Moulton, 71–72). Some manuscripts (see Aune, 2.484) have ὡς instead of εἰς. Even if not original this brings out the apparent sense of the vision, since the sea is not turned into wormwood but becomes bitter *like* it. This is consistent with ἐκ τῶν ὑδάτων ὅτι ἐπικράνθησαν where the waters are turned bitter.
πολλοί. Nominative subject of ἀπέθανον.
τῶν ἀνθρώπων. Partitive genitive.
ἀπέθανον. Aor act ind 3rd pl ἀποθνῄσκω.
ἐκ τῶν ὑδάτων. Cause.
ὅτι. Introduces a causal clause, introducing not just the reason they died, but why they died because of the water.
ἐπικράνθησαν. Aor pass ind 3rd pl πικραίνω. The implied subject is the "waters" from the preceding PP (ἐκ τῶν ὑδάτων).

8:12 Καὶ ὁ τέταρτος ἄγγελος ἐσάλπισεν· καὶ ἐπλήγη τὸ τρίτον τοῦ ἡλίου καὶ τὸ τρίτον τῆς σελήνης καὶ τὸ τρίτον τῶν ἀστέρων, ἵνα σκοτισθῇ τὸ τρίτον αὐτῶν καὶ ἡ ἡμέρα μὴ φάνῃ τὸ τρίτον αὐτῆς καὶ ἡ νὺξ ὁμοίως.

ὁ τέταρτος ἄγγελος. Nominative subject of ἐσάλπισεν.
ἐσάλπισεν. Aor act ind 3rd sg σαλπίζω.
ἐπλήγη. Aor pass ind 3rd sg πλήσσω.
τὸ τρίτον ... καὶ τὸ τρίτον ... καὶ τὸ τρίτον. Nominative subject of ἐπλήγη. There is incongruity between the singular verb and the plural (compound) subject. Most likely the neuter gender of τρίτον can account for this, since it is a common pattern for neuter plural subjects (the threefold τρίτον) to take a singular verb.
τοῦ ἡλίου ... τῆς σελήνης ... τῶν ἀστέρων. Partitive genitive.
ἵνα. Introduces a result clause.
σκοτισθῇ. Aor pass subj 3rd sg σκοτίζω. Subjunctive with ἵνα.
τὸ τρίτον. Nominative subject of σκοτισθῇ.
αὐτῶν. Partitive genitive.
ἡ ἡμέρα. Nominative subject of φάνῃ.
φάνῃ. Aor act subj 3rd sg φαίνω. Subjunctive with ἵνα.
τὸ τρίτον. Like the other examples of τὸ τρίτον followed by a partitive genitive above, τὸ τρίτον should be taken as a substantive (BDAG,

1016.2) and is probably a nominative in apposition to ἡ ἡμέρα rather than an accusative of time (contra Osborne, 356 n. 16).

αὐτῆς. Partitive genitive.

ἡ νύξ. Nominative subject of implied φάνῃ.

ὁμοίως. Comparision: "pert. to being similar in some respect" (BDAG, 707).

8:13 Καὶ εἶδον, καὶ ἤκουσα ἑνὸς ἀετοῦ πετομένου ἐν μεσουρανήματι λέγοντος φωνῇ μεγάλῃ· οὐαὶ οὐαὶ οὐαὶ τοὺς κατοικοῦντας ἐπὶ τῆς γῆς ἐκ τῶν λοιπῶν φωνῶν τῆς σάλπιγγος τῶν τριῶν ἀγγέλων τῶν μελλόντων σαλπίζειν.

This verse can be seen as an introduction to ch. 9, which begins to narrate the three woes announced in this verse.

εἶδον. Aor act ind 1st sg ὁράω.

ἤκουσα. Aor act ind 1st sg ἀκούω.

ἑνὸς ἀετοῦ. Genitive direct object of ἤκουσα. Though it is possible that John hears the eagle flying in the heavens, the reference to what John heard (ἤκουσα) introduces what the eagle says (λέγοντος). Osborne (359 n. 1) understands this as the use of ἑνός (from εἷς) as an indefinitive article (see also Smalley, 224–25; Aune, 2.485). The difficulty with this is that Greek does not have an indefinite article, though it has various ways of expressing indefiniteness. Though "an" might be an appropriate *translation*, this is more of a matter of English translation than Greek grammar. More likely is Caragounis who notes that in the "NT the cardinal numbers, εἷς, μία, ἕν, are losing their numerical value and are being reduced to an indefinite pronoun" (113), though Revelation's use of εἷς, μία, ἕν still retains its numerical value, especially when εἷς is followed by a partitive construction. See e.g., 6:1.

πετομένου. Pres mid ptc masc gen sg πέτομαι (attributive).

ἐν μεσουρανήματι. Locative. "[A] point or region in the sky directly above the earth" (LN 1.10).

λέγοντος. Pres act ptc masc gen sg λέγω. Complement in an object-complement double genitive construction with ἀετοῦ. On the use of the participle λέγοντος to introduce speech, see 1:17 on λέγων.

φωνῇ μεγάλῃ. Dative of instrument or dative of manner.

οὐαὶ οὐαὶ οὐαὶ. An interjection that denotes "a state of intense hardship or distress" (LN 22.9). Here the hardship or distress is caused by the plagues associated with the last three trumpet judgements. The threefold repetition is emphatic.

τοὺς κατοικοῦντας. Pres act ptc masc acc pl κατοικέω (substantival). Accusative of person with οὐαί (BDAG, 734.1.c). Robertson (487) labels it an adverbial accusative. The interjection οὐαί is usually found in the NT with the dative case (Robertson, 1193), and here A 1006 1841 2329 𝔐^A read the dative τοῖς κατοικοῦσιν. The accusative with οὐαί also occurs in 12:12.

ἐπὶ τῆς γῆς. Locative.

ἐκ τῶν λοιπῶν φωνῶν. Introduces the cause of the threefold οὐαί.

τῆς σάλπιγγος. Genitive of source or subjective genitive.

τῶν τριῶν ἀγγέλων. Possessive genitive.

τῶν μελλόντων. Pres act ptc masc gen pl μέλλω (attributive).

σαλπίζειν. Pres act inf σαλπίζω (complementary).

Revelation 9:1-12

¹And the fifth angel sounded (his) trumpet, and I saw a star falling from heaven onto the earth, and the key to the pit of the abyss was given to it. ²And (the star) opened the pit of the abyss, and smoke came up out of the pit as smoke from a great furnace and the sun and the sky were darkened from the smoke from the pit. ³And locusts came out of the smoke upon the earth, and authority was given to them as scorpions have authority over the earth. ⁴And they were told not to harm the grass of the earth nor any green plant nor any tree, except the people who do not have the seal of God upon their foreheads. ⁵And (the authority) to kill people was not given to them, but only to torment them for five months; and their torment was like the torment of a scorpion, whenever they strike a person. ⁶And in those days people will seek death and they will not find it, and they will desire to die and death will flee from them. ⁷And the likeness of the locusts was as horses prepared for battle, and upon their heads was something as crowns like gold, and their faces were as human faces, ⁸and they had hair as the hair of women, and their teeth were like the teeth of lions. ⁹And they had breastplates as breastplates of iron, and the sound of their wings was like the sound of the chariots of many horses rushing into battle. ¹⁰And they had tails like scorpions, and stingers, and in their tails (they had) the authority to harm people for five months. ¹¹They had a king over them, the angel of the abyss; his name in Hebrew is Abaddon, and in Greek he has the name, Apollyon. ¹²The first woe has passed. Look, there are still two woes after these things.

9:1 Καὶ ὁ πέμπτος ἄγγελος ἐσάλπισεν· καὶ εἶδον ἀστέρα ἐκ τοῦ οὐρανοῦ πεπτωκότα εἰς τὴν γῆν, καὶ ἐδόθη αὐτῷ ἡ κλεὶς τοῦ φρέατος τῆς ἀβύσσου

In this section the fifth and sixth trumpet sounds receive the greatest elaboration (vv. 1-11) and therefore are prominent in the trumpet sequence. The fifth and sixth trumpets are also to be identified as the first two woes of the three woes anticipated in 8:13 (cf. 9:12).

ὁ πέμπτος ἄγγελος. Nominative subject of ἐσάλπισεν.
ἐσάλπισεν. Aor act ind 3rd sg σαλπίζω.
εἶδον. Aor act ind 1st sg ὁράω.
ἀστέρα. Accusative direct object of εἶδον.
ἐκ τοῦ οὐρανοῦ. Source. The PP modifies πεπτωκότα.
πεπτωκότα. Prf act ptc masc acc sg πίπτω. The participle may be attributive, but more likely should be taken as the complement in an object-complement double accusative construction with ἀστέρα. Based on the usage of the perfect tense, Aune concludes that John "says only that he saw the star *after* it had fallen" (525; see also Smalley, 225: "John does not see a star actually falling from heaven, but witnesses the effects of its ascent."). However, this conception depends too much on an understanding of the perfect that assumes "present results based on a prior action" (see "Verbal Aspect" in the Introduction). Rather, what John apparently sees is the star in the state of falling (Mathewson 2010, 134). The perfect participle seems to draw attention to the state of the star (falling) in preparation for the act that is to follow: the loosing of the locusts.

εἰς τὴν γῆν. Locative.
ἐδόθη. Aor pass ind 3rd sg δίδωμι. The passive of δίδωμι, which is used throughout this section, suggests that the characters act only with permission.
αὐτῷ. Dative indirect object of ἐδόθη. The antecedent is ἀστέρα.
ἡ κλεὶς. Nominative subject of ἐδόθη.
τοῦ φρέατος. The idea of the genitive here is the key that opens the pit ("the key to the pit").
τῆς ἀβύσσου. Epexegetical genitive. An ἀβύσσος is literally "a pit, or deep hole," but as BDAG indicates the term often indicates "a transcendent place associated with the dead and hostile powers" (2.2). In Revelation the ἀβύσσος is the source of demonic powers (see also 9:2; 11:7; 20:1, 3).

9:2 καὶ ἤνοιξεν τὸ φρέαρ τῆς ἀβύσσου, καὶ ἀνέβη καπνὸς ἐκ τοῦ φρέατος ὡς καπνὸς καμίνου μεγάλης, καὶ ἐσκοτώθη ὁ ἥλιος καὶ ὁ ἀὴρ ἐκ τοῦ καπνοῦ τοῦ φρέατος.

ἤνοιξεν. Aor act ind 3rd sg ἀνοίγω.
τὸ φρέαρ. Accusative direct object of ἤνοιξεν.
τῆς ἀβύσσου. Epexegetical genitive. See also verse 1 on τῆς ἀβύσσου.
ἀνέβη. Aor act ind 3rd sg ἀναβαίνω.
καπνὸς. Nominative subject of ἀνέβη.

ἐκ τοῦ φρέατος. Source.
ὡς καπνὸς. Comparison.
καπνὸς. Nominative subject of an implied form of ἀναβαίνω.
καμίνου μεγάλης. Genitive of source.
ἐσκοτώθη. Aor pass ind 3rd sg σκοτόω. There is an incongruity in number between the singular verb ἐσκοτώθη and plural subject ὁ ἥλιος καὶ ὁ ἀήρ. As Turner notes, "The verb, if it stands first, usually agrees with the first subject" (313; Charles, 1.cxli). This could also be because the author treats ὁ ἥλιος καὶ ὁ ἀήρ as a single entity (see McKay 1994, 18).
ὁ ἥλιος καὶ ὁ ἀήρ. Nominative subject of ἐσκοτώθη.
ἐκ τοῦ καπνοῦ. Cause.
τοῦ φρέατος. Genitive of source.

9:3 καὶ ἐκ τοῦ καπνοῦ ἐξῆλθον ἀκρίδες εἰς τὴν γῆν, καὶ ἐδόθη αὐταῖς ἐξουσία ὡς ἔχουσιν ἐξουσίαν οἱ σκορπίοι τῆς γῆς.

ἐκ τοῦ καπνοῦ. Source.
ἐξῆλθον. Aor act ind 3rd pl ἐξέρχομαι.
ἀκρίδες. Nominative subject of ἐξῆλθον.
εἰς τὴν γῆν. Locative.
ἐδόθη. Aor pass ind 3rd sg δίδωμι.
αὐταῖς. Dative indirect object of ἐδόθη.
ἐξουσία. Nominative subject of ἐδόθη.
ὡς. Comparison or manner.
ἔχουσιν. Pres act ind 3rd pl ἔχω.
ἐξουσίαν. Accusative direct object of ἔχουσιν.
οἱ σκορπίοι. Nominative subject of ἔχουσιν.
τῆς γῆς. Genitive of source ("from the earth") or location ("upon the earth").

9:4 καὶ ἐρρέθη αὐταῖς ἵνα μὴ ἀδικήσουσιν τὸν χόρτον τῆς γῆς οὐδὲ πᾶν χλωρὸν οὐδὲ πᾶν δένδρον, εἰ μὴ τοὺς ἀνθρώπους οἵτινες οὐκ ἔχουσι τὴν σφραγῖδα τοῦ θεοῦ ἐπὶ τῶν μετώπων.

καὶ. Aune interprets the καί as adversative and suggests that it should be translated "but" (2.485; also Smalley, 228). While this may be true at the level of translation due to the relationship between verses 3 and 4, grammatically the καί simply indicates continuity.
ἐρρέθη. Aor pass ind 3rd sg εἶπον.
αὐταῖς. Dative indirect object of ἐρρέθη.
ἵνα. Introduces a content clause that functions as the subject of ἐρρέθη. Here the clause introduced by ἵνα followed by μή functions as a

prohibition. A ἵνα clause often functions as a command or prohibition when following a verb of perception (Porter 1992, 223).

ἀδικήσουσιν. Fut act ind 3rd pl ἀδικέω. On the use of the future in place of the subjunctive with ἵνα, see 3:9 on ἥξουσιν. ℵ 0207 𝔐 predictably have the aorist subjunctive ἀδικήσωσιν.

τὸν χόρτον ... οὐδὲ πᾶν χλωρὸν οὐδὲ πᾶν δένδρον. Accusative direct object of ἀδικήσουσιν.

τῆς γῆς. Genitive of possession or genitive of location.

μὴ ... οὐδὲ πᾶν ... οὐδὲ πᾶν. "Not ... nor any ... nor any."

εἰ μή. According to Louw and Nida this expression can be understood as "a marker of contrast by designating an exception" and can be translated "except that, but, however, instead, but only" (89.131).

τοὺς ἀνθρώπους. Accusative direct object of an implied ἀδικήσουσιν.

οἵτινες. Nominative subject of ἔχουσι.

ἔχουσι. Pres act ind 3rd pl ἔχω.

τὴν σφραγῖδα. Accusative direct object of ἔχουσι.

τοῦ θεοῦ. Possessive genitive or subjective genitive.

ἐπὶ τῶν μετώπων. Locative.

9:5 καὶ ἐδόθη αὐτοῖς ἵνα μὴ ἀποκτείνωσιν αὐτούς, ἀλλ' ἵνα βασανισθήσονται μῆνας πέντε, καὶ ὁ βασανισμὸς αὐτῶν ὡς βασανισμὸς σκορπίου ὅταν παίσῃ ἄνθρωπον.

ἐδόθη. Aor pass ind 3rd sg δίδωμι.

αὐτοῖς. Dative indirect object of ἐδόθη. The antecedent is ἀκρίδες from verse 3. The mismatch in gender (masculine αὐτοῖς and feminine ἀκρίδες) is probably due to the fact that the feminine locusts would have symbolized male persons (in v. 7 they are identified as warriors) (Mussies, 138).

ἵνα. Introduces a content clause that functions as the subject of ἐδόθη. The clause may function as an indirect prohibition.

ἀποκτείνωσιν. Pres act subj 3rd pl ἀποκτείνω. Subjunctive with ἵνα.

αὐτούς. Accusative direct object of ἀποκτείνωσιν. The antecedent is τοὺς ἀνθρώπους in verse 4.

ἀλλ'. Introduces a contrast between the two ἵνα clauses.

ἵνα. Introduces a content clause that functions as the subject of ἐδόθη. According to McKay (1994, 116) it functions as an indirect command.

βασανισθήσονται. Fut pass ind 3rd pl βασανίζω. On the future in place of the subjunctive, see 3:9 on ἥξουσιν. Here the future is used to emphasize what the locusts/scorpions are permitted to do, whereas the subjunctive (ἀποκτείνωσιν) is used of what they may not do. The assumed subject of βασανισθήσονται is those whom the locusts are not permitted to kill (αὐτούς; or ἀνθρώπους of v. 4). Predictably, a number of manuscripts read the aorist subjunctive βασανισθῶσιν (𝔓¹¹⁵ᵛⁱᵈ 1006 1611 1841 2351 𝔐ᴷ).

μῆνας πέντε. Accusative indicating extent of time.
ὁ βασανισμὸς. Nominative subject of a verbless clause.
αὐτῶν. Subjective genitive. The antecedent is the locusts (v. 3).
ὡς βασανισμὸς. Comparison. Functions as the predicate of a verbless clause.
σκορπίου. Subjective genitive.
ὅταν. Introduces a temporal clause. Though elsewhere in the Apocalypse ὅταν with the aorist subjunctive refers to a specific event (see on 4:9), here it appears to refer generally to any time that a scorpion stings a human being, in the context of a comparison (ὡς), and thus can be rendered "whenever." Turner (113) argues that it refers to action that is indefinite or iterative.
παίσῃ. Aor act subj 3rd sg παίω. Subjunctive with ὅταν.
ἄνθρωπον. Accusative direct object of παίσῃ.

9:6 καὶ ἐν ταῖς ἡμέραις ἐκείναις ζητήσουσιν οἱ ἄνθρωποι τὸν θάνατον καὶ οὐ μὴ εὑρήσουσιν αὐτόν, καὶ ἐπιθυμήσουσιν ἀποθανεῖν καὶ φεύγει ὁ θάνατος ἀπ' αὐτῶν.

ἐν ταῖς ἡμέραις ἐκείναις. Temporal. The antecedent of ταῖς ἡμέραις ἐκείναις is probably the events in 9:5. The demonstrative ἐκεῖνος occurs only here and in 11:13 in Revelation.
ζητήσουσιν. Fut act ind 3rd pl ζητέω.
οἱ ἄνθρωποι. Nominative subject of ζητήσουσιν.
τὸν θάνατον. Accusative direct object of ζητήσουσιν.
εὑρήσουσιν. Fut act ind 3rd pl εὑρίσκω. οὐ μή with the future tense is a strong way of denying that something will happen. On the use of the future in place of the subjunctive, see 3:9 on ἥξουσιν.
αὐτόν. Accusative direct object of εὑρήσουσιν.
ἐπιθυμήσουσιν. Fut act ind 3rd pl ἐπιθυμέω.
ἀποθανεῖν. Aor act inf ἀποθνῄσκω (direct object of ἐπιθυμήσουσιν).
φεύγει. Pres act ind 3rd sg φεύγω. The present tense is future referring, following a string of future tense forms and deictically limited by ἐν ταῖς ἡμέραις ἐκείναις. The future tense form φεύξεται is attested in 1854 2329 2351 𝔐ᴷ. The present tense, as a departure from the pattern of futures, is used to draw attention to the awful irony: Death fleeing so as to thwart the very thing that humanity desires (Mathewson 2010, 136). Osborne (369 n.20) denies this is a future-referring use of the present and incorrectly concludes that the present tense indicates that death "keeps on fleeing," which illegitimately assumes a "continuous" or "durative" meaning for the present tense (see "Verbal Aspect" in the Introduction).

ὁ θάνατος. Nominative subject of φεύγει. To give personal qualities to an abstract idea (death can flee) is an example of the rhetorical figure of speech, personification.

ἀπ' αὐτῶν. Separation.

9:7 Καὶ τὰ ὁμοιώματα τῶν ἀκρίδων ὅμοια ἵπποις ἡτοιμασμένοις εἰς πόλεμον, καὶ ἐπὶ τὰς κεφαλὰς αὐτῶν ὡς στέφανοι ὅμοιοι χρυσῷ, καὶ τὰ πρόσωπα αὐτῶν ὡς πρόσωπα ἀνθρώπων,

τὰ ὁμοιώματα. Nominative subject of a verbless clause.
τῶν ἀκρίδων. Possessive genitive.
ὅμοιοι. Predicate adjective of a verbless clause.
ἵπποις. Dative complement of ὅμοιος.
ἡτοιμασμένοις. Prf pass ptc masc dat pl ἑτοιμάζω (attributive). The perfect tense form emphasizes their state of preparedness.
εἰς πόλεμον. Purpose.
ἐπὶ τὰς κεφαλὰς. Locative.
αὐτῶν. Possessive genitive.
ὡς στέφανοι. Comparison. This seems to be part of a clause with an implied subject: "And upon their heads (was something) like crowns."
χρυσῷ. Dative complement of ὅμοιος.
τὰ πρόσωπα. Nominative subject of a verbless clause.
αὐτῶν. Possessive genitive.
ὡς πρόσωπα. Comparison. Functions as the predicate of a verbless clause.
ἀνθρώπων. Possessive genitive.

9:8 καὶ εἶχον τρίχας ὡς τρίχας γυναικῶν, καὶ οἱ ὀδόντες αὐτῶν ὡς λεόντων ἦσαν,

εἶχον. Impf act ind 3rd pl ἔχω. On the significance of the imperfect tense, see verse 10 on ἔχουσιν.
τρίχας. Accusative direct object of εἶχον.
ὡς τρίχας. Comparison.
γυναικῶν. Possessive genitive.
οἱ ὀδόντες. Nominative subject of ἦσαν.
αὐτῶν. Possessive genitive.
ὡς λεόντων. Comparison. The entire phrase functions as the predicate of ἦσαν.
λεόντων. Genitive of possession modifying an implied ὀδόντες.
ἦσαν. Impf act ind 3rd pl εἰμί.

9:9 καὶ εἶχον θώρακας ὡς θώρακας σιδηροῦς, καὶ ἡ φωνὴ τῶν πτερύγων αὐτῶν ὡς φωνὴ ἁρμάτων ἵππων πολλῶν τρεχόντων εἰς πόλεμον,

εἶχον. Impf act ind 3rd pl ἔχω. On the significance of the imperfect tense, see verse 10 on ἔχουσιν.

θώρακας. Accusative direct object of εἶχον.

ὡς θώρακας σιδηροῦς. Comparison. The term σιδηροῦς indicates "pertaining to being made or consisting of iron" (LN 2.59).

ἡ φωνὴ. Nominative subject of a verbless clause.

τῶν πτερύγων. Genitive of source or subjective genitive.

αὐτῶν. Possessive genitive.

ὡς φωνὴ. Comparison. The entire phrase functions as the predicate of the verbless clause.

ἁρμάτων. Genitive of source or subjective genitive.

ἵππων πολλῶν. The entire expression ἁρμάτων ἵππων πολλῶν is difficult to analyze grammatically. Aune (2.487) suggests that ἵππων πολλῶν is either a genitive of association ("chariots *with many horses*") or that both genitives should be taken independently as modifying φωνή ("the sound of chariots, of many horses"). Overall, the notion communicated by the genitive seems to be something like "chariots drawn by horses" (Osborne, 372 n. 24).

τρεχόντων. Pres act ptc masc gen pl τρέχω (attributive).

εἰς πόλεμον. Goal.

9:10 καὶ ἔχουσιν οὐρὰς ὁμοίας σκορπίοις καὶ κέντρα, καὶ ἐν ταῖς οὐραῖς αὐτῶν ἡ ἐξουσία αὐτῶν ἀδικῆσαι τοὺς ἀνθρώπους μῆνας πέντε,

ἔχουσιν. Pres act ind 3rd pl ἔχω. Historical or narrative present (see 4:5 on ἐκπορεύονται). The present tense here contrasts with the two previous imperfect forms of the same verb in verses 8 and 9 (εἶχον). The verb ἔχω throughout Revelation occurs exclusively in the present and imperfect tenses (imperfective aspect). The reason for the switch here to the present tense may be that the two remote imperfect forms (vv. 8, 9) describe features of the locusts that form the background for and set the stage for the two present forms, which focus on the locusts' ability to harm humanity under their nefarious leader (vv. 10, 11). See Mathewson 2010, 136.

οὐρὰς ... καὶ κέντρα. Accusative direct object of ἔχουσιν.

σκορπίοις. Dative complement of ὁμοίας.

ἐν ταῖς οὐραῖς αὐτῶν ἡ ἐξουσία αὐτῶν ἀδικῆσαι τοὺς ἀνθρώπους μῆνας πέντε. Lit. "Their authority to harm people for five months was in their tails."

ἐν ταῖς οὐραῖς. Locative.
αὐτῶν. Possessive genitive.
ἡ ἐξουσία. Nominative subject of a verbless clause.
αὐτῶν. Subjective genitive.
ἀδικῆσαι. Aor act inf ἀδικέω (epexegetical to ἐξουσία).
τοὺς ἀνθρώπους. Accusative direct object of ἀδικῆσαι.
μῆνας πέντε. Accusative indicating extent of time.

9:11 ἔχουσιν ἐπ' αὐτῶν βασιλέα τὸν ἄγγελον τῆς ἀβύσσου, ὄνομα αὐτῷ Ἑβραϊστὶ Ἀβαδδὼν, καὶ ἐν τῇ Ἑλληνικῇ ὄνομα ἔχει Ἀπολλύων.

ἔχουσιν. Pres act ind 3rd pl ἔχω. On the present tense, see verse 10 on ἔχουσιν.

ἐπ' αὐτῶν. Used with βασιλέα, ἐπί is a marker of "power, authority, control of or over someone or someth." (BDAG 365.9.a).

βασιλέα. Accusative direct object of ἔχουσιν.

τὸν ἄγγελον. Accusative in apposition to βασιλέα.

τῆς ἀβύσσου. Genitive of subordination ("the angel over/in charge of the abyss").

ὄνομα. This is often labeled as a parenthetical nominative (BDF §144; Aune, 1.clxix), but it could also be analyzed as a nominative of a verbless clause forming its own clause (Porter 1992, 85). In support of the parenthetical view is the lack of a καί, which John uses to introduce and link clauses. It appears to stand "all by itself" (Robertson, 460) or functions as an explanatory clause inserted within another clause (Wallace, 53; see also 6:8 on ὄνομα).

αὐτῷ. Dative of respect or possession (see Porter 1992, 97–98).

Ἑβραϊστὶ. Dative of reference, referring to the language in which the name is written.

Ἀβαδδὼν. Nominative in apposition to ὄνομα. Lit. "with respect to Hebrew, there was a name to him, Abaddon."

ἐν τῇ Ἑλληνικῇ. See Ἑβραϊστί above.

ὄνομα. Accusative direct object of ἔχει.

ἔχει. Pres act ind 3rd sg ἔχω.

Ἀπολλύων. Ἀπολλύων stands in apposition to the accusative ὄνομα. On the apposition of the nominative to the accusative case, "As the name-case the nominative is sometimes left unaltered in the sentence instead of being put in the case of the word with which it is in apposition" (cf. Robertson, 458).

9:12 Ἡ οὐαὶ ἡ μία ἀπῆλθεν· ἰδοὺ ἔρχεται ἔτι δύο οὐαὶ μετὰ ταῦτα.

Ἡ οὐαὶ ἡ μία. Nominative subject of ἀπῆλθεν. Here μία is used with the sense of the ordinal "first" (BDAG, 293.4.b; BDF §247). For the meaning of οὐαί, see 8:13.

ἀπῆλθεν. Aor act ind 3rd sg ἀπέρχομαι.

ἰδού. A marker of attention that deictically functions to make the following statement emphatic (the coming of two more woes). On the form, see 1:7.

ἔρχεται. Pres mid ind 3rd sg ἔρχομαι. The present tense here is future referring, as is often true with ἔρχομαι (see 1:7 on ἔρχεται).

δύο οὐαί. Nominative subject of ἔρχεται. The plural number does not match the singular verb (ἔρχεται). Sometimes a singular verb can be used with a plural subject when the latter is seen as a single entity (McKay 1994, 18). Perhaps, following Aune (2.488), we should see δύο as multiplicative, meaning "twice." If this is the case, οὐαί would still be considered singular (Mussies, 217, translates it "there is to come yet twice a Woe"). Robertson (405) argues that John would have considered the woe neuter, so that the neuter plural would take a singular verb, but the fact that it occurs as a feminine at the beginning of the verse (Ἡ οὐαὶ ἡ μία) renders this solution unlikely.

μετὰ ταῦτα. Temporal. The antecedent of ταῦτα is the first woe, the locusts of 9:1-11.

Revelation 9:13-21

¹³And the sixth angel sounded (his) trumpet. And I heard the first voice from the four horns of the golden altar that is before God ¹⁴saying to the sixth angel who has the trumpet, "Release the four angels that are bound at the great river, Euphrates." ¹⁵And the four angels were released, who were prepared for the hour and day and month and year, in order that they might kill a third of humanity. ¹⁶And the number of the mounted soldiers was twenty thousand times tens of thousands; I heard their number. ¹⁷And in this way I saw the horses in the vision and those who were sitting upon them; they had breastplates of fire and sapphire and sulphur, and the heads of the horses were like the heads of lions, and from their mouths poured forth fire and smoke and sulphur. ¹⁸From these three plagues a third of humanity was killed, from the fire and the smoke and the sulphur that poured forth from their mouths. ¹⁹For the authority of the horses was in their mouths and in their tails, for their tails were like serpents, having heads, and with them they inflict harm. ²⁰And the rest of humanity, who were not killed by these plagues, still did not repent from the works of their hands, in order that they should not worship demons and idols of gold and silver and copper and stone and wood, which can neither see nor hear nor walk about. ²¹And they

did not repent from their murders nor from their sorcery nor from their adultery nor from their stealing.

9:13 Καὶ ὁ ἕκτος ἄγγελος ἐσάλπισεν· καὶ ἤκουσα φωνὴν μίαν ἐκ τῶν [τεσσάρων] κεράτων τοῦ θυσιαστηρίου τοῦ χρυσοῦ τοῦ ἐνώπιον τοῦ θεοῦ,

ὁ ἕκτος ἄγγελος. Nominative subject of ἐσάλπισεν. The sixth trumpet corresponds to the second woe (8:13; 9:12).
ἐσάλπισεν. Aor act ind 3rd sg σαλπίζω.
ἤκουσα. Aor act ind 1st sg ἀκούω.
φωνὴν μίαν. Accusative direct object of ἤκουσα. On the function of μίαν as an indefinite pronoun, see 8:13 on ἑνὸς ἀετοῦ.
ἐκ τῶν [τεσσάρων] κεράτων. Source.
τοῦ θυσιαστηρίου. Possessive genitive or partitive genitive. On the meaning of θυσιαστήριον, see 6:9.
τοῦ χρυσοῦ. Attributive genitive.
τοῦ ἐνώπιον τοῦ θεοῦ. The article functions as an adjectivizer, turning the PP into an attributive modifier of τοῦ θυσιαστηρίου: Lit. "the before-God altar."
ἐνώπιον τοῦ θεοῦ. Locative.

9:14 λέγοντα τῷ ἕκτῳ ἀγγέλῳ, ὁ ἔχων τὴν σάλπιγγα· λῦσον τοὺς τέσσαρας ἀγγέλους τοὺς δεδεμένους ἐπὶ τῷ ποταμῷ τῷ μεγάλῳ Εὐφράτῃ.

λέγοντα. Pres act ptc fem acc sg λέγω. The participle is possibly attributive, but more likely it functions as the complement in an object-complement double accusative construction with φωνήν. On the use of the participle to introduce speech, see 1:17 on λέγων.
τῷ ἕκτῳ ἀγγέλῳ. Dative indirect object of λέγοντα.
ὁ ἔχων. Pres act ptc masc nom sg ἔχω (substantival). ὁ ἔχων could stand in apposition to τῷ ἕκτῳ ἀγγέλῳ, which would create grammatical incongruity, since a nominative participle stands in apposition to a dative substantive. However, this may be a parenthetical statement: ". . . saying to the sixth angel (the one who has the trumpet): release the four angels."
τὴν σάλπιγγα. Accusative direct object of ἔχων.
λῦσον. Aor act impv 2nd sg λύω. While aorist imperatives do not necessarily indicate a single event, in this context that is clearly the case (the angel is commanded to perform a one-time act).
τοὺς τέσσαρας ἀγγέλους. Accusative direct object of λῦσον.
τοὺς δεδεμένους. Prf pass ptc masc acc pl δέω (attributive).

ἐπὶ τῷ ποταμῷ τῷ μεγάλῳ. Locative. For ἐπί meaning "at," see 8:3 on ἐπὶ τοῦ θυσιαστηρίου.
Εὐφράτῃ. Dative in apposition to τῷ ποταμῷ.

9:15 καὶ ἐλύθησαν οἱ τέσσαρες ἄγγελοι οἱ ἡτοιμασμένοι εἰς τὴν ὥραν καὶ ἡμέραν καὶ μῆνα καὶ ἐνιαυτόν, ἵνα ἀποκτείνωσιν τὸ τρίτον τῶν ἀνθρώπων.

ἐλύθησαν. Aor pass ind 3rd pl λύω. The passive form focuses attention on the new topic, the τέσσαρες ἄγγελοι.
οἱ τέσσαρες ἄγγελοι. Nominative subject of ἐλύθησαν.
οἱ ἡτοιμασμένοι. Prf pass ptc masc nom pl ἑτοιμάζω (attributive).
εἰς τὴν ὥραν καὶ ἡμέραν καὶ μῆνα καὶ ἐνιαυτόν. Goal (extensive). On this use of εἰς, see Porter (1992, 152).
τὴν. Here the article with multiple substantives connected by καί is used where each item is a subset of the next: hour → day → month → year (Wallace, 287).
ἵνα. Introduces a purpose clause.
ἀποκτείνωσιν. Pres act subj 3rd pl ἀποκτείνω. Subjunctive with ἵνα.
τὸ τρίτον. Accusative direct object of ἀποκτείνωσιν.
τῶν ἀνθρώπων. Partitive genitive.

9:16 καὶ ὁ ἀριθμὸς τῶν στρατευμάτων τοῦ ἱππικοῦ δισμυριάδες μυριάδων, ἤκουσα τὸν ἀριθμὸν αὐτῶν.

ὁ ἀριθμὸς. Nominative subject of a verbless clause.
τῶν στρατευμάτων. Objective genitive (the soldiers are numbered). Aune (2.489) labels this a genitive of quantity, though Wallace (122) says that that usage usually occurs with verbs.
τοῦ ἱππικοῦ. The genitive could be taken as epexegetical genitive ("the soldiers, that is, the calvary"; BDAG, 480) or perhaps better as attributive genitive ("the mounted soldiers").
δισμυριάδες μυριάδων. Nominative predicate of a verbless clause. δισμυριάδες indicates literally, "a double myriad" or twenty thousand (BDAG, 252). According to BDAG, the entire expression would then indicate "several units of twenty-thousand multiplied by 10,000" (252). Aune renders the phrase "twice ten thousands times ten thousand" (2.538). δισμυριάς could also be written separately (δὶς μυριάς/δύο μυριάδες) as is evident in the textual tradition: Λ 025 (δεὶς μυριάδες μυριάδων); ℵ (δύο μυριάδων μυριάδας); 𝔓⁴⁷ 2042 (δύο μυριάδες μυριάδων). Mussies (224–25) argues that the expression is a Hebraism, so that the δισ- literally renders the dual of the Hebrew רבותים. In this case the expression should be translated "ten thousand times tens of

thousands." However, it is doubtful that δισ- is simply an attempt to literally (mis)translate the Hebrew dual. In any case, this expression is to be taken as indicating "an indefinite number of incalculable immensity" (BDAG, 252; cf. Beale, 509: "an incalculable immensity").

ἤκουσα. Aor act ind 1st sg ἀκούω.

τὸν ἀριθμὸν. Accusative direct object of ἤκουσα.

αὐτῶν. Objective genitive (see above on τῶν στρατευμάτων).

9:17 Καὶ οὕτως εἶδον τοὺς ἵππους ἐν τῇ ὁράσει καὶ τοὺς καθημένους ἐπ' αὐτῶν, ἔχοντας θώρακας πυρίνους καὶ ὑακινθίνους καὶ θειώδεις, καὶ αἱ κεφαλαὶ τῶν ἵππων ὡς κεφαλαὶ λεόντων, καὶ ἐκ τῶν στομάτων αὐτῶν ἐκπορεύεται πῦρ καὶ καπνὸς καὶ θεῖον.

οὕτως. Here οὕτως seems to "pert[ain] to what follows in discourse material, *in this way, as follows*" (BDAG, 742.2). It indicates that the author will now describe the manner in which he saw the horses just referred to in verse 16.

εἶδον. Aor act ind 1st sg ὁράω.

τοὺς ἵππους . . . καὶ τοὺς καθημένους. Accusative direct object of εἶδον.

ἐν τῇ ὁράσει. Indicates the manner in which John saw the horses or the context or circumstances in which he saw them: in a vision.

τοὺς καθημένους. Pres mid ptc masc acc pl κάθημαι (substantival).

ἐπ' αὐτῶν. Locative.

ἔχοντας. Pres act ptc masc acc pl ἔχω. The participle may be attributive, describing the horses, or it may function as the complement in an object-complement double accusative construction with ἵππους. There is some initial ambiguity as to what the participle is describing, the horses, or those seated upon them. The clear mention of ἵππων in the next clause seems to indicate that it is the horses and not the riders that are being described.

θώρακας πυρίνους καὶ ὑακινθίνους καὶ θειώδεις. Accusative direct object of ἔχοντας. Osborne (382) incorrectly labels πυρίνους, ὑακινθίνους, and θειώδεις as genitives.

αἱ κεφαλαὶ. Nominative subject of a verbless clause.

τῶν ἵππων. Partitive genitive.

ὡς κεφαλαὶ. Comparison. Functions as the predicate of a verbless clause.

λεόντων. Possessive genitive.

ἐκ τῶν στομάτων. Source.

αὐτῶν. Possessive genitive.

ἐκπορεύεται. Pres mid ind 3rd sg ἐκπορεύομαι. Historical or narrative present (see 4:5 on ἐκπορεύονται). Here it gives prominence to this particular feature of the horses.

πῦρ καὶ καπνὸς καὶ θεῖον. Nominative subject of ἐκπορεύεται. A singular verb is followed by a plural subject (πῦρ καὶ καπνὸς καὶ θεῖον). A verb, when it stands first before the subjects, often agrees in number with the first subject (Turner, 313; Charles, 1.cxli).

9:18 ἀπὸ τῶν τριῶν πληγῶν τούτων ἀπεκτάνθησαν τὸ τρίτον τῶν ἀνθρώπων, ἐκ τοῦ πυρὸς καὶ τοῦ καπνοῦ καὶ τοῦ θείου τοῦ ἐκπορευομένου ἐκ τῶν στομάτων αὐτῶν.

ἀπὸ τῶν τριῶν πληγῶν τούτων. Source or means.
ἀπεκτάνθησαν. Aor pass ind 3rd pl ἀποκτείνω.
τὸ τρίτον. Nominative subject of ἀπεκτάνθησαν. The singular subject with the plural verb can be explained as the use of the plural with a collective noun (τρίτον), which here is used with a partitive genitive plural construction.
τῶν ἀνθρώπων. Partitive genitive.
ἐκ τοῦ πυρὸς καὶ τοῦ καπνοῦ καὶ τοῦ θείου. Source or means. The PP here stands in apposition to ἀπὸ τῶν τριῶν πληγῶν τούτων. ἐκ is used similarly to ἀπό at the beginning of the verse; but ἀπό seems to summarize the source of death, while the ἐκ specifies the source in more detail: the fire, smoke, and sulphur.
τοῦ ἐκπορευομένου. Pres mid ptc neut gen sg ἐκπορεύομαι (attributive). There is grammatical incongruity in number in that a singular participle modifies a compound noun phrase (τοῦ πυρὸς καὶ τοῦ καπνοῦ καὶ τοῦ θείου). This may be because the author sees these three as a single entity (cf. McKay 1994, 18).
ἐκ τῶν στομάτων. Source. This phrase forms an inclusio with ἐκ τῶν στομάτων in verse 17. Smalley (240) notes the chiastic structure in verses 17-18: out of their mouths/comes/fire, smoke, brimstone//fire, smoke, brimstone/coming/out of their mouths.
αὐτῶν. Possessive genitive.

9:19 ἡ γὰρ ἐξουσία τῶν ἵππων ἐν τῷ στόματι αὐτῶν ἐστιν καὶ ἐν ταῖς οὐραῖς αὐτῶν, αἱ γὰρ οὐραὶ αὐτῶν ὅμοιαι ὄφεσιν, ἔχουσαι κεφαλὰς καὶ ἐν αὐταῖς ἀδικοῦσιν.

ἡ ... ἐξουσία. Nominative subject of ἐστιν.
γὰρ. Causal.
τῶν ἵππων. Subjective genitive.
ἐν τῷ στόματι. Locative. The PP functions as the predicate of ἐστιν.

αὐτῶν. Possessive genitive.
ἐστιν. Pres act ind 3rd sg εἰμί. On the loss of accent, see 1:8.
ἐν ταῖς οὐραῖς. Locative.
αὐτῶν. Possessive genitive.
γὰρ. Causal.
αἱ ... οὐραί. Nominative subject of a verbless clause.
αὐτῶν. Possessive genitive.
ὅμοιαι. Predicate adjective of a verbless clause.
ὄφεσιν. Dative complement of ὅμοιος.
ἔχουσαι. Pres act ptc fem nom pl ἔχω. While the participle may function attributively, it is also possible that this is an example of a participle functioning similar to a main verb. On this use of the participle, see 1:16 on ἔχων.
κεφαλὰς. Accusative direct object of ἔχουσαι.
ἐν αὐταῖς. Instrumental.
ἀδικοῦσιν. Pres act ind 3rd pl ἀδικέω. Historical or narrative present (see 4:5 on ἐκπορεύονται).

9:20 Καὶ οἱ λοιποὶ τῶν ἀνθρώπων, οἳ οὐκ ἀπεκτάνθησαν ἐν ταῖς πληγαῖς ταύταις, οὐδὲ μετενόησαν ἐκ τῶν ἔργων τῶν χειρῶν αὐτῶν, ἵνα μὴ προσκυνήσουσιν τὰ δαιμόνια καὶ τὰ εἴδωλα τὰ χρυσᾶ καὶ τὰ ἀργυρᾶ καὶ τὰ χαλκᾶ καὶ τὰ λίθινα καὶ τὰ ξύλινα, ἃ οὔτε βλέπειν δύνανται οὔτε ἀκούειν οὔτε περιπατεῖν,

οἱ λοιποὶ. Nominative subject of μετενόησαν.
τῶν ἀνθρώπων. Partitive genitive.
οἵ. Nominative subject of ἀπεκτάνθησαν.
ἀπεκτάνθησαν. Aor pass ind 3rd pl ἀποκτείνω.
ἐν ταῖς πληγαῖς ταύταις. Instrumental.
οὐδὲ. "Not even" (BDAG, 735.3). Rather than the simple negative οὐ, the compound form is more emphatic and emphasizes the refusal of humanity to repent even in the face of these plagues.
μετενόησαν. Aor act ind 3rd pl μετανοέω.
ἐκ τῶν ἔργων. Separation. On ἐκ + genitive following μετανοέω, see 2:21 on ἐκ τῆς πορνείας.
τῶν χειρῶν. Subjective genitive.
αὐτῶν. Possessive genitive.
ἵνα. Introduces a purpose or result clause (Zerwick §352).
προσκυνήσουσιν. Fut act ind 3rd pl προσκυνέω. Future with ἵνα. On the use of the future in place of the subjunctive, see 3:9 on ἥξουσιν.
τὰ δαιμόνια καὶ τὰ εἴδωλα ... τὰ ξύλινα. Accusative direct object of προσκυνήσουσιν.
ἅ. Nominative subject of δύνανται.

οὔτε . . . οὔτε . . . οὔτε. "Neither . . . nor . . . nor."

βλέπειν. Pres act inf βλέπω (complementary). The placing of the infinitive before the verb it complements (while the other complementary infinitives follow it) would seem to lend it prominence. Perhaps this is because Revelation is a record of what John "saw" through an Ἀποκάλυψις, and so now he contrasts the inability of demons and idols to "see."

δύνανται. Pres mid ind 3rd sg δύναμαι. Neuter plural subjects (ἅ) regularly take a singular verb form.

ἀκούειν. Pres act inf ἀκούω (complementary).

περιπατεῖν. Pres act inf περιπατέω (complementary).

9:21 καὶ οὐ μετενόησαν ἐκ τῶν φόνων αὐτῶν οὔτε ἐκ τῶν φαρμάκων αὐτῶν οὔτε ἐκ τῆς πορνείας αὐτῶν οὔτε ἐκ τῶν κλεμμάτων αὐτῶν.

οὐ . . . οὔτε . . . οὔτε . . . οὔτε. "Not . . . neither . . . neither . . . nor." (BDF §445.1).

μετενόησαν. Aor act ind 3rd pl μετανοέω.

ἐκ τῶν φόνων. Separation (see also 9:20 on ἐκ τῶν ἔργων).

αὐτῶν. Subjective genitive.

ἐκ τῶν φαρμάκων. Separation (see 9:20 on ἐκ τῶν ἔργων).

αὐτῶν. Subjective genitive.

ἐκ τῆς πορνείας. Separation (see 9:20 on ἐκ τῶν ἔργων).

αὐτῶν. Subjective genitive.

ἐκ τῶν κλεμμάτων. Separation (see 9:20 on ἐκ τῶν ἔργων).

αὐτῶν. Subjective genitive.

Revelation 10:1-11

¹And I saw another strong angel coming down out of heaven, dressed with a cloud, and a rainbow was on his head and his face was like the sun and his feet like pillars of fire. ²And in his hand he had an open scroll. And he placed his right foot on the sea, and his left foot on the earth, ³and he cried out in a great voice just like a lion roaring. And when he cried out, the seven thunders spoke their sounds. ⁴And when the seven thunders spoke I was about to write it, and I heard a voice from heaven saying, "Seal up what the seven thunders spoke, and do not write it." ⁵And the angel that I saw standing upon the sea and upon the earth raised his right hand to heaven ⁶and swore an oath by the one who lives forever, who created heaven and the things in it and the earth and the things in it and the sea and the things in it, that time shall be no more. ⁷But in those days of the voice of the seventh angel, when he is about to sound (his) trumpet, the mystery of God will be accomplished, as he

proclaimed to his servants, the prophets. ⁸And the voice that I heard from heaven again spoke with me and said, "Go, take the scroll that is open in the right hand of the angel standing upon the sea and upon the earth." ⁹And I went to the angel, telling him to give me the scroll. And he said to me, "Take and consume it, and it will embitter your stomach, but in your mouth it will be sweet like honey." ¹⁰And I took the scroll from the hand of the angel and consumed it, and in my mouth it was as sweet as honey, and when I ate it, my stomach became bitter. ¹¹And he said to me, "It is necessary for you again to prophesy against people and nations and tongues and many kings."

10:1 Καὶ εἶδον ἄλλον ἄγγελον ἰσχυρὸν καταβαίνοντα ἐκ τοῦ οὐρανοῦ περιβεβλημένον νεφέλην, καὶ ἡ ἶρις ἐπὶ τῆς κεφαλῆς αὐτοῦ καὶ τὸ πρόσωπον αὐτοῦ ὡς ὁ ἥλιος καὶ οἱ πόδες αὐτοῦ ὡς στῦλοι πυρός,

εἶδον. Aor act ind 1st sg ὁράω.

ἄλλον ἄγγελον ἰσχυρὸν. Accusative direct object of εἶδον. This angel could be related to the angel in 5:2, since these are the only two places where an angel is described as ἰσχυρός and as crying out with a great voice (φωνῇ μεγάλῃ), and both are related to a scroll (Smalley, 256). Yet we should probably see this as a different angel than 5:2 due to the use of ἄλλον ("another," "other") to describe it here in 10:1.

καταβαίνοντα. Pres act ptc masc acc sg καταβαίνω. The participle could be attributive, or more likely it functions as the complement in an object-complement double accusative construction.

ἐκ τοῦ οὐρανοῦ. Source.

περιβεβλημένον. Prf mid ptc masc acc sg περιβάλλω (attributive).

νεφέλην. Accusative direct object of περιβεβλημένον.

ἡ ἶρις. Nominative subject of a verbless clause.

ἐπὶ τῆς κεφαλῆς. Locative.

αὐτοῦ. Possessive genitive.

τὸ πρόσωπον. Nominative subject of a verbless clause.

αὐτοῦ. Possessive genitive.

ὡς ὁ ἥλιος. Comparison. Functions as the predicate of a verbless clause.

οἱ πόδες. Nominative subject of a verbless clause. πόδες is probably a synecdoche for the "legs" of the angel (cf. NRSV, NIV).

αὐτοῦ. Possessive genitive.

ὡς στῦλοι. Comparison. Functions as the predicate of a verbless clause.

πυρός. Attributive genitive.

10:2 καὶ ἔχων ἐν τῇ χειρὶ αὐτοῦ βιβλαρίδιον ἠνεῳγμένον. καὶ ἔθηκεν τὸν πόδα αὐτοῦ τὸν δεξιὸν ἐπὶ τῆς θαλάσσης, τὸν δὲ εὐώνυμον ἐπὶ τῆς γῆς,

ἔχων. Pres act ptc masc nom sg ἔχω. This is an example of a participle functioning as a finite verb, perhaps as a predicate of or periphrastic with a form of an implied εἰμί. On this use of the participle, see 1:16 on ἔχων. There is grammatical incongruity between the accusative ἄγγελον and the nominative case of ἔχων. This may indicate that the participle functions as a finite verb. Beale (529–30) argues that the incongruity is to draw attention to an OT allusion to Dan 10:6.

ἐν τῇ χειρὶ. Locative.

αὐτοῦ. Possessive genitive.

βιβλαρίδιον. Accusative direct object of ἔχων. βιβλαρίδιον is the diminutive form ("little scroll") of βίβλος (BDAG, 176). βιβλίον, another diminutive form, is found here in verse 8 and is the term used to refer to the scroll in 5:1, 2, 3, 4, 5, 8, 9. However, most think that βιβλίον has lost its diminutive force (see, e.g., Mussies, 116–17). This is also true of other diminutive forms in Revelation, such as ἀρνίον in 5:6 (Mussies, 108; Aune, 2.558). Something similar could be said about θηρίον (11:7; 13:1-4, 11, 12, 14, 15, 17, 18; 14:9, 11; 15:2; 16:2, 10, 13; 17:3, 7, 8, 11-13, 16, 17; 19:19, 20; 20:10), which clearly has no diminutive force. Commentators, however, typically acknowledge that βιβλαρίδιον still carries diminuative force: "a little scroll" (Smalley, 258; Beale, 526; Mussies, 116–17), which is actually a "double" diminutive form (-αρίδιον combines both diminutive endings—άριον and -ίδιον). The different forms would seem to distinguish the two scrolls in chs. 5 and 10. However, as already noted in verse 8, the author uses βιβλίον for the same scroll that he designates here as a βιβλαρίδιον. This suggests that the two terms can apparently be used interchangeably to *refer to* the same scroll (cf. Hermas *Vis.* βιβλίον [2.4.2], βιβλαρίδιον [2.1.3; 2.4.3], βιβλίδιον [2.1.3, 4; 2.4.1]). Therefore, the scrolls in chs. 5 and 10 cannot be neatly distinguished based only on the different forms. However, the double diminutive ending suggests that βιβλαρίδιον carries diminutive meaning (BDAG, 176; LN 6.65), even though it still *refers to* the same scroll. The reason for the use of the diminutive βιβλαρίδιον here is probably related to the need for the seer to eat it (Mussies, 116), while the use of βιβλίον in verse 8 may serve to identify it as a scroll similar to or identical to the scroll of ch. 5. In addition, the following consideration might suggest that the two scrolls are the same scroll: (1) the same OT intertext lies behind both chs. 5 and 10: Ezek 2:9, 10; (2) whereas the scroll is sealed (perfect κατεσφραγισμένον) in ch. 5, now it is presented to John as opened (perfect ἠνεῳγμένον);

and (3) both scrolls are associated with an angel with a "loud voice." See further Bauckham (243–57).

ἠνεῳγμένον. Prf pass ptc neut acc sg ἀνοίγω (attributive). The stative aspect of this participle may recall the stative aspect of the participle describing the "sealed" scroll in 5:1: κατεσφραγισμένον. Its state of openness draws attention to the contrast with its previous state of being sealed.

ἔθηκεν. Aor act ind 3rd sg τίθημι.

τὸν πόδα . . . τὸν δεξιὸν. Accusative direct object of ἔθηκεν.

αὐτοῦ. Possessive genitive.

ἐπὶ τῆς θαλάσσης. Locative.

δὲ. Development. Draws a contrast between the location of the right and left foot of the angel.

τὸν εὐώνυμον. Accusative direct object of ἔθηκεν.

ἐπὶ τῆς γῆς. Locative. Placing his feet on the sea and the earth signifies the universal authority of the angel (Smalley, 260).

10:3 καὶ ἔκραξεν φωνῇ μεγάλῃ ὥσπερ λέων μυκᾶται. καὶ ὅτε ἔκραξεν, ἐλάλησαν αἱ ἑπτὰ βρονταὶ τὰς ἑαυτῶν φωνάς.

ἔκραξεν. Aor act ind 3rd sg κράζω.

φωνῇ μεγάλῃ. Dative of instrument or manner.

ὥσπερ. Introduces a comparison. This is the only place where ὥσπερ is used in Revelation.

λέων. Nominative subject of μυκᾶται.

μυκᾶται. Pres mid ind 3rd sg μυκάομαι. The present tense here is timeless, used in a gnomic-type of statement. The verb μυκάομαι is an onomatopoeic word (the pronounciation resembles the sound it represents, e.g., "swish"; see BDAG, 660).

ὅτε. Introduces a temporal clause.

ἔκραξεν. Aor act ind 3rd sg κράζω.

ἐλάλησαν. Aor act ind 3rd pl λαλέω.

αἱ ἑπτὰ βρονταὶ. Nominative subject of ἐλάλησαν.

τὰς . . . φωνάς. Accusative direct object of ἐλάλησαν.

ἑαυτῶν. Genitive of source or subjective genitive.

10:4 καὶ ὅτε ἐλάλησαν αἱ ἑπτὰ βρονταί, ἤμελλον γράφειν, καὶ ἤκουσα φωνὴν ἐκ τοῦ οὐρανοῦ λέγουσαν· σφράγισον ἃ ἐλάλησαν αἱ ἑπτὰ βρονταί, καὶ μὴ αὐτὰ γράψῃς.

ὅτε. Introduces a temporal clause.

ἐλάλησαν. Aor act ind 3rd pl λαλέω.

αἱ ἑπτὰ βρονταὶ. Nominative subject of ἐλάλησαν.

ἤμελλον. Impf act ind 1st sg μέλλω.
γράφειν. Pres act inf γράφω (complementary).
καί. Blount (192) incorrectly labels this an adversative use of καί. Any adversative notion, if present at all, is due to the semantic relationship between the clauses and is not the meaning of καί itself. The καί simply indicates continuity.
ἤκουσα. Aor act ind 1st sg ἀκούω.
φωνὴν. Accusative direct object of ἤκουσα.
ἐκ τοῦ οὐρανοῦ. Source.
λέγουσαν. Pres act ptc fem acc sg λέγω. The participle is either attributive or functions as the complement in an object-complement double accusative construction with φωνήν. On the use of the participle λέγουσαν to introduce speech, see 1:17 on λέγων.
σφράγισον. Aor act impv 2nd sg σφραγίζω. The act of sealing something is "to keep the message secret by not writing it down" (Aune, 2.562).
ἅ. Accusative direct object of ἐλάλησαν. ἅ introduces a headless relative clause. The entire clause functions as the direct object of σφράγισον.
ἐλάλησαν. Aor act ind 3rd pl λαλέω.
αἱ ἑπτὰ βρονταὶ. Nominative subject of ἐλάλησαν.
αὐτὰ. Accusative direct object of γράψῃς.
γράψῃς. Aor act subj 2nd sg γράφω (prohibition). On the aorist prohibition, see 6:6 on ἀδικήσῃς. Though the aorist prohibition by itself does not indicate the forbidding of the beginning of an action ("Don't start"), in this *context*, where the author is about to write what he hears in the seven thunders, μὴ γράψῃς does prohibit the beginning of an activity.

10:5 Καὶ ὁ ἄγγελος, ὃν εἶδον ἑστῶτα ἐπὶ τῆς θαλάσσης καὶ ἐπὶ τῆς γῆς, ἦρεν τὴν χεῖρα αὐτοῦ τὴν δεξιὰν εἰς τὸν οὐρανὸν

ὁ ἄγγελος. Nominative subject of ἦρεν. The nominative subject switches the topic back to the ἄγγελος.
ὅν. Accusative direct object of εἶδον.
εἶδον. Aor act ind 1st sg ὁράω.
ἑστῶτα. Prf act ptc masc acc sg ἵστημι. Complement in an object-complement double accusative construction with ὅν.
ἐπὶ τῆς θαλάσσης καὶ ἐπὶ τῆς γῆς. Locative.
ἦρεν. Aor act ind 3rd sg αἴρω.
τὴν χεῖρα ... τὴν δεξιὰν. Accusative direct object of ἦρεν.
αὐτοῦ. Possessive genitive.
εἰς τὸν οὐρανὸν. Locative. εἰς is used in a directive sense of "movement toward" (Porter 1992, 152).

10:6 καὶ ὤμοσεν ἐν τῷ ζῶντι εἰς τοὺς αἰῶνας τῶν αἰώνων, ὃς ἔκτισεν τὸν οὐρανὸν καὶ τὰ ἐν αὐτῷ καὶ τὴν γῆν καὶ τὰ ἐν αὐτῇ καὶ τὴν θάλασσαν καὶ τὰ ἐν αὐτῇ, ὅτι χρόνος οὐκέτι ἔσται,

ὤμοσεν. Aor act ind 3rd sg ὀμνύω.

ἐν τῷ ζῶντι. "A preposition sometimes replaces the simple accusative for the person or thing by whom or which one swears" (Wallace, 205). Perhaps this phrase also reflects Dan Theod. 12:7 which has ἐν τῷ ζῶντι.

τῷ ζῶντι. Pres act ptc masc dat sg ζάω (substantival).

εἰς τοὺς αἰῶνας τῶν αἰώνων. Temporal. On this construction, see 1:18.

ὅς. Nominative subject of ἔκτισεν.

ἔκτισεν. Aor act ind 3rd sg κτίζω.

τὸν οὐρανὸν καὶ τὰ ἐν αὐτῷ καὶ τὴν γῆν καὶ τὰ ἐν αὐτῇ καὶ τὴν θάλασσαν καὶ τὰ ἐν αὐτῇ. Accusative direct object of ἔκτισεν.

τὰ ἐν αὐτῇ. The article τά functions as a nominalizer turning the locative PPs (ἐν αὐτῷ, ἐν αὐτῇ, ἐν αὐτῇ) into substantives.

ὅτι. Introduces a clausal complement that functions as the object of ὤμοσεν (i.e., the content of the oath).

χρόνος οὐκέτι ἔσται. This clause (lit. "time will be no longer") should be taken not in the sense of "time will cease to exist" in some philosophical sense, but in the sense of "the period of waiting will be up." While several have taken it in the sense of "there will be no more delay" (Mounce, 205–6; Beale, 539), the emphasis in this context is not on the delay or postponement of eschatological events (Aune, 2.568)—and χρόνος rarely means "delay." Rather, the idea is that time is up and the mystery is about to unfold. That is, the time of waiting will come to an end.

χρόνος. Nominative subject of ἔσται.

οὐκέτι. Temporal ("no longer"). Functions as the predicate of ἔσται.

ἔσται. Fut act ind 3rd sg εἰμί.

10:7 ἀλλ' ἐν ταῖς ἡμέραις τῆς φωνῆς τοῦ ἑβδόμου ἀγγέλου, ὅταν μέλλῃ σαλπίζειν, καὶ ἐτελέσθη τὸ μυστήριον τοῦ θεοῦ, ὡς εὐηγγέλισεν τοὺς ἑαυτοῦ δούλους τοὺς προφήτας.

ἀλλ'. Runge says that ἀλλά provides a corrective to "some aspect of what precedes" (93). Rather than there being any more time of waiting ("time will be no longer"), the mystery of God is now going to be fulfilled.

ἐν ταῖς ἡμέραις. Temporal.

τῆς φωνῆς. Here the genitive should be understood as "in the days when the voice of the eighth angel sounded."

τοῦ ἑβδόμου ἀγγέλου. Genitive of source or subjective genitive.
ὅταν. Introduces a temporal clause.
μέλλῃ. Pres act subj 3rd sg μέλλω. Subjunctive with ὅταν. μέλλω followed by an infinitive is virtually equivalent to a future tense and refers to action that will occur in the future. Therefore, this construction should not be taken to suggest that the mystery will be completed just before the sounding of the trumpet (Beale, 540–41). Rather, the mystery will be fulfilled when the trumpet will sound.
σαλπίζειν. Pres act inf σαλπίζω (complementary).
ἐτελέσθη. Aor pass ind 3rd sg τελέω. Though not very common, the aorist here is future referring. There have been different ways to explain this, most of the explanations based on the assumption that the aorist tense must refer to past-time action. First, Osborne (400 n. 13), following Wallace (564), explains this as an aorist used of a future event as if it had already taken place. Smalley (265) calls it "proleptic." Fanning explains it as involving "a rhetorical transfer of viewpoint, envisaging an event yet future as though it had already occurred" (269). Furthermore, Fanning (274) says that the effect of the future-referring aorist is to lend vividness and certainty to the vision. However, it is difficult to think that the future tense verbs or the construction μέλλω + infinitive are any less vivid or certain. Second, Charles (1.265) labels it a Semitism and understands it to reflect the so-called Hebrew "prophetic perfect" (also Beale, 547), though Fanning (273) correctly observes that this use of the aorist is not un-Greek. Third, Mussies (337) sees it influenced by Mishnaic Hebrew or Aramaic. It is better, however, to understand this construction in light of verbal aspect (see "Verbal Aspect" in the Introduction), with the aorist simply portraying a future event as a complete whole. The PP ἐν ταῖς ἡμέραις and ὅταν μέλλῃ σαλπίζειν serve to establish the temporal frame of reference (Mathewson 2010, 59). Some witnesses read the aorist subjunctive τελέσθῇ (1854 2351 𝔐ᴬ), probably connecting it with the preceding ὅταν.

τὸ μυστήριον. Nominative subject of ἐτελέσθη. The term μυστήριον suggests "God's salvific purposes in Christ for his creation, hidden for a time but now fully manifest" (Smalley, 265). The mystery concerns the eschatological plan of God for the consummation of all things.
τοῦ θεοῦ. Possessive genitive or possibly genitive of source.
ὡς. Comparative particle indicating manner.
εὐηγγέλισεν. Aor act ind 3rd sg εὐαγγελίζω.
τοὺς ... δούλους. Accusative direct object of εὐηγγέλισεν. It is also possible that this is an example of "advancement," where the indirect object (which would be dative; note translation above) has advanced to the direct object slot, and therefore takes the accusative case.

ἑαυτοῦ. Possessive genitive.
τοὺς προφήτας. Accusative in apposition to τοὺς δούλους.

10:8 Καὶ ἡ φωνὴ ἣν ἤκουσα ἐκ τοῦ οὐρανοῦ πάλιν λαλοῦσαν μετ' ἐμοῦ καὶ λέγουσαν· ὕπαγε λάβε τὸ βιβλίον τὸ ἠνεῳγμένον ἐν τῇ χειρὶ τοῦ ἀγγέλου τοῦ ἑστῶτος ἐπὶ τῆς θαλάσσης καὶ ἐπὶ τῆς γῆς.

ἡ φωνὴ. As Aune (2.551) acknowledges, the syntax of the verse is awkward. The nominative φωνή is not linked grammatically with anything in the proceeding clause, but is followed by a relative clause (ἥν) that modifies it. The two participles that follow (λαλοῦσαν, λέγουσαν) take their case from the relative pronoun ἥν. The nominative φωνή appears to be a nominative absolute, which specifies the nominal idea and forms its own clause (Porter 1992, 85). Or perhaps there is an implied form of εἰμί: "(There was) a voice . . ."
ἥν. Accusative direct object of ἤκουσα.
ἤκουσα. Aor act ind 1st sg ἀκούω.
ἐκ τοῦ οὐρανοῦ. Source.
λαλοῦσαν. Pres act ptc fem acc sg λαλέω. Complement in an object-complement double accusative construction with ἥν.
μετ' ἐμοῦ. Accompaniment.
λέγουσαν. Pres act ptc fem acc sg λέγω. Complement in an object-complement double accusative construction with ἥν. Both participle clauses linked by καί form a compound complement. On the use of the participle λέγουσαν to introduce speech, see 1:17 on λέγων.
ὕπαγε. Pres act impv 2nd sg ὑπάγω.
λάβε. Aor act impv 2nd sg λαμβάνω.
τὸ βιβλίον. Accusative direct object of λάβε.
τὸ ἠνεῳγμένον. Prf pass ptc neut acc sg ἀνοίγω (attributive). Smalley (266) reads too much into the force of the perfect by saying that it indicates a completed action that cannot be reversed (see v. 2 above).
ἐν τῇ χειρὶ. Locative.
τοῦ ἀγγέλου. Possessive genitive.
τοῦ ἑστῶτος. Prf act ptc masc gen sg ἵστημι (attributive).
ἐπὶ τῆς θαλάσσης καὶ ἐπὶ τῆς γῆς. Locative.

10:9 καὶ ἀπῆλθα πρὸς τὸν ἄγγελον λέγων αὐτῷ δοῦναί μοι τὸ βιβλαρίδιον. καὶ λέγει μοι· λάβε καὶ κατάφαγε αὐτό, καὶ πικρανεῖ σου τὴν κοιλίαν, ἀλλ' ἐν τῷ στόματί σου ἔσται γλυκὺ ὡς μέλι.

ἀπῆλθα. Aor act ind 1st sg ἀπέρχομαι. The aorist form here shows the tendency for some 2nd aorist verbs to take 1st aorist endings (-α).

This perhaps reflects the tendency in Koine Greek toward simplification (see also 21:1, 4). Some scribes (ℵ C) used the more common ἀπῆλθον.

πρὸς τὸν ἄγγελον. Locative.

λέγων. Pres act ptc masc nom sg λέγω (manner). On the use of the participle λέγων to introduce speech, see 1:17 on λέγων.

αὐτῷ. Dative indirect object of λέγων.

δοῦναί. Aor act inf δίδωμι (indirect discourse, functioning as an indirect command). The accenting is due to the enclitic μοι that follows.

μοι. Dative indirect object of δοῦναί.

βιβλαρίδιον. Accusative direct object of δοῦναί. On the meaning, see verse 2 on βιβλαρίδιον.

λέγει. Pres act ind 3rd sg λέγω. Historical or narrative present (see 4:5 on ἐκπορεύονται). The present may be used to draw attention to the following words of the angel.

μοι. Dative indirect object of λέγει.

λάβε. Aor act impv 2nd sg λαμβάνω.

κατάφαγε. Aor act impv 2nd sg κατεσθίω. The preposition κατά has a perfectivizing (telicizing) force on the verb, meaning "to devour something completely" (LN 23.11).

αὐτό. Accusative direct object of λάβε καὶ κατάφαγε.

πικρανεῖ. Fut act ind 3rd sg πικραίνω.

σου. Possessive genitive. Placed before the head term it modifies for prominence. Its position may also function to produce a chiastic arrangement with the following clause: embitter/your/stomach//mouth/your/will be sweet.

τὴν κοιλίαν. Accusative direct object of πικρανεῖ.

ἀλλ'. Introduces a contrast with the scroll embittering the stomach.

ἐν τῷ στόματί. Locative. The accenting is due to the enclitic σου that follows.

σου. Possessive genitive.

ἔσται. Fut act ind 3rd sg εἰμί.

γλυκὺ. Predicate adjective.

ὡς μέλι. Comparison. The metaphor of sweetness probably refers to the initial reaction to the scroll, while the bitterness refers to its message of judgment that comes upon further contemplation of its contents (Beale, 551–52). The order here may be another example of the literary device of hysteron-proteron (see 3:3 on εἴληφας), since the scroll should be in the mouth first, then in the stomach. This may draw attention to the first element of bitterness/judgment. The reversal may also function to produce a chiastic arrangement with verse 10, which reverses the order: bitter in stomach/sweet in mouth (v. 9)//sweet in mouth/bitter in stomach (v. 10). See also verse 10 on ἐπικράνθη.

10:10 Καὶ ἔλαβον τὸ βιβλαρίδιον ἐκ τῆς χειρὸς τοῦ ἀγγέλου καὶ κατέφαγον αὐτό, καὶ ἦν ἐν τῷ στόματί μου ὡς μέλι γλυκὺ καὶ ὅτε ἔφαγον αὐτό, ἐπικράνθη ἡ κοιλία μου.

ἔλαβον. Aor act ind 1st sg λαμβάνω.
τὸ βιβλαρίδιον. Accusative direct object of ἔλαβον. On the meaning, see verse 2 on βιβλαρίδιον.
ἐκ τῆς χειρὸς. Separation.
τοῦ ἀγγέλου. Possessive genitive.
κατέφαγον. Aor act ind 1st sg κατεσθίω. On the meaning, see verse 9 on κατάφαγε.
αὐτό. Accusative direct object of κατέφαγον.
ἦν. Impf act ind 3rd sg εἰμί.
ἐν τῷ στόματί. Locative. The accenting of στόματί is due to the enclitic μου that follows.
μου. Possessive genitive.
ὡς μέλι γλυκὺ. Comparison. The entire phrase functions as the predicate of ἦν.
ὅτε. Introduces a temporal clause.
ἔφαγον. Aor act ind 1st sg ἐσθίω. Robertson (563) incorrectly says that the dropping of the preposition with the repetition of the verb (see κατέφαγον) still retains the sense of the compound form.
αὐτό. Accusative direct object of ἔφαγον.
ἐπικράνθη. Aor pass ind 3rd sg πικραίνω. The metaphors of sweetness and bitterness form a chiastic structure in verses 9-10: bitterness/sweetness//sweetness/bitterness. The effect is probably to emphasize the message of judgment contained within the scroll (see also v. 9 on ὡς μέλι).
ἡ κοιλία. Nominative subject of ἐπικράνθη.
μου. Possessive genitive.

10:11 καὶ λέγουσίν μοι· δεῖ σε πάλιν προφητεῦσαι ἐπὶ λαοῖς καὶ ἔθνεσιν καὶ γλώσσαις καὶ βασιλεῦσιν πολλοῖς.

λέγουσίν. Pres act ind 3rd pl λέγω. Historical or narrative present (see 4:5 on ἐκπορεύονται). The present may be used to draw attention to the following words of the angel. The accenting is due to the enclitic μοι that follows. Though a single angel has been speaking to John until this point, here the verb is plural. This is probably an impersonal use of a plural verb, which can be translated as a passive: "It was said to me" (see McKay, 1994, 19; Aune, 2.553; Osborne, 404; Smalley, 268; see also 2:24 on ὡς λέγουσιν). In an apparent attempt to "correct" the text some manuscripts (1611 1854 2053 𝔐^A) read λέγει.

μοι. Dative indirect object of λέγουσίν.
δεῖ. Pres act ind 3rd sg δεῖ (impersonal).
σε. Accusative subject of προφητεῦσαι.
προφητεῦσαι. Aor act inf προφητεύω (complementary). It is also possible to view the infinitive as the subject of δεῖ: "To prophesy is necessary" (see Wallace, 600–601).
ἐπὶ λαοῖς καὶ ἔθνεσιν καὶ γλώσσαις καὶ βασιλεῦσιν πολλοῖς. ἐπί is a "marker indicating the one to whom, for whom, or about whom someth. is done" (BDAG, 366). It is also possible that it is a "marker of hostile opposition, *against*" (BDAG, 366; see Robertson, 605). In the first case, John is being instructed to prophesy a positive message to the nations as a witness to them. In the second case, John is being instructed to prophesy a negative message of judgment toward the nations. It is also possible to take ἐπί in the sense of "about," and to see both positive and negative elements in the message, depending on whether the nations repent or not (Osborne, 405). However, within the context of the affect of bitterness in the seer's stomach (vv. 9, 10) and the judgment by the two witnesses in ch. 11 it is better to take it negatively in the sense of "against."

Revelation 11:1-2

¹And a measuring reed like a rod was given to me, and I was told, "Arise and measure the temple of God and the altar and those worshiping in it. ²And leave out the outer court of the temple and do not measure it, for it will be given over to the Gentiles, and they will trample the holy city for forty-two months."

11:1 Καὶ ἐδόθη μοι κάλαμος ὅμοιος ῥάβδῳ, λέγων· ἔγειρε καὶ μέτρησον τὸν ναὸν τοῦ θεοῦ καὶ τὸ θυσιαστήριον καὶ τοὺς προσκυνοῦντας ἐν αὐτῷ.

ἐδόθη. Aor pass ind 3rd sg δίδωμι.
μοι. Dative indirect object of ἐδόθη.
κάλαμος. Nominative subject of ἐδόθη.
ὅμοιος. Comparison.
ῥάβδῳ. Dative complement of ὅμοιος.
λέγων. Pres act ptc masc nom sg λέγω (manner). On the use of the participle λέγων to introduce speech, see 1:17 on λέγων. While adverbial participles generally take the same subject as the verb they modify, here the subject of the participle is not the subject κάλαμος, but the implied agent of ἐδόθη, probably an angelic being who now speaks to John. This is probably the reason for the addition of καὶ εἱστήκει ὁ ἄγγελος in some

manuscripts (ℵ² 046 1854 2329 2351 *al*). It is not clear where the speech, which begins here, ends in the subsequent verses, though some translations conclude the speech at the end of verse 3 (NRSV; NIV), which I have very tentatively followed. Verse 3 begins with a first singular verb, indicating that the voice is apparently still speaking. Beyond this it is not clear where the speech actually ends. Aune (2.585) thinks that at verse 8 ("where *their* Lord was crucified") the speech has apparently already concluded with the shift from the first and second to the third person, and suggests that it ends with verse 4.

ἔγειρε. Pres act impv 2nd sg ἐγείρω.

μέτρησον. Aor act impv 2nd sg μετρέω. The idea communicated by the act of measuring is preservation and protection.

τὸν ναὸν . . . καὶ τὸ θυσιαστήριον καὶ τοὺς προσκυνοῦντας. Accusative direct object of μέτρησον.

τοῦ θεοῦ. Possessive genitive.

τοὺς προσκυνοῦντας. Pres act ptc masc acc pl προσκυνέω (substantival).

ἐν αὐτῷ. Locative. There are two possible antecedents of αὐτῷ: θυσιαστήριον or ναόν. The nearest possible antecedent is θυσιαστήριον, which would indicate that those worshiping do so "at the altar" (Osborne, 411 n. 4). However, it is more likely that the antecedent is the temple (ναόν) and the ἐν is taken as the location of the worshipers "in" the temple. It is doubtful that we should follow Smalley (273) in concluding that it could be both, since this is more a matter of grammatical ambiguity.

11:2 καὶ τὴν αὐλὴν τὴν ἔξωθεν τοῦ ναοῦ ἔκβαλε ἔξωθεν καὶ μὴ αὐτὴν μετρήσῃς, ὅτι ἐδόθη τοῖς ἔθνεσιν, καὶ τὴν πόλιν τὴν ἁγίαν πατήσουσιν μῆνας τεσσαράκοντα [καὶ] δύο.

τὴν αὐλὴν τὴν ἔξωθεν. Accusative direct object of ἔκβαλε. The outer court probably refers to the outer court of the worshipers from Ezek 40–42, a text that lies behind John's vision and reference to the act of measuring here (see Beale, 559–64).

τοῦ ναοῦ. Partitive genitive.

ἔκβαλε. Aor act impv 2nd sg ἐκβάλλω. The verb followed by ἔξωθεν is difficult to translate (lit. "to cast outside"). It is probably best to translate the entire expression along the lines of "leave out (of consideration)" (BDAG, 299.4). Aune (2.577) translates it "exclude."

ἔξωθεν. Locative.

αὐτήν. Accusative direct object of μετρήσῃς.

μετρήσῃς. Aor act subj 2nd sg μετρέω (prohibition). On the aorist prohibition, see 6:6 on ἀδικήσῃς. Here the traditional understanding of the aorist prohibition, which construes it as forbidding the beginning of an action, works, but only because the *context* makes it clear that the activity has not started yet (the seer has just been given the measuring reed). The aorist itself simply looks at the action prohibited as a complete whole.

ὅτι. Introduces a causal clause.

ἐδόθη. Aor pass ind 3rd sg δίδωμι. The aorist here is probably future referring. On this usage, see 10:7 on ἐτελέσθη.

τοῖς ἔθνεσιν. Dative indirect object of ἐδόθη.

τὴν πόλιν τὴν ἁγίαν. Accusative direct object of πατήσουσιν.

πατήσουσιν. Fut act ind 3rd pl πατέω. The implied subject is τὰ ἔθνη. The literal meaning of πατέω "to trample" can by metaphorical extension suggest "to conquer and keep under subjection" (LN 39.54).

μῆνας τεσσαράκοντα [καὶ] δύο. Accusative indicating extent of time.

Revelation 11:3-14

³"And I will give (authority) to my two witnesses and they will prophesy for twelve hundred and sixty days, clothed in sackcloth." ⁴These are the two olive trees and the two lampstands that are standing before the Lord of the earth. ⁵And if anyone wants to harm them, fire will come out of their mouths and devour their enemies; indeed if anyone desires to harm them, so it is necessary for that person to be put to death. ⁶They have authority to close up the sky so that it will not rain for the days of their prophecy, and they have authority over the waters to turn them into blood and to strike the earth with every plague as often as they desire. ⁷And whenever they complete their witness, the beast that comes out of the abyss will make war with them and will conquer them and kill them. ⁸And their bodies (will lie) on the street of the great city, which is called, spiritually, Sodom and Egypt, where also their Lord was crucified. ⁹And (those) from peoples and tribes and tongues and nations will see their bodies for three and one half days, and they will not permit the bodies to be buried in a tomb. ¹⁰And those who dwell on the earth will rejoice over them and celebrate and send gifts to each other because these two prophets tormented those who dwell on the earth. ¹¹And after the three and one half days the Spirit of life from God entered them and they stood on their feet and great fear fell on those who saw them. ¹²And they (the two witnesses) heard a great voice from heaven saying to them, "Come up here!" And they went up into heaven in a cloud, and their enemies saw them. ¹³And at that hour there was a great earthquake and a tenth of the city fell and seven thousand people died in the earthquake, and the rest became afraid and gave glory to the God of heaven. ¹⁴The second woe has passed. Look, the third woe is coming soon.

11:3 Καὶ δώσω τοῖς δυσὶν μάρτυσίν μου καὶ προφητεύσουσιν ἡμέρας χιλίας διακοσίας ἑξήκοντα περιβεβλημένοι σάκκους.

Verses 1-13 reveal an interesting pattern of tense usage with indicative verbs, where it begins with a series of future tense forms (v. 3), then switches to predominantly present tenses (vv. 4-10) with further future forms (v. 7), and then ends with a group of aorist tense forms (vv. 11-13). The shifting in tense forms is an indication that the tenses are not used for temporal purposes in this section (see Mathewson 2010, 137–38; Porter 1989a, 236). The future and present tense forms serve to establish the prophetic quality of this section, as well as to describe important features of the two witnesses, their activity, and their rejection. The present tense forms are either timeless/descriptive or perhaps future referring and are used to make certain assertions about the two witnesses (Porter 1989a, 236). "The present tense forms function to describe the witnesses and their activities, while the future emphasizes what can be expected to take place" (Mathewson 2010, 140). The aorist tense forms then serve to resume the narrative of the vision from verse 1a (from the standpoint of the description of the two witnesses) and to move the narrative to its conclusion. This analysis is to be preferred over Mussies' temporal scheme (334–39; followed by Beale, 608), which sees the tenses reflecting shifts of time, where the mixing of aorist, present, and future tenses is interpreted to reflect the past time when the visions were actually seen, what he again sees before his eyes, and the fact that he is predicting future events. Such a scheme cannot account for why the author shifts between tenses, and why certain tenses are used at certain places in the narrative.

δώσω. Fut act ind 1st sg δίδωμι. The verb δώσω is difficult to render. It is probably necessary to add an assumed word, such as "authority" (ἐξουσίαν, see v. 6 below) in the translation ("I will give authority to my two witnesses"). As BDAG (243.13) note, δίδωμι can be used in the sense of to "*grant someone the power* or *authority, give someone the right*."

τοῖς δυσὶν μάρτυσίν. Dative indirect object of δώσω. The accenting of μάρτυσίν is due to the enclitic μου that follows.

μου. Objective genitive (witness about me).

καί. Aune (2.579) thinks that the καί here is used consecutively ("so that they will prophesy"). While this may be true semantically, grammatically the καί simply indicates continuity.

προφητεύσουσιν. Fut act ind 3rd pl προφητεύω. On the future tense, see above.

ἡμέρας χιλίας διακοσίας ἑξήκοντα. Accusative indicating extent of time.

περιβεβλημένοι. Prf mid ptc masc nom pl περιβάλλω (manner).

σάκκους. Accusative direct object of περιβεβλημένοι.

11:4 οὗτοί εἰσιν αἱ δύο ἐλαῖαι καὶ αἱ δύο λυχνίαι αἱ ἐνώπιον τοῦ κυρίου τῆς γῆς ἑστῶτες.

οὗτοί. Nominative subject of εἰσιν. The accenting is due to the enclitic εἰσιν that follows. The use of the demonstrative οὗτοι here and in verse 6 is emphatic and foregrounds the two witnesses. As Levinsohn notes, "The 'near' nature of οὗτος manifests itself by being used in reference to animate participants that are *thematic*: the centre of attention" (2009, 210).

εἰσιν. Pres act ind 3rd pl εἰμί. On the loss of accent, see 1:8.

αἱ δύο ἐλαῖαι καὶ αἱ δύο λυχνίαι. Predicate nominative.

αἱ ... ἑστῶτες. Prf act ptc masc nom pl ἵστημι (attributive). The masculine gender of the participle lacks grammatical concord with the feminine αἱ δύο ἐλαῖαι καὶ αἱ δύο λυχνίαι. This can be explained by the fact that the two feminine metaphors refer to the two witnesses who are males, or it takes its gender from οὗτοί.

ἐνώπιον τοῦ κυρίου. Locative.

τῆς γῆς. Genitive of subordination.

11:5 καὶ εἴ τις αὐτοὺς θέλει ἀδικῆσαι πῦρ ἐκπορεύεται ἐκ τοῦ στόματος αὐτῶν καὶ κατεσθίει τοὺς ἐχθροὺς αὐτῶν· καὶ εἴ τις θελήσῃ αὐτοὺς ἀδικῆσαι, οὕτως δεῖ αὐτὸν ἀποκτανθῆναι.

εἴ. Introduces the protasis of a first-class conditional sentence. The accent is due to the enclitic τις that follows. Against Smalley, the first-class condition does not suggest that "the situtation is real" (278). Rather, the first-class condition only makes an assertion for the sake of argument (Porter 1992, 256). Only the context can determine whether the protasis is a reality. Boyer (1981) has determined, based on context, that only 37% of first-class conditions are obviously true, while 12% were false and 51% were undetermined. The context here is undetermined.

τις. Nominative subject of θέλει.

αὐτοὺς. Accusative direct object of ἀδικῆσαι.

θέλει. Pres act ind 3rd sg θέλω. On the present tense, see above on verse 3.

ἀδικῆσαι. Aor act inf ἀδικέω (complementary).

πῦρ. Nominative subject of ἐκπορεύεται.

ἐκπορεύεται. Pres mid ind 3rd sg ἐκπορεύομαι. On the present tense, see above on verse 3.

ἐκ τοῦ στόματος. Source. The singular στόματος is modified by a plural pronoun αὐτῶν. According to Turner this is a "distributive singular," where "[s]omething belonging to each person in a group of people is placed in the sing" (23).

αὐτῶν. Possessive genitive.

κατεσθίει. Pres act ind 3rd sg κατεσθίω. On the present tense, see above on verse 3.

τοὺς ἐχθροὺς. Accusative direct object of κατεσθίει.

αὐτῶν. Genitive of relationship.

εἴ. Introduces the protasis of a third-class conditional sentence (see below on θελήσῃ). The accenting is due to the enclitic τις that follows.

τις. Nominative subject of θελήσῃ.

θελήσῃ. Aor act subj 3rd sg θέλω. The subjunctive follows εἰ rather than the expected ἐάν. As BDF note (§372.3), εἰ is already encroaching upon the sphere of ἐάν in the Koine period (cf. Porter 1989a, 309). However, the fact that the author uses ἐάν with the subjunctive θελήσωσιν in verse 5 suggests that the choice of εἰ here is intentional. This construction should be treated as a third-class conditional sentence on the basis of the subjunctive mood of θελήσῃ in the protasis. Many manuscripts (C P 046 1854 2053 2344 𝔐) read the indicative θέλει, while others ($\mathfrak{P}^{47}$ 1006 1611 1841 2329 2351) read the future θελήσει. Both could be seen as attempts to alleviate the perceived difficulty of a subjunctive following εἰ, though the latter reading could have arisen from confusion regarding the sound of the endings: ῃ and ει. The repetition of the conditional construction with nearly identical protases requires explanation. The εἴ with the subjunctive θελήσῃ in the second half of the verse, and the εἴ with the indicative θέλει in the first half of the verse has been explained by Swete as "the former must be held to state a hypothetical case, whilst the latter posits the θέλησις as a fact" (136). However, this is based on a misunderstanding of the first-class conditional with the indicative mood as establishing a fact. The first-class conditional sentence (εἰ with θέλει) makes an assertion in the protasis for the sake of the argument (with no indication as to the certainty of it taking place). The following conditional construction (εἰ with θελήσῃ) repeats the first, but with the subjunctive mood projects a hypothetical action (Porter 1992, 262), perhaps to express some doubt whether anyone could harm the witnesses. The use of εἰ with the subjunctive θελήσῃ is perhaps to continue the conditional from the first part of the verse. The first-class condition would make an assertion about what anyone intends to do; the third-class condition projects what someone might want to do. The contrast could be captured in the translation: "If anyone desires . . . if anyone should want to. . . ." The repeated conditional construction is emphatic and "intensifies the terrifying nature of the judgment (death by incineration) which the witnesses are capable of inflicting on the enemies of God and his gospel" (Smalley, 279).

αὐτούς. Accusative direct object of ἀδικῆσαι.
ἀδικῆσαι. Aor act inf ἀδικέω (complementary).
οὕτως. Manner. Introduces the apodosis of the conditional sentence.
δεῖ. Pres act ind 3rd sg δεῖ (impersonal). On the present tense, see above on verse 3.
αὐτὸν. Accusative subject of ἀποκτανθῆναι.
ἀποκτανθῆναι. Aor pass inf ἀποκτείνω (complementary). It is also possible to view ἀποκτανθῆναι as the subject of δεῖ: "To be killed is necessary" (Wallace, 600–601).

11:6 οὗτοι ἔχουσιν τὴν ἐξουσίαν κλεῖσαι τὸν οὐρανόν, ἵνα μὴ ὑετὸς βρέχῃ τὰς ἡμέρας τῆς προφητείας αὐτῶν, καὶ ἐξουσίαν ἔχουσιν ἐπὶ τῶν ὑδάτων στρέφειν αὐτὰ εἰς αἷμα καὶ πατάξαι τὴν γῆν ἐν πάσῃ πληγῇ ὁσάκις ἐὰν θελήσωσιν.

οὗτοι. Nominative subject of ἔχουσιν. On the use of the demonstrative, see verse 4.
ἔχουσιν. Pres act ind 3rd pl ἔχω. On the present tense, see verse 3.
τὴν ἐξουσίαν. Accusative direct object of ἔχουσιν.
κλεῖσαι. Aor act inf κλείω (epexegetical to ἐξουσίαν).
τὸν οὐρανόν. Accusative direct object of κλεῖσαι.
ἵνα. Introduces a result clause.
ὑετὸς. Nominative subject of βρέχῃ.
βρέχῃ. Pres act subj 3rd sg βρέχω. Subjunctive with ἵνα.
τὰς ἡμέρας. Accusative indicating extent of time.
τῆς προφητείας. The idea communicated by the genitive is "the days when they prophesied."
αὐτῶν. Subjective genitive.
ἐξουσίαν. Accusative direct object of ἔχουσιν.
ἔχουσιν. Pres act ind 3rd pl ἔχω. On the present tense, see verse 3.
ἐπὶ τῶν ὑδάτων. The preposition ἐπί indicates the extent of the authority of the two witnesses.
στρέφειν. Pres act inf στρέφω (epexegetical to ἐξουσίαν).
αὐτὰ. Accusative direct object of στρέφειν.
εἰς αἷμα. Goal. BDAG notes that εἰς with verbs of changing (such as στρέφω) indicates "a change from one state to another" (290 4.b).
πατάξαι. Aor act inf πατάσσω (epexegetical to ἐξουσίαν).
τὴν γῆν. Accusative direct object of πατάξαι.
ἐν πάσῃ πληγῇ. Instrumental.
ὁσάκις ἐὰν. "As often as" (BDAG, 728).
θελήσωσιν. Aor act subj 3rd pl θέλω. Subjunctive with ἐάν.

11:7 Καὶ ὅταν τελέσωσιν τὴν μαρτυρίαν αὐτῶν, τὸ θηρίον τὸ ἀναβαῖνον ἐκ τῆς ἀβύσσου ποιήσει μετ' αὐτῶν πόλεμον καὶ νικήσει αὐτοὺς καὶ ἀποκτενεῖ αὐτούς.

Καὶ. According to Smalley (280) the καί introducing this verse is adversative. However, any adversative notion is present in the broader context of the relationship between the two clauses. The καί simply expresses continuity.

ὅταν. Introduces a temporal clause.

τελέσωσιν. Aor act subj 3rd pl τελέω. Subjunctive with ὅταν.

τὴν μαρτυρίαν. Accusative direct object of τελέσωσιν.

αὐτῶν. Subjective genitive.

τὸ θηρίον. Nominative subject of ποιήσει. The subject introduces a new topic in this clause.

τὸ ἀναβαῖνον ἐκ τῆς ἀβύσσου. This construction is probably timeless and descriptive. It simply describes the beast as "the one who comes up out of the abyss" without specifying when this takes place. Therefore, it is unnecessary to deduce with Beale that it includes "the idea that the beast has been characterized as rising from the abyss throughout the period of the church's witness" (589).

τὸ ἀναβαῖνον. Pres act ptc neut nom sg ἀναβαίνω (attributive).

ἐκ τῆς ἀβύσσου. Source. See also 9:1 on τῆς ἀβύσσου.

ποιήσει. Fut act ind 3rd sg ποιέω. On the future tense, see verse 3. The three future tense forms in this verse, ποιήσει, νικήσει, ἀποκτενεῖ, indicate what can be expected to take place once the condition of the ὅταν clause (ὅταν τελέσωσιν τὴν μαρτυρίαν αὐτῶν) is fulfilled (Mathewson 2010, 140–41).

μετ' αὐτῶν. Accompaniment. Harris (164) is probably incorrect in concluding that "against" is one of the nuances of μετά if by this he means that it is one of its "meanings." However, this is an appropriate *translation* of the preposition here based on the implication in the context. The implication of the preposition is "to engage in battle with."

πόλεμον. Accusative direct object of ποιήσει.

νικήσει. Fut act ind 3rd sg νικάω. On the future tense, see verse 3.

αὐτοὺς. Accusative direct object of νικήσει.

ἀποκτενεῖ. Fut act ind 3rd sg ἀποκτείνω. On the future tense, see verse 3.

αὐτούς. Accusative direct object of ἀποκτενεῖ.

11:8 καὶ τὸ πτῶμα αὐτῶν ἐπὶ τῆς πλατείας τῆς πόλεως τῆς μεγάλης, ἥτις καλεῖται πνευματικῶς Σόδομα καὶ Αἴγυπτος, ὅπου καὶ ὁ κύριος αὐτῶν ἐσταυρώθη.

τὸ πτῶμα. Nominative subject of a verbless clause. On the singular noun (distributive) modified by a plural pronoun, see 11:5 on ἐκ τοῦ στόματος.

αὐτῶν. Possessive genitive.

ἐπὶ τῆς πλατείας. Locative. The πλατείας could mean "wide road, street" (BDAG, 823) or the "public square" or "plaza" in a city (Aune, 2.581; Smalley, 281). See also 21:21; 22:2.

τῆς πόλεως τῆς μεγάλης. Partitive genitive.

ἥτις. Nominative subject of καλεῖται.

καλεῖται. Pres pass ind 3rd sg καλέω. The present tense is gnomic or timeless here.

πνευματικῶς. Manner. This word suggests the idea that the city is to be understood not literally but figuratively as a reference to its spiritual character, or through spiritual eyes (Beale, 592). Aune (2.581) thinks that it should be understood as meaning "prophetically" (see also BDAG, 837.2).

Σόδομα καὶ Αἴγυπτος. Along with ἥτις this is part of a double nominative construction with a passive verb from a double accusative construction: "I call it (the city) Sodom and Egypt" (see Culy 2009, 83–87).

ὅπου. Locative. Functions as a relative adverb.

ὁ κύριος. Nominative subject of ἐσταυρώθη.

αὐτῶν. Genitive of subordination.

ἐσταυρώθη. Aor pass ind 3rd sg σταυρόω.

11:9 καὶ βλέπουσιν ἐκ τῶν λαῶν καὶ φυλῶν καὶ γλωσσῶν καὶ ἐθνῶν τὸ πτῶμα αὐτῶν ἡμέρας τρεῖς καὶ ἥμισυ καὶ τὰ πτώματα αὐτῶν οὐκ ἀφίουσιν τεθῆναι εἰς μνῆμα.

βλέπουσιν. Pres act ind 3rd pl βλέπω. On the present tense, see verse 3.

ἐκ τῶν λαῶν καὶ φυλῶν καὶ γλωσσῶν καὶ ἐθνῶν. Partitive. This construction functions as the subject of βλέπουσιν (see 2:7 on ἐκ τοῦ ξύλου). It modifies an assumed τίνες ("some"). The partitive construction "should not be pressed to indicate a specific representative group" (Mounce, 227 n. 31).

τὸ πτῶμα. Accusative direct object of βλέπουσιν. On the singular noun (distributive) modified by a plural pronoun, see 11:5 on ἐκ τοῦ στόματος above.

αὐτῶν. Possessive genitive.

ἡμέρας τρεῖς καὶ ἥμισυ. Accusative indicating extent of time.

τὰ πτώματα. Accusative subject of τεθῆναι.

αὐτῶν. Possessive genitive.

ἀφίουσιν. Pres act ind 3rd pl ἀφίημι. On the present tense, see verse 3.
τεθῆναι. Prf pass inf τίθημι (direct object).
εἰς μνῆμα. Locative.

11:10 καὶ οἱ κατοικοῦντες ἐπὶ τῆς γῆς χαίρουσιν ἐπ' αὐτοῖς καὶ εὐφραίνονται καὶ δῶρα πέμψουσιν ἀλλήλοις, ὅτι οὗτοι οἱ δύο προφῆται ἐβασάνισαν τοὺς κατοικοῦντας ἐπὶ τῆς γῆς.

οἱ κατοικοῦντες. Pres act ptc masc nom pl κατοικέω (substantival). Nominative subject of χαίρουσιν.
ἐπὶ τῆς γῆς. Locative.
χαίρουσιν. Pres act ind 3rd pl χαίρω. On the present tense, see verse 3.
ἐπ' αὐτοῖς. Indicates the basis for the feeling expressed in χαίρουσιν (BDAG, 365.6.c).
εὐφραίνονται. Pres mid ind 3rd pl εὐφραίνω. On the present tense, see verse 3.
δῶρα. Accusative direct object of πέμψουσιν.
πέμψουσιν. Fut act ind 3rd pl πέμπω. On the future tense, see verse 3.
ἀλλήλοις. Dative indirect object of πέμψουσιν. The notion communicated by ἀλλήλοις is that they exchange gifts with each other.
ὅτι. Introduces a causal clause.
οὗτοι οἱ δύο προφῆται. Nominative subject of ἐβασάνισαν. The demonstrative οὗτοι picks up the occurrence of the pronoun with reference to the two witnesses in verses 4 and 6, and perhaps draws attention to them as thematic and their activity as the source of the earth-dwellers' rejoicing.
ἐβασάνισαν. Aor act ind 3rd pl βασανίζω. The aorist functions to summarize the activity of the two witnesses from verses 3-6.
τοὺς κατοικοῦντας. Pres act ptc masc acc pl κατοικέω (substantival). Accusative direct object of ἐβασάνισαν.
ἐπὶ τῆς γῆς. Locative.

11:11 Καὶ μετὰ τὰς τρεῖς ἡμέρας καὶ ἥμισυ πνεῦμα ζωῆς ἐκ τοῦ θεοῦ εἰσῆλθεν ἐν αὐτοῖς, καὶ ἔστησαν ἐπὶ τοὺς πόδας αὐτῶν, καὶ φόβος μέγας ἐπέπεσεν ἐπὶ τοὺς θεωροῦντας αὐτούς.

μετὰ τὰς τρεῖς ἡμέρας καὶ ἥμισυ. Temporal.
πνεῦμα. Nominative subject of εἰσῆλθεν.
ζωῆς. Attributive genitive or perhaps the notion is something like "the Spirit who gives life."
ἐκ τοῦ θεοῦ. Source.

εἰσῆλθεν. Aor act ind 3rd sg εἰσέρχομαι. The aorist tense dominates throughout the rest of this section. This is in marked contrast to the present and future tenses that have dominated up until this point. The significance may be that the previous section was primarily descriptive of the nature and activities of the two witnesses and their mistreatment. Now the narrative is resumed with the aorist tense, as the main narrative tense that simply moves the story along to its conclusion. The aorist tenses in this verse may also be a result of an allusion to Ezek 37:10: *εἰσῆλθεν εἰς αὐτοὺς τὸ πνεῦμα* (Mathewson 2010, 141–42).

ἐν αὐτοῖς. Locative. Here the preposition follows a verb with a prefixed εἰς. Moule (75) suggests that this is an example of the overlapping of ἐν with εἰς. A number of manuscripts ($\mathfrak{P}^{47}$ ℵ $\mathfrak{M}^K$) read εἰς αὐτούς.

ἔστησαν. Aor act ind 3rd pl ἵστημι. On the function of the aorist, see εἰσῆλθεν above. The aorist may also be explained by an allusion to Ezek 37:10: *ἔστησαν ἐπὶ τῶν ποδῶν αὐτῶν*.

ἐπὶ τοὺς πόδας. Locative.

αὐτῶν. Possessive genitive.

φόβος μέγας. Nominative subject of ἐπέπεσεν.

ἐπέπεσεν. Aor act ind 3rd sg πίπτω.

ἐπὶ τοὺς θεωροῦντας. Locative.

τοὺς θεωροῦντας. Pres act ptc masc acc pl θεωρέω (substantival). Accusative object of the preposition.

αὐτούς. Accusative direct object of θεωροῦντας.

11:12 καὶ ἤκουσαν φωνῆς μεγάλης ἐκ τοῦ οὐρανοῦ λεγούσης αὐτοῖς· ἀνάβατε ὧδε. καὶ ἀνέβησαν εἰς τὸν οὐρανὸν ἐν τῇ νεφέλῃ, καὶ ἐθεώρησαν αὐτοὺς οἱ ἐχθροὶ αὐτῶν.

ἤκουσαν. Aor act ind 3rd pl ἀκούω. Many manuscripts ($\mathfrak{P}^{47}$ ℵ^c $\mathfrak{M}$) read ἤκουσα, probably due to the use of the 1st singular elsewhere with reference to John hearing a voice from heaven (e.g., 1:10; 4:1 with ἀνάβα ὧδε; 6:1; 10:8). Here it is the two witnesses who hear the voice (Charles, 1.290; Metzger, 672).

φωνῆς μεγάλης. Genitive direct object of ἤκουσαν.

ἐκ τοῦ οὐρανοῦ. Source.

λεγούσης. Pres act ptc fem gen sg λέγω. Complement in an object-complement double genitive construction with φωνῆς μεγάλης. On the use of the participle λεγούσης to introduce speech, see 1:17 on λέγων.

αὐτοῖς. Dative indirect object of λεγούσης.

ἀνάβατε. Aor act impv 2nd pl ἀναβαίνω.

ὧδε. Locative. Indicates a location from the standpoint of the speaker.

ἀνέβησαν. Aor act ind 3rd pl ἀναβαίνω.

εἰς τὸν οὐρανὸν. Locative.

ἐν τῇ νεφέλῃ. Locative or possibly means.
ἐθεώρησαν. Aor act ind 3rd pl θεωρέω.
αὐτούς. Accusative direct object of ἐθεώρησαν.
οἱ ἐχθροί. Nominative subject of ἐθεώρησαν.
αὐτῶν. Genitive of relationship.

11:13 Καὶ ἐν ἐκείνῃ τῇ ὥρᾳ ἐγένετο σεισμὸς μέγας καὶ τὸ δέκατον τῆς πόλεως ἔπεσεν καὶ ἀπεκτάνθησαν ἐν τῷ σεισμῷ ὀνόματα ἀνθρώπων χιλιάδες ἑπτὰ καὶ οἱ λοιποὶ ἔμφοβοι ἐγένοντο καὶ ἔδωκαν δόξαν τῷ θεῷ τοῦ οὐρανοῦ.

ἐν ἐκείνῃ τῇ ὥρᾳ. Temporal. BDAG defines ὥρᾳ here as "a point of time as an occasion for an event" (1103.3).
ἐγένετο. Aor mid ind 3rd sg γίνομαι.
σεισμὸς μέγας. Nominative subject of ἐγένετο.
τὸ δέκατον. Nominative subject of ἔπεσεν.
τῆς πόλεως. Partitive genitive.
ἔπεσεν. Aor act ind 3rd sg πίπτω.
ἀπεκτάνθησαν. Aor act ind 3rd pl ἀποκτείνω.
ἐν τῷ σεισμῷ. Locative or instrumental.
ὀνόματα ... χιλιάδες ἑπτά. Nominative subject of ἀπεκτάνθησαν. The construction ὀνόματα ἀνθρώπων carries the meaning "people" (BDAG, 714.2; LN 9.19). The neuter plural subject occurs with a plural verb. This is due to the fact that ὀνόματα stands for persons (see 3:4 on ὀνόματα).
ἀνθρώπων. Possessive genitive.
οἱ λοιποί. Nominative subject of ἐγένοντο.
ἔμφοβοι. Predicate adjective of ἐγένοντο.
ἐγένοντο. Aor mid ind 3rd pl γίνομαι.
ἔδωκαν. Aor act ind 3rd pl δίδωμι.
δόξαν. Accusative direct object of ἔδωκαν.
τῷ θεῷ. Dative indirect object of ἔδωκαν.
τοῦ οὐρανοῦ. Genitive of source or possibly genitive expressing location.

11:14 Ἡ οὐαὶ ἡ δευτέρα ἀπῆλθεν· ἰδοὺ ἡ οὐαὶ ἡ τρίτη ἔρχεται ταχύ.

Ἡ οὐαὶ ἡ δευτέρα. Nominative subject of ἀπῆλθεν. The second woe refers back to the sixth trumpet in 9:13-21. The third woe (ἡ οὐαὶ ἡ τρίτη) probably refers to the seventh trumpet narrated in 11:15-19 (Beale, 609–10).
ἀπῆλθεν. Aor act ind 3rd sg ἀπέρχομαι.

ἰδού. A marker of attention that deictically functions to make the following statement emphatic. On the form, see 1:7. Here it draws attention to the coming of the third and final woe.

ἡ οὐαὶ ἡ τρίτη. Nominative subject of ἔρχεται.

ἔρχεται. Pres mid ind 3rd sg ἔρχομαι. The present tense is future referring.

ταχύ. Temporal. ταχύ could be translated either "soon" or "quickly." On the translation "soon," see 2:16. Here it stresses the imminence of judgment (see BDAG, 993.1.b.β).

Revelation 11:15-19

¹⁵And the seventh angel sounded (his) trumpet. And there came about great voices in heaven saying, "The kingdom of the world has become (the kingdom) of our Lord and of his Christ, and he shall reign forever and ever." ¹⁶And the twenty-four elders who were before God seated on their thrones fell upon their faces and worshiped God ¹⁷saying, "We give thanks to you, Lord God Almighty, the one who is and who was, because you have received your great power, and you reign. ¹⁸And the nations were angry and your wrath has come, and the time for the dead to be judged and to give the reward to your servants (has come), the prophets and the saints and those who fear your name, to the small and to the great, and to destroy those who destroy the earth." ¹⁹And the temple of God in heaven was opened and his ark of the covenant was seen in his temple, and there were lightenings and sounds and thunders and an earthquake and large hail.

11:15 Καὶ ὁ ἕβδομος ἄγγελος ἐσάλπισεν· καὶ ἐγένοντο φωναὶ μεγάλαι ἐν τῷ οὐρανῷ λέγοντες· ἐγένετο ἡ βασιλεία τοῦ κόσμου τοῦ κυρίου ἡμῶν καὶ τοῦ Χριστοῦ αὐτοῦ, καὶ βασιλεύσει εἰς τοὺς αἰῶνας τῶν αἰώνων.

ὁ ἕβδομος ἄγγελος. Nominative subject of ἐσάλπισεν.

ἐσάλπισεν. Aor act ind 3rd sg σαλπίζω.

ἐγένοντο. Aor mid ind 3rd pl γίνομαι.

φωναὶ μεγάλαι. Nominative subject of ἐγένοντο.

ἐν τῷ οὐρανῷ. Locative.

λέγοντες. Pres act ptc masc nom pl (manner). The feminine subject is followed by a masculine participle. Perhaps this is a construction according to sense, since the voices could come from angels or the multitude of saints (7:9; Beale, 611).

ἐγένοντο. Aor mid ind 3rd sg γίνομαι. It is doubtful that this is to be taken as a "proleptic aorist" similar to a Hebrew so-called "prophetic perfect" (Aune, 2.638). Rather, from the standpoint of the speakers of this hymn, this is an example of an aorist used of an event that has just taken place, but which also overlaps with present time (Porter 1989a, 226; Wallace, 565; Fanning, 275). God's kingdom has arrived. Mounce says that throughout this section (vv. 15-17) "the extensive use of the aorist tense conveys a sense of absolute certainty" (230). However, the absolute certainty of the events yet to take place comes from the context and the one speaking, not from any specific tense usage. It is difficult to think that events portrayed in the present, perfect, or future tense are any less certain.

ἡ βασιλεία. Nominative subject of ἐγένοντο.

τοῦ κόσμου. Objective genitive. The term κόσμος occurs only here and in 13:8 and 17:8. In all three places it probably carries a negative sense of the entire system of human existence that is in conflict with and opposed to God and his purposes and kingdom (see BDAG, 562.7.b).

τοῦ κυρίου. Possessive genitive, functioning as the predicate of ἐγένοντο.

ἡμῶν. Genitive of subordination.

τοῦ Χριστοῦ. Possessive genitive, functioning as the predicate of ἐγένοντο.

αὐτοῦ. Genitive of relationship.

βασιλεύσει. Fut act ind 3rd sg βασιλεύω. The subject of the singular here is ambiguous, since it could be either κυρίου or Χριστοῦ (the antecedent of αὐτοῦ, which modifies Χριστοῦ, is κυρίου, suggesting that two different persons are being referred to here). Since the kingdom belongs to both the Lord and his Christ, it is likely that the ambiguity is deliberate, and is due to the trinitarian nature of the author's theology (see ch. 5 where God and the Lamb are both objects of the same worship, and both sit on the one throne [5:11-13]). Therefore, the singular represents the unity of God and Christ as the "one" who will rule. On "Trinitarian Ambiguity" in 1–3 John, see Culy (2004, xxvii).

εἰς τοὺς αἰῶνας τῶν αἰώνων. Temporal. On this construction, see 1:18.

11:16 Καὶ οἱ εἴκοσι τέσσαρες πρεσβύτεροι [οἱ] ἐνώπιον τοῦ θεοῦ καθήμενοι ἐπὶ τοὺς θρόνους αὐτῶν ἔπεσαν ἐπὶ τὰ πρόσωπα αὐτῶν καὶ προσεκύνησαν τῷ θεῷ

οἱ εἴκοσι τέσσαρες πρεσβύτεροι. Nominative subject of ἔπεσαν.
[οἱ] . . . καθήμενοι. Pres mid ptc masc nom pl κάθημαι (attributive).
ἐνώπιον τοῦ θεοῦ. Locative.
ἐπὶ τοὺς θρόνους. Locative.
αὐτῶν. Possessive genitive.

ἔπεσαν. Aor act ind 3rd pl πίπτω.
ἐπὶ τὰ πρόσωπα. Locative.
αὐτῶν. Possessive genitive.
προσεκύνησαν. Aor act ind 3rd pl προσκυνέω.
τῷ θεῷ. Dative direct object of προσεκύνησαν.

11:17 λέγοντες· εὐχαριστοῦμέν σοι, κύριε ὁ θεὸς ὁ παντοκράτωρ, ὁ ὢν καὶ ὁ ἦν, ὅτι εἴληφας τὴν δύναμίν σου τὴν μεγάλην καὶ ἐβασίλευσας.

λέγοντες. Pres act ptc masc nom pl λέγω (manner). On the use of the participle λέγοντες to introduce speech, see 1:17 on λέγων.

εὐχαριστοῦμέν. Pres act ind 1st pl εὐχαριστέω. The accenting is due to the enclitic σοι that follows.

σοι. Dative indirect object of εὐχαριστοῦμέν.

κύριε. Vocative of address.

ὁ θεὸς. Nominative for vocative in apposition to κύριε.

ὁ παντοκράτωρ. Nominative for vocative in apposition to κύριε.

ὁ ὢν. Pres act ptc masc nom sg εἰμί (substantival). Nominative in apposition to κύριε.

ὁ ἦν. Nominative in apposition to κύριε.

ἦν. Impf act ind 3rd sg εἰμί. On the imperfect form, see 1:7. The formula here lacks the ὁ ἐρχόμενος of the threefold formula in 1:7, 8. The reason, no doubt, is because in this poem God has received power and his kingdom has already come (v. 15). Thus the reference to the future coming (ὁ ἐρχόμενος) is no longer necessary. Some manuscripts (051 1006 1841 *al*) add ὁ ἐρχόμενος to conform with the earlier threefold form of this formula.

ὅτι. Introduces a causal clause.

εἴληφας. Prf act ind 2nd sg λαμβάνω. The perfect tense here may be used to emphasize the state of reception of power by God as the basis for his ruling.

τὴν δύναμίν . . . τὴν μεγάλην. Accusative direct object of εἴληφας.

σου. Possessive genitive or subjective genitive.

ἐβασίλευσας. Aor act ind 2nd sg βασιλεύω. The aorist here is timeless, though it is possible that in the context of receiving power it carries an ingressive notion ("you have become king" or "you have begun to reign"; so Robertson, 834; Osborne, 443 n. 7; Blount, 220; Smalley, 290). This notion, if present at all, comes from the context and is not the "meaning" of the aorist tense (see "Verbal Aspect" in the Introduction). However, rather than an ingressive notion, it is more likely that the aorist here only suggests the present or the timeless notion that God reigns ("you reign").

11:18 καὶ τὰ ἔθνη ὠργίσθησαν, καὶ ἦλθεν ἡ ὀργή σου καὶ ὁ καιρὸς τῶν νεκρῶν κριθῆναι καὶ δοῦναι τὸν μισθὸν τοῖς δούλοις σου τοῖς προφήταις καὶ τοῖς ἁγίοις καὶ τοῖς φοβουμένοις τὸ ὄνομά σου, τοὺς μικροὺς καὶ τοὺς μεγάλους, καὶ διαφθεῖραι τοὺς διαφθείροντας τὴν γῆν.

τὰ ἔθνη. Nominative subject of ὠργίσθησαν.

ὠργίσθησαν. Aor mid ind 3rd pl ὀργίζω. The -θη form here functions as a middle. On the voice, see "Deponency" in the Series Introduction. Here the plural neuter subject (ἔθνη) is found with a plural verb, rather than the more commom singular verb. In Revelation, words in the neuter with reference to personal beings often take a plural verb (Turner, 313).

ἦλθεν. Aor act ind 3rd sg ἔρχομαι. The singular verb is followed by multiple subjects. The verb ἦλθεν takes its number from the first subject mentioned (Turner, 313).

ἡ ὀργή. Nominative subject of ἦλθεν.

σου. Subjective genitive.

ὁ καιρὸς. Nominative subject of ἦλθεν.

τῶν νεκρῶν. Possessive genitive.

κριθῆναι. Aor pass inf κρίνω (epexegetical to καιρός).

δοῦναι. Aor act inf δίδωμι (epexegetical to καιρός).

τὸν μισθὸν. Accusative direct object of δοῦναι.

τοῖς δούλοις . . . καὶ τοῖς ἁγίοις καὶ τοῖς φοβουμένοις. Dative indirect object of δοῦναι.

σου. Possessive genitive.

τοῖς προφήταις. Dative in apposition to δούλοις.

τοῖς φοβουμένοις. Pres mid ptc masc dat pl φοβέομαι (substantival). This is not an additional group to τοῖς δούλοις . . . καὶ τοῖς ἁγίοις. Rather, the καί preceding it may be epexegetical, further identifying τοῖς δούλοις . . . καὶ τοῖς ἁγίοις.

τὸ ὄνομά. Accusative direct object of τοῖς φοβουμένοις. The accenting is due to the enclitic σου that follows.

σου. Possessive genitive.

τοὺς μικροὺς καὶ τοὺς μεγάλους. There is a grammatical incongruity with this accusative noun phrase standing in apposition to the dative τοῖς φοβουμένοις. An explanation for the accusative case here is difficult (Robertson, 414), but it may be due to an allusion to the identical wording in LXX Ps 113:21 (τοὺς μικροὺς καὶ τοὺς μεγάλους). The variant τοῖς μικροῖς καὶ τοῖς μεγάλοις is found in ℵ² 𝔐.

διαφθεῖραι. Aor act inf διαφθείρω (epexegetical to καιρός).

τοὺς διαφθείροντας. Pres act ptc masc acc pl διαφθείρω (substantival). Accusative direct object of διαφθεῖραι.

τὴν γῆν. Accusative direct object of διαφθείροντας.

11:19 Καὶ ἠνοίγη ὁ ναὸς τοῦ θεοῦ ὁ ἐν τῷ οὐρανῷ καὶ ὤφθη ἡ κιβωτὸς τῆς διαθήκης αὐτοῦ ἐν τῷ ναῷ αὐτοῦ, καὶ ἐγένοντο ἀστραπαὶ καὶ φωναὶ καὶ βρονταὶ καὶ σεισμὸς καὶ χάλαζα μεγάλη.

ἠνοίγη. Aor pass ind 3rd sg ἀνοίγω.
ὁ ναὸς. Nominative subject of ἠνοίγη.
τοῦ θεοῦ. Possessive genitive.
ὁ. The article functions as an adjectivizer that turns the PP into an attributive modifier of ὁ ναός: Lit. "the in-the-heaven temple."
ἐν τῷ οὐρανῷ. Locative.
ὤφθη. Aor pass ind 3rd sg ὁράω.
ἡ κιβωτὸς. Nominative subject of ὤφθη.
τῆς διαθήκης. Genitive of description.
αὐτοῦ. Possessive genitive. There is some ambiguity as to which word this modifies: the entire expression ἡ κιβωτός τῆς διαθήκης ("his ark of the covenant") or only διαθήκης ("the ark of his covenant"). Both Aune (2.677) and Smalley (294) appeal to OT evidence to support the first and second option respectively. Thus, one can find references to "my (God's) covenant," but also to "the ark of God" or "the ark of Yahweh" (Aune, 2.677). The meaning of the text is not significantly affected either way, but given the focus on the ark in this context, the first option, that αὐτοῦ modifies the entire expression, is likely. Aune (2.677) says that there are thirty references in the OT to the "ark of the covenant of Yahweh" or "ark of the covenant of God" where the possessive phrase "of Yahweh/God" seems to modify the entire phrase "the ark of the covenant" (e.g., Num 10:33; 14:44; Deut 10:8; 31:9; Josh 3:3; 4:7; 6:6; 1 Sam 4:3; 1 Kgs 3:15; 1 Chr 15:25-26; 2 Chr 5:7).
ἐν τῷ ναῷ. Locative.
αὐτοῦ. Possessive genitive.
ἐγένοντο. Aor mid ind 3rd pl γίνομαι.
ἀστραπαὶ καὶ φωναὶ καὶ βρονταὶ καὶ σεισμὸς καὶ χάλαζα μεγάλη. Nominative subject of ἐγένοντο.

Revelation 12:1-6

[1]And a great sign was seen in heaven, a woman clothed with the sun, and the moon was under her feet and upon her head was a crown of twelve stars. [2]And she was pregnant, and she cried out suffering birth pangs and in the throes of giving birth. [3]And another sign was seen in heaven, and look a large red dragon having seven heads and ten horns and upon his heads were seven crowns, [4]and his tail dragged a third of the stars

of heaven and he threw them onto the earth. And the dragon stood before the woman who was about to give birth, in order that whenever she gives birth to her child he might devour it. ⁵And she gave birth to a son, a male, who is about to shepherd all the nations with an iron rod. And her child was snatched up to God and to his throne. ⁶And the woman fled into the desert where there is a place prepared by God, in order that she might be nourished there for twelve hundred and sixty days.

12:1 Καὶ σημεῖον μέγα ὤφθη ἐν τῷ οὐρανῷ, γυνὴ περιβεβλημένη τὸν ἥλιον, καὶ ἡ σελήνη ὑποκάτω τῶν ποδῶν αὐτῆς καὶ ἐπὶ τῆς κεφαλῆς αὐτῆς στέφανος ἀστέρων δώδεκα,

σημεῖον μέγα. Nominative subject of ὤφθη.

ὤφθη. Aor pass ind 3rd sg ὁράω.

ἐν τῷ οὐρανῷ. Locative.

γυνὴ. Nominative in apposition to σημεῖον μέγα.

περιβεβλημένη. Prf mid ptc fem nom sg περιβάλλω (attributive).

τὸν ἥλιον. Accusative direct object of περιβεβλημένη.

ἡ σελήνη. Nominative subject of a verbless clause.

ὑποκάτω τῶν ποδῶν. Locative.

αὐτῆς. Possessive genitive.

ἐπὶ τῆς κεφαλῆς. Locative.

αὐτῆς. Possessive genitive.

στέφανος. Nominative subject of a verbless clause. In contrast to the διαδήματα (see below on v. 3), the στέφανος was a wreath signifying honor or victory or high office (LN 6.192).

ἀστέρων δώδεκα. Epexegetical genitive. "A crown consisting of twelve stars."

12:2 καὶ ἐν γαστρὶ ἔχουσα, καὶ κράζει ὠδίνουσα καὶ βασανιζομένη τεκεῖν.

ἐν γαστρὶ ἔχουσα. Lit. "having in the belly." This is "a technical phrase for a pregnant woman" (Aune, 2.682; see also Matt 1:18, 23; 1 Thess 5:3).

ἔχουσα. Pres act ptc fem nom sg ἔχω. This is an example of the participle functioning independently as a finite verb (Mussies, 325; Wallace, 653; see also 1:16 on ἔχων).

κράζει. Pres act ind 3rd sg κράζω. Historical or narrative present (see 4:5 on ἐκπορεύονται). Here it probably highlights the agony of the woman. Some manuscripts (C 2351 𝔐ᵏ) change the verb to the imperfect ἔκραζεν, while 046 has the aorist ἔκραξεν.

ὠδίνουσα. Pres act ptc fem nom sg ὠδίνω (manner or cause).

βασανιζομένη. Pres mid ptc fem nom sg βασανίζω (manner or cause). Smalley (316) incorrectly labels this as a historical present, since the label should only be applied to present indicative verbs in narrative (see 4:5 on ἐκπορεύονται).

τεκεῖν. Aor act inf τίκτω. The function of the infinitive here and what it modifies are unclear. It seems to explain the reason for her crying out (κράζει), but it is also possible that τεκεῖν modifies βασανιζομένη, giving the reason or the purpose for her being tormented (Swete, 149).

12:3 καὶ ὤφθη ἄλλο σημεῖον ἐν τῷ οὐρανῷ, καὶ ἰδοὺ δράκων μέγας πυρρὸς ἔχων κεφαλὰς ἑπτὰ καὶ κέρατα δέκα καὶ ἐπὶ τὰς κεφαλὰς αὐτοῦ ἑπτὰ διαδήματα,

ὤφθη. Aor pass ind 3rd sg ὁράω.
ἄλλο σημεῖον. Nominative subject of ὤφθη.
ἐν τῷ οὐρανῷ. Locative.
ἰδοὺ. A marker of attention that deictically functions to make the following statement emphatic. On the form of ἰδού, see 1:7. Here it draws attention to the dragon figure.
δράκων πυρρὸς μέγας. Nominative subject of a verbless clause.
ἔχων. Pres act ptc masc nom sg ἔχω (attributive).
κεφαλὰς ἑπτὰ καὶ κέρατα δέκα. Accusative direct object of ἔχων.
ἐπὶ τὰς κεφαλὰς. Locative.
αὐτοῦ. Possessive genitive.
ἑπτὰ διαδήματα. Accusative direct object of ἔχων. In contrast to the στέφανος (see above on v. 1), the διαδήμα was "a type of crown employed as a symbol of the highest ruling power in a particular area and therefore often associated with kingship" (LN 6.196). Besides here and in 13:1 to refer to the dragon and the beast, the only other place this term occurs is in 19:12 on the rider on the white horse.

12:4 καὶ ἡ οὐρὰ αὐτοῦ σύρει τὸ τρίτον τῶν ἀστέρων τοῦ οὐρανοῦ καὶ ἔβαλεν αὐτοὺς εἰς τὴν γῆν. Καὶ ὁ δράκων ἕστηκεν ἐνώπιον τῆς γυναικὸς τῆς μελλούσης τεκεῖν, ἵνα ὅταν τέκῃ τὸ τέκνον αὐτῆς καταφάγῃ.

ἡ οὐρὰ. Nominative subject of σύρει.
αὐτοῦ. Possessive genitive.
σύρει. Pres act ind 3rd sg σύρω. Historical or narrative present (see 4:5 on ἐκπορεύονται). In the midst of narrative aorists, the use of the present tense here functions "to draw attention to one particularly salient [defiant] action of the dragon" (Mathewson 2010, 144).
τὸ τρίτον. Accusative direct object of σύρει.
τῶν ἀστέρων. Partitive genitive.
τοῦ οὐρανοῦ. Genitive of location (stars in heaven).

ἔβαλεν. Aor act ind 3rd sg βάλλω. The author switches from the present (σύρει) to the aorist (ἔβαλεν) to the perfect (ἕστηκεν) in verse 4, and then back to the aorist in verse 5 (ἔτεκεν). This is not a "strange concantenation" of tenses as Osborne claims (461 n. 5). Rather, from the standpoint of verbal aspect, the aorists carry along the storyline, summarizing the main events, while the present and perfect select certain elements of the story to foreground (see "Verbal Aspect" in the Introduction).

αὐτοὺς. Accusative direct object of ἔβαλεν.

εἰς τὴν γῆν. Locative.

ὁ δράκων. Nominative subject of ἕστηκεν. The article is anaphoric referring back to the first mention of δράκων in verse 3.

ἕστηκεν. Prf act ind 3rd sg ἵστημι. The perfect tense may function to highlight the malicious intent of the dragon. It might also serve to contrast with the posture of the Lamb and his followers who also stand (e.g., 5:6; 7:9; 11:4). See also above on ἔβαλεν.

ἐνώπιον τῆς γυναικὸς. Locative. The article is anaphoric referring back to the first mention of the γυνή in verse 1.

τῆς μελλούσης. Pres act ptc fem gen sg μέλλω (attributive).

τεκεῖν. Aor act inf τίκτω (complementary).

ἵνα. Introduces a purpose clause.

ὅταν. Introduces an indefinite temporal clause within the ἵνα clause.

τέκῃ. Aor act subj 3rd sg τίκτω. Subjunctive with ὅταν.

τὸ τέκνον. Accusative direct object of τέκῃ.

αὐτῆς. Genitive of relationship.

καταφάγῃ. Aor act subj 3rd sg κατεσθίω. Subjunctive with ἵνα. The prefixed preposition κατά intensifies the meaning of the verb (φάγῃ—"eat"; καταφάγῃ—"devour"; see Porter 1992, 140–41). The assumed object of καταφάγῃ is τέκνον.

12:5 καὶ ἔτεκεν υἱὸν ἄρσεν, ὃς μέλλει ποιμαίνειν πάντα τὰ ἔθνη ἐν ῥάβδῳ σιδηρᾷ. καὶ ἡρπάσθη τὸ τέκνον αὐτῆς πρὸς τὸν θεὸν καὶ πρὸς τὸν θρόνον αὐτοῦ.

ἔτεκεν. Aor act ind 3rd sg τίκτω. On the tense, see also verse 4 on ἔβαλεν.

υἱόν. Accusative direct object of ἔτεκεν.

ἄρσεν. Accusative in apposition to υἱόν. The neuter adjective stands in apposition to the masculine υἱόν. Later in 12:13 the author uses the masculine ἄρσενα. Beale (640–41) suggests that the neuter here draws attention to the OT allusion to LXX Isa 66:7 (ἄρσεν). The masculine accusative ἄρσενα or ἄρρενα is found in $\mathfrak{P}^{47}$ ℵ P 046 051 1006 1611 1841 1854 2053 2329 2344 2351 𝔐, probably in conformity to ἄρσενα in verse 13. However, given the strong external support for the masculine reading, it is possible that a scribe altered it to the neuter to conform to Isa 66:7, or that the final vowel on ἄρσενα was inadvertently dropped out, perhaps if the scribe was hearing it read with the following ὅς.

ὅς. Nominative subject of μέλλει.
μέλλει. Pres act ind 3rd sg μέλλω.
ποιμαίνειν. Pres act inf ποιμαίνω (complementary). On the meaning, see 2:27 on ποιμανεῖ (the use in 7:17 contrasts).
πάντα τὰ ἔθνη. Accusative direct object of ποιμαίνειν.
ἐν ῥάβδῳ σιδηρᾷ. Instrumental.
ἡρπάσθη. Aor pass ind 3rd sg ἁρπάζω.
τὸ τέκνον. Nominative subject of ἡρπάσθη.
αὐτῆς. Genitive of relationship.
πρὸς τὸν θεὸν καὶ πρὸς τὸν θρόνον. Here πρός is a "marker of movement or orientation toward someone/someth." (BDAG, 874.3).
αὐτοῦ. Possessive genitive.

12:6 καὶ ἡ γυνὴ ἔφυγεν εἰς τὴν ἔρημον, ὅπου ἔχει ἐκεῖ τόπον ἡτοιμασμένον ἀπὸ τοῦ θεοῦ, ἵνα ἐκεῖ τρέφωσιν αὐτὴν ἡμέρας χιλίας διακοσίας ἑξήκοντα.

ἡ γυνὴ. Nominative subject of ἔφυγεν. The nominative γυνή switches the topic from the son in verse 5 back to the woman. On the use of the article, see verse 4.
ἔφυγεν. Aor act ind 3rd sg φεύγω.
εἰς τὴν ἔρημον. Locative.
ὅπου. Locative. The local adverb ὅπου substitutes for a relative pronoun (Caragounis, 193). The entire clause ὅπου ἔχει ἐκεῖ τόπον modifies ἔρημον.
ἔχει. Pres act ind 3rd sg ἔχω. Historical or narrative present (see 4:5 on ἐκπορεύονται).
ἐκεῖ. Locative. The ἐκεῖ here is redundant following ὅπου ("where she has a place there"). Like the redundant use of the pronoun (see Rev 3:8) this construction probably highlights the antecedent, the location of the woman's protection.
τόπον. Accusative direct object of ἔχει.
ἡτοιμασμένον. Prf pass ptc masc acc sg ἑτοιμάζω (attributive).
ἀπὸ τοῦ θεοῦ. Agency is sometimes expressed by ἀπό rather than by ὑπό (Wallace, 433), as here.
ἵνα. Introduces a purpose clause.
ἐκεῖ. Locative.
τρέφωσιν. Pres act subj 3rd pl τρέφω. Subjunctive with ἵνα. Osborne reads too much into the present tense by concluding that it is used here "to stress God's continual care of the church during that period" (464).

The present tense simply looks at the action as a process seen as unfolding (see "Verbal Aspect" in the Introduction). The plural number should probably be explained as an impersonal use of the verb with a plural subject, which can be translated as a passive: "She might be nourished" (see Robertson, 820; McKay, 19; see also 2:24 on ὡς λέγουσιν).

αὐτὴν. Accusative direct object of τρέφωσιν.

ἡμέρας χιλίας διακοσίας ἑξήκοντα. Accusative indicating extent of time.

Revelation 12:7-18

⁷And a war took place in heaven, Michael and the angels fighting with the dragon. And the dragon and his angels made war, ⁸and they were not strong enough, nor was there a place found for them in heaven any longer. ⁹And the great dragon was thrown down, the ancient serpent, the one called the Devil and Satan, the one who deceives the entire inhabited world, was thrown onto the earth and his angels were also thrown down with him. ¹⁰And I heard a loud voice in heaven saying, "Now has come the salvation and power and kingdom of our God and the authority of his Christ, for the accuser of our brothers has been thrown down, the one who accuses them before the throne of God day and night. ¹¹And they overcame him because of the blood of the Lamb and because of the word of their testimony. And they did not love their lives even in the face of death. ¹²For this reason rejoice, Oh heavens and those dwelling in them. Woe to the earth and to the sea, for the accuser has come down to you, having great wrath, knowing that he has only a short time." ¹³And when the dragon saw that he had been thrown down onto the earth, he pursued the woman who gave birth to the male son. ¹⁴And two wings of a great eagle were given to the woman, in order that she might fly into the desert into her place, where she will be nurtured for a time, times, and half a time from the presence of the serpent. ¹⁵And the serpent poured out water as a river from its mouth behind the woman, in order that he might cause her to be swept away by the river. ¹⁶And the earth helped the woman, and the earth opened its mouth and drank up the river that the dragon poured out of its mouth. ¹⁷And the dragon was angered by the woman and it went away to make war with the rest of her offspring who keep the commands of God and who hold their witness about Jesus. ¹⁸And the dragon stood on the sand of the seashore.

12:7 Καὶ ἐγένετο πόλεμος ἐν τῷ οὐρανῷ, ὁ Μιχαὴλ καὶ οἱ ἄγγελοι αὐτοῦ τοῦ πολεμῆσαι μετὰ τοῦ δράκοντος. καὶ ὁ δράκων ἐπολέμησεν καὶ οἱ ἄγγελοι αὐτοῦ,

ἐγένετο. Aor mid ind 3rd sg γίνομαι.

πόλεμος. Nominative subject of ἐγένετο. The nominative introduces a new topic.

ἐν τῷ οὐρανῷ. Locative.

ὁ Μιχαὴλ καὶ οἱ ἄγγελοι αὐτοῦ τοῦ πολεμῆσαι μετὰ τοῦ δράκοντος. The entire phrase stands in apposition to πόλεμος ἐν τῷ οὐρανῷ.

ὁ Μιχαὴλ καὶ οἱ ἄγγελοι ... τοῦ πολεμῆσαι. There are two difficult grammatical issues in this clause. (1) ὁ Μιχαὴλ καὶ οἱ ἄγγελοι apparently functions as the nominative subject of the infinitive πολεμῆσαι, where an accusative subject would normally be expected. Moule (129) thinks this is an example of John's "barbarous Greek." However, there are at least two ways that this has been explained. First, this could be an example of Semitic influence, where in Hebrew a subject precedes a *lamed* (ל) prefix with an infinitive (Charles, 1.322; Mussies, 96; Thompson, 62–63; Aune, 2.654; Beale, 654; Smalley, 322–23). There are clear examples of this construction in the LXX (see Hos 9:13; 1 Chr 9:25; Ps 24:14; Ecc 3:15; Aune, 2.654). Second, some have attempted to solve the difficulty by postulating an ellipsis of ἦλθον preceding the infinitive (Beale, 654): "Michael and his angels *came* to make war," or by an ellipsis of ἐγένετο (from the beginning of the verse) before ὁ Μιχαὴλ: "There *came* Michael and his angels to make war" (Swete, 153). In both of these proposals the nominative would function naturally as the subject of the elided verbs, thus solving the problem. A third possibility is that the nominative case as the subject of the infinitive is meant to draw attention to Michael and his angels as the ones who do battle with Satan and his angels. (2) There is uncertainty as to how to classify the infinitive τοῦ πολεμῆσαι (omitted by 2351). If an elided ἦλθον or ἐγένετο is assumed, then the infinitive functions to indicate purpose or result. Several scholars think that the infinitive τοῦ πολεμῆσαι is in apposition to or epexegetical to πόλεμος. Turner, for example, notes that τοῦ with the infinitive can function epexegetically (141; see also Robertson, 1066; Porter 1992, 199). The most likely explanations are either that the infinitive is epexegetical to πόλεμος and that the nominative subject of the infinitive is meant to draw attention to Michael (perhaps to draw attention to an OT allusion in Dan 10:13, 21; 12:1) and his angels, or that ἐγένετο (from the beginning of the verse) is to be supplied before the mention of Michael. Fortunately, the sense of the construction is not affected by the grammatical difficulty.

αὐτοῦ. Possessive genitive.

πολεμῆσαι. Aor act inf πολεμέω (epexegetical; see above on ὁ Μιχαὴλ καὶ οἱ ἄγγελοι ... τοῦ πολεμῆσαι).

μετὰ τοῦ δράκοντος. Accompaniment. Harris (164) is correct that μετά can be *translated* "against," but is probably incorrect in suggesting that semantically this is one of the meanings of the preposition. On the article with δράκοντος, see verse 4.

ὁ δράκων . . . καὶ οἱ ἄγγελοι. Nominative subject of ἐπολέμησεν. On the article with δράκων, see verse 4.

ἐπολέμησεν. Aor act ind 3rd sg πολεμέω. The plural subject ὁ δράκων . . . καὶ οἱ ἄγγελοι is used with a singular verb. As McKay (1994) notes, "If one of the subjects is more important than the others [here, ὁ δράκων] a singular verb may be attached to it" (18).

αὐτοῦ. Possessive genitive.

12:8 καὶ οὐκ ἴσχυσεν οὐδὲ τόπος εὑρέθη αὐτῶν ἔτι ἐν τῷ οὐρανῷ.

ἴσχυσεν. Aor act ind 3rd sg ἰσχύω.
τόπος. Nominative subject of εὑρέθη.
εὑρέθη. Aor pass ind 3rd sg εὑρίσκω.
αὐτῶν. Possessive genitive. The genitive is separated from its head noun (τόπος) by the verb.
ἔτι. With a negative οὐδέ the adverb ἔτι should be translated "no longer" (BDAG, 400.1.b.β).
ἐν τῷ οὐρανῷ. Locative.

12:9 καὶ ἐβλήθη ὁ δράκων ὁ μέγας, ὁ ὄφις ὁ ἀρχαῖος, ὁ καλούμενος Διάβολος καὶ ὁ Σατανᾶς, ὁ πλανῶν τὴν οἰκουμένην ὅλην, ἐβλήθη εἰς τὴν γῆν, καὶ οἱ ἄγγελοι αὐτοῦ μετ' αὐτοῦ ἐβλήθησαν.

ἐβλήθη. Aor pass ind 3rd sg βάλλω. The passive keeps the focus on the grammatical subject ὁ δράκων.

ὁ δράκων ὁ μέγας. Nominative subject of ἐβλήθη. On the article, see verse 4.

ὁ ὄφις ὁ ἀρχαῖος. Nominative in apposition to ὁ δράκων ὁ μέγας.

ὁ καλούμενος. Pres pass ptc masc nom sg καλέω (substantival). Nominative in apposition to ὁ δράκων ὁ μέγας.

Διάβολος καὶ ὁ Σατανᾶς. With ὁ δράκων ὁ μέγας this forms a double nominative construction with a passive verb from a double accusative construction (Culy 2009, 83–87): "I call the dragon the devil and Satan."

ὁ πλανῶν. Pres act ptc masc nom sg πλανάω (substantival). Nominative in apposition to ὁ δράκων ὁ μέγας. This piling up of nominative constructions in apposition to ὁ δράκων is what is often referred to by linguists as "overspecification" (Runge, 317–23), providing more information than is necessary. Here it functions to focus attention on the dragon, and to draw attention to the OT background (Gen 3).

τὴν οἰκουμένην ὅλην. Accusative direct object of ὁ πλανῶν. "All the inhabitants of the earth" (BDAG, 699.3).

ἐβλήθη. Aor pass ind 3rd sg βάλλω. ἐβλήθη here is resumptive, picking up the initial ἐβλήθη, which was cut off by the string of appositional phrases.

εἰς τὴν γῆν. Locative.

οἱ ἄγγελοι. Nominative subject of ἐβλήθησαν.

αὐτοῦ. Possessive genitive.

μετ' αὐτοῦ. Accompaniment.

ἐβλήθησαν. Aor pass ind 3rd spl βάλλω.

12:10 καὶ ἤκουσα φωνὴν μεγάλην ἐν τῷ οὐρανῷ λέγουσαν· ἄρτι ἐγένετο ἡ σωτηρία καὶ ἡ δύναμις καὶ ἡ βασιλεία τοῦ θεοῦ ἡμῶν καὶ ἡ ἐξουσία τοῦ χριστοῦ αὐτοῦ, ὅτι ἐβλήθη ὁ κατήγωρ τῶν ἀδελφῶν ἡμῶν, ὁ κατηγορῶν αὐτοὺς ἐνώπιον τοῦ θεοῦ ἡμῶν ἡμέρας καὶ νυκτός.

ἤκουσα. Aor act ind 1st sg ἀκούω.

φωνὴν μεγάλην. Accusative direct object of ἤκουσα.

ἐν τῷ οὐρανῷ. Locative.

λέγουσαν. Pres act ptc fem acc sg λέγω. Complement in an object-complement double accusative construction. On the use of the participle λέγουσαν to introduce speech, see 1:17 on λέγων.

ἐγένετο. Aor mid ind 3rd sg γίνομαι. This is an example of an aorist used to refer to an action that has just occurred in the immediate past, which overlaps with present time. As Wallace says, "It is sometimes difficult to tell whether the aorist refers to the immediate past or to the present (dramatic)" (565). Note the temporal adverb ἄρτι, which helps establish the temporal frame of reference. When a verb precedes multiple subjects (plural) it often takes the number of the first subject (ἡ σωτηρία) (Turner, 313; Charles, 1.cxli).

ἡ σωτηρία καὶ ἡ δύναμις καὶ ἡ βασιλεία. Nominative subject of ἐγένετο.

τοῦ θεοῦ. Subjective genitive. The genitive modifies all three preceding nouns.

ἡμῶν. Genitive of subordination.

ἡ ἐξουσία. Nominative subject of ἐγένετο.

τοῦ χριστοῦ. Subjective genitive.

αὐτοῦ. Genitive of relationship.

ὅτι. Introduces a causal clause.

ἐβλήθη. Aor pass ind 3rd sg βάλλω.

ὁ κατήγωρ. Nominative subject of ἐβλήθη.

τῶν ἀδελφῶν. Objective genitive.

ἡμῶν. Genitive of relationship.

ὁ κατηγορῶν. Pres act ptc masc nom sg κατηγορέω (substantival). Nominative in apposition to ὁ κατήγωρ. The verb means "to bring serious charges or accusations against someone, with the possible connotation of a legal or court context" (LN 33.427). Mussies (341) and Aune (2.655) think that the participle is past-time referring, since the accuser has now been cast out of heaven and can no longer accuse God's people. However, the present participle is often used in Revelation simply to refer to a characteristic of one who is identified as one who does the action of the participle ("the one who accuses").

αὐτούς. Accusative direct object of ὁ κατηγορῶν.
ἐνώπιον τοῦ θεοῦ. Locative.
ἡμῶν. Genitive of subordination.
ἡμέρας καὶ νυκτός. Genitive of time (see 4:8).

12:11 καὶ αὐτοὶ ἐνίκησαν αὐτὸν διὰ τὸ αἷμα τοῦ ἀρνίου καὶ διὰ τὸν λόγον τῆς μαρτυρίας αὐτῶν καὶ οὐκ ἠγάπησαν τὴν ψυχὴν αὐτῶν ἄχρι θανάτου.

αὐτοί. Nominative subject of ἐνίκησαν.
ἐνίκησαν. Aor act ind 3rd pl νικάω.
αὐτόν. Accusative direct object of ἐνίκησαν.
διὰ τὸ αἷμα. Cause, although most English versions translate this as indicating means. "Blood" is a metonymy for "death" by substituting the means (shedding of blood) for the effect (death).
τοῦ ἀρνίου. Possessive genitive.
διὰ τὸν λόγον. Cause.
τῆς μαρτυρίας. Objective genitive ("the word about their witness") or epexegetical genitive ("the word, which is their testimony"; Aune, 2.703; Smalley, 328).
αὐτῶν. Subjective genitive.
ἠγάπησαν. Aor act ind 3rd pl ἀγαπάω.
τὴν ψυχήν. Accusative direct object of ἠγάπησαν.
αὐτῶν. Possessive genitive. A singular noun is modified by a plural pronoun. According to Turner this is a "distributive singular," where "[s]omething belonging to each person in a group of people is placed in the sing" (23).
ἄχρι θανάτου. Extent. ἄχρι functions as "a marker of extension up to a certain point, *as far as*" (BDAG, 161.2).

12:12 διὰ τοῦτο εὐφραίνεσθε, [οἱ] οὐρανοὶ καὶ οἱ ἐν αὐτοῖς σκηνοῦντες. οὐαὶ τὴν γῆν καὶ τὴν θάλασσαν, ὅτι κατέβη ὁ διάβολος πρὸς ὑμᾶς ἔχων θυμὸν μέγαν, εἰδὼς ὅτι ὀλίγον καιρὸν ἔχει.

διὰ τοῦτο. Cause. The antecedent of τοῦτο is the content of verses 10-11: the coming of God's kingdom, the overthrow of Satan, and the overcoming of the saints. Typically, neuter demonstrative pronouns have as their antecedent a syntactical unit larger than a single word. This connector, along with the imperative εὐφραίνεσθε and the nominatives of address οὐρανοὶ καὶ οἱ ... σκηνοῦντες, marks this verse as prominent. Here it contrasts with the woe pronounced on the sphere of earth and sea.

εὐφραίνεσθε. Pres mid impv 2nd pl εὐφραίνω.

[οἱ] οὐρανοὶ καὶ οἱ ... σκηνοῦντες. Nominative used as a vocative. This is the only place in the Apocalypse where οὐρανός occurs in the plural. This is probably due to an OT allusion; in a number of places the LXX contains a call to the heavens (οὐρανοί) to rejoice (Beale, 666; see Deut 32:43; 1 Chron 16:31; Ps 95[96]:11; Isa 44:23; 45:8; 49:13).

οἱ ... σκηνοῦντες. Pres act ptc masc nom pl σκηνόω (substantival). The word used here, σκηνόω (rather than οἰκέω), recalls the status of the saints as those who dwell in the heavenly temple (Beale, 666). See also 7:15; 13:6; 21:3, where God and/or the saints dwell in the heavenly tabernacle/temple.

ἐν αὐτοῖς. Locative.

οὐαί. An interjection that denotes "a state of intense hardship or distress" (LN 22.9).

τὴν γῆν καὶ τὴν θάλασσαν. Accusative with οὐαί. Only here and in 8:13 does the simple accusative occur with οὐαί. Usually the dative is found after οὐαί (Robertson, 1193). Since the Latin *uae* can be used with an accusative or a dative, Aune thinks that οὐαί with the accusative here could be a Latinism (2.656).

ὅτι. Introduces a causal clause.

κατέβη. Aor mid ind 3rd sg καταβαίνω.

ὁ διάβολος. Nominative subject of κατέβη.

πρὸς ὑμᾶς. Locative. The PP indicates movement toward someone (BDAG, 874.3.a).

ἔχων. Pres act ptc masc nom sg ἔχω (manner, modifying κατέβη).

θυμὸν μέγαν. Accusative direct object of ἔχων.

εἰδώς. Prf act ptc masc nom sg οἶδα (causal).

ὅτι. Introduces a content clause that is the clausal complement of εἰδώς.

ὀλίγον καιρὸν. Accusative direct object of ἔχει.

ἔχει. Pres act ind 3rd sg ἔχω.

12:13 Καὶ ὅτε εἶδεν ὁ δράκων ὅτι ἐβλήθη εἰς τὴν γῆν, ἐδίωξεν τὴν γυναῖκα ἥτις ἔτεκεν τὸν ἄρσενα.

ὅτε. Introduces a temporal clause.

εἶδεν. Aor act ind 3rd sg ὁράω.
ὁ δράκων. Nominative subject of εἶδεν. On the article, see verse 4.
ὅτι. Introduces a content clause that is the clausal complement of εἶδεν.
ἐβλήθη. Aor pass ind 3rd sg βάλλω.
εἰς τὴν γῆν. Locative.
ἐδίωξεν. Aor act ind 3rd sg διώκω.
τὴν γυναῖκα. Accusative direct object of ἐδίωξεν. On the article, see verse 4.
ἥτις. Nominative subject of ἔτεκεν.
ἔτεκεν. Aor act ind 3rd sg τίκτω.
τὸν ἄρσενα. Accusative direct object of ἔτεκεν. The article is anaphoric referring back to the ἄρσεν in verse 5.

12:14 καὶ ἐδόθησαν τῇ γυναικὶ αἱ δύο πτέρυγες τοῦ ἀετοῦ τοῦ μεγάλου, ἵνα πέτηται εἰς τὴν ἔρημον εἰς τὸν τόπον αὐτῆς, ὅπου τρέφεται ἐκεῖ καιρὸν καὶ καιροὺς καὶ ἥμισυ καιροῦ ἀπὸ προσώπου τοῦ ὄφεως.

ἐδόθησαν. Aor pass ind 3rd pl δίδωμι.
τῇ γυναικί. Dative indirect object of ἐδόθησαν. On the article, see verse 4.
αἱ δύο πτέρυγες. Nominative subject of ἐδόθησαν.
τοῦ ἀετοῦ τοῦ μεγάλου. Possessive genitive.
ἵνα. Introduces a purpose clause.
πέτηται. Pres mid subj 3rd sg πέτομαι. Subjunctive with ἵνα.
εἰς τὴν ἔρημον. Locative.
εἰς τὸν τόπον. Locative. The PP further specifies εἰς τὴν ἔρημον.
αὐτῆς. Possessive genitive.
ὅπου. Introduces a local clause (denoting space) that functions like a relative clause.
τρέφεται. Pres pass ind 3rd sg τρέφω. The present tense, along with the resumptive ὅπου . . . ἐκεῖ construction, highlights the protection of the woman.
ἐκεῖ. Locative. Resumes ὅπου. On the redundant use of ὅπου with ἐκεῖ, see verse 6 on ἐκεῖ.
καιρὸν καὶ καιροὺς καὶ ἥμισυ καιροῦ. Accusative indicating extent of time. Lit. "time and times and half of a time."
καιροῦ. Partitive genitive.
ἀπὸ προσώπου. Separation.
τοῦ ὄφεως. Possessive genitive.

12:15 καὶ ἔβαλεν ὁ ὄφις ἐκ τοῦ στόματος αὐτοῦ ὀπίσω τῆς γυναικὸς ὕδωρ ὡς ποταμόν, ἵνα αὐτὴν ποταμοφόρητον ποιήσῃ.

ἔβαλεν. Aor act ind 3rd sg βάλλω.
ὁ ὄφις. Nominative subject of ἔβαλεν.
ἐκ τοῦ στόματος. Source.
αὐτοῦ. Possessive genitive.
ὀπίσω τῆς γυναικὸς. Locative. On the article, see verse 4.
ὕδωρ. Accusative direct object of ἔβαλεν.
ὡς ποταμόν. Comparison.
ἵνα. Introduces a purpose clause.
αὐτὴν. Accusative direct object of ποιήσῃ.
ποταμοφόρητον. Complement in an object-complement double accusative construction with αὐτήν. The adjective means "pertaining to being carried away by a river or flood" (LN 15.205). A hapax legomenon in the NT.

ποιήσῃ. Aor act subj 3rd sg ποιέω. Subjunctive with ἵνα. Here ποιήσῃ is probably used in a causative sense ("he might cause her to be carried away by a river").

12:16 καὶ ἐβοήθησεν ἡ γῆ τῇ γυναικὶ καὶ ἤνοιξεν ἡ γῆ τὸ στόμα αὐτῆς καὶ κατέπιεν τὸν ποταμὸν ὃν ἔβαλεν ὁ δράκων ἐκ τοῦ στόματος αὐτοῦ.

ἐβοήθησεν. Aor act ind 3rd sg βοηθέω.
ἡ γῆ. Nominative subject of ἐβοήθησεν.
τῇ γυναικὶ. Dative direct object of ἐβοήθησεν.
ἤνοιξεν. Aor act ind 3rd sg ἀνοίγω.
ἡ γῆ. Nominative subject of ἤνοιξεν.
τὸ στόμα. Accusative direct object of ἤνοιξεν.
αὐτῆς. Possessive genitive.
κατέπιεν. Aor act ind 3rd sg καταπίνω. The prefixed κατά probably has an intensifying effect: "to drink down, *swallow, swallow up*" (BDAG, 524.1).
τὸν ποταμὸν. Accusative direct object of κατέπιεν.
ὃν. Accusative direct object of ἔβαλεν.
ἔβαλεν. Aor act ind 3rd sg βάλλω.
ὁ δράκων. Nominative subject of ἔβαλεν. On the article, see verse 4.
ἐκ τοῦ στόματος. Source.
αὐτοῦ. Possessive genitive.

12:17 καὶ ὠργίσθη ὁ δράκων ἐπὶ τῇ γυναικὶ καὶ ἀπῆλθεν ποιῆσαι πόλεμον μετὰ τῶν λοιπῶν τοῦ σπέρματος αὐτῆς τῶν τηρούντων τὰς ἐντολὰς τοῦ θεοῦ καὶ ἐχόντων τὴν μαρτυρίαν Ἰησοῦ.

ὠργίσθη. Aor pass or mid ind 3rd sg ὀργίζομαι. On the voice, see "Deponency" in the Series Introduction.

ὁ δράκων. Nominative subject of ὠργίσθη. On the article, see verse 4.

ἐπὶ τῇ γυναικὶ. "After verbs which express feelings" ἐπί can indicate the basis for those emotions and can be translated "*at, because of*" (BDAG, 365.6.c).

ἀπῆλθεν. Aor act ind 3rd sg ἀπέρχομαι.

ποιῆσαι. Aor act inf ποιέω (purpose).

πόλεμον. Accusative direct object of ποιῆσαι.

μετὰ τῶν λοιπῶν. Accompaniment (see also v. 7).

τοῦ σπέρματος. Partitive genitive. The term σπέρμα (lit. "seed") can be translated "descendants" here (BDAG, 937.2.a).

αὐτῆς. Genitive of relationship or genitive of source.

τῶν τηρούντων. Pres act ptc masc gen pl τηρέω (attributive to τῶν λοιπῶν).

τὰς ἐντολὰς. Accusative direct object of τηρούντων.

τοῦ θεοῦ. Genitive of source or subjective genitive.

ἐχόντων. Pres act ptc masc gen pl ἔχω (attributive τῶν λοιπῶν).

τὴν μαρτυρίαν. Accusative direct object of ἐχόντων.

Ἰησοῦ. Objective genitive.

12:18 Καὶ ἐστάθη ἐπὶ τὴν ἄμμον τῆς θαλάσσης.

ἐστάθη. Aor mid ind 3rd sg ἵστημι. On the voice, see "Deponency" in the Series Introduction. The reading ἐστάθη is well supported by 𝔓⁴⁷ ℵ A C 1854 2344 2351. However, the first person ἐστάθην is supported by P 046 051 1006 1611 1841 2053 2329 𝔐. This latter reading probably arose in an attempt to conform it to the first person εἶδον in 13:1 (Metzger, 673). If ἐστάθη is accepted as the correct reading, then it is the beast and not John who stands on the shore of the sea. This reading makes good contextual sense, since the dragon now stands on the sea in preparation for enlisting the help of two other draconic type figures in ch. 13 in his attack against the woman's offspring.

ἐπὶ τὴν ἄμμον. Locative.

τῆς θαλάσσης. Possessive genitive or descriptive genitive.

Revelation 13:1-8

¹And I saw a beast coming up out of the sea, having ten horns and seven heads, and upon his horns ten crowns, and upon his heads blasphemous names. ²And the beast that I saw was like a leopard and his feet were like a bear's and his mouth like the mouth of a lion. And the dragon gave to him his power and his throne and great authority. ³And one of his heads was as slain unto death, and his mortal wound was healed. And the whole earth marveled after the beast ⁴and they

worshiped the dragon because he gave authority to the beast, and they worshiped the beast, saying, "Who is like the beast, and who is able to make war with him?" ⁵And a mouth to speak great and blasphemous things was given to him, and authority was given to him to be active for forty-two months. ⁶And he opened his mouth for the purpose of blaspheming against God, to blaspheme his name and his dwelling place, that is, those dwelling in heaven. ⁷And the ability to make war with the saints and to overcome them was given to him, and authority over every tribe, people, language, and nation was given to him. ⁸And all those who live on the earth will worship him, whose names are not written in the Lamb's book of life, who was slain from the foundation of the world.

13:1 Καὶ εἶδον ἐκ τῆς θαλάσσης θηρίον ἀναβαῖνον, ἔχον κέρατα δέκα καὶ κεφαλὰς ἑπτὰ καὶ ἐπὶ τῶν κεράτων αὐτοῦ δέκα διαδήματα καὶ ἐπὶ τὰς κεφαλὰς αὐτοῦ ὀνόμα[τα] βλασφημίας.

Καὶ εἶδον. Introduces a new scene and character in the vision.
εἶδον. Aor act ind 1st sg ὁράω.
ἐκ τῆς θαλάσσης. Source.
θηρίον. Accusative direct object of εἶδον.
ἀναβαῖνον. Pres act ptc neut acc sg ἀναβαίνω. Complement in an object-complement double accusative construction with θηρίον.
ἔχον. Pres act ptc neut acc sg ἔχω (attributive).
κέρατα δέκα καὶ κεφαλὰς ἑπτὰ καὶ . . . δέκα διαδήματα. Accusative direct object of ἔχον.
ἐπὶ τῶν κεράτων. Locative.
αὐτοῦ. Possessive genitive.
ἐπὶ τὰς κεφαλὰς. Locative.
αὐτοῦ. Possessive genitive.
ὀνόμα[τα]. Accusative direct object of ἔχον. The manuscript evidence is fairly evenly divided between the singular (ὀνόμα) and the plural (ὀνόματα). 𝔓⁴⁷ ℵ C P 1006 1841 2329 𝔐ᴬ have ὀνόμα, while A 046 051 1611 1854 2053 2344 2351 𝔐ᴷ have ὀνόματα. It is possible that the singular ὀνόμα was made to conform to the other two descriptive elements of the beast in the plural, κέρατα and διαδήματα. However, it is also possible that the plural ὀνόμα[τα] is the correct reading due to the parallel in 17:3 (ὀνόματα βλασφημίας). The difference would be that with the plural, several names were written on each head, while with the singular, one name is written on each of the seven heads. As Beale recognizes, "The difference does not significantly alter the meaning" (685).
βλασφημίας. Attributive genitive.

13:2 καὶ τὸ θηρίον ὃ εἶδον ἦν ὅμοιον παρδάλει καὶ οἱ πόδες αὐτοῦ ὡς ἄρκου καὶ τὸ στόμα αὐτοῦ ὡς στόμα λέοντος. καὶ ἔδωκεν αὐτῷ ὁ δράκων τὴν δύναμιν αὐτοῦ καὶ τὸν θρόνον αὐτοῦ καὶ ἐξουσίαν μεγάλην.

τὸ θηρίον. Nominative subject of ἦν. The article is anaphoric, pointing back to the first mention of the beast in verse 1.
ὅ. Accusative direct object of εἶδον.
εἶδον. Aor act ind 1st sg ὁράω.
ἦν. Impf act ind 3rd sg εἰμί. The imperfect is used for explanatory background material.
ὅμοιον. Predicate adjective.
παρδάλει. Dative complement of ὅμοιος.
οἱ πόδες. Nominative subject of a verbless clause.
αὐτοῦ. Possessive genitive.
ὡς ἄρκου. Comparison. The entire construction functions as the predicate of a verbless clause.
ἄρκου. Possessive genitive ("as belonging to a bear").
τὸ στόμα. Nominative subject of a verbless clause.
αὐτοῦ. Possessive genitive.
ὡς στόμα. Comparison. The entire construction functions as the predicate of a verbless clause.
λέοντος. Possessive genitive. Some manuscripts (ℵ 1611 2351) have the plural λέοντων. The fact that the other animals mentioned are singular argues for the singular reading here, though it is possible that the plural is the original reading and a scribe changed it to singular to conform to the singular of the other animals.
ἔδωκεν. Aor act ind 3rd sg δίδωμι.
αὐτῷ. Dative indirect object of ἔδωκεν.
ὁ δράκων. Nominative subject of ἔδωκεν.
τὴν δύναμιν . . . καὶ τὸν θρόνον . . . καὶ ἐξουσίαν μεγάλην. Accusative direct object of ἔδωκεν.
αὐτοῦ. Subjective genitive.
αὐτοῦ. Possessive genitive.

13:3 καὶ μίαν ἐκ τῶν κεφαλῶν αὐτοῦ ὡς ἐσφαγμένην εἰς θάνατον, καὶ ἡ πληγὴ τοῦ θανάτου αὐτοῦ ἐθεραπεύθη. Καὶ ἐθαυμάσθη ὅλη ἡ γῆ ὀπίσω τοῦ θηρίου

μίαν. Accusative probably functioning as the direct object of an implied εἶδον (Charles, 1.348).
ἐκ τῶν κεφαλῶν. Partitive.
αὐτοῦ. Possessive genitive. The antecedent is θηρίον (v. 2).

ὡς ἐσφαγμένην. Comparison, functioning as the predicate of a verbless clause. English translations of the clause introduced by ὡς often translate this phrase in a way that seems to indicate that the beast only appeared to be, but was not really, slain. NASB: "as if it had been slain"; NRSV: "seems to have received a death blow"; ESV: "seemed to have a mortal wound"; NIV: "seemed to have a fatal wound." However, ὡς is used throughout the Apocalypse to describe what John saw, drawing a comparison with something (BDAG, 1104.2). It does not suggest that the beast only appeared to receive a death blow when in reality it did not, any more than the use of the identical phrase in 5:6 suggests that Christ was not really slain, but only appeared that way.

ἐσφαγμένην. Prf pass ptc fem acc sg σφάζω (substantival). The perfect passive participle contrasts the slain head of the beast with Christ who was described as slain in 5:6 (ἐσφαγμένον).

εἰς θάνατον. Result (BDAG, 290.4.e).

ἡ πληγὴ τοῦ θανάτου αὐτοῦ. Lit. "the plague of his death."

ἡ πληγή. Nominative subject of ἐθεραπεύθη. πληγή here is to be understood as a "blow" or a "wound" (LN 19.1, 20.29; BDAG, 825.2: "wound caused by a blow").

τοῦ θανάτου. Attributive genitive (NIV: "fatal wound").

αὐτοῦ. Subjective genitive (he/it dies). Charles (1.349) thinks that the antecedent is μίαν ἐκ τῶν κεφαλῶν. However, one would expect the feminine αὐτῆς if this were the case (Mounce, 253 n. 13). Rather, the pronoun αὐτοῦ parallels the αὐτοῦ after ἐκ τῶν κεφαλῶν earlier in the verse and refers back to the beast (θηρίον) in verse 2.

ἐθεραπεύθη. Aor pass ind 3rd sg θεραπεύω.

ἐθαυμάσθη. Aor mid ind 3rd sg θαυμάζω. On the voice, see "Deponency" in the Series Introduction.

ὅλη ἡ γῆ. Nominative subject of ἐθαυμάσθη.

ὀπίσω τοῦ θηρίου. Here ὀπίσω functions as a "marker of one who is followed as a leader" (LN 36.35).

13:4 καὶ προσεκύνησαν τῷ δράκοντι, ὅτι ἔδωκεν τὴν ἐξουσίαν τῷ θηρίῳ, καὶ προσεκύνησαν τῷ θηρίῳ λέγοντες· τίς ὅμοιος τῷ θηρίῳ καὶ τίς δύναται πολεμῆσαι μετ' αὐτοῦ;

προσεκύνησαν. Aor act ind 3rd pl προσκυνέω. The plural refers back to the singular ὅλη ἡ γῆ. This is another example of a construction according to sense, where ὅλη ἡ γῆ would have been regarded collectively by the author (Aune, 2.717).

τῷ δράκοντι. Dative direct object of προσεκύνησαν.

ὅτι. Introduces a causal clause.

ἔδωκεν. Aor act ind 3rd sg δίδωμι.

τὴν ἐξουσίαν. Accusative direct object of ἔδωκεν.
τῷ θηρίῳ. Dative indirect object of ἔδωκεν.
προσεκύνησαν. Aor act ind 3rd pl προσκυνέω.
τῷ θηρίῳ. Dative direct object of προσεκύνησαν. Some manuscripts (A 1876 2014 2043 2066 2344) have the accusative τὸ θηρίον. It is possible that a scribe could have changed the dative to the accusative to conform to the use of the accusative with neuter nouns following προσκυνέω elsewhere in Revelation (see 4:10 on τῷ ζῶντι).

λέγοντες. Pres act ptc masc nom pl λέγω (manner). On the use of λέγοντες to introduce speech, see 1:17 on λέγων.
τίς. Nominative subject of a verbless clause. Introduces a question.
ὅμοιος. Predicate adjective of a verbless clause.
τῷ θηρίῳ. Dative complement of ὅμοιος.
τίς. Nominative subject of δύναται. Introduces a question.
δύναται. Pres mid ind 3rd sg δύναμαι.
πολεμῆσαι. Aor act inf πολεμέω (complementary).
μετ' αὐτοῦ. Accompaniment (see also 12:7).

13:5 Καὶ ἐδόθη αὐτῷ στόμα λαλοῦν μεγάλα καὶ βλασφημίας καὶ ἐδόθη αὐτῷ ἐξουσία ποιῆσαι μῆνας τεσσαράκοντα [καὶ] δύο.

ἐδόθη. Aor pass ind 3rd sg δίδωμι.
αὐτῷ. Dative indirect object of ἐδόθη.
στόμα. Nominative subject of ἐδόθη.
λαλοῦν. Pres act ptc neut nom sg λαλέω (attributive).
μεγάλα καὶ βλασφημίας. Accusative direct object of λαλοῦν.
ἐδόθη. Aor pass ind 3rd sg δίδωμι.
αὐτῷ. Dative indirect object of ἐδόθη.
ἐξουσία. Nominative subject of ἐδόθη.
ποιῆσαι. Aor act inf (epexegetical to ἐξουσία). The verb lacks a direct object. Some manuscripts (051 2329 𝔐ᴷ; ὃ θέλει in ℵ) attempt to make sense of this by adding πόλεμον (see v. 7 below), but ποιῆσαι should probably be understood to mean something like "to be active in some way, *work, be active*" (BDAG, 841.6). BDAG notes that this use occurs with an accusative of time.
μῆνας τεσσαράκοντα [καὶ] δύο. Accusative indicating extent of time.

13:6 καὶ ἤνοιξεν τὸ στόμα αὐτοῦ εἰς βλασφημίας πρὸς τὸν θεὸν βλασφημῆσαι τὸ ὄνομα αὐτοῦ καὶ τὴν σκηνὴν αὐτοῦ, τοὺς ἐν τῷ οὐρανῷ σκηνοῦντας.

ἤνοιξεν. Aor act ind 3rd sg ἀνοίγω.

τὸ στόμα. Accusative direct object of ἤνοιξεν.
αὐτοῦ. Possessive genitive.
εἰς βλασφημίας. Purpose.
πρὸς τὸν θεὸν. Indicates a hostile relationship ("against").
βλασφημῆσαι. Aor act inf βλασφημέω. Since the previous εἰς βλασφημίας expresses the purpose of opening his mouth, the infinitive can be taken as epexegetical, further specifying the blasphemy against God (see also Aune, 2.717).
τὸ ὄνομα. Accusative direct object of βλασφημῆσαι.
αὐτοῦ. Possessive genitive.
τὴν σκηνὴν. Accusative direct object of βλασφημῆσαι.
αὐτοῦ. Possessive genitive or subjective genitive.
τοὺς ... σκηνοῦντας. Pres act ptc masc acc pl σκηνόω (substantival). Accusative in apposition to τὴν σκηνὴν αὐτοῦ. For the notion of God's dwelling identified with the people who reside there with him, see 12:12; 21:3.
ἐν τῷ οὐρανῷ. Locative.

13:7 καὶ ἐδόθη αὐτῷ ποιῆσαι πόλεμον μετὰ τῶν ἁγίων καὶ νικῆσαι αὐτούς, καὶ ἐδόθη αὐτῷ ἐξουσία ἐπὶ πᾶσαν φυλὴν καὶ λαὸν καὶ γλῶσσαν καὶ ἔθνος.

ἐδόθη. Aor pass ind 3rd sg δίδωμι.
αὐτῷ. Dative indirect object of ἐδόθη.
ποιῆσαι. Aor act inf ποιέω (substantival, subject of ἐδόθη). One of the difficulties in understanding this chapter is the various ways in which the verb ποιέω is used (vv. 7, 12, 13, 14, 15, 16). Here ποιῆσαι is used in the sense of "to undertake or do someth. that brings about an event" (BDAG, 839.2) and with πόλεμον could be translated "to make/wage war."
πόλεμον. Accusative direct object of ποιῆσαι.
μετὰ τῶν ἁγίων. Accompaniment (see also 12:7).
νικῆσαι. Aor act inf νικάω (subject of ἐδόθη).
αὐτούς. Accusative direct object of νικῆσαι.
ἐδόθη. Aor pass ind 3rd sg δίδωμι.
αὐτῷ. Dative indirect object of ἐδόθη.
ἐξουσία. Nominative subject of ἐδόθη.
ἐπὶ πᾶσαν φυλὴν καὶ λαὸν καὶ γλῶσσαν καὶ ἔθνος. Following ἐξουσία the preposition ἐπί indicates "authority ... or control of or over someone or someth." (BDAG, 365.9).

13:8 καὶ προσκυνήσουσιν αὐτὸν πάντες οἱ κατοικοῦντες ἐπὶ τῆς γῆς, οὗ οὐ γέγραπται τὸ ὄνομα αὐτοῦ ἐν τῷ βιβλίῳ τῆς ζωῆς τοῦ ἀρνίου τοῦ ἐσφαγμένου ἀπὸ καταβολῆς κόσμου.

προσκυνήσουσιν. Fut act ind 3rd pl προσκυνέω.
αὐτὸν. Accusative direct object of προσκυνήσουσιν. The antecedent is not entirely clear. It could be the first beast, or it could be the dragon. If it refers to the θηρίον, the masculine αὐτόν would be used due to the beast symbolizing a male figure (Aune, 2.718).
πάντες. Nominative subject of προσκυνήσουσιν.
οἱ κατοικοῦντες. Pres act ptc masc nom pl κατοικέω (attributive). It is also possible that οἱ κατοικοῦντες is substantival and functions as the grammatical subject of προσκυνήσουσιν so that πάντες modifies it as an attributive adjective.
ἐπὶ τῆς γῆς. Locative.
οὗ. Possessive genitive. The relative pronoun modifies τὸ ὄνομα and is picked up at the end of the clause by the resumptive αὐτοῦ. The antecedent of the singular pronoun is the plural πάντες. Most likely this is due to the author focusing on each individual person who worships the beast as part of the larger group (Mounce, 256).
γέγραπται. Prf pass ind 3rd sg γράφω.
τὸ ὄνομα. Nominative subject of γέγραπται.
αὐτοῦ. Possessive genitive. Redundant use of the pronoun with οὗ (see also 3:8). This construction could reflect Semitic style, and probably functions to draw attention to the antecedent: the one whose name is not written in the book of life.
ἐν τῷ βιβλίῳ. Locative.
τῆς ζωῆς. Attributive genitive.
τοῦ ἀρνίου. Possessive genitive.
τοῦ ἐσφαγμένου. Prf pass ptc neut gen sg σφαγίζω (attributive). The perfect passive participle highlights the connection to the description of the Lamb from 5:6 (ἐσφαγμένον). Mussies (348) thinks that the participle has been influenced by the "Semitic gerundive qāṭul." However, there is nothing "un-Greek" about this construction, and Mussies too quickly assumes an underlying Semitic influence on John's grammar (see the Introduction on "the Language of Revelation").
ἀπὸ καταβολῆς. Temporal. Indicates the time from which an event occurred (Porter 1992, 147). There is some question as to what this phrase modifies. On the one hand, it could modify ἐσφαγμένου, which is its closest antecedent (Charles, 1.354; Mounce, 256; Osborne, 503). This would suggest that Christ's death was ordained from the foundation of the world (Charles, 1.354). Scholars that hold this position point to 1 Pet 1:19, 20. However, Swete (167) has argued that it should modify

γέγραπται based on the parallel with 17:8 (see also Smalley, 343; Aune, 2.746–47; Beale, 702). While either view is possible, it is preferrable to take ἀπὸ καταβολῆς as modifying ἐσφαγμένου, which is the closest antecedent ("it is unlikely that the concluding temporal clause goes with 'written,' since twelve words separate them"; Beale, 702), suggesting that the author is referring to God's plan of redemption being determined "from the foundation of the world."

κόσμου. Objective genitive.

Revelation 13:9-10

⁹If anyone has an ear, that person should listen. ¹⁰If anyone is to go into captivity, into captivity they will go; if anyone is to be put to death with the sword, they will be put to death with the sword. Here is the endurance and the faithfulness of the saints.

13:9 Εἴ τις ἔχει οὖς ἀκουσάτω.

The imperative mood, along with the conditional sentences, marks this section out as of a different character than verses 1-8 and 11-18. Verses 9-10 constitute a hortatory section that "describe[s] the response that believers are to have to the situation of deception and persecution depicted in vv. 1-8" (Beale, 704).

Εἴ. Introduces the protasis of a first-class conditional sentence. It assumes the truth of the protasis for the sake of argument.

τις. Nominative subject of ἔχει.

ἔχει. Pres act ind 3rd sg ἔχω.

οὖς. Accusative direct object of ἔχει.

ἀκουσάτω. Aor act impv 3rd sg ἀκούω. On the force of the third person imperative, see 2:7 on ἀκουσάτω.

13:10 εἴ τις εἰς αἰχμαλωσίαν, εἰς αἰχμαλωσίαν ὑπάγει· εἴ τις ἐν μαχαίρῃ ἀποκτανθῆναι αὐτὸν ἐν μαχαίρῃ ἀποκτανθῆναι. Ὧδέ ἐστιν ἡ ὑπομονὴ καὶ ἡ πίστις τῶν ἁγίων.

εἴ. Introduces the protasis of a first-class conditional sentence. The accenting is due to the enclitic τις that follows.

τις. Nominative subject of a verbless clause. Lit. "if anyone into captivity." It is possible that a verb such as ὑπάγει found in the apodosis is assumed here (2351 has ἀπάγει), although this may be more of a need in English translation than for Greek. The elliptical nature of this statement may be due to its proverbial character.

εἰς αἰχμαλωσίαν, εἰς αἰχμαλωσίαν. Goal.

ὑπάγει. Pres act ind 3rd sg ὑπάγω. The present tense is timeless or gnomic, used in a proverbial type of saying.

εἴ. Introduces the protasis of a first-class conditional sentence. The accenting is due to the enclitic τις that follows.

τις. Nominative subject of a verbless clause. See below on ἀποκτανθῆναι.

ἐν μαχαίρῃ. Instrumental.

ἀποκτανθῆναι. Aor pass inf ἀποκτείνω (predicate in a verbless clause): "If anyone *is* to be put to death" (Smalley, 344). Several manuscripts have changed the first passive infinitive to a future active ἀποκτενεῖ (C 051 [2053] 2329 2351 𝔐ᴬ) or a present active ἀποκτένει (ℵ 1006 1611 1841 1854) in the protasis, with δεῖ beginning the protasis (see Aune, 2.719, for a full list of readings). The effect of these readings would be to suggest vindication of the saints through the assurance that their persecutors will be punished ("if anyone will kill/kills [the saints] with a sword, it will be necessary for that person to be killed with a sword"). That is, the subject of the active verb in the protasis and the passive infinitive in the apodosis is the one persecuting the saints. However, it is possible that the latter two readings can be accounted for by a scribe assimilating this saying to that of Jesus in Matt 26:52 (Beale, 707–8). Furthermore, it appears to introduce an element at odds with the emphasis on encouragement and perseverance of the readers. Osborne is correct that "the context is one of persecution rather than vindication" (509). Therefore, NA[28]/UBS[5], though only attested in codex A, is to be preferred.

αὐτόν. Accusative subject of the second ἀποκτανθῆναι. Charles' (1.356) speculation, that αὐτόν is a corruption of αὐτός, is unnecessary.

ἐν μαχαίρῃ. Instrumental.

ἀποκτανθῆναι. Aor pass inf ἀποκτείνω. Syntactically, the infinitive is either complementary to an implied δεῖ ("*It is necessary* for him to be put to death") or is to be understood in the same way as the first part of the sentence: "He *is* to be put to death with a sword." This is to be preferred over those who interpret the infinitive as imperatival (Turner, 78; Smalley, 344).

Ὧδε. An adverb of place that functions substantivally as the subject of ἐστιν. Here it functions like a demonstrative pronoun and points back to the preceding part of verse 10. The accenting is due to the enclitic ἐστιν that follows. BDAG (1101.2) says that it functions as "a ref. to a present event, object, or circumstance, *in this case, at this point, on this occasion, under these circumstances*." They translate it "here is (an opportunity for) endurance."

ἐστιν. Pres act ind 3rd sg εἰμί. On the loss of accent, see 1:8.

ἡ ὑπομονὴ καὶ ἡ πίστις. Predicate nominative of ἐστιν.

τῶν ἁγίων. Subjective genitive modifying ἡ ὑπομονὴ καὶ ἡ πίστις.

Revelation 13:11-18

[11]And I saw another beast coming up from the earth, and it had two horns like a lamb and it spoke like a dragon. [12]And it exercised all the authority of the first beast on his behalf, and he caused the earth and those dwelling in it to worship the first beast, whose mortal wound was healed. [13]And he performed great signs, that is, he even caused fire to come down from heaven onto the earth in the presence of humanity. [14]And he deceived those who dwell upon the earth by the signs that were given to him to perform on behalf of the beast, telling those who dwell upon the earth to make an image to the beast, who has the wound from the sword and lives. [15]And (authority) was given to him to give a spirit to the image of the beast, in order that also the image of the beast might speak, and to cause whoever does not worship the image of the beast to be put to death. [16]And he caused all, the small and the great, the rich and the poor, the free and the slave, to receive a mark on their right hand or on their forehead, [17]and for no one to be able to buy or sell, except the one who has the mark, the name of the beast or the number of his name. [18]Here is wisdom: the one who has a mind should calculate the number of the beast, for it is the number of man, and his number is six hundred and sixty-six.

13:11 Καὶ εἶδον ἄλλο θηρίον ἀναβαῖνον ἐκ τῆς γῆς, καὶ εἶχεν κέρατα δύο ὅμοια ἀρνίῳ καὶ ἐλάλει ὡς δράκων.

Καὶ εἶδον. This phrase here introduces a new character in the vision in ch. 13: the second beast.

εἶδον. Aor act ind 1st sg ὁράω.

ἄλλο θηρίον. Accusative direct object of εἶδον. While grammars frequently draw attention to the distinction between ἄλλος and ἕτερος, as indicating "another of the same kind" and "another of a different kind," it is doubtful that this distinction can be maintained consistently in the NT (see LN 58.36, 37) and it should not be pressed.

ἀναβαῖνον. Pres act ptc neut acc sg ἀναβαίνω. Complement in an object-complement double accusative construction.

ἐκ τῆς γῆς. Source or locative (Charles, 1.357).

εἶχεν. Impf act ind 3rd sg ἔχω. The imperfect aspect is appropriate for introducing offline, supporting material. Along with ἐλάλει that follows, the imperfects "function to provide the setting for the description of the second beast with present tense forms" (Mathewson 2010, 147). In light of this function, Osborne reads too much into the imperfects in seeing them as "stressing the ongoing nature of the beast" (511 n. 2).

κέρατα δύο. Accusative direct object of εἶχεν.

ὅμοια. "[P]ertaining to being similar to something else in some respect" (LN 64.1).

ἀρνίῳ. Dative complement of ὅμοιος.

ἐλάλει. Impf act ind 3rd sg λαλέω. On the significance of the aspect, see εἶχεν above.

ὡς δράκων. Manner. δράκων is the nominative subject of an implied ἐλάλει.

13:12 καὶ τὴν ἐξουσίαν τοῦ πρώτου θηρίου πᾶσαν ποιεῖ ἐνώπιον αὐτοῦ, καὶ ποιεῖ τὴν γῆν καὶ τοὺς ἐν αὐτῇ κατοικοῦντας ἵνα προσκυνήσουσιν τὸ θηρίον τὸ πρῶτον, οὗ ἐθεραπεύθη ἡ πληγὴ τοῦ θανάτου αὐτοῦ.

τὴν ἐξουσίαν ... πᾶσαν. Accusative direct object of ποιεῖ.

τοῦ πρώτου θηρίου. Subjective genitive.

ποιεῖ. Pres act ind 3rd sg ποιέω. Here ποιεῖ with τὴν ἐξουσίαν should be understood in the sense of "to carry out or to excercize the authority of the first beast." This is the first in a series of "historical" or narrative present (see 4:5 on ἐκπορεύονται) tense forms (imperfective aspect) in 13:11-18. While aorist tense forms in the indicative mood dominate the narrative in 13:1-8, here present tense verbs in the indicative mood are more frequent. The present ποιεῖ is found here in verses 12 (2×), 13, and 16. The present subjunctive of the same verb (ποιῇ) is found in verse 13. Two further present tense forms are found in verse 14: πλανᾷ and ἔχει. The concentration of present tense indicative forms in this section over against the aorist forms in verses 1-8 suggests that this material is of a different character in the narrative. The present tense forms serve to make this section of the discourse prominent. Perhaps the reason for this is that this section is the most relevant for the readers of Revelation. If the second beast represents the local authorities who are keen to enforce the imperial cult in local cities (chs. 2-3; see Blount, 257), then the present tense functions to draw attention to the significance of this section for the readers. It is this last beast that acutely affects the readers and through which they directly experience the persecuting activities of the dragon and the first beast (see Mathewson 2010, 148-50). This is not to suggest that the present tenses are used because the action is present from the standpoint of the readers (contra Osborne, 512). Rather, the imperfective aspect describes and foregrounds the action as of particular significance for the readers. The present tense form ποιεῖ also plays a role in structuring this section, dividing it up into further subunits: verses 12, 13-15, 16-17.

ἐνώπιον αὐτοῦ. Here ἐνώπιον is used in the sense of "*by the authority of, on behalf of*" (BDAG, 342.4.b).

ποιεῖ. Pres act ind 3rd sg ποιέω. On the aspect, see above on ποιεῖ. Here ποιεῖ connotes causality and is complemented by a ἵνα clause (BDAG, 840.2.h). See below.

τὴν γῆν καὶ τοὺς . . . κατοικοῦντας. Accusative direct object of ποιεῖ.

τοὺς . . . κατοικοῦντας. Pres act ptc masc acc pl κατοικέω (substantival).

ἐν αὐτῇ. Locative.

ἵνα. Introduces a content clause that is the complement to ποιεῖ in a causative construction. "He causes the earth and those dwelling it it to worship." It is also possible to understand this ἵνα clause substantivally as the complement in an object-complement construction with τὴν γῆν and τοὺς . . . κατοικοῦντας.

προσκυνήσουσιν. Fut act ind 3rd pl προσκυνέω. Future with ἵνα. On the use of the future in place of the subjunctive, see 3:9 on ἥξουσιν. Many manuscripts (P 046 051 1006 1611 1841 1854 2329 2377 𝔐) have the aorist subjunctive προσκυνήσωσιν.

τὸ θηρίον τὸ πρῶτον. Accusative direct object of προσκυνήσουσιν.

οὗ. Possessive genitive. The relative pronoun gets picked up by the αὐτοῦ at the end of the verse.

ἐθεραπεύθη. Aor pass ind 3rd sg θεραπεύω.

ἡ πληγή. Nominative subject of ἐθεραπεύθη. ἡ πληγή indicates "the condition resulting from being severely hurt or wounded" (LN 20.29). ἡ πληγὴ τοῦ θανάτου then should be rendered "a mortal wound."

τοῦ θανάτου. Attributive genitive.

αὐτοῦ. Objective genitive (the plague kills him). αὐτοῦ resumes the relative οὗ. On this redundant construction, see verse 8 above.

13:13 καὶ ποιεῖ σημεῖα μεγάλα, ἵνα καὶ πῦρ ποιῇ ἐκ τοῦ οὐρανοῦ καταβαίνειν εἰς τὴν γῆν ἐνώπιον τῶν ἀνθρώπων,

ποιεῖ. Pres act ind 3rd sg ποιέω. Here ποιεῖ is used in the sense of to "*do, perform* miracles" (BDAG, 839.2.b). On the aspect, see verse 12 above on ποιεῖ.

σημεῖα μεγάλα. Accusative direct object of ποιεῖ.

ἵνα. While BDF (§391.5) and Charles (1.359) think that the ἵνα clause expresses a result, more likely ἵνα introduces a clause that functions epexegetically (Mussies, 245; Aune, 2.720; Osborne, 513 n. 4), to further define ποιεῖ σημεῖα μεγάλα. It seems redundant to say that the fire coming down out of heaven is the result of the great signs, while it makes better sense to see the fire coming down out of heaven *as* a great sign.

πῦρ. Accusative subject of καταβαίνειν.

ποιῇ. Pres act subj 3rd sg ποιέω. Subjunctive with ἵνα. Here ποιῇ connotes causality and is complemented by an infinitive (BDAG, 840.2.h). See below.

ἐκ τοῦ οὐρανοῦ. Source.

καταβαίνειν. Pres act inf καταβαίνω. Complementary to ποιεῖ in a causative construction. "He causes fire to come down."

εἰς τὴν γῆν. Locative.

ἐνώπιον τῶν ἀνθρώπων. ἐνώπιον is used with the meaning "*in the sight of, in the presence of*" (BDAG, 342.2).

13:14 καὶ πλανᾷ τοὺς κατοικοῦντας ἐπὶ τῆς γῆς διὰ τὰ σημεῖα ἃ ἐδόθη αὐτῷ ποιῆσαι ἐνώπιον τοῦ θηρίου, λέγων τοῖς κατοικοῦσιν ἐπὶ τῆς γῆς ποιῆσαι εἰκόνα τῷ θηρίῳ, ὃς ἔχει τὴν πληγὴν τῆς μαχαίρης καὶ ἔζησεν.

πλανᾷ. Pres act ind 3rd sg πλανάω. On the significance of the aspect, see verse 12.

τοὺς κατοικοῦντας. Pres act ptc masc acc pl κατοικέω (substantival). Accusative direct object of πλανᾷ.

ἐπὶ τῆς γῆς. Locative.

διὰ τὰ σημεῖα. Causal.

ἅ. Nominative subject of ἐδόθη.

ἐδόθη. Aor pass ind 3rd sg δίδωμι.

αὐτῷ. Dative indirect object of ἐδόθη.

ποιῆσαι. Aor act inf ποιέω (purpose). On the meaning of ποιῆσαι, see verse 13 above on ποιεῖ.

ἐνώπιον τοῦ θηρίου. On the meaning of this expression, see verse 12 above on ἐνώπιον αὐτοῦ.

λέγων. Pres act ptc masc nom sg λέγω (manner or attendant circumstance). On the use of the participle λέγων to introduce speech, see 1:17 on λέγων. Here it introduces indirect discourse (see ποιῆσαι below). The masculine participle here is an example of a construction according to sense, since the noun from which it would take its gender is neuter: τοῦ θηρίου. The fact that the beast probably stands for a male person has influenced the masculine gender of λέγων.

τοῖς κατοικοῦσιν. Pres act ptc masc dat pl κατοικέω (substantival). Dative indirect object of λέγων.

ἐπὶ τῆς γῆς. Locative.

ποιῆσαι. Aor act inf ποιέω (indirect discourse; here an indirect command). Here ποιῆσαι carries the sense of "to make or fashion" (LN 42.29; BDAG, 839.1.a).

εἰκόνα. Accusative direct object of ποιῆσαι.

τῷ θηρίῳ. Dative of advantage. The image is made "in honor of the beast" (Smalley, 347; see also the translation in Aune, 2.715).

ὅς. Nominative subject of ἔχει. The masculine pronoun, modifying the neuter θηρίῳ, reflects the gender of the beast, who is considered a male (Robertson, 713).

ἔχει. Pres act ind 3rd sg ἔχω. On the significance of the aspect, see verse 12.

τὴν πληγὴν. Accusative direct object of ἔχει.

τῆς μαχαίρης. Genitive of source, or the idea may be the plague that is caused by the sword.

ἔζησεν. Aor act ind 3rd sg ζάω. While the aorist here is frequently understood as ingressive ("came to life"; Smalley, 347; Wallace, 559), it is also possible to simply read it as summarizing the state of the beast ("he lives"). See the Introduction on "Verbal Aspect."

13:15 Καὶ ἐδόθη αὐτῷ δοῦναι πνεῦμα τῇ εἰκόνι τοῦ θηρίου, ἵνα καὶ λαλήσῃ ἡ εἰκὼν τοῦ θηρίου καὶ ποιήσῃ [ἵνα] ὅσοι ἐὰν μὴ προσκυνήσωσιν τῇ εἰκόνι τοῦ θηρίου ἀποκτανθῶσιν.

ἐδόθη. Aor pass ind 3rd sg δίδωμι.

αὐτῷ. Dative indirect object of ἐδόθη.

δοῦναι. Aor act inf δίδωμι (subject of ἐδόθη).

πνεῦμα. Accusative direct object of δοῦναι.

τῇ εἰκόνι. Dative indirect object of δοῦναι.

τοῦ θηρίου. The genitive indicates the form or likeness that the image represents or reflects.

ἵνα. Introduces a purpose clause.

λαλήσῃ. Aor act subj 3rd sg λαλέω. Subjunctive with ἵνα.

ἡ εἰκὼν. Nominative subject of λαλήσῃ . . . καὶ ποιήσῃ.

τοῦ θηρίου. On the function of the genitive after εἰκών, see above.

ποιήσῃ. Aor act subj 3rd sg ποιέω. Subjunctive with ἵνα. Here ποιήσῃ connotes causality and is complemented by a ἵνα clause (BDAG, 840.2.h). See below.

[ἵνα] . . . ἀποκτανθῶσιν. The ἵνα introduces a content clause that is complementary to ποιεῖ in a causative construction. "He causes them (as many as do not worship the image of the beast) to die." The bracketed ἵνα is included by A P 1006 1841 2329 2344, but omitted in ℵ 046 1611 2053 2351 2377 𝔐.

ὅσοι ἐὰν μὴ προσκυνήσωσιν τῇ εἰκόνι τοῦ θηρίου. The entire clause functions as the subject of ἀποκτανθῶσιν: "that as many as did not worship the beast might be put to death."

ὅσοι ἐάν. Nominative subject of προσκυνήσωσιν. Lit. "as many as ever." The ἐάν makes the statement more general (BDAG, 729.2).

προσκυνήσωσιν. Aor act subj 3rd pl προσκυνέω. Subjunctive with ἐάν.

τῇ εἰκόνι. Dative direct object of προσκυνήσωσιν.

τοῦ θηρίου. On the function of the genitive after εἰκών, see above.

ἀποκτανθῶσιν. Aor pass subj 3rd pl ἀποκτείνω. Subjunctive with [ἵνα].

13:16 καὶ ποιεῖ πάντας, τοὺς μικροὺς καὶ τοὺς μεγάλους, καὶ τοὺς πλουσίους καὶ τοὺς πτωχούς, καὶ τοὺς ἐλευθέρους καὶ τοὺς δούλους, ἵνα δῶσιν αὐτοῖς χάραγμα ἐπὶ τῆς χειρὸς αὐτῶν τῆς δεξιᾶς ἢ ἐπὶ τὸ μέτωπον αὐτῶν

ποιεῖ. Pres act ind 3rd sg ποιέω. Here ποιεῖ connotes causality and is complemented by a ἵνα clause (BDAG, 840.2.h).

πάντας. Accusative direct object of ποιεῖ.

τοὺς μικροὺς καὶ τοὺς μεγάλους, καὶ τοὺς πλουσίους καὶ τοὺς πτωχούς, καὶ τοὺς ἐλευθέρους καὶ τοὺς δούλους. Accusative in apposition to πάντας, if the punctuaton of NA[28] is followed. These three pairings constitute a merism. That is, the pairings express totality or the entire range of socio-economic relationships.

ἵνα. Introduces a content clause that is complementary to ποιεῖ in a causative construction: "He causes all to be given a mark."

δῶσιν. Aor act subj 3rd pl δίδωμι. Subjunctive with ἵνα. This is probably an impersonal use of the verb with a plural subject, which can be translated as a passive: "they might be given a mark" (McKay 1994, 19; see also 2:24 on ὡς λέγουσιν).

αὐτοῖς. Dative indirect object of δῶσιν.

χάραγμα. Accusative direct object of δῶσιν. χάραγμα suggests a mark that is engraved, branded, or etched (BDAG, 1077.1). Louw and Nida suggest that in relationship to "beast" χάραγμα probably indicates something like "'a mark showing one's relationship to the beast' or 'a mark of loyalty to the beast' or 'a mark of the party of the beast'" (33.482).

ἐπὶ τῆς χειρὸς . . . τῆς δεξιᾶς. Locative.

αὐτῶν. Possessive genitive. The plural pronoun modifies a singular noun. The singular τῆς χειρός is what Turner calls a "distributive singular," where "[s]omething belonging to each person in a group of people is placed in the sing" (23; see also Mussies, 84).

ἐπὶ τὸ μέτωπον. Locative. The switch to ἐπί with the accusative rather than the genitive (ἐπὶ τῆς χειρὸς) does not appear to carry any difference in meaning.

αὐτῶν. Possessive genitive. On the plural pronoun modifying the singular τὸ μέτωπον, see above on αὐτῶν.

13:17 καὶ ἵνα μή τις δύνηται ἀγοράσαι ἢ πωλῆσαι εἰ μὴ ὁ ἔχων τὸ χάραγμα τὸ ὄνομα τοῦ θηρίου ἢ τὸν ἀριθμὸν τοῦ ὀνόματος αὐτοῦ.

ἵνα. Introduces a purpose clause.
τις. Nominative subject of δύνηται.
δύνηται. Pres mid subj 3rd sg δύναμαι. Subjunctive with ἵνα.
ἀγοράσαι. Aor act inf ἀγοράζω (complementary).
πωλῆσαι. Aor act inf πωλέω (complementary).
εἰ μὴ. An expression meaning "except, if not" (BDAG, 278.6.i.α).
ὁ ἔχων. Pres act ptc masc nom sg ἔχω (substantival). Nominative subject of a verbless clause.
τὸ χάραγμα. Accusative direct object of ἔχων.
τὸ ὄνομα . . . ἢ τὸν ἀριθμὸν. Accusative in apposition to τὸ χάραγμα.
τοῦ θηρίου. Possessive genitive.
τοῦ ὀνόματος. Possessive genitive or epexegetical genitive (Swete, 174: "The number of the name is probably the name itself").
αὐτοῦ. Possessive genitive.

13:18 Ὧδε ἡ σοφία ἐστίν. ὁ ἔχων νοῦν ψηφισάτω τὸν ἀριθμὸν τοῦ θηρίου, ἀριθμὸς γὰρ ἀνθρώπου ἐστίν, καὶ ὁ ἀριθμὸς αὐτοῦ ἑξακόσιοι ἑξήκοντα ἕξ.

Ὧδε. An adverb of place that functions substantivally as the subject of ἐστίν, and refers cataphorically to the rest of v. 18 (contra Osborne, 519). On the meaning, see verse 10 above on Ὧδε.
ἡ σοφία. Predicate nominative of ἐστίν.
ἐστίν. Pres act ind 3rd sg εἰμί.
ὁ ἔχων. Pres act ptc masc nom sg ἔχω (substantival). Nominative subject of ψηφισάτω.
νοῦν. Accusative direct object of ἔχων. The νοῦς is "the psychological faculty of understanding, reasoning, thinking and deciding" (LN 26.14).
ψηφισάτω. Aor act impv 3rd sg ψηφίζω. On the force of the third person imperative, see 2:7 on ἀκουσάτω.
τὸν ἀριθμὸν. Accusative direct object of ψηφισάτω.
τοῦ θηρίου. Possessive genitive.
ἀριθμὸς. Nominative subject of ἐστίν.
γὰρ. Introduces a causal clause.

ἀνθρώπου. Attributive genitive ("human number") or possessive genitive ("belonging to a human"). The idea may be "a number referring to a human being" (Aune, 2.722). Part of the difficulty in interpreting this verse is deciding whether ἀνθρώπου is understood more generically (human) or more specifically (person). If the latter, the number 666 could be referring to a specific person, such as Nero (Osborne, 520). If the former (Wallace, 254), the number 666 is "humanly calculable" (Smalley, 351) or refers to "the number of humankind" (Wallace, 254), "a number *of humanity*" as fallen humanity (Beale, 724).

ἐστίν. Pres act ind 3rd sg εἰμί.

ὁ ἀριθμὸς. Nominative subject of a verbless clause.

αὐτοῦ. Possessive genitive.

ἑξακόσιοι ἑξήκοντα ἕξ. Predicate nominative of a verbless clause. ἑξακόσιοι is a declinable adjective that takes its masculine gender from ἀνθρώπου, while the adjectives ἑξήκοντα and ἕξ are indeclinable. The reading ἑξακόσιοι ἑξήκοντα ἕξ followed by NA[28] and UBS[5] is found in codex A. A number of other manuscripts ($\mathfrak{P}^{47}$ 051 $\mathfrak{M}$) read three letters that function numerically, χξς, which add up to 666: χ = 600; ξ = 60; ς = (digamma) 6 (see Aune, 2.722). Codex ℵ has the feminine ἑξακόσιαι, while P 1006 1841 1854 2053[vid] have the neuter ἑξακόσια. The latter is probably due to the neuter of θηρίον, which may also be due to the fact that 666 is the numerical value of the letters in θηρίον. Both of these readings support the number 666. Two interesting variations are ἑξακόσια ἑξήκοντα πέντε (665) in 2344, and ἑξακόσιαι δέκα ἕξ (616) in C (χιϛ in $\mathfrak{P}^{115}$), the latter possibly reflecting either the numerical value of the Latin spelling of "Nero Caesar" (transliterated into Hebrew) or the name Gaius Caesar (Caligula). The weight of the manuscript evidence argues for one of the readings 666.

Revelation 14:1-5

[1]And I saw, and look, the Lamb standing on Mount Zion and with him the one hundred and forty-four thousand who have his name and the name of his Father written upon their foreheads. [2]And I heard a sound from heaven like a sound of many waters and like a sound of loud thunder, and the sound that I heard was like (the sound of) harpists playing on their harps. [3]And they were singing a new song before the throne and before the four living creatures and the elders, and no one was able to learn the song except the one hundred and forty four thousand who were redeemed from the earth. [4]These are the ones who did not defile themselves with women, for they are virgins, these who follow

the Lamb wherever he goes. These were redeemed from humanity to be firstfruits to God and to the Lamb, ⁵and in their mouth no lie was found; they are blameless.

14:1 Καὶ εἶδον, καὶ ἰδοὺ τὸ ἀρνίον ἑστὸς ἐπὶ τὸ ὄρος Σιὼν καὶ μετ' αὐτοῦ ἑκατὸν τεσσαράκοντα τέσσαρες χιλιάδες ἔχουσαι τὸ ὄνομα αὐτοῦ καὶ τὸ ὄνομα τοῦ πατρὸς αὐτοῦ γεγραμμένον ἐπὶ τῶν μετώπων αὐτῶν.

εἶδον. Aor act ind 1st sg ὁράω. This chapter can be divided up into three sections based on the use of Καὶ εἶδον in verses 1, 6, 14, which functions to divide the larger vision up into visionary segments.

ἰδοὺ. A marker of attention that deictically functions to make the following statement emphatic. On the form, see 1:7. Here it draws attention to the Lamb standing on Mount Zion.

τὸ ἀρνίον. Nominative subject of a verbless clause.

ἑστὸς. Prf act ptc neut nom sg ἵστημι. If attributive, the articular noun is followed by an anarthrous participle (cf. Porter 1989a, 395). It is also possible that the participle functions as a finite verb (Mussies, 325; Aune, 2.784; Smalley, 353). For this function of the participle, see 1:16 on ἔχων. The stative aspect of the participle recalls the description of the posture of the Lamb from 5:6.

ἐπὶ τὸ ὄρος. Locative.

Σιών. Accusative in apposition to ὄρος.

μετ' αὐτοῦ. Accompaniment.

ἑκατὸν τεσσαράκοντα τέσσαρες χιλιάδες. Nominative subject of a verbless clause.

ἔχουσαι. Pres act ptc fem nom pl ἔχω (attributive).

τὸ ὄνομα ... τὸ ὄνομα. Accusative direct object of ἔχουσαι.

αὐτοῦ. Possessive genitive.

τοῦ πατρὸς. Possessive genitive.

αὐτοῦ. Genitive of relationship.

γεγραμμένον. Prf pass ptc neut acc sg γράφω (attributive). The singular participle modifies ὄνομα, which occurs twice, and may suggest that John did not strictly distinguish the two names, given the fact that he equates God and the Lamb elsewhere (see chs. 4–5) and does not always distinguish them grammatically (11:15; 22:3, 4). The singular would then point to the unity of God and the Lamb.

ἐπὶ τῶν μετώπων. Locative.

αὐτῶν. Possessive genitive.

14:2 καὶ ἤκουσα φωνὴν ἐκ τοῦ οὐρανοῦ ὡς φωνὴν ὑδάτων πολλῶν καὶ ὡς φωνὴν βροντῆς μεγάλης, καὶ ἡ φωνὴ ἣν ἤκουσα ὡς κιθαρῳδῶν κιθαριζόντων ἐν ταῖς κιθάραις αὐτῶν.

ἤκουσα. Aor act ind 1st sg ἀκούω.
φωνὴν. Accusative direct object of ἤκουσα. Throughout verse 2 φωνή should be understood as "sound" rather than a singular "voice" (Aune, 2.784).
ἐκ τοῦ οὐρανοῦ. Source.
ὡς φωνὴν. Comparison.
ὑδάτων πολλῶν. Genitive of source or subjective genitive.
ὡς φωνὴν. Comparison.
βροντῆς μεγάλης. Genitive of source or subjective genitive.
ἡ φωνὴ. Nominative subject of a verbless clause.
ἣν. Accusative direct object of ἤκουσα.
ἤκουσα. Aor act ind 1st sg ἀκούω.
ὡς κιθαρῳδῶν κιθαριζόντων ἐν ταῖς κιθάραις αὐτῶν. Comparison. Functions as the predicate of a verbless clause. Lit. "as of harpists harping with/on their harps."
κιθαριζόντων. Pres act ptc masc gen pl κιθαρίζω (substantival). Genitive of source or subjective genitive. The genitive κιθαρῳδῶν probably modifies an implied "sound" (a sound as the sound of harpists).
ἐν ταῖς κιθάραις. Instrumental.
αὐτῶν. Possessive genitive.

14:3 καὶ ᾄδουσιν [ὡς] ᾠδὴν καινὴν ἐνώπιον τοῦ θρόνου καὶ ἐνώπιον τῶν τεσσάρων ζῴων καὶ τῶν πρεσβυτέρων, καὶ οὐδεὶς ἐδύνατο μαθεῖν τὴν ᾠδὴν εἰ μὴ αἱ ἑκατὸν τεσσαράκοντα τέσσαρες χιλιάδες, οἱ ἠγορασμένοι ἀπὸ τῆς γῆς.

ᾄδουσιν. Pres act ind 3rd pl ᾄδω. Historical or narrative present (see 4:5 on ἐκπορεύονται). Here it functions to draw attention to the song sung by the 144,000. Mussies's (334) suggestion, that the switch from the aorist in verse 2 to the present tense here due to recalling what he saw in the past and reliving the experience in his mind's eye, is misguided and overly dependent on a strict temporal view of Greek tense forms (see "Verbal Aspect" in the Introduction). The grammatical subject of the plural ᾄδουσιν is not clear. The subject may be angelic hosts (see 5:9-12), but seems to include the redeemed 144,000 from verse 1 and the end of verse 3.

[ὡς]. The manuscript evidence is fairly evenly divided for inclusion or omission of the comparative particle. 𝔓⁴⁷ ℵ P 1611 1854 2053 2329 2344 2377 𝔐ᴷ *al* include ὡς, while A C 051 1006 1841 𝔐ᴬ omit it. In favor of inclusion, the use of ὡς and a noun functioning substantivally is consistent with Revelation's style elsewhere (4:6; 6:6; 9:7; 15:2; 19:1, 6). But it is possible that ὡς was added here in conformity with ὡς and a noun functioning substantivally elsewhere in Revelation, perhaps in conformity with its usage in verse 2 (Metzger, 677). In some of these instances (4:6; 6:6; 19:1, 6) there is a textual issue regarding the omission of ὡς (Aune, 2.784). Reflecting the difficulty, the NA[28]/UBS[5] include it in brackets. In either case, ᾠδὴν καινήν with or without ὡς functions as the direct object of ᾄδουσιν.

ᾠδὴν καινήν. Accusative direct object of ᾄδουσιν. Grammarians frequently label this a "cognate accusative" (Wallace, 189–90), though this label is not strictly a grammatical label, since it does not function any differently than a direct object.

ἐνώπιον τοῦ θρόνου καὶ ἐνώπιον τῶν τεσσάρων ζῴων καὶ τῶν πρεσβυτέρων. Locative.

οὐδεὶς. Nominative subject of ἐδύνατο.

ἐδύνατο. Impf mid ind 3rd sg δύναμαι.

μαθεῖν. Aor act inf μανθάνω (complementary).

τὴν ᾠδὴν. Accusative direct object of μαθεῖν.

εἰ μὴ. "Except, if not."

αἱ ἑκατὸν τεσσαράκοντα τέσσαρες χιλιάδες. Nominative subject of a verbless clause. The article is anaphoric, referring back to the first mention of the group in verse 1.

οἱ ἠγορασμένοι. Prf pass ptc masc nom pl ἀγοράζω (attributive). The perfect tense focuses on their status as "redeemed." Though modifying αἱ ἑκατὸν τεσσαράκοντα τέσσαρες χιλιάδες the masculine gender of the participle is an example of construction according to sense, since the 144,000 are identified as males in verse 4. The term ἀγοράζω literally means to buy or purchase (LN 57.188), but by metaphorical extension can connote "to cause the release or freedom of someone by a means that proves costly to the individual causing the release" (LN 37.131). The broader context of Revelation suggests that the cost is the sacrificial death (blood) of the Lamb (see 1:5).

ἀπὸ τῆς γῆς. Separation.

14:4 οὗτοί εἰσιν οἳ μετὰ γυναικῶν οὐκ ἐμολύνθησαν, παρθένοι γάρ εἰσιν, οὗτοι οἱ ἀκολουθοῦντες τῷ ἀρνίῳ ὅπου ἂν ὑπάγῃ. οὗτοι ἠγοράσθησαν ἀπὸ τῶν ἀνθρώπων ἀπαρχὴ τῷ θεῷ καὶ τῷ ἀρνίῳ,

οὗτοί. Nominative subject of εἰσιν. The accenting is due to the enclitic εἰσιν that follows. The use of the demonstrative οὗτοι here and in verse 6 is emphatic. As Levinsohn notes, "The 'near' nature of οὗτος manifests itself by being used in reference to animate participants that are *thematic*: the centre of attention" (2009, 210). The triple repetition of οὗτοι in this section is highly emphatic and foregrounds the 144,000 who have been redeemed from the earth.

εἰσιν. Pres act ind 3rd pl εἰμί. On the loss of accent, see 1:8.

οἵ. Nominative subject of ἐμολύνθησαν. The relative pronoun introduces a headless relative clause. The entire clause functions as the predicate of εἰσιν.

μετὰ γυναικῶν. Association or accompaniment.

ἐμολύνθησαν. Aor pass or mid ind 3rd pl μολύνω. On the voice, see on "Deponency" in the Series Introduction.

παρθένοι. Predicate nominative. The imagery here is not of literal virgins, but reflects either the nuptial imagery of the people of God as the bride of the Lamb (21:2, 9) or perhaps the stipulations under OT law that soldiers abstain from sexual relationships during times of war (Deut 23:9-11; 2 Sam 11:8-11; Bauckham, 230–31). In either case the term is used metaphorically of the people of God who refuse to compromise with the idolatrous world. παρθένοι is masculine to agree with the masculine οὗτοί.

γάρ. Explanatory.

εἰσιν. Pres act ind 3rd pl εἰμί. On the loss of accent, see 1:8.

οὗτοι. Nominative in apposition to παρθένοι. On the function of the demonstrative, see above.

οἱ ἀκολουθοῦντες. Pres act ptc masc nom pl ἀκολουθέω (attributive). It is also possible that οἱ ἀκολουθοῦντες is substantival and stands in apposition to παρθένοι and οὗτοι functions as its modifier. Smalley (358) overinterprets the present tense by saying that the present participle "suggests an ongoing commitment to the discipleship of Christ" (see the Introduction on "Verbal Aspect").

τῷ ἀρνίῳ. Dative direct object of ἀκολουθοῦντες.

ὅπου ἄν. Locative. With the subjunctive ὅπου ἄν is translated "wherever" (BDAG, 717.1.a.β).

ὑπάγῃ. Pres act subj 3rd sg ὑπάγω. Subjunctive with ὅπου ἄν. A C 2329 *al* read the present indicative ὑπάγει (on ἄν with the indicative, see Porter, 1989a, 125–26; Robertson, 969). If this is the correct reading, it would be the only place in the NT where ἄν is used with a *present* indicative. For this reason, Aune (2.785) and Smalley (307) are more inclined to see the weight slightly on the side of the subjunctive reading. It is likely that the issue reflects an unintentional error where the two endings would have been pronounced identically (η and ει).

οὗτοι. Nominative subject of ἠγοράσθησαν. On the function of the demonstrative, see above.

ἠγοράσθησαν. Aor pass ind 3rd pl ἀγοράζω.

ἀπὸ τῶν ἀνθρώπων. Separation.

ἀπαρχὴ. Nominative in apposition to οὗτοι. The term "firstfruits" is a cultic term that refers to the first portion of something (harvest) that was consecrated to God, so that the remaining could be put to daily use (BDAG, 98.1; Beale, 742). The "firstfruits" signified that the entire crop belonged to God. The term could be used in the OT and the NT metaphorically to refer to the people of God themselves (BDAG, 98). The image could suggest that what is in view here in 14:4 is a portion of the people of God who foreshadow a larger gathering of the people of God (Osborne, 531). The term is used this way in Rom 11:16; 16:5; 1 Cor 16:15; and James 1:18; and it is used of Christ's resurrection as the "firstfruits" of the resurrection of Christians at the end of history in 1 Cor 15:20, 23. However, "firstfruits" could also be used to refer to the entirety of God's people. In the OT, Jer 2:3 identifies the entire nation of Israel who were redeemed from Egypt as the first of God's harvest (Beale, 743). This is most likely the sense here: the entire people of God are the ἀπαρχή, not a select group within them, who have been redeemed from the earth and are now presented to God and the Lamb. The singular suggests that the entire group, rather than just the individuals, are the "firstfruits." Therefore, the focus is on the entire group as an offering to God and the Lamb (Mounce, 271).

τῷ θεῷ καὶ τῷ ἀρνίῳ. Dative of advantage.

14:5 καὶ ἐν τῷ στόματι αὐτῶν οὐχ εὑρέθη ψεῦδος, ἄμωμοί εἰσιν.

ἐν τῷ στόματι. Locative. The prepositional phrase is fronted for emphasis.

αὐτῶν. Possessive genitive. The singular στόματι is a distributive noun modified by a plural αὐτῶν (Aune, 2.785). On this construction, see 13:16 on τῆς χειρὸς αὐτῶν τῆς δεξιᾶς and τὸ μέτωπον αὐτῶν.

εὑρέθη. Aor pass ind 3rd sg εὑρίσκω.

ψεῦδος. Nominative subject of εὑρέθη.

ἄμωμοί. Predicate adjective of εἰσιν. The accenting is due to the enclitic εἰσιν that follows. A term that is used of the absence of defects or blemishes in sacrificial animals, ἄμωμος is also used to refer to persons who are "without fault and therefore morally blameless" (BDAG, 56.2; Charles, 2.10-11).

εἰσιν. Pres act ind 3rd pl εἰμί. On the loss of accent, see 1:8.

Revelation 14:6-13

⁶And I saw another angel flying in mid heaven, having an eternal gospel to preach to those living upon the earth and to every nation and tribe and tongue and people, ⁷saying in a loud voice, "Fear God and give

him glory, for the time of his judgment has come, and worship the one who made heaven and earth and sea and the springs of water." ⁸And another angel, a second one, followed saying, "Fallen, fallen is Babylon the great, which has caused all the nations to drink from the wine of the wrath of her adulteries." ⁹And another angel, a third one, followed them saying in a loud voice, "If anyone worships the beast and his image and receives the mark upon their forehead or upon their hand, ¹⁰they will drink from the wine of the wrath of God, which is mixed without being diluted in the cup of his wrath and they shall be tormented with fire and sulfur before the holy angels and before the Lamb. ¹¹And the smoke of their torment will go up forever and ever, and those who worship the beast and its image, and if any one receives the mark of his name, they will not have rest day and night." ¹²Here is the endurance of the saints, those who keep the commandments of God and faith in Jesus. ¹³And I heard a voice from heaven saying, "Write: Blessed are the dead who die in the Lord from now." "Yes," says the Spirit, "they shall rest from their labors, for their works follow after them."

14:6 Καὶ εἶδον ἄλλον ἄγγελον πετόμενον ἐν μεσουρανήματι, ἔχοντα εὐαγγέλιον αἰώνιον εὐαγγελίσαι ἐπὶ τοὺς καθημένους ἐπὶ τῆς γῆς καὶ ἐπὶ πᾶν ἔθνος καὶ φυλὴν καὶ γλῶσσαν καὶ λαόν,

εἶδον. Aor act ind 1st sg ὁράω. On the function, see verse 1 above.

ἄλλον ἄγγελον. Accusative direct object of εἶδον. The term ἄλλον ("another," "other") is difficult since it is not clear to what preceding angel or group of angels this one is being compared. This is probably the reason why 𝔓⁴⁷ ℵ 𝔐 omit ἄλλον. Perhaps Smalley (361) is correct that in a book latent with angelic beings the force of ἄλλον should not be pressed here.

πετόμενον. Pres mid ptc masc acc sg πέτομαι. Complement in an object-complement double accusative construction.

ἐν μεσουρανήματι. Locative.

ἔχοντα. Pres act ptc masc acc sg ἔχω (attributive).

εὐαγγέλιον αἰώνιον. Accusative direct object of ἔχοντα.

εὐαγγελίσαι. Aor act inf εὐαγγελίζω (purpose or epexegetical to εὐαγγέλιον αἰώνιον).

ἐπὶ τοὺς καθημένους. ἐπί here functions as a "marker indicating the one to whom, for whom, or about whom somth. is done" (BDAG, 366.14).

τοὺς καθημένους. Pres mid ptc masc acc pl κάθημαι (substantival). 𝔓¹¹⁵ᵛⁱᵈ A 051 *pc* have the reading κατοικοῦντας. Charles (2.12-13) speculates that a scribe may have substituted this for καθημένους to create a more neutral expression, since κατοικοῦντας elsewhere in the Apocalypse has negative connotations. However, this could also have been the reasoning of the author of the Apocalypse himself. That καθημένους is the correct reading is also suggested by the OT allusion to Jer 32(25):29. Here καθημένους carries the notion of "to be a resident in a place, *stay, be, live, reside, settle*" (BDAG, 491.2).

ἐπὶ τῆς γῆς. Locative.

ἐπὶ πᾶν ἔθνος καὶ φυλὴν καὶ γλῶσσαν καὶ λαόν. On the function of ἐπί, see above on ἐπὶ τοὺς καθημένους.

14:7 λέγων ἐν φωνῇ μεγάλῃ· φοβήθητε τὸν θεὸν καὶ δότε αὐτῷ δόξαν, ὅτι ἦλθεν ἡ ὥρα τῆς κρίσεως αὐτοῦ, καὶ προσκυνήσατε τῷ ποιήσαντι τὸν οὐρανὸν καὶ τὴν γῆν καὶ θάλασσαν καὶ πηγὰς ὑδάτων.

λέγων. Pres act ptc masc nom sg λέγω (manner). On the use of the participle λέγων to introduce speech, see 1:17. The nominative case is another example of John's well-known grammatical irregularities. One would have expected the accusative case rather than the nominative here, since it modifies an infinitive εὐαγγελίσαι (v. 6). The nominative case of the participle λέγων may be used because it modifies the unexpressed subject of the infinitive. Beale (754) thinks it has been enhanced by the LXX.

ἐν φωνῇ μεγάλῃ. Instrumental.

φοβήθητε. Aor mid impv 2nd pl φοβέομαι. On the voice, see on "Deponency" in the Series Introduction.

τὸν θεόν. Accusative direct object of φοβήθητε.

δότε. Aor act impv 2nd pl δίδωμι.

αὐτῷ. Dative indirect object of δότε.

δόξαν. Accusative direct object of δότε.

ὅτι. Introduces a causal clause.

ἦλθεν. Aor act ind 3rd sg ἔρχομαι.

ἡ ὥρα. Nominative subject of ἦλθεν.

τῆς κρίσεως. Descriptive genitive: "The hour when his judgment takes place."

αὐτοῦ. Subjective genitive.

προσκυνήσατε. Aor act impv 2nd pl προσκυνέω.

τῷ ποιήσαντι. Aor act ptc masc dat sg ποιέω (substantival). Dative direct object of προσκυνήσατε.

τὸν οὐρανὸν καὶ τὴν γῆν καὶ θάλασσαν καὶ πηγάς. Accusative direct object of ποιήσαντι. The article is used with οὐρανόν and γῆν because they are viewed as distinct, while θάλασσαν and πηγάς are anarthrous because they are a subset of τὴν γῆν (Wallace, 287).

ὑδάτων. Genitive of description or content.

14:8 Καὶ ἄλλος ἄγγελος δεύτερος ἠκολούθησεν λέγων· ἔπεσεν ἔπεσεν Βαβυλὼν ἡ μεγάλη ἣ ἐκ τοῦ οἴνου τοῦ θυμοῦ τῆς πορνείας αὐτῆς πεπότικεν πάντα τὰ ἔθνη.

ἄλλος ἄγγελος δεύτερος. Nominative subject of ἠκολούθησεν.
ἠκολούθησεν. Aor act ind 3rd sg ἀκολουθέω.
λέγων. Pres act ptc masc nom sg λέγω (manner). On the use of the participle λέγων to introduce speech, see 1:17.
ἔπεσεν ἔπεσεν. Aor act ind 3rd sg πίπτω. The aorist tense is probably future referring (Fanning, 274; Porter 1992, 37–38; Beale, 754; Aune, 2.829; Osborne, 537; Smalley, 363, who incorrectly says that because it is aorist it refers to a future event as if it has already happened). On this usage of the aorist, see 10:7 on ἐτελέσθη. It is also possible that the aorist could be taken as present referring from the standpoint of the angelic pronouncment of judgment: it refers to the *verdict of judgment* by the angel given in advance of the *execution* of the verdict in the actual fall of Babylon in 16:19; 18:2 (Mathewson 2010, 62). "[T]he destruction of Babylon has now been decided" (Mussies, 338). We might say, "Babylon is as good as fallen." The repetition of ἔπεσεν adds emphasis to the pronouncement and also reflects the OT allusion to Isa 21:9.
Βαβυλὼν ἡ μεγάλη. Nominative subject of ἔπεσεν ἔπεσεν.
ἣ. Nominative subject of πεπότικεν.
ἐκ τοῦ οἴνου. Source.
τοῦ θυμοῦ. Epexegetical genitive. On the meaning, see πορνείας below. The piling up of genitives lends prominence to this section, highlighting the reason (crimes) for Babylon's fall, and this observation may be more important than giving a precise label to each genitive. As Turner (218) notes, in this kind of construction usually each genitive depends on the preceding one to form an accumulative chain.
τῆς πορνείας. The genitive is somewhat difficult. The difficulty centers on the image of God's wrath (θυμοῦ) and Babylon's adultery (πορνείας) and their relationship to one another. It is possible to understand θυμοῦ as a reference to God's own wrath, as is clearly the case in verse 10 below. If this is the case, the relationship between God's wrath and adultery could be a causal one, so that the genitive πορνείας expresses the cause of God's wrath (θυμοῦ). According to Mounce, the combining of the two images suggests "that the heady potion of Rome's seductive practices inevitably involves the wrath of God" (274). However, it is preferable to take θυμοῦ not as a reference to God's wrath as in verse 10, but as meaning "an intense passionate desire of an overwhelming and possibly destructive character" (LN 25.19). In this case, τῆς πορνείας should probably be understood as an attributive genitive (Smalley, 364; Aune, 2.786): "Her immoral passion." BDAG (461.1) reverses the genitives in

their translation: "The wine of her passionate immorality." The connection with verse 10, αὐτὸς πίεται ἐκ τοῦ οἴνου τοῦ θυμοῦ τοῦ θεοῦ, is rhetorical. Those who drink from the wine of the *passion* of Babylon's immorality (v. 8) will also drink of the wine of the *anger* of God (v. 10).

αὐτῆς. Subjective genitive.

πεπότικεν. Prf act ind 3rd sg ποτίζω. The perfect tense may lend further prominence to the reason for Babylon's fall. Rather than the accusative of thing, ποτίζω is here followed by ἐκ τοῦ οἴνου (BDAG, 857.1.a). See above.

πάντα τὰ ἔθνη. Accusative direct object of πεπότικεν.

14:9 Καὶ ἄλλος ἄγγελος τρίτος ἠκολούθησεν αὐτοῖς λέγων ἐν φωνῇ μεγάλῃ· εἴ τις προσκυνεῖ τὸ θηρίον καὶ τὴν εἰκόνα αὐτοῦ καὶ λαμβάνει χάραγμα ἐπὶ τοῦ μετώπου αὐτοῦ ἢ ἐπὶ τὴν χεῖρα αὐτοῦ,

ἄλλος ἄγγελος τρίτος. Nominative subject of ἠκολούθησεν.

ἠκολούθησεν. Aor act ind 3rd sg ἀκολουθέω.

αὐτοῖς. Dative direct object of ἠκολούθησεν.

λέγων. Pres act ptc masc nom sg λέγω (manner). On the use of the participle λέγων to introduce speech, see 1:17.

ἐν φωνῇ μεγάλῃ. Instrumental.

εἴ. Introduces the protasis of a first-class conditional sentence. The accenting is due to the enclitic τις that follows.

τις. Nominative subject of προσκυνεῖ.

προσκυνεῖ. Pres act ind 3rd sg προσκυνέω.

τὸ θηρίον καὶ τὴν εἰκόνα. Accusative direct object of προσκυνεῖ.

αὐτοῦ. On the function of the genitive after εἰκόνα, see 13:15.

λαμβάνει. Pres act ind 3rd sg λαμβάνω.

χάραγμα. Accusative direct object of λαμβάνει.

ἐπὶ τοῦ μετώπου. Locative.

αὐτοῦ. Possessive genitive.

ἐπὶ τὴν χεῖρα. Locative. It is difficult to detect a difference in meaning between the genitive and the switch to the accusative following ἐπί (Robertson, 601).

αὐτοῦ. Possessive genitive.

14:10 καὶ αὐτὸς πίεται ἐκ τοῦ οἴνου τοῦ θυμοῦ τοῦ θεοῦ τοῦ κεκερασμένου ἀκράτου ἐν τῷ ποτηρίῳ τῆς ὀργῆς αὐτοῦ καὶ βασανισθήσεται ἐν πυρὶ καὶ θείῳ ἐνώπιον ἀγγέλων ἁγίων καὶ ἐνώπιον τοῦ ἀρνίου.

καί. Ascensive ("even").

αὐτός. Nominative subject of πίεται. The pronoun here is emphatic (though Robertson, 680, says any emphasis is very slight).

πίεται. Fut mid ind 3rd sg πίνω.
ἐκ τοῦ οἴνου. Source.
τοῦ θυμοῦ. Epexegetical genitive. On the piling up of genitives, see verse 8 above. While in verse 8 θυμοῦ meant "passionate desire," here it means "fury" (LN 88.178).
τοῦ θεοῦ. Subjective genitive.
τοῦ κεκερασμένου. Prf pass ptc masc gen sg κεράννυμι (attributive). The word suggests "to mix liquid components, mostly water with wine" (BDAG, 540.1).
ἀκράτου. The adjective means "pertaining to being pure in the sense of not being diluted and hence at full strength" (LN 79.99). The two notions of "mixed" (κεκερασμένου) and "undiluted" (ἀκράτου) appear paradoxical (lit. "mixed unmixed"). Smalley may be correct that "the wine of God's wrath is both (lit.) 'mixed', so as to increase its strength, and 'unmixed', because its potency is not diluted by water" (366). Therefore, it refers to God's wrath at full strength (BDAG, 38). In any case, the concept of mixing (κεκερασμένου) should not be taken to imply diluting.
ἐν τῷ ποτηρίῳ. Locative.
τῆς ὀργῆς. Genitive of content ("the cup full of wrath").
αὐτοῦ. Subjective genitive.
βασανισθήσεται. Fut pass ind 3rd sg βασανίζω.
ἐν πυρὶ καὶ θείῳ. Instrumental.
ἐνώπιον ἀγγέλων ἁγίων καὶ ἐνώπιον τοῦ ἀρνίου. Locative.

14:11 καὶ ὁ καπνὸς τοῦ βασανισμοῦ αὐτῶν εἰς αἰῶνας αἰώνων ἀναβαίνει, καὶ οὐκ ἔχουσιν ἀνάπαυσιν ἡμέρας καὶ νυκτὸς οἱ προσκυνοῦντες τὸ θηρίον καὶ τὴν εἰκόνα αὐτοῦ καὶ εἴ τις λαμβάνει τὸ χάραγμα τοῦ ὀνόματος αὐτοῦ.

ὁ καπνός. Nominative subject of ἀναβαίνει.
τοῦ βασανισμοῦ. Attributive genitive.
αὐτῶν. Objective genitive.
εἰς αἰῶνας αἰώνων. Temporal. On this construction, see 1:18.
ἀναβαίνει. Pres act ind 3rd sg ἀναβαίνω. The present tense is future referring.
ἔχουσιν. Pres act ind 3rd pl ἔχω.
ἀνάπαυσιν. Accusative direct object of ἔχουσιν. On ἀνάπαυσιν with ἔχουσιν, see 4:8.
ἡμέρας καὶ νυκτός. Genitive of time (see 4:8).
οἱ προσκυνοῦντες. Pres act ptc masc nom pl προσκυνέω (substantival). Nominative subject of ἔχουσιν.
τὸ θηρίον καὶ τὴν εἰκόνα. Accusative direct object of προσκυνοῦντες.

αὐτοῦ. On the function of the genitive with εἰκόνα, see 13:15.

εἴ. Introduces the protasis of a first-class conditional sentence. The accenting is due to the enclitic τις that follows. The καὶ that introduces the conditional clause links it with the previous clause (οἱ προσκυνοῦντες) and suggests that it functions as the subject of ἔχουσιν. Rhetorically, the conditional sentence has the effect of drawing attention to worship of and identification with the beast as the overarching reason for judgment.

τις. Nominative subject of λαμβάνει.
λαμβάνει. Pres act ind 3rd sg λαμβάνω.
τὸ χάραγμα. Accusative direct object of λαμβάνει.
τοῦ ὀνόματος. Epexegetical genitive.
αὐτοῦ. Possessive genitive.

14:12 Ὧδε ἡ ὑπομονὴ τῶν ἁγίων ἐστίν, οἱ τηροῦντες τὰς ἐντολὰς τοῦ θεοῦ καὶ τὴν πίστιν Ἰησοῦ.

Although NA[28] marks this verse as part of the speech of the third angel, following Swete (186) verse 12 should probably be treated as a comment by the author himself (cf. the NRSV). This would be consistent with similar comments by the seer introduced by Ὧδε elsewhere (13:10, 18; 17:9).

Ὧδε. An adverb of place that functions substantivally like a demonstrative as the subject of ἐστίν and cataphorically (like 13:10, 18) points forward to the rest of verse 12. "Here is the endurance of the saints: those who keep the comands of God and the faith in Jesus." On the meaning, see 13:10.

ἡ ὑπομονὴ. Predicate nominative of ἐστίν.
τῶν ἁγίων. Subjective genitive.
ἐστίν. Pres act ind 3rd sg εἰμί.
οἱ τηροῦντες. Pres act ptc masc nom pl τηρέω (substantival). There is apparent incongruity between the genitive case of τῶν ἁγίων and οἱ τηροῦντες, which is in the nominative case and to which the participle seems to refer (א 1006 1611 1841 pc read τῶν τηρῶντων). But this assumes that οἱ τηροῦντες is grammatically in apposition to τῶν ἁγίων. Robertson (414) says that it "is a loose addition." However, the participle construction οἱ τηροῦντες does not only define ἁγίων. Rather, it seems to stand in apposition to Ὧδε.

τὰς ἐντολὰς. Accusative direct object of τηροῦντες.
τοῦ θεοῦ. Genitive of source or subjective genitive.
τὴν πίστιν. Accusative direct object of τηροῦντες.
Ἰησοῦ. Objective genitive ("faith in Jesus").

14:13 Καὶ ἤκουσα φωνῆς ἐκ τοῦ οὐρανοῦ λεγούσης· γράψον· μακάριοι οἱ νεκροὶ οἱ ἐν κυρίῳ ἀποθνῄσκοντες ἀπ' ἄρτι. ναί, λέγει τὸ πνεῦμα, ἵνα ἀναπαήσονται ἐκ τῶν κόπων αὐτῶν, τὰ γὰρ ἔργα αὐτῶν ἀκολουθεῖ μετ' αὐτῶν.

ἤκουσα. Aor act ind 1st sg ἀκούω.
φωνῆς. Genitive direct object of ἤκουσα.
ἐκ τοῦ οὐρανοῦ. Source.
λεγούσης. Pres act ptc fem gen sg λέγω. Complement in an object-complement double genitive construction with φωνῆς. On the use of the participle λεγούσης to introduce speech, see 1:17 on λέγων.
γράψον. Aor act impv 2nd sg γράφω. This is an example of several commands for John to write found in Revelation. Though these commands may sometimes refer to the content of the entire book (1:11, 19; 21:5), here it refers to the rest of the beatitude in verse 13. The command "emphasizes the importance of the message which follows" (Smalley, 369).
μακάριοι. Predicate nominative of a verbless clause.
οἱ νεκροί. Nominative subject of a verbless clause.
ἐν κυρίῳ. Locative, in a metaphorical sense.
ἀποθνῄσκοντες. Pres act ptc masc nom pl ἀποθνῄσκω (attributive).
ἀπ' ἄρτι. Temporal, indicating "the point from which someth. begins" here used "of time" (BDAG, 105.2). There is some difficulty in determining what this expression modifies. There are three principal options for understanding this expression. (1) Aune (2.788) thinks that ἀπ' ἄρτι should be taken as ἀπαρτί meaning "certainly, exactly, truly." Further, he argues that the punctuation of NA[28] should be changed so that ἀπαρτί goes with the following clause. This, however, overlooks the fact that an expression of certainty is already present with the ναί, and taking it this way is somewhat awkward if the ναί is retained ($\mathfrak{P}^{47}$ ℵ* 336 582 620 628 1918). (2) Retaining the reading as a temporal expression (contra Aune), ἀπ' ἄρτι could go with the following ναί, λέγει τὸ πνεῦμα ἵνα ἀναπαήσονται ἐκ τῶν κόπων αὐτῶν: "From now on, yes, says the Spirit, they will rest from their labors" (Smalley, 369). (3) Following the punctuation found in NA[28], ἀπ' ἄρτι could modify the preceding clause, since it immediately follows it, emphasizing the eternal blessing for those who die: "Blessed are those who die from now on." The difficulty is whether this leaves out others who have died prior to this statement (Smalley, 369). One way of solving this is to take the temporal expression as modifying μακάριοι rather than ἀποθνῄσκοντες: "The dead who die in the Lord are blessed from now on." Beale (769) suggests that the temporal ἀπ' ἄρτι could also be understood as a reference to the redemptive work of Christ, as the point from which the saints are

blessed. In any case, the blessing that the dead experience from now on is resting from their labors.

ναί. A particle that expresses affirmation or agreement (if original; see Metzger, 678–79), "*certainly, indeed, quite so*" (BDAG, 665). Functions as the content of the speech introduced by λέγει. NA²⁸ presents the rest of verse 13 as part of the speech of the voice from heaven. However, this should probably be taken as the Spirit responding to the voice from heaven (Swete, 187; Osborne, 545; NRSV, NIV) reported by the author, rather than as part of what the voice from heaven said (see the translation above).

λέγει. Pres act ind 3rd sg λέγω.

τὸ πνεῦμα. Nominative subject of λέγει.

ἵνα. Caragounis (222 n. 303) understands the ἵνα to introduce a causal clause, which may find some support in 𝔓⁴⁷, which reads ὅτι rather than ἵνα (see also BDF §369.2; Swete, 187). On the other hand, the ὅτι reading may not have been intended to signal a causal clause. It could introduce a content clause after λέγει or function as an epexegetical clause. Another option would be to take the ἵνα clause as a content clause further describing the blessing (μακάριοι) in the earlier part of the verse (Osborne, 545; Beale, 768). Smalley (370) says that it gives the content of the blessing, but labels it a consecutive use of ἵνα. The latter is probably to be preferred: Those who die in the Lord do so *so that* they rest from their labors.

ἀναπαήσονται. Fut mid ind 3rd pl ἀναπαύω. Future with ἵνα. On the use of the future in place of the subjunctive, see 3:9 on ἥξουσιν.

ἐκ τῶν κόπων. Separation.

αὐτῶν. Subjective genitive.

γὰρ. Explanatory.

τὰ ... ἔργα. Nominative subject of ἀκολουθεῖ.

αὐτῶν. Subjective genitive.

ἀκολουθεῖ. Pres act ind 3rd sg ἀκολουθέω. It is common for plural neuter subjects to be found with singular verbs (Porter 1992, 73).

μετ' αὐτῶν. Association.

Revelation 14:14-20

¹⁴And I saw and look, a white cloud, and upon the cloud was someone seated like a son of man, having on his head a gold crown and in his hand a sharp sickle. ¹⁵And another angel came out of the temple, crying out in a loud voice to the one seated upon the cloud, "Send your sickle and reap, for the hour to harvest has come, for the harvest of the earth is ripe." ¹⁶And the one seated upon the cloud threw out his sickle upon the earth and the earth was harvested. ¹⁷And another angel came out

from the temple that is in heaven, and he too had a sharp sickle. ¹⁸And another angel who has authority over the fire came out from the altar, and he called with a loud voice to the one who had the sharp sickle saying, "Send your sharp sickle and harvest the grapes of the vine of the earth, for its grapes are ripe." ¹⁹And the angel threw out his sickle onto the earth and harvested the vineyard of the earth and threw it into the great winepress of the wrath of God. ²⁰And the winepress was trampled outside of the city and blood flowed from the winepress up to the bridles of the horses for sixteen hundred stadia.

14:14 Καὶ εἶδον, καὶ ἰδοὺ νεφέλη λευκή, καὶ ἐπὶ τὴν νεφέλην καθήμενον ὅμοιον υἱὸν ἀνθρώπου, ἔχων ἐπὶ τῆς κεφαλῆς αὐτοῦ στέφανον χρυσοῦν καὶ ἐν τῇ χειρὶ αὐτοῦ δρέπανον ὀξύ.

Καὶ εἶδον. Introduces a new element in the vision.

εἶδον. Aor act ind 1st sg ὁράω. On the function, see verse 1 above.

ἰδού. A marker of attention that deictically functions to make the following statement emphatic. Here it draws attention to the Son of Man. On the form, see 1:7.

νεφέλη λευκή. Nominative subject of a verbless clause.

ἐπὶ τὴν νεφέλην. Locative.

καθήμενον. Pres mid ptc masc acc sg κάθημαι (substantival). Accusative direct object of an implied εἶδον.

ὅμοιον υἱὸν. Comparison. On the grammatical issue, see 1:13 on ὅμοιον υἱὸν.

ἀνθρώπου. Genitive of relationship.

ἔχων. Pres act ptc masc nom sg ἔχω. The participle seems to function attributively. This is another example of a solecism, since one would expect the accusative in order to conform to καθήμενον ὅμοιον υἱὸν ($\mathfrak{P}^{47}$ ℵ* pc read ἔχοντα). This usage is common with ἔχων in Revelation. The nominative may be due to the author's desire to draw attention to this descriptive feature of the Son of Man.

ἐπὶ τῆς κεφαλῆς. Locative.

αὐτοῦ. Possessive genitive.

στέφανον χρυσοῦν καὶ ... δρέπανον ὀξύ. Accusative direct object of ἔχων.

ἐν τῇ χειρὶ. Locative.

αὐτοῦ. Possessive genitive.

14:15 καὶ ἄλλος ἄγγελος ἐξῆλθεν ἐκ τοῦ ναοῦ κράζων ἐν φωνῇ μεγάλῃ τῷ καθημένῳ ἐπὶ τῆς νεφέλης· πέμψον τὸ δρέπανόν σου καὶ θέρισον, ὅτι ἦλθεν ἡ ὥρα θερίσαι, ὅτι ἐξηράνθη ὁ θερισμὸς τῆς γῆς.

ἄλλος ἄγγελος. Nominative subject of ἐξῆλθεν.
ἐξῆλθεν. Aor act ind 3rd sg ἐξέρχομαι.
ἐκ τοῦ ναοῦ. Source.
κράζων. Pres act ptc masc nom sg κράζω (manner).
ἐν φωνῇ μεγάλῃ. Instrumental.
τῷ καθημένῳ. Pres mid ptc masc dat sg κάθημαι (substantival). Dative indirect object of κράζων.
ἐπὶ τῆς νεφέλης. Locative.
πέμψον. Aor act impv 2nd sg πέμπω.
τὸ δρέπανόν. Accusative direct object of πέμψον. The accenting is due to the enclitic σου that follows.
σου. Possessive genitive.
θέρισον. Aor act impv 2nd sg θερίζω. It is not necessary to treat the aorist as ingressive ("begin to reap") following Osborne (552). The aorist simply summarizes the entire act of reaping.
ὅτι. Introduces a causal clause.
ἦλθεν. Aor act ind 3rd sg ἔρχομαι.
ἡ ὥρα. Nominative subject of ἦλθεν.
θερίσαι. Aor act inf θερίζω (epexegetical to ἡ ὥρα).
ὅτι. Introduces a causal clause.
ἐξηράνθη. Aor pass ind 3rd sg ξηραίνω. The term ξηραίνω typically simply means "to become dry," but here suggests "to become dry and therefore ready for harvesting" (BDAG, 685.3).
ὁ θερισμὸς. Nominative subject of ἐξηράνθη.
τῆς γῆς. Objective genitive.

14:16 καὶ ἔβαλεν ὁ καθήμενος ἐπὶ τῆς νεφέλης τὸ δρέπανον αὐτοῦ ἐπὶ τὴν γῆν καὶ ἐθερίσθη ἡ γῆ.

ἔβαλεν. Aor act ind 3rd sg βάλλω.
ὁ καθήμενος. Pres mid ptc masc nom sg κάθημαι (substantival). Nominative subject of ἔβαλεν.
ἐπὶ τῆς νεφέλης. Locative.
τὸ δρέπανον. Accusative direct object of ἔβαλεν.
αὐτοῦ. Possessive genitive.
ἐπὶ τὴν γῆν. Locative.
ἐθερίσθη. Aor pass ind 3rd sg θερίζω. The passive shifts the focus to the subject ἡ γῆ.
ἡ γῆ. Nominative subject of ἐθερίσθη.

14:17 Καὶ ἄλλος ἄγγελος ἐξῆλθεν ἐκ τοῦ ναοῦ τοῦ ἐν τῷ οὐρανῷ ἔχων καὶ αὐτὸς δρέπανον ὀξύ.

ἄλλος ἄγγελος. Nominative subject of ἐξῆλθεν.
ἐξῆλθεν. Aor act ind 3rd sg ἐξέρχομαι.
ἐκ τοῦ ναοῦ. Source.
τοῦ ἐν τῷ οὐρανῷ. The article functions as an adjectivizer, turning the entire PP into an attributive modifier of τοῦ ναοῦ. Lit. "the in-the-heaven temple."
ἐν τῷ οὐρανῷ. Locative.
ἔχων. Pres act ptc masc nom sg ἔχω (manner, modifying ἐξῆλθεν).
καὶ. Adverbial: "also."
αὐτὸς. Nominative subject of ἔχων. The use of the pronoun here is emphatic.
δρέπανον ὀξύ. Accusative direct object of ἔχων.

14:18 καὶ ἄλλος ἄγγελος [ἐξῆλθεν] ἐκ τοῦ θυσιαστηρίου [ὁ] ἔχων ἐξουσίαν ἐπὶ τοῦ πυρός, καὶ ἐφώνησεν φωνῇ μεγάλῃ τῷ ἔχοντι τὸ δρέπανον τὸ ὀξὺ λέγων· πέμψον σου τὸ δρέπανον τὸ ὀξὺ καὶ τρύγησον τοὺς βότρυας τῆς ἀμπέλου τῆς γῆς, ὅτι ἤκμασαν αἱ σταφυλαὶ αὐτῆς.

ἄλλος ἄγγελος. Nominative subject of ἐξῆλθεν. If ἐξῆλθεν is absent, it functions as the subject of a verbless clause.
[ἐξῆλθεν]. Aor act ind 3rd sg ἐξέρχομαι. ℵ C (051 1854) have ἐξῆλθεν, while 𝔓⁴⁷ A 1611 2053 *pc* omit it. It is difficult to determine whether ἐξῆλθεν was added by a scribe to bring this verse into conformity with verses 15 and 17, or whether it was inadvertantly or intentionally dropped out by a scribe due to the repetition of ἐξῆλθεν in the space of just a few sentences. In any case, the PP ἐκ τοῦ θυσιαστηρίου expresses what is implied in ἐξῆλθεν.
ἐκ τοῦ θυσιαστηρίου. Source.
[ὁ] ἔχων. Pres act ptc masc nom sg ἔχω. The participle (without the article) could function as a finite verb if ἐξῆλθεν is omitted. However, it may function attributively, modifying ἄλλος ἄγγελος, especially if one accepts the presence of the article, which is attested in A C 2329. The article may have been added to make the attributive function of the participle explicit.
ἐξουσίαν. Accusative direct object of ἔχων.
ἐπὶ τοῦ πυρός. The preposition ἐπί indicates that over which someone exercizes authority (BDAG, 365.9).
ἐφώνησεν. Aor act ind 3rd sg φωνέω. The implied subject is the angel who comes from the altar.
φωνῇ μεγάλῃ. Dative of instrument.

τῷ ἔχοντι. Pres act ptc masc dat sg ἔχω (substantival). Dative indirect object of ἐφώνησεν. The referent is the angel in verse 17 (contra Aune, 2.790, who thinks it is a solecism because he apparently connects it to the wrong angel).

τὸ δρέπανον τὸ ὀξύ. Accusative direct object of ἔχοντι. The article is anaphoric, referring back to the first mention in verse 17.

λέγων. Pres act ptc masc nom sg λέγω (manner). On the use of the participle λέγων to introduce speech, see 1:17 on λέγων.

πέμψον. Aor act impv 2nd sg πέμπω.

σου. Possessive genitive. Placed before the head term it modifies for prominence.

τὸ δρέπανον τὸ ὀξύ. Accusative direct object of πέμψον. The article is anaphoric, referring back to the first mention in verse 17.

τρύγησον. Aor act impv 2nd sg τρυγάω.

τοὺς βότρυας. Accusative direct object of τρύγησον.

τῆς ἀμπέλου. Possessive genitive or genitive of source.

τῆς γῆς. Epexegetical genitive.

ὅτι. Introduces a causal clause.

ἤκμασαν. Aor act ind 3rd pl ἀκμάζω. Mussies (338) labels this an aorist with perfective value. However, this is probably influenced more by English translation than the semantics of the aorist tense form (see "Verbal Aspect" in the Introduction).

αἱ σταφυλαί. Nominative subject of ἤκμασαν.

αὐτῆς. Possessive genitive.

14:19 καὶ ἔβαλεν ὁ ἄγγελος τὸ δρέπανον αὐτοῦ εἰς τὴν γῆν καὶ ἐτρύγησεν τὴν ἄμπελον τῆς γῆς καὶ ἔβαλεν εἰς τὴν ληνὸν τοῦ θυμοῦ τοῦ θεοῦ τὸν μέγαν.

ἔβαλεν. Aor act ind 3rd sg βάλλω.

ὁ ἄγγελος. Nominative subject of ἔβαλεν.

τὸ δρέπανον. Accusative direct object of ἔβαλεν.

αὐτοῦ. Possessive genitive.

εἰς τὴν γῆν. Goal.

ἐτρύγησεν. Aor act ind 3rd sg τρυγάω.

τὴν ἄμπελον. Accusative direct object of ἐτρύγησεν. On the meaning, see verse 18 above on τῆς ἀμπέλου.

τῆς γῆς. Epexegetical genitive.

ἔβαλεν. Aor act ind 3rd sg βάλλω.

εἰς τὴν ληνὸν ... τὸν μέγαν. Goal. Note the masculine τὸν μέγαν modifying the feminine second declension τὴν ληνόν (BDF §136.3). The author was probably influenced by the intervening τοῦ θυμοῦ τοῦ θεοῦ, which the ληνόν symbolizes. The readings τὴν μεγάλην (א 1006 1841

1854 2053 *al*) and τοῦ μεγάλου (𝔓⁴⁷ 1611 *pc*) can be seen as attempts to "correct" the grammar. Beale (779–80) argues that the masculine is meant to highlight the OT allusion to Isa 63:2.

τοῦ θυμοῦ. Epexegetical genitive or genitive of content.

τοῦ θεοῦ. Subjective genitive.

14:20 καὶ ἐπατήθη ἡ ληνὸς ἔξωθεν τῆς πόλεως καὶ ἐξῆλθεν αἷμα ἐκ τῆς ληνοῦ ἄχρι τῶν χαλινῶν τῶν ἵππων ἀπὸ σταδίων χιλίων ἑξακοσίων.

ἐπατήθη. Aor pass ind 3rd sg πατέω.

ἡ ληνὸς. Nominative subject of ἐπατήθη.

ἔξωθεν τῆς πόλεως. Locative.

ἐξῆλθεν. Aor act ind 3rd sg ἐξέρχομαι.

αἷμα. Nominative subject of ἐξῆλθεν.

ἐκ τῆς ληνοῦ. Source.

ἄχρι τῶν χαλινῶν. Extent. Here ἄχρι is used to indicate extension up to a goal ("up to" or "as far as" the horses' bridles; see LN 84.19).

τῶν ἵππων. Possessive genitive.

ἀπὸ σταδίων χιλίων ἑξακοσίων. According to BDAG (106.4) ἀπό can be used "to indicate distance from a point" (cf. Charles, 1.cxxviii: "at a distance from"). However, Zerwick (§71) notes that the preposition indicates not the point from which the distance is measured, but the distance itself. A στάδιον was a unit of measurement that was equivalent to about 200 yards or 192 meters or one eighth of a mile (see BDAG, 940.1). 1600 stadia = approximately 184 miles (Beale, 782).

Revelation 15:1-8

¹And I saw another great and marvelous sign in heaven, seven angels having the seven last plagues, because with them the wrath of God will be completed. ²And I saw something like a glassy sea mixed with fire and those who overcame the beast and his image and the number of his name standing by the glassy sea, having harps from God. ³And they were singing the song of Moses, the servant of God, and the song of the Lamb, saying, "Great and marvelous are your works, Lord, God Almighty; righteous and true are your ways, King of the nations; ⁴who will not fear you and glorify your name, Lord? For you alone are holy, for all the nations will come and worship before you, for your righteous deeds have been made known." ⁵And after these things I saw, and the temple of the tent of witness in heaven was opened, ⁶and the seven angels who have the seven plagues came out of the temple, clothed with clean bright linen with golden belts girded around their chests. ⁷And one of the four living creatures gave to the seven angels seven golden bowls full of the wrath of

God who lives forever and ever. ⁸And the temple was filled with smoke from the glory of God and from his power, and no one was able to enter the temple until the seven plagues of the seven angels were completed.

15:1 Καὶ εἶδον ἄλλο σημεῖον ἐν τῷ οὐρανῷ μέγα καὶ θαυμαστόν, ἀγγέλους ἑπτὰ ἔχοντας πληγὰς ἑπτὰ τὰς ἐσχάτας, ὅτι ἐν αὐταῖς ἐτελέσθη ὁ θυμὸς τοῦ θεοῦ.

Καὶ εἶδον. Introduces a new major scene within the visionary narrative.

εἶδον. Aor act ind 1st sg ὁράω.

ἄλλο σημεῖον ... μέγα καὶ θαυμαστόν. Accusative direct object of εἶδον.

ἐν τῷ οὐρανῷ. Locative.

ἀγγέλους ἑπτὰ. Accusative in apposition to σημεῖον.

ἔχοντας. Pres act ptc masc acc pl ἔχω (attributive).

πληγὰς ἑπτὰ τὰς ἐσχάτας. Accusative direct object of ἔχοντας.

ὅτι. Introduces a causal clause, indicating why the seven plagues are last (ἐσχάτας).

ἐν αὐταῖς. Instrumental.

ἐτελέσθη. Aor pass ind 3rd sg τελέω. This is an example of the aorist tense form that seems to refer to action that is future (Porter 1992, 38; Fanning, 274), since the plagues have not yet been unleashed. Beale (788) thinks that the aorist emphasizes the certainty of the event; but it is difficult to see how the aorist used of a future event makes it any more certain than the future or present tense forms used of future events. This observation is based on an overly temporal understanding of the tense (a future action seen as if it were already past). The aorist simply looks at the event as a complete whole. On this use of the aorist, see 10:7 on ἐτελέσθη.

ὁ θυμὸς. Nominative subject of ἐτελέσθη.

τοῦ θεοῦ. Subjective genitive.

15:2 Καὶ εἶδον ὡς θάλασσαν ὑαλίνην μεμιγμένην πυρὶ καὶ τοὺς νικῶντας ἐκ τοῦ θηρίου καὶ ἐκ τῆς εἰκόνος αὐτοῦ καὶ ἐκ τοῦ ἀριθμοῦ τοῦ ὀνόματος αὐτοῦ ἑστῶτας ἐπὶ τὴν θάλασσαν τὴν ὑαλίνην ἔχοντας κιθάρας τοῦ θεοῦ.

Καὶ εἶδον. Introduces a new feature within the vision.

εἶδον. Aor act ind 1st sg ὁράω.

ὡς θάλασσαν ὑαλίνην. Comparison. Functions as the direct object of εἶδον. It is probably part of an elided clause: "I saw *something* like a glassy sea."

μεμιγμένην. Prf pass ptc fem acc sg μίγνυμι (attributive). It is also possible that it functions as the complement in an object-complement double accusative construction.

πυρί. Dative of association (Robertson, 529).

τοὺς νικῶντας. Pres act ptc masc acc pl νικάω (substantival). Accusative direct object of εἶδον.

ἐκ τοῦ θηρίου. Separation. The preposition ἐκ with the genitive is a mark of disassociation from someone or something (Aune, 1.clxxx). Here it follows νικῶντας. The expression τοὺς νικῶντας ἐκ τοῦ θηρίου seems to be used in the sense of "those who are victorious over" (Aune, 2.872) or in an equivalent way to τηρήσαντες ἑαυτοὺς ἐκ τοῦ θηρίου (BDF §212; BDAG, 673.1.a).

ἐκ τῆς εἰκόνος. On the function, see ἐκ τοῦ θηρίου above.

αὐτοῦ. On the function of the genitive with εἰκόνα, see 13:15.

ἐκ τοῦ ἀριθμοῦ. On the function, see ἐκ τοῦ θηρίου above.

τοῦ ὀνόματος. On the function, see 13:17 on ὀνόματος.

αὐτοῦ. Possessive genitive.

ἑστῶτας. Prf act ptc masc acc pl ἵστημι. The participle functions as the complement in an object-complement double accusative construction with τοὺς νικῶντας.

ἐπὶ τὴν θάλασσαν τὴν ὑαλίνην. Locative. With the accusative ἐπί can sometimes indicate "at, by, near someone or someth." (BDAG, 363.1.c.γ). Though since what John sees is something *like* a sea (ὡς θάλασσαν ὑαλίνην) the saints could be seen as standing *upon* it (Swete, 195; Beale, 791; Smalley, 385).

ἔχοντας. Pres act ptc masc acc pl ἔχω (manner).

κιθάρας. Accusative direct object of ἔχοντας.

τοῦ θεοῦ. The idea could be "harps given to them by God" (genitive of source). Beale (791), however, says that the genitive communicates the idea "harps for playing to God."

15:3 καὶ ᾄδουσιν τὴν ᾠδὴν Μωϋσέως τοῦ δούλου τοῦ θεοῦ καὶ τὴν ᾠδὴν τοῦ ἀρνίου λέγοντες· μεγάλα καὶ θαυμαστὰ τὰ ἔργα σου, κύριε ὁ θεὸς ὁ παντοκράτωρ· δίκαιαι καὶ ἀληθιναὶ αἱ ὁδοί σου, ὁ βασιλεὺς τῶν ἐθνῶν·

ᾄδουσιν. Pres act ind 3rd pl ᾄδω. Historical or narrative present (see 4:5 on ἐκπορεύονται). Here it functions to draw attention to the song that is sung in verses 3-4. On the shift from a participle (v. 2) to a finite verb, see 1:6 on ἐποίησεν.

τὴν ᾠδήν. Accusative (cognate) direct object of ᾄδουσιν. See also 14:3 on ᾠδὴν καινήν.

Μωϋσέως. Possessive genitive or subjective genitive: "the song that Moses sung" (cf. Exod 15).

τοῦ δούλου. Genitive in apposition to Μωϋσέως.
τοῦ θεοῦ. Possessive genitive.
τὴν ᾠδὴν. Accusative (cognate) direct object of ᾄδουσιν.
τοῦ ἀρνίου. Possessive genitive or objective genitive: "the song about the Lamb" (Smalley, 386). If one understands Μωϋσέως above to be subjective ("the song sung by Moses"), it is possible to take ἀρνίου in parallel fashion as subjective (Beale, 793): "the song sung by the Lamb," which the Lamb's followers now sing. However, there are no other examples of the Lamb singing a song in Revelation, and it is not necessary to understand the two genitives in the same way.
λέγοντες. Pres act ptc masc nom pl λέγω (manner). On the use of λέγοντες to introduce speech, see 1:17.
μεγάλα καὶ θαυμαστὰ. Predicate adjectives in a verbless clause.
τὰ ἔργα. Nominative subject of a verbless clause.
σου. Subjective genitive.
κύριε. Vocative of address.
ὁ θεός. Nominative in apposition to κύριε. Zerwick notes that the nominative used in apposition to a vocative is always articular (§33).
ὁ παντοκράτωρ. Nominative in apposition to κύριε.
δίκαιαι καὶ ἀληθιναί. Predicate adjectives of a verbless clause.
αἱ ὁδοί. Nominative subject in a verbless clause. Here ὁδοί means *way of life, way of acting, conduct*" and refers to "the *ways* of God, referring . . . to the ways that God initiates" (BDAG, 691–92.3.b).
σου. Possessive genitive or subjective genitive.
ὁ βασιλεὺς. Nominative functioning as a vocative.
τῶν ἐθνῶν. Genitive of subordination. Some manuscripts read τῶν αἰώνων ($\mathfrak{P}^{47}$ ℵ* C 1006 1611 1841 *pc*). The reading τῶν ἐθνῶν (ℵ¹ A P 𝔐 *pm*) is probably to be preferred due to the OT background of this verse (Jer 10:7).

15:4 τίς οὐ μὴ φοβηθῇ, κύριε, καὶ δοξάσει τὸ ὄνομά σου ; ὅτι μόνος ὅσιος, ὅτι πάντα τὰ ἔθνη ἥξουσιν καὶ προσκυνήσουσιν ἐνώπιόν σου, ὅτι τὰ δικαιώματά σου ἐφανερώθησαν.

τίς. Nominative subject of φοβηθῇ and δοξάσει. Introduces a deliberative question.
φοβηθῇ. Aor mid subj 3rd sg φοβέομαι. The subjunctive is used with οὐ μή, which expresses emphatic negation. Here it is used in a deliberative question. On the voice see, "Deponency" in the Series Introduction.
κύριε. Vocative of address.
δοξάσει. Fut act ind 3rd sg δοξάζω. The future tense is used parallel to the subjunctive φοβηθῇ with οὐ μή. Here it is used in a deliberative question. On the use of the future in place of the subjunctive, see 3:9 on

ἥξουσιν. Predictably, some manuscripts read the subjunctive δοξάσῃ (ℵ 1006 1611 1841 2062 𝔐ᴷ). Furthermore, the endings would have been pronounced (and heard by a scribe) identically (-σει and -σῃ).

τὸ ὄνομά. Accusative direct object of δοξάσει. The accenting is due to the enclitic σου that follows.

σου. Possessive genitive.

ὅτι. Introduces a causal clause. This is the first of three ὅτι clauses following the deliberative question. All three ὅτι clauses probably are to be seen as parallel to each other and all three provide reasons for why God should be feared and glorified. However, it is possible that the last ὅτι clause, ὅτι τὰ δικαιώματά σου ἐφανερώθησαν, provides the reason for why the nations will come and worship in the second ὅτι clause. Beale (797, following BDAG, 732.5.c) suggests that the second ὅτι clause, ὅτι πάντα τὰ ἔθνη ἥξουσιν καὶ προσκυνήσουσιν ἐνώπιόν σου, should be taken consecutively ("so that") indicating the effect of God's incomparable holiness indicated in the first ὅτι clause, though he thinks the last ὅτι clause is parallel to the first one, and hence causal. However, treating it as consecutive seems to be more of a reflection of the possible semantic relationship between the two clauses, rather than based on the meaning of ὅτι. Furthermore, there is no need to take the ὅτι clause in any way other than its usual causal sense when it is seen as providing a further reason for why God should be feared and glorified expressed in the rhetorical question.

μόνος ὅσιος. Predicate adjective of a verbless clause. μόνος indicates that the Lord "alone" or "only" is holy (BDAG, 658–59.1.a.δ). The term ὅσιος is used only here and in 16:15 in Revelation, in contrast to the more common ἅγιος. The usage of ὅσιος here may be due to OT influence (LXX Ps 145:17).

ὅτι. Introduces a second causal clause (see also above).

πάντα τὰ ἔθνη. Nominative subject of ἥξουσιν καὶ προσκυνήσουσιν.

ἥξουσιν. Fut act ind 3rd pl ἥκω.

προσκυνήσουσιν. Fut act ind 3rd pl προσκυνέω. Aune (2.853), following Thompson (99), proposes that καὶ προσκυνήσουσιν functions as a final clause. However, this depends more upon the possible semantic relationship of the two clauses and not on the grammatical relationship. The καί simply indicates continuity.

ἐνώπιόν σου. Locative.

ὅτι. Introduces a third causal clause (see also above).

τὰ δικαιώματά. Nominative subject of ἐφανερώθησαν. The accenting is due to the enclitic σου that follows.

σου. Subjective genitive.

ἐφανερώθησαν. Aor pass ind 3rd pl φανερόω.

15:5 Καὶ μετὰ ταῦτα εἶδον, καὶ ἠνοίγη ὁ ναὸς τῆς σκηνῆς τοῦ μαρτυρίου ἐν τῷ οὐρανῷ,

μετὰ ταῦτα. Temporal. Like other uses of this phrase the reference is to the order in which John sees things, not the chronological order in which the events in the visions actually occur (see 4:1).
εἶδον. Aor act ind 1st sg ὁράω. Here εἶδον is not followed by an accusative direct object, but by an entire clause that describes the content of what John saw.
ἠνοίγη. Aor pass ind 3rd sg ἀνοίγω.
ὁ ναὸς. Nominative subject of ἠνοίγη.
τῆς σκηνῆς. Epexegetical genitive ("the temple, that is, the tabernacle").
τοῦ μαρτυρίου. Genitive of description.
ἐν τῷ οὐρανῷ. Locative.

15:6 καὶ ἐξῆλθον οἱ ἑπτὰ ἄγγελοι [οἱ] ἔχοντες τὰς ἑπτὰ πληγὰς ἐκ τοῦ ναοῦ ἐνδεδυμένοι λίνον καθαρὸν λαμπρὸν καὶ περιεζωσμένοι περὶ τὰ στήθη ζώνας χρυσᾶς.

ἐξῆλθον. Aor act ind 3rd pl ἐξέρχομαι.
οἱ ἑπτὰ ἄγγελοι. Nominative subject of ἐξῆλθον. The article is anaphoric, referring back to the first mention of the seven angels in verse 1.
[οἱ] ἔχοντες. Pres act ptc masc nom pl ἔχω (attributive). Even if not original, the bracketed article (attested in A C 1611 1841 2329 *pm*) makes explicit the function of the participle.
τὰς ἑπτὰ πληγὰς. Accusative direct object of ἔχοντες.
ἐκ τοῦ ναοῦ. Separation.
ἐνδεδυμένοι. Prf mid ptc masc nom pl ἐνδύω. The participle functions adverbially, modifying ἐξῆλθον and indicating manner. The two perfect participles, ἐνδεδυμένοι and περιεζωσμένοι, draw attention to the status of the seven angels.
λίνον καθαρὸν λαμπρὸν. Accusative direct object of ἐνδεδυμένοι. Instead of λίνον, fairly strong manuscript evidence supports the reading λίθον (A C 2053 2062). However, the latter reading makes less sense in the context (Metzger, 680) and may have arisen due to the unusual meaning of λίνον ("linen *garment*") here (Aune, 2.854). The word λίνον is used only here in Revelation (if orginal). A similar expression occurs in 19:8, but with βύσσινον rather than λίνον.
περιεζωσμένοι. Prf mid ptc masc nom pl περιζώννυμι. On the function, see above on ἐνδεδυμένοι.

περὶ τὰ στήθη. Locative. The preposition περί is repeated from the verb περιεζωσμένοι.
ζώνας χρυσᾶς. Accusative direct object of περιεζωσμένοι.

15:7 καὶ ἓν ἐκ τῶν τεσσάρων ζῴων ἔδωκεν τοῖς ἑπτὰ ἀγγέλοις ἑπτὰ φιάλας χρυσᾶς γεμούσας τοῦ θυμοῦ τοῦ θεοῦ τοῦ ζῶντος εἰς τοὺς αἰῶνας τῶν αἰώνων.

ἕν. Nominative subject of ἔδωκεν.
ἐκ τῶν τεσσάρων ζῴων. Partitive.
ἔδωκεν. Aor act ind 3rd sg δίδωμι.
τοῖς ἑπτὰ ἀγγέλοις. Dative indirect object of ἔδωκεν. The article is anaphoric, referring back to the first mention of the seven angels in verse 1.
ἑπτὰ φιάλας χρυσᾶς. Accusative direct object of ἔδωκεν.
γεμούσας. Pres act ptc masc acc pl γέμω (attributive).
τοῦ θυμοῦ. Genitive complement of γεμούσας.
τοῦ θεοῦ. Subjective genitive.
τοῦ ζῶντος. Pres act ptc masc gen sg ζάω (attributive).
εἰς τοὺς αἰῶνας τῶν αἰώνων. Temporal (see also 1:18).

15:8 καὶ ἐγεμίσθη ὁ ναὸς καπνοῦ ἐκ τῆς δόξης τοῦ θεοῦ καὶ ἐκ τῆς δυνάμεως αὐτοῦ, καὶ οὐδεὶς ἐδύνατο εἰσελθεῖν εἰς τὸν ναὸν ἄχρι τελεσθῶσιν αἱ ἑπτὰ πληγαὶ τῶν ἑπτὰ ἀγγέλων.

ἐγεμίσθη. Aor pass ind 3rd sg γέμω.
ὁ ναὸς. Nominative subject of ἐγεμίσθη.
καπνοῦ. Genitive complement of ἐγεμίσθη.
ἐκ τῆς δόξης. Source or cause.
τοῦ θεοῦ. Subjective genitive.
ἐκ τῆς δυνάμεως. Source or cause.
αὐτοῦ. Subjective genitive.
καί. Attempts to label the καί as consecutive (cf. Beale, 807) are due more to the semantic relationship between the two clauses than to the grammatical function of καί. The καί simply indicates continuation.
οὐδεὶς. Nominative subject of ἐδύνατο.
ἐδύνατο. Impf mid ind 3rd sg δύναμαι.
εἰσελθεῖν. Aor act inf εἰσέρχομαι (complementary).
εἰς τὸν ναὸν. Locative.
ἄχρι. Introduces a temporal clause. With the aorist subjunctive, ἄχρι is used of a "future event preceded in time by the action of the main clause" (Turner, 111).
τελεσθῶσιν. Aor pass subj 3rd pl τελέω. Subjunctive with ἄχρι.

αἱ ἑπτὰ πληγαί. Nominative subject of τελεσθῶσιν.
τῶν ἑπτὰ ἀγγέλων. Possessive genitive. The article is anaphoric, referring back to the first mention of the seven angels in verse 1.

Revelation 16:1-11

¹And I heard a loud voice from the temple saying to the seven angels, "Go and pour out the seven bowls of the wrath of God upon the earth." ²And the first (angel) went and poured out his bowl upon the earth; and there came about bad and evil sores on people who have the mark of the beast and who worship his image. ³And the second (angel) poured out his bowl upon the sea, and there was blood as from a dead person, and every living thing that was in the sea died. ⁴And the third (angel) poured out his bowl upon the rivers and the springs of water, and they became blood. ⁵And I heard the angel in charge of the waters saying, "You are just, the one who is and who was, the holy one, because you judge these things, ⁶for they have shed the blood of the saints and the prophets, and you have given them blood to drink; they are worthy (of this)." ⁷And I heard the altar saying, "Yes, Lord, God Almighty, true and just are your judgments." ⁸And the fourth (angel) poured out his bowl upon the sun, and the sun was given the ability to burn people with fire. ⁹And people were burned with great heat and they blasphemed the name of God who has authority over these plagues, and they did not repent in order to give him glory. ¹⁰And the fifth (angel) poured out his bowl upon the throne of the beast, and his kingdom was darkened, and they gnawed their tongues because of the pain, ¹¹and they blasphemed the God of heaven because of their pain and because of their sores, and they did not repent from their works.

16:1 Καὶ ἤκουσα μεγάλης φωνῆς ἐκ τοῦ ναοῦ λεγούσης τοῖς ἑπτὰ ἀγγέλοις· ὑπάγετε καὶ ἐκχέετε τὰς ἑπτὰ φιάλας τοῦ θυμοῦ τοῦ θεοῦ εἰς τὴν γῆν.

ἤκουσα. Aor act ind 1st sg ἀκούω.
μεγάλης φωνῆς. Genitive direct object of ἤκουσα.
ἐκ τοῦ ναοῦ. Source.
λεγούσης. Pres act ptc fem gen sg λέγω (substantival). Complement in an object-complement double genitive construction with μεγάλης φωνῆς. On the use of the participle λεγούσης to introduce speech, see 1:17 on λέγων.
τοῖς ἑπτὰ ἀγγέλοις. Dative indirect object of λεγούσης.
ὑπάγετε. Pres act impv 2nd sg ὑπάγω.
καί. Smalley (400) and Aune (2.855) think the καί with ἐκχέετε functions consecutively (Smalley) or to show purpose (Aune), and is the

equivalent of ἵνα and the subjunctive. While a consecutive idea is true semantically, grammatically the καί simply indicates continuity.

ἐκχέετε. Pres act impv 2nd sg ἐκχέω. The imperative here refers to a specific command (see also ὑπάγετε above). Further, Osborne is incorrect to suggest that it pictures the "ongoing outpouring of judgment in the bowls" (579 n. 1). The present tense simply looks at the action as a process (see the Introduction on "Verbal Aspect").

τὰς ἑπτὰ φιάλας. Accusative direct object of ἐκχέετε.

τοῦ θυμοῦ. Genitive of content (the bowls contain God's wrath).

τοῦ θεοῦ. Subjective genitive.

εἰς τὴν γῆν. Goal. The preposition εἰς can have a directional sense (motion toward; Porter 1992, 152). According to BDAG εἰς can indicate "extension involving goal or place" (288.1) and more specifically "of movement directed at a surface of an area, *on* . . ." (289.1.a.γ).

16:2 Καὶ ἀπῆλθεν ὁ πρῶτος καὶ ἐξέχεεν τὴν φιάλην αὐτοῦ εἰς τὴν γῆν, καὶ ἐγένετο ἕλκος κακὸν καὶ πονηρὸν ἐπὶ τοὺς ἀνθρώπους τοὺς ἔχοντας τὸ χάραγμα τοῦ θηρίου καὶ τοὺς προσκυνοῦντας τῇ εἰκόνι αὐτοῦ.

ἀπῆλθεν. Aor act ind 3rd sg ἀπέρχομαι.

ὁ πρῶτος. Nominative subject of ἀπῆλθεν. The specific referent (ἄγγελος) is left implicit.

ἐξέχεεν. Aor act ind 3rd sg ἐκχέω.

τὴν φιάλην. Accusative direct object of ἐξέχεεν.

αὐτοῦ. Possessive genitive.

εἰς τὴν γῆν. Goal. On the meaning of εἰς, see verse 1. 051 2053 2062 $\mathfrak{M}^A$ read ἐπί instead of εἰς.

ἐγένετο. Aor mid ind 3rd sg γίνομαι. Aune (2.868) notes that the effects of the pouring out of each of the bowls is expressed with the repeated καὶ ἐγένετο (v. 2, 4, 10, 18, 19).

ἕλκος κακὸν καὶ πονηρὸν. Nominative subject of ἐγένετο. The singular is collective, and refers to the sores that come upon all humanity (ἐπὶ τοὺς ἀνθρώπους). Note the plural ἐκ τῶν ἑλκῶν in verse 11 below.

ἐπὶ τοὺς ἀνθρώπους. Locative.

τοὺς ἔχοντας. Pres act ptc masc acc pl ἔχω (attributive).

τὸ χάραγμα. Accusative direct object of ἔχοντας.

τοῦ θηρίου. Possessive genitive, or perhaps "the mark that the beast gives."

τοὺς προσκυνοῦντας. Pres act ptc masc acc pl προσκυνέω (attributive).

τῇ εἰκόνι. Dative direct object of προσκυνοῦντας.

αὐτοῦ. On the function of the genitive with εἰκόνι, see 13:15.

16:3 Καὶ ὁ δεύτερος ἐξέχεεν τὴν φιάλην αὐτοῦ εἰς τὴν θάλασσαν, καὶ ἐγένετο αἷμα ὡς νεκροῦ, καὶ πᾶσα ψυχὴ ζωῆς ἀπέθανεν τὰ ἐν τῇ θαλάσσῃ.

ὁ δεύτερος. Nominative subject of ἐξέχεεν. 051 2344 𝔐 add the substantive ἄγγελος making explicit what is implicit. The same textual variant occurs in verses 4, 8, 10, 12, 17.
ἐξέχεεν. Aor act ind 3rd sg ἐκχέω.
τὴν φιάλην. Accusative direct object of ἐξέχεεν.
αὐτοῦ. Possessive genitive.
εἰς τὴν θάλασσαν. Goal. On the meaning of εἰς, see verse 1.
ἐγένετο. Aor mid ind 3rd sg γίνομαι.
αἷμα. Nominative subject of ἐγένετο.
ὡς νεκροῦ. Comparison.
νεκροῦ. Possessive genitive or genitive of source. Lit. "as of/from a dead (person)."
πᾶσα ψυχὴ. Nominative subject of ἀπέθανεν.
ζωῆς. Attributive genitive.
ἀπέθανεν. Aor act ind 3rd sg ἀποθνῄσκω.
τὰ. The article functions as a nominalizer, turning the entire PP into a substantive. The entire construction stands in apposition to πᾶσα ψυχή. The plural article is due to the sense of πᾶσα ψυχή. Probably to avoid an awkward construction, 𝔓⁴⁷ ℵ 𝔐 omit the article (Beale, 816).
ἐν τῇ θαλάσσῃ. Locative.

16:4 Καὶ ὁ τρίτος ἐξέχεεν τὴν φιάλην αὐτοῦ εἰς τοὺς ποταμοὺς καὶ τὰς πηγὰς τῶν ὑδάτων, καὶ ἐγένετο αἷμα.

ὁ τρίτος. Nominative subject of ἐξέχεεν.
ἐξέχεεν. Aor act ind 3rd sg ἐκχέω.
τὴν φιάλην. Accusative direct object of ἐξέχεεν.
αὐτοῦ. Possessive genitive.
εἰς τοὺς ποταμοὺς καὶ τὰς πηγὰς. Goal. On the meaning of εἰς, see verse 1.
τῶν ὑδάτων. Genitive of content or genitive of source (springs that produce water) or epexegetical genitive (Aune, 2.855). See also 7:17.
ἐγένετο. Aor mid ind 3rd sg γίνομαι. The singular is used here with an assumed plural subject (τοὺς ποταμοὺς καὶ τὰς πηγὰς). This may be because the author treats the rivers and springs as a single entity (McKay 1994, 18). To harmonize with the plural bodies of water, 𝔓⁴⁷ A 1006 1611 1841 1854 2053 2329 *pc* change to the plural ἐγένοντο. As the harder reading, the singular is probably original.
αἷμα. Predicate nominative of ἐγένετο.

16:5 Καὶ ἤκουσα τοῦ ἀγγέλου τῶν ὑδάτων λέγοντος· δίκαιος εἶ, ὁ ὢν καὶ ὁ ἦν, ὁ ὅσιος, ὅτι ταῦτα ἔκρινας,

ἤκουσα. Aor act ind 1st sg ἀκούω.
τοῦ ἀγγέλου. Genitive direct object of ἤκουσα.
τῶν ὑδάτων. Genitive of subordination (NIV: "the angel in charge of the waters").
λέγοντος. Pres act ptc masc gen sg λέγω (substantival). Complement in an object-complement double genitive construction with τοῦ ἀγγέλου. On the use of the participle λέγοντος to introduce speech, see 1:17 on λέγων.
δίκαιος. Predicate adjective.
εἶ. Pres act ind 2nd sg εἰμί.
ὁ ὤν. Pres act ptc masc nom sg εἰμί (substantival). Nominative in apposition to the implied subject ("you") of εἶ, or nominative of address.
ὁ ἦν. The article serves as a nominalizer (as with ὁ ὤν above), but here turns a finite verb into a substantive. On the function of the case, see ὁ ὤν.
ἦν. Impf act ind 3rd sg εἰμί. On the lack of ὁ ἐρχόμενος from the threefold formula in 1:4, 8; 4:8, see 11:17 on ἦν.
ὁ ὅσιος. Nominative in apposition to the implied subject ("you") of εἶ.
ὅτι. Introduces a causal clause.
ταῦτα. Accusative direct object of ἔκρινας. The antecedent of ταῦτα is not clear. Within the bowl sequence the antecedent is probably the seven bowl judgments (Smalley, 403) or perhaps only the preceding three plagues (Aune, 2.856).
ἔκρινας. Aor act ind 2nd sg κρίνω.

16:6 ὅτι αἷμα ἁγίων καὶ προφητῶν ἐξέχεαν καὶ αἷμα αὐτοῖς [δ]έδωκας πιεῖν, ἄξιοί εἰσιν.

ὅτι. There is some ambiguity as to the syntactical function of this ὅτι clause (Swete, 202–3). (1) The ὅτι clause could be parallel to the ὅτι clause that ends verse 5 (ὅτι ταῦτα ἔκρινας), providing a further reason for why God is righteous and holy (so Beale, 818, though he still thinks it is a further elucidation of the first ὅτι clause). (2) The ὅτι clause could function to further explain or give the reason for the previous ὅτι clause, explaining God's judgment of "all things" (see Osborne, 583). (3) The ὅτι clause could begin a new sentence and provide the reason for why God gives the followers of the beast blood to drink in the rest of the verse: they have shed the blood of the saints (see 3:10 for a sentence-initial ὅτι clause).

Revelation 16:5-7

αἷμα. Accusative direct object of ἐξέχεαν. A synecdoche for "death," substituting the means (shedding of blood) for the effect (death).

ἁγίων καὶ προφητῶν. Possessive genitive.

ἐξέχεαν. Aor act ind 3rd pl ἐκχέω. The subject of the plural verb here is unclear from the context. It is possible that this should be seen as an impersonal construction, which can be translated as passive (Aune, 2.856): "Blood was poured out." For this construction, see 2:24 on ὡς λέγουσιν.

αἷμα. Accusative direct object of δέδωκας.

αὐτοῖς. Dative indirect object of δέδωκας.

[δ]έδωκας. Prf act ind 2nd sg δίδωμι. The perfect δέδωκας is found in A C 1611 2329. However, the aorist ἔδωκας has strong manuscript support in 𝔓⁴⁷ ℵ P 046 051 1006 1841 2053 2062 𝔐 and is perhaps to be preferred.

πιεῖν. Aor act inf πίνω (purpose).

ἄξιοί εἰσιν. It is unclear what this modifies. It is possible that it refers to the saints and the prophets being worthy (see 3:4). However, it is probably better to take it as referring to the previous and closest clause regarding those who have been given blood to drink since it immediately follows καὶ αἷμα αὐτοῖς δέδωκας πιεῖν. "Those who have shed the blood of the faithful are said to be 'worthy' of receiving blood to drink" (Mounce, 295–96). Due to the apparent abruptness of ἄξιοί εἰσιν and lack of a clear connection to the preceding clause, a number of readings arose in an attempt to indicate more precisely its connection with the preceding clause: ὅπερ (ℵ); ἄρα (2329); γάρ (2053 2062); ὅτι (2019).

ἄξιοί. Predicate adjective. The accenting is due to the enclitic εἰσιν that follows.

εἰσιν. Pres act ind 3rd pl εἰμί. On the loss of accent, see 1:8.

16:7 Καὶ ἤκουσα τοῦ θυσιαστηρίου λέγοντος· ναὶ κύριε ὁ θεὸς ὁ παντοκράτωρ, ἀληθιναὶ καὶ δίκαιαι αἱ κρίσεις σου.

ἤκουσα. Aor act ind 1st sg ἀκούω.

τοῦ θυσιαστηρίου. Genitive direct object of ἤκουσα. It is possible that this is an elliptical expression, with τινά/ός or φωνήν, as reflected in the textual variants. ἐκ τοῦ θυσιαστηρίου is found in 046 2329 *pc* and φωνὴν ἐκ τοῦ θυσιαστηρίου is found in 2019.

λέγοντος. Pres act ptc masc gen sg λέγω. Complement in an object-complement double genitive construction. On the use of the participle λέγοντος to introduce speech, see 1:17 on λέγων.

ναί. A particle that expresses affirmation or agreement, "*certainly, indeed, quite so*" (BDAG, 665).

κύριε. Vocative of address.

ὁ θεός. Nominative in apposition to κύριε. Aune (1.clxxvi–vii; 2.853) notes this construction where the articular nominative stands in apposition to a vocative form found here and in 11:17; 15:3. For articular nominatives following a vocative form, see also 18:20.

ὁ παντοκράτωρ. Nominative in apposition to κύριε.

ἀληθιναὶ καὶ δίκαιαι. Predicate adjective of a verbless clause.

αἱ κρίσεις. Nominative subject of a verbless clause.

σου. Subjective genitive.

16:8 Καὶ ὁ τέταρτος ἐξέχεεν τὴν φιάλην αὐτοῦ ἐπὶ τὸν ἥλιον, καὶ ἐδόθη αὐτῷ καυματίσαι τοὺς ἀνθρώπους ἐν πυρί.

ὁ τέταρτος. Nominative subject of ἐξέχεεν.

ἐξέχεεν. Aor act ind 3rd sg ἐκχέω.

τὴν φιάλην. Accusative direct object of ἐξέχεεν.

αὐτοῦ. Possessive genitive.

ἐπὶ τὸν ἥλιον. Locative. The remainder of the bowl judgments use ἐπί to indicate the direction of the pouring toward a goal (Porter 1992, 160; BDAG, 364.4).

ἐδόθη. Aor pass ind 3rd sg δίδωμι.

αὐτῷ. Dative indirect object of ἐδόθη. The antecedent is ἥλιον.

καυματίσαι. Aor act inf καυματίζω (substantival). Nominative subject of ἐδόθη. This is to be preferred over Aune's (2.857) suggestion that the sun, or the angel is the subject.

τοὺς ἀνθρώπους. Accusative direct object of καυματίσαι.

ἐν πυρί. Instrumental.

16:9 καὶ ἐκαυματίσθησαν οἱ ἄνθρωποι καῦμα μέγα καὶ ἐβλασφήμησαν τὸ ὄνομα τοῦ θεοῦ τοῦ ἔχοντος τὴν ἐξουσίαν ἐπὶ τὰς πληγὰς ταύτας καὶ οὐ μετενόησαν δοῦναι αὐτῷ δόξαν.

ἐκαυματίσθησαν. Aor pass ind 3rd pl καυματίζω.

οἱ ἄνθρωποι. Nominative subject of ἐκαυματίσθησαν.

καῦμα μέγα. Accusative direct object of the passive verb ἐκαυματίσθησαν (Aune calls it a cognate accusative; 2.857), or perhaps it should be understood as an example of "advancement" (the instrument normally in the dative ["with," "by"] advances to the direct object slot and hence takes the accusative case; see Culy 2009, 92–99).

ἐβλασφήμησαν. Aor act ind 3rd pl βλασφημέω.

τὸ ὄνομα. Accusative direct object of ἐβλασφήμησαν.

τοῦ θεοῦ. Possessive genitive.

τοῦ ἔχοντος. Pres act ptc masc gen sg ἔχω (attributive).

τὴν ἐξουσίαν. Accusative direct object of ἔχοντος.

ἐπὶ τὰς πληγὰς ταύτας. The preposition ἐπί indicates that over which the ἐξουσίαν is exercised.
μετενόησαν. Aor act ind 3rd pl μετανοέω.
δοῦναι. Aor act inf δίδωμι (result).
αὐτῷ. Dative indirect object of δοῦναι.
δόξαν. Accusative direct object of δοῦναι.

16:10 Καὶ ὁ πέμπτος ἐξέχεεν τὴν φιάλην αὐτοῦ ἐπὶ τὸν θρόνον τοῦ θηρίου, καὶ ἐγένετο ἡ βασιλεία αὐτοῦ ἐσκοτωμένη, καὶ ἐμασῶντο τὰς γλώσσας αὐτῶν ἐκ τοῦ πόνου,

ὁ πέμπτος. Nominative subject of ἐξέχεεν.
ἐξέχεεν. Aor act ind 3rd sg ἐκχέω.
τὴν φιάλην. Accusative direct object of ἐξέχεεν.
αὐτοῦ. Possessive genitive.
ἐπὶ τὸν θρόνον. Locative.
τοῦ θηρίου. Possessive genitive.
ἐγένετο. Aor mid ind 3rd sg γίνομαι.
ἡ βασιλεία. Nominative subject of ἐγένετο.
αὐτοῦ. Subjective genitive.
ἐσκοτωμένη. Prf pass ptc fem nom sg σκοτόω (predicate adjective of ἐγένετο).
ἐμασῶντο. Impf mid ind 3rd pl μασάομαι. The implied subject of the plural verb is probably the subjects of the kingdom (βασιλεία).
τὰς γλώσσας. Accusative direct object of ἐμασῶντο.
αὐτῶν. Possessive genitive. For the antecedent, see ἐμασῶντο above.
ἐκ τοῦ πόνου. Causal. ἐκ may still carry the notion of "source." Their pain was the source, and hence the cause, of their biting.

16:11 καὶ ἐβλασφήμησαν τὸν θεὸν τοῦ οὐρανοῦ ἐκ τῶν πόνων αὐτῶν καὶ ἐκ τῶν ἑλκῶν αὐτῶν καὶ οὐ μετενόησαν ἐκ τῶν ἔργων αὐτῶν.

ἐβλασφήμησαν. Aor act ind 3rd pl βλασφημέω. On the implied subject of the verb, see verse 10 above on ἐμασῶντο.
τὸν θεὸν. Accusative direct object of ἐβλασφήμησαν.
τοῦ οὐρανοῦ. Genitive of subordination or genitive of location.
ἐκ τῶν πόνων. Causal. See ἐκ τοῦ πόνου in verse 10.
αὐτῶν. Possessive genitive.
ἐκ τῶν ἑλκῶν. Causal. See ἐκ τοῦ πόνου in verse 10.
αὐτῶν. Possessive genitive.
μετενόησαν. Aor act ind 3rd pl μετανοέω. On the implied subject of the verb, see verse 10 above on ἐμασῶντο.

ἐκ τῶν ἔργων. Separation. On ἐκ + genitive following μετανοέω, see 2:21 on ἐκ τῆς πορνείας.

αὐτῶν. Subjective genitive.

Revelation 16:12-16

¹²And the sixth (angel) poured out his bowl upon the great river Euphrates, and its water was dried up in order to prepare the way for the kings from the east. ¹³And I saw three unclean spirits like frogs come out of the mouth of the dragon and out of the mouth of the beast and out of the mouth of the false prophet. ¹⁴For they are demonic spirits who perform signs, who come upon the kings of the whole inhabited world in order to gather them for the battle of the great day of God, Almighty. ¹⁵Look, I am coming like a thief; blessed is the one who watches and who keeps their garments on, in order that they might not walk around naked and that their shame might be seen. ¹⁶And they gathered them together to a place that is called, in Hebrew, Armageddon.

16:12 Καὶ ὁ ἕκτος ἐξέχεεν τὴν φιάλην αὐτοῦ ἐπὶ τὸν ποταμὸν τὸν μέγαν τὸν Εὐφράτην, καὶ ἐξηράνθη τὸ ὕδωρ αὐτοῦ, ἵνα ἑτοιμασθῇ ἡ ὁδὸς τῶν βασιλέων τῶν ἀπὸ ἀνατολῆς ἡλίου.

ὁ ἕκτος. Nominative subject of ἐξέχεεν.

ἐξέχεεν. Aor act ind 3rd sg ἐκχέω.

τὴν φιάλην. Accusative direct object of ἐξέχεεν.

αὐτοῦ. Possessive genitive.

ἐπὶ τὸν ποταμὸν τὸν μέγαν. Locative.

τὸν Εὐφράτην. Accusative in apposition to τὸν ποταμὸν τὸν μέγαν.

ἐξηράνθη. Aor pass ind 3rd sg ξηραίνω.

τὸ ὕδωρ. Nominative subject of ἐξηράνθη.

αὐτοῦ. Possessive genitive.

ἵνα. Introduces a purpose clause.

ἑτοιμασθῇ. Aor pass subj 3rd sg ἑτοιμάζω. Subjunctive with ἵνα.

ἡ ὁδὸς. Nominative subject of ἑτοιμασθῇ.

τῶν βασιλέων. The force of the genitive should be taken to indicate something like "the way *for* the kings" or "the way that the kings travel."

τῶν. The article functions as an adjectivizer, turning the entire PP into an attributive modifier of τῶν βασιλέων: Lit. "the from-the-east kings."

ἀπὸ ἀνατολῆς ἡλίου. Source. Lit. "from the rising of the sun." On this expression meaning "east," see 7:2.

16:13 Καὶ εἶδον ἐκ τοῦ στόματος τοῦ δράκοντος καὶ ἐκ τοῦ στόματος τοῦ θηρίου καὶ ἐκ τοῦ στόματος τοῦ ψευδοπροφήτου πνεύματα τρία ἀκάθαρτα ὡς βάτραχοι·

Καὶ εἶδον. Focuses on a new or important feature in the vision.
εἶδον. Aor act ind 1st sg ὁράω.
ἐκ τοῦ στόματος ... ἐκ τοῦ στόματος ... ἐκ τοῦ στόματος. Source.
τοῦ δράκοντος ... τοῦ θηρίου ... τοῦ ψευδοπροφήτου. Possessive genitive. See Rev 12–13 for the order of these three figures.
πνεύματα τρία ἀκάθαρτα. Accusative direct object of εἶδον. It is not clear whether one of the three spirits comes out of the mouth of the dragon, beast, and false prophet each, or whether all three spirits come out of all three mouths. Perhaps the symbolism should not be pressed in too literal of a manner.
ὡς βάτραχοι. Comparison. βάτραχος ("frog") is a hapax legomenon in the NT.

16:14 εἰσὶν γὰρ πνεύματα δαιμονίων ποιοῦντα σημεῖα, ἃ ἐκπορεύεται ἐπὶ τοὺς βασιλεῖς τῆς οἰκουμένης ὅλης συναγαγεῖν αὐτοὺς εἰς τὸν πόλεμον τῆς ἡμέρας τῆς μεγάλης τοῦ θεοῦ τοῦ παντοκράτορος.

εἰσὶν. Pres act ind 3rd pl εἰμί. Though neuter plural nouns often take singular verbs, neuter plurals that refer to personal beings often take plural verbs in Revelation.
γὰρ. Introduces a clause that strengthens the previous clause.
πνεύματα. Predicate nominative.
δαιμονίων. Attributive genitive or epexegetical genitive.
ποιοῦντα. Pres act ptc neut nom pl ποιέω (attributive). On the number, see εἰσίν above.
σημεῖα. Accusative direct object of ποιοῦντα.
ἃ. Nominative subject of ἐκπορεύεται. Though the antecedent could be the demons, it is also possible that the antecedent is σημεῖα. The latter would fit the tendency in Revelation observed by Aune (2.858) that the neuter plural of animate beings often takes a third person plural verb (πνεύματα with εἰσὶν above), while inanimate things in the plural tend to take third person singular verbs (ἐκπορεύεται), though the author does not always follow this pattern. However, it is more likely that the demonic beings rather than the signs would be responsible for "gathering" the kings for battle (see v. 16 below).
ἐκπορεύεται. Pres mid ind 3rd sg ἐκπορεύομαι. Neuter plural subjects (ἃ) often take singular verbs.
ἐπὶ τοὺς βασιλεῖς. Locative.

τῆς οἰκουμένης ὅλης. Genitive of subordination: "The whole inhabited world."
συναγαγεῖν. Aor act inf συνάγω (purpose).
αὐτούς. Accusative direct object of συναγαγεῖν.
εἰς τὸν πόλεμον. Goal or purpose.
τῆς ἡμέρας τῆς μεγάλης. Genitive of description. Or the idea may be temporal: "The battle that takes place on the great day."
τοῦ θεοῦ. Possessive genitive.
τοῦ παντοκράτορος. Genitive in apposition to θεοῦ.

16:15 Ἰδοὺ ἔρχομαι ὡς κλέπτης. μακάριος ὁ γρηγορῶν καὶ τηρῶν τὰ ἱμάτια αὐτοῦ, ἵνα μὴ γυμνὸς περιπατῇ καὶ βλέπωσιν τὴν ἀσχημοσύνην αὐτοῦ.

Ἰδού. A marker of attention that deictically functions to make the following statement emphatic. Here it draws attention to the statement on the manner of Christ's coming. On the form, see 1:7.
ἔρχομαι. Pres mid ind 1st sg ἔρχομαι. Here the present tense is used of action that is future referring (see 1:7).
ὡς κλέπτης. Manner. κλέπτης is the nominative subject of an implied ἔρχεται.
μακάριος. Predicate adjective of a verbless clause.
ὁ γρηγορῶν. Pres act ptc masc nom sg γρηγορέω (substantival). Nominative subject of a verbless clause.
τηρῶν. Pres act ptc masc nom sg τηρέω (substantival). The article ὁ before γρηγορῶν also governs τηρῶν so that both function substantivally as conjoined nominative subjects of the verbless clause.
τὰ ἱμάτια. Accusative direct object of τηρῶν.
αὐτοῦ. Possessive genitive.
ἵνα. Introduces a purpose clause.
γυμνός. Adjective functioning as an adverb, indicating manner.
περιπατῇ. Pres act subj 3rd sg περιπατέω. Subjunctive with ἵνα.
βλέπωσιν. Pres act subj 3rd pl βλέπω. Subjunctive with ἵνα. This is probably an example of an impersonal verb in the plural without a subject, which could be translated as a passive: "They might not be seen" (see McKay 1994, 19; see also 2:24 on ὡς λέγουσιν). Thompson (21–22) incorrectly thinks God is the subject based on the third person plural being used to express an Aramaic passive.
τὴν ἀσχημοσύνην. Accusative direct object of βλέπωσιν. This word translated "nakedness" refers to a state of shamefulness (LN 25.202) and is a euphemism for the genitals (BDAG, 147.4).
αὐτοῦ. Possessive genitive. The antecedent is ὁ γρηγορῶν καὶ τηρῶν.

16:16 Καὶ συνήγαγεν αὐτοὺς εἰς τὸν τόπον τὸν καλούμενον Ἑβραϊστὶ Ἁρμαγεδών.

συνήγαγεν. Aor act ind 3rd sg συνάγω. The verb resumes the reference to συναγαγεῖν in verse 14 following the hortatory saying in verse 15. The implied subject is the πνεύματα δαιμονίων from verse 15. Plural neuter subjects often take singular verbs.
αὐτοὺς. Accusative direct object of συνήγαγεν. The antecedent is τοὺς βασιλεῖς from verse 14.
εἰς τὸν τόπον. Locative.
τὸν καλούμενον. Pres pass ptc masc acc sg καλέω (attributive).
Ἑβραϊστὶ. Dative of reference, referring to the language by which the name is called.
Ἁρμαγεδών. Lit. "mountain of Megiddo." An accusative functioning in a double accusative construction with τόπον and the passive verb form καλούμενον from the construction: "I call the mountain Armageddon." The accusative form is due to τὸν τόπον being the object of the preposition εἰς. 046 1611 2053 2062 𝔐ᴷ have Μαγε(δ)δων. The reason for this may be the lack of any reference in the OT to a mountain of Megiddo (Beale, 839).

Revelation 16:17-21

¹⁷And the seventh (angel) poured out his bowl upon the air, and there came a loud voice out of the temple from the throne, saying, "It has been accomplished." ¹⁸And there was lightening and sounds and thunderings and a great earthquake happened, so very great an earthquake such as had not occurred since the time people have been on the earth. ¹⁹And the great city was (split) into three parts and the cities of the nations fell. And Babylon the great was remembered before God so that he gave it the cup of the wine of the anger of his wrath. ²⁰And every island fled and no mountains were found. ²¹And great hailstones, each weighing a talent, came down from heaven upon the people, and the people blasphemed God because of the plague of hail, for the harm caused by it was very great.

16:17 Καὶ ὁ ἕβδομος ἐξέχεεν τὴν φιάλην αὐτοῦ ἐπὶ τὸν ἀέρα, καὶ ἐξῆλθεν φωνὴ μεγάλη ἐκ τοῦ ναοῦ ἀπὸ τοῦ θρόνου λέγουσα· γέγονεν.

ὁ ἕβδομος. Nominative subject of ἐξέχεεν.
ἐξέχεεν. Aor act ind 3rd sg ἐκχέω.
τὴν φιάλην. Accusative direct object of ἐξέχεεν.
αὐτοῦ. Possessive genitive.

ἐπὶ τὸν ἀέρα. Locative.
ἐξῆλθεν. Aor act ind 3rd sg ἐξέρχομαι.
φωνὴ μεγάλη. Nominative subject of ἐξῆλθεν.
ἐκ τοῦ ναοῦ. Source.
ἀπὸ τοῦ θρόνου. Source. The preposition ἐκ indicates the general source of the voice, τοῦ ναοῦ, and the preposition ἀπό specifies the specific item (τοῦ θρόνου) within the temple from which the voice comes. For this construction, see also 3:12 on ἀπὸ τοῦ θεοῦ.
λέγουσα. Pres act ptc fem nom sg λέγω (manner). On the use of the participle λέγουσα to introduce speech, see 1:17 on λέγων.
γέγονεν. Prf act ind 3rd sg γίνομαι. Perhaps the perfect tense is used to lend prominence to the climax of God's judgments in the series of bowl plagues. See 21:6 on γέγοναν with reference to the consummation of God's new creation.

16:18 καὶ ἐγένοντο ἀστραπαὶ καὶ φωναὶ καὶ βρονταὶ καὶ σεισμὸς ἐγένετο μέγας, οἷος οὐκ ἐγένετο ἀφ' οὗ ἄνθρωπος ἐγένετο ἐπὶ τῆς γῆς τηλικοῦτος σεισμὸς οὕτως μέγας.

ἐγένοντο. Aor mid ind 3rd pl γίνομαι.
ἀστραπαὶ καὶ φωναὶ καὶ βρονταί. Nominative subject of ἐγένοντο.
σεισμὸς ... μέγας. Nominative subject of ἐγένετο.
ἐγένετο. Aor mid ind 3rd sg γίνομαι.
οἷος. The correlative pronoun ("such as") is picked up with τηλικοῦτος σεισμὸς below.
ἐγένετο. Aor mid ind 3rd sg γίνομαι.
ἀφ' οὗ. Temporal: "Since."
ἄνθρωπος. Nominative subject of ἐγένετο.
ἐγένετο. Aor mid ind 3rd sg γίνομαι
ἐπὶ τῆς γῆς. Locative.
τηλικοῦτος σεισμὸς. A correlative adjective used like a demonstrative pronoun suggesting "a degree which is comparable to some other expression of degree—'so great'" (LN 78.36). Here it picks up the correlative οἷος above and further highlights the magnitude of the earthquake.
οὕτως μέγας. The expression is redundant and adds further emphasis.

16:19 καὶ ἐγένετο ἡ πόλις ἡ μεγάλη εἰς τρία μέρη καὶ αἱ πόλεις τῶν ἐθνῶν ἔπεσαν. καὶ Βαβυλὼν ἡ μεγάλη ἐμνήσθη ἐνώπιον τοῦ θεοῦ δοῦναι αὐτῇ τὸ ποτήριον τοῦ οἴνου τοῦ θυμοῦ τῆς ὀργῆς αὐτοῦ.

ἐγένετο. Aor mid ind 3rd sg γίνομαι.
ἡ πόλις ἡ μεγάλη. Nominative subject of ἐγένετο.

εἰς τρία μέρη. Goal or end result of an action (BDAG, 290.4). Functions as the predicate of ἐγένετο.
αἱ πόλεις. Nominative subject of ἔπεσαν.
τῶν ἐθνῶν. Possessive genitive or attributive genitive.
ἔπεσαν. Aor act ind 3rd pl πίπτω.
Βαβυλὼν ἡ μεγάλη. Nominative subject of ἐμνήσθη.
ἐμνήσθη. Aor pass ind 3rd sg μιμνήσκομαι.
ἐνώπιον τοῦ θεοῦ. Locative.
δοῦναι. Aor act inf δίδωμι (result).
αὐτῇ. Dative indirect object of δοῦναι.
τὸ ποτήριον. Accusative direct object of δοῦναι.
τοῦ οἴνου. Genitive of content.
τοῦ θυμοῦ. Epexegetical genitive.
τῆς ὀργῆς. Attributive genitive.
αὐτοῦ. Subjective genitive. The piling up of genitives (see 14:8 on τοῦ θυμοῦ) lends prominence to the expression of God's wrath.

16:20 καὶ πᾶσα νῆσος ἔφυγεν καὶ ὄρη οὐχ εὑρέθησαν.

πᾶσα νῆσος. Nominative subject of ἔφυγεν.
ἔφυγεν. Aor act ind 3rd sg φεύγω.
ὄρη. Nominative subject of εὑρέθησαν.
εὑρέθησαν. Aor pass ind 3rd pl εὑρίσκω. The passive voice places the focus on the geographical objects (ὄρη) as the topic of this clause.

16:21 καὶ χάλαζα μεγάλη ὡς ταλαντιαία καταβαίνει ἐκ τοῦ οὐρανοῦ ἐπὶ τοὺς ἀνθρώπους, καὶ ἐβλασφήμησαν οἱ ἄνθρωποι τὸν θεὸν ἐκ τῆς πληγῆς τῆς χαλάζης, ὅτι μεγάλη ἐστὶν ἡ πληγὴ αὐτῆς σφόδρα.

χάλαζα μεγάλη. Nominative subject of καταβαίνει.
ὡς ταλαντιαία. Comparison. A "talent" was a measure of weight that was 125 Roman pounds (a pound being twelve ounces) or roughly ninety pounds in English weight (LN 86.5). NRSV: "each weighing about a hundred pounds"; ESV, NIV.
καταβαίνει. Pres act ind 3rd sg καταβαίνω. Historical or narrative present (see 4:5 on ἐκπορεύονται). Here it functions to highlight the climactic judgment from God, to which humanity still responds with refusal to repent.
ἐκ τοῦ οὐρανοῦ. Source.
ἐπὶ τοὺς ἀνθρώπους. Locative.
ἐβλασφήμησαν. Aor act ind 3rd pl βλασφημέω.
οἱ ἄνθρωποι. Nominative subject of ἐβλασφήμησαν.
τὸν θεὸν. Accusative direct object of ἐβλασφήμησαν.

ἐκ τῆς πληγῆς. Cause.
τῆς χαλάζης. Epexegetical genitive.
ὅτι. Introduces a causal clause.
μεγάλη. Predicate adjective of ἐστὶν.
ἐστὶν. Pres act ind 3rd sg εἰμί.
ἡ πληγὴ. Nominative subject of ἐστὶν.
αὐτῆς. Possessive genitive or subjective genitive ("the blow it caused").
σφόδρα. Louw and Nida define the adverb as "a very high point on a scale of extent and in many contexts implying vehemence or violence" (78.19). Its placement at the end of the clause is for emphasis.

Revelation 17:1-6

¹And one of the seven angels who hold the seven bowls came and spoke with me, saying, "Come. I will show you the judgment of the great prostitute who sits upon many waters, ²with whom the kings of the earth have committed adultery and those who dwell upon the earth have become drunk from the wine of her adultery." ³And he carried me away in the Spirit into the desert. And I saw a woman seated upon a scarlet beast, full of blasphemous names, having seven heads and ten horns. ⁴And the woman was dressed in purple and scarlet and she was adorned with gold and precious stone and pearls, and she had a golden cup in her hand full of abominations and the unclean things of her adultery. ⁵And upon her forehead was a name written, "Mystery, Babylon the Great, Mother of prostitutes and of abominations of the earth." ⁶And I saw the women drunk from the blood of the saints and from the blood of the witnesses of Jesus. And I was greatly astonished at seeing her.

17:1 Καὶ ἦλθεν εἷς ἐκ τῶν ἑπτὰ ἀγγέλων τῶν ἐχόντων τὰς ἑπτὰ φιάλας καὶ ἐλάλησεν μετ' ἐμοῦ λέγων· δεῦρο, δείξω σοι τὸ κρίμα τῆς πόρνης τῆς μεγάλης τῆς καθημένης ἐπὶ ὑδάτων πολλῶν,

ἦλθεν. Aor act ind 3rd sg ἔρχομαι.
εἷς. Nominative subject of ἦλθεν.
ἐκ τῶν ἑπτὰ ἀγγέλων. Partitive.
τῶν ἐχόντων. Pres act ptc masc gen pl ἔχω (attributive).
τὰς ἑπτὰ φιάλας. Accusative direct object of ἐχόντων.
ἐλάλησεν. Aor act ind 3rd sg λαλέω.
μετ' ἐμοῦ. Accompaniment.
λέγων. Pres act ptc masc nom sg λέγω (manner). On the use of the participle λέγων to introduce speech, see 1:17.

δεῦρο. An adverb of place that functions as an interjecton meaning "*over here, (come) here, come!*" (BDAG, 220.1; see also 21:9).

δείξω. Fut act ind 1st sg δείκνυμι. The future tense may function to express the intention of the angelic guide. However, it is also possible, along with Wallace (465; also BDAG, 220.1), to take this as a hortatory subjunctive (aor act subj 1st sg; "let me show you"), since according to BDAG (220.1) δεῦρο is usually followed by an imperative.

σοι. Dative indirect object of δείξω.

τὸ κρίμα. Accusative direct object of δείξω.

τῆς πόρνης τῆς μεγάλης. Objective genitive.

τῆς καθημένης. Pres mid ptc fem gen sg κάθημαι (attributive). The use of κάθημαι to refer to the prostitute may be a deliberate contrast to God and the Lamb who are seated on the throne (e.g., 4:2; 5:13) (Smalley, 427).

ἐπὶ ὑδάτων πολλῶν. Locative. Aune (3.907) suggests that since it is difficult to visualize the woman sitting "upon" many waters, ἐπὶ should be translated "beside." While possible, this overlooks the metaphorical nature of the imagery depicting the woman. Furthermore, the description of the woman "seated upon many waters" suggests her position of authority over them.

17:2 μεθ' ἧς ἐπόρνευσαν οἱ βασιλεῖς τῆς γῆς καὶ ἐμεθύσθησαν οἱ κατοικοῦντες τὴν γῆν ἐκ τοῦ οἴνου τῆς πορνείας αὐτῆς.

μεθ' ἧς. Association.

ἐπόρνευσαν. Aor act ind 3rd pl πορνεύω. On the meaning of πορνεύω, see 2:15 on πορνεῦσαι.

οἱ βασιλεῖς. Nominative subject of ἐπόρνευσαν.

τῆς γῆς. Genitive of subordination.

ἐμεθύσθησαν. Aor pass ind 3rd pl μεθύσκω.

οἱ κατοικοῦντες. Pres act ptc masc nom pl κατοικέω (substantival). Nominative subject of ἐμεθύσθησαν.

τὴν γῆν. Accusative direct object of κατοικοῦντες.

ἐκ τοῦ οἴνου. Means or cause.

τῆς πορνείας. Epexegetical genitive.

αὐτῆς. Subjective genitive. The relative clause is apparently continued with a clause ending with a pronoun. Robertson notes that a relative clause can be continued with καί and the pronoun αὐτός (724). According to McKay, "It is quite normal Greek, although not very common (partly due to the prevalence of participles), for a clause following a relative clause and referring to the same antecedent to have a personal pronoun instead of a relative pronoun" (1994, 150).

17:3 καὶ ἀπήνεγκέν με εἰς ἔρημον ἐν πνεύματι. Καὶ εἶδον γυναῖκα καθημένην ἐπὶ θηρίον κόκκινον, γέμον[τα] ὀνόματα βλασφημίας, ἔχων κεφαλὰς ἑπτὰ καὶ κέρατα δέκα.

ἀπήνεγκέν. Aor act ind 3rd sg ἀποφέρω. The accenting is due to the enclitic με that follows.

με. Accusative direct object of ἀπήνεγκέν.

εἰς ἔρημον. Locative.

ἐν πνεύματι. Manner or instrumental. See 21:10.

Καὶ εἶδον. Focuses on a new feature of the vision, the woman sitting on the beast.

εἶδον. Aor act ind 1st sg ὁράω.

γυναῖκα. Accusative direct object of εἶδον.

καθημένην. Pres mid ptc fem acc sg κάθημαι. Complement in an object-complement double accusative construction. On the significance of the use of καθημένην, see verse 1 on καθημένης.

ἐπὶ θηρίον κόκκινον. Locative.

γέμον[τα]. Pres act ptc neut/masc acc pl/sg γέμω (attributive). The reading γέμοντα (either neut acc pl or masc acc sg) is found in ℵ* A P 2053 2062 2329 *pc*, while the neuter singular γέμον is found in ℵ² 051 𝔐. The plural reading is difficult, since the word that it modifies is the singular θηρίον. It is possible that the plural ending –τα was substituted due to the influence of the plural ὀνόματα that follows. It is also possible that the τα should be seen as an article that goes with ὀνόματα. However, it may be preferable to take -οντα as a masculine accusative singular ending and understand this as an example of a construction according to sense, where the neuter θηρίον is understood as referring to a human figure (Aune, 3.908). See also ἔχων below.

ὀνόματα. Accusative complement of γέμον[τα]. γέμω usually takes the genitive (see v. 4 below on βδελυγμάτων). The accusative expressing the content of γέμω is found only here and in verse 4 (see τὰ ἀκάθαρτα below) in Revelation. It is possible that this reflects a Hebrew construction מלא with the accusative of content (Aune, 3.908). However, seeing the accusative as the result of Semitic influence does not account for the use of the genitive of the same word in verse 4 (which is also followed by an accusative; see βδελυγμάτων καὶ τὰ ἀκάθαρτα). It is also possible that this reflects the fact that the accusative was being found in Koine Greek in places where other cases were expected, including after verbs of filling (Robertson, 455, 474, 506). The reading ὀνομάτων in 051 2344 𝔐^A is clearly an attempt to "amend" the text.

βλασφημίας. Attributive genitive.

ἔχων. Pres act ptc masc nom sg ἔχω (attributive). The gender and case do not match up with its antecedent, which is neuter and accusative (θηρίον). The masculine gender may be the result of a construction according to sense, treating the beast as referring (symbolically) to a human figure. The nominative of ἔχων lacking concord with the noun it modifies is common and should perhaps be seen as a deliberate grammatical departure to draw attention to the following description. Beale (854) thinks that it reflects an allusion to Dan 7:7. Some manuscripts have the accusative ἔχοντα (אP) or ἔχον (046 051 𝔐 *pc*).

κεφαλὰς ἑπτὰ καὶ κέρατα δέκα. Accusative direct object of ἔχων.

17:4 καὶ ἡ γυνὴ ἦν περιβεβλημένη πορφυροῦν καὶ κόκκινον καὶ κεχρυσωμένη χρυσίῳ καὶ λίθῳ τιμίῳ καὶ μαργαρίταις, ἔχουσα ποτήριον χρυσοῦν ἐν τῇ χειρὶ αὐτῆς γέμον βδελυγμάτων καὶ τὰ ἀκάθαρτα τῆς πορνείας αὐτῆς

ἡ γυνὴ. Nominative subject of ἦν. The article is anaphoric pointing back to the first mention of the woman (γυναῖκα) in verse 3.

ἦν. Impf act ind 3rd sg εἰμί.

περιβεβλημένη. Prf mid ptc fem nom sg περιβάλλω (pluperfect periphrastic; see Porter 1992, 42).

πορφυροῦν καὶ κόκκινον. Accusative direct object of περιβεβλημένη.

κεχρυσωμένη. Prf pass ptc fem nom sg χρυσόω (periphrastic). The two perfect participles, περιβεβλημένη and κεχρυσωμένη, draw attention to the state of the woman who is a key figure in this vision, while the present participle ἔχουσα describes her holding a cup.

χρυσίῳ καὶ λίθῳ τιμίῳ καὶ μαργαρίταις. Dative of instrument.

ἔχουσα. Pres act ptc fem nom sg ἔχω (manner).

ποτήριον χρυσοῦν. Accusative direct object of ἔχουσα.

ἐν τῇ χειρὶ Locative.

αὐτῆς. Possessive genitive.

γέμον. Pres act ptc neut acc sg γέμω (attributive).

βδελυγμάτων. Genitive complement of γέμον. The word generally means something that is disgusting and detestable to God (BDAG, 172.1) and here probably refers to idolatry (Smalley, 430–31).

τὰ ἀκάθαρτα. Accusative complement of γέμον. One would expect the genitive after γέμον, as with βδελυγμάτων. On the accusative, see verse 3 on ὀνόματα. Aune (3.909) points to a parallel in 2 Kgdms 23:7, where the adjective πλῆρες is followed by a noun in the genitive and then the accusative, though Rev 17:4 has the participle γέμον. It is unlikely that Beale (857) is correct that τὰ ἀκάθαρτα may be an accusative direct object of ἔχουσα, since semantically it more naturally goes with βδελυγμάτων as the content of the cup, rather than as a separate item that the woman holds in her hand. Furthermore, the καὶ which precedes it links it to βδελυγμάτων so that both function as complements of γέμον.

τῆς πορνείας. Possessive genitive or genitive of source.
αὐτῆς. Subjective genitive.

17:5 καὶ ἐπὶ τὸ μέτωπον αὐτῆς ὄνομα γεγραμμένον, μυστήριον, Βαβυλὼν ἡ μεγάλη, ἡ μήτηρ τῶν πορνῶν καὶ τῶν βδελυγμάτων τῆς γῆς.

ἐπὶ τὸ μέτωπον. Locative.
αὐτῆς. Possessive genitive.
ὄνομα. Nominative subject of a verbless clause.
γεγραμμένον. Prf pass ptc neut nom sg γράφω (attributive).
μυστήριον. Nominative in apposition to ὄνομα. It is not clear whether μυστήριον is part of the title itself or an introduction to the title (Beale, 859). Compare the punctuation in the NRSV (introducton to the title: "A mystery, 'Babylon the Great'"; see also NASB; ESV) with the NIV (part of the title: "'MYSTERY BABYLON THE GREAT'"; though the NIV 2011 has repunctuated the text to reflect the same reading as the NRSV; cf. KJV). For the term μυστήριον, Beale says, "The disclosure of the mystery is not merely the revelation of end-time events hitherto hidden in the decretive counsels of God, but the revelation of the unexpected or ironic manner in which such events will unravel" (858). The mystery concerns the eschatological plan of God for the consummation of all things (see 10:7). In light of this, BDAG's (662.1.c) suggestion that it means "*allegorical significance*" is insufficient.

Βαβυλὼν ἡ μεγάλη. Nominative in apposition to ὄνομα.
ἡ μήτηρ. Nominative in apposition to Βαβυλὼν ἡ μεγάλη.
τῶν πορνῶν καὶ τῶν βδελυγμάτων. The genitive may communicate a superlative idea (she is a prostitute and abominator above all others) or the idea that all prostitutes and abominations derive from or are inspired by her. As Beale says, probably the phrase "mother of prostitutes and of abominations" "connotes her authoritative influence over and inspiration of the system of idolatry" (858).

τῆς γῆς. Attributive genitive (earthly abominations) or genitive of location.

17:6 καὶ εἶδον τὴν γυναῖκα μεθύουσαν ἐκ τοῦ αἵματος τῶν ἁγίων καὶ ἐκ τοῦ αἵματος τῶν μαρτύρων Ἰησοῦ. Καὶ ἐθαύμασα ἰδὼν αὐτὴν θαῦμα μέγα.

καὶ εἶδον. Introduces a new scene in the visionary segment.
εἶδον. Aor act ind 1st sg ὁράω.

τὴν γυναῖκα. Accusative direct object of εἶδον. The article is anaphoric pointing back to the first mention in verse 3.

μεθύουσαν. Pres act ptc fem acc sg μεθύω. Complement in an object-complement double accusative construction.

ἐκ τοῦ αἵματος. Source.

τῶν ἁγίων. Possessive genitive.

ἐκ τοῦ αἵματος. Source.

τῶν μαρτύρων. Possessive genitive.

Ἰησοῦ. Objective genitive: "who testified about Jesus."

ἐθαύμασα. Aor act ind 1st sg θαυμάζω. Though the word usually means "to wonder, to be amazed, to marvel" (LN 25.213), Thompson (12) has argued that due to Semitic influence the word means "to be appalled," a meaning that Thompson says is unattested in secular Greek. However, the difference between being astonished and appalled appears minimal, since as Louw and Nida (25.213) note, θαυμάζω can have positive or negative connotations depending on the context. Porter(1989b, 585) cites an example from Chariton 6.3.6, where θαυμάζω could be translated "appalled." Ultimately, this appears to be more of a translational issue than an issue of the semantics of θαυμάζω.

ἰδών. Aor act ptc masc nom sg ὁράω (temporal or causal).

αὐτήν. Accusative direct object of ἰδών.

θαῦμα μέγα. Accusative (cognate, Aune, 3.910) direct object of ἐθαύμασα.

Revelation 17:7-18

⁷And the angel said to me, "Why are you astonished? I will tell you the mystery of the woman and the beast that bears her and has seven heads and ten horns. ⁸The beast that you saw was and is not, and it is about to come up from the abyss and go into destruction. And those who dwell upon the earth will marvel—that is, those whose name is not written in the book of life from the foundation of the world—seeing the beast, because he was and is not and is coming. ⁹Here is the mind that has wisdom: The seven heads are seven mountains, upon which the woman is seated. And they are seven kings. ¹⁰Five have fallen, one is, and another has not yet come, and when he comes it is necessary that he remains for a short time. ¹¹And the beast that was and is not, he is both an eighth and is of the seven, and he is going into destruction. ¹²And the ten horns that you saw are ten kings who have not yet received a kingdom, but they will receive authority as kings for one hour along with the beast. ¹³These possess one mind and they will give power and their authority to the beast. ¹⁴These will make war with the Lamb, and the Lamb will overcome them, for he is the Lord of lords and King of kings,

and the called, chosen and faithful are with him." ¹⁵And he said to me, "The waters that you saw where the prostitute is seated are peoples and multitudes and nations and tongues. ¹⁶And the ten horns that you saw and the beast, these will hate the prostitute and will make her desolate and naked, and they will eat her flesh and burn her with fire. ¹⁷For God placed it in their hearts to accomplish his purpose, that is to accomplish one purpose, to give their kingdom to the beast, until the words of God are fulfilled. ¹⁸And the woman that you saw is the great city that has authority over the kings of the earth."

17:7 Καὶ εἶπέν μοι ὁ ἄγγελος· διὰ τί ἐθαύμασας; ἐγὼ ἐρῶ σοι τὸ μυστήριον τῆς γυναικὸς καὶ τοῦ θηρίου τοῦ βαστάζοντος αὐτὴν τοῦ ἔχοντος τὰς ἑπτὰ κεφαλὰς καὶ τὰ δέκα κέρατα.

Verses 1-6 lack finite verbs to describe the woman and the beast, which are mainly depicted with participial forms (the indicative verbs refer to John and the angel and John's response). The vision of the woman and the beast is static (Aune, 3. 919) and sets up the description in verses 7-18. In these verses, where the angel interprets the vision, present and future tense forms predominate to describe what the beast, woman, and other metaphorical elements of the vision (ten horns) actually do or what happens to them (Mathewson 2010, 154).

εἶπέν. Aor act ind 3rd sg εἶπον. The accenting is due to the enclitic μοι that follows.

μοι. Dative indirect object of εἶπέν.

ὁ ἄγγελος. Nominative subject of εἶπέν. The nominative subject indicates a switch in topic from the seer in the first person to the angel who will interpret the details of the vision.

διὰ τί. Cause. Introduces an interrogative. Lit. "because of why."

ἐθαύμασας. Aor act ind 2nd sg θαυμάζω. On the meaning, see verse 6 on ἐθαύμασα.

ἐγώ. Nominative subject of ἐρῶ. The pronoun functions to bring out the contrast between the seer's astonishment and the response of the angel.

ἐρῶ. Fut act ind 1st sg λέγω.

σοι. Dative indirect object of ἐρῶ.

τὸ μυστήριον. Accusative direct object of ἐρῶ.

τῆς γυναικὸς. Epexegetical genitive. The article is anaphoric referring back to the first mention in verse 3.

τοῦ θηρίου. Epexegetical genitive. The article is anaphoric referring back to the first mention in verse 3.

τοῦ βαστάζοντος. Pres act ptc neut gen sg βαστάζω (attributive).

αὐτήν. Accusative direct object of βαστάζοντος.

τοῦ ἔχοντος. Pres act ptc neut gen sg ἔχω (attributive).
τὰς ἑπτὰ κεφαλὰς καὶ τὰ δέκα κέρατα. Accusative direct object of ἔχοντος.

17:8 Τὸ θηρίον ὃ εἶδες ἦν καὶ οὐκ ἔστιν καὶ μέλλει ἀναβαίνειν ἐκ τῆς ἀβύσσου καὶ εἰς ἀπώλειαν ὑπάγει, καὶ θαυμασθήσονται οἱ κατοικοῦντες ἐπὶ τῆς γῆς, ὧν οὐ γέγραπται τὸ ὄνομα ἐπὶ τὸ βιβλίον τῆς ζωῆς ἀπὸ καταβολῆς κόσμου, βλεπόντων τὸ θηρίον ὅτι ἦν καὶ οὐκ ἔστιν καὶ παρέσται.

Τὸ θηρίον. Nominative subject of ἦν καὶ . . . ἔστιν καὶ μέλλει . . . καὶ . . . ὑπάγει.

ὅ. Accusative direct object of εἶδες.

εἶδες. Aor act ind 2nd sg ὁράω. The phrase ὃ εἶδες is used throughout this section to summarize and itemize the elements from the vision in verses 1-6, which are now taken up by the interpreting angel (see vv. 12, 15, 16, 18).

ἦν. Impf act ind 3rd sg εἰμί. Here the imperfect tense has probably been chosen for temporal reasons. The entire phrase ἦν καὶ οὐκ ἔστιν καὶ μέλλει ἀναβαίνειν grammatically and conceptually is probably meant to be a parody of the threefold divine name found throughout Revelation: ὁ ὢν καὶ ὁ ἦν καὶ ὁ ἐρχόμενος (1:4, 8; 4:8; see Mathewson 2010, 152).

ἔστιν. Pres act ind 3rd sg εἰμί.

μέλλει. Pres act ind 3rd sg μέλλω. This verb with an infinitive often functions in place of a future tense form. McKay says that "there seems to be little difference in meaning between the simple future and the periphrasis of the present tense of μέλλειν with the infinitive (mostly imperfective, but future and aorist are also found), except that μέλλειν may sometimes seem more emphatic" (1994, 52).

ἀναβαίνειν. Pres act inf ἀναβαίνω (complementary). The present μέλλει followed by the present tense infinitive ἀναβαίνειν does not suggest that the beast comes up out of the abyss throughout history (Mounce, 312). Rather, the construction is equivalent to a future tense verb (McKay 1994, 12; see also above on μέλλει).

ἐκ τῆς ἀβύσσου. Source.

εἰς ἀπώλειαν. Goal.

ὑπάγει. Pres act ind 3rd sg ὑπάγω. The present tense with verbs of coming and going often has future force temporally, as here. Some manuscripts (ℵ P 046 051 1006 1841 1854 2030 2329 2344 𝔐) read the infinitive ὑπάγειν (indicating purpose), the difference being only the final letter. As Metzger (682) notes, the final ν was often indicated in some manuscripts by a horizontal stroke of the preceding letter. However, it is probably more explicable as an attempt to conform to the preceding infinitive ἀναβαίνειν following μέλλει.

θαυμασθήσονται. Fut mid ind 3rd pl θαυμάζω. On the voice, see "Deponency" in the Series Introduction, though Robertson (819) still thinks it is possible to find a passive sense here.

οἱ κατοικοῦντες. Pres act ptc masc nom pl κατοικέω (substantival). Nominative subject of θαυμασθήσονται.

ἐπὶ τῆς γῆς. Locative.

ὧν. Possessive genitive (modifying τὸ ὄνομα).

γέγραπται. Prf pass ind 3rd sg γράφω.

τὸ ὄνομα. Nominative subject of γέγραπται.

ἐπὶ τὸ βιβλίον. Locative.

τῆς ζωῆς. Attributive genitive.

ἀπὸ καταβολῆς. Temporal. Indicates the point from which the action (writing of the name) takes place.

κόσμου. Objective genitive.

βλεπόντων. Pres act ptc masc gen pl βλέπω (temporal, modifying θαυμασθήσονται). The genitive case of the participle, where one would expect the nominative βλέποντες congruent with οἱ κατοικοῦντες, is probably due to attraction to the case of the relative pronoun ὧν, which further restricts "those who dwell upon the earth." This is preferable to Aune's suggestion (3.910; followed by Smalley, 435) that this is a genitive absolute construction, since genitive absolutes do not normally have the same subject as the main verb (Wallace, 655), as is the case with the participle here.

τὸ θηρίον. Accusative direct object of βλεπόντων.

ὅτι. Introduces a causal clause. It is possible that the ὅτι is to be understood as the clausal complement of βλεπόντων. However, since βλεπόντων already has a direct object (θηρίον) it is preferable to understand it as introducing a causal clause.

ἦν. Impf act ind 3rd sg εἰμί.

ἔστιν. Pres act ind 3rd sg εἰμί.

παρέσται. Pres act ind 3rd sg πάρειμι. The present tense is future referring.

17:9 ὧδε ὁ νοῦς ὁ ἔχων σοφίαν. Αἱ ἑπτὰ κεφαλαὶ ἑπτὰ ὄρη εἰσίν, ὅπου ἡ γυνὴ κάθηται ἐπ' αὐτῶν. καὶ βασιλεῖς ἑπτά εἰσιν·

ὧδε. An adverb of place that functions substantivally as the subject of a verbless clause and points back anaphorically to the riddle of the beast in verse 8 (Aune, 3.941; see the division of the verse in NA[28]; see also 13:18).

ὁ νοῦς. Predicate nominative of a verbless clause.

ὁ ἔχων. Pres act ptc masc nom sg ἔχω (attributive).
σοφίαν. Accusative direct object of ἔχων.
Αἱ ἑπτὰ κεφαλαὶ. Nominative subject of εἰσίν.
ἑπτὰ ὄρη. Predicate nominative. The term ὄρος has some flexibility and could mean either a "mountain" or a "hill" (BDAG, 724).
εἰσίν. Pres act ind 3rd pl εἰμί.
ὅπου. Introduces a local clause (denoting space), with ὅπου functioning like a relative pronoun (Robertson, 683). ὅπου is resumed by the redundant personal pronoun αὐτῶν ("where [referring to the seven mountains] ... upon them"). This construction draws attention to the antecedent, ἑπτὰ ὄρη (see also 3:8 on αὐτήν).
ἡ γυνὴ. Nominative subject of κάθηται.
κάθηται. Pres mid ind 3rd sg κάθημαι.
ἐπ' αὐτῶν. Locative. Resumptive of ὅπου.
βασιλεῖς ἑπτά. Predicate nominative.
εἰσιν. Pres act ind 3rd pl εἰμί. On the loss of accent, see 1:8. The implied subject is Αἱ ἑπτὰ κεφαλαί.

17:10 οἱ πέντε ἔπεσαν, ὁ εἷς ἔστιν, ὁ ἄλλος οὔπω ἦλθεν, καὶ ὅταν ἔλθῃ ὀλίγον αὐτὸν δεῖ μεῖναι.

οἱ πέντε. Nominative subject of ἔπεσαν. The article functions as a nominalizer.
ἔπεσαν. Aor act ind 3rd pl πίπτω.
ὁ εἷς. Nominative subject of ἔστιν. The article functions as a nominalizer.
ἔστιν. Pres act ind 3rd sg εἰμί.
ὁ ἄλλος. Nominative subject of ἦλθεν. The article functions as a nominalizer. Robertson (750) says that ὁ εἷς and ὁ ἄλλος function contrastively: "the one ... the other."
ἦλθεν. Aor act ind 3rd sg ἔρχομαι.
ὅταν. Introduces a temporal clause.
ἔλθῃ. Aor act subj 3rd sg ἔρχομαι. Subjunctive with ὅταν.
ὀλίγον. Accusative adjective functioning adverbially (temporal).
αὐτὸν. Accusative subject of μεῖναι.
δεῖ. Pres act ind 3rd sg δεῖ (impersonal).
μεῖναι. Aor act inf μένω (complementary). It is also possible that it functions as the subject of δεῖ: "To remain is necessary."

17:11 καὶ τὸ θηρίον ὃ ἦν καὶ οὐκ ἔστιν καὶ αὐτὸς ὄγδοός ἐστιν καὶ ἐκ τῶν ἑπτά ἐστιν, καὶ εἰς ἀπώλειαν ὑπάγει.

τὸ θηρίον. Nominative subject of ἐστιν ... ἐστιν ... ὑπάγει.

ὃ ἦν. See on 1:8.
ἦν. Impf act ind 3rd sg εἰμί.
ἔστιν. Pres act ind 3rd sg εἰμί.
καὶ . . . καὶ. "Both . . . and."
αὐτὸς. Nominative subject of the following ἐστιν. The pronoun is emphatic (not intensive, contra Charles, 1.cxxii). The masculine pronoun, which modifies the neuter θηρίον, is probably a construction according to sense, since the beast refers to a human being.
ὄγδοός. Predicate nominative of the following ἐστιν. The accenting is due to the enclitic ἐστιν that follows.
ἐστιν. Pres act ind 3rd sg εἰμί. On the loss of accent, see 1:8.
ἐκ τῶν ἑπτά. Partitive.
ἐστιν. Pres act ind 3rd sg εἰμί. On the loss of accent, see 1:8.
εἰς ἀπώλειαν. Goal.
ὑπάγει. Pres act ind 3rd sg ὑπάγω. On the temporal significance, see verse 8.

17:12 Καὶ τὰ δέκα κέρατα ἃ εἶδες δέκα βασιλεῖς εἰσιν, οἵτινες βασιλείαν οὔπω ἔλαβον, ἀλλ' ἐξουσίαν ὡς βασιλεῖς μίαν ὥραν λαμβάνουσιν μετὰ τοῦ θηρίου.

τὰ δέκα κέρατα. Nominative subject of εἰσιν.
ἃ. Accusative direct object of εἶδες.
εἶδες. Aor act ind 2nd sg ὁράω. On its function see verse 8.
δέκα βασιλεῖς. Predicate nominative.
εἰσιν. Pres act ind 3rd pl εἰμί. On the loss of accent see 1:8.
οἵτινες. Nominative subject of ἔλαβον.
βασιλείαν. Accusative direct object of ἔλαβον.
ἔλαβον. Aor act ind 3rd pl λαμβάνω. According to Aune (3.911), βασιλείαν . . . ἔλαβον (lit. "to receive a kingdom") is an idiom meaning "to become king."
ἀλλ'. Contrast. ἀλλά provides a correction to the previous clause (cf. Runge, 93).
ἐξουσίαν. Accusative direct object of λαμβάνουσιν.
ὡς βασιλεῖς. Manner. βασιλεῖς is the nominative subject of an elliptical clause: "as a king *has authority*."
μίαν ὥραν. Temporal. Adverbial accusative of time.
λαμβάνουσιν. Pres act ind 3rd pl λαμβάνω. The aorist tense ἔλαβον summarizes what the kings have not yet received, while the present tenses (λαμβάνουσιν, ἔχουσιν, διδόασιν) in verses 12b-13 foreground the authority they will receive in collusion with the beast (Mathewson 2010, 153).
μετὰ τοῦ θηρίου. Association.

17:13 οὗτοι μίαν γνώμην ἔχουσιν καὶ τὴν δύναμιν καὶ ἐξουσίαν αὐτῶν τῷ θηρίῳ διδόασιν.

οὗτοι. Nominative subject of ἔχουσιν. As Levinsohn notes, "The 'near' nature of οὗτος manifests itself by being used in reference to animate participants that are *thematic*: the centre of attention" (2009, 210). The use of the near demonstrative here and in verse 14 draws attention to the ten kings who carry out their will in conjunction with the beast, but are defeated by the Lamb.

μίαν γνώμην. Accusative direct object of ἔχουσιν. The idiom μίαν γνώμην comes from the sphere of politics and refers to the concord or agreement within a city or state (Aune, 3.952).

ἔχουσιν. Pres act ind 3rd pl ἔχω.

τὴν δύναμιν καὶ ἐξουσίαν. Accusative direct object of διδόασιν. The direct object is fronted to draw attention to the power and authority given to the beast.

αὐτῶν. Subjective genitive.

τῷ θηρίῳ. Dative indirect object of διδόασιν.

διδόασιν. Pres act ind 3rd pl δίδωμι.

17:14 οὗτοι μετὰ τοῦ ἀρνίου πολεμήσουσιν καὶ τὸ ἀρνίον νικήσει αὐτούς, ὅτι κύριος κυρίων ἐστὶν καὶ βασιλεὺς βασιλέων καὶ οἱ μετ' αὐτοῦ κλητοὶ καὶ ἐκλεκτοὶ καὶ πιστοί.

οὗτοι. Nominative subject of πολεμήσουσιν. The antecedent is δέκα βασιλεῖς and probably also τῷ θηρίῳ in verses 12 and 13 respectively. On the significance of οὗτοι, see verse 13 above.

μετὰ τοῦ ἀρνίου. Accompaniment.

πολεμήσουσιν. Fut act ind 3rd pl πολεμέω. Here the author shifts from present tense forms in verses 12-13 to two future tense forms in verse 14. The shift is from a description of what is the case, to an expectation of what will happen (see also Porter 1989a, 231), reflecting the prophetic nature of this section of the vision. See also the future tense verbs in verses 15-17.

τὸ ἀρνίον. Nominative subject of νικήσει.

νικήσει. Fut act ind 3rd sg νικάω.

αὐτούς. Accusative direct object of νικήσει.

ὅτι. Introduces a causal clause.

κύριος. Nominative subject of ἐστίν.

κυρίων. Genitive of subordination. The construction κύριος κυρίων indicates the idea of "Lord above all other lords" or a superlative idea, "The greatest of all lords" (Aune, 3.911).

ἐστὶν. Pres act ind 3rd sg εἰμί.

βασιλεὺς. Nominative subject of ἐστίν.
βασιλέων. On the genitive, see κυρίων above.
οἱ μετ' αὐτοῦ. Accompaniment. The article functions as a nominalizer, which turns the entire PP into a substantive that functions as the nominative subject of a verbless clause.
κλητοὶ καὶ ἐκλεκτοὶ καὶ πιστοί. Predicate adjective of a verbless clause.

17:15 Καὶ λέγει μοι· τὰ ὕδατα ἃ εἶδες οὗ ἡ πόρνη κάθηται, λαοὶ καὶ ὄχλοι εἰσὶν καὶ ἔθνη καὶ γλῶσσαι.

λέγει. Pres act ind 3rd sg λέγω. Historical or narrative present (see 4:5 on ἐκπορεύονται). Here it draws attention to the following speech.
μοι. Dative indirect object of λέγει.
τὰ ὕδατα. Nominative subject of εἰσίν.
ἃ. Accusative direct object of εἶδες.
εἶδες. Aor act ind 2nd sg ὁράω. On its function see verse 8.
οὗ. Locative.
ἡ πόρνη. Nominative subject of κάθηται.
κάθηται. Pres mid ind 3rd sg κάθημαι.
λαοὶ καὶ ὄχλοι ... καὶ ἔθνη καὶ γλῶσσαι. Predicate nominative of εἰσίν. The verb εἰσίν divides the first two and last two items in the fourfold list. The dividing of the noun clause may function to indicate prominence.
εἰσὶν. Pres act ind 3rd pl εἰμί.

17:16 καὶ τὰ δέκα κέρατα ἃ εἶδες καὶ τὸ θηρίον οὗτοι μισήσουσιν τὴν πόρνην καὶ ἠρημωμένην ποιήσουσιν αὐτὴν καὶ γυμνὴν καὶ τὰς σάρκας αὐτῆς φάγονται καὶ αὐτὴν κατακαύσουσιν ἐν πυρί.

τὰ δέκα κέρατα. Topic construction. τὰ δέκα κέρατα ἃ εἶδες καὶ τὸ θηρίον anticipates and is resumed by the demonstrative pronoun οὗτοι. This construction (left dislocation) functions to draw attention to the topic of ten horns and the beast (see 1:5 on Τῷ ἀγαπῶντι ... καὶ λύσαντι).
ἃ. Accusative direct object of εἶδες.
εἶδες. Aor act ind 2nd sg ὁράω. On its function see verse 8.
τὸ θηρίον. Topic construction. See τὰ δέκα κέρατα above.
οὗτοι. Nominative subject of μισήσουσιν ... ποιήσουσιν ... φάγονται ... κατακαύσουσιν. Resumes τὰ δέκα κέρατα ... καὶ τὸ θηρίον, which are neuter, while the demonstrative οὗτοι is masculine. This is most likely a construction according to sense, where the horns and the beast are understood to represent human rulers.

μισήσουσιν. Fut act ind 3rd pl μισέω. The string of future tenses reflect the prophetic quality of the interpretation of the vision.

τὴν πόρνην. Accusative direct object of μισήσουσιν.

ἠρημωμένην ... καὶ γυμνὴν. Complement in an object-complement double accusative construction with αὐτήν.

ἠρημωμένην. Prf pass ptc fem acc sg ἐρημόω. See above on ἠρημωμένην ... καὶ γυμνὴν. The fronting of the participle makes the prostitute's desolation more prominent.

ποιήσουσιν. Fut act ind 3rd pl ποιέω.

αὐτὴν. Accusative direct object of ποιήσουσιν.

τὰς σάρκας. Accusative direct object of φάγονται.

αὐτῆς. Possessive genitive.

φάγονται. Fut mid ind 3rd pl ἐσθίω.

αὐτὴν. Accusative direct object of κατακαύσουσιν.

κατακαύσουσιν. Fut act ind 3rd pl κατακαίω.

ἐν πυρί. Instrumental.

17:17 ὁ γὰρ θεὸς ἔδωκεν εἰς τὰς καρδίας αὐτῶν ποιῆσαι τὴν γνώμην αὐτοῦ καὶ ποιῆσαι μίαν γνώμην καὶ δοῦναι τὴν βασιλείαν αὐτῶν τῷ θηρίῳ ἄχρι τελεσθήσονται οἱ λόγοι τοῦ θεοῦ.

ὁ ... θεὸς. Nominative subject of ἔδωκεν.

γὰρ. Introduces the cause of the events in verse 16.

ἔδωκεν. Aor act ind 3rd sg δίδωμι.

εἰς τὰς καρδίας. Locative.

αὐτῶν. Possessive genitive. The antecedent is the ten horns (v. 16). This could also include the beast, but since they give their kingdom to the beast, it is better to restrict the antecedent to the ten horns (= kings).

ποιῆσαι. Aor act inf ποιέω (direct object of ἔδωκεν).

τὴν γνώμην. Accusative direct object of ποιῆσαι.

αὐτοῦ. Subjective genitive. The antecedent is ὁ θεός. Some manuscripts (א² 2329) have the genitive plural αὐτῶν. This may be due to conformity to the other usages of αὐτῶν in this verse, or the desire to soften God's responsibility for the evil actions of the kings (Beale, 888).

ποιῆσαι. Aor act inf ποιέω (direct object of ἔδωκεν).

μίαν γνώμην. Accusative direct object of ποιῆσαι.

δοῦναι. Aor act inf δίδωμι (direct object of ἔδωκεν). Smalley (441) notes that the last two infinitive clauses (ποιῆσαι μίαν γνώμην καὶ δοῦναι τὴν βασιλείαν αὐτῶν τῷ θηρίῳ) are more specific descriptions of the first more general clause (ποιῆσαι τὴν γνώμην αὐτοῦ). While this may be true and makes good sense semantically, grammatically the three infinitives function as the direct objects of ἔδωκεν, and all three clauses are linked with καί, which expresses continuity between the three expressions.

τὴν βασιλείαν. Accusative direct object of δοῦναι.
αὐτῶν. Subjective genitive. The antecedent is the ten horns.
τῷ θηρίῳ. Dative indirect object of δοῦναι.
ἄχρι. Introduces a temporal clause. A "marker of continuous extent of time up to a point" (BDAG, 160.1).
τελεσθήσονται. Fut pass ind 3rd pl τελέω. Future with ἄχρι. On the use of the future in place of the subjunctive, see 3:9 on ἥξουσιν. Predictably, some manuscripts have the aorist subjunctive τελεσθῶσιν (1006 1611 1841 2030 𝔐ᴷ).
οἱ λόγοι. Nominative subject of τελεσθήσονται.
τοῦ θεοῦ. Genitive of source or subjective genitive.

17:18 καὶ ἡ γυνὴ ἣν εἶδες ἔστιν ἡ πόλις ἡ μεγάλη ἡ ἔχουσα βασιλείαν ἐπὶ τῶν βασιλέων τῆς γῆς.

ἡ γυνὴ. Nominative subject of ἔστιν. Here γυνὴ is the subject (rather than ἡ πόλις ἡ μεγάλη). Since the two substantives with εἰμί both have an article, word order determines function (Wallace, 44).
ἣν. Accusative direct object of εἶδες.
εἶδες. Aor act ind 2nd sg ὁράω. On the function, see verse 8.
ἔστιν. Pres act ind 3rd sg εἰμί.
ἡ πόλις ἡ μεγάλη. Predicate nominative of ἔστιν.
ἡ ἔχουσα. Pres act ptc fem nom sg ἔχω (attributive).
βασιλείαν. Accusative direct object of ἔχουσα.
ἐπὶ τῶν βασιλέων. Here, ἐπί is a marker indicating the extent of the authority of βασιλείαν.
τῆς γῆς. Genitive of subordination.

Revelation 18:1-8

¹After these things I saw another angel coming down from heaven, having great authority, and the earth was illuminated by his glory. ²And he cried out with a strong voice, saying, "Fallen, fallen is Babylon the Great, and it has become a dwelling place for demons and a prison for every unclean spirit and a prison for every unclean bird and a prison for every unclean and detestable beast, ³for all the nations have drunk from the wine of the passion of her adultery, and the kings of the earth have committed adultery with her, and the merchants of the earth have become rich from the power of her luxury." ⁴And I heard another voice from heaven saying, "Come out of her, my people, so that you will not participate in her sins and that you will not receive her plagues; ⁵for her

sins have touched the heavens, and God has remembered her unrighteous deeds. ⁶Pay back to her just as she paid out, and give her duplicate according to her works, and in the cup which she mixed mix for her a double portion. ⁷To the degree that she glorified herself and lived in luxury, give her the same degree of torment and mourning; for in her heart she says, 'I am seated as queen, and I am not a widow, and I will certainly not see mourning.' ⁸For this reason, in one hour her plagues will come, death and mourning and famine, and she will be burned up with fire; for the God who judges her is a strong Lord."

18:1 Μετὰ ταῦτα εἶδον ἄλλον ἄγγελον καταβαίνοντα ἐκ τοῦ οὐρανοῦ ἔχοντα ἐξουσίαν μεγάλην, καὶ ἡ γῆ ἐφωτίσθη ἐκ τῆς δόξης αὐτοῦ.

Μετὰ ταῦτα. Temporal (see 4:1).
εἶδον. Aor act ind 1st sg ὁράω.
ἄλλον ἄγγελον. Accusative direct object of εἶδον.
καταβαίνοντα. Pres act ptc masc acc sg καταβαίνω. Complement in an object-complement double accusative construction.
ἐκ τοῦ οὐρανοῦ. Source.
ἔχοντα. Pres act ptc masc acc sg ἔχω (attributive).
ἐξουσίαν μεγάλην. Accusative direct object of ἔχοντα.
ἡ γῆ. Nominative subject of ἐφωτίσθη.
ἐφωτίσθη. Aor pass ind 3rd sg φωτίζω.
ἐκ τῆς δόξης. Source.
αὐτοῦ. Subjective genitive.

18:2 καὶ ἔκραξεν ἐν ἰσχυρᾷ φωνῇ λέγων· ἔπεσεν ἔπεσεν Βαβυλὼν ἡ μεγάλη, καὶ ἐγένετο κατοικητήριον δαιμονίων καὶ φυλακὴ παντὸς πνεύματος ἀκαθάρτου καὶ φυλακὴ παντὸς ὀρνέου ἀκαθάρτου [καὶ φυλακὴ παντὸς θηρίου ἀκαθάρτου] καὶ μεμισημένου,

ἔκραξεν. Aor act ind 3rd sg κράζω.
ἐν ἰσχυρᾷ φωνῇ. Instrumental.
λέγων. Pres act ptc masc nom sg λέγω (manner). On the use of the participle λέγων to introduce speech, see 1:17 on λέγων.
ἔπεσεν ἔπεσεν. Aor act ind 3rd sg πίπτω. The temporal reference of the aorist is difficult to pin down here, especially since the city apparently has not yet fallen in verses 4-8, while the fall of the city seems to be assumed in verse 9 (the fall of Babylon is not explicitly narrated in this section). If verse 2 anticipates the fall of Babylon (cf. 14:8), it is possible to see the aorists as future referring (Swete, 227; Smalley, 444). However, it is important to realize that it is unlikely that the material in ch. 18 is arranged chronologically (see Aune, 3.975; Beale, 891;

Mussies, 338–39). With some justification, Ressiguie (227) posits the following temporal division: verses 1-3 take place immediately after the fall of Babylon; verses 4-8 take place before the fall of Babylon; verses 9-20 take place after the fall of Babylon. It is possible, then, that verse 2 summarizes the fall of Babylon that presumably has already taken place between chs. 17 and 18:2. Hence, the aorists are past referring here (see also ἐγένετο). Verses 4-8 revert back to a hortatory call to come out of Babylon. Verses 9-20 then revert to a description of the effects of the fall of the great city (see also Mathewson 2010, 154–56). The repetition of the verb is for emphasis, and also reflects the OT allusion to Isa 21:9.

Βαβυλὼν ἡ μεγάλη. Nominative subject of ἔπεσεν ἔπεσεν. Reference to Babylon the great city is reduced to pronominal forms in the rest of this section (e.g., αὐτῆς) or implicitly marked in the verb ending, except when the three different groups address her in mourning in verses 10, 16, and 19, and when heaven and the saints rejoice in verse 21.

ἐγένετο. Aor mid ind 3rd sg γίνομαι.
κατοικητήριον. Predicate nominative.
δαιμονίων. Subjective genitive.
φυλακὴ. Predicate nominative.
παντὸς πνεύματος ἀκαθάρτου. Objective genitive.
φυλακὴ. Predicate nominative.
παντὸς ὀρνέου ἀκαθάρτου. Objective genitive.
[καὶ φυλακὴ παντὸς θηρίου ἀκαθάρτου]. This phrase is omitted by ℵ C 051 𝔐. The omission could be accounted for through an error of eyesight—the previous line begins and ends with the same words (φυλακὴ ἀκαθάρτου), causing a scribe to accidentally omit the latter phrase (haplography). If this portion is absent, we would translate the final part of the verse: "a prison for every unclean and detestable bird."
μεμισημένου. Prf pass ptc neut gen sg μισέω (attributive).

18:3 ὅτι ἐκ τοῦ οἴνου τοῦ θυμοῦ τῆς πορνείας αὐτῆς πέπωκαν πάντα τὰ ἔθνη καὶ οἱ βασιλεῖς τῆς γῆς μετ' αὐτῆς ἐπόρνευσαν καὶ οἱ ἔμποροι τῆς γῆς ἐκ τῆς δυνάμεως τοῦ στρήνους αὐτῆς ἐπλούτησαν.

ὅτι. Introduces a causal clause, giving the reason for Babylon's fall and its status as a dwelling for everything unclean.
ἐκ τοῦ οἴνου. Source. The string of genitives (τοῦ θυμοῦ τῆς πορνείας αὐτῆς) function to give prominence to this reason for her fall. This may be more important than the precise labels given to each genitive.
τοῦ θυμοῦ. Epexegetical genitive.
τῆς πορνείας. Attributive genitive: "Immoral passions" (Aune, 3.966).
αὐτῆς. Subjective genitive.

πέπωκαν. Prf act ind 3rd pl πίνω. In the midst of the string of aorists the perfect tense may function to draw further attention to the reason for Babylon's fall. Despite weak manuscript support, πέπωκαν (1006ᶜ 2329) is followed by the NA²⁸/UBS⁵ (the latter gives this reading a D rating). This reading is often preferred because it supposedly makes the best sense in the context (Smalley, 422). Furthermore, the OT prophetic background (see Jer 25:15; Isa 51:7, 39) may suggest some form of the word "to drink" or "to make drunk" (Metzger, 683). However, Aune (3.965–66) argues for the plausibility of the reading πέπτωκαν or πεπτώκασιν ("have fallen," from πίπτω) based on superior manuscript evidence (א A C 046 1006 1611 1841 2030 𝔐ᵏ al), and this reading should probably be preferred: "For from the wine of the passion all the nations *have fallen*." This would also make sense of the context following the reference to Babylon's fall in verse 2 (ἔπεσεν ἔπεσεν): now the nations also fall in judgment. The reading πεπότικεν (94 2042 2065 2432) is probably due to assimilation to 14:8. For a more detailed discussion of the different variants, see Aune (3.965–66).

πάντα τὰ ἔθνη. Nominative subject of πέπωκαν.

καί. Smalley (445) says that the conjunction is causal (see also Aune, 3.966). While this may or may not be valid at a semantic level, at the grammatical level the καί simply indicates continuity.

οἱ βασιλεῖς. Nominative subject of ἐπόρνευσαν.

τῆς γῆς. Genitive of subordination.

μετ' αὐτῆς. Association.

ἐπόρνευσαν. Aor act ind 3rd pl πορνεύω. While the word could indicate literally committing sexually immoral acts, it can also be used metaphorically of engaging in idolatrous practices. Here it is used of nations who participate in the unjust practices, particularly economical, of Babylon. While the language of committing adultery is frequently used in the OT of Israel's unfaithfulness to Yahweh, it could also be used of other cities and their seductive economic practices (Nah 3:4; Isa 23:17), which is how John uses it here with reference to Babylon's seduction of the kings of the earth (see Hauck and Schultz, 587, for this use of πορνεύω).

οἱ ἔμποροι. Nominative subject of ἐπλούτησαν.

τῆς γῆς. Genitive of description or genitive expressing location.

ἐκ τῆς δυνάμεως. Means or cause.

τοῦ στρήνους. Genitive of source or subjective genitive. The word suggests "to live sensually by gratifying the senses with sexual immorality" (LN 88.254). It may also carry the idea of living in luxury (Beale, 895–96) as a metaphorical meaning.

αὐτῆς. Possessive genitive.

ἐπλούτησαν. Aor act ind 3rd pl πλουτέω. Mussies (338) thinks that this (and ἐπόρνευσαν) is an aorist with the value of a perfect tense (see also Smalley, 445). However, this seems to be influenced more by English translation than the semantics of the aorist tense and depends on Mussies' assumption that the meaning of the aorist tense derives from an underlying Semitic construction. Fanning (93) incorrectly thinks that the aorist carries an ingressive notion ("they got wealthy"), since this is a verb that indicates a state or condition, so that the aorist emphasizes the entrance into that condition. However, it is more likely that the aorist looks at the entire state or condition of being wealthy. An ingressive notion should not be pressed here and certainly is not being emphasized (see the Introduction on "Verbal Aspect").

18:4 Καὶ ἤκουσα ἄλλην φωνὴν ἐκ τοῦ οὐρανοῦ λέγουσαν· ἐξέλθατε ὁ λαός μου ἐξ αὐτῆς ἵνα μὴ συγκοινωνήσητε ταῖς ἁμαρτίαις αὐτῆς, καὶ ἐκ τῶν πληγῶν αὐτῆς ἵνα μὴ λάβητε,

Once more, throughout verses 4-20 the author shifts between aorist, present, and future indicative verb forms. This shifting in tenses should be understood along the lines of verbal aspect. The aorist carries along the main storyline; the present selects specific features on which to dwell; the future indicates action that can be expected to take place and points to the prophetic quality of the narrative (Mathewson 2010, 156; see also "Verbal Aspect" in the Introduction).

ἤκουσα. Aor act ind 1st sg ἀκούω.

ἄλλην φωνὴν. Accusative direct object of ἤκουσα. The "strong voice" seems to encompass the entirety of 18:4-20, though other voices are embedded within the angelic voice (Mathewson 2010, 154).

ἐκ τοῦ οὐρανοῦ. Source.

λέγουσαν. Pres act ptc masc acc sg λέγω. Complement in an object-complement double accusative construction. On the use of the participle λέγουσαν to introduce speech, see 1:17 on λέγων.

ἐξέλθατε. Aor act impv 2nd pl ἐξέρχομαι. The plural here is followed by a singular subject λαός for those who are addressed. This is a construction according to sense due to the fact that λαός is collective (cf. McKay 1994, 18).

ὁ λαός. Nominative functioning as a vocative.

μου. Possessive genitive or genitive of relationship.

ἐξ αὐτῆς. Separation.

ἵνα. Introduces a purpose clause.

συγκοινωνήσητε. Aor act subj 2nd pl συγκοινωνέω. Subjunctive with ἵνα.

ταῖς ἁμαρτίαις. συγκοινωνέω can take the dative indicating the thing with which someone associates or participates (cf. BDAG, 952.1).

αὐτῆς. Subjective genitive.

ἐκ τῶν πληγῶν. Partitive. It is unusual that the partitive construction occurs before the ἵνα clause, rather than following it. This may be because, as Aune (3.991; followed by Osborne, 639) has suggested, the author achieves a chiastic structure with the previous ἵνα clause: in order that you might not share/in her sins—from her plagues/in order that you might not receive.

αὐτῆς. The genitive should be understood as "the plagues that come upon her" (objective genitive).

ἵνα. Introduces a purpose clause.

λάβητε. Aor act subj 2nd pl λαμβάνω. Subjunctive with ἵνα.

18:5 ὅτι ἐκολλήθησαν αὐτῆς αἱ ἁμαρτίαι ἄχρι τοῦ οὐρανοῦ καὶ ἐμνημόνευσεν ὁ θεὸς τὰ ἀδικήματα αὐτῆς.

ὅτι. Introduces a causal clause. Beale (900) sees the ὅτι clause as providing the reason for Babylon being punished with such "plagues" in verse 4. However, all the verbs in the speech of the angel in verse 4 refer to the readers in the second person, focusing not on Babylon's fall, but on the need of the readers to leave, so that following the two purpose clauses (v. 14), the ὅτι clause should be seen as providing the reason for the imperative ἐξέλθατε. They are to "come out" precisely because God is about to judge Babylon for her sins.

ἐκολλήθησαν. Aor mid ind 3rd pl κολλάω. On the voice, see "Deponency" in the Series Introduction. The verb κολλάω carries the meaning of "to be closely associated, cling to, attach to" or "come in close contact with" (BDAG, 556.2.a.β). With ἄχρι τοῦ οὐρανοῦ (see below) it seems to form an idiom meaning something like "her sins have touched the heavens" (BDAG, 556.2.a.β) or "her sins have become very, very many" (LN 59.66).

αὐτῆς. Subjective genitive. Placed before the head term it modifies for prominence.

αἱ ἁμαρτίαι. Nominative subject of ἐκολλήθησαν.

ἄχρι τοῦ οὐρανοῦ. Extent. BDAG (161.2) defines it as a "marker of extension up to a certain point, *as far as*." "The metaphor 'to the heavens' is a hyperbolic way of emphasizing the magnitude of something" (Aune, 3.992).

ἐμνημόνευσεν. Aor act ind 3rd sg μνημονεύω. Elsewhere in the OT (Ps 109:14; Hos 9:9) the act of God "remembering" is an expression of judgment (Beale, 900).

ὁ θεὸς. Nominative subject of ἐμνημόνευσεν.

τὰ ἀδικήματα. Accusative direct object of ἐμνημόνευσεν.

αὐτῆς. Subjective genitive.

18:6 ἀπόδοτε αὐτῇ ὡς καὶ αὐτὴ ἀπέδωκεν καὶ διπλώσατε τὰ διπλᾶ κατὰ τὰ ἔργα αὐτῆς, ἐν τῷ ποτηρίῳ ᾧ ἐκέρασεν κεράσατε αὐτῇ διπλοῦν,

ἀπόδοτε. Aor act impv 2nd pl ἀποδίδωμι. The subject of the imperatives in this verse is probably God (Beale, 900).
αὐτῇ. Dative indirect object of ἀπόδοτε.
ὡς. Comparison.
αὐτὴ. Nominative subject of ἀπέδωκεν.
ἀπέδωκεν. Aor act ind 3rd sg ἀποδίδωμι.
διπλώσατε τὰ διπλᾶ. Lit. "double the double." Although this construction is sometimes taken to suggest that Babylon will receive twice the amount of punishment that she gave out, the idea is of reduplication or equivalency: "Produce a duplicate" (Beale, 901), or "repay Babylon the equivalent of what she has done" (Smalley, 447–48). The punishment will match the crime. God will pay Babylon back fully for what she has done. This fits with the emphasis in the previous clause on "giving back to her as she gave out" and in verse 7: "To the degree that she has glorified herself, give her the same degree of torment and mourning."
διπλώσατε. Aor act impv 2nd pl διπλόω.
τὰ διπλᾶ. Accusative direct object of διπλώσατε.
κατὰ τὰ ἔργα. Standard.
αὐτῆς. Subjective genitive.
ἐν τῷ ποτηρίῳ. Locative.
ᾧ. Direct object. Rather than the expected accusative case, the dative occurs due to attraction to its antecedent ποτηρίῳ.
ἐκέρασεν. Aor act ind 3rd sg κεράννυμι.
κεράσατε. Aor act impv 2nd pl κεράννυμι.
αὐτῇ. Dative of disadvantage.
διπλοῦν. Accusative direct object of κεράσατε. Lit. "a double portion" (but see above on διπλώσατε τὰ διπλᾶ).

18:7 ὅσα ἐδόξασεν αὐτὴν καὶ ἐστρηνίασεν, τοσοῦτον δότε αὐτῇ βασανισμὸν καὶ πένθος. ὅτι ἐν τῇ καρδίᾳ αὐτῆς λέγει ὅτι κάθημαι βασίλισσα καὶ χήρα οὐκ εἰμὶ καὶ πένθος οὐ μὴ ἴδω.

ὅσα ἐδόξασεν αὐτὴν καὶ ἐστρηνίασεν. Topic construction (see 1:5 on Τῷ ἀγαπῶντι . . . καὶ λύσαντι). The correlative ὅσα is resumed by the τοσοῦτον. According to BDAG (729.3) this construction ὅσα . . . τοσοῦτον indicates "degree of correlative extent" and should be translated "to the degree that . . . to the same degree." This topic construction draws attention to the self-glorification of Babylon as the standard for her judgment.

ἐδόξασεν. Aor act ind 3rd sg δοξάζω.

αὐτὴν. Accusative direct object of ἐδόξασεν. Here the personal pronoun αὐτός functions in a reflexive sense ("herself"). The reflexive ἑαυτήν is found in ℵ² 1006 1841 1854 (2329 𝔐ᴬ).

ἐστρηνίασεν. Aor act ind 3rd sg στρηνιάω. On the meaning, see verse 3 on στρήνους.

τοσοῦτον ... βασανισμὸν καὶ πένθος. Accusative direct object of δότε. Resumes the topic ὅσα ἐδόξασεν αὐτὴν καὶ ἐστρηνίασεν. On the meaning of τοσοῦτον, see ὅσα above.

δότε. Aor act impv 2nd pl δίδωμι.

αὐτῇ. Dative indirect object of δότε.

ὅτι. Introduces a causal clause. Provides a further reason for Babylon's fall.

ἐν τῇ καρδίᾳ. Locative, used metaphorically.

αὐτῆς. Possessive genitive.

λέγει. Pres act ind 3rd sg λέγω.

ὅτι. Introduces a content clause that is the clausal complement (direct discourse) of λέγει.

κάθημαι. Pres mid ind 1st sg κάθημαι.

βασίλισσα. Nominative absolute, used as a title: "As queen, I sit" (Aune, 3.967).

χήρα. Predicate nominative of εἰμί.

εἰμὶ. Pres act ind 1st sg εἰμί.

πένθος. Accusative direct object of ἴδω.

ἴδω. Aor act subj 1st sg εἶδον. The subjunctive is used with οὐ μὴ, which expresses emphatic negation. Here it draws attention to the contrast between Babylon's claim in this verse and the judgment (θάνατος καὶ πένθος καὶ λιμός) that befalls her in the next verse.

18:8 διὰ τοῦτο ἐν μιᾷ ἡμέρᾳ ἥξουσιν αἱ πληγαὶ αὐτῆς, θάνατος καὶ πένθος καὶ λιμός, καὶ ἐν πυρὶ κατακαυθήσεται, ὅτι ἰσχυρὸς κύριος ὁ θεὸς ὁ κρίνας αὐτήν.

διὰ τοῦτο. Causal (lit. "because of this"). The antecedent is everything following the second ὅτι clause in verse 7 above: "Because of Rome's pride and self-confidence she shall be overthrown suddenly" (Charles, 2.99).

ἐν μιᾷ ἡμέρᾳ. Temporal.

ἥξουσιν. Fut act ind 3rd pl ἥκω.

αἱ πληγαὶ. Nominative subject of ἥξουσιν.

αὐτῆς. The genitive communicates the idea "the plagues that come upon her."

θάνατος καὶ πένθος καὶ λιμός. Nominative in apposition to αἱ πληγαί.

ἐν πυρὶ. Instrumental.

κατακαυθήσεται. Fut pass ind 3rd sg κατακαίω. The compound form carries the notion of "burn up" or "consume" (BDAG, 517).

ὅτι. Introduces a causal clause.

ἰσχυρὸς κύριος. Predicate nominative of a verbless clause.

ὁ θεὸς. Nominative in apposition to κύριος.

ὁ κρίνας. Aor act ptc masc nom sg κρίνω (attributive). It is also possible that the participle is substantival and stands in apposition to θεός.

αὐτήν. Accusative direct object of κρίνας.

Revelation 18:9-20

⁹"And the kings of the earth who committed adultery with her and lived in luxury, shall weep and mourn over her, when they see the smoke from her burning, ¹⁰standing from far off because of fear of her torment, saying, 'Woe woe, great city, Babylon the mighty city, for in one hour your judgment has come.' ¹¹And the merchants of the earth will weep and mourn over her, because no one buys their cargo ever again, ¹²cargo of gold and silver, and precious stone and pearls and fine linen and purple cloth and silk and scarlet cloth, and every aromatic wood and every ivory vessel and every vessel of costly wood and copper and iron and marble, ¹³and cinnamon and amomum and incense and perfume and frankincense and wine and olive oil and fine flour and wheat and animals and sheep and horses and carriages and bodies, and the souls of men. ¹⁴And the fruit of your soul's longings has gone away from you, and all your luxury and splendor has perished from you, and they will never again be found. ¹⁵The merchants of these things, who have become rich from her, will stand far off because of fear of her torment, weeping and mourning, ¹⁶saying, 'Woe woe, great city, clothed in fine linen and purple and scarlet, and adorned with gold and precious stone and pearl. ¹⁷For in one hour so much wealth has been laid waste.' And every shipmaster and everyone who sails over the region and sailors and as many as work the sea stood from far off ¹⁸and they cried out seeing the smoke from its burning, saying, 'Who is like the great city?' ¹⁹And they threw dust on their heads, and they cried out weeping and mourning, saying, 'Woe woe, great city, in which all who have boats in the sea have become rich from her prosperity, for in one hour she has been laid waste.' ²⁰Rejoice over her, heaven and the saints and apostles and prophets, for God has rendered judgment because of her judgment of you."

18:9 Καὶ κλαύσουσιν καὶ κόψονται ἐπ' αὐτὴν οἱ βασιλεῖς τῆς γῆς οἱ μετ' αὐτῆς πορνεύσαντες καὶ στρηνιάσαντες, ὅταν βλέπωσιν τὸν καπνὸν τῆς πυρώσεως αὐτῆς,

κλαύσουσιν. Fut act ind 3rd pl κλαίω. On the significance of the future tense, see verse 11 on κλαίουσιν.
κόψονται. Fut mid ind 3rd pl κόπτω. On the voice and meaning, see 1:7. On the significance of the future tense, see verse 11 on κλαίουσιν.
ἐπ' αὐτήν. The preposition ἐπί can indicate the object toward which feelings or actions are directed (BDAG, 366.15). Here it indicates the object of the mourning.
οἱ βασιλεῖς. Nominative subject of κλαύσουσιν καὶ κόψονται.
τῆς γῆς. Genitive of subordination.
οἱ ... πορνεύσαντες. Aor act ptc masc nom pl πορνεύω (attributive).
οἱ ... στρηνιάσαντες. Aor act ptc masc nom pl στρηνιάω (attributive). On the meaning, see verse 3 on στρήνους.
μετ' αὐτῆς. Association.
ὅταν. Introduces a temporal clause.
βλέπωσιν. Pres act subj 3rd pl βλέπω. Subjunctive with ὅταν.
τὸν καπνόν. Accusative direct object of βλέπωσιν.
τῆς πυρώσεως. Genitive of source.
αὐτῆς. Subjective genitive.

18:10 ἀπὸ μακρόθεν ἑστηκότες διὰ τὸν φόβον τοῦ βασανισμοῦ αὐτῆς λέγοντες· οὐαὶ οὐαί, ἡ πόλις ἡ μεγάλη, Βαβυλὼν ἡ πόλις ἡ ἰσχυρά, ὅτι μιᾷ ὥρᾳ ἦλθεν ἡ κρίσις σου.

ἀπὸ μακρόθεν. Locative/spatial. Here ἀπό is used "to indicate distance fr. a point" (BDAG, 106.4): "from a great distance."
ἑστηκότες. Prf act ptc masc nom pl ἵστημι (temporal or manner). Modifes κλαύσουσιν καὶ κόψονται (v. 9). The perfect tense may draw further attention to the distance from the city at which the kings ironically now stand, upon which they were so closely dependent.
διὰ τὸν φόβον. Cause.
τοῦ βασανισμοῦ. Objective genitive.
αὐτῆς. Objective genitive.
λέγοντες. Pres act ptc masc nom pl λέγω (manner). Although this participle could modify the preceding participle ἑστηκότες, it probably modifies κλαύσουσιν καὶ κόψονται (v. 9), expressing the manner of their crying and mourning. On the use of the participle λέγοντες to introduce speech, see 1:17 on λέγων.

οὐαὶ οὐαί. An interjection that denotes "a state of intense hardship or distress" (LN 22.9). Here the distress is caused by the judgment that comes upon the great city.

ἡ πόλις ἡ μεγάλη. Nominative functioning as a vocative.

Βαβυλὼν. Nominative in apposition to ἡ πόλις ἡ μεγάλη.

ἡ πόλις ἡ ἰσχυρά. Nominative in apposition to Βαβυλὼν. The piling up of phrases to refer to Babylon (overspecification) draws attention to the contrast between her previous status and her present judgment.

ὅτι. Introduces a causal clause.

μιᾷ ὥρᾳ. Dative of time. The common understanding of the dative of time as expressing a point in time (Wallace, 155) would seem to fit here, though this is primarily dependent lexically on μιᾷ ὥρᾳ.

ἦλθεν. Aor act ind 3rd sg ἔρχομαι.

ἡ κρίσις. Nominative subject of ἦλθεν.

σου. Objective genitive.

18:11 Καὶ οἱ ἔμποροι τῆς γῆς κλαίουσιν καὶ πενθοῦσιν ἐπ' αὐτήν, ὅτι τὸν γόμον αὐτῶν οὐδεὶς ἀγοράζει οὐκέτι

οἱ ἔμποροι. Nominative subject of κλαίουσιν καὶ πενθοῦσιν.

τῆς γῆς. Genitive of description or genitive expressing location.

κλαίουσιν. Pres act ind 3rd pl κλαίω. The two present tense forms, κλαίουσιν καὶ πενθοῦσιν, are probably future referring (see κλαύσουσιν καὶ κόψονται in v. 9). Together the future and present tense forms function to make prominent the response of those to the fall of Bablylon upon which they had depended for their livlihood. Beale's suggestion (909), following Mussies (335), that the present tense indicates that the vision is still present to the eye is overly dependent on a strictly temporal meaning for the present tense (see "Verbal Aspect"in the Introduction).

πενθοῦσιν. Pres act ind 3rd pl πενθέω. On the significance of the present tense, see above on κλαίουσιν. The two terms κλαίουσιν and πενθοῦσιν from the same semantic domain may be used for effect to emphasize the response of those who depended upon Babylon to her destruction. The distinction between the two terms may be that κλαίω suggests "to weep or wail, with emphasis upon the noise accompanying the weeping" (LN 25.138), while πενθέω means "to experience sadness or grief as the result of depressing circumstances or the condition of persons" (LN 25.142). Both together would express the sound of weeping and wailing and the grief and deep sorrow of which the weeping is an expression.

ἐπ' αὐτήν. On the meaning of the preposition, see verse 9.

ὅτι. Introduces a causal clause.

τὸν γόμον. Direct object of ἀγοράζει. The term refers to "freight" or "cargo" (BDAG, 205).

αὐτῶν. Possessive genitive.

οὐδεὶς. Nominative subject of ἀγοράζει.

ἀγοράζει. Pres act ind 3rd pl ἀγοράζω.

οὐκέτι. The addition of οὐκέτι after οὐδείς is emphatic and suggests "never again" (BDAG, 736.1).

18:12 γόμον χρυσοῦ καὶ ἀργύρου καὶ λίθου τιμίου καὶ μαργαριτῶν καὶ βυσσίνου καὶ πορφύρας καὶ σιρικοῦ καὶ κοκκίνου, καὶ πᾶν ξύλον θύϊνον καὶ πᾶν σκεῦος ἐλεφάντινον καὶ πᾶν σκεῦος ἐκ ξύλου τιμιωτάτου καὶ χαλκοῦ καὶ σιδήρου καὶ μαρμάρου,

γόμον... μαρμάρου. The entire verse along with the next one (v. 13) stands in apposition to τὸν γόμον in the previous verse (v. 11), which is picked up by γόμον here. For a description of each of the cargoes enumerated in verses 12-13, see Bauckham (350–66) and Charles (2.102–5).

γόμον. Accusative in apposition to τὸν γόμον in verse 11.

χρυσοῦ... κοκκίνου. Genitive of content.

πᾶν ξύλον θύϊνον καὶ πᾶν σκεῦος ἐλεφάντινον καὶ πᾶν σκεῦος. Accusative direct object of ἀγοράζει (v. 11).

σκεῦος. The term is "a highly generic term for any kind of jar, bowl, basket, or vase—'vessel, container'" (LN 6.118).

ἐκ ξύλου τιμιωτάτου καὶ χαλκοῦ καὶ σιδήρου καὶ μαρμάρου. The PP expresses the material makeup or the contents of the σκεῦος. Some manuscripts (A 1006 1841) read λίθου rather than ξύλου, most likely because ξύλου was thought to be out of place with the other items in the list following it (Metzger, 684). Furthermore, elsewhere in Revelation τίμιος modifies a reference to a stone (17:4; 18:12, 16; 21:11, 19).

τιμιωτάτου. The superlative adjective, which is probably elative in force, means "very" or "exceedingly" precious (Robertson, 670).

18:13 καὶ κιννάμωμον καὶ ἄμωμον καὶ θυμιάματα καὶ μύρον καὶ λίβανον καὶ οἶνον καὶ ἔλαιον καὶ σεμίδαλιν καὶ σῖτον καὶ κτήνη καὶ πρόβατα, καὶ ἵππων καὶ ῥεδῶν καὶ σωμάτων, καὶ ψυχὰς ἀνθρώπων.

κιννάμωμον... πρόβατα. Accusative direct object of ἀγοράζει (v. 11).

ἵππων καὶ ῥεδῶν καὶ σωμάτων. The genitives seem to modify an assumed noun in the accusative case, perhaps γόμον. The genitives then function to express the content of the cargo. This is to be preferred to Charles' suggestion (2.104) that these words are to be excised because it is awkward to find the genitive inserted in the midst of accusative constructions. While Aune (3.969) may be right that σωμάτων can be translated "slaves," he seems to confuse sense and reference. That is, σωμάτων does not *mean* "slaves," though it can *refer to* slaves as it does here in a list of cargoes.

καὶ ψυχὰς ἀνθρώπων. The comma before καὶ ψυχὰς ἀνθρώπων in the NA[28]/UBS[5] suggests that the editors have understood the καί to function as introducing a clause that is epexegetical, with the "souls of men" further defining σωμάτων (see Aune, 3.969), but the accusative case of ψυχὰς and the genitive of σωμάτων argue against this. It is simply a further direct object of ἀγοράζει (v. 11).

ψυχὰς. Accusative direct object of ἀγοράζει (v. 11). The "seat and center of the inner human life in its many and varied aspects" (BDAG, 1099.2). This serves to distinguish the σωμάτων from the rest of the cargo. In contrast to the common dehumanizing of slaves, John reminds his readers that they have "souls."

ἀνθρώπων. Possessive genitive or attributive genitive ("human souls").

18:14 καὶ ἡ ὀπώρα σου τῆς ἐπιθυμίας τῆς ψυχῆς ἀπῆλθεν ἀπὸ σοῦ, καὶ πάντα τὰ λιπαρὰ καὶ τὰ λαμπρὰ ἀπώλετο ἀπὸ σοῦ καὶ οὐκέτι οὐ μὴ αὐτὰ εὑρήσουσιν.

ἡ ὀπώρα. Nominative subject of ἀπῆλθεν. The term ὀπώρα literally means "the mature fruit of plants" or "ripe fruit," but metaphorically it can mean "good things" (LN 3.34).

σου. Possessive genitive, modifying τῆς ψυχῆς. Placed before the head term it modifies for prominence. The entire expression ἡ ὀπώρα σου τῆς ἐπιθυμίας τῆς ψυχῆς can be translated "the fruit your soul longed for."

τῆς ἐπιθυμίας. Subjective genitive, modifying ἡ ὀπώρα.

τῆς ψυχῆς. Subjective genitive, modifying τῆς ἐπιθυμίας.

ἀπῆλθεν. Aor act ind 3rd sg ἀπέρχομαι.

ἀπὸ σοῦ. Separation.

πάντα τὰ λιπαρὰ καὶ τὰ λαμπρὰ. Nominative subject of ἀπώλετο.

ἀπώλετο. Aor mid ind 3rd sg ἀπόλλυμι. Plural neuter subjects commonly take a singular verb.

ἀπὸ σοῦ. Separation.

αὐτὰ. Accusative direct object of εὑρήσουσιν. The antecedent is at least the rest of verse 14, but probably also the entire list of cargo including verses 12-13.

εὑρήσουσιν. Fut act ind 3rd pl εὑρίσκω. The future with οὐ μή is an emphatic way of expressing negation. Here it emphasizes the complete absence of the things listed in this verse. On the use of the future in place of the subjunctive, see 3:9 on ἥξουσιν. The combination of οὐκέτι οὐ μή is an even stronger way of expressing negation and can be translated "never again" (BDAG, 736.1). This is probably an example of an impersonal verb in the plural without a subject, which could be translated as a passive: "These things will not be found" (see McKay 1994, 19). For this construction, see 2:24 on ὡς λέγουσιν.

18:15 Οἱ ἔμποροι τούτων οἱ πλουτήσαντες ἀπ' αὐτῆς ἀπὸ μακρόθεν στήσονται διὰ τὸν φόβον τοῦ βασανισμοῦ αὐτῆς κλαίοντες καὶ πενθοῦντες

Οἱ ἔμποροι. Nominative subject of στήσονται.

τούτων. Objective genitive (see also Aune, 3.970). The demonstrative is anaphoric, referring back to the list of cargoes in verses 12-13.

οἱ πλουτήσαντες. Aor act ptc masc nom pl πλουτέω (attributive). Mussies (338) thinks that the aorist participle has the value of a perfect tense since (1) the aorist and perfect are being confused, and (2) the meaning of the participle has been influenced semitically. However, Mussies' observation should be rejected since it is not clear that the aorist and perfect were entirely confused and should not be distinguished (see 5:7 on εἴληφεν), and it incorrectly assumes that the meaning of the aorist participle has been influenced by an underlying Semitic construction.

ἀπ' αὐτῆς. Source.

ἀπὸ μακρόθεν. Spatial. On the meaning, see verse 11.

στήσονται. Fut mid ind 3rd pl ἵστημι.

διὰ τὸν φόβον. Cause.

τοῦ βασανισμοῦ. Objective genitive.

αὐτῆς. Objective genitive.

κλαίοντες. Pres act ptc masc nom pl κλαίω (manner).

πενθοῦντες. Pres act ptc masc nom pl πενθέω (manner). On the possible difference between the two terms, see verse 11 on πενθοῦσιν.

18:16 λέγοντες· οὐαὶ οὐαί, ἡ πόλις ἡ μεγάλη, ἡ περιβεβλημένη βύσσινον καὶ πορφυροῦν καὶ κόκκινον καὶ κεχρυσωμένη [ἐν] χρυσίῳ καὶ λίθῳ τιμίῳ καὶ μαργαρίτῃ,

λέγοντες. Pres act ptc masc nom pl λέγω (manner). Modifies κλαίοντες καὶ πενθοῦντες. On the use of the participle λέγοντες to introduce speech, see 1:17 on λέγων.

οὐαὶ οὐαί. See verse 10 above.

ἡ πόλις ἡ μεγάλη. Nominative functioning as a vocative.

ἡ περιβεβλημένη. Prf mid ptc fem nom sg περιβάλλω (attributive).

βύσσινον καὶ πορφυροῦν καὶ κόκκινον. Accusative direct object of περιβεβλημένη.

κεχρυσωμένη. Prf pass ptc fem nom sg χρυσόω (attributive). Probably the article ἡ governs both περιβεβλημένη and κεχρυσωμένη, which are connected by καί. The piling up of stative participles draws attention to the status of the city and recalls the city's description from 17:4.

[ἐν] χρυσίῳ καὶ λίθῳ τιμίῳ καὶ μαργαρίτῃ. Instrumental.

18:17 ὅτι μιᾷ ὥρᾳ ἠρημώθη ὁ τοσοῦτος πλοῦτος. Καὶ πᾶς κυβερνήτης καὶ πᾶς ὁ ἐπὶ τόπον πλέων καὶ ναῦται καὶ ὅσοι τὴν θάλασσαν ἐργάζονται, ἀπὸ μακρόθεν ἔστησαν

ὅτι. Introduces a causal clause.
μιᾷ ὥρᾳ. Dative of time. On the construction, see verse 10.
ἠρημώθη. Aor pass ind 3rd sg ἐρημόω.
ὁ τοσοῦτος πλοῦτος. Nominative subject of ἠρημώθη.
πᾶς κυβερνήτης καὶ πᾶς ὁ ἐπὶ τόπον πλέων καὶ ναῦται καὶ ὅσοι τὴν θάλασσαν ἐργάζονται. This entire expression functions as the subject of ἔστησαν (despite the comma in NA[28] and UBS[5]).

κυβερνήτης. This term describes "one who is responsible for the management of a ship, *shipmaster*" (BDAG, 574.1), or a "captain" according to Charles (2.105).

ὁ ἐπὶ τόπον πλέων. Lit. "the one sailing upon the place/region." This is an unusual phrase. According to Louw and Nida, the expression means "one who frequently travels by sea" (54.27). τόπον can indicate "an area of any size, gener. specified as a place of habitation" (BDAG, 1011.1). In this case, the term used along with πλέων (travel by sea, sail) would appear to refer to the sea, the place over which the sailors ply their trade. However, it may be better to follow Swete (237) who says the phrase should be understood as "he who sails for (any) part," keeping the usual meaning of τόπον (also Smalley, 458). Though this phrase does not occur elsewhere in the NT, see Acts 27:2.

ὁ ... πλέων καὶ ναῦται. Pres act ptc masc nom sg πλέω (substantival). Nominative subject of ἔστησαν.
ἐπὶ τόπον. Locative.
ὅσοι. Nominative subject of ἐργάζονται.
τὴν θάλασσαν. Accusative direct object of ἐργάζονται.
ἐργάζονται. Pres mid ind 3rd pl ἐργάζομαι.
ἀπὸ μακρόθεν. Locative. On the meaning, see verse 10.
ἔστησαν. Aor act ind 3rd pl ἵστημι.

18:18 καὶ ἔκραζον βλέποντες τὸν καπνὸν τῆς πυρώσεως αὐτῆς λέγοντες· τίς ὁμοία τῇ πόλει τῇ μεγάλῃ;

ἔκραζον. Impf act ind 3rd pl κράζω. In contrast to the previous two groups, the kings and merchants, whose oral response was recorded in the future and present tense indicative forms (kings, vv. 9-10: κλαύσουσιν, κόψονται; merchants, vv. 11-16: κλαίουσιν, πενθοῦσιν), the final group's (shipowners) response is recorded in the imperfect tense forms: ἔκραζον (twice in vv. 18-19). The more remote imperfect form may be used here in order to bring the response of the onlookers to a close and to transition to and highlight the response of heaven and the saints to the fall of Babylon in verse 20 (Mathewson 2010, 157). Grammatically, the response of mourning from the three groups in verses 9-19 contrasts with the rejoicing of heaven in verse 20 (see below).

βλέποντες. Pres act ptc masc nom pl βλέπω (temporal or causal).

τὸν καπνὸν. Accusative direct object of βλέποντες.

τῆς πυρώσεως. Genitive of source.

αὐτῆς. Objective genitive.

λέγοντες. Pres act ptc masc nom pl λέγω (manner). Modifies ἔκραζον. On the use of the participle λέγοντες to introduce speech, see 1:17 on λέγων.

τίς. Nominative subject of a verbless clause. Introduces a deliberative type of question.

ὁμοία. Predicate adjective of a verbless clause.

τῇ πόλει τῇ μεγάλῃ. Dative complement of ὅμοιος.

18:19 καὶ ἔβαλον χοῦν ἐπὶ τὰς κεφαλὰς αὐτῶν καὶ ἔκραζον κλαίοντες καὶ πενθοῦντες, λέγοντες· οὐαὶ οὐαί, ἡ πόλις ἡ μεγάλη, ἐν ᾗ ἐπλούτησαν πάντες οἱ ἔχοντες τὰ πλοῖα ἐν τῇ θαλάσσῃ ἐκ τῆς τιμιότητος αὐτῆς, ὅτι μιᾷ ὥρᾳ ἠρημώθη.

ἔβαλον. Aor act ind 3rd pl βάλλω.

χοῦν. Accusative direct object of ἔβαλον.

ἐπὶ τὰς κεφαλὰς. Locative.

αὐτῶν. Possessive genitive.

ἔκραζον. Impf act ind 3rd pl κράζω. On the aspect, see verse 18.

κλαίοντες. Pres act ptc masc nom pl κλαίω (manner).

πενθοῦντες. Pres act ptc masc nom pl πενθέω (manner).

λέγοντες. Pres act ptc masc nom pl λέγω (manner). On the use of the participle λέγοντες to introduce speech, see 1:17 on λέγων.

οὐαὶ οὐαί. See verse 10 above.

ἡ πόλις ἡ μεγάλη. Nominative functioning as a vocative.

ἐν ᾗ. Means.

ἐπλούτησαν. Aor act ind 3rd pl πλουτέω.

πάντες. Nominative subject of ἐπλούτησαν.

οἱ ἔχοντες. Pres act ptc masc nom pl ἔχω (attributive). It is also possible to take ἔχοντες as substantival with πάντες functioning as an attributive modifier.

τὰ πλοῖα. Accusative direct object of οἱ ἔχοντες.

ἐν τῇ θαλάσσῃ. Locative.

ἐκ τῆς τιμιότητος. Source or cause, modifying ἐπλούτησαν.

αὐτῆς. Possessive genitive.

ὅτι. Introduces a causal clause.

μιᾷ ὥρᾳ. Dative of time (see v. 10).

ἠρημώθη. Aor pass ind 3rd sg ἐρημόω.

18:20 Εὐφραίνου ἐπ' αὐτῇ, οὐρανὲ καὶ οἱ ἅγιοι καὶ οἱ ἀπόστολοι καὶ οἱ προφῆται, ὅτι ἔκρινεν ὁ θεὸς τὸ κρίμα ὑμῶν ἐξ αὐτῆς.

Εὐφραίνου. Pres act impv 2nd sg εὐφραίνω. The shift in mood to the imperative, the present tense, and the vocative form all mark this out as a prominent section that stands in contrast (rejoicing over Babylon's fall) to the response of the three previous groups (mourning over Babylon's fall). Though the subject of the verb is plural (οὐρανέ καὶ οἱ ἅγιοι καὶ οἱ ἀπόστολοι καὶ οἱ προφῆται) the verb is singular. As Turner notes, "The verb, if it stands first, usually agrees with the first subject" (313; cf. Charles, 1.cxli).

ἐπ' αὐτῇ. Basis or cause for the rejoicing.

οὐρανὲ καὶ οἱ ἅγιοι καὶ οἱ ἀπόστολοι καὶ οἱ προφῆται. Vocative (οὐρανέ) and nominatives functioning as vocatives. The article is always used with nominatives when they function as vocatives in Revelation (Aune, 3.972). It is probable that the groups are to be distinguished along the lines of those who are in heaven (οὐρανέ) and those upon the earth (οἱ ἅγιοι καὶ οἱ ἀπόστολοι καὶ οἱ προφῆται) (Beale, 916).

ὅτι ἔκρινεν ὁ θεὸς τὸ κρίμα ὑμῶν ἐξ αὐτῆς. Lit. "For God judged the judgment of you from her." The meaning seems to be that "God judged her because she has judged you" (LN 90.16: "God condemned her for what she did to you").

ὅτι. Introduces a causal clause.

ἔκρινεν. Aor act ind 3rd sg κρίνω.

ὁ θεὸς. Nominative subject of ἔκρινεν.

τὸ κρίμα. Accusative direct object of ἔκρινεν.

ὑμῶν. Objective genitive.

ἐξ αὐτῆς. Source, modifying κρίμα.

Revelation 18:21-24

²¹And a strong angel took a stone like a large millstone and threw it into the sea saying, "Thus with violence Babylon the great city will be thrown down and it will not be found any longer. ²²And the sound of harpists and musicians and flute players and trumpeters will never be heard in you again, and every craftsman of every trade will never be found in you again, and the sound of the mill will not be heard in you any longer, ²³and the light of the lamp will not shine in you any longer, and the sound of the bridegroom and the bride will not be heard in you any longer; for your merchants were the great ones of the earth, for by your sorcery all the nations were led astray, ²⁴and in it was found the blood of the prophets and saints and of all who were slain upon the earth."

18:21 Καὶ ἦρεν εἷς ἄγγελος ἰσχυρὸς λίθον ὡς μύλινον μέγαν καὶ ἔβαλεν εἰς τὴν θάλασσαν λέγων· οὕτως ὁρμήματι βληθήσεται Βαβυλὼν ἡ μεγάλη πόλις καὶ οὐ μὴ εὑρεθῇ ἔτι.

ἦρεν. Aor act ind 3rd sg αἴρω.

εἷς ἄγγελος ἰσχυρὸς. Nominative subject of ἦρεν. On the function of εἷς here, Caragounis notes that in the "NT the cardinal numbers, εἷς, μία, ἕν, are losing their numerical value and are being reduced to an indefinite pronoun" (113).

λίθον. Accusative direct object of ἦρεν.

ὡς μύλινον μέγαν. Comparison.

ἔβαλεν. Aor act ind 3rd sg βάλλω.

εἰς τὴν θάλασσαν. Locative.

λέγων. Pres act ptc masc nom sg λέγω (manner). On the use of the participle λέγων to introduce speech, see 1:17 on λέγων.

οὕτως. Manner.

ὁρμήματι. Dative of manner.

βληθήσεται. Fut pass ind 3rd sg βάλλω.

Βαβυλὼν. Nominative subject of βληθήσεται.

ἡ μεγάλη πόλις. Nominative in apposition to Βαβυλὼν.

οὐ μὴ ... ἔτι. With a negative the adverb ἔτι should be translated "no longer" or "not ... any longer" (BDAG, 400.1.b.β).

εὑρεθῇ. Aor pass subj 3rd sg εὑρίσκω. The subjunctive is used with οὐ μή, which expresses emphatic negation.

18:22 καὶ φωνὴ κιθαρῳδῶν καὶ μουσικῶν καὶ αὐλητῶν καὶ σαλπιστῶν οὐ μὴ ἀκουσθῇ ἐν σοὶ ἔτι, καὶ πᾶς τεχνίτης πάσης τέχνης οὐ μὴ εὑρεθῇ ἐν σοὶ ἔτι, καὶ φωνὴ μύλου οὐ μὴ ἀκουσθῇ ἐν σοὶ ἔτι,

φωνὴ. Nominative subject of ἀκουσθῇ.

κιθαρῳδῶν καὶ μουσικῶν καὶ αὐλητῶν καὶ σαλπιστῶν. Genitive of source or subjective genitive.

οὐ μὴ ... ἔτι. See verse 21.

ἀκουσθῇ. Aor pass subj 3rd sg ἀκούω. The subjunctive is used with οὐ μὴ, which expresses emphatic negation.

ἐν σοὶ. Locative.

πᾶς τεχνίτης. Nominative subject of εὑρεθῇ.

πάσης τέχνης. Objective genitive.

οὐ μὴ ... ἔτι. See verse 21.

εὑρεθῇ. Aor pass subj 3rd sg εὑρίσκω. The subjunctive is used with οὐ μὴ, which expresses emphatic negation.

ἐν σοὶ. Locative.

φωνὴ. Nominative subject of ἀκουσθῇ.

μύλου. Genitive of source or subjective genitive.

οὐ μὴ ... ἔτι. See verse 21.

ἀκουσθῇ. Aor pass subj 3rd sg ἀκούω. The subjunctive is used with οὐ μὴ, which expresses emphatic negation.

ἐν σοὶ. Locative.

18:23 καὶ φῶς λύχνου οὐ μὴ φάνῃ ἐν σοὶ ἔτι, καὶ φωνὴ νυμφίου καὶ νύμφης οὐ μὴ ἀκουσθῇ ἐν σοὶ ἔτι· ὅτι οἱ ἔμποροί σου ἦσαν οἱ μεγιστᾶνες τῆς γῆς, ὅτι ἐν τῇ φαρμακείᾳ σου ἐπλανήθησαν πάντα τὰ ἔθνη,

φῶς. Nominative subject of φάνῃ.

λύχνου. Genitive of source.

οὐ μὴ ... ἔτι. See verse 21.

φάνῃ. Aor act subj 3rd sg φαίνω. The subjunctive is used with οὐ μὴ, which expresses emphatic negation.

ἐν σοὶ. Locative.

φωνὴ. Nominative subject of ἀκουσθῇ.

νυμφίου καὶ νύμφης. Genitive of source or subjective genitive.

οὐ μὴ ... ἔτι. See verse 21.

ἀκουσθῇ. Aor pass subj 3rd sg ἀκούω. The subjunctive is used with οὐ μὴ, which expresses emphatic negation.

ἐν σοὶ. Locative.

ὅτι. Introduces a causal clause, providing a reason for the removal of all these things as a judgment on the great city. That is, Rome is judged because of its economic exploitation of the rest of the empire.

οἱ ἔμποροί. Nominative subject of ἦσαν. The accenting is due to the enclitic σου that follows.

σου. Genitive of relationship.

ἦσαν. Impf act ind 3rd pl εἰμί.

οἱ μεγιστᾶνες. Predicate nominative. This noun refers to "a person of particularly great importance and high status" (LN 87.41).

τῆς γῆς. Genitive of subordination or genitive expressing location.

ὅτι. Introduces a causal clause. While this could provide a reason for the previous ὅτι clause (Swete, 264), this would suggest that the "great ones" became rich because of the city's sorcery and all the nations were deluded. Instead, it makes better sense to interpret the sorcery and delusion of the nations as providing a further reason for the removal of all these things as a judgment on the great city.

ἐν τῇ φαρμακείᾳ. Instrumental.

σου. Subjective genitive.

ἐπλανήθησαν. Aor pass ind 3rd pl πλανάω.

πάντα τὰ ἔθνη. Nominative subject of ἐπλανήθησαν. Neuter plural subjects commonly take plural verbs in Revelation when they refer to personal beings.

18:24 καὶ ἐν αὐτῇ αἷμα προφητῶν καὶ ἁγίων εὑρέθη καὶ πάντων τῶν ἐσφαγμένων ἐπὶ τῆς γῆς.

ἐν αὐτῇ. Locative. The antecedent is Βαβυλὼν ἡ μεγάλη πόλις in verse 21. As part of the ὅτι clause (v. 23), this verse provides a further reason for the removal of all these things as a judgment on the great city (Blount, 337).

αἷμα. Nominative subject of εὑρέθη. "Blood" is a metonymy for "death" by substituting the means (shedding of blood) for the effect (death).

προφητῶν καὶ ἁγίων … καὶ πάντων τῶν ἐσφαγμένων. Possessive genitive.

εὑρέθη. Aor pass ind 3rd sg εὑρίσκω.

τῶν ἐσφαγμένων. Prf pass ptc masc gen pl σφάζω (attributive). It is also possible to take ἐσφαγμένων as substantival with πάντων in attributive relation to it.

ἐπὶ τῆς γῆς. Locative.

Revelation 19:1-10

¹After these things I heard as a great voice of a large multitude in heaven saying, "Hallelujah! Salvation and glory and power belong to our God, ²for true and just are his judgments, for he has judged the great prostitute who corrupted the earth with her fornication, and he has avenged the blood of his servants shed by her hand." ³And a second time the voice said, "Hallelujah! Indeed her smoke rises forever and ever." ⁴And the twenty four elders and the four living creatures fell down and

worshiped God who is seated on the throne, saying, "Amen. Hallelujah!" ⁵And a voice came out from the throne saying, "Praise to our God, all his slaves and those who fear him, the small and the great." ⁶And I heard as a voice of a large multitude and the sound of many waters and the sound of strong thunder saying, "Hallelujah, for the Lord God Almighty reigns. ⁷Let us rejoice and let us exalt and let us give him glory, for the marriage of the Lamb has come and his bride has prepared herself"; ⁸and it was given to her to clothe herself in fine, clean pure linen; for the fine linen is the righteous deeds of the saints. ⁹And he said to me, "Write. Blessed are those who have been invited to the marriage supper of the Lamb." And he said to me, "These are the true words of God." ¹⁰And I fell down before his feet to worship him. And he said to me, "See that you do not. I am your fellow slave and of your brothers who have the testimony of Jesus. Worship God. For the testimony of Jesus is the spirit of prophecy."

19:1 Μετὰ ταῦτα ἤκουσα ὡς φωνὴν μεγάλην ὄχλου πολλοῦ ἐν τῷ οὐρανῷ λεγόντων· ἁλληλουϊά· ἡ σωτηρία καὶ ἡ δόξα καὶ ἡ δύναμις τοῦ θεοῦ ἡμῶν,

Μετὰ ταῦτα. Temporal (see 4:1).

ἤκουσα. Aor act ind 1st sg ἀκούω.

ὡς φωνὴν μεγάλην. Comparison. Fills the slot of the direct object of ἤκουσα and assumes an implied direct object: "I heard *something* like a loud voice."

ὄχλου πολλοῦ. Genitive of source or subjective genitive.

ἐν τῷ οὐρανῷ. Locative.

λεγόντων. Pres act ptc masc gen pl λέγω. Complement in an object-complement double genitive construction with ὡς φωνὴν μεγάλην. The genitive case (rather than the expected accusative) and masculine gender probably come from ὄχλου πολλοῦ (it is the voice of the great crowd that John hears). The plural participle is a construction according to sense reflecting the collective (plural) sense of ὄχλου πολλοῦ (Mussies, 138). On the use of the participle λεγόντων to introduce speech, see 1:17 on λέγων.

ἁλληλουϊά. An exclamation. A Greek transliteration of the Hebrew הללו־יה meaning "praise Yahweh."

ἡ σωτηρία καὶ ἡ δόξα καὶ ἡ δύναμις. Nominative subject of a verbless clause.

τοῦ θεοῦ. Possessive genitive in a doxology (NIV: "belong to our God").

ἡμῶν. Genitive of subordination.

19:2 ὅτι ἀληθιναὶ καὶ δίκαιαι αἱ κρίσεις αὐτοῦ· ὅτι ἔκρινεν τὴν πόρνην τὴν μεγάλην ἥτις ἔφθειρεν τὴν γῆν ἐν τῇ πορνείᾳ αὐτῆς, καὶ ἐξεδίκησεν τὸ αἷμα τῶν δούλων αὐτοῦ ἐκ χειρὸς αὐτῆς.

ὅτι. Introduces a causal clause.
ἀληθιναὶ καὶ δίκαιαι. Predicate adjective of a verbless clause.
αἱ κρίσεις. Nominative subject of a verbless clause.
αὐτοῦ. Subjective genitive.
ὅτι. Introduces a causal clause. It is not clear what this ὅτι clause modifies. It is possible that it is parallel with the previous ὅτι clause and provides a further reason for the celebration in verse 1 (Mounce, 337 n. 4). However, due to the emphasis in this clause on judging and avenging, it seems more natural to take it as modifying the first ὅτι clause and providing the basis for God's judgments being true and righteous by introducing a specific instance of those judgments.
ἔκρινεν. Aor act ind 3rd sg κρίνω.
τὴν πόρνην τὴν μεγάλην. Accusative direct object of ἔκρινεν.
ἥτις. Nominative subject of ἔφθειρεν.
ἔφθειρεν. Impf act ind 3rd sg φθείρω. Smalley says that the imperfect tense "is a reminder of the continuous, as well as pernicious, influence of Babylon on the world" (477). However, it is inappropriate to interpret the imperfect as denoting continuous or pernicious action; rather, it conceives of the action as in progress and remote, hence providing supporting or explanatory material (see "Verbal Aspect" in the Introduction).
τὴν γῆν. Accusative direct object of ἔφθειρεν.
ἐν τῇ πορνείᾳ. Instrumental.
αὐτῆς. Subjective genitive.
ἐξεδίκησεν. Aor act ind 3rd sg ἐκδικέω.
τὸ αἷμα. Accusative direct object of ἐξεδίκησεν. "Blood" is a metonomy for death substituting the means (shedding blood) for the effect (death).
τῶν δούλων. Possessive genitive.
αὐτοῦ. Possessive genitive.
ἐκ χειρὸς. The PP may designate the persons "*on* whom vengeance is taken, or who is punished" (BDAG, 301.2). However, it is also possible to take it as the *cause* or *means* of the shedding of blood: "The blood shed by her hands." This would fit the accusation against Babylon and reason for her judgment in 18:24: the blood of those slain was found in her.
αὐτῆς. Possessive genitive.

19:3 Καὶ δεύτερον εἴρηκαν· ἁλληλουϊά· καὶ ὁ καπνὸς αὐτῆς ἀναβαίνει εἰς τοὺς αἰῶνας τῶν αἰώνων.

δεύτερον. Temporal. This is not a reference to a second voice. The neuter is used to indicate time: "A second time" (Mussies, 220).
εἴρηκαν. Prf act ind 3rd pl λέγω. Fanning (303) thinks that this is an example of the perfect tense used with an aoristic sense (see also BDF §343.1; Wallace, 579; Beale, 929). The fact that εἴρηκα is used in 7:14, however, immediately followed by the aorist εἶπεν, makes it unlikely that εἴρηκαν is simply the semantic equivalent of an aorist.
ἁλληλουϊά. See verse 1. "[T]he second Hallelujah is not merely formal, but adds strength to the first" (Swete, 243).
καὶ. Smalley (478) interprets the conjunction as providing the basis for the praise (cf. Aune, 3.1015). While this may be true conceptually, the καί should probably been seen as adverbial ("indeed").
ὁ καπνὸς. Nominative subject of ἀναβαίνει.
αὐτῆς. Genitive of source.
ἀναβαίνει. Pres act ind 3rd sg ἀναβαίνω.
εἰς τοὺς αἰῶνας τῶν αἰώνων. Temporal (see 1:18).

19:4 καὶ ἔπεσαν οἱ πρεσβύτεροι οἱ εἴκοσι τέσσαρες καὶ τὰ τέσσαρα ζῷα καὶ προσεκύνησαν τῷ θεῷ τῷ καθημένῳ ἐπὶ τῷ θρόνῳ λέγοντες· ἀμὴν ἁλληλουϊά.

ἔπεσαν. Aor act ind 3rd pl πίπτω.
οἱ πρεσβύτεροι οἱ εἴκοσι τέσσαρες καὶ τὰ τέσσαρα ζῷα. Nominative subject of ἔπεσαν and προσεκύνησαν.
προσεκύνησαν. Aor act ind 3rd pl προσκυνέω.
τῷ θεῷ. Dative direct object of προσεκύνησαν.
καθημένῳ. Pres mid ptc masc dat sg κάθημαι (attributive).
ἐπὶ τῷ θρόνῳ. Locative.
λέγοντες. Pres act ptc masc nom pl λέγω (manner). On the use of the participle λέγοντες to introduce speech, see 1:17 on λέγων.
ἀμὴν ἁλληλουϊά. An exclamation. See 7:12 on ἀμήν . . . ἀμήν, and 19:1, 3 on ἁλληλουϊά.

19:5 Καὶ φωνὴ ἀπὸ τοῦ θρόνου ἐξῆλθεν λέγουσα· αἰνεῖτε τῷ θεῷ ἡμῶν πάντες οἱ δοῦλοι αὐτοῦ [καὶ] οἱ φοβούμενοι αὐτόν, οἱ μικροὶ καὶ οἱ μεγάλοι.

φωνὴ. Nominative subject of ἐξῆλθεν.
ἀπὸ τοῦ θρόνου. Source or direction from which the voice came.
ἐξῆλθεν. Aor act ind 3rd sg ἐξέρχομαι.

λέγουσα. Pres act ptc fem nom sg λέγω (manner). On the use of the participle λέγουσα to introduce speech, see 1:17 on λέγων.

αἰνεῖτε. Pres act impv 2nd pl αἰνέω.

τῷ θεῷ. Dative direct object of αἰνεῖτε.

ἡμῶν. Genitive of subordination.

πάντες οἱ δοῦλοι. Nominative functioning as a vocative.

αὐτοῦ. Possessive genitive.

οἱ φοβούμενοι. Pres mid ptc masc nom pl φοβέομαι (attributive). If the [καί] is accepted as the correct reading (found in A 051 [0229] 𝔐), φοβούμενοι would function substantivally ("those fearing") and would perhaps constitute an additional group to οἱ δοῦλοι. It is difficult to think that the author would conceive of two separate groups, one that serves God, and the other that fears him (contra Swete, 244). If the καί is accepted, it probably functions in an epexegetical manner to further describe οἱ δοῦλοι.

αὐτόν. Accusative direct object of φοβούμενοι.

οἱ μικροὶ καὶ οἱ μεγάλοι. If the [καί] is accepted as the correct reading, then φοβούμενοι could be construed as a substantival participle (see above) and οἱ μικροὶ καὶ οἱ μεγάλοι would stand in apposition to φοβούμενοι. If the [καί] is absent, then οἱ μικροὶ καὶ οἱ μεγάλοι would stand in apposition to πάντες οἱ δοῦλοι. The phrase constitutes a merism referring to people of every social and economic status.

19:6 Καὶ ἤκουσα ὡς φωνὴν ὄχλου πολλοῦ καὶ ὡς φωνὴν ὑδάτων πολλῶν καὶ ὡς φωνὴν βροντῶν ἰσχυρῶν λεγόντων· ἁλληλουϊά, ὅτι ἐβασίλευσεν κύριος ὁ θεὸς [ἡμῶν] ὁ παντοκράτωρ.

ἤκουσα. Aor act ind 1st sg ἀκούω.

ὡς φωνὴν ... ὡς φωνὴν ... ὡς φωνὴν. Comparison. The comparative phrase assumes an implied direct object of ἤκουσα: "I heard *something* like a voice."

ὄχλου πολλοῦ. Genitive of source or subjective genitive.

ὑδάτων πολλῶν. Genitive of source or subjective genitive.

βροντῶν ἰσχυρῶν. Genitive of source or subjective genitive.

λεγόντων. Pres act ptc masc gen pl λέγω. Complement in an object-complement double genitive construction with φωνήν. While the accusative case and singular number is expected, so that the genitive plural is grammatically incongruent, the genitive case and plural number have been influenced by the genitive ὄχλου πολλοῦ and ὑδάτων πολλῶν καὶ ὡς φωνὴν βροντῶν ἰσχυρῶν. On the use of the participle λεγόντων to introduce speech, see 1:17 on λέγων.

ἁλληλουϊά. See verses 1 and 3.

ὅτι. Introduces a causal clause.

ἐβασίλευσεν. Aor act ind 3rd sg βασιλεύω. Though this could be construed as a so-called ingressive aorist ("became king" or "began to reign"), preferred by most commentaries (Aune, 3.1016; Blount, 340; Smalley, 481; Osborne, 672; Beale, 932), it may be preferrable to understand it with present temporal or even timeless reference simply summarizing God's activity of reigning: "the Lord reigns." There is no reason to limit this to an ingressive notion (the entrance into the state of reigning); rather, the entire state is being summarized by the aorist.

κύριος. Nominative subject of ἐβασίλευσεν.

ὁ θεὸς. Nominative in apposition to κύριος.

[ἡμῶν]. If original, a genitive of subordination. Some manuscripts (A 1006 1841) do not include ἡμῶν. The fact that the pronoun is not included in other usages of the title (κύριος ὁ θεὸς ὁ παντοκράτωρ) in Revelation (4:8; 11:17; 15:3; 16:7; 21:22) may suggest that it was omitted here to conform to the other instances. However, it could also have been added to conform to the use of the pronoun with the two other instances of "God" in verses 1 and 5 (Metzger, 685).

ὁ παντοκράτωρ. Nominative in apposition to κύριος.

19:7 χαίρωμεν καὶ ἀγαλλιῶμεν καὶ δώσωμεν τὴν δόξαν αὐτῷ, ὅτι ἦλθεν ὁ γάμος τοῦ ἀρνίου καὶ ἡ γυνὴ αὐτοῦ ἡτοίμασεν ἑαυτὴν

χαίρωμεν. Pres act subj 1st pl χαίρω (hortatory subjunctive). The three hortatory subjunctives suggest that this section is particularly prominent (foregrounded) as the climax to the response to Babylon's fall in 19:1-8. Verses 1-8 indicate a progression from the voice of a great multitude (v. 1) to another voice (v. 3) to the voice of the twenty-four elders and four living creatures (v. 4) to a voice depicted with the threefold great crowd, many waters, and strong thunder (v. 6). The last voice calls for everyone to join in a climactic celebration in the form of three hortatory subjunctives (with the 1st pl) of the arrival of the wedding supper of the Lamb and his bride, which stands in stark contrast to the judgment of the prostitute.

ἀγαλλιῶμεν. Pres act subj 1st pl ἀγαλλιάω (hortatory subjunctive).

δώσωμεν. Aor act subj 1st pl δίδωμι (hortatory subjunctive).

τὴν δόξαν. Accusative direct object of δώσωμεν.

αὐτῷ. Dative indirect object of δώσωμεν.

ὅτι. Introduces a causal clause.

ἦλθεν. Aor act ind 3rd sg ἔρχομαι. Aune labels this an "aorist used with perfective value" (3.1017). However, this is more dependent on English translation than on a valid meaning and usage of the aorist tense. The aorist is used here of an action that has just taken place, and which probably has some overlap with present time (Mathewson 2010,

55–56). As Fanning (275) and Wallace (565) note, it is often difficult to distinguish an event in the recent past from the immediate present.

ὁ γάμος. Nominative subject of ἦλθεν.
τοῦ ἀρνίου. Subjective genitive.
ἡ γυνὴ. Nominative subject of ἡτοίμασεν.
αὐτοῦ. Genitive of relationship.
ἡτοίμασεν. Aor act ind 3rd sg ἑτοιμάζω.
ἑαυτὴν. Accusative direct object of ἡτοίμασεν.

19:8 καὶ ἐδόθη αὐτῇ ἵνα περιβάληται βύσσινον λαμπρὸν καθαρόν· τὸ γὰρ βύσσινον τὰ δικαιώματα τῶν ἁγίων ἐστίν.

ἐδόθη. Aor pass ind 3rd sg δίδωμι. The implied agent here is probably God or the Lamb.
αὐτῇ. Dative indirect object of ἐδόθη.
ἵνα. Introduces a substantive clause that in its entirety functions as the subject of ἐδόθη.
περιβάληται. Aor mid subj 3rd pl περιβάλλω. Subjunctive with ἵνα.
βύσσινον λαμπρὸν καθαρόν. Accusative direct object of περιβάληται.
τὸ . . . βύσσινον. Nominative subject of ἐστίν.
γὰρ. Explanatory.
τὰ δικαιώματα. Predicate nominative.
τῶν ἁγίων. Subjective genitive.
ἐστίν. Pres act ind 3rd sg εἰμί.

19:9 Καὶ λέγει μοι· γράψον· μακάριοι οἱ εἰς τὸ δεῖπνον τοῦ γάμου τοῦ ἀρνίου κεκλημένοι. καὶ λέγει μοι· οὗτοι οἱ λόγοι ἀληθινοὶ τοῦ θεοῦ εἰσιν.

λέγει. Pres act ind 3rd sg λέγω. Historical or narrative present (see 4:5 on ἐκπορεύονται). Here it functions to highlight the angel's command to John to write (v. 9) and the command not to worship him (the angel) but to worship God (v. 10). The implied subject is the angel who begins this visionary segment in 17:1-2.
μοι. Dative indirect object of λέγει.
γράψον. Aor act impv 2nd sg γράφω. The content of what John is to write is μακάριοι οἱ εἰς τὸ δεῖπνον τοῦ γάμου τοῦ ἀρνίου κεκλημένοι.
μακάριοι. Predicate nominative of a verbless clause.
οἱ . . . κεκλημένοι. Prf pass ptc masc nom pl καλέω (substantival). Nominative subject of a verbless clause.
εἰς τὸ δεῖπνον. Direction or goal.
τοῦ γάμου. Attributive genitive.
τοῦ ἀρνίου. Subjective genitive.

λέγει. Pres act ind 3rd sg λέγω. On the significance of the present tense, see λέγει above.

μοι. Dative indirect object of λέγει.

οὗτοι. Nominative subject of εἰσιν. The antecedent of οὗτοι is at least the previous saying, "Blessed are those who are called to the wedding supper of the Lamb." But in analogy to the similar saying in 21:5b, it probably encompasses a much larger section, perhaps all of verses 1-9a and the speeches there, or it may refer only to verses 7-9a and the marriage metaphor (Beale, 945).

οἱ λόγοι ἀληθινοί. Predicate adjective.

τοῦ θεοῦ. Genitive of source or subjective genitive.

εἰσιν. Pres act ind 3rd pl εἰμί. On the loss of accent, see 1:8.

19:10 καὶ ἔπεσα ἔμπροσθεν τῶν ποδῶν αὐτοῦ προσκυνῆσαι αὐτῷ. καὶ λέγει μοι· ὅρα μή· σύνδουλός σού εἰμι καὶ τῶν ἀδελφῶν σου τῶν ἐχόντων τὴν μαρτυρίαν Ἰησοῦ· τῷ θεῷ προσκύνησον. ἡ γὰρ μαρτυρία Ἰησοῦ ἐστιν τὸ πνεῦμα τῆς προφητείας.

ἔπεσα. Aor act ind 1st sg πίπτω.

ἔμπροσθεν τῶν ποδῶν. Locative.

αὐτοῦ. Possessive genitive.

προσκυνῆσαι. Aor act inf προσκυνέω (purpose).

αὐτῷ. Dative direct object of προσκυνῆσαι.

λέγει. Pres act ind 3rd sg λέγω. On the significance of the present tense, see verse 9. The angel's response introduced with the present tense λέγει is foregrounded over against John's incorrect response recorded in the aorist (ἔπεσα).

μοι. Dative indirect object of λέγει.

ὅρα μή. This is probably an elliptical expression for something like ὅρα μὴ ποιήσῃς τοῦτο (Swete, 249).

ὅρα. Aor act impv 2nd sg ὁράω.

σύνδουλός. Nominative subject of εἰμι. The accenting is due to the enclitic εἰμι that follows.

σού. With the σύν- compound noun, σύνδουλός, the genitive here indicates association: "Fellow servant with you" (Wallace, 129). The accenting is due to the enclitic εἰμι that follows.

εἰμι. Pres act ind 3rd sg εἰμί. On the loss of accent, see 1:8.

τῶν ἀδελφῶν. See σού above.

σου. Genitive of relationship.

τῶν ἐχόντων. Pres act ptc masc gen pl ἔχω (attributive).

τὴν μαρτυρίαν. Accusative direct object of ἐχόντων.

Ἰησοῦ. Objective genitive. It is possible that this should be understood as a subjective genitive (the testimony that Jesus bore). However, the fact that the testimony is something that they have (ἐχόντων) along with the clear references to the saints testifying/having testimony elsewhere (6:9; 11:7; 12:11; 17:6) as a cause for their death, suggests that the genitive Ἰησοῦ here should be taken as objective (the testimony about Jesus). Beale (947) opts for both a subjective and objective genitive reading (cf. Smalley, 487). However, this confuses grammatical ambiguity with semantic "fullness" of interpretation.

τῷ θεῷ. Dative direct object of προσκύνησον. The fronting of the complement is for emphasis, to draw attention to the proper object of John's worship over against his worship of the angel.

προσκύνησον. Aor act impv 2nd sg προσκυνέω.

ἡ ... μαρτυρία. Nominative subject of ἐστιν.

γὰρ. Broadly strengthens the entire preceding response of the angel (cf. Runge, 52).

Ἰησοῦ. Objective genitive. See above.

ἐστιν. Pres act ind 3rd sg εἰμί. On the loss of accent, see 1:8.

τὸ πνεῦμα. Predicate nominative.

τῆς προφητείας. The genitive here could be taken as "the prophetic Spirit" (Aune, 3.1038) or in the sense of "the Spirit that produces/inspires prophecy." The entire phrase ἡ ... μαρτυρία Ἰησοῦ ἐστιν τὸ πνεῦμα τῆς προφητείας could be be understood as "it is ultimately the Spirit of God who moves the faithful to give needed testimony to the truth about the Lamb" (Smalley, 487).

Revelation 19:11-16

[11]And I saw heaven opened, and look, a white horse and one seated upon it called faithful and true, and in righteousness he judges and makes war. [12]And his eyes are [as] flames of fire, and upon his head are many crowns; he has a name written that no one knows except him, [13]and he is clothed with a garment dipped in blood, and his name is called "the Word of God." [14]And the armies in heaven were following him on white horses, clothed in fine linen, white and clean. [15]And out of his mouth comes a sharp sword, in order that with it he might strike down the nations, and he will shepherd them with an iron rod, and he tramples the winepress of the wine of the wrath of the anger of God the Almighty, [16]and he has upon his garment and upon his thigh a name written: "King of kings and Lord of lords."

19:11 Καὶ εἶδον τὸν οὐρανὸν ἠνεῳγμένον, καὶ ἰδοὺ ἵππος λευκὸς καὶ ὁ καθήμενος ἐπ' αὐτὸν [καλούμενος] πιστὸς καὶ ἀληθινός, καὶ ἐν δικαιοσύνῃ κρίνει καὶ πολεμεῖ.

The concentration of present and perfect tense forms in both indicative verbs and participles in such a short textual space suggests that this section functions as a peak in the discourse (Mathewson 2010, 164). Here the "open heaven" *(οὐρανὸν ἠνεῳγμένον,* perfect) announces the coming of the Messiah to bring the visionary narrative to its resolution in a climactic scene of judgment and salvation, much like the same language in 4:1 inaugurates the vision. The present and perfect verb forms in verses 11-16 function in a highly descriptive manner to depict important features of the rider, not necessarily to refer to any specific activities. Following the description of the rider in verses 11-16, where the present and perfect tense forms serve to slow the narrative down and focus on the rider on the white horse, verses 19-21 are of a different character, shifting to a series of aorist tense forms that depict in summary fashion the actual end-time battle and move the narrative forward to its conslusion.

Καὶ εἶδον. This phrase begins a new visionary unit. This is also confirmed by οὐρανὸν ἠνεῳγμένον, which parallels the beginning of John's vision in 4:1.

εἶδον. Aor act ind 1st sg ὁράω.

τὸν οὐρανὸν. Accusative direct object of εἶδον.

ἠνεῳγμένον. Prf pass ptc masc acc sg ἀνοίγω. Complement in an object-complement double accusative construction. The perfect aspect draws attention to heaven in the state of being open in preparation for the vision, and recalls the open door to heaven in 4:1 (θύρα ἠνεῳγμένη ἐν τῷ οὐρανῷ).

ἰδού. A marker of attention that deictically functions to make the following statement emphatic. On the form, see 1:7. Here it draws attention to the rider on the white horse, who will be described in detail.

ἵππος λευκός. Nominative subject of a verbless clause.

ὁ καθήμενος. Pres mid ptc masc nom sg κάθημαι (substantival). Nominative subject of a verbless clause.

ἐπ' αὐτὸν. Locative.

[καλούμενος]. Pres pass ptc masc nom sg καλέω. The participle καλούμενος can be found in different locations in relationship to πιστὸς ... καὶ ἀληθινός in ℵ (1006) 1611 1841 1854 2028 2030 2053 2062 𝔐ᴷ, while A 051 𝔐ᴬ omit it. Most likely, καλούμενος was inserted with πιστὸς καὶ ἀληθινός to make clear that it is a title, consistent with Rev 3:14, rather than just a description of the rider (Aune, 3.1042; contra Metzger, 685–86).

πιστὸς καὶ ἀληθινός. Predicate adjective of a verbless clause. If καλούμενος is read (see above), it functions as a double nominative construction with the passive verb from a double accusative construction: "I call the one sitting upon (the horse) faithful and true" (see Culy 2009, 83–87).

ἐν δικαιοσύνῃ. Manner.

κρίνει. Pres act ind 3rd sg κρίνω. Historical or narrative present (see 4:5 on ἐκπορεύονται). The present tense κρίνει and πολεμεῖ function to highlight important characteristic features of the rider on the horse. The present tense here is timeless, in that it describes what is always true of the rider rather than referring to any specific event (Smalley, 488, calls them gnomic).

πολεμεῖ. Pres act ind 3rd sg πολεμέω. On the significance of the present tense, see above on κρίνει.

19:12 οἱ δὲ ὀφθαλμοὶ αὐτοῦ [ὡς] φλὸξ πυρός, καὶ ἐπὶ τὴν κεφαλὴν αὐτοῦ διαδήματα πολλά, ἔχων ὄνομα γεγραμμένον ὃ οὐδεὶς οἶδεν εἰ μὴ αὐτός,

οἱ ... ὀφθαλμοί. Nominative subject of a verbless clause.

δέ. Development. The conjunction δέ departs from the commonly used καί in Revelation. δέ is used to indicate that the author signals a new or distinct development in the story (Runge, 31). Here the δέ is used to shift the focus to a description of the appearance and dress of the rider (Swete, 251).

αὐτοῦ. Possessive genitive.

[ὡς] φλόξ. Functions as the predicate of a verbless clause.

πυρός. Attributive genitive or epexegetical genitive.

ἐπὶ τὴν κεφαλὴν. Locative.

αὐτοῦ. Possessive genitive.

διαδήματα πολλά. Nominative subject of verbless clause.

ἔχων. Pres act ptc masc nom sg ἔχω. The gender of the participle ἔχων is probably dependent on ὁ καθήμενος in verse 11. The participle may function to further describe the one seated (ὁ καθήμενος) on the white horse, or it may function like a finite verb (Aune, 3.1042; Wallace, 653; see 1:16 on ἔχων).

ὄνομα. Accusative direct object of ἔχων.

γεγραμμένον. Prf pass ptc neut acc sg γράφω (attributive). This is the first of a string of five perfect participles in verses 12-16 used to refer to the rider (γεγραμμένον, περιβεβλημένος, βεβαμμένον, ἐνδεδυμένοι, γεγραμμένον). This cluster of participles draws attention to the status and dress of the rider on the horse (see v. 11).

ὅ. Accusative direct object of οἶδεν.

οὐδείς. Nominative subject of οἶδεν.
οἶδεν. Prf act ind 3rd sg οἶδα.
εἰ μὴ. "If not, except."
αὐτός. Nominative subject of implied οἶδεν.

19:13 καὶ περιβεβλημένος ἱμάτιον βεβαμμένον αἵματι, καὶ κέκληται τὸ ὄνομα αὐτοῦ ὁ λόγος τοῦ θεοῦ.

περιβεβλημένος. Prf mid ptc masc nom sg περιβάλλω. The participle is difficult to classify. Most likely it further describes the one sitting (ὁ καθήμενος) on the white horse. On the perfect tense form, see verse 12 on γεγραμμένον.
ἱμάτιον. Accusative direct object of περιβεβλημένος.
βεβαμμένον. Prf pass ptc neut acc sg βάπτω (attributive). On the perfect tense form, see verse 12 on γεγραμμένον. On the complicated text-critical issue and arguments for βεβαμμένον as the correct reading, see Aune (3.1043).
αἵματι. Dative of location.
κέκληται. Prf pass ind 3rd sg καλέω. On the significance of the perfect tense form, see verse 11.
τὸ ὄνομα. Nominative subject of κέκληται.
αὐτοῦ. Possessive genitive.
ὁ λόγος. Along with ὄνομα the nominative λόγος forms a double nominative construction with a passive verb from a double accusative construction: "I called his name the word" (Culy 2009, 83–87).
τοῦ θεοῦ. Genitive of source or subjective genitive.

19:14 Καὶ τὰ στρατεύματα [τὰ] ἐν τῷ οὐρανῷ ἠκολούθει αὐτῷ ἐφ' ἵπποις λευκοῖς, ἐνδεδυμένοι βύσσινον λευκὸν καθαρόν.

τὰ στρατεύματα. Nominative subject of ἠκολούθει.
[τὰ]. If original the article functions as an adjectivizer, turning the entire PP into an attributive modifier of στρατεύματα: Lit. "the in-the-heaven armies."
ἐν τῷ οὐρανῷ. Locative.
ἠκολούθει. Impf act ind 3rd sg ἀκολουθέω. Neuter plural subjects commonly take a singular verb. The function of the imperfect to indicate offline material suggests that the army here serves a background purpose. It keeps the focus on the rider, and possibly reflects the fact that the army plays no real role in the actual battle later in verses 20-21. The Lamb himself defeats their enemies.
αὐτῷ. Dative direct object of ἠκολούθει.
ἐφ' ἵπποις λευκοῖς. Locative.

ἐνδεδυμένοι. Prf mid ptc masc nom pl ἐνδύω (manner). The masculine gender is a construction according to sense (στρατεύματα refers to persons) (Robertson, 412).

βύσσινον λευκὸν καθαρόν. Accusative direct object of ἐνδεδυμένοι.

19:15 καὶ ἐκ τοῦ στόματος αὐτοῦ ἐκπορεύεται ῥομφαία ὀξεῖα, ἵνα ἐν αὐτῇ πατάξῃ τὰ ἔθνη, καὶ αὐτὸς ποιμανεῖ αὐτοὺς ἐν ῥάβδῳ σιδηρᾷ, καὶ αὐτὸς πατεῖ τὴν ληνὸν τοῦ οἴνου τοῦ θυμοῦ τῆς ὀργῆς τοῦ θεοῦ τοῦ παντοκράτορος,

ἐκ τοῦ στόματος. Source. The fronting of the PP draws attention to the rider's mouth as the source of judgment (cf. v. 21 below).

αὐτοῦ. Possessive genitive.

ἐκπορεύεται. Pres mid ind 3rd sg ἐκπορεύομαι. On the significance of the present tense, see verse 11 on κρίνει.

ῥομφαία ὀξεῖα. Nominative subject of ἐκπορεύεται.

ἵνα. Introduces a purpose clause.

ἐν αὐτῇ. Instrumental.

πατάξῃ. Aor act subj 3rd sg πατάσσω. Subjunctive with ἵνα.

τὰ ἔθνη. Accusative direct object of πατάξῃ.

αὐτὸς. Nominative subject of ποιμανεῖ. The pronoun is emphatic.

ποιμανεῖ. Fut act ind 3rd sg ποιμαίνω. Although the term can positively mean "to shepherd or lead and provide for" (LN 44.3, 36.2), it can also mean "to rule over or govern" (LN, 37.57) with more negative connotations (BDAG, 842.2.a.γ). The latter is the case here given the context of judgment.

αὐτοὺς. Accusative direct object of ποιμανεῖ. The antecedent is ἔθνη. This is another example of a construction according to sense, with a masculine pronoun having as its antecedent a neuter noun. The nations refer to people, hence the masculine αὐτοὺς.

ἐν ῥάβδῳ σιδηρᾷ. Instrumental.

αὐτὸς. Nominative subject of πατεῖ. The pronoun is emphatic.

πατεῖ. Pres act ind 3rd sg πατέω. On the significance of the present tense, see verse 11 on κρίνει.

τὴν ληνὸν. Accusative direct object of πατεῖ.

τοῦ οἴνου. The notion indicated by the genitive may be that the wine is contained in the winepress (genitive of content). As Aune (3.1043) notes, "This string of five gens. is the longest such string in Revelation." This piling up of genitives functions to lend prominence to the display of God's wrath. This is more important than the labels given to each individual genitive.

τοῦ θυμοῦ. Genitive of apposition.

τῆς ὀργῆς. Attributive genitive.

τοῦ θεοῦ. Genitive of source or subjective genitive.

τοῦ παντοκράτορος. Genitive in apposition to τοῦ θεοῦ or epexegetical genitive.

19:16 καὶ ἔχει ἐπὶ τὸ ἱμάτιον καὶ ἐπὶ τὸν μηρὸν αὐτοῦ ὄνομα γεγραμμένον· Βασιλεὺς βασιλέων καὶ κύριος κυρίων.

ἔχει. Pres act ind 3rd sg ἔχω. On the significance of the present tense, see verse 11 on κρίνει.

ἐπὶ τὸ ἱμάτιον. Locative.

ἐπὶ τὸν μηρὸν. Locative.

αὐτοῦ. Possessive genitive.

ὄνομα. Accusative direct object of ἔχει.

γεγραμμένον. Prf pass ptc neut acc sg γράφω (attributive).

Βασιλεὺς. Nominative of appellation. The name Βασιλεύς seems to stand in apposition to ὄνομα, so that one would expect the accusative case. However, names frequently appear in the nominative case even when another case is expected. But here it may be the predicate of a verbless clause: "(It is) King of kings."

βασιλέων. The genitive could function as a genitive of subordination, with the idea being that the Βασιλεύς is superior over the βασιλέων in the genitive ("king over and above all other kings"). More specifically, it seems to carry a superlative idea: The head noun is supreme above the group indicated by the genitive (Wallace, 103 n. 84).

κύριος. Nominative of appellation. See Βασιλεύς above.

κυρίων. See βασιλέων above.

Revelation 19:17-21

[17]And I saw an angel standing in the sun and he cried out with a loud voice saying to all the birds flying in the mid-heaven: "Come. Gather for the great supper of God [18]in order that you might eat the flesh of kings and the flesh of commanders and the flesh of the strong and the flesh of horses and of those seated on them and the flesh of both all the free and slaves and the small and the great." [19]And I saw the beast and the kings of the earth and their soldiers gathered to make war with the one seated on the horse and with his army. [20]And the beast was seized and with him the false prophet, who performed the signs before him, by which he deceived those who received the mark of the beast and who worshiped his image. While living, the two were thrown into the lake of fire burning with sulfur. [21]And the rest were killed with the sword that comes out of the mouth of the one seated upon the horse. And all the birds were gorged from their flesh.

19:17 Καὶ εἶδον ἕνα ἄγγελον ἑστῶτα ἐν τῷ ἡλίῳ καὶ ἔκραξεν [ἐν] φωνῇ μεγάλῃ λέγων πᾶσιν τοῖς ὀρνέοις τοῖς πετομένοις ἐν μεσουρανήματι· Δεῦτε συνάχθητε εἰς τὸ δεῖπνον τὸ μέγα τοῦ θεοῦ

Καὶ εἶδον. This phrase introduces a new character and scene within the ongoing vision. Here, and in verse 19 it marks subsections of verses 17-21 (Smalley, 496).

εἶδον. Aor act ind 1st sg ὁράω.

ἕνα ἄγγελον. Accusative direct object of εἶδον. On ἕνα, Caragounis notes that in the "NT the cardinal numbers, εἷς, μία, ἕν, are losing their numerical value and are being reduced to an indefinite pronoun" (3.1043).

ἑστῶτα. Prf act ptc masc acc sg ἵστημι (substantival). Complement in an object-complement double accusative construction.

ἐν τῷ ἡλίῳ. Locative.

ἔκραξεν. Aor act ind 3rd sg κράζω.

[ἐν] φωνῇ μεγάλῃ. Dative of instrument or manner; with the preposition, instrumental or manner.

λέγων. Pres act ptc masc nom sg λέγω (manner). On the use of the participle λέγων to introduce speech, see 1:17 on λέγων.

πᾶσιν τοῖς ὀρνέοις. Dative indirect object of λέγων.

τοῖς πετομένοις. Pres mid ptc neut dat pl πέτομαι (attributive).

ἐν μεσουρανήματι. Locative.

Δεῦτε. An adverb meaning "come." BDAG (220) describes it as a hortatory particle. It is often followed by an imperative or aorist subjunctive.

συνάχθητε. Aor mid impv 2nd pl συνάγω. On the voice, see "Deponency" in the Series Introduction.

εἰς τὸ δεῖπνον τὸ μέγα. Locative.

τοῦ θεοῦ. Possessive genitive.

19:18 ἵνα φάγητε σάρκας βασιλέων καὶ σάρκας χιλιάρχων καὶ σάρκας ἰσχυρῶν καὶ σάρκας ἵππων καὶ τῶν καθημένων ἐπ' αὐτῶν καὶ σάρκας πάντων ἐλευθέρων τε καὶ δούλων καὶ μικρῶν καὶ μεγάλων.

ἵνα. Introduces a purpose clause.

φάγητε. Aor act subj 2nd pl ἐσθίω. Subjunctive with ἵνα.

σάρκας ... σάρκας ... σάρκας ... σάρκας ... σάρκας. Accusative direct object of φάγητε.

βασιλέων ... χιλιάρχων ... ἰσχυρῶν ... ἵππων καὶ τῶν καθημένων ... πάντων ἐλευθέρων ... δούλων καὶ μικρῶν καὶ μεγάλων. Possessive genitive.

τῶν καθημένων. Pres mid ptc masc gen pl κάθημαι (substantival). Possessive genitive.

ἐπ' αὐτῶν. Locative.
τε καί. "Both . . . and."

19:19 Καὶ εἶδον τὸ θηρίον καὶ τοὺς βασιλεῖς τῆς γῆς καὶ τὰ στρατεύματα αὐτῶν συνηγμένα ποιῆσαι τὸν πόλεμον μετὰ τοῦ καθημένου ἐπὶ τοῦ ἵππου καὶ μετὰ τοῦ στρατεύματος αὐτοῦ.

Καὶ εἶδον. Introduces a new division in the visionary segment.
εἶδον. Aor act ind 1st sg ὁράω.
τὸ θηρίον καὶ τοὺς βασιλεῖς . . . καὶ τὰ στρατεύματα. Accusative direct object of εἶδον.
τῆς γῆς. Genitive of subordination ("the kings who rule over the earth").
αὐτῶν. Possessive genitive. The antecedent is τὸ θηρίον καὶ τοὺς βασιλεῖς. The reading αὐτοῦ is found in A *pc*, to indicate that the army belongs only to the beast.
συνηγμένα. Prf pass ptc neut acc pl συνάγω (substantival). Complement in an object-complement double accusative construction with τὰ στρατεύματα. The perfect tense emphasizes their state of preparedness for battle and picks up the reference to their being gathered in 16:14, 16.
ποιῆσαι. Aor act inf ποιέω (purpose).
τὸν πόλεμον. Accusative direct object of ποιῆσαι.
μετὰ τοῦ καθημένου. Association (see also 12:7).
τοῦ καθημένου. Pres mid ptc masc gen sg κάθημαι (substantival).
ἐπὶ τοῦ ἵππου. Locative.
μετὰ τοῦ στρατεύματος. Accompaniment (see also 12:7).
αὐτοῦ. Possessive genitive.

19:20 καὶ ἐπιάσθη τὸ θηρίον καὶ μετ' αὐτοῦ ὁ ψευδοπροφήτης ὁ ποιήσας τὰ σημεῖα ἐνώπιον αὐτοῦ, ἐν οἷς ἐπλάνησεν τοὺς λαβόντας τὸ χάραγμα τοῦ θηρίου καὶ τοὺς προσκυνοῦντας τῇ εἰκόνι αὐτοῦ· ζῶντες ἐβλήθησαν οἱ δύο εἰς τὴν λίμνην τοῦ πυρὸς τῆς καιομένης ἐν θείῳ.

ἐπιάσθη. Aor pass ind 3rd sg πιάζω. This verb means "to seize with intent to overpower or gain control" (BDAG, 812.2). The cluster of aorist tense forms functions to summarize the battle scene and move the narrative forward to its conclusion. The singular verb is followed by a plural subject (τὸ θηρίον καὶ μετ' αὐτοῦ ὁ ψευδοπροφήτης). As Turner notes, "The verb, if it stands first, usually agrees with the first subject" (313; cf. Charles, 1.cxli).
τὸ θηρίον καὶ . . . ὁ ψευδοπροφήτης. Nominative subject of ἐπιάσθη.
μετ' αὐτοῦ. Accompaniment.

ὁ ποιήσας. Aor act ptc masc nom sg ποιέω (attributive).
τὰ σημεῖα. Accusative direct object of ποιήσας.
ἐνώπιον αὐτοῦ. According to BDAG (342.4.b), ἐνώπιον should be understood here in the sense of "*by the authority of, on behalf of.*" The antecedent of αὐτοῦ is θηρίον.
ἐν οἷς. Instrumental. The antecedent is σημεῖα.
ἐπλάνησεν. Aor act ind 3rd sg πλανάω.
τοὺς λαβόντας. Aor act ptc masc acc pl λαμβάνω (substantival). Accusative direct object of ἐπλάνησεν.
τὸ χάραγμα. Accusative direct object of λαβόντας.
τοῦ θηρίου. Possessive genitive or genitive of source.
τοὺς προσκυνοῦντας. Pres act ptc masc acc pl προσκυνέω (substantival). Accusative direct object of ἐπλάνησεν.
τῇ εἰκόνι. Dative direct object of προσκυνοῦντας.
αὐτοῦ. Possessive genitive or the genitive indicates the form or likeness that the image represents or reflects (see 13:18).
ζῶντες. Pres act ptc masc nom pl ζάω (temporal or manner).
ἐβλήθησαν. Aor pass ind 3rd pl βάλλω.
οἱ δύο. Nominative subject of ἐβλήθησαν.
εἰς τὴν λίμνην. Locative.
τοῦ πυρὸς. Attributive genitive or possibly genitive of content.
τῆς καιομένης. Pres mid ptc fem gen sg καίω (attributive, of λίμνην or πυρός). The gender of the participle comes from λίμνην, but its case is dependent on πυρός. The participle καιομένης may modify the entire construction τὴν λίμνην τοῦ πυρὸς. Beale (969) thinks the incongruity may be intentional to highlight an allusion to Ezek 38 and Dan 7:11.
ἐν θείῳ. Association.

19:21 καὶ οἱ λοιποὶ ἀπεκτάνθησαν ἐν τῇ ῥομφαίᾳ τοῦ καθημένου ἐπὶ τοῦ ἵππου τῇ ἐξελθούσῃ ἐκ τοῦ στόματος αὐτοῦ, καὶ πάντα τὰ ὄρνεα ἐχορτάσθησαν ἐκ τῶν σαρκῶν αὐτῶν.

οἱ λοιποί. Nominative subject of ἀπεκτάνθησαν.
ἀπεκτάνθησαν. Aor pass ind 3rd pl ἀποκτείνω.
ἐν τῇ ῥομφαίᾳ. Instrumental.
τοῦ καθημένου. Pres mid ptc masc gen sg κάθημαι (substantival). Possessive genitive.
ἐπὶ τοῦ ἵππου. Locative.
τῇ ἐξελθούσῃ. Aor act ptc fem dat sg ἐξέρχομαι (attributive to ῥομφαίᾳ).
ἐκ τοῦ στόματος. Source.
αὐτοῦ. Possessive genitive.
πάντα τὰ ὄρνεα. Nominative subject of ἐχορτάσθησαν.

ἐχορτάσθησαν. Aor mid or pass ind 3rd pl χορτάζω. On the voice, see "Deponency" in the Series Introduction. Often neuter plural subjects that refer to living beings take a plural verb in Revelation (Mussies, 231).

ἐκ τῶν σαρκῶν. Source or means.
αὐτῶν. Possessive genitive.

Revelation 20:1-10

¹And I saw an angel coming down out of heaven having the key to the abyss and a great chain in his hand. ²And he seized the dragon, the ancient serpent, who is the Devil and Satan, and he bound him for a thousand years ³and threw him into the abyss and locked and sealed it over him, in order that he might not deceive the nations any longer until the thousand years are completed. After these things it is necessary for him to be released for a short time. ⁴And I saw thrones and people sat upon them and judgment was given in their favor, (and I saw) the souls of those beheaded because of their testimony for Jesus and because of the word of God and who did not worship the beast nor his image and did not receive the mark upon their foreheads and upon their hands. And they came to life and reigned with Christ for a thousand years. ⁵The rest of the dead did not come to life until the thousand years were completed. This is the first resurrection. ⁶Blessed and holy is the one who takes part in the first resurrection; over these the second death does not have authority, but they will be priests of God and of Christ and they shall reign with him for a thousand years. ⁷And when the thousand years are completed, Satan will be released from his prison ⁸and he will go out to deceive the nations that are in the four corners of the earth, Gog and Magog, to gather them together for the battle, whose number is as the sand of the sea. ⁹And they went up upon the breadth of the earth and surrounded the camp of the saints and the beloved city, and fire came down from heaven and devoured them. ¹⁰And the devil who deceived them was thrown into the lake of fire and sulfur where the beast and false prophet were also, and they will be tormented day and night for ever and ever.

20:1 Καὶ εἶδον ἄγγελον καταβαίνοντα ἐκ τοῦ οὐρανοῦ ἔχοντα τὴν κλεῖν τῆς ἀβύσσου καὶ ἅλυσιν μεγάλην ἐπὶ τὴν χεῖρα αὐτοῦ.

Καὶ εἶδον. This phrase introduces a new scene within the vision, linking together a series of visionary units, but as Smalley (501) notes it does not denote a chronological progression.

εἶδον. Aor act ind 1st sg ὁράω.

ἄγγελον. Accusative direct object of εἶδον.
καταβαίνοντα. Pres act ptc masc acc sg καταβαίνω. Complement in an object-complement double accusative construction.
ἐκ τοῦ οὐρανοῦ. Source.
ἔχοντα. Pres act ptc masc acc sg ἔχω (attributive).
τὴν κλεῖν ... καὶ ἅλυσιν μεγάλην. Accusative direct object of ἔχοντα.
τῆς ἀβύσσου. The idea of the genitive seems to be "the key that opens/locks the abyss," or "the key to the abyss" (see also 9:1 on τῆς ἀβύσσου).
ἐπὶ τὴν χεῖρα. Locative.
αὐτοῦ. Possessive genitive.

20:2 καὶ ἐκράτησεν τὸν δράκοντα, ὁ ὄφις ὁ ἀρχαῖος, ὅς ἐστιν Διάβολος καὶ ὁ Σατανᾶς, καὶ ἔδησεν αὐτὸν χίλια ἔτη

ἐκράτησεν. Aor act ind 3rd sg κρατέω.
τὸν δράκοντα. Accusative direct object of ἐκράτησεν.
ὁ ὄφις ὁ ἀρχαῖος. Nominative in apposition to τὸν δράκοντα. There is a grammatical incongruity with the noun (and adjective) in the nominative standing in apposition to a noun in the accusative case. Most likely this is an example of the nominative being used as a title. It may also serve to recall the introduction of the serpent with the identical phrase in 12:9. ℵ 046 051 1006 1611 1841 1854 2030 2050 2053 2062 2329 2377 𝔐 correct the text to the expected accusative τὸν ὄφιν τὸν ἀρχαῖον.
ὅς. Nominative subject of ἐστιν.
ἐστιν. Pres act ind 3rd sg εἰμί. On the loss of the accent, see 1:8.
Διάβολος καὶ ὁ Σατανᾶς. Predicate nominative of ἐστιν. The piling up of terms with reference to τὸν δράκοντα is an example of what linguists call "overspecification." Here it places the focus on the dragon and also "reactivates" the dragon from 12:9.
ἔδησεν. Aor act ind 3rd sg δέω.
αὐτόν. Accusative direct object of ἔδησεν.
χίλια ἔτη. Accusative indicating extent of time.

20:3 καὶ ἔβαλεν αὐτὸν εἰς τὴν ἄβυσσον καὶ ἔκλεισεν καὶ ἐσφράγισεν ἐπάνω αὐτοῦ, ἵνα μὴ πλανήσῃ ἔτι τὰ ἔθνη ἄχρι τελεσθῇ τὰ χίλια ἔτη. μετὰ ταῦτα δεῖ λυθῆναι αὐτὸν μικρὸν χρόνον.

ἔβαλεν. Aor act ind 3rd sg βάλλω.
αὐτόν. Accusative direct object of ἔβαλεν.
εἰς τὴν ἄβυσσον. Locative. See also 9:1 on τῆς ἀβύσσου.
ἔκλεισεν. Aor act ind 3rd sg κλείω.
ἐσφράγισεν. Aor act ind 3rd sg σφραγίζω.

ἐπάνω αὐτοῦ. Locative.
ἵνα. Introduces a purpose clause.
πλανήσῃ. Aor act subj 3rd sg λανάω. Subjunctive with ἵνα.
μὴ . . . ἔτι. "No longer."
τὰ ἔθνη. Accusative direct object of πλανήσῃ.
ἄχρι. Introduces a temporal clause. ἄχρι indicates "extent of time up to a point" (BDAG, 160.1).
τελεσθῇ. Aor pass subj 3rd sg τελέω. Subjunctive with ἄχρι.
τὰ χίλια ἔτη. Nominative subject of τελεσθῇ. The article functions anaphorically, pointing back to the first (anarthrous) mention of the thousand years (see v. 2) as the time of Satan's binding. Neuter plural subjects are commonly found with a singular verb.
μετὰ ταῦτα. Temporal.
δεῖ. Pres act ind 3rd sg δεῖ (impersonal).
λυθῆναι. Aor pass inf λύω (complementary). It is also possible that the infinitive functions as the subject of δεῖ: "To be loosed is necessary."
αὐτὸν. Accusative subject of λυθῆναι.
μικρὸν χρόνον. Accusative indicating extent of time.

20:4 Καὶ εἶδον θρόνους καὶ ἐκάθισαν ἐπ᾽ αὐτοὺς καὶ κρίμα ἐδόθη αὐτοῖς, καὶ τὰς ψυχὰς τῶν πεπελεκισμένων διὰ τὴν μαρτυρίαν Ἰησοῦ καὶ διὰ τὸν λόγον τοῦ θεοῦ καὶ οἵτινες οὐ προσεκύνησαν τὸ θηρίον οὐδὲ τὴν εἰκόνα αὐτοῦ καὶ οὐκ ἔλαβον τὸ χάραγμα ἐπὶ τὸ μέτωπον καὶ ἐπὶ τὴν χεῖρα αὐτῶν. καὶ ἔζησαν καὶ ἐβασίλευσαν μετὰ τοῦ Χριστοῦ χίλια ἔτη.

Καὶ εἶδον. Introduces a new feature of the vision.
εἶδον. Aor act ind 1st sg ὁράω.
θρόνους. Accusative direct object of εἶδον.
ἐκάθισαν. Aor act ind 3rd pl καθίζω. The implied subject is the group referred to with αὐτοῖς below.
ἐπ᾽ αὐτοὺς. Locative.
κρίμα. Nominative subject of ἐδόθη.
ἐδόθη. Aor pass ind 3rd sg δίδωμι.
αὐτοῖς. Dative indirect object. Most translations and commentaries interpret the dative pronoun as a dative indirect object in the sense of "judgment was given *to them*," that is "the authority to judge was given to them" (NIV; see also KJV, NRSV, NASB, ESV, NET). The emphasis would then be on the judging role that they play during the thousand year period. It could also be understood as a dative of advantage in the sense of "judgment was given for them/on their behalf," that is "a favorable verdict was rendered on their behalf" (Smalley, 506; CEB: "judgment was given in their favor"). This reading would fit with the theme of

Satan's judgment in Rev 20. The corollary of Satan's judgment is the vindication of the saints. Satan ruled over them, killed them, and accused them. Now they are vindicated, come to life, and reign.

καί. The καί introduces a clause that is epexegetical, further defining those who sit on the thrones.

τὰς ψυχάς. Accusative direct object of εἶδον (see also 6:9 on τὰς ψυχάς).

τῶν πεπελεκισμένων. Prf pass ptc masc gen pl πελεκίζω (substantival). Possessive genitive.

διὰ τὴν μαρτυρίαν. Cause.

Ἰησοῦ. Objective genitive.

διὰ τὸν λόγον. Cause.

τοῦ θεοῦ. Genitive of source or subjective genitive.

οἵτινες. Nominative subject of προσεκύνησαν. Grammatically, there is ambiguity as to how many groups John envisions here. There are some who think that καὶ οἵτινες introduces a second group in addition to those who have been beheaded (Swete, 262; Beale, 1000–1001; Smalley, 507). "The triumph of Christ is shared not by the martyrs only but by all who under the sway of the Beast and the False Prophet suffered reproach" (Swete, 262). However, others understand this as a further description of the martyrs, rather than a second group (Mounce, 355–56; Osborne, 706; Blount, 365), taking the καί before οἵτινες as epexegetical. There may be a slight advantage to taking this as a further reference to the same group just mentioned, the martyrs, since refusal to worship the beast and martyrdom are closely linked in 13:15-16 (Osborne, 706). Beale (1001) objects to the identification of the group introduced by οἵτινες with the souls (ψυχάς) of those beheaded because (1) οἵτινες is masculine rather than feminine as is ψυχάς; and (2) if οἵτινες further defined ψυχάς we would expect οἵτινες to be accusative rather than nominative (Smalley, 507, also thinks that the use of the nominative pronoun οἵτινες suggests a different group). However, John may have used the masculine because he understood the "souls" as those belonging to persons (a construction according to sense), or it could get its gender from πεπελεκισμένων. More importantly, we should not expect the accusative case for οἵτινες since, while the gender and number of a pronoun are determined by the antecedent, the case of the pronoun is determined by its function within its own clause; here it is nominative because it functions as the subject of προσεκύνησαν. Aune (3.1088) plausibly suggests that verse 4 looks at the same group from two different perspectives: They "had been executed for positive reasons (v 4b: their obedience to the commands of God and their witness to Jesus) and negative reasons (v 4c: their refusal to worship the beast or its image and to receive its brand on their foreheads and right hands)."

προσεκύνησαν. Aor act ind 3rd pl προσκυνέω.

τὸ θηρίον οὐδὲ τὴν εἰκόνα. Accusative direct object of προσεκύνησαν.

αὐτοῦ. Possessive genitive, or the genitive indicates the form or likeness that the image represents or reflects (see 13:18).

ἔλαβον. Aor act ind 3rd pl λαμβάνω.

τὸ χάραγμα. Accusative direct object of ἔλαβον.

ἐπὶ τὸ μέτωπον καὶ ἐπὶ τὴν χεῖρα. Locative. The "forehead" and "hand" are distributive and apply to each person in the group (hence the plural translation).

αὐτῶν. Possessive genitive.

ἔζησαν. Aor act ind 3rd pl ζάω. I have translated the aorist in an ingressive sense ("came to life") due to the contextual contrast between their description as those beheaded (τῶν πεπελεκισμένων) and now living (ἔζησαν). This is not the same as saying that there is a category of "ingressive aorist" (e.g., Robertson, 833; Wallace, 558–59; Turner, 71; Aune, 3.1073). See "Verbal Aspect" in the Introduction. Rather, the aorist summarizes an action that could be understood as ingressive in this context. However, we should probably not make too much of the ingressive nuance, and recognize that the aorist could simply summarize their state of being alive (Fanning, 257).

ἐβασίλευσαν. Aor act ind 3rd pl βασιλεύω.

μετὰ τοῦ Χριστοῦ. Accompaniment.

χίλια ἔτη. See on verse 3. The rhetorical significance of this number is that it contrasts with the much shorter time periods that designate the reign of Satan and the beast: three and one half years, forty-two months, twelve-hundred and sixty days (see Rev 12–13).

20:5 οἱ λοιποὶ τῶν νεκρῶν οὐκ ἔζησαν ἄχρι τελεσθῇ τὰ χίλια ἔτη. Αὕτη ἡ ἀνάστασις ἡ πρώτη.

οἱ λοιποὶ. Nominative subject of ἔζησαν.

τῶν νεκρῶν. Partitive genitive.

ἔζησαν. Aor act ind 3rd pl ζάω. On the semantics and function of the aorist, see verse 4 on ἔζησαν.

ἄχρι. Temporal (see v. 3).

τελεσθῇ. Aor pass subj 3rd sg τελέω. Subjunctive with ἄχρι. Neuter plural subjects are commonly found with a singular verb.

τὰ χίλια ἔτη. Nominative subject of τελεσθῇ.

Αὕτη. Nominative subject of a verbless clause. Functions anaphorically to refer back to verse 4 (the saints coming to life at the beginning of the thousand years). This means that the first part of verse 5, οἱ λοιποὶ τῶν νεκρῶν οὐκ ἔζησαν ἄχρι τελεσθῇ τὰ χίλια ἔτη, is a "parenthetical remark [that] refers to the brief narrative in Rev 20:12-13" (Aune, 3.1090).

ἡ ἀνάστασις ἡ πρώτη. Predicate nominative of a verbless clause.

20:6 μακάριος καὶ ἅγιος ὁ ἔχων μέρος ἐν τῇ ἀναστάσει τῇ πρώτῃ· ἐπὶ τούτων ὁ δεύτερος θάνατος οὐκ ἔχει ἐξουσίαν, ἀλλ' ἔσονται ἱερεῖς τοῦ θεοῦ καὶ τοῦ Χριστοῦ καὶ βασιλεύσουσιν μετ' αὐτοῦ [τὰ] χίλια ἔτη.

μακάριος καὶ ἅγιος. Predicate nominative of a verbless clause.

ὁ ἔχων. Pres act ptc masc nom sg ἔχω (substantival). Nominative subject of a verbless clause.

μέρος. Accusative direct object of ἔχων.

ἐν τῇ ἀναστάσει τῇ πρώτῃ. The PP indicates that in which someone has a share after μέρος.

ἐπὶ τούτων. Indicates the persons over which something has authority (BDAG, 365.9). This is a construction according to sense, with the plural τούτων referring to the collective group consisting of each one who has a share (ὁ ἔχων μέρος) in the first resurrection. The PP is fronted for emphasis. Semantically, this clause seems to indicate the reason why those who share in the first resurrection are blessed.

ὁ δεύτερος θάνατος. Nominative subject of ἔχει.

ἔχει. Pres act ind 3rd sg ἔχω. The present tense is future referring. See the future ἔσονται below, which provides a contrast (ἀλλ') to ἔχει.

ἐξουσίαν. Accusative direct object of ἔχει.

ἀλλ'. Contrast. Provides a correction to the previous statement (cf. Runge, 56).

ἔσονται. Fut act ind 3rd pl εἰμί.

ἱερεῖς. Predicate nominative.

τοῦ θεοῦ καὶ τοῦ Χριστοῦ. Possessive genitive, or possibly an objective genitive (as priests they serve God and Christ).

βασιλεύσουσιν. Fut act ind 3rd pl βασιλεύω.

μετ' αὐτοῦ. Accompaniment.

[τὰ] χίλια ἔτη. See verse 3.

20:7 Καὶ ὅταν τελεσθῇ τὰ χίλια ἔτη, λυθήσεται ὁ σατανᾶς ἐκ τῆς φυλακῆς αὐτοῦ

ὅταν. Introduces a temporal clause.

τελεσθῇ. Aor pass subj 3rd sg τελέω. Subjunctive with ὅταν.

τὰ χίλια ἔτη. Nominative subject of τελεσθῇ. It is common for a neuter plural subject to be used with a singular verb.

λυθήσεται. Fut pass ind 3rd sg λύω.
ὁ σατανᾶς. Nominative subject of λυθήσεται.
ἐκ τῆς φυλακῆς. Separation.
αὐτοῦ. Possessive genitive or objective genitive.

20:8 καὶ ἐξελεύσεται πλανῆσαι τὰ ἔθνη τὰ ἐν ταῖς τέσσαρσιν γωνίαις τῆς γῆς, τὸν Γὼγ καὶ Μαγώγ, συναγαγεῖν αὐτοὺς εἰς τὸν πόλεμον, ὧν ὁ ἀριθμὸς αὐτῶν ὡς ἡ ἄμμος τῆς θαλάσσης.

ἐξελεύσεται. Fut mid ind 3rd sg ἐξέρχομαι.
πλανῆσαι. Aor act inf πλανάω (purpose).
τὰ ἔθνη. Accusative direct object of πλανῆσαι.
τὰ. The article functions as an adjectivizer, turning the PP into an attributive modifier of τὰ ἔθνη. Lit. "the in-the-four-corners-of-the-earth nations."
ἐν ταῖς τέσσαρσιν γωνίαις. Locative.
τῆς γῆς. Epexegetical genitive or possibly partitive genitive.
τὸν Γὼγ καὶ Μαγώγ. Accusative in apposition to τὰ ἔθνη.
συναγαγεῖν. Aor act inf συνάγω (purpose, modifying πλανῆσαι).
αὐτοὺς. Accusative direct object of συναγαγεῖν.
εἰς τὸν πόλεμον. Purpose.
ὧν. Objective genitive, modifying ὁ ἀριθμός.
ὁ ἀριθμὸς. Nominative subject of a verbless clause.
αὐτῶν. Objective genitive. The redundant pronoun is resumptive of ὧν. Lit. "*of whom* the number *of them* is as the sand of the sea." The function of this construction is to draw attention to the antecedent.
ὡς ἡ ἄμμος. Comparison. Functions as the predicate of a verbless clause.
τῆς θαλάσσης. Possessive genitive.

20:9 καὶ ἀνέβησαν ἐπὶ τὸ πλάτος τῆς γῆς καὶ ἐκύκλευσαν τὴν παρεμβολὴν τῶν ἁγίων καὶ τὴν πόλιν τὴν ἠγαπημένην, καὶ κατέβη πῦρ ἐκ τοῦ οὐρανοῦ καὶ κατέφαγεν αὐτούς.

ἀνέβησαν. Aor act ind 3rd pl ἀναβαίνω.
ἐπὶ τὸ πλάτος. Locative. The meaning of πλάτος τῆς γῆς is something like "the broad plain of the earth" (BDAG, 823).
τῆς γῆς. Epexegetical genitive or genitive expressing location.
ἐκύκλευσαν. Aor act ind 3rd pl κυκλεύω.
τὴν παρεμβολὴν. Accusative direct object of ἐκύκλευσαν.
τῶν ἁγίων. Subjective genitive or possessive genitive.
καὶ. Epexegetical. The τὴν πόλιν τὴν ἠγαπημένην does not appear to be something separate from τὴν παρεμβολήν.

τὴν πόλιν. Accusative direct object of ἐκύκλευσαν.
τὴν ἠγαπημένην. Prf pass ptc fem acc sg ἀγαπάω (attributive).
κατέβη. Aor mid ind 3rd sg καταβαίνω. Rhetorically, κατέβη provides a contrast to ἀνέβησαν at the beginning of the verse.
πῦρ. Nominative subject of κατέβη.
ἐκ τοῦ οὐρανοῦ. Source.
κατέφαγεν. Aor act ind 3rd sg κατεσθίω. On the meaning, see 10:9 on κατάφαγε.
αὐτούς. Accusative direct object of κατέφαγεν. The antecedent is only τὰ ἔθνη from verse 8, since the Devil is disposed of in the next verse. This is another example a mismatch of gender between the masculine αὐτούς and its neuter antecedent τὰ ἔθνη. This is to be explained as a construction according to sense: The nations consist of people.

20:10 καὶ ὁ διάβολος ὁ πλανῶν αὐτοὺς ἐβλήθη εἰς τὴν λίμνην τοῦ πυρὸς καὶ θείου ὅπου καὶ τὸ θηρίον καὶ ὁ ψευδοπροφήτης, καὶ βασανισθήσονται ἡμέρας καὶ νυκτὸς εἰς τοὺς αἰῶνας τῶν αἰώνων.

ὁ διάβολος. Nominative subject of ἐβλήθη.
ὁ πλανῶν. Pres act ptc masc nom sg πλανάω (attributive). The present tense participle apparently refers to action that is temporally past (BDF §339.3).
αὐτούς. Accusative direct object of πλανῶν. The antecedent is τὰ ἔθνη (see v. 7). On the mismatch of gender, see verse 9 on αὐτούς.
ἐβλήθη. Aor pass ind 3rd sg βάλλω.
εἰς τὴν λίμνην. Locative.
τοῦ πυρὸς καὶ θείου. Attributive genitive or genitive of content.
ὅπου. Introduces a local clause (denoting space) that functions like a relative clause and further describes τὴν λίμνην τοῦ πυρὸς καὶ θείου.
καὶ. Adverbial: "Also."
τὸ θηρίον καὶ ὁ ψευδοπροφήτης. Nominative subject of a verbless clause or of an assumed ἐβλήθησαν.
βασανισθήσονται. Fut pass ind 3rd pl βασανίζω.
ἡμέρας καὶ νυκτὸς. Genitive of time.
εἰς τοὺς αἰῶνας τῶν αἰώνων. Temporal (see 1:18).

Revelation 20:11-15

[11]And I saw a large white throne and one seated on it, from whose presence the earth and the heaven fled, and no place was found for them. [12]And I saw the dead, the great and the insignificant standing before the throne. And books were opened, and another book was opened, which is (the book) of life, and the dead were judged from the things written

in the books according to their works. ¹³And the sea gave up the dead that were in it and Death and Hades gave up the dead that were in them, and each person was judged according to their works. ¹⁴And Death and Hades were thrown into the lake of fire. This is the second death, the lake of fire. ¹⁵And if anyone was not found written in the book of life, they were thrown into the lake of fire.

20:11 Καὶ εἶδον θρόνον μέγαν λευκὸν καὶ τὸν καθήμενον ἐπ' αὐτόν, οὗ ἀπὸ τοῦ προσώπου ἔφυγεν ἡ γῆ καὶ ὁ οὐρανὸς καὶ τόπος οὐχ εὑρέθη αὐτοῖς.

Καὶ εἶδον. Introduces a new scene within the vision.
εἶδον. Aor act ind 1st sg ὁράω.
θρόνον μέγαν λευκὸν. Accusative direct object of εἶδον.
τὸν καθήμενον. Pres mid ptc masc acc sg κάθημαι (substantival). Accusative direct object of εἶδον.
ἐπ' αὐτόν. Locative.
οὗ. Possessive genitive, modifying προσώπου (lit. "from whose face"). The antecedent is τὸν καθήμενον.
ἀπὸ τοῦ προσώπου. Separation.
ἔφυγεν. Aor act ind 3rd sg φεύγω.
ἡ γῆ καὶ ὁ οὐρανός. Nominative subject of ἔφυγεν. The plural subject follows a singular verb. As Turner notes, "The verb, if it stands first, usually agrees with the first subject" (313; cf. Charles, 1.cxli).
καὶ. Aune (3.1075) interprets the καί adversatively. However, grammatically the καί simply indicates continuity.
τόπος. Nominative subject of εὑρέθη.
εὑρέθη. Aor pass ind 3rd sg εὑρίσκω.
αὐτοῖς. Dative of advantage.

20:12 καὶ εἶδον τοὺς νεκρούς, τοὺς μεγάλους καὶ τοὺς μικρούς, ἑστῶτας ἐνώπιον τοῦ θρόνου. καὶ βιβλία ἠνοίχθησαν, καὶ ἄλλο βιβλίον ἠνοίχθη, ὅ ἐστιν τῆς ζωῆς, καὶ ἐκρίθησαν οἱ νεκροὶ ἐκ τῶν γεγραμμένων ἐν τοῖς βιβλίοις κατὰ τὰ ἔργα αὐτῶν.

καὶ εἶδον. Introduces a new participant in the present scene.
εἶδον. Aor act ind 1st sg ὁράω.
τοὺς νεκρούς. Accusative direct object of εἶδον.
τοὺς μεγάλους καὶ τοὺς μικρούς. Accusative in apposition to νεκρούς. The phrase constitutes a merism, which covers the various levels of society.
ἑστῶτας. Prf act ptc masc acc pl ἵστημι. Complement in an object-complement double accusative construction with νεκρούς.

ἐνώπιον τοῦ θρόνου. Locative/spatial.
βιβλία. Nominative subject of ἠνοίχθησαν.
ἠνοίχθησαν. Aor pass ind 3rd pl ἀνοίγω.
ἄλλο βιβλίον. Nominative subject of ἠνοίχθη.
ἠνοίχθη. Aor pass ind 3rd sg ἀνοίγω.
ὅ. Nominative subject of ἐστιν.
ἐστιν. Pres act ind 3rd sg εἰμί. On the loss of accent, see 1:8.
τῆς ζωῆς. Attributive genitive modifying an implied βιβλίον.
ἐκρίθησαν. Aor pass ind 3rd pl κρίνω.
οἱ νεκροί. Nominative subject of ἐκρίθησαν.
ἐκ τῶν γεγραμμένων. Cause, providing the basis for judgment.
τῶν γεγραμμένων. Prf pass ptc masc gen pl γράφω (substantival).
ἐν τοῖς βιβλίοις. Locative.
κατὰ τὰ ἔργα. Standard.
αὐτῶν. Subjective genitive.

20:13 καὶ ἔδωκεν ἡ θάλασσα τοὺς νεκροὺς τοὺς ἐν αὐτῇ καὶ ὁ θάνατος καὶ ὁ ᾅδης ἔδωκαν τοὺς νεκροὺς τοὺς ἐν αὐτοῖς, καὶ ἐκρίθησαν ἕκαστος κατὰ τὰ ἔργα αὐτῶν.

ἔδωκεν. Aor act ind 3rd sg δίδωμι.
ἡ θάλασσα. Nominative subject of ἔδωκεν.
τοὺς νεκρούς. Accusative direct object of ἔδωκαν.
τούς. The article functions as an adjectivizer, turning the entire PP into an attributive modifier of νεκρούς. Lit. "the in-it dead."
ἐν αὐτῇ. Locative.
ὁ θάνατος καὶ ὁ ᾅδης. Nominative subject of ἔδωκαν.
ἔδωκαν. Aor act ind 3rd pl δίδωμι.
τοὺς νεκρούς. Accusative direct object of ἔδωκαν.
τούς. The article functions as an adjectivizer, turning the entire PP into an attributive modifier of νεκρούς. Lit. "the in-them dead."
ἐν αὐτοῖς. Locative. The antecedent is ὁ θάνατος καὶ ὁ ᾅδης.
ἐκρίθησαν. Aor pass ind 3rd pl κρίνω.
ἕκαστος. Nominative subject of ἐκρίθησαν. The singular ἕκαστος is used with a plural verb. This can be explained by the fact that ἕκαστος carries a distributive sense (BDAG, 298).
κατὰ τὰ ἔργα. Standard.
αὐτῶν. Subjective genitive.

20:14 καὶ ὁ θάνατος καὶ ὁ ᾅδης ἐβλήθησαν εἰς τὴν λίμνην τοῦ πυρός. οὗτος ὁ θάνατος ὁ δεύτερός ἐστιν, ἡ λίμνη τοῦ πυρός.

ὁ θάνατος καὶ ὁ ᾅδης. Nominative subject of ἐβλήθησαν.

ἐβλήθησαν. Aor pass ind 3rd pl βάλλω.
εἰς τὴν λίμνην. Locative.
τοῦ πυρός. Attributive genitive or genitive of content.
οὗτος. Nominative subject of ἐστιν. The demonstrative οὗτος can functon anaphorically (pointing back) or cataphorically (pointing forward). Here it functions cataphorically and points forward to ἡ λίμνη τοῦ πυρός.
ὁ θάνατος ὁ δεύτερός. Predicate nominative of ἐστιν. The accenting of δεύτερός is due to the enclitic ἐστιν that follows.
ἐστιν. Pres act ind 3rd sg εἰμί. On the loss of accent, see 1:8.
ἡ λίμνη. Nominative in apposition to οὗτος.
τοῦ πυρός. Genitive of description or genitive of content.

20:15 καὶ εἴ τις οὐχ εὑρέθη ἐν τῇ βίβλῳ τῆς ζωῆς γεγραμμένος, ἐβλήθη εἰς τὴν λίμνην τοῦ πυρός.

εἴ. Introduces the protasis of a first-class conditional sentence.
τις. Nominative subject of εὑρέθη.
εὑρέθη. Aor pass ind 3rd sg εὑρίσκω.
ἐν τῇ βίβλῳ. Locative.
τῆς ζωῆς. Attributive genitive.
γεγραμμένος. Prf pass ptc masc nom sg γράφω. Along with τις this is part of a double nominative construction with a passive verb from a double accusative construction: "I found someone written" (Culy 2009, 83–87).
ἐβλήθη. Aor pass ind 3rd sg βάλλω.
εἰς τὴν λίμνην. Locative.
τοῦ πυρός. Attributive genitive or genitive of content.

Revelation 21:1-8

¹And I saw a new heaven and a new earth. For the first heaven and the first earth passed away, and the sea was no more. ²And I saw the holy city, the New Jerusalem, coming down out of heaven from God, prepared as a bride adorned for her husband. ³And I heard a loud voice from the throne saying, "Look, the dwelling of God is with people, and he will dwell with them, and they will be his people, and God himself will be their God with them, ⁴and he will wipe every tear from their eyes, and there will no longer be death or mourning or crying or pain, for the first things have passed away." ⁵And the one seated upon the throne said, "Look, I make all things new." And he said, "Write, for these words are faithful and true." ⁶And he said to me, "It has been accomplished. I am the Alpha and the Omega, the beginning and the end. To the one who

is thirsty I will give from the spring of the water of life freely. ⁷The one who overcomes will inherit these things and I will be his God and he will be my son. ⁸But for the cowardly and unbelieving and abominators and murderers and fornicators and sorcerers and idolaters and to every liar, their share is in the lake that burns with fire and sulfur, which is the second death."

21:1 Καὶ εἶδον οὐρανὸν καινὸν καὶ γῆν καινήν. ὁ γὰρ πρῶτος οὐρανὸς καὶ ἡ πρώτη γῆ ἀπῆλθαν καὶ ἡ θάλασσα οὐκ ἔστιν ἔτι.

21:1-5a form a chiastic structure, with the references to "new" (καινός) in verses 1 and 5a bracketing the entire section. The reference to the sea being οὐκ ἔτι (v. 1c) parallels the reference to the features that will be οὐκ ἔτι in verse 4. At the center of the chiasm is the New Jerusalem (v. 2) and the beginning of the speech in verse 3.

A New heavens and earth (1a-b)
  B The sea is no more (1c)
    C The Holy City New Jerusalem (v. 2)
    C´ The dwelling of God with his people (v. 3)
  B´ Suffering and crying are no more (4)
A´ New creation (5a)

Καὶ εἶδον. Introduces a new visionary segment.
εἶδον. Aor act ind 1st sg ὁράω.
οὐρανὸν καινὸν καὶ γῆν καινήν. Accusative direct object of εἶδον.
ὁ ... πρῶτος οὐρανὸς καὶ ἡ πρώτη γῆ. Nominative subject of ἀπῆλθαν.
γὰρ. Explanation.
ἀπῆλθαν. Aor act ind 3rd pl ἀπέρχομαι. See also 10:9 on ἀπῆλθα.
ἡ θάλασσα. Nominative subject of ἔστιν.
οὐκ ... ἔτι. "No longer."
ἔστιν. Pres act ind 3rd sg εἰμί.

21:2 καὶ τὴν πόλιν τὴν ἁγίαν Ἰερουσαλὴμ καινὴν εἶδον καταβαίνουσαν ἐκ τοῦ οὐρανοῦ ἀπὸ τοῦ θεοῦ ἡτοιμασμένην ὡς νύμφην κεκοσμημένην τῷ ἀνδρὶ αὐτῆς.

τὴν πόλιν τὴν ἁγίαν. Accusative direct object of εἶδον. This is the only other place in Revelation besides 21:22 (see below) where the object of the vision precedes the εἶδον. Perhaps this is to give it more prominence in preparation for the attention that it will receive in 21:9–22:5.
Ἰερουσαλὴμ καινήν. Accusative in apposition to τὴν πόλιν τὴν ἁγίαν.
εἶδον. Aor act ind 1st sg ὁράω.

καταβαίνουσαν. Pres act ptc fem acc sg καταβαίνω. Complement in an object-complement double accusative construction with τὴν πόλιν τὴν ἁγίαν.

ἐκ τοῦ οὐρανοῦ. Source.

ἀπὸ τοῦ θεοῦ. Source. In contrast to ἐκ, ἀπό can be used of the originator of an action (BDAG, 106.5.d).

ἡτοιμασμένην. Prf pass ptc fem acc sg ἑτοιμάζω (attributive). The expansion through the two perfect participles in this verse draws attention to the introduction of the bride/New Jerusalem particularly to contrast it with the harlot/Babylon (17:4: περιβεβλημένη, κεχρυσωμένη).

ὡς νύμφην. Comparison.

κεκοσμημένην. Prf pass ptc fem acc sg κοσμέω (attributive).

τῷ ἀνδρὶ. Dative of advantage.

αὐτῆς. Genitive of relationship.

21:3 καὶ ἤκουσα φωνῆς μεγάλης ἐκ τοῦ θρόνου λεγούσης· ἰδοὺ ἡ σκηνὴ τοῦ θεοῦ μετὰ τῶν ἀνθρώπων, καὶ σκηνώσει μετ' αὐτῶν, καὶ αὐτοὶ λαοὶ αὐτοῦ ἔσονται, καὶ αὐτὸς ὁ θεὸς μετ' αὐτῶν ἔσται [αὐτῶν θεός],

ἤκουσα. Aor act ind 1st sg ἀκούω.

φωνῆς μεγάλης. Genitive direct object of ἤκουσα.

ἐκ τοῦ θρόνου. Source.

λεγούσης. Pres act ptc fem gen sg λέγω. Complement in an object-complement double genitive construction with φωνῆς. On the use of the participle λεγούσης to introduce speech, see 1:17 on λέγων.

ἰδοὺ. A marker of attention that deictically functions to make the following statement emphatic. Here it draws attention to the significance of what the voice says. On the form, see 1:7.

ἡ σκηνὴ. Nominative subject of a verbless clause.

τοῦ θεοῦ. Subjective genitive.

μετὰ τῶν ἀνθρώπων. Association.

σκηνώσει. Fut act ind 3rd sg σκηνόω.

μετ' αὐτῶν. Association.

αὐτοὶ. Nominative subject of ἔσονται.

λαοί. Predicate nominative. Some manuscripts (P 051 1006 1611 1841 1854 2062 𝔐ᴷ) have the singular λαός while others (ℵ A 046 2030 2050 2053 2062ᵗˣᵗ 2329 𝔐ᴬ) support the plural λαοί. It is possible that the singular was the original reading and the plural reading was influenced by the preceding plural pronoun αὐτοί (Metzger, 688). But the plural reading has a slight advantage due to its somewhat better manuscript evidence and its conformity with John's more universal perspective (the people of God are from every tribe, tongue, language, and nation; see also the plural ἀνθρώπων above). Furthermore, the singular can be explained as an attempt of scribes to conform the covenant formula here in 21:3 to the standard OT covenant formula (Beale, 1048), which contains the singular "people" (cf. Lev 26:12; Jer 31:1, 33; Ezek 36:28; 37:27, 28; Zech 8:8).

αὐτοῦ. Possessive genitive or genitive of relationship.
ἔσονται. Fut act ind 3rd pl εἰμί.
αὐτὸς ὁ θεός. Nominative subject of ἔσται. The pronoun is intensive.
μετ' αὐτῶν. Association or accompaniment. Functions as the predicate of ἔσται.
ἔσται. Fut act ind 3rd sg εἰμί.
[αὐτῶν θεός]. It is difficult to determine whether these words should be included or not (ℵ 046 𝔐ᴷ omit them). The issue comes down to whether a scribe would have omitted them because it seemed redundant, or whether a scribe added them to bring this statement into conformity with the OT covenant formula (for those that include it: A P 2030 2050 2053 2329 𝔐ᴬ [025 051 1854 have θεὸς αὐτῶν]). Further, while the reference to λαοὶ αὐτοῦ lends itself to a corresponding, balancing αὐτῶν θεός, the genitive pronoun does not preceed θεός elsewhere in Revelation as it does here, also making it the more difficult reading. Fortunately, the meaning of the clause is not altered significantly by the presence or absence of this reading. If original, αὐτῶν θεός seems to function in apposition to αὐτὸς ὁ θεὸς μετ' αὐτῶν.

21:4 καὶ ἐξαλείψει πᾶν δάκρυον ἐκ τῶν ὀφθαλμῶν αὐτῶν, καὶ ὁ θάνατος οὐκ ἔσται ἔτι οὔτε πένθος οὔτε κραυγὴ οὔτε πόνος οὐκ ἔσται ἔτι, [ὅτι] τὰ πρῶτα ἀπῆλθαν.

ἐξαλείψει. Fut act ind 3rd sg ἐξαλείφω.
πᾶν δάκρυον. Accusative direct object of ἐξαλείψει.
ἐκ τῶν ὀφθαλμῶν. Separation.
αὐτῶν. Possessive genitive.
ὁ θάνατος. Nominative subject of ἔσται.
οὐκ ἔσται ἔτι . . . οὐκ ἔσται ἔτι. "Will be no longer."
οὐκ . . . οὔτε . . . οὔτε . . . οὔτε. "Not . . . neither . . . neither . . . nor" (BDF, §445.1).
ἔσται. Fut act ind 3rd sg εἰμί.
πένθος . . . κραυγὴ . . . πόνος. Nominative subject of ἔσται.
[ὅτι]. If original, it introduces a causal clause. It is possible that the ὅτι, absent in ℵ A 025 052 al, was omitted due to an error of sight following the ἔτι preceding it (see Aune, 3.1111). It may also have been added to clarify the relationship of τὰ πρῶτα ἀπῆλθαν to the preceding clause.

The ὅτι makes explicit grammatically the apparent semantic relationship (causal).

τὰ πρῶτα. Nominative subject of ἀπῆλθαν. The neuter plural subject here occurs with a plural verb, which normally only occurs with subjects referring to personal beings.

ἀπῆλθαν. Aor act ind 3rd pl ἀπέρχομαι. See also 10:9 on ἀπῆλθα.

21:5 Καὶ εἶπεν ὁ καθήμενος ἐπὶ τῷ θρόνῳ· ἰδοὺ καινὰ ποιῶ πάντα καὶ λέγει· γράψον, ὅτι οὗτοι οἱ λόγοι πιστοὶ καὶ ἀληθινοί εἰσιν.

εἶπεν. Aor act ind 3rd sg λέγω.

ὁ καθήμενος. Pres mid ptc masc nom sg κάθημαι (substantival). Nominative subject of εἶπεν.

ἐπὶ τῷ θρόνῳ. Locative.

ἰδοὺ. A marker of attention that deictically functions to make the following statement emphatic. Here it draws attention to the act of making all things new. On the form, see 1:7.

καινὰ. Complement in an object-complement double accusative construction with πάντα. The fronting of the complement is emphatic and, along with ἰδού, further draws attention to the theme of newness (see 21:1, 2).

ποιῶ. Pres act ind 1st sg ποιέω. The present tense is future referring.

πάντα. Accusative direct object of ποιῶ.

λέγει. Pres act ind 3rd sg λέγω. Historical or narrative present (see 4:5 on ἐκπορεύονται). It is difficult to discern a reason for the alternation between the aorist εἶπέν (vv. 5, 6) and the present tense λέγει here, unless perhaps the author wants to draw more attention to the reliability of the words of the book (see also 19:9). It is unlikely that Swete (279) is correct that the shift to the present λέγει indicates a new speaker without a clearer indication of a different speaker, since in verse 6 God is clearly still the one speaking.

γράψον. Aor act impv 2nd sg γράφω.

ὅτι. Introduces a causal clause. It is also possible, though less likely, that the ὅτι functions to introduce the clausal complement of γράψον, indicating what the seer is commanded to write.

οὗτοι οἱ λόγοι. Nominative subject of εἰσιν. The antecedent is probably the speech of the one seated on the throne in verse 5a or possibly the entire new creation prophecy of 21:1-5a (contra Osborne, 737, who takes it as referring to the entire book).

πιστοὶ καὶ ἀληθινοί. Predicate adjective.

εἰσιν. Pres act ind 3rd pl εἰμί. On the loss of accent, see 1:8.

21:6 καὶ εἶπέν μοι· γέγοναν. ἐγώ [εἰμι] τὸ ἄλφα καὶ τὸ ὦ, ἡ ἀρχὴ καὶ τὸ τέλος. ἐγὼ τῷ διψῶντι δώσω ἐκ τῆς πηγῆς τοῦ ὕδατος τῆς ζωῆς δωρεάν.

εἶπέν. Aor act ind 3rd sg λέγω. The accenting is due to the enclitic μοι that follows.

μοι. Dative indirect object of εἶπέν.

γέγοναν. Prf act ind 3rd pl γίνομαι. The perfect tense may be used to highlight the state of completion of God's plan for salvation that is finally reached in 21:1-8 in contrast to the parallel expression in 16:17 in relationship to God's climactic judgment. At this point in the history of Greek the perfect ending -ασι was in the process of being replaced by the 1st aorist 3rd plural ending -αν (Mussies, 265).

ἐγώ. Nominative subject of a verbless clause. But see on [εἰμι] below.

[εἰμι]. Some manuscripts (ℵ 025 046 051 1611 1854 2050 2229) omit εἰμι. The inclusion of εἰμι merely makes explicit what is implicit in the equative clause. Its inclusion could have been influenced by the occurrence of this phrase in 1:8 (Aune, 3.1111).

τὸ ἄλφα καὶ τὸ ὦ. Predicate nominative of a verbless clause. But see on [εἰμι] above. For this phrase, see also 1:8.

ἡ ἀρχὴ καὶ τὸ τέλος. Nominative in apposition to τὸ ἄλφα καὶ τὸ ὦ.

ἐγώ. Nominative subject of δώσω.

τῷ διψῶντι. Aor act ptc masc dat sg διψάω (substantival). Dative indirect object of δώσω. Fronted for emphasis.

δώσω. Fut act ind 1st sg δίδωμι.

ἐκ τῆς πηγῆς. Source. Modifies an assumed direct object of δώσω: "I will give *to drink* from the spring of the water of life."

τοῦ ὕδατος. Genitive of content or epexegetical genitive.

τῆς ζωῆς. Attributive genitive or epexegetical genitive.

δωρεάν. Adverbial accusative of manner.

21:7 ὁ νικῶν κληρονομήσει ταῦτα καὶ ἔσομαι αὐτῷ θεὸς καὶ αὐτὸς ἔσται μοι υἱός.

ὁ νικῶν. Pres act ptc masc nom sg νικάω (substantival). Nominative subject of κληρονομήσει.

κληρονομήσει. Fut act ind 3rd sg κληρονομέω.

ταῦτα. Accusative direct object of κληρονομήσει. The antecedent is probably all the blessings of the new creation depicted in verses 1-6.

ἔσομαι. Fut act ind 1st sg εἰμί. The first person verb and pronoun μοι demonstrate that this verse still belongs to the speech of the one sitting on the throne (vv. 5, 6).

αὐτῷ. Dative of reference or possession. The antecedent is ὁ νικῶν.

θεός. Predicate nominative of ἔσομαι.
αὐτὸς. Nominative subject of ἔσται.
ἔσται. Fut act ind 3rd sg εἰμί.
μοι. Dative of reference or possession.
υἱός. Predicate nominative.

21:8 τοῖς δὲ δειλοῖς καὶ ἀπίστοις καὶ ἐβδελυγμένοις καὶ φονεῦσιν καὶ πόρνοις καὶ φαρμάκοις καὶ εἰδωλολάτραις καὶ πᾶσιν τοῖς ψευδέσιν τὸ μέρος αὐτῶν ἐν τῇ λίμνῃ τῇ καιομένῃ πυρὶ καὶ θείῳ, ὅ ἐστιν ὁ θάνατος ὁ δεύτερος.

τοῖς ... δειλοῖς καὶ ... πᾶσιν τοῖς ψευδέσιν. Dative of reference (contrasts with the dative αὐτῷ in v. 7 above). Topic construction. The list of datives anticipates and is resumed by the pronoun αὐτῶν. This construction (left dislocation) draws attention to those who participate in these vices (see also 1:5 on Τῷ ἀγαπῶντι ... καὶ λύσαντι).

δὲ. Development. Within this context the inheritance of God's people is contrasted with the fate of those characterized by this vice list.

δειλοῖς. This term (lit. "cowards") refers to those who "for fear of losing social standing, economic wealth, physical well-being, and perhaps even life, they surrender their witness to God's lordship and testify to the lordship of Caesar and Rome instead" (Blount, 383).

ἐβδελυγμένοις. Pres mid ptc masc dat pl βδελύσσομαι (substantival). The term suggests "to strongly detest something on the basis that it is abominable" (LN 25.186). While Beale (1059) may be correct that idolatry is in mind, it is probably better to understand it as more broadly referring to one who engages in any practice that is destestable.

φαρμάκοις. This term refers to one who practices magic and sorcery (LN 53.101).

τὸ μέρος. Nominative subject of a verbless clause.

αὐτῶν. Possessive genitive. "The αὐτῶν resumes the eight classes mentioned in the preceding datives" (Charles, 2.217).

ἐν τῇ λίμνῃ. Locative.

τῇ καιομένῃ. Pres mid ptc fem dat sg καίω (attributive).

πυρὶ καὶ θείῳ. Dative of manner or means.

ὅ. Nominative subject of ἐστιν. The neuter gender of ὅ is incongruent with λίμνῃ. However, it may function to refer to the entire phrase τῇ λίμνῃ τῇ καιομένῃ πυρὶ καὶ θείῳ, or it may modify the neuter τὸ μέρος (Smalley, 544). On the other hand, it is likely that ὅ ἐστιν is a common way of explaining an idea.

ἐστιν. Pres act ind 3rd sg εἰμί. On the loss of accent, see 1:8.

ὁ θάνατος ὁ δεύτερος. Predicate nominative.

Revelation 21:9-21

⁹And one of the seven angels who had the seven bowls full of the seven last plagues came and spoke with me saying, "Come, I will show you the bride, the wife of the Lamb." ¹⁰And he led me away in the Spirit upon a large and high mountain, and he showed me the holy city Jerusalem coming down out of heaven from God, ¹¹having the glory of God, its splendor like a precious stone, as a jasper stone shining like crystal; ¹²it had a large and high wall, and had twelve gates and upon the twelve gates were twelve angels and names were written on the gates, which were the names of the twelve tribes of Israel; ¹³from the east three gates and from the south three gates and from the north three gates and from the west three gates. ¹⁴And the wall of the city had twelve foundations and upon them were the twelve names of the twelve apostles of the Lamb. ¹⁵And the one who was speaking with me had a gold measuring reed in order to measure the city and its gates and its wall. ¹⁶And the city was laid out foursquare and its length was as great as its width, and he measured the city with the reed at twelve thousand stadia; its length and breadth and height were equal. ¹⁷And he measured its wall, one hundred and forty cubits, the measure of a man, which is of an angel. ¹⁸And the material of its wall was jasper and the city was pure gold like pure glass. ¹⁹The foundations of the wall of the city were adorned with every precious stone: the first foundation jasper, the second sapphire, the third chalcedony, the fourth emerald, ²⁰the fifth sadonyx, the sixth sardius, the seventh chrysolite, the eighth beryl, the ninth topaz, the tenth chrysoprase, the eleventh hyacinth, the twelfth amethyst, ²¹and the twelve gates were twelve pearls, each one of the gates was from a single pearl. And the broad street of the city was pure gold as transparent glass.

21:9 Καὶ ἦλθεν εἷς ἐκ τῶν ἑπτὰ ἀγγέλων τῶν ἐχόντων τὰς ἑπτὰ φιάλας τῶν γεμόντων τῶν ἑπτὰ πληγῶν τῶν ἐσχάτων καὶ ἐλάλησεν μετ' ἐμοῦ λέγων· δεῦρο, δείξω σοι τὴν νύμφην τὴν γυναῖκα τοῦ ἀρνίου.

ἦλθεν. Aor act ind 3rd sg ἔρχομαι.

εἷς. Nominative subject of ἦλθεν.

ἐκ τῶν ἑπτὰ ἀγγέλων. Partitive.

τῶν ἐχόντων. Pres act ptc masc gen pl ἔχω (attributive). The participles ἐχόντων and γεμόντων are timeless (descriptive) or past, since the angels have already poured out their bowls in ch. 16 (Swete, 283).

τὰς ἑπτὰ φιάλας. Accusative direct object of ἐχόντων.

τῶν γεμόντων. Pres act ptc fem gen pl γέμω (attributive). There is grammatical incongruence between the case (genitive) of γεμόντων and the case (accusative) of τὰς ἑπτὰ φιάλας, which it modifies. The genitive ending may be influenced by the following τῶν ἑπτὰ πληγῶν τῶν ἐσχάτων. Predictably, a number of manuscripts (1 1006 1611 1841 1854 2030 2377 𝔐ᴷ) correct it to the accusative τὰς γεμούσας.

τῶν ἑπτὰ πληγῶν τῶν ἐσχάτων. Genitive complement of γεμόντων.
ἐλάλησεν. Aor act ind 3rd sg λαλέω.
μετ' ἐμοῦ. Accompaniment.
λέγων. Pres act ptc masc nom sg λέγω (manner). On the use of the participle λέγων to introduce speech, see 1:17 on λέγων.
δεῦρο. See 17:1.
δείξω. Fut act ind 1st sg δείκνυμι. It is also possible, along with Wallace (465) and Turner (94), to take this as a first person singular hortatory subjunctive following δεῦρο ("let me show you"). See also 17:1.
σοι. Dative indirect object of δείξω.
τὴν νύμφην. Accusative direct object of δείξω.
τὴν γυναῖκα. Accusative in apposition to τὴν νύμφην.
τοῦ ἀρνίου. Genitive of relationship.

21:10 καὶ ἀπήνεγκέν με ἐν πνεύματι ἐπὶ ὄρος μέγα καὶ ὑψηλόν, καὶ ἔδειξέν μοι τὴν πόλιν τὴν ἁγίαν Ἰερουσαλὴμ καταβαίνουσαν ἐκ τοῦ οὐρανοῦ ἀπὸ τοῦ θεοῦ

ἀπήνεγκέν. Aor act ind 3rd sg ἀπάγω. The accenting is due to the enclitic με that follows.
με. Accusative direct object of ἀπήνεγκέν.
ἐν πνεύματι. Manner or instrumental. On this phrase, see 17:3.
ἐπὶ ὄρος μέγα καὶ ὑψηλόν. Locative. Since the PP modifies ἀπήνεγκέν, the mountain is the vantage point from which John sees the vision rather than the location of the city.
ἔδειξέν. Aor act ind 3rd sg δείκνυμι. The accenting is due to the enclitic μοι that follows.
μοι. Dative indirect object of ἔδειξέν.
τὴν πόλιν τὴν ἁγίαν. Accusative direct object of ἔδειξέν.
Ἰερουσαλήμ. Accusative in apposition to τὴν πόλιν τὴν ἁγίαν.
καταβαίνουσαν. Pres act ptc fem acc sg καταβαίνω. It is possible that the participle is attributive. However, it likely functions as the complement in an object-complement double accusative construction with τὴν πόλιν τὴν ἁγίαν.
ἐκ τοῦ οὐρανοῦ. Source.
ἀπὸ τοῦ θεοῦ. Source. ἀπό can be used of the one who originates an action (BDAG, 106.5.d).

21:11 ἔχουσαν τὴν δόξαν τοῦ θεοῦ, ὁ φωστὴρ αὐτῆς ὅμοιος λίθῳ τιμιωτάτῳ ὡς λίθῳ ἰάσπιδι κρυσταλλίζοντι.

ἔχουσαν. Pres act ptc fem acc sg ἔχω. It is possible that the participle functions attributively to further describe the city, the New Jerusalem. However, it is also possible that it functions adverbially to modify the preceding participle καταβαίνουσαν, indicating manner.

τὴν δόξαν. Accusative direct object of ἔχουσαν.

τοῦ θεοῦ. Subjective genitive.

ὁ φωστήρ. Nominative subject of a verbless clause. The term can mean either a "light-giving body" or the "state of brightness or shining, *splendor, radiance*" (BDAG, 1073.2). If the latter, it refers to the appearance of the city; if the former, it refers to that which gives it light, presumably a reference to God himself. Supporting the latter is the fact that in 4:3 the appearance of the one seated upon the throne is likened to ἰάσπιδι, the same precious stone describing the φωστήρ here.

αὐτῆς. Subjective genitive.

ὅμοιος. Predicate nominative of a verbless clause.

λίθῳ τιμιωτάτῳ. Dative complement of ὅμοιος. The superlative is used with an elative meaning: "Most precious or valuable" (Turner, 31).

ὡς λίθῳ ἰάσπιδι. Comparison.

κρυσταλλίζοντι. Pres act ptc masc dat sg κρυσταλλίζω (attributive).

21:12 ἔχουσα τεῖχος μέγα καὶ ὑψηλόν, ἔχουσα πυλῶνας δώδεκα καὶ ἐπὶ τοῖς πυλῶσιν ἀγγέλους δώδεκα καὶ ὀνόματα ἐπιγεγραμμένα, ἅ ἐστιν [τὰ ὀνόματα] τῶν δώδεκα φυλῶν υἱῶν Ἰσραήλ·

ἔχουσα. Pres act ptc fem nom sg ἔχω. This participle may be further describing the holy city or be adverbial, parallel with ἔχουσαν in verse 11, but, given its case, it probably functions as a predicate of a verbless clause.

τεῖχος μέγα καὶ ὑψηλόν. Accusative direct object of ἔχουσα.

ἔχουσα. Pres act ptc fem nom sg ἔχω. On the function, see above on ἔχουσα.

πυλῶνας δώδεκα. Accusative direct object of ἔχουσα.

ἐπὶ τοῖς πυλῶσιν. Locative.

ἀγγέλους δώδεκα καὶ ὀνόματα. Accusative direct object of ἔχουσα.

ἐπιγεγραμμένα. Prf pass ptc neut acc pl ἐπιγράφω (attributive).

ἅ. Nominative subject of ἐστιν.

ἐστιν. Pres act ind 3rd sg εἰμί. On the loss of accent, see 1:8. Neuter plural subjects commonly take a singular verb.

[τὰ ὀνόματα]. These words, omitted by ℵ 051 𝔐ᴬ, seem to make explicit what is implied from the preceding clause, though it is possible that they were omitted because they were thought unnecessary in light of ὀνόματα above (Metzger, 689).

τῶν δώδεκα φυλῶν. Possessive genitive, modifying ὀνόματα whether implied or included.

υἱῶν. Epexegetical genitive.

Ἰσραήλ. Genitive of relationship.

21:13 ἀπὸ ἀνατολῆς πυλῶνες τρεῖς καὶ ἀπὸ βορρᾶ πυλῶνες τρεῖς καὶ ἀπὸ νότου πυλῶνες τρεῖς καὶ ἀπὸ δυσμῶν πυλῶνες τρεῖς.

ἀπὸ ἀνατολῆς … καὶ ἀπὸ βορρᾶ … καὶ ἀπὸ νότου … καὶ ἀπὸ δυσμῶν. Here ἀπό indicates "the point from which something begins, lit. or fig." (BDAG, 105.2). The entire clause further describes the τῶν δώδεκα φυλῶν by associating them with the four directions of the compass.

πυλῶνες τρεῖς … πυλῶνες τρεῖς … πυλῶνες τρεῖς … πυλῶνες τρεῖς. Nominative subject of a verbless clause.

21:14 καὶ τὸ τεῖχος τῆς πόλεως ἔχων θεμελίους δώδεκα καὶ ἐπ' αὐτῶν δώδεκα ὀνόματα τῶν δώδεκα ἀποστόλων τοῦ ἀρνίου.

τὸ τεῖχος. Nominative subject of ἔχων.

τῆς πόλεως. Partitive genitive.

ἔχων. Pres act ptc masc nom sg ἔχω. Again, the syntax of the participle is difficult. Robertson (412) calls it a mere slip. The fact that the case and gender do not "fit" any of the nouns it could modify, πόλιν or τεῖχος, may suggest that it is used to draw attention to this descriptive feature of the city. However, it may indicate that this is an example of the participle functioning independently as a main verb (cf. Porter 1989a, 376) or as the predicate of an implied verb. On this use of the participle, see 1:16 on ἔχων.

θεμελίους δώδεκα. Accusative direct object of ἔχων.

ἐπ' αὐτῶν. Locative.

δώδεκα ὀνόματα. Accusative direct object of ἔχων.

τῶν δώδεκα ἀποστόλων. Possessive genitive.

τοῦ ἀρνίου. Possessive genitive.

21:15 Καὶ ὁ λαλῶν μετ' ἐμοῦ εἶχεν μέτρον κάλαμον χρυσοῦν, ἵνα μετρήσῃ τὴν πόλιν καὶ τοὺς πυλῶνας αὐτῆς καὶ τὸ τεῖχος αὐτῆς.

ὁ λαλῶν. Pres act ptc masc nom sg λαλέω (substantival). Nominative subject of εἶχεν.

μετ' ἐμοῦ. Accompaniment.

εἶχεν. Impf act ind 3rd sg ἔχω. The "offline" imperfect tense form probably provides further supplemental information.

μέτρον κάλαμον χρυσοῦν. Accusative direct object of εἶχεν.

ἵνα. Introduces a purpose clause.
μετρήσῃ. Aor act subj 3rd sg μετρέω. Subjunctive with ἵνα.
τὴν πόλιν καὶ τοὺς πυλῶνας . . . καὶ τὸ τεῖχος. Accusative direct object of μετρήσῃ.
αὐτῆς . . . αὐτῆς. Partitive genitive.

21:16 καὶ ἡ πόλις τετράγωνος κεῖται καὶ τὸ μῆκος αὐτῆς ὅσον [καὶ] τὸ πλάτος. καὶ ἐμέτρησεν τὴν πόλιν τῷ καλάμῳ ἐπὶ σταδίων δώδεκα χιλιάδων, τὸ μῆκος καὶ τὸ πλάτος καὶ τὸ ὕψος αὐτῆς ἴσα ἐστίν.

ἡ πόλις. Nominative subject of κεῖται.
τετράγωνος. Predicate adjective with κεῖται. However, if κεῖται is understood as passive (Robertson, 813), then τετράγωνος could be part of a double nominative construction with a passive verb from a double accusative construction (cf. Culy 2009, 83–87).
κεῖται. Pres mid or pass ind 3rd sg κεῖμαι.
τὸ μῆκος. Nominative subject of a verbless clause.
αὐτῆς. Possessive genitive or partitive genitive.
ὅσον τὸ πλάτος. Predicate nominative of a verbless clause.
ἐμέτρησεν. Aor act ind 3rd sg μετρέω.
τὴν πόλιν. Accusative direct object of ἐμέτρησεν.
τῷ καλάμῳ. Dative of instrument.
ἐπὶ σταδίων δώδεκα χιλιάδων. Measure: "a degree extending to a particular point as marked by the context—'to the point of, to the extent of, to the degree that, up to'" (LN 78.51). On σταδίων as a unit of measurement, see 14:20. However, Beale provides the important reminder that we should not be too concerned to convert the unit of measurements into modern-day equivalents, "since the figurative nature and intention of the original numbers would become distorted" (1077).
τὸ μῆκος καὶ τὸ πλάτος καὶ τὸ ὕψος. Nominative subject of ἐστίν.
αὐτῆς. Partitive genitive (Young, 29).
ἴσα. Predicate adjective.
ἐστίν. Pres act ind 3rd sg εἰμί. It is common for a neuter plural subject (τὸ μῆκος καὶ τὸ πλάτος καὶ τὸ ὕψος) to be found with a singular verb.

21:17 καὶ ἐμέτρησεν τὸ τεῖχος αὐτῆς ἑκατὸν τεσσαράκοντα τεσσάρων πηχῶν μέτρον ἀνθρώπου, ὅ ἐστιν ἀγγέλου.

ἐμέτρησεν. Aor act ind 3rd sg μετρέω.
τὸ τεῖχος. Accusative direct object of ἐμέτρησεν.
αὐτῆς. Partitive genitive.
ἑκατὸν τεσσαράκοντα τεσσάρων πηχῶν. Genitive of content ("its measurement consisting of 144 cubits"). ἑκατὸν τεσσαράκοντα is indeclineable, its case being determined by the context.

μέτρον. Predicate nominative of a verbless clause: "(It is) a human measurement."
ἀνθρώπου. Attributive genitive ("human measurement").
ὅ. Nominative subject of ἐστιν.
ἐστιν. Pres act ind 3rd sg εἰμί. On the loss of accent, see 1:8.
ἀγγέλου. Attributive genitive ("angelic measurement"). Modifies an implied μέτρον.

21:18 καὶ ἡ ἐνδώμησις τοῦ τείχους αὐτῆς ἴασπις καὶ ἡ πόλις χρυσίον καθαρὸν ὅμοιον ὑάλῳ καθαρῷ.

ἡ ἐνδώμησις. Nominative subject of a verbless clause. Though this word can mean "a foundation" (LN 7.41), since the foundations are already mentioned (θεμέλιοι) most likely the word connotes "the material used in the construction" (LN 7.77; see BDAG, 334). That is, ἴασπις is to be understood as the material out of which the wall is constructed (Swete, 290).
τοῦ τείχους. The entire construction ἡ ἐνδώμησις τοῦ τείχους seems to indicate "the material from which the wall was constructed."
αὐτῆς. Partitive genitive. The antecedent is the city.
ἴασπις. Predicate nominative of a verbless clause.
ἡ πόλις. Nominative subject of a verbless clause.
χρυσίον καθαρὸν. Predicate nominative of a verbless clause.
ὅμοιον. Introduces a comparison.
ὑάλῳ καθαρῷ. Dative complement of ὅμοιος.

21:19 οἱ θεμέλιοι τοῦ τείχους τῆς πόλεως παντὶ λίθῳ τιμίῳ κεκοσμημένοι· ὁ θεμέλιος ὁ πρῶτος ἴασπις, ὁ δεύτερος σάπφιρος, ὁ τρίτος χαλκηδών, ὁ τέταρτος σμάραγδος,

οἱ θεμέλιοι. Nominative subject of a verbless clause, or possibly subject of the participle κεκοσμημένοι, if it is understood as an independent use of the participle.
τοῦ τείχους. Partitive genitive.
τῆς πόλεως. Partitive genitive.
παντὶ λίθῳ τιμίῳ. Dative of instrument or manner.
κεκοσμημένοι. Prf pass ptc masc nom pl κοσμέω. It is possible to understand this as a predicate use of the participle in a verbless clause ("the foundations [were] adorned"). However, it could also function independently as the main verb of the clause (Wallace, 653). Given the parallel with the previous clause depicting the makeup of the wall, the participle here should be understood as a predicate of a verbless clause.

ὁ θεμέλιος ὁ πρῶτος. Nominative subject of a verbless clause. The list of stones with which each foundation is identified also elaborates on παντὶ λίθῳ τιμίῳ.
ἴασπις. Predicate nominative of a verbless clause.
ὁ δεύτερος. Nominative subject of a verbless clause (ὁ θεμέλιος is implied with the remaining subjects).
σάπφιρος. Predicate nominative of a verbless clause.
ὁ τρίτος. Nominative subject of a verbless clause.
χαλκηδών. Predicate nominative of a verbless clause.
ὁ τέταρτος. Nominative subject of a verbless clause.
σμάραγδος. Predicate nominative of a verbless clause.

21:20 ὁ πέμπτος σαρδόνυξ, ὁ ἕκτος σάρδιον, ὁ ἕβδομος χρυσόλιθος, ὁ ὄγδοος βήρυλλος, ὁ ἔνατος τοπάζιον, ὁ δέκατος χρυσόπρασος, ὁ ἑνδέκατος ὑάκινθος, ὁ δωδέκατος ἀμέθυστος,

ὁ πέμπτος. Nominative subject of a verbless clause.
σαρδόνυξ. Predicate nominative of a verbless clause.
ὁ ἕκτος. Nominative subject of a verbless clause.
σάρδιον. Predicate nominative of a verbless clause.
ὁ ἕβδομος. Nominative subject of a verbless clause.
χρυσόλιθος. Predicate nominative of a verbless clause.
ὁ ὄγδοος. Nominative subject of a verbless clause.
βήρυλλος. Predicate nominative of a verbless clause.
ὁ ἔνατος. Nominative subject of a verbless clause.
τοπάζιον. Predicate nominative of a verbless clause.
ὁ δέκατος. Nominative subject of a verbless clause.
χρυσόπρασος. Predicate nominative of a verbless clause.
ὁ ἑνδέκατος. Nominative subject of a verbless clause.
ὑάκινθος. Predicate nominative of a verbless clause.
ὁ δωδέκατος. Nominative subject of a verbless clause.
ἀμέθυστος. Predicate nominative of a verbless clause.

21:21 καὶ οἱ δώδεκα πυλῶνες δώδεκα μαργαρῖται, ἀνὰ εἷς ἕκαστος τῶν πυλώνων ἦν ἐξ ἑνὸς μαργαρίτου. καὶ ἡ πλατεῖα τῆς πόλεως χρυσίον καθαρὸν ὡς ὕαλος διαυγής.

οἱ δώδεκα πυλῶνες. Nominative subject of a verbless clause.
δώδεκα μαργαρῖται. Predicate nominative of a verbless clause.
ἀνὰ εἷς ἕκαστος. Nominative subject of ἦν. Here ἀνά is used as an adverb (Robertson, 571; BDF §204; Charles, 1.cxxviii). With εἷς it is used in a distributive sense (lit. "up to one"), "each, apiece" (BDAG, 58.3; Moule, 66).

τῶν πυλώνων. Partitive genitive.

ἦν. Impf act ind 3rd sg εἰμί.

ἐξ ἑνὸς μαργαρίτου. ἐκ here indicates "the material out of which someth. is made" (BDAG, 297.3.h). The PP functions as the predicate of ἦν.

ἡ πλατεῖα. Nominative subject of a verbless clause. While this word is usually taken as a reference to the main, broad street running down the center of the city (BDAG, 823; LN 1.103), it could also be understood as the plaza or square in the center of the city (Aune, 3.1166).

τῆς πόλεως. Possessive genitive or partitive genitive.

χρυσίον καθαρὸν. Predicate nominative of a verbless clause.

ὡς ὕαλος διαυγής. Comparison.

Revelation 21:22-27

[22]And I did not see a temple in it, for the Lord God Almighty is its temple, and the Lamb (is its temple). [23]And the city did not have need of the sun nor the moon in order that they might give it light, for the glory of God enlightens it, and its lamp is the Lamb. [24]And the nations will walk through its light, and the kings of the earth will bring their glory into it, [25]and its gates will never be shut during the day, for there will no longer be night, [26]and they will bring the glory and honor of the nations into it. [27]And there will not enter into it anything unclean and the one who does abominations and the liar, but only those written in the Lamb's book of life.

21:22 Καὶ ναὸν οὐκ εἶδον ἐν αὐτῇ, ὁ γὰρ κύριος ὁ θεὸς ὁ παντοκράτωρ ναὸς αὐτῆς ἐστιν καὶ τὸ ἀρνίον.

As elsewhere in John's visions, the author mixes aorist, present, and future tense forms. The reason for this is not to reflect temporal concerns, as if the author narrated past events that depict future realities but then portrayed some events as if the author were present at the time they took place (Mussies, 336; Beale, 1101). Rather, the verb tenses (aspects) indicate the author's perspective on the various events that he saw (εἶδον) in his vision (see "Verbal Aspect" in the Introduction).

ναὸν. Accusative direct object of εἶδον. The accusative direct object precedes the verb εἶδον (see also 21:2 on τὴν πόλιν τὴν ἁγίαν). This may be to draw attention to the startling fact that there was no temple in the city.

εἶδον. Aor act ind 1st sg ὁράω.

ἐν αὐτῇ. Locative. The antecedent is "the city."

ὁ ... κύριος. Nominative subject of ἐστιν. The article functions to indicate that κύριος is the subject of ἐστιν.

γὰρ. Causal.

ὁ θεὸς. Nominative in apposition to κύριος.

ὁ παντοκράτωρ. Nominative in apposition to κύριος.

ναὸς. Predicate nominative of ἐστιν.

αὐτῆς. Possessive genitive.

ἐστιν. Pres act ind 3rd sg εἰμί. On the loss of accent, see 1:8.

τὸ ἀρνίον. Nominative subject of ἐστιν. The article indicates that ἀρνίον is (part of) the subject. There is lack of concord with the plural (compound) subject and the singular verb ἐστιν. A frequent pattern is to find the singular verb agreeing with the first mentioned subject (Porter 1992, 75). Wallace (401) suggests that the force of this construction is to stress the first-named subject. But it is highly doubtful that God is being stressed over the Lamb here.

21:23 καὶ ἡ πόλις οὐ χρείαν ἔχει τοῦ ἡλίου οὐδὲ τῆς σελήνης ἵνα φαίνωσιν αὐτῇ, ἡ γὰρ δόξα τοῦ θεοῦ ἐφώτισεν αὐτήν, καὶ ὁ λύχνος αὐτῆς τὸ ἀρνίον.

ἡ πόλις. Nominative subject of ἔχει. The explicit subject is mentioned to shift the topic back from God and the Lamb in verse 22 to the city.

οὐ ... οὐδὲ. "Not ... nor" (BDF §445.1).

χρείαν. Accusative direct object of ἔχει.

ἔχει. Pres act ind 3rd sg ἔχω. Historical or narrative present (see 4:5 on ἐκπορεύονται).

τοῦ ἡλίου οὐδὲ τῆς σελήνης. Genitive after χρείαν indicates that which is needed or is to be supplied (BDAG, 1088.1).

ἵνα. Introduces a purpose clause.

φαίνωσιν. Pres act subj 3rd pl φαίνω. Subjunctive with ἵνα. φαίνω is intransitive ("to shine or produce light"; BDAG, 1046.1) and is followed by a dative indicating location.

αὐτῇ. Dative of location.

ἡ ... δόξα. Nominative subject of ἐφώτισεν.

γὰρ. Causal.

τοῦ θεοῦ. Subjective genitive.

ἐφώτισεν. Aor act ind 3rd sg φωτίζω.

αὐτήν. Accusative direct object of ἐφώτισεν.

ὁ λύχνος. Nominative subject of a verbless clause.

αὐτῆς. Possessive genitive or objective genitive.

τὸ ἀρνίον. Predicate nominative of a verbless clause. It is possible that τὸ ἀρνίον should be understood as the subject in parallel with the subject ἡ δόξα τοῦ θεοῦ in the previous clause (Charles, 2.172) in a sort of chiastic construction. "The glory of God enlightens it" / "Its lamp is the Lamb."

21:24 καὶ περιπατήσουσιν τὰ ἔθνη διὰ τοῦ φωτὸς αὐτῆς, καὶ οἱ βασιλεῖς τῆς γῆς φέρουσιν τὴν δόξαν αὐτῶν εἰς αὐτήν,

περιπατήσουσιν. Fut act ind 3rd pl περιπατέω.

τὰ ἔθνη. Nominative subject of περιπατήσουσιν. In Revelation it is common for a neuter plural subject referring to persons to occur with a plural verb (Porter 1992, 73–74).

διὰ τοῦ φωτὸς. Locative.

αὐτῆς. Genitive of source.

οἱ βασιλεῖς. Nominative subject of φέρουσιν.

τῆς γῆς. Genitive of subordination.

φέρουσιν. Pres act ind 3rd pl φέρω. In the context of other future tense forms, the present tense here is probably future referring (Mathewson 2010, 73).

τὴν δόξαν. Accusative direct object of φέρουσιν.

αὐτῶν. Possessive genitive.

εἰς αὐτήν. Locative.

21:25 καὶ οἱ πυλῶνες αὐτῆς οὐ μὴ κλεισθῶσιν ἡμέρας, νὺξ γὰρ οὐκ ἔσται ἐκεῖ,

οἱ πυλῶνες. Nominative subject of κλεισθῶσιν.

αὐτῆς. Partitive genitive.

κλεισθῶσιν. Aor pass subj 3rd pl κλείω. The subjunctive is used with οὐ μὴ, which expresses emphatic negation.

ἡμέρας. Genitive of time (time during which).

νὺξ. Nominative subject of ἔσται.

γὰρ. A causal sense is to be preferred over Beale's (1096) suggestion that it is emphatic and to be translated "indeed," since the following clause naturally provides the reason why the gates do not need to be shut: There will be no more night, the time when city gates were shut to keep out anything/anyone unwanted (Osborne, 764).

ἔσται. Fut act ind 3rd sg εἰμί.

ἐκεῖ. Locative.

21:26 καὶ οἴσουσιν τὴν δόξαν καὶ τὴν τιμὴν τῶν ἐθνῶν εἰς αὐτήν.

οἴσουσιν. Fut act ind 3rd pl φέρω. The implied subject of this verb is unclear. It is possible to take the third plural construction as an indefinite plural (Aune, 3.1139), which could be translated as a passive ("the glory and honor of the nations will be brought into it"); or the subject could be οἱ βασιλεῖς from verse 24 (Mounce, 385). However, in verse 24 the kings are already depicted as bringing their wealth into the city. Beale (1100) argues that the text is not concerned with the precise subject, only that the glory and honor of the nations come into the city. Given that verses 25-26 are likely an allusion to Isa 60:11, where the open gates accommodate the influx of nations into the city, it is likely that the assumed subject of οἴσουσιν is the nations (Fekkes, 272).

τὴν δόξαν καὶ τὴν τιμὴν. Accusative direct object of οἴσουσιν.
τῶν ἐθνῶν. Possessive genitive or genitive of source.
εἰς αὐτήν. Locative.

21:27 καὶ οὐ μὴ εἰσέλθῃ εἰς αὐτὴν πᾶν κοινὸν καὶ [ὁ] ποιῶν βδέλυγμα καὶ ψεῦδος εἰ μὴ οἱ γεγραμμένοι ἐν τῷ βιβλίῳ τῆς ζωῆς τοῦ ἀρνίου.

καί. Blount (392) and Aune (3.1139) label this "adversative." However, this is a semantic rather than a grammatical judgment dependent on the relationship of the clauses. The καί simply indicates continuity.

εἰσέλθῃ. Aor act subj 3rd sg εἰσέρχομαι. The subjunctive is used with οὐ μή, which expresses emphatic negation.

εἰς αὐτήν. Locative.

πᾶν κοινὸν καὶ [ὁ] ποιῶν βδέλυγμα καὶ ψεῦδος. Nominative subject of εἰσέλθῃ. There is lack of concord with a plural subject and singular verb (εἰσέλθῃ). "A frequent pattern is to find a singular element closest to the singular verb" (Porter 1992, 75).

[ὁ] ποιῶν. Pres act ptc masc nom sg ποιέω (substantival). Nominative subject of εἰσέλθῃ.

εἰ μή. "Except, if not" (BDAG, 278.6.i.a).

οἱ γεγραμμένοι. Prf pass ptc masc nom pl γράφω (substantival). Nominative subject of an implied εἰσέλθῃ.

ἐν τῷ βιβλίῳ. Locative.
τῆς ζωῆς. Attributive genitive.
τοῦ ἀρνίου. Possessive genitive.

Revelation 22:1-5

¹And he showed me the river of the water of life shining like crystal, coming from the throne of God and of the Lamb. ²In the midst of the city's broad street and on either side of the river was the tree of life producing twelve fruits, giving its fruit according to each month; and the leaves of the tree were for the healing of the nations. ³And there will no longer be any curse. And the throne of God and of the Lamb will be in it, and his servants will serve him ⁴and they will see his face, and his name

will be on their foreheads. ⁵And there will no longer be night, and they will not have need of the light of the lamp and the light of the sun, for the Lord God will shine upon them, and they will rule forever and ever.

22:1 Καὶ ἔδειξέν μοι ποταμὸν ὕδατος ζωῆς λαμπρὸν ὡς κρύσταλλον, ἐκπορευόμενον ἐκ τοῦ θρόνου τοῦ θεοῦ καὶ τοῦ ἀρνίου.

ἔδειξέν. Aor act ind 3rd sg δείκνυμι. The accenting is due to the enclitic μοι that follows.
μοι. Dative indirect object of ἔδειξέν.
ποταμὸν . . . λαμπρὸν. Accusative direct object of ἔδειξέν.
ὕδατος. Genitive of content or epexegetical genitive.
ζωῆς. Attributive genitive or epexegetical genitive.
ὡς κρύσταλλον. Comparison.
ἐκπορευόμενον. Pres mid ptc masc acc sg ἐκπορεύομαι. The participle may function attributively modifying ποταμόν, or as the complement in an object-complement double accusative construction with ποταμὸν.
ἐκ τοῦ θρόνου. Source.
τοῦ θεοῦ καὶ τοῦ ἀρνίου. Possessive genitive.

22:2 ἐν μέσῳ τῆς πλατείας αὐτῆς καὶ τοῦ ποταμοῦ ἐντεῦθεν καὶ ἐκεῖθεν ξύλον ζωῆς ποιοῦν καρποὺς δώδεκα, κατὰ μῆνα ἕκαστον ἀποδιδοῦν τὸν καρπὸν αὐτοῦ, καὶ τὰ φύλλα τοῦ ξύλου εἰς θεραπείαν τῶν ἐθνῶν.

ἐν μέσῳ. Locative. Syntactically, there are two possibilities for what ἐν μέσῳ could modify (Charles, 2.176): (1) it could go with the verse that precedes; in this case the river of life is pictured as flowing down through the middle of the street/plaza (NRSV, NIV, ESV, Osborne, 770; Smalley, 562); (2) it could go with what follows; in this case the tree is found in the middle of the street/plaza (see the punctuation of the NA²⁸/UBS⁵, which place a full stop after τοῦ ἀρνίου in v. 1). While either is syntactically possible, the latter may be the more probable since having the tree in the midst of the street/plaza is consistent with an allusion to Gen 2:9 where the tree of life is in the midst (LXX ἐν μέσῳ) of the Garden. There is no need to try to make sense literally of the symbolism of the vision where the tree of life is in the midst of the street/plaza and on both sides of the river. More important than a precise visual reconstruction is the OT texts that the author evokes in his vision.
τῆς πλατείας. Partitive genitive. On the meaning, see 21:21 on πλατεῖα.
αὐτῆς. Possessive genitive or partitive genitive.

τοῦ ποταμοῦ. Partitive genitive.

ἐντεῦθεν καὶ ἐκεῖθεν. Locative. This expression (lit. "from here and from there") can be translated "on each side" (BDAG, 339.1, 301).

ξύλον. Nominative subject of a verbless clause.

ζωῆς. Attributive genitive. However, the idea communicated by the genitive seems to be "the tree that gives life" (see 2:7).

ποιοῦν. Pres act ptc neut acc sg ποιέω (attributive).

καρποὺς δώδεκα. Accusative direct object of ποιοῦν. Thompson (17) considers ποιοῦν καρποὺς to be a possible Hebrew idiom, found also in Aramaic. However, the expression is not entirely un-Greek (LSJ, 1428).

κατὰ μῆνα ἕκαστον. Temporal. Here κατά is used distributively (BDAG, 512.2.c): Lit. "according to each month."

ἀποδιδοῦν. Pres act ptc neut acc sg ἀποδίδωμι (manner, modifies ποιοῦν).

τὸν καρπὸν. Accusative direct object of ἀποδιδοῦν.

αὐτοῦ. Possessive genitive or genitive of source.

τὰ φύλλα. Nominative subject of a verbless clause.

τοῦ ξύλου. Possessive genitive or partitive genitive.

εἰς θεραπείαν. Purpose. Functions as the predicate of a verbless clause (Thompson, 85).

τῶν ἐθνῶν. Objective genitive. Some manuscripts omit τῶν ἐθνῶν (א 2053 2062 pc), perhaps in an effort to conform the text to Ezek 47:17, which says only that the leaves were for healing (Beale, 1108).

22:3 καὶ πᾶν κατάθεμα οὐκ ἔσται ἔτι. καὶ ὁ θρόνος τοῦ θεοῦ καὶ τοῦ ἀρνίου ἐν αὐτῇ ἔσται, καὶ οἱ δοῦλοι αὐτοῦ λατρεύσουσιν αὐτῷ

πᾶν . . . οὐκ . . . ἔτι. "No longer any."

πᾶν κατάθεμα. Nominative subject of ἔσται. While κατάθεμα could mean "a curse," more likely it means "an accursed thing" (BDAG, 517) here and has its background in the Hebrew חרם (cf. Zech 14:11) referring to the total destruction pronounced on an apostate nation (Osborne, 773; Beale, 1112; Aune, 3.1179: "curse of war"; BDAG, 517). This would be the corollary to the leaves that heal the nations in verse 2: their healing means they no longer need to fear destruction.

ἔσται. Fut act ind 3rd sg εἰμί.

ὁ θρόνος. Nominative subject of ἔσται.

τοῦ θεοῦ καὶ τοῦ ἀρνίου. Possessive genitive.

ἐν αὐτῇ. Locative.

ἔσται. Fut act ind 3rd sg εἰμί.

οἱ δοῦλοι. Nominative subject of λατρεύσουσιν.

αὐτοῦ. Possessive genitive. The antecedent of αὐτοῦ is ambiguous, since it could be either θεοῦ or ἀρνίου from the preceding clause. The ambiguity may be intentional and indicates the heightened Christology and reflects the trinitarian nature of the author's theology. "The two are conceived so much as a unity that the singular pronoun can refer to both" (Beale, 1113). See 11:15 on βασιλεύσει. On "Trinitarian Ambiguity" in 1–3 John, see Culy 2004, xxvii.

λατρεύσουσιν. Fut act ind 3rd pl λατρεύω. On the meaning of λατρεύουσιν, see 7:15.

αὐτῷ. Dative direct object of λατρεύσουσιν. On the ambiguity of the antecedent, see on αὐτοῦ above

22:4 καὶ ὄψονται τὸ πρόσωπον αὐτοῦ, καὶ τὸ ὄνομα αὐτοῦ ἐπὶ τῶν μετώπων αὐτῶν.

ὄψονται. Fut mid ind 3rd pl ὁράω.

τὸ πρόσωπον. Accusative direct object of ὄψονται.

αὐτοῦ. Possessive genitive. On the ambiguity of the antecedent, see on αὐτοῦ in verse 3.

τὸ ὄνομα. Nominative subject of a verbless clause.

αὐτοῦ. Possessive genitive. On the ambiguity of the antecedent, see on αὐτοῦ in verse 3.

ἐπὶ τῶν μετώπων. Locative. Functions as the predicate of a verbless clause.

αὐτῶν. Possessive genitive. The antecedent is οἱ δοῦλοι in verse 3.

22:5 καὶ νὺξ οὐκ ἔσται ἔτι καὶ οὐκ ἔχουσιν χρείαν φωτὸς λύχνου καὶ φωτὸς ἡλίου, ὅτι κύριος ὁ θεὸς φωτίσει ἐπ' αὐτούς, καὶ βασιλεύσουσιν εἰς τοὺς αἰῶνας τῶν αἰώνων.

νὺξ. Nominative subject of ἔσται.

οὐκ ... ἔτι. "No longer."

ἔσται. Fut act ind 3rd sg εἰμί.

ἔχουσιν. Pres act ind 3rd pl ἔχω. The implied subject is οἱ δοῦλοι from verse 3. In the midst of future tense forms, the present tense is future referring, as many scribes made explicit by substituting the future ἕξουσιν (A 1006 1841 2050 2053 2062 2329 *pc*).

χρείαν. Accusative direct object of ἔχουσιν.

φωτὸς ... φωτὸς. Genitive after χρείαν indicating that which is needed or to be supplied (BDAG, 1088.1).

λύχνου. Genitive of source.

ἡλίου. Genitive of source.

ὅτι. Introduces a causal clause.

κύριος. Nominative subject of φωτίσει.

ὁ θεὸς. Nominative in apposition to κύριος.

φωτίσει. Fut act ind 3rd sg φωτίζω. The verb φωτίζω can be used intransitively or transitively. Here it is used intransitively, "to function as a source of light, *to shine*" (BDAG, 1074.1).

ἐπ' αὐτούς. Locative ("upon/over them").

βασιλεύσουσιν. Fut act ind 3rd pl βασιλεύω.

εἰς τοὺς αἰῶνας τῶν αἰώνων. Temporal (see 1:18).

Revelation 22:6-9

⁶And he said to me, "These words are faithful and true, and the Lord God of the spirits of the prophets has sent his angel to show to his servants what is necessary to take place soon." ⁷"And look, I am coming soon. Blessed is the one who keeps the words of the prophecy of this book." ⁸And I, John, am the one who heard and saw these things. And when I heard and saw, I fell down to worship before the feet of the angel who showed me these things. ⁹And he said to me, "See that you do not! I am a fellow servant of you and of your brothers, the prophets, and of those who keep the words of this book; worship God."

22:6 Καὶ εἶπέν μοι· οὗτοι οἱ λόγοι πιστοὶ καὶ ἀληθινοί, καὶ ὁ κύριος ὁ θεὸς τῶν πνευμάτων τῶν προφητῶν ἀπέστειλεν τὸν ἄγγελον αὐτοῦ δεῖξαι τοῖς δούλοις αὐτοῦ ἃ δεῖ γενέσθαι ἐν τάχει.

εἶπέν. Aor act ind 3rd sg λέγω. The accenting is due to the enclitic μοι that follows. Some manuscripts (1611 1854 𝔐ᴷ) read λέγει, probably in conformity with the other present tense forms in this section (vv. 9, 10) and perhaps also with the corresponding account of John worshiping the angel in 19:9-10.

μοι. Dative indirect object of εἶπέν.

οὗτοι οἱ λόγοι. Nominative subject of a verbless clause. The antecedent could be the entire book of Revelation (Swete, 302; Smalley, 569), or at least beginning with 4:1. However, it is more likely that it refers specifically to the New Jerusalem vision in 21:9–22:5, which the angel, speaking here, has just shown (ἔδειξέν) to John.

πιστοὶ καὶ ἀληθινοί. Predicate nominative of a verbless clause. The two words together express the trust in and certainty of the fulfillment of God's act of bringing about a new creation (Beale, 1123).

ὁ κύριος. Nominative subject of ἀπέστειλεν.

ὁ θεὸς. Nominative in apposition to κύριος.

τῶν πνευμάτων. Genitive of subordination. Beale (1124) labels the genitive objective, but translates it "the Lord God (ruling) over (or inspiring?) the spirits." According to Aune, the point here is that "God sovereignly determines and controls the utterances of the prophetic servants so that what they say and write is both reliable and true" (3.1182).

τῶν προφητῶν. Possessive genitive.
ἀπέστειλεν. Aor act ind 3rd sg ἀποστέλλω.
τὸν ἄγγελον. Accusative direct object of ἀπέστειλεν.
αὐτοῦ. Possessive genitive or genitive of source.
δεῖξαι. Aor act inf δείκνυμι (purpose).
τοῖς δούλοις. Dative indirect object of δεῖξαι.
αὐτοῦ. Possessive genitive.
ἅ. Accusative subject of γενέσθαι. The relative pronoun ἅ introduces a headless relative clause. The entire clause functions as the direct object of δεῖξαι.
δεῖ. Pres act ind 3rd sg δεῖ (impersonal).
γενέσθαι. Aor mid inf γίνομαι (complementary). It is also possible that γενέσθαι is the subject of δεῖ: "To come about is necessary."
ἐν τάχει. Temporal. On the meaning of this phrase, see 1:1 on ἐν τάχει.

22:7 καὶ ἰδοὺ ἔρχομαι ταχύ. μακάριος ὁ τηρῶν τοὺς λόγους τῆς προφητείας τοῦ βιβλίου τούτου.

ἰδοὺ. A marker of attention that deictically makes the following statement emphatic. Here it draws attention to the following saying of Jesus. On the form, see 1:7.
ἔρχομαι. Pres mid ind 1st sg ἔρχομαι.
ταχύ. On ταχύ indicating imminence, see 1:1 on ἐν τάχει (see also BDAG, 993.2).
μακάριος. Predicate adjective of a verbless clause.
ὁ τηρῶν. Pres act ptc masc nom sg τηρέω (substantival). Nominative subject of a verbless clause.
τοὺς λόγους. Accusative direct object of τηρῶν.
τῆς προφητείας. Epexegetical genitive.
τοῦ βιβλίου τούτου. The idea communicated by the genitive is probably "the prophecy contained in this book."

22:8 Κἀγὼ Ἰωάννης ὁ ἀκούων καὶ βλέπων ταῦτα. καὶ ὅτε ἤκουσα καὶ ἔβλεψα, ἔπεσα προσκυνῆσαι ἔμπροσθεν τῶν ποδῶν τοῦ ἀγγέλου τοῦ δεικνύοντός μοι ταῦτα.

Κἀγὼ. On the form of this word, see 2:6. The ἐγώ in Κἀγώ functions as nominative subject of a verbless clause.
Ἰωάννης. Nominative in apposition to ἐγώ in Κἀγώ.
ὁ ἀκούων. Pres act ptc masc nom sg ἀκούω (substantival). Predicate nominative of a verbless clause. The two present participles ἀκούων and βλέπων are probably past referring (Mussies, 341), since John has already

seen and heard the visions recorded in the book (see ἤκουσα and ἔβλεψα below). Osborne (783 n. 7) overinterprets the present tense of the participles when he concludes that they "emphasize the ongoing reception of the visions throughout the Apocalypse." The present tense depicts the action as a process (see also "Verbal Aspect" in the Introduction).

βλέπων. Pres act ptc masc nom sg βλέπω (substantival). Predicate nominative of a verbless clause. On the function, see ἀκούων above.

ταῦτα. Accusative direct object of ὁ ἀκούων καὶ βλέπων. The antecedent is probably the contents of the entire book, though it may refer specifically to the vision of the New Jerusalem in 21:9–22:5.

ὅτε. Introduces a temporal clause.

ἤκουσα. Aor act ind 1st sg ἀκούω.

ἔβλεψα. Aor act ind 1st sg βλέπω. If original, this is the only place in the Apocalypse where John uses the aorist of βλέπω (supported by ℵ 1006 1841 2329 𝔐^A). Several manuscripts (A 2053 2062 2329) have the imperfect ἔβλεπον.

ἔπεσα. Aor act ind 1st sg πίπτω.

προσκυνῆσαι. Aor act inf προσκυνέω (purpose).

ἔμπροσθεν τῶν ποδῶν. Locative.

τοῦ ἀγγέλου. Possessive genitive.

τοῦ δεικνύοντός. Pres act ptc masc gen sg δείκνυμι (attributive). The accenting is due to the enclitic μοι that follows. The participle has past temporal reference, since the angel has already shown John the vision.

μοι. Dative indirect object of δεικνύοντός.

ταῦτα. Accusative direct object of δεικνύοντός. On the antecedent, see above on ταῦτα.

22:9 καὶ λέγει μοι· ὅρα μή· σύνδουλός σού εἰμι καὶ τῶν ἀδελφῶν σου τῶν προφητῶν καὶ τῶν τηρούντων τοὺς λόγους τοῦ βιβλίου τούτου· τῷ θεῷ προσκύνησον.

λέγει. Pres act ind 3rd sg λέγω. Historical or narrative present (see 4:5 on ἐκπορεύονται). Here the present tense may foreground the angel's response in contrast to the incorrect response of John in the aorist tense (ἔπεσα) in verse 8.

μοι. Dative indirect object of λέγει.

ὅρα μή. See 19:10.

ὅρα. Aor act impv 2nd sg ὁράω.

σύνδουλός. Predicate nominative of εἰμι. The accenting is due to the enclitic σού that follows.

σού. With the σύν- compound noun, the genitive here indicates association (Wallace, 129): "Fellow servant with you." The accenting is due to the enclitic εἰμι that follows.

εἰμι. Pres act ind 1st sg εἰμί. On the loss of accent, see 1:8.
τῶν ἀδελφῶν. On the function of the genitive, see σού above.
σου. Genitive of relationship.
τῶν προφητῶν. Genitive in apposition to τῶν ἀδελφῶν.
τῶν τηρούντων. Pres act ptc masc gen pl τηρέω (substantival). On the function of the genitive, see σού above.
τοὺς λόγους. Accusative direct object of τῶν τηρούντων.
τοῦ βιβλίου τούτου. The idea communicated by the genitive is probably "the words contained in this book." Here the antecedent is the entire book of Revelation.
τῷ θεῷ. Dative complement of προσκύνησον.
προσκύνησον. Aor act impv 2nd sg προσκυνέω.

Revelation 22:10-21

[10]And he said to me, "Do not seal up the words of the prophecy of this book, for the time is near. [11]The unjust person should continue to act unjustly and the defiled person should continue to be defiled, and the righteous person should continue to practice righteousness and the holy person should continue to be holy." [12]"Look, I am coming soon, and my reward is with me to give to each according to their work. [13]I am the Alpha and the Omega, the first and the last, the beginning and the end." [14]Blessed are those who wash their robes, in order that their authority might be over the tree of life and that they might enter into the city by the gates. [15]Outside are the dogs and sorcerers and the fornicators and murderers and idolaters and everyone who loves and practices lying. [16]"I, Jesus, sent my angel to testify about these things to you for the churches. I am the root and offspring of David, the bright morning star." [17]Both the Spirit and the bride say, "Come." And the one who hears must say, "Come." And the one who is thirsting must come; the one who desires must receive the water of life freely. [18]I testify to everyone who hears the words of the prophecy of this book: If anyone adds to these things, God will add to that person the plagues that are written in this book, [19]and if anyone takes away from the words of the book of this prophecy, God will take away that person's share in the tree of life and of the holy city, which are written about in this book. [20]The one who testifies about these things says, "Yes, I am coming soon." Amen, come Lord Jesus.
[21]The grace of the Lord Jesus be with everyone.

22:10 Καὶ λέγει μοι· μὴ σφραγίσῃς τοὺς λόγους τῆς προφητείας τοῦ βιβλίου τούτου, ὁ καιρὸς γὰρ ἐγγύς ἐστιν.

λέγει. Pres act ind 3rd sg λέγω. Historical or narrative present (see 4:5 on ἐκπορεύονται). Here it draws attention to the words of the angel that follow.

μοι. Dative indirect object of λέγει.

σφραγίσῃς. Aor act subj 2nd sg σφραγίζω (prohibition). Here the implication of the prohibition in this context is to forbid an action from beginning.

τοὺς λόγους. Accusative direct object of σφραγίσῃς.

τῆς προφητείας. Epexegetical genitive.

τοῦ βιβλίου τούτου. The idea communicated by the genitive is probably "the prophecy contained in this book."

ὁ καιρὸς. Nominative subject of ἐστιν.

γὰρ. Cause. Provides the reason for the command to not seal up the book.

ἐγγύς. The adverb functions as the predicate of ἐστιν.

ἐστιν. Pres act ind 3rd sg εἰμί. On the loss of accent, see 1:8.

22:11 ὁ ἀδικῶν ἀδικησάτω ἔτι καὶ ὁ ῥυπαρὸς ῥυπανθήτω ἔτι, καὶ ὁ δίκαιος δικαιοσύνην ποιησάτω ἔτι καὶ ὁ ἅγιος ἁγιασθήτω ἔτι.

ὁ ἀδικῶν. Pres act ptc masc nom sg ἀδικέω (substantival). Nominative subject of ἀδικησάτω. The term ἀδικέω here means "to do injustice" (Beale, 1134).

ἀδικησάτω. Aor act impv 3rd sg ἀδικέω. On the force of the third person imperative, see 2:7 on ἀκουσάτω.

ἔτι ... ἔτι ... ἔτι ... ἔτι. Expresses the notion of continuance (BDAG, 400.1.a).

ὁ ῥυπαρὸς. Nominative subject of ῥυπανθήτω.

ῥυπανθήτω. Aor pass impv 3rd sg ῥυπαρεύω. This word is a hapax legomenon in the NT. On the force of the third person imperative, see 2:7 on ἀκουσάτω.

ὁ δίκαιος. Nominative subject of ποιησάτω.

δικαιοσύνην. Accusative direct object of ποιησάτω.

ποιησάτω. Aor act impv 3rd sg ποιέω. On the force of the third person imperative, see 2:7 on ἀκουσάτω.

ὁ ἅγιος. Nominative subject of ἁγιασθήτω.

ἁγιασθήτω. Aor pass impv 3rd sg ἁγιάζω. On the force of the third person imperative, see 2:7 on ἀκουσάτω.

22:12 Ἰδοὺ ἔρχομαι ταχύ, καὶ ὁ μισθός μου μετ' ἐμοῦ ἀποδοῦναι ἑκάστῳ ὡς τὸ ἔργον ἐστὶν αὐτοῦ.

Ἰδού. A marker of attention that deictically functions to make the following statement emphatic. Here it draws attention to the following saying of Jesus (see also 22:7). On the form, see 1:7.

ἔρχομαι. Pres mid ind 1st sg ἔρχομαι. The present tense here is future referring.

ταχύ. Temporal. On ταχύ as an expression of imminence, see 1:1 on ἐν τάχει.

ὁ μισθός. Nominative subject of a verbless clause.

μου. Possessive genitive or genitive of source.

μετ' ἐμοῦ. Accompaniment. Functions as the predicate of a verbless clause.

ἀποδοῦναι. Aor act inf ἀποδίδωμι (purpose). The term means "to recompense, whether in a good or bad sense" (BDAG, 110.4). The focus here seems to be on recompense in a positive sense as the reward of eschatological salvation, though recompense in a negative sense in terms of judgment may also be in mind as well.

ἑκάστῳ. Dative indirect object of ἀποδοῦναι.

ὡς τὸ ἔργον ἐστὶν αὐτοῦ. Lit. "as is his/her work." The ὡς could be interpreted as "according to" (BDAG, 1104.1.b.γ), and is probably parallel to Jesus' statement in 2:23: δώσω ὑμῖν ἑκάστῳ κατὰ τὰ ἔργα ὑμῶν.

ἐστίν. Pres act ind 3rd sg εἰμί.

αὐτοῦ. Subjective genitive (modifying ἔργον).

22:13 ἐγὼ τὸ ἄλφα καὶ τὸ ὦ, ὁ πρῶτος καὶ ὁ ἔσχατος, ἡ ἀρχὴ καὶ τὸ τέλος.

These words probably still belong to the speech of Christ beginning in verse 12.

ἐγώ. Nominative subject of a verbless clause. The referent is probably still the speaker from verse 12, Christ.

τὸ ἄλφα καὶ τὸ ὦ. Predicate nominative of a verbless clause. On the meaning, see 1:8 on τὸ ἄλφα καὶ τὸ ὦ.

ὁ πρῶτος καὶ ὁ ἔσχατος. Nominative in apposition to τὸ ἄλφα καὶ τὸ ὦ.

ἡ ἀρχὴ καὶ τὸ τέλος. Nominative in apposition to τὸ ἄλφα καὶ τὸ ὦ.

22:14 Μακάριοι οἱ πλύνοντες τὰς στολὰς αὐτῶν, ἵνα ἔσται ἡ ἐξουσία αὐτῶν ἐπὶ τὸ ξύλον τῆς ζωῆς καὶ τοῖς πυλῶσιν εἰσέλθωσιν εἰς τὴν πόλιν.

It is not clear who the speaker is in verses 14-15. It could be John, since Jesus is reintroduced in verse 16 as the speaker.

Μακάριοι. Predicate nominative of a verbless clause.

οἱ πλύνοντες. Pres act ptc masc nom pl πλύνω (substantival). Nominative subject of a verbless clause. The words οἱ πλύνοντες τὰς στολὰς αὐτῶν are replaced by οἱ ποιοῦντες τὰς ἐντολὰς αὐτοῦ in 𝔐. The former reading ("those washing their robes") is probably original, and the latter reading ("those keeping his commands") could have arisen due to both phrases in Greek sounding similar (Metzger, 690). Further, elsewhere the author uses the expression τηρεῖν τὰς ἐντολάς in 12:17 and 14:12, though τὰς ἐντολάς does not occur with ποιέω (Aune, 3.1198). Perhaps the similar wording in 12:17 and 14:12 facilitated the change here (Beale, 1140). The variant "those who keep the commandments of God" may serve as an early interpretation of what "those who wash their robes" entails (Beale, 1140).

τὰς στολὰς. Accusative direct object of πλύνοντες.

αὐτῶν. Possessive genitive.

ἵνα. Introduces a purpose clause.

ἔσται. Fut act ind 3rd sg εἰμί. Future with ἵνα. On the use of the future in place of the subjunctive, see 3:9 on ἥξουσιν. Here the future and subjunctive (εἰσέλθωσιν) are used side-by-side after ἵνα.

ἡ ἐξουσία. Nominative subject of ἔσται. Here ἐξουσία seems to mean "a state of control over someth., *freedom of choice, right*" (BDAG, 352.1).

αὐτῶν. Subjective genitive.

ἐπὶ τὸ ξύλον. With ἐξουσία, ἐπί is a "marker of power, authority, control of or over someone or someth." (BDAG, 365.9).

τῆς ζωῆς. Attributive genitive. Or the idea of the genitive could be "the tree that gives life" (see also 22:2).

τοῖς πυλῶσιν. Dative of means or manner.

εἰσέλθωσιν. Aor act subj 3rd pl εἰσέρχομαι. Subjunctive with ἵνα.

εἰς τὴν πόλιν. Locative.

22:15 ἔξω οἱ κύνες καὶ οἱ φάρμακοι καὶ οἱ πόρνοι καὶ οἱ φονεῖς καὶ οἱ εἰδωλολάτραι καὶ πᾶς φιλῶν καὶ ποιῶν ψεῦδος.

ἔξω. Locative. Functions as the predicate in a verbless clause.

οἱ κύνες καὶ οἱ φάρμακοι ... καὶ ποιῶν ψεῦδος. Nominative subject of a verbless clause. Robertson (757) says that the repetition of the article can function to distinguish classes from other classes.

φιλῶν. Pres act ptc masc nom sg φιλέω (substantival). Nominative subject of a verbless clause. It is also possible to take πᾶς as the substantive and the participle as attributive.

ποιῶν. Pres act ptc masc nom sg ποιέω (substantival). On the function, see φιλῶν above.

ψεῦδος. Accusative direct object of ποιῶν.

22:16 Ἐγὼ Ἰησοῦς ἔπεμψα τὸν ἄγγελόν μου μαρτυρῆσαι ὑμῖν ταῦτα ἐπὶ ταῖς ἐκκλησίαις. ἐγώ εἰμι ἡ ῥίζα καὶ τὸ γένος Δαυίδ, ὁ ἀστὴρ ὁ λαμπρὸς ὁ πρωϊνός.

Ἐγώ. Nominative subject of ἔπεμψα.

Ἰησοῦς. Nominative in apposition to Ἐγώ.

ἔπεμψα. Aor act ind 1st sg πέμπω. Though Thompson (40) thinks this is an example of the aorist referring to present time, it is more likely that it has past reference in this context, summarizing the angel's role in showing John the previous vision. Furthermore, Thompson attributes such a usage of the aorist to Semitic influence from the Hebrew perfect, though it is not uncommon for the aorist tense to be used in non-past contexts (Porter 1992, 36–40). This does not preclude Semitic influence. See also "Verbal Aspect" in the Introduction.

τὸν ἄγγελόν. Accusative direct object of ἔπεμψα. The accenting is due to the enclitic μου that follows.

μου. Possessive genitive.

μαρτυρῆσαι. Aor act inf μαρτυρέω (purpose).

ὑμῖν. Dative indirect object.

ταῦτα. Accusative direct object of μαρτυρῆσαι. The antecedent is probably the contents of the entire book.

ἐπὶ ταῖς ἐκκλησίαις. "[A] marker of persons benefited by an event, with the implication of their being in a dependent relationship" (LN 90.40). Beale (1145) argues that ὑμῖν and ἐπὶ ταῖς ἐκκλησίαις refer to the same group, but this requires him to take ἐπὶ ταῖς ἐκκλησίαις unnaturally in the sense of "in/among the churches." We should probably understand ὑμῖν as referring to a specific group, perhaps church authorities or prophets, or possibly the angels of the seven churches (Rev 2–3), who witness "to" or "for the benefit of" the church (Aune, 3.1225-26; followed also by Osborne, 792; Smalley, 576).

ἐγώ. Nominative subject of εἰμι.

εἰμι. Pres act ind 1st sg εἰμί. On the loss of accent, see on 1:7.

ἡ ῥίζα καὶ τὸ γένος. Predicate nominative.

Δαυίδ. Genitive of source. "The root and offspring from David."

ὁ ἀστὴρ ὁ λαμπρὸς ὁ πρωϊνός. Nominative in apposition to ἡ ῥίζα καὶ τὸ γένος.

22:17 Καὶ τὸ πνεῦμα καὶ ἡ νύμφη λέγουσιν· ἔρχου. καὶ ὁ ἀκούων εἰπάτω· ἔρχου. καὶ ὁ διψῶν ἐρχέσθω, ὁ θέλων λαβέτω ὕδωρ ζωῆς δωρεάν.

Καὶ ... καὶ. "Both ... and."
τὸ πνεῦμα καὶ ἡ νύμφη. Nominative subject of λέγουσιν.
λέγουσιν. Pres act ind 3rd pl λέγω.
ἔρχου. Pres mid impv 2nd sg ἔρχομαι.
ὁ ἀκούων. Pres act ptc masc nom sg ἀκούω (substantival). Nominative subject of εἰπάτω.
εἰπάτω. Aor act impv 3rd sg λέγω. On the force of the third person imperative, see 2:7 on ἀκουσάτω.
ἔρχου. Pres mid impv 2nd sg ἔρχομαι.
ὁ διψῶν. Pres act ptc masc nom sg διψάω (substantival). Nominative subject of ἐρχέσθω.
ἐρχέσθω. Pres mid impv 3rd sg ἔρχομαι. On the force of the third person imperative, see 2:7 on ἀκουσάτω.
ὁ θέλων. Pres act ptc masc nom sg θέλω (substantival). Nominative subject of λαβέτω.
λαβέτω. Aor act impv 3rd sg λαμβάνω. On the force of the third person imperative, see 2:7 on ἀκουσάτω.
ὕδωρ. Accusative direct object of λαβέτω.
ζωῆς. Attributive genitive or epexegetical genitive.
δωρεάν. Manner.

22:18 Μαρτυρῶ ἐγὼ παντὶ τῷ ἀκούοντι τοὺς λόγους τῆς προφητείας τοῦ βιβλίου τούτου· ἐάν τις ἐπιθῇ ἐπ' αὐτά, ἐπιθήσει ὁ θεὸς ἐπ' αὐτὸν τὰς πληγὰς τὰς γεγραμμένας ἐν τῷ βιβλίῳ τούτῳ,

Μαρτυρῶ. Pres act ind 1st sg μαρτυρέω.
ἐγώ. Nominative subject of Μαρτυρῶ. The referent of the pronoun is difficult to determine. It could be Jesus speaking again (so Swete, 311; Charles, 2.218–19; Mounce, 396; Aune, 3.1229), or John (so Smalley, 583; Beale, 1154). The former view finds support in that the one who testifies in verse 20 is Jesus. The latter view possibly finds support in the multiple witnesses in this section: the angel (v. 16), Jesus (v. 20), and then John (vv. 18-19) (Beale, 1154). Perhaps a precise identification is difficult (and unnecessary?) since all the different voices within the book are ultimately embedded within the revelation of Jesus Christ (1:1).

τῷ ἀκούοντι. Pres act ptc masc dat sg ἀκούω (substantival). Dative indirect object of Μαρτυρῶ.
τοὺς λόγους. Accusative direct object of ἀκούοντι.
τῆς προφητείας. Epexegetical genitive.

τοῦ βιβλίου τούτου. The idea communicated by the genitive is probably "the prophecy contained in this book."

ἐάν. Introduces the protasis of a third-class conditional sentence. It is likely that the third-class condition here functions in a hortatory manner ("Don't add to"), or to support the hortatory intentions of the author in this section. The third-class condition only occurs elsewhere in the messages to the churches in 2:5, 22; 3:3, 20 in hortatory sections.

τις. Nominative subject of ἐπιθῇ.

ἐπιθῇ. Aor act subj 3rd sg ἐπιτίθημι. Subjunctive with ἐάν. The use of ἐπιθῇ and ἐπιθήσει in slightly different senses is an example of a rhetorical figure of speech known as paronomasia, a play on two different senses of the same word. This is meant to draw attention to the statement (Caragounis, 455–56).

ἐπ' αὐτά. A "marker of addition to what is already in existence" (BDAG, 365.7; LN 89.101). There is no neuter noun that could function as the antecedent for αὐτά in this verse. However, it is likely that the antecedent is the entire phrase τοὺς λόγους τῆς προφητείας τοῦ βιβλίου τούτου, perhaps accounting for the neuter gender of αὐτά.

ἐπιθήσει. Fut act ind 3rd sg ἐπιτίθημι. Mussies (323) incorrectly attributes to the future tense a Hebrew jussive or an imperatival sense: "God may (must) add." However, the future tense simply indicates what God can be expected to do, conditioned upon the fulfillment of the action in the protasis ("if anyone adds to these things"). See also ἐπιθῇ above.

ὁ θεὸς. Nominative subject of ἐπιθήσει.

ἐπ' αὐτὸν. On the meaning of ἐπί, see above on ἐπ' αὐτά.

τὰς πληγὰς. Accusative direct object of ἐπιθήσει. The variant, which includes ἑπτά (046 051 2377 𝔐^A) is no doubt secondary, intentionally or unintentionally conforming to earlier references to the seven plagues in the book (15:1; [17:1]; 21:9).

τὰς γεγραμμένας. Prf pass ptc fem acc pl γράφω (attributive).

ἐν τῷ βιβλίῳ τούτῳ. Locative.

22:19 καὶ ἐάν τις ἀφέλῃ ἀπὸ τῶν λόγων τοῦ βιβλίου τῆς προφητείας ταύτης, ἀφελεῖ ὁ θεὸς τὸ μέρος αὐτοῦ ἀπὸ τοῦ ξύλου τῆς ζωῆς καὶ ἐκ τῆς πόλεως τῆς ἁγίας τῶν γεγραμμένων ἐν τῷ βιβλίῳ τούτῳ.

ἐάν. Introduces the protasis of a third-class conditional sentence. On the function, see verse 18 on ἐάν.

τις. Nominative subject of ἀφέλῃ.

ἀφέλῃ. Aor act subj 3rd sg ἀφαιρέω. Subjunctive with ἐάν. On the figure of speech (ἀφέλῃ . . . ἀφελεῖ), see verse 18 on ἐπιθῇ.

ἀπὸ τῶν λόγων. Separation.

τοῦ βιβλίου. The idea communicated by the genitive seems to be the words "contained in this book."

τῆς προφητείας ταύτης. Epexegetical genitive or genitive of content.

ἀφελεῖ. Fut act ind 3rd sg ἀφαιρέω. See also ἀφέλῃ above.

ὁ θεὸς. Nominative subject of ἀφελεῖ.

τὸ μέρος. Accusative direct object of ἀφελεῖ.

αὐτοῦ. Possessive genitive.

ἀπὸ τοῦ ξύλου. Partitive. The PP is meant to provide a rhetorical contrast to ἀπὸ τῶν λόγων above, though the two expressions function in slightly different ways (one expressing separation, and the other being partitive).

τῆς ζωῆς. Attributive genitive. The idea communicated by the genitive may also be "the tree that gives life" (see 22:2).

ἐκ τῆς πόλεως τῆς ἁγίας. Partitive.

τῶν γεγραμμένων. Prf pass ptc masc or neut acc pl γράφω (attributive, modifying τοῦ ξύλου τῆς ζωῆς and τῆς πόλεως τῆς ἁγίας).

ἐν τῷ βιβλίῳ τούτῳ. Locative.

22:20 Λέγει ὁ μαρτυρῶν ταῦτα· ναί, ἔρχομαι ταχύ. Ἀμήν, ἔρχου, κύριε Ἰησοῦ.

Λέγει. Pres act ind 3rd sg λέγω.

ὁ μαρτυρῶν. Pres act ptc masc nom sg μαρτυρέω (substantival). Nominative subject of Λέγει.

ταῦτα. Accusative direct object of μαρτυρῶν. The antecedent could be the warning in verses 18-19, since verse 18 begins with Μαρτυρῶ. However, a reference to "witness" occurs in verse 16 (μαρτυρῆσαι), and the demonstrative ταῦτα occurs in verse 8 (twice) and verse 16 with reference to the entire book. Thus it is likely that ταῦτα refers to the entire book here also.

ναί. An exclamation that provides an emphatic affirmative response to a question or statement (Young, 201).

ἔρχομαι. Pres mid ind 1st sg ἔρχομαι. The present tense here is future referring.

ταχύ. Temporal.

Ἀμήν. An exclamation. See also 7:12 on ἀμήν … ἀμήν.

ἔρχου. Pres mid impv 2nd sg ἔρχομαι. The imperative may function to indicate an entreaty or polite command (see Wallace, 488).

κύριε Ἰησοῦ. Vocative of address.

22:21 Ἡ χάρις τοῦ κυρίου Ἰησοῦ μετὰ πάντων.

Ἡ χάρις. The nominative functions as the subject of an implied optative verb from εἰμί expressing a wish.
τοῦ κυρίου Ἰησοῦ. Genitive of source.
μετὰ πάντων. Accompaniment.

GLOSSARY

Adjectivizer—In Greek syntax, this term refers to an article that is used to change a non-adjective into an adjectival modifier. Thus, in the phrase, ἀπὸ παντὸς ἔθνους τῶν ὑπὸ τὸν οὐρανόν, the article τῶν changes the prepositional phrase, ὑπὸ τὸν οὐρανόν, into an attributive modifier of παντὸς ἔθνους.

Aktionsart—A term used in relation to verb tense that refers to the supposed objective quality of the action of the verb, e.g., whether it is punctiliar, durative, iterative, inceptive, etc.

Anaphoric—Referring back to, i.e., coreferential with, a preceding word or group of words. Thus, pronouns are anaphoric references to participants that have already been introduced into the discourse.

Anarthrous—Lacking an article.

Antecedent—An element that is referred to by another expression that follows it. Thus, the antecedent of a relative pronoun is that element in the preceding context to which the relative clause provides additional information.

Apodosis—The second part ("then" clause) in a conditional construction.

Arthrous/Articular—Including an article.

Ascensive—In Greek, this term is most often used in relation to conjunctions, especially καί. It refers to a usage that is intensive or expresses a final addition or point of focus. In such instances, the conjunction is typically translated, "even."

Aspect—This term is used in relation to verb tense and refers to the writer's/speaker's subjective choice of how to portray the verbal action, e.g., perfective or imperfective.

Attraction—Relative pronouns at times take on or "attract" to the case of their antecedent. For example, in the text, Πάντων δὲ θαυμαζόντων ἐπὶ πᾶσιν οἷς ἐποίει εἶπεν πρὸς τοὺς μαθητὰς αὐτοῦ ("While everyone was marveling at all that he was doing, he said to his disciples"), the expected case for the relative pronoun would be accusative (οὕς), since it functions as the direct object of ἐποίει. Instead, it has been attracted to the case of its antecedent (πᾶσιν).

Background—This term is used to refer to information that is off the event line, or storyline, i.e., those events or material that do not move the narrative forward. Instead, background information comments on, amplifies, or otherwise supports the narration.

Cataphoric—Referring forward to, i.e., coreferential with, a following word or group of words. The demonstrative οὗτος is frequently used in this manner.

Causative—Causative verbs or constructions denote that a new state of affairs is brought about or "caused" by the action of the verb or construction. Both δίδωμι and ποιέω are examples of verbs that can be used to form a causative construction. For example, in the text, δὸς τοῖς δούλοις σου μετὰ παρρησίας πάσης λαλεῖν τὸν λόγον σου (lit. "Give to your servants to speak your word with all boldness") the imperative and infinitive verbs (δὸς and λαλεῖν) form a causative verb phrase ("cause to speak").

Clausal complement—This type of complement is structurally a direct object, but since it is a clause rather than a noun phrase scholars often use the language of "complement" rather than "direct object." For example, ὅτι is often used to introduce complement clauses with verbs of speech that represent what was said: λέγω γὰρ ὑμῖν ὅτι δύναται ὁ θεὸς ἐκ τῶν λίθων τούτων ἐγεῖραι τέκνα τῷ Ἀβραάμ ("For I tell you that God is able to raise up children for Abraham from these stones.")

Clitic—A word that is written as a separate word in the syntax but is pronounced and accented as if it were part of another word. There are two types. Enclitics give their accent to the preceding word; proclitics shift the accent to the following word.

Complement—In the handbook, this term is used in two ways in addition to its use in the phrase, "clausal complement": (1) A constituent, other than an accusative direct object, that is required to complete a verb phrase. Verbs that include a prepositional prefix often take a complement whose case is determined by the prefix. E.g., verbs with the prefix συν- characteristically take a dative complement. (2) The second element in a double accusative construction, which completes the verbal idea. In the sentence, "I call my son Superman," Superman would be the complement.

Copula/Copular Clause—A copula is a linking verb that joins a subject and predicate into an equative or copular clause. In the copular clause, Ἡ γενεὰ αὕτη γενεὰ πονηρά ἐστιν ("This generation is a wicked generation"), the copula is ἐστιν.

Crasis—The merging of two words through the use of contraction, e.g., κἀμοί for καὶ ἐμοί.

Deictic—In this handbook the term deictic is used to refer to discourse deixis, which concerns "the use of expressions within some utterance to refer to some portion of the discourse that contains that utterance (including the utterance itself)" (Levinson, 85).

Elative—An adjectival form that denotes intensity or superiority.

Enclitic—A clitic is a word that appears as a discreet word in the syntax but is pronounced as if it were part of another word. *En*clitics "give" their accent to the *preceding* word.

Equative verb/clause—An equative verb, like εἰμί, γίνομαι, or ὑπάρχω, is a verb that joins a subject and predicate to form an equative clause ("something is something"), e.g., Ἡ γενεὰ αὕτη γενεὰ πονηρά ἐστιν ("This generation is a wicked generation").

External evidence—In textual criticism the evidence available from manuscripts and versions is described as external evidence. See also *internal evidence*.

Final (clause)—An older term for a purpose clause; it may also be applied to the function of individual elements such as the infinitive or participle.

Foreground—This term is used to refer to information that is on the event line, or storyline, i.e., those events that move the narrative forward.

Fronting—Placing a constituent earlier in the sentence than its default order, most commonly in a preverbal position.

Genitive of relationship—Wallace (83) prefers to limit this label to *familial* relationships, but we have followed Young (25–26) in applying it to a variety of *social* relationships as well, including slaves, friends, and enemies.

Hapax legomenon—A word that occurs only once in Greek literature or in the NT.

Haplography—The accidental omission of text.

Headless relative clause—A relative clause with no expressed antecedent, e.g., "He is doing *that which is not lawful*."

Hysteron-proteron—A stylistic device ("last-"first") where the author places the results before the process (e.g., "open-unseal").

Imperfective (aspect)—The semantic value of the present and imperfect tenses that indicates that the writer/speaker is portraying the situation as a process.

Inclusio—An "envelope" or "bookend" structure in which the same or similar language is used to begin and end a unit of discourse.

Intransitive—A type of verb that does not require a direct object. Some verbs may be either transitive or intransitive depending on the statement in which they are used.

Left Dislocation—This literary device introduces "the next primary topic of the discourse" (Runge 2009, §14.2) by placing it at the beginning of the sentence and then picking it up with a resumptive pronoun in the actual sentence. E.g., "The struggling student in my Greek class, he passed his mid-term exam with flying colors." Sometimes referred to as a "topic construction."

Litotes—A figure of speech in which a statement is made by negating the opposite idea. E.g., "she is *not* a *bad* tennis player" means "she is a *good* tennis player."

Marked—Departing from the normal or neutral pattern, or having additive features. At various levels of grammar, speakers/writers have a choice between various options. One option will typically be viewed as the "default" or "unmarked" member of the set. The other members are "marked." Something that is "marked" may be more prominent, in focus, emphatic, etc.

Merism—a literary device that mentions the extremes of a spectrum in order to portray everything in between the extremes ("the least to the greatest").

Metonymy/Metonym—Metonymy is a figure of speech in which one term is used in place of another with which it is associated. In the expression, "he was reading the prophet Isaiah," the writer ("the prophet Isaiah") is used as a metonym for his writings ("the book that the prophet Isaiah wrote").

Nominal (clause)—A nominal is a noun or something that functions like a noun. In a nominal clause, a nominative noun stands alone in the clause without a verb, and sometimes without any other elements.

Nominalizer—In Greek syntax, this term refers to an article that is used to change a word, phrase, or clause into a substantive. Most commonly, nominalizers are used to make an adjective or participle substantival.

Perfective (aspect)—The semantic value of the aorist tense that indicates that the writer/speaker is portraying the situation in summary as a whole with no reference to any process that might be involved. See also *imperfective aspect* and *stative aspect.*

Peak—A climactic development within a discourse.

Personification—A device whereby an author attributes a human characteristic to a nonhuman entity (inanimate object or abstract idea).

Prominence—The "semantic and grammatical elements of discourse that serve to set aside certain subjects, ideas or motifs of the author as more or less semantically or pragmatically significant than others" (Reed, 75–76).

Protasis—The first part ("if" clause) in a conditional construction.

Semitism—The influence of a Semitic language (Hebrew or Aramaic) on a Greek writer sometimes produces a form of expression that is atypical of a native Greek speaker. Sometimes this influence is indirect, mediated through the Septuagint (thus a Septuagintism).

Stative (aspect)—The semantic value of the perfect and pluperfect tenses that indicates that the writer/speaker is portraying a situation as a state or condition with no reference to any process or expenditure of energy. See also *imperfective aspect* and *perfective aspect*.

Storyline (discourse structure)—This term is used to refer to information that moves the narrative forward. In the narrative genre of the NT this is most commonly expressed with aorist tense forms or sometimes narrative presents.

Synecdoche—A figure of speech in which one term is used in place of another with which it is associated, specifically involving a part-whole relationship. In the sentence, "Do you have your own *wheels*?" the word "wheels" stands for the entire "vehicle" of which it is a part.

Topic construction—In the handbook, this term is used in relation to the phenomenon that linguists refer to as left dislocation. This literary device introduces "the next primary topic of the discourse" (Runge §14.2) by placing it at the beginning of the sentence and then picking it up with a resumptive pronoun in the actual sentence. E.g., "The struggling student in my Greek class, he passed his mid-term exam with flying colors."

Unmarked—The unmarked or default choice between two or more options refers to a writer choosing not to signal the presence of some feature (Runge §9.2).

WORKS CITED

Aune, David. *Revelation 1–5*. Word Biblical Commentary 52a. Dallas: Word, 1997.

———. *Revelation 6–16*. Word Biblical Commentary 52b. Nashville: Thomas Nelson, 1998.

———. *Revelation 17–22*. Word Biblical Commentary 52c. Nashville: Thomas Nelson, 1998.

Bakker, Egbert J. "Voice, Aspect, and Aktionsart: Middle and Passive in Ancient Greek." Pages 23–47 in *Voice: Form and Function*. Edited by B. Fox and P. Hopper. Typological Studies in Language 27. Philadelphia: Benjamins, 1994.

Bauckham, Richard J. *The Climax of Prophecy: Studies in the Book of Revelation*. Edinburgh: T&T Clark, 1993.

Beale, Gregory K. *The Book of Revelation*. New International Greek Testament Commentary. Grand Rapids: Eerdmans, 1999.

Black, David A. *Linguistics for Students of New Testament Greek: A Survey of Basic Concepts and Applications*. 2nd ed. Grand Rapids: Baker Academic, 1995.

Blount, Brian K. *Revelation*. New Testament Library. Louisville: Westminster John Knox, 2009.

Boyer, James L. "First-class Conditions: What Do They Mean?" *Grace Theological Journal* 2 (1981): 75–114.

———. "A Classification of Imperatives: A Statistical Study." *Grace Theological Journal* 8 (1987): 35–54.

Campbell, Constantine R. *Verbal Aspect, the Indicative Mood, and Narrative: Soundings in the Greek of the New Testament*. Studies in Biblical Greek 13. New York: Peter Lang, 2007.

———. *Verbal Aspect and Non-Indicative Verbs: Further Soundings in the Greek of the New Testament*. Studies in Biblical Greek 15. New York: Peter Lang, 2008.

Caragounis, Chrys C. *The Development of Greek and the New Testament: Morphology, Syntax, Phonology, and Textual Transmission.* Grand Rapids: Baker Academic, 2006.

Charles, R. H. *A Critical and Exegetical Commentary on the Revelation of St. John.* 2 vols. International Critical Commentary. New York: Charles Scribner's, 1920.

Conrad, Carl. "New Observations on Voice in the Ancient Greek Verb." Unpublished Paper, November, 2002. www.artsci.wustl.edu?~cw conrad/docs/NewObsAncGrkVv.pdf.

Culy, Martin M. *I, II, III John: A Handbook on the Greek Text.* Waco, Tex.: Baylor University Press, 2004.

———. "Double Case Constructions in Koine Greek." *Journal of Greco-Roman Christianity and Judaism* 6 (2009): 82–106.

Decker, Rodney J. *Temporal Deixis of the Greek Verb in the Gospel of Mark with Reference to Verbal Aspect.* Studies in New Testament Greek 10. New York: Peter Lang, 2001.

Fanning, Buist W. *Verbal Aspect in New Testament Greek.* Oxford: Clarendon, 1990.

Fekkes, Jan. *Isaiah and Prophetic Traditions in the Book of Revelation: Visionary Antecedents and Their Development.* Journal for the Study of the New Testament Supplement Series 93. Sheffield: Sheffield Academic, 1994.

Harris, Murray J. *Prepositions and Theology in the Greek New Testament.* Grand Rapids: Zondervan, 2012.

Hauck, F. and S. Schultz. "πόρνη κτλ." Pages 579–95 in vol. 6 of *Theological Dictionary of the New Testament.* Edited by G. Kittel and G. Friedrich. Translated by G. Bromiley. 10 vols. Grand Rapids: Eerdmans, 1964–1976.

Hemer, Colin. *The Letters to the Seven Churches of Asia in their Local Setting.* Grand Rapids: Eerdmans, 1986 (reprint 2001).

Levinson, Stephen C. *Pragmatics.* Cambridge Textbooks in Linguistics. Cambridge: Cambridge University Press, 1983.

Levinsohn, Stephen H. *Discourse Features of New Testament Greek: A Coursebook on the Information Structure of New Testament Greek.* 2nd ed. Dallas: SIL, 2000.

———. "Toward a Unified Linguistic Description of οὗτος and ἐκεῖνος." Pages 204–16 in *The Linguist as Pedagogue: Trends in the Teaching and Linguistic Analysis of the Greek New Testament.* Edited by S. E. Porter and M. B. O'Donnell. Sheffield: Sheffield Phoenix, 2009.

McKay, K. L. "On the Perfect and Other Aspects in New Testament Greek." *Novum Testamentum* 23 (1981): 289–329.

———. "Time and Aspect in New Testament Greek." *Novum Testamentum* 34 (1992): 209–28.

———. *A New Syntax of the Verb in New Testament Greek: An Aspectual Approach*. Studies in Biblical Greek 5. New York: Peter Lang, 1994.

Mathewson, David. "Verbal Aspect in Imperatival Constructions in Pauline Ethical Injunctions." *Filologia Neotestamentaria* 17 (1996): 21–35.

———. *Verbal Aspect in the Book of Revelation: The Function of Greek Verb Tenses in John's Apocalypse*. Linguistic Biblical Studies 4. Leiden: Brill, 2010.

Metzger, Bruce M. *A Textual Commentary on the Greek New Testament*. 2nd ed. Stuttgart: United Bible Society, 1994.

Moule, C. F. D. *An Idiom Book of New Testament Greek*. 2nd ed. Cambridge: Cambridge University Press, 1959.

Moulton, James H. *A Grammar of New Testament Greek. I. Prolegomena*. 3rd ed. Edinburgh: T&T Clark, 1908.

Moulton, James H., and George Milligan. *The Vocabulary of the Greek New Testament Illustrated from the Papyri and Other Non-Literary Sources*. Grand Rapids: Eerdmans, 1930 (reprint 1980).

Mounce, Robert H. *The Book of Revelation*. New International Commentary on the New Testament. Grand Rapids: Eerdmans, 1977.

Mussies, G. *The Morphology of Koine Greek as Used in the Apocalypse of John: A Study in Bilingualism*. Novum Testamentum Supplement 27. Leiden: Brill, 1971.

Nida, E. A. et al. *Style and Discourse, with Special Reference to the Text of the Greek New Testament*. Cape Town: Bible Society, 1983.

Osborne, Grant R. *Revelation*. Baker Exegetical Commentary on the New Testament. Grand Rapids: Baker Academic, 2002.

Pennington, Jonathan T. "Deponency in Koine Greek: The Grammatical Question and the Lexicographical Dilemma." *Trinity Journal* 24 (2003): 55–76.

Porter, Stanley E. *Verbal Aspect in the Greek of the New Testament, with Reference to Tense and Mood*. Studies in Biblical Greek 1. New York: Peter Lang, 1989a.

———. "The Language of the Apocalypse in Recent Discussion." *New Testament Studies* 35 (1989b): 582–603.

———. *Idioms of the Greek New Testament*. Biblical Language: Greek 2. Sheffield: Sheffield Academic, 1992.

Reed, Jeffrey T. *Discourse Analysis of Philippians: Method and Rhetoric in the Debate over Literary Integrity*. Journal for the Study of the New Testament Supplement Series 136. Sheffield: Sheffield Academic, 1997.

Resseguie, James L. *The Revelation of John: A Narrative Commentary*. Grand Rapids: Baker Academic, 2009.

Robertson, A. T. *A Grammar of the Greek New Testament in the Light of Historical Research*. 4th ed. Nashville: Broadman, 1934.

Runge, Steven E. *Discourse Grammar of the Greek New Testament*. Peabody, Mass.: Hendrickson, 2010.

Schmidt, Daryl D. "Semitisms and Septuagintalisms in the Book of Revelation." *New Testament Studies* 37 (1991): 592–603.

Smalley, Stephen S. *The Revelation to John: A Commentary on the Greek Text of the Apocalypse*. Downers Grove, Ill.: InterVarsity, 2005.

Strathmann, H. "λατρεύω, λατρεία." Pages 58–65 in vol. 4 of *Theological Dictionary of the New Testament*. Edited by G. Kittel and G. Friedrich. Translated by G. Bromiley. 10 vols. Grand Rapids: Eerdmans, 1964–1976.

Swete, Henry Barclay. *The Apocalypse of St. John*. Grand Rapids: Eerdmans, 1968 (reprint).

Taylor, Bernard A. "Deponency and Greek Lexicography." Pages 167–76 in *Biblical Greek Language and Lexicography: Essays in Honor of Frederick W. Danker*. Edited by B. A. Taylor et al. Grand Rapids: Eerdmans, 2004.

Thompson, Steven. *The Apocalypse and Semitic Syntax*. Cambridge: Cambridge University Press, 1985.

Turner, Nigel. *A Grammar of New Testament Greek. III: Syntax*. Edinburgh: T&T Clark, 1963.

Wallace, Daniel B. *Greek Grammar Beyond the Basics: An Exegetical Syntax of the New Testament*. Grand Rapids: Zondervan, 1996.

Young, Richard A. *Intermediate New Testament Greek: A Linguistic and Exegetical Approach*. Nashville: Broadman & Holman, 1994.

Zerwick, Maximilian. *Biblical Greek Illustrated by Examples*. Rome: Pontifical Biblical Institute, 1963.

GRAMMAR INDEX

Accusative absolute, 1:20
Accusative complement, 17:3, 4
Accusative direct object, 1:1, 2^2, 3^2,
  5², 6, 7², 10, 11, 12², 13³, 16, 17², 18,
  19, 20², 2:1², 2:2⁵, 3, 4, 5², 6³, 7², 8,
  9², 10³, 11², 12², 13², 14⁵, 15², 17³,
  18², 19, 20⁴, 21, 22², 23², 24³, 25,
  26², 27, 28, 29², 3:1⁴, 2², 4², 5², 6², 7²,
  8⁷, 9², 10³, 11², 12⁴, 13², 14, 15, 16,
  17, 18⁴, 19, 22², 4:1, 7, 8², 9, 10, 11²,
  5:1, 2³, 3², 4², 5, 6², 8², 9³, 10, 11, 12,
  13², 6:1, 2, 3, 4², 5², 6, 7², 9³, 10, 12,
  13, 15, 16, 7:1², 2³, 3², 9², 13, 14²,
  17³, 8:1, 2, 3, 5², 6², 9, 9:1, 2, 3, 4²,
  5², 6², 8, 9, 10², 11², 14², 15, 17³, 19,
  20, 10:1², 2³, 3, 4², 5², 6, 7, 8, 9³, 10³,
  11:1, 2³, 3, 5³, 6⁵, 7⁴, 9, 10², 11, 12,
  13, 17, 18⁴, 12:1, 3², 4³, 5², 6², 9, 10,
  11², 12², 13², 15², 16³, 17³, 13:1³, 2²,
  3, 4, 5, 6³, 7², 8, 9, 11², 12³, 13, 14³,
  15, 16², 17, 18², 14:1, 3², 6², 7³, 8,
  9², 11³, 12², 14, 15, 16, 17, 18⁴, 19²,
  15:1², 2², 3², 4, 6³, 7, 16:1, 2², 3, 4,
  5, 6², 8², 9⁴, 10², 11, 12, 13, 14², 15²,
  16, 17, 19, 21, 17:1², 2, 3³, 4², 6³, 7³,
  8², 9, 12³, 13², 14, 15, 16⁵, 17³, 18²,
  18:1², 4, 5, 6², 7³, 8, 9, 11, 12, 13²,
  14, 16, 17, 18, 19², 20, 21, 19:2³, 5,
  7², 8, 10, 11, 12², 13, 14, 15³, 16, 17,
  18, 19², 20⁴, 20:1², 2², 3³, 4⁴, 6², 8²,
  9³, 10, 11², 12, 13², 21:1, 2, 4, 5, 7,
  9², 10², 11, 12³, 14², 15², 16, 17, 22,
  23², 24, 26, 22:1, 2², 4, 5, 6, 7, 8², 9,
  10, 11, 14, 15, 16², 17, 18², 19, 20
Accusative direct object of implied
  verb, 1:20, 4:4³, 9:4, 14:14
Accusative in apposition, 1:6, 2:20,
  9:11, 10:7, 11:18, 12:5, 13:6, 16, 17,
  14:1, 15:1, 16:12, 18:12, 20:8, 12,
  21:2, 9
Accusative indicating extent of time,
  3:3, 9:5, 10, 11:2, 3, 6, 9, 12:6, 14,
  13:5, 20:2, 3
Accusative with οὐαί, 8:13, 12:12
Accusative of respect, 1:20
Accusative subject of the infinitive,
  1:1, 2:9. 3:9, 4:1, 10:11, 11:5, 9,
  13:10, 13, 17:10, 22:6
Adjectivizer, 1:4, 2:24, 5:5, 7:17, 8:3,
  9, 9:13, 11:19, 14:17, 16:12, 19:14,
  20:8, 13²
Adverbial accusative, 2:10, 3:17, 9:5,
  17:10, 21:6
ἀκούω with genitive vs. accusative,
  1:3, 10, 3:20, 4:1, 5:11, 13, 6:1, 3, 5,
  7, 7:4, 8:13, 9:13, 16, 10:4, 8, 11:12,
  12:10, 14:2², 13, 16:1, 5, 7, 21:3

ἀλλά (corrective, adversative), 2:4, 6, 9², 14, 20, 3:4, 9, 9:5, 10:7, 9, 17:12, 20:6
ἀνά (distributive), 4:8
ἀνά (spatial), 7:17
Anaphoric article, 2:12, 4:2², 3², 5:1², 6, 6:1, 7:2, 12:4, 13, 13:2, 14:3, 18², 15:6, 7, 8, 17:6, 7², 20:3
ἀπό (agency), 12:6
ἀπό (locative, distance), 14:20, 18:10, 15, 17
ἀπό (means), 9:18
ἀπό (partitive), 22:19
ἀπό ("point from which"), 21:13
ἀπό (separation), 6:16², 9:6, 12:14, 14:3, 4, 18:14², 20:11, 22:19
ἀπό (source), 1:4², 5, 3:12, 7:2, 9:18, 16:12, 17, 18:15, 19:5, 21:2, 10
ἀπό (temporal), 13:8, 14:13, 16:18, 17:8
Attraction (accusative),
Attraction (dative), 18:6
Attraction (genitive), 4:1
Attributive genitive, 1:3, 14, 2:18, 3:5, 18, 4:5, 6:1, 8, 12, 7:17, 9:13, 16, 10:1, 11:11, 13:1, 3, 8, 12, 18, 14:11, 16:3, 14, 19², 17:3, 5, 8, 18:3, 13, 19:9, 12, 15, 20, 20:6, 10, 12, 14², 15², 21:6, 17², 27, 22:1, 2, 14, 17, 19
αὐτός (intensive),
ἄχρι (extent), 12:11, 14:20, 18:5
ἄχρι(ς) (temporal), 2:10, 25, 26, 7:3, 15:8, 17:17, 20:3, 5

Chiasm, 3:7, 10:9, 10, 21:1
Cognate accusative, 5:9, 14:3, 15:3², 17:6
Cognate dative, 5:1, 12
Complement in double accusative, 1:6, 11
Complement in double dative, 1:9

Construction according to sense, 4:1, 14:3, 16:3, 17:3², 16, 18:4, 19:1, 14, 15, 20:9
Crasis, 2:6

Dative complement, 1:15, 2:18, 4:3², 6, 7³, 9:7², 10, 19, 11:1, 13:2, 4, 11, 18:18, 21:11, 18
Dative in apposition, 1:1, 2:24, 9:14, 11:18
Dative of advantage/disadvantage, 1:4, 6, 5:9, 10, 8:3, 13:14, 14:4, 18:6, 20:4, 11, 21:2
Dative of association, 15:2
Dative direct object, 3:18, 4:10, 7:11, 15, 11:16, 12:16, 13:4², 15, 14:4, 7, 9, 16:2, 19:4, 5, 10², 14, 20, 22:3, 9
Dative indirect object, 1:1³, 11, 2:1, 7³, 8, 10, 11, 12, 14, 17³, 18, 21, 23, 24, 26, 28, 29, 3:1, 6, 7, 13, 14, 21, 22, 4:1, 9, 5:5, 6:2, 4³, 8, 11², 16, 7:2², 13, 14², 8:2, 3, 9:1, 3, 4, 5, 13, 10:9³, 11, 11:1, 2, 3, 10, 12, 13, 17, 18, 12:14, 13:2, 4, 5², 7², 14², 15², 16, 14:7, 15, 18, 15:7, 16:1, 6, 8, 9, 19, 17:1, 7, 13, 15, 17, 18:6, 7, 19:7, 8, 9², 10, 17, 20:4, 21:6², 9, 10, 22:1, 6², 8, 9, 10, 12, 16, 18
Dative of location, 2:5, 16, 19:13, 21:23
Dative of manner, 6:10, 7:2, 10, 8:8, 13, 10:3, 18:21, 19:17, 21:8, 19, 22:14
Dative of means/instrument, 5:1, 12, 6:10, 7:2, 10, 8:8, 13, 10:3, 14:18, 17:4, 18:16, 19:17, 21:8, 16, 19, 22:14
Dative of possession, 1:5², 6, 5:13², 6:8, 7:10, 12, 9:11, 21:7²,
Dative of recipient, 1:4
Dative of respect/reference, 4:3², 6:8, 8:3, 9:11², 16:16, 21:7², 8
Dative of time, 8:3, 18:10, 17, 19

Grammar Index

δέ (development), 1:14, 2:24, 10:2, 19:12, 21:8
διά (cause), 1:9, 2:3, 4:11, 6:9², 7:15, 12:11², 12, 13:14, 17:7, 18:8, 10, 15, 20:4²,
διά (intermediate agent), 1:1
διά (spatial), 21:24
Diminutive, 5:6, 10:2
Double accusative construction, 1:6, 2:2², 20, 3:2, 12, 4:1, 4, 5:1, 2, 4, 6, 10, 13, 6:1, 6, 7:1, 2, 9:1, 14, 17, 10:1, 4, 5, 8, 12:9, 10, 15, 13:1, 11, 14:6, 15:2, 16:16, 17:3, 6, 16, 18:1, 4, 19:11, 17, 19, 20:1, 12, 21:2, 5, 10, 22:1
Double dative construction, 1:9
Double diminutive, 10:2
Double genitive construction, 6:3, 5, 8:13, 11:12, 14:13, 16:1, 5, 7, 19:6, 21:3
Double nominative construction, 5:4, 7:9, 8:11, 11:8, 12:9, 19:11, 13, 20:15, 21:16

εἰς (direction), 1:11, 5:6, 10:5, 19:9
εἰς (goal), 9:9, 15, 11:6, 13:10, 14:19², 16:1, 2, 3, 4, 14, 19, 17:8, 11, 19:9
εἰς (locative), 1:11, 2:10, 22², 5:6, 6:13, 15, 8:5, 7, 8, 9:1, 3, 10:5, 11:9, 12, 12:4, 6, 9, 13, 14², 13:13, 15:8, 16:16, 17:3, 17, 18:21, 19:17, 20:3, 10, 14, 15, 21:24, 26, 27, 22:14
εἰς (predicate after linking verb), 8:11
εἰς (purpose), 9:7, 13:6, 16:14, 20:8, 22:2
εἰς (result), 13:3, 16:19
εἰς (temporal), 1:6, 18, 4:9, 10, 5:13, 7:12, 10:6, 11:15, 14:11, 15:7, 19:3, 20:10, 22:5
ἐκ (cause), 6:10, 8:11, 13, 9:2, 15:8, 16:10, 11², 21, 17:2, 18:3, 19, 19:2, 20:12

ἐκ (content), 18:12
ἐκ (instrumental), 2:11
ἐκ ("material out of which"), 21:21
ἐκ (means), 3:18, 9:18, 17:2, 18:3, 19:2, 21
ἐκ (partitive), 2:7, 10, 3:9, 5:5, 9, 6:1², 7:4, 9, 13, 11:9, 13:3, 15:7, 17:1, 11, 18:4, 21:9, 22:19
ἐκ (separation), 1:5, 2:5, 21, 22, 3:5, 10, 16, 5:7, 6:4, 14, 7:14, 17, 9:20, 21⁴, 10:10, 14:13, 15:2, 6, 16:11, 18:4, 20:7, 21:4
ἐκ (source), 1:16, 2:7, 9, 3:12, 4:5, 6:10, 7:4, 9, 8:4, 5, 10, 9:1, 2, 3, 13, 17, 18², 10:1, 4, 8, 11:5, 7, 11, 12, 12:15, 16, 13:1, 11, 13, 14:2, 8, 10, 13, 15, 17, 18, 20, 15:8, 16:1, 10, 13, 17, 21, 17:6², 8, 18:1², 3, 4, 19, 20, 19:15, 21², 20:1, 9, 21:2, 3, 6, 10, 22:1
ἐκεῖ (locative), 2:14, 12:6², 14, 21:25
ἐκεῖθεν (locative), 22:2
Elative, 21:11
Emphatic negation, 2:11, 3:5, 12, 7:16, 9:6, 15:4, 18:7, 14, 21, 22³, 23², 21:25, 27
ἔμπροσθεν (locative), 4:6, 19:10, 22:8
ἐν (association/accompaniment), 8:7, 19:20
ἐν (instrumental), 1:5, 2:16, 23, 27, 3:5, 5:2, 9, 6:8, 7:14, 9:19, 20, 11:6, 13, 12:5, 13:10², 14:2, 9, 10, 15, 15:1, 16:8, 17:3, 16, 18:2, 8, 16, 23, 19:2, 15², 17, 20, 21, 21:10
ἐν (locative), 1:3, 9², 10, 13, 16, 2:1³, 7, 8, 12, 18, 3:1, 4, 7, 12, 14, 21², 4:1, 2², 6, 5:3, 6², 13², 6:5, 6, 7:9, 14, 15, 8:1, 9, 13, 9:10, 19², 10:2, 8, 9, 10, 11:1, 11, 12, 13, 15, 19², 12:1, 3, 7, 8, 10, 12, 13:6, 8, 12, 14:5, 6, 7, 10, 13, 14, 17, 15:1, 5, 16:3, 17:4,

18:6, 7, 19, 22³, 23², 24, 19:1, 14, 17², 20:8, 12, 13², 15, 21:8, 22, 27, 22:2, 3, 18, 19
ἐν (manner), 1:15, 16, 2:23, 27, 3:4, 5, 4:4, 9:17, 17:3, 19:11, 17, 21:10
ἐν (means), 1:15, 11:12, 18:19
ἐν (temporal), 1:1, 10, 2:13, 9:6, 10:7, 11:13, 18:8, 22:6
ἐντεῦθεν, 22:2
ἐνώπιον (locative), 1:4, 2:14, 3:2, 5², 8, 9, 4:5, 6, 10², 5:8, 7:9, 11, 15, 8:2, 3, 4, 9:13, 11:4, 16, 12:4, 10, 13:13, 14:3, 10, 15:4, 16:19, 20:12
ἐνώπιον (on behalf of), 13:12, 19:20
ἐνώπιον (viewpoint), 3:2
ἐπάνω (locative), 6:8, 20:3
Epexegetical genitive, 1:3, 20, 2:10, 5:5, 7:4, 17, 9:1, 2, 16, 12:1, 11, 13:17, 14:8, 10, 11, 18, 19², 15:5, 16:14, 19, 21, 17:2, 7², 18:3, 19:12, 15², 20:8, 9, 21:6², 12, 22:1², 7, 10, 17, 18, 19
ἐπί (addition), 22:18
ἐπί (basis), 18:20
ἐπί ("control or authority"), 2:26, 5:10, 6:8, 9:11, 11:6, 13:7, 14:18, 16:9, 17:18, 20:6, 22:14
ἐπί ("feelings and actions"), 1:7, 11:10, 12:17, 18:9
ἐπί (locative), 1:17, 20, 2:17, 24, 3:10², 12, 20, 4:2, 4², 9, 10, 5:1², 3, 7, 10, 13³, 6:2, 4, 5, 10, 16², 7:1², 3, 10, 11, 15², 17, 8:3², 10, 13, 9:4, 7, 14, 17, 10:1, 2², 5, 8, 11:8, 10², 11², 16², 12:1, 3, 18, 13:1², 8, 14², 16², 14:1², 6, 9², 14², 15, 16², 15:2, 16:2, 8, 10, 12, 14, 17, 18, 21, 17:1, 3, 5, 8², 9, 18:17, 19, 24, 19:4, 11, 12, 14, 16², 18, 19, 21, 20:1, 4², 9, 11, 21:5, 10, 12, 14, 22:4, 5
ἐπί (measure), 21:16
ἐπί (opposition), 3:3, 10:11

ἐπί (person benefited), 22:16
ἐπί ("to whom something is done"), 14:6
ἔσωθεν (locative), 4:8, 5:1
ἔτι (temporal), 6:11, 7:16
Euphemism, 16:15
ἔξω/ἔξωθεν (locative), 3:12, 11:2, 14:20, 22:15
ἕως (temporal), 6:11

First-class condition, 11:5, 13:9, 10², 14:9, 11, 20:15
Fronting, 2:24, 3:10, 5:13, 17:13, 19:15, 20:6, 21:5, 6

γάρ (causal), 1:3, 9:19², 13:18, 17:17, 21:22, 23, 25, 22:10
γάρ (explanatory), 3:2, 14:4, 13, 19:8, 21:1
γάρ (strengtheing), 19:10
Genitive absolute (temporal), 1:15
Genitive of association, 9:9, 19:10, 22:9
Genitive in apposition, 3:9, 12, 15:3, 16:14, 19:15, 22:9
Genitive of comparison, 2:19
Genitive complement, 4:6, 5:8, 15:7, 8, 17:4, 21:9
Genitive of content/quality, 2:18, 6:6², 7:17, 8:10, 14:7, 10, 19, 16:1, 4, 19, 18:12, 13, 19:15, 20, 20:10, 14², 15, 21:6, 17, 22:1, 19
Genitive of description, 6:15, 11:19, 12:18, 14:7², 8, 15:5, 16:14, 18:3, 11
Genitive indicating location, 1:7, 6:8, 13, 15², 7:1, 8:5, 9:3, 4, 11:13, 12:4, 16:11, 18:3, 11, 23, 20:9
Genitive of price, 6:6²
Genitive of product, 2:7
Genitive of quality, 9:16
Genitive of relationship, 1:6, 9, 13, 2:14, 18, 23, 28, 3:5, 21, 6:11, 7:4², 11:5, 12, 15, 12:4, 5, 10², 17, 14:1,

14, 18:4, 23, 19:7, 10, 21:2, 3, 9, 12, 22:9
Genitive of separation, 1:5
Genitive of source, 1:1, 2, 9, 10, 15, 2:16, 24, 3:1, 8, 18, 20, 4:5, 5:5, 6, 11, 6:7, 9, 8:4, 5, 13, 9:2^2, 3, 9^2, 10:3, 7^2, 11:13, 12:17^2, 13:14, 14:2^3, 12, 18, 16:3, 4, 17:4, 17, 18:3, 9, 18, 22, 23^2, 19:1, 3, 6^2, 9, 13, 15, 20:4, 21:24, 26, 22:2, 5^2, 6, 12, 16, 21
Genitive of subordination, 1:5^2, 20, 2:1, 8, 12, 18, 3:1, 2, 7, 12^4, 14^2, 4:11, 5:10, 7:3, 10, 12, 14, 9:11, 11:4, 8, 15, 12:10^2, 15:3, 16:5, 11, 14, 17:2, 14, 18, 18:3, 9, 23, 19:1, 5, 6, 16, 19, 20, 21:24, 22:6
Genitive of time, 2:10, 4:8, 7:15, 12:10, 14:11, 20:10, 21:25

Headless relative clause, 1:1, 7, 11, 19^3, 2:10, 25, 3:11, 19, 4:1, 10:4, 14:4, 22:6
Historical (narrative) present, 4:5, 5:5, 5:9, 9:10, 17, 19, 10:9, 11, 12:2, 4, 6, 13:12, 14:3, 15:3, 16:21, 17:15, 19:9, 11, 21:5, 22:9, 10
Hortatory subjunctive, 17:1, 19:7^3, 21:9
Hysteron proteron, 3:3^2, 4:11, 10:9

ἵνα (content), 3:9, 9:4, 52, 13:12, 15, 16, 14:13
ἵνα (epexegetical), 2:21, 13:13
ἵνα (indirect discourse), 6:11
ἵνα (purpose/final), 2:10, 21, 3:9, 11, 18^3, 6:2, 7:1, 8:3, 6, 9:15, 20, 12:4, 6, 14, 15, 13:15, 17, 16:12, 15, 18:4^2, 19:15, 18, 20:3, 21:15, 23, 22:14
ἵνα (result), 8:12, 9:20, 11:6, 13:13, 14:13
ἵνα (subject), 6:4, 19:8
Independent nominative, 8:11

Infinitive (complementary), 1:1, 19, 2:2, 10^2, 21, 3:2, 8, 10, 16, 4:1, 5:3^2, 6:11, 17, 7:9, 8:13, 9:20^3, 10:4, 7, 11, 11:5^3, 12:4, 5, 13:4, 10, 13, 17^2, 14:3, 15:8, 17:8, 10, 20:3, 22:6
Infinitive (direct object), 2:7, 14, 20, 3:21, 11:9, 17:17^3,
Infinitive (epexegetical), 2:14^2, 4:11, 5:2^2, 4^2, 9^2, 12, 6:8, 7:2, 9:10, 11:6^3, 18^3, 12:7^2, 13:5, 6, 14:6
Infinitive (indirect discourse), 2:9, 3:9, 10:9, 13:14
Infinitive (predicate), 13:10
Infinitive (purpose), 1:1, 12, 2:14^2, 3:10, 18, 12:2, 7, 17, 13:14, 14:6, 16:6, 14, 19:10, 19, 20:8^2, 22:8, 12, 16
Infinitive (result), 2:20, 5:5, 12:7, 16:9, 19
Infinitive (subject), 1:1, 4:1, 6:4, 7:2, 10:11, 13:7^2, 15, 16:8, 17:10, 20:3, 22:6

καί (adversative), 2:2, 21, 3:1, 9:4, 10:4, 11:7, 20:11, 21:27
καί (ascensive), 1:7, 2:13, 15, 28, 3:21, 6:11, 14:10, 17, 20:10
καί (consecutive), 11:3, 15:8, 16:1
καί (epexegetical), 1:19, 2:2, 19, 18:13, 19:5, 20:4, 9
καί (result), 8:7
κατά (distributive), 22:2
κατά (opposition), 2:4, 14, 20
κατά (standard), 2:23, 18:6, 20:12, 13
κυκλόθεν (locative), 4:3, 4, 8
κύκλῳ (locative), 4:6, 5:11, 7:11

Litotes, 3:5

Marker of attention, 1:7, 18, 2:10, 22, 3:8, 9^2, 20, 4:1^2, 2, 5:5, 6:2, 5, 8, 7:9, 9:12, 11:14, 12:3, 14:1, 14, 16:15, 19:11, 21:3, 5, 22:7, 12
Merism, 1:8, 13:16, 19:5, 20:12

μετά (accompaniment), 3:20², 21², 4:1, 6:8, 10:8, 11:7, 12:7, 9, 17, 13:4, 7, 14:1, 4, 17:1, 14², 19:19, 20, 20:4, 6, 21:3, 9, 15, 22:12, 21

μετά (association), 1:7, 12, 2:16, 22, 3:4, 4:1, 14:4, 13, 17:2, 12, 18:3, 9, 19:19, 21:3³

μετά (manner), 1:7

μετά (temporal), 1:19, 4:1², 7:1, 9, 9:12, 11:11, 15:5, 18:1, 19:1, 20:3

Metaphor, 1:16, 2:10, 14, 23, 27, 10:10, 11:2, 14:3, 4², 17:1, 18:3

Metonymy, 1:5, 5:9², 6:10, 19:2

Nominalizer, 10:6, 16:3, 5, 17:10³, 14

Nominative absolute, 1:1, 4², 10:8, 12:3, 18:7

Nominative of appellation, 19:16²

Nominative in apposition, 1:5³, 8³, 9², 2:1, 13, 18, 3:7⁴, 14², 4:8³, 5:5, 6:10, 7:4, 8:9, 12, 9:11², 11:17², 12:1, 7, 9³, 10, 14:4³, 12, 15:3², 16:5², 7², 17:5³, 18:8², 10², 21, 19:5, 6², 20:2, 14, 21:6, 22², 22:5, 6, 8, 13², 16²

Nominative subject, 1:1, 2, 7³, 8², 9, 12, 16², 17, 19², 20², 2:1, 6, 7², 8², 10, 11³, 12, 13², 14, 15, 17³, 18, 23², 24², 27, 29², 3:1, 2, 3, 4, 5, 6², 7³, 8, 9, 10, 11, 13², 14, 18, 19, 20², 21, 22², 4:2, 5², 8, 9, 10, 11, 5:3, 4, 5², 6, 8³, 10, 11, 12, 14², 6:1, 2, 4², 8², 11², 12³, 13², 14², 15, 17², 7:1, 9, 11, 13², 14², 15, 16, 17², 8:1, 2², 3², 4, 5², 6, 7⁵, 8², 9², 10², 11³, 12⁴, 9:1², 2², 3³, 4, 6², 8, 12², 13, 15, 17, 18, 19, 20³, 10:3², 4², 5, 6², 7, 10, 11:1, 4, 5³, 6², 7, 8³, 10², 11², 12, 13⁴, 14², 15³, 16, 18³, 19³, 12:1, 3, 4², 5², 6, 7³, 8, 9², 10³, 11, 12, 13², 14, 15, 16³, 17, 13:2², 3², 4, 5², 7, 8², 9, 12, 14², 15², 17, 18², 14:3, 4³, 5, 7, 8³, 9², 10, 11³, 13², 15³, 16², 17², 18², 19, 20², 15:1, 4³, 5, 6, 7, 8³, 16:2², 3³, 4, 8, 9, 10², 12³, 14, 15, 17², 18³, 19³, 20², 21³, 17:1, 2², 4, 7², 8², 9², 10³, 11², 12², 13, 14⁴, 15², 16, 17², 18, 18:1, 2, 3³, 5², 6, 8, 9, 10, 11², 14², 15, 17³, 19, 20, 21², 22³, 23⁴, 24, 19:2, 3, 4, 5, 6, 7², 8, 9, 10², 12, 13, 14, 15³, 20², 21², 20:2, 3, 4², 5², 6, 7², 9, 10, 11², 12⁴, 13³, 14², 15, 21:1², 3², 4³, 5², 6, 7², 8, 9, 12, 14, 15, 16², 17, 19, 21, 22², 23³, 24², 25², 27³, 22:3³, 5², 6, 10, 11⁴, 14, 16², 17⁴, 18³, 19², 20

Nominative subject of an implied verb, 2:17, 6:11, 14, 8:12, 9:2, 12:7, 13:11, 17:12, 19:12, 20:10, 22:21

Nominative subject of a verbless equative clause, 1:3², 4, 6, 14², 15², 16, 2:13, 17, 18, 19, 4:1², 2, 3², 5, 6, 7⁴, 8, 5:2, 13², 6:2², 5², 6², 8², 12, 7:4, 5, 9², 10, 12, 9:5, 7², 9, 10, 11, 16, 17, 10:1³, 12:1², 13:2², 4, 10², 17, 18, 14:1², 2, 3, 13, 14, 18, 15:3², 16:7, 17:5, 14, 18:18, 19:1, 2, 9, 11², 12², 20:5, 6, 8, 10, 21:3, 6, 8, 11, 13, 16, 18², 19⁵, 20⁸, 21², 23, 22:2², 4, 6, 7, 8, 12, 12, 14, 15²

Nominative as vocative, 4:11, 6:10, 11:17², 12:12, 15:3, 18:4, 10, 16, 19, 20, 19:5

Objective genitive, 1:1, 2, 9, 2:13², 14, 3:10, 14, 5:2, 5, 9, 11, 7:4, 9:16², 11:3, 15, 12:10, 11, 17, 13:8, 12, 14:11, 12, 15, 17:1, 6, 8, 18:2², 4, 10³, 15³, 18, 20, 22, 19:10², 20:4, 7, 8², 21:23, 22:2, 6

ὅμοιος/ὁμοίως (comparison), 8:12, 11:1, 14:14, 21:18

ὀπίσω/ὄπισθεν (locative), 1:10, 4:6, 5:1, 12:15, 13:3

ὅπου/ποῦ (locative), 2:13³, 19, 11:8, 12:6, 14, 14:4, 17:9, 20:10

ὅταν (temporal), 4:9, 8:1, 9:5, 10:7, 11:7, 12:4, 17:10, 18:9, 20:7

ὅτε (temporal), 1:17, 5:8, 6:1, 3, 5, 6, 9, 12, 10:3, 4, 10, 12:13, 22:8

ὅτι (causal), 3:4, 8, 10, 16, 17, 4:11, 5:4, 9, 6:17, 7:17, 8:11, 11:2, 10, 17, 12:10, 12, 13:4, 14:7, 15², 18, 15:1, 4³, 16:5, 6, 21, 17:8, 14, 18:3, 5, 7, 8, 10, 11, 17, 19, 20, 23², 19:2², 6, 7, 21:4, 5, 22:5

ὅτι (clausal complement), 2:2, 4, 20, 23, 3:17, 10:6, 12:12, 13, 17:8, 21:5

ὅτι (clausal complement; direct discourse), 2:23; 3:17, 18:7

ὅτι (clausal complement; indirect discourse with a verb of cognition), 3:9

ὅτι (epexegetical), 2:6, 14, 3:1², 15

οὗ (locative), 17:15

οὐκέτι (temporal), 10:6

οὖν (inferential), 1:19, 2:5, 16, 3:3, 19

οὖν (resumptive), 3:3

οὕτως (manner), 2:15, 3:5, 9:17, 11:5, 18:21

οὕτως (inference), 3:16

παρά (locative), 2:13
παρά (source), 2:28, 3:18
Paranomasia, 22:18
Parenthetical nominative, 6:8
Participle (attendant circumstance), 13:14
Participle (attributive), 1:9, 13, 2:17², 3:8, 10, 4:1, 4², 5, 6, 7, 8, 9, 5:1, 6, 8², 12, 6:2, 5, 11, 13, 14, 7:2, 4, 5, 8, 9, 10, 13, 8:6, 7, 8, 10, 13², 9:1, 9, 14², 15, 17, 18, 19, 10:1², 2, 4, 8², 11:4, 7, 11, 16, 12:1, 3, 4, 6, 17², 13:1, 5, 8², 14:1³, 3, 4, 6, 10, 13, 14, 18, 15:1, 2, 6, 7², 16:2², 9, 14, 16, 17:1², 3², 4, 7², 9, 18, 18:1, 2, 8, 9², 15, 16², 19, 24, 19:4, 5, 10, 12, 13, 16, 17, 20², 21, 20:1, 9, 10, 21:2², 8, 9², 10, 11², 12, 22:1, 2, 8, 18, 19

Participle (causal), 12:2², 12, 17:6, 18:18
Participle (finite verb), 1:16, 4:1, 7, 8, 6:2, 5, 9:19, 10:2, 12:2, 14:1, 18, 19:12, 21:14, 19
Participle (manner), 1:17, 4:1, 8, 10, 5:8, 9, 12, 6:2, 10, 7:1, 2, 3, 10, 12, 13, 8:3, 10:9, 11:1, 3, 15, 17, 12:2², 12, 13:4, 14, 14:7, 8, 9, 15, 17, 18, 15:2, 3, 6, 16:17, 17:1, 4, 5, 18:2, 10², 15², 16, 18, 19², 21, 19:4, 5, 14, 17, 20, 21:9, 11, 22:2
Participle (means), 1:1
Participle (parenthetical), 1:16, 2:20, 3:12, 4:8, 9:14
Participle (periphrastic), 1:16², 18, 3:2, 10:2, 17:4²
Participle (predicate), 1:16, 10:2, 21:14, 19
Participle (substantival), 1:3⁴, 4², 5², 13, 18, 2:1², 2, 7², 9, 11², 12, 14, 15, 17³, 18, 20, 22, 23, 26², 29, 3:1, 5, 6, 7³, 9, 10, 12², 13, 21, 22, 4:2, 3, 9, 10², 5:1, 6, 7, 13, 6:2, 4, 5, 8, 9, 10, 16, 7:4, 5, 8, 14, 15, 8:9, 13, 9:14, 17, 10:6, 11:1, 10², 17, 18², 12:9², 10, 12, 13:3, 6, 8, 12, 14², 17, 18, 14:2, 4, 6, 7, 11, 12, 14, 15, 16, 18, 15:2, 16:5, 15², 17:2, 8, 18:8, 17, 19, 24, 19:9, 11, 17, 18, 19², 20², 21, 20:4, 6, 11, 12, 21:5, 6, 7, 8, 15, 27², 22:7, 8², 9, 11, 14, 15², 17, 18, 20
Participle (temporal), 1:12, 6:13, 17:6, 8, 18:10, 18, 19:20
Partitive genitive, 1:5, 2:1, 17, 4:8, 5:11, 6:8, 7:1, 8:7², 9², 10, 11², 12³, 9:13, 15, 17, 18, 20, 11:2, 8, 13, 12:4, 14, 17, 20:5, 8, 21:14, 15, 16², 17, 18, 19², 21², 25, 22:2⁴
Pendent/Hanging nominative, 2:26, 3:21, 6:8
περί (spatial), 15:6

Periphrastic (present), 1:18, 3:2
Personification, 6:16
πλήν (adversative), 2:25
πόθεν (interrogative), 2:5
πόθεν (locative), 7:13
Possessive genitive, 1:1², 4, 5, 14², 15, 16², 17², 18, 2:1², 3, 5², 7, 8, 9, 12, 13², 16, 18³, 3:1², 4, 5³, 7², 8, 9², 11, 12⁵, 14, 16, 18², 20, 21², 4:4, 5, 7, 10, 5:1, 2, 5, 6, 7, 9², 6:5, 9, 10, 13, 14, 15, 16, 7:1, 2, 3², 9, 11, 14², 15², 17, 8:4, 11, 13, 9:4², 7⁴, 8², 9, 10, 13, 17², 18, 19³, 20, 10:1³, 2², 5, 7², 8, 9², 10³, 11:1, 5, 8, 9², 11, 13, 15², 16², 17, 18³, 19³, 12:1², 3, 4, 5, 7², 8, 9, 11², 14³, 15, 16², 18, 13:1², 2⁵, 3, 6³, 8³, 12, 16², 17³, 18³, 14:1³, 2, 5, 9², 11, 14², 15, 16, 18³, 19, 20, 15:2, 3⁴, 4, 8, 16:2², 3², 4, 6, 8, 9, 10³, 11², 12², 13, 14, 15², 17, 19, 21, 17:4², 5, 6², 8, 16, 17, 18:3, 4, 7, 11, 13, 14, 19², 24, 19:1, 2³, 5, 10, 12², 13, 15, 16, 17, 18², 19², 20², 21³, 20:1, 4³, 6, 7, 8, 11, 21:3, 4, 8, 12, 14², 16, 21, 22, 23, 24, 26, 27, 22:1, 2³, 3², 4³, 6³, 8, 12, 14, 16, 19
Predicate accusative, 2:9, 3:9
Predicate adjective, 1:18, 2:10, 3:1, 15³, 16³, 17², 4:11, 6:12, 10:9, 11:13, 13:2, 14:5, 16:5, 6, 10, 21, 19:9, 21:5, 16²
Predicate adjective of a verbless clause, 1:3², 14, 15, 2:18, 19, 4:3², 7³, 8, 5:2, 9:7, 19, 13:4, 15:3², 4, 18:18, 19:2, 11, 16, 22:7
Predicate nominative, 1:8, 17, 18, 20², 2:8, 9, 23, 3:4, 4:1, 5, 5:6, 8, 9, 11, 12, 7:14, 8:8, 11:4, 13:10, 18, 14:4, 12, 16:4, 14, 17:9², 11, 12, 15, 18, 18:2³, 7, 23, 19:8, 10, 20:2, 6, 14, 21:3, 7², 8, 22, 22:9, 16

Predicate nominative of a verbless equative clause, 1:16, 2:9, 13, 6:8, 9:16, 13:18, 14:13, 16:7, 15³, 17:9, 14, 18:8, 19:9, 12, 20:5, 6, 21:6, 11, 12, 16, 17, 18², 19⁴, 20⁸, 21², 23, 22:6, 8², 13, 14
Prominence/prominent, 2:9, 19, 3:1, 2, 8², 15, 5:1, 6, 13, 7:13, 9:1, 17, 20, 10:9, 12:12, 13:12, 14:8², 18, 16:17, 19, 17:15, 16, 18:3, 5, 11, 14, 20, 19:7, 15, 21:2
πρός (extension towards goal), 3:20
πρός (locative), 1:13, 17, 10:9, 12:12
πρός (opposition), 13:6
πρός (orientation), 12:5
πῶς (manner), 3:3

Semitic influence, 1:17, 2:7, 23, 24, 3:8, 9, 20
Solecism, 1:4, 13, 15, 14:14
Subjective genitive, 1:1, 2², 9, 15, 16, 2:2, 4, 6, 9, 13, 14, 15, 19³, 21, 22, 23, 26, 3:1, 2, 8², 10, 14, 15, 4:11, 5:8, 11, 6:7, 9, 16, 17, 7:2², 8:3, 4, 13, 9:4, 5², 9², 10, 19, 20, 21⁴, 10:3, 7, 11:6, 7, 17, 18, 12:10², 11, 17, 13:2, 3, 6, 10, 12, 14:2³, 7, 8, 10², 12, 13², 19, 15:1, 3⁴, 4, 7, 8, 16:1, 7, 10, 11, 19, 21, 17:2, 4, 13, 17³, 18:1, 2, 3², 4, 5², 6, 9, 14², 22², 23², 19:1, 2, 6², 7, 8, 9², 13, 15, 20:4, 9, 12, 13, 21:3, 11², 23, 22:12, 14
Synecdoche, 3:4, 10:1

ταχύ (temporal), 2:16, 3:11, 11:14, 22:12, 20
Third-class condition, 2:5, 22, 3:3, 20, 11:5, 22:18, 19
Topic construction, 1:5, 2:7, 17, 26, 3:12, 21, 6:4, 8, 7:13, 17:16², 18:7, 21:8

ὑπό (means), 6:13
ὑπό (ultimate agency), 6:8

ὑποκάτω (locative), 5:3, 13, 6:9, 12:1

Vocative, 7:14, 11:17, 15:3, 4, 16:7, 18:20, 22:20
Vocative in apposition, 11:17^2

ὡς ("according to"), 22:12
ὡς (approximation), 8:1
ὡς (comparative), 1:10, 14^3, 15, 16, 2:18, 27, 28, 3:21, 4:1, 6, 7, 5:6, 6:6, 12^2, 13, 14, 8:8, 10, 9:2, 3, 5, 7^2, 8^2, 9^2, 17, 10:1^2, 7, 9, 10, 12:15, 13:2^2, 3, 14:2^3, 3, 15:2, 16:3, 13, 21, 18:6, 21, 19:1, 6, 20:8, 21:2, 11, 21, 22:1
ὡς (manner), 1:15, 17, 24, 3:3, 5:6, 6:1, 11, 9:3, 13:11, 16:15, 17:12
ὥσπερ (comparative), 10:3

AUTHOR INDEX

Aune, David, xxii, xxiii, xxiv, 2, 3, 8, 9, 10, 11, 13, 17, 18, 19, 23, 29, 34, 35, 40, 45, 46, 47, 48, 49, 51, 64, 66, 68, 69, 70, 73, 74, 77, 82, 83, 86, 87, 88, 89, 92, 95, 96, 98, 99, 102, 103, 106, 107, 111, 112, 113, 114, 116, 117, 121, 122, 123, 125, 131, 133, 134, 136, 138, 140, 142, 147, 152, 155, 156, 161, 164, 165, 171, 173, 174, 175, 179, 181, 184, 185, 186, 187, 188, 189, 192, 196, 201, 204, 206, 207, 209, 210, 211, 212, 213, 214, 217, 223, 224, 225, 227, 228, 230, 232, 233, 237, 238, 239, 241, 243, 248, 249, 252, 258, 260, 263, 264, 265, 266, 267, 275, 276, 277, 280, 285, 287, 296, 298, 299, 301, 302, 309, 310, 311

Bauckham, Richard J., 99, 106, 132, 188, 247

BDAG (Bauer, Danker, Arndt, and Gingrich), 7, 9, 11, 12, 13, 15, 21, 25, 30, 37, 42, 47, 51, 54, 55, 56, 57, 64, 65, 69, 73, 77, 79, 81, 84, 86, 87, 88, 89, 91, 92, 93, 95, 96, 102, 104, 105, 107, 113, 114, 116, 122, 123, 125, 126, 128, 131, 132, 139, 140, 142, 145, 147, 148, 150, 151, 152, 159, 162, 163, 164, 165, 167, 168, 171, 172, 173, 176, 179, 180, 181, 182, 183, 188, 189, 190, 191, 192, 193, 194, 196, 197, 199, 200, 202, 204, 205, 206, 210, 213, 214, 218, 221, 223, 225, 226, 231, 236, 240, 241, 242, 244, 245, 247, 248, 249, 250, 253, 257, 267, 269, 270, 271, 274, 277, 278, 281, 284, 290, 291, 292, 294, 295, 296, 297, 299, 301, 302, 303, 304, 307, 308, 309, 312

BDF (Blass, Debrunner, and Funk), 6, 21, 47, 48, 75, 82, 87, 95, 102, 107, 108, 112, 122, 123, 129, 144, 179, 197, 201, 204, 258, 279, 285, 295, 297

Beale, Gregory K., 1, 2, 4, 5, 8, 9, 13, 16, 18, 20, 29, 31, 33, 45, 49, 52, 59, 66, 69, 73, 75, 78, 81, 83, 87, 93, 94, 112, 126, 131, 134, 135, 137, 140, 142, 146, 147, 150, 151, 158, 161, 165, 169, 175, 176, 184, 189, 191, 192, 196, 197, 202, 203, 204, 205, 206, 208, 211, 212, 219, 225, 226, 235, 236, 239, 241, 242, 246, 252, 258, 260, 262, 263, 271, 275, 285, 288, 293, 296, 298, 299, 301, 302, 303, 307, 309, 310, 311

Black, David A., 43
Blount, Brian K., 94, 133, 153, 178, 255, 260, 275, 288, 299
Boyer, James L., 15, 143

Campbell, Constantine R., xxv, xxvi, xxvii, 63
Caragounis, Chrys C., 24, 27, 46, 48, 61, 75, 106, 108, 114, 159, 197, 253, 269, 312
Charles, R. H., xxiv, 6, 15, 16, 17, 19, 24, 30, 35, 45, 47, 49, 66, 78, 79, 89, 99, 103, 107, 110, 117, 127, 135, 149, 161, 163, 170, 171, 174, 176, 177, 179, 190, 202, 232, 243, 247, 250, 252, 270, 280, 288, 295, 298, 300, 311
Culy, Martin M., 9, 21, 71, 112, 147, 152, 162, 214, 265, 266, 282, 293, 302

Decker, Rodney J., xxv

Fanning, Buist W., xxv, 75, 102, 108, 135, 152, 192, 203, 240, 258, 261, 276
Fekkes, Jan, 299

Harris, Murray J., 30, 61, 64, 105, 146, 162
Hauck, F., 239
Hemer, Colin, 13

Levinson, Stephen C., 317
Levinsohn, Stephen H., 3, 61, 143, 187, 233
LSJ (Liddell, Scott, and Jones), 8, 301
LN (Louw and Nida), 2, 3, 12, 15, 26, 31, 39, 40, 42, 47, 52, 57, 60, 73, 81, 85, 87, 89, 91, 92, 101, 106, 107, 112, 114, 118, 121, 131, 137, 141, 150, 156, 157, 164, 165, 167, 171, 177, 178, 179, 181, 182, 183, 187, 192, 194, 202, 218, 220, 221, 222, 227, 239, 241, 246, 247, 248, 250, 252, 255, 267, 288, 293, 294, 296, 310, 312

McKay, K. L., xxv, xxvi, 7, 15, 19, 35, 36, 48, 53, 76, 77, 90, 96, 117, 118, 123, 127, 138, 160, 162, 182, 211, 218, 223, 229, 240, 249
Mathewson, David L., xxiii, xxv, xxvi, xxix, 15, 41, 47, 56, 66, 75, 93, 98, 101, 103, 104, 116, 119, 121, 135, 142, 146, 149, 157, 178, 192, 228, 229, 232, 238, 240, 251, 260, 264, 298
Metzger, Bruce M., 23, 78, 79, 83, 93, 149, 168, 187, 197, 207, 229, 239, 247, 260, 264, 284, 291, 309
Milligan, George, 12
Moule, C. F. D., 11, 61, 64, 78, 82, 103, 108, 149, 161, 295
Moulton, James H., 12, 113
Mounce, Robert H., 45, 64, 89, 103, 107, 134, 147, 152, 171, 174, 189, 192, 213, 229, 257, 275, 299, 311
Mussies, G., xxiv, 6, 17, 33, 41, 48, 66, 73, 75, 98, 101, 102, 107, 118, 123, 125, 131, 135, 142, 156, 161, 164, 174, 179, 182, 185, 186, 192, 201, 238, 239, 240, 246, 249, 256, 258, 272, 287, 296, 304, 312

Nida, E. A., 65

Osborne, Grant R., xxii, 2, 11, 13, 20, 29, 35, 40, 41, 45, 49, 50, 60, 64, 71, 72, 73, 79, 88, 92, 95, 101, 102, 104, 107, 108, 109, 114, 119, 121, 126, 135, 138, 139, 140, 153, 158, 159, 174, 176, 178, 179, 183, 184, 189, 192, 197, 199, 210, 212, 241, 260, 275, 286, 298, 300, 301, 305, 310

Porter, Stanley E., xxiv, xxv, xxvi, xxviii, 1, 6, 12, 14, 15, 21, 26, 35,

37, 40, 48, 49, 53, 55, 58, 61, 63, 75, 87, 88, 91, 92, 96, 97, 100, 102, 103, 110, 118, 122, 125, 133, 136, 142, 143, 144, 152, 158, 161, 174, 185, 188, 192, 197, 203, 210, 214, 225, 227, 233, 292, 297, 298, 299, 310

Reed, Jeffrey T., 319
Resseguie, James L., 41, 70, 238
Robertson, A. T., xxviii, 4, 5, 13, 33, 42, 46, 48, 56, 64, 74, 78, 79, 99, 102, 106, 107, 113, 114, 115, 122, 123, 138, 139, 153, 154, 160, 161, 165, 181, 188, 193, 195, 204, 223, 224, 230, 231, 247, 267, 276, 292, 293, 295, 309
Runge, Steven E., xxiii, xxviii, xxix, 6, 12, 20, 24, 31, 40, 49, 63, 87, 134, 162, 232, 263, 265, 277, 318, 319

Schmidt, Daryl D., xxiv
Schultz, S., 239
Smalley, Stephen S., 2, 17, 20, 27, 41, 45, 46, 56, 66, 69, 71, 72, 73, 74, 77, 79, 84, 86, 95, 102, 107, 108, 114, 116, 117, 127, 130, 131, 132, 135, 136, 138, 140, 143, 144, 146, 147, 153, 155, 156, 161, 164, 175, 176, 181, 185, 188, 190, 192, 194, 196, 197, 204, 205, 209, 212, 223, 225, 230, 235, 236, 239, 240, 242, 250, 257, 258, 260, 263, 265, 269, 272, 274, 275, 288, 300, 303, 310, 311
Strathmann, H., 104
Swete, Henry Barclay, 3, 5, 41, 45, 49, 63, 70, 71, 76, 107, 109, 111, 144, 157, 161, 174, 183, 195, 197, 204, 212, 236, 250, 255, 258, 259, 262, 265, 275, 286, 289, 294, 303, 311

Thompson, Steven, xxiv, 6, 15, 22, 35, 49, 56, 59, 66, 103, 161, 206, 218, 301, 319
Turner, Nigel, xxvi, 22, 46, 63, 102, 110, 117, 119, 127, 143, 154, 163, 164, 176, 192, 208, 252, 270, 276, 280, 290, 291

Wallace, Daniel B., xxviii, 1, 2, 4, 5, 15, 17, 22, 23, 56, 60, 67, 68, 69, 75, 80, 81, 88, 101, 107, 108, 113, 122, 125, 134, 135, 139, 145, 152, 156, 159, 163, 181, 184, 187, 191, 223, 230, 236, 246, 258, 261, 262, 265, 268, 276, 290, 294, 297, 305, 313, 317

Young, Richard A., 75, 105, 110, 293, 313, 317

Zerwick, Maximilian, 46, 75, 107, 128, 202, 205